Lecture Notes in Computer Science 2618

Edited by G. Goos, J. Hartmanis, and J. van Leeuwen

T0226263

Springer
Berlin
Heidelberg
New York
Barcelona
Hong Kong
London
Milan
Paris
Tokyo

Pierpaolo Degano (Ed.)

Programming Languages and Systems

12th European Symposium on Programming, ESOP 2003
Held as Part of the Joint European Conferences
on Theory and Practice of Software, ETAPS 2003
Warsaw, Poland, April 7-11, 2003
Proceedings

 Springer

Series Editors

Gerhard Goos, Karlsruhe University, Germany
Juris Hartmanis, Cornell University, NY, USA
Jan van Leeuwen, Utrecht University, The Netherlands

Volume Editor

Pierpaolo Degano
Università di Pisa, Dipartimento di Informatica
Via F. Buonarroti, 2, 56127 Pisa, Italy
E-mail: degano@di.unipi.it

Cataloging-in-Publication Data applied for

A catalog record for this book is available from the Library of Congress.

Bibliographic information published by Die Deutsche Bibliothek.
Die Deutsche Bibliothek lists this publication in the Deutsche Nationalbibliografie;
detailed bibliographic data is available in the Internet at <http://dnb.ddb.de>.

CR Subject Classification (1998): D.3, D.1-2, F.3-4, E.1

ISSN 0302-9743
ISBN 3-540-00886-1 Springer-Verlag Berlin Heidelberg New York

Springer-Verlag Berlin Heidelberg New York
a member of BertelsmannSpringer Science+Business Media GmbH

http://www.springer.de

© Springer-Verlag Berlin Heidelberg 2003
Printed in Germany

Typesetting: Camera-ready by author, data conversion by PTP-Berlin GmbH
Printed on acid-free paper   SPIN: 10872938   06/3142   5 4 3 2 1 0

Foreword

ETAPS 2003 was the sixth instance of the European Joint Conferences on Theory and Practice of Software. ETAPS is an annual federated conference that was established in 1998 by combining a number of existing and new conferences. This year it comprised five conferences (FOSSACS, FASE, ESOP, CC, TACAS), 14 satellite workshops (AVIS, CMCS, COCV, FAMAS, Feyerabend, FICS, LDTA, RSKD, SC, TACoS, UniGra, USE, WITS and WOOD), eight invited lectures (not including those that are specific to the satellite events), and several tutorials. We received a record number of submissions to the five conferences this year: over 500, making acceptance rates fall below 30% for every of them. Congratulations to all the authors who made it to the final program! I hope that all the other authors still found a way of participating in this exciting event and I hope you will continue submitting.

A special event was held to honor the 65th birthday of Prof. Wlad Turski, one of the pioneers of our young science. The deaths of some of our "fathers" in the summer of 2002 — Dahl, Dijkstra and Nygaard — reminded us that Software Science and Technology is, perhaps, no longer that young. Against this sobering background, it is a treat to celebrate one of our most prominent scientists and his lifetime of achievements. It gives me particular personal pleasure that we are able to do this for Wlad during my term as chairman of ETAPS.

The events that comprise ETAPS address various aspects of the system development process, including specification, design, implementation, analysis and improvement. The languages, methodologies and tools which support these activities are all well within its scope. Different blends of theory and practice are represented, with an inclination towards theory with a practical motivation on the one hand and soundly based practice on the other. Many of the issues involved in software design apply to systems in general, including hardware systems, and the emphasis on software is not intended to be exclusive.

ETAPS is a loose confederation in which each event retains its own identity, with a separate program committee and independent proceedings. Its format is open-ended, allowing it to grow and evolve as time goes by. Contributed talks and system demonstrations are in synchronized parallel sessions, with invited lectures in plenary sessions. Two of the invited lectures are reserved for "unifying" talks on topics of interest to the whole range of ETAPS attendees. The aim of cramming all this activity into a single one-week meeting is to create a strong magnet for academic and industrial researchers working on topics within its scope, giving them the opportunity to learn about research in related areas, and thereby to foster new and existing links between work in areas that were formerly addressed in separate meetings.

ETAPS 2003 was organized by Warsaw University, Institute of Informatics, in cooperation with the Foundation for Information Technology Development, as well as:

- European Association for Theoretical Computer Science (EATCS);
- European Association for Programming Languages and Systems (EAPLS);
- European Association of Software Science and Technology (EASST); and

– ACM SIGACT, SIGSOFT and SIGPLAN.

The organizing team comprised:

Mikołaj Bojańczyk, Jacek Chrząszcz, Piotr Chrząstowski-Wachtel, Grzegorz Grudziński, Kazimierz Grygiel, Piotr Hoffman, Janusz Jabłonowski, Mirosław Kowaluk, Marcin Kubica (publicity), Sławomir Leszczyński (www), Wojciech Moczydłowski, Damian Niwiński (satellite events), Aleksy Schubert, Hanna Sokołowska, Piotr Stańczyk, Krzysztof Szafran, Marcin Szczuka, Łukasz Sznuk, Andrzej Tarlecki (co-chair), Jerzy Tiuryn, Jerzy Tyszkiewicz (book exhibition), Paweł Urzyczyn (co-chair), Daria Walukiewicz-Chrząszcz, Artur Zawłocki.

ETAPS 2003 received support from:[1]

– Warsaw University
– European Commission, High-Level Scientific Conferences and Information Society Technologies
– US Navy Office of Naval Research International Field Office,
– European Office of Aerospace Research and Development, US Air Force
– Microsoft Research

Overall planning for ETAPS conferences is the responsibility of its Steering Committee, whose current membership is:

Egidio Astesiano (Genoa), Pierpaolo Degano (Pisa), Hartmut Ehrig (Berlin), José Fiadeiro (Leicester), Marie-Claude Gaudel (Paris), Evelyn Duesterwald (IBM), Hubert Garavel (Grenoble), Andy Gordon (Microsoft Research, Cambridge), Roberto Gorrieri (Bologna), Susanne Graf (Grenoble), Görel Hedin (Lund), Nigel Horspool (Victoria), Kurt Jensen (Aarhus), Paul Klint (Amsterdam), Tiziana Margaria (Dortmund), Ugo Montanari (Pisa), Mogens Nielsen (Aarhus), Hanne Riis Nielson (Copenhagen), Fernando Orejas (Barcelona), Mauro Pezzè (Milano), Andreas Podelski (Saarbrücken), Don Sannella (Edinburgh), David Schmidt (Kansas), Bernhard Steffen (Dortmund), Andrzej Tarlecki (Warsaw), Igor Walukiewicz (Bordeaux), Herbert Weber (Berlin).

I would like to express my sincere gratitude to all of these people and organizations, the program committee chairs and PC members of the ETAPS conferences, the organizers of the satellite events, the speakers themselves, and Springer-Verlag for agreeing to publish the ETAPS proceedings. The final votes of thanks must go, however, to Andrzej Tarlecki and Paweł Urzyczyn. They accepted the risk of organizing what is the first edition of ETAPS in Eastern Europe, at a time of economic uncertainty, but with great courage and determination. They deserve our greatest applause.

Leicester, January 2003   José Luiz Fiadeiro
                                           ETAPS Steering Committee Chair

---

[1] The contents of this volume do not necessarily reflect the positions or the policies of these organizations and no official endorsement should be inferred.

Preface

This volume contains the 27 papers presented at ESOP 2003, the 12th European Symposium on Programming, which took place in Warsaw, Poland, April 5–13, 2003. The ESOP series began in 1986 with the goal of bridging the gap between theory and practice. The conferences are devoted to fundamental issues in the specification, analysis and implementation of programming languages and systems.

The call for ESOP 2003 encouraged papers addressing the topics traditionally covered by ESOP (but not limited to):

- programming paradigms and their integration;
- semantics;
- calculi of computation;
- security;
- advanced type systems;
- program analysis and transformation;
- practical algorithms based on theoretical developments.

The volume begins with two invited contributions, both in the area of security. The first belongs to ETAPS as a whole, and accompanies its "unifying invited lecture" entitled *Computer Security from a Programming Language and Static Analysis Perspective*, delivered by Xavier Leroy. The second contribution is *What Makes a Cryptographic Protocol Secure? The Evolution of Requirements Specification in Formal Cryptographic Protocol Analysis*, by the ESOP invited speaker Catherine Meadows. The remaining 25 papers were selected by the Programme Committee from the 99 submissions.

Each submission was reviewed by at least three referees, and papers were selected in the latter stages of a one-week electronic discussion phase. I would like to sincerely thank all members of the ESOP 2003 Programme Committee for the excellent job they did in the very difficult selection process, always carried on in a kind, agreeable atmosphere. Also, I would like to thank all the subreferees for their invaluable contribution. I am also grateful to Michele Curti for the help with the conference management software. Finally, many thanks to the ETAPS Organising Committee, chaired by Andrzej Tarlecki and Pawel Urzyczyn, and to the Steering Committee of ETAPS, in particular to José Luiz Fiadeiro, for their efficient coordination of all the activities leading up to ESOP 2003.

Pisa, January 2003   Pierpaolo Degano

Programme Chair

Pierpaolo Degano   Univ. Pisa, Italy

Programme Committee

Patrick Cousot   ENS Paris, France
Mariangiola Dezani-Ciancaglini   Univ. Torino, Italy
Cedric Fournet   Microsoft Research Cambridge, UK
John Hughes   Chalmers Univ., Sweden
Joshua Guttman   MITRE, USA
John Mitchell   Stanford Univ., USA
Alan Mycroft   Univ. Cambridge, UK
Hanne Riis Nielson   IMM Copenhagen, Denmark
Oscar Nierstrasz   Univ. Berne, Switzerland
Catuscia Palamidessi   INRIA Paris, France & Penn State Univ.,
           USA

Dave Schmidt   Kansas State Univ., USA
Helmut Seidl   Univ. Trier, Germany
Perdita Stevenson   Univ. Edinburgh, UK

Referees

Adriana Compagnoni
Agostino Cortesi
Alan Lawrence
Alessandra Di Pierro
Alexandru Berlea
Allen Stoughton
Andrew Kennedy
Andrew Pitts
Antoine Miné
Anupam Datta
Arnaud Venet
Bertrand Jeannet
Bruno Blanchet
Carlo Montangero
Charles Consel
Charles Hymans
Chiara Bodei
Chris Hankin
Christian Haack
Christopher Anderson
Christoph Kessler
Claudio Russo
Corrado Priami
Dale Miller
Dario Colazzo
Davide Ancona
Davide Sangiorgi
David Monniaux
Don Syme
Elodie Sims
Elvira Albert
Emilio Tuosto
Fabio Gadducci
Felice Cardone
Francesco Logozzo
Francesco Ranzato
Francois Maurel
Francois Pottier
Frank S. de Boer
Frank Valencia
Gabriela Arévalo
German Puebla
Giancarlo Mauri
GianLuigi Ferrari

Giorgio Delzanno
Giorgio Ghelli
Gregory Morrisett
Hans Huttel
Henning Christiansen
Henrik Pilegaard
Hongwei Xi
Hongyan Sun
Ian Gent
Ian Stark
Iliano Cervesato
Ivano Salvo
James Riely
Jeremy Singer
Jerome Feret
John Boyland
John Longley
Karol Ostrovsky
Keith Wansbrough
Kurt Sieber
Kurt Stenzel
Laura Ponisio
Laurence Melloul
Laurent Mauborgne
Luca Becchetti
Luca Cardelli
Luigi Liquori
Marcin Benke
Marco Danelutto
Mark Shinwell
Markus Mueller-Olm
Martin Abadi
Martin Elsman
Martin Fränzle
Martin Grohe
Martin Sulzmann
Massimo Bartoletti
Matthew Parkinson
Maurizio Gabbrielli
Michael Hanus
Michael O'Boyle
Michael R. Hansen
Michal Konecny
Michele Lanza

Table of Contents

Invited Talks

Contributed Papers

Computer Security from a Programming Language and Static Analysis Perspective
(Extended Abstract of Invited Lecture)

Xavier Leroy

INRIA Rocquencourt and Trusted Logic S.A.
Domaine de Voluceau, B.P. 105, 78153 Le Chesnay, France
Xavier.Leroy@inria.fr

1 Introduction

Computer security [16,5] is usually defined as ensuring integrity, confidentiality, and availability requirements even in the presence of a determined, malicious opponent. Sensitive data must be modified and consulted by authorized users only (integrity, confidentiality); moreover, the system should resist "denial of service" attacks that attempt to render it unusable (availability). In more colorful language, computer security has been described as "programming Satan's computer" [6]: the implementor must assume that every weakness that can be exploited will be.

Security is a property of a complete system, and involves many different topics, both computer-related (hardware, systems, networks, programming, cryptography) and user-related (organizational and social policies and laws). In this talk, we discuss the impact of programming languages and static program analysis on the implementation of access control security policies, with special emphasis on smart cards. By lack of time, we will not discuss other relevant examples of programming language concepts being used for computer security, such as type systems for information flow [42,41,20,2,34,35] and validation of cryptographic protocols using process algebras and types [4,1,3].

2 Access Control

Access control is the most basic and widespread security policy. An access control policy provides yes/no answers to the question "is this principal (user, program, role, ...) allowed to perform this operation (read, write, creation, deletion, ...) on this resource (file, network connection, database record, ...)?". Access control is effective to ensure integrity, and can also ensure simple confidentiality properties.

2.1 Preventing Direct Access to a Resource

Access control is performed by fragments of code (OS kernel, reference monitor, privileged library) that check that access to a logical resource (file, network

P. Degano (Ed.): ESOP 2003, LNCS 2618, pp. 1–9, 2003.

connection) is allowed before performing the operation on the underlying low-level resource (disk or network controller). Of course, access control is moot if the program can bypass this code and operate directly on the low-level resource.

The traditional answer to this issue relies on hardware-enforced mechanisms: the low-level resources can only be accessed while the processor is in supervisor mode, and switching from user mode to supervisor mode can only be performed through specific entry points that branch to the access control code. On the user side, resources are represented indirectly by "handles", e.g. indices into kernel tables. Hardware memory management prevents user code from accessing kernel data directly.

This model, while effective, is not always suitable. Sometimes, user-mode programs must be further partitioned into relatively trusted (Web browser) and completely untrusted (Web applets). Switching between user and supervisor modes can be expensive. The required hardware support may not be present, e.g. in small embedded devices.

An alternate, language-based approach executes all code within the same memory space, without hardware protections, but relies on strong typing to restrict direct access to sensitive resources. These resources are directly represented by pointers, but strong typing prevents these pointers from being forged, e.g. by guessing their addresses. Thus, the typing discipline of the language can be used to enforce security invariants on the resources.[1]

As a trivial example, if a resource is not reachable from the initial memory roots of a piece of code, memory safety, also called garbage collection safety, ensures that this code can never access this resource. As a less trivial example, two standard type-based encapsulation techniques can be used to provide controlled access to a resource: procedural encapsulation and type abstraction [27].

- With procedural encapsulation, the resource is a free variable of a function closure, or a private field of an object, and only the closure or the object are given to the untrusted code. The latter, then, cannot fetch the resource pointers directly from the object or the closure (this would be ill-typed), and must call the function or a method of the object to operate on the resource; the code of the function or the method will then perform the required access checks before performing the operation.
- With type abstraction, the resource pointer itself can be given to the untrusted code, but its type is made abstract, preventing the code from operating directly on it; to use the resource, the code must call one of the operations provided in the signature of the abstract type, and this code will then perform access checks as described before.

As outlined above, strong typing can be exploited to enforce access control. The remaining question, then, is how to enforce a strong typing discipline during execution of (untrusted) code. A simple approach is to perform type checks dynamically, during program execution. This can be achieved in many ways: direct

---

[1] Strong typing is also effective at preventing other kinds of attacks such as buffer overflows that cause attacker-provided data to be executed as privileged code.

interpretation of the program source (if available); compilation of the source with insertion of run-time checks; bytecode interpretation of virtual machine code such as the JVM [28]; just-in-time compilation of said virtual machine code; and instrumentation of precompiled machine code with additional checks (software fault isolation) [43].

To reduce the run-time overhead of dynamic type checking, it is desirable to perform some of the type checks statically, during a program analysis pass prior to actual execution. Static typing of source code is common and well understood [8]. However, source for untrusted code is not always available. Moreover, bugs in the source-to-executable compiler could introduce type violations after type checking; in other terms, the compiler is part of the trusted computing base. These drawbacks can be avoided by performing static type-checking on lower-level, compiled code. A famous example is Java bytecode verification [18,28, 25], which performs static type-checking on JVM bytecode at dynamic loading time. Typed Assembly Language [31,30] goes several steps below virtual machine code: it statically type-checks assembly code for an actual microprocessor (the Intel $x86$ family), including many advanced idioms such as stack unwinding for exception handling.

Java bytecode verification and typed assembly language leave certain checks relevant to type safety to be performed at run-time: typically, array bound checks, or Java's downcasts. More advanced type systems based on dependent types were proposed to allow static verification of array bound checks (and more) [47,46,38,13]. Proof-carrying code [32] takes this approach to the extreme by re-placing static type checking with static proof checking in a general program logic: the provider of the code provides not only compiled code, but also a proof that it satisfies a certain security property; the user of the code, then, checks this proof to make sure that the code meets the property. The property typically includes type correctness and memory safety, but can also capture finer behavioral aspects of the code [33].

2.2   Implementing Access Control

The security policy implemented by access control checks is traditionally represented as an access control matrix, giving for each resource and each principal the allowed operations. This matrix is often represented as access control lists (each resource carries information on which principals can access it) or as capabilities (each principal carries a set of resources that it can access). The yes/no nature of access control matrices is sometimes too coarse: security automata [37] can be used instead to base access control decisions on the history of the program execution, e.g. to allow an applet to read local files or make network connections, but not both (to prevent information leaks).

Determining the principal that is about to perform a sensitive operation is often difficult. In particular, shared library code that performs operations on behalf of an untrusted user must have lower privileges than when performing operations on behalf of a trusted user. The Java security manager [17] uses stack inspection to address this problem: each method is associated with a principal, and the permissions granted are those of the least privileged principal appearing in the method call stack leading to the current operation. This model is sometimes too restrictive: an applet is typically allowed to draw text on the screen, but not to read files; yet, to draw text on behalf of the applet, the system may need to read fonts from files. Privilege amplification mechanisms are provided to address this need, whereas system code can assert a permission (e.g. read a file for the font loading code) regardless of whether its caller has it.

Access control checks are traditionally performed dynamically, during execution. The run-time overhead of these checks is generally tolerable, and can be further reduced by partial evaluation techniques allowing for instance inline expansion and specialization of security automata [15,12,40].

Still, it is desirable to perform static approximations of access control checks: to guide and validate optimizations such as removal of redundant checks, but also to help programmers determine whether their code works correctly under a given security policy. Jensen *et al.* [7] develop a static approximation of the Java stack inspection mechanism, where the (infinitely many) call stacks are abstracted as a finite automaton, and security properties described as temporal formulae are model-checked against this automaton. Pottier *et al.* [36] compose the security-passing interpretation of stack inspection (proposed in [45] as a dynamic implementation technique) with conventional type systems described in the $HM(X)$ framework to obtain type-based static security analyses. Finally, Walker [44] describes a type system for typed assembly language where the states of security automata are expressed within the types themselves, allowing fine static control of the program security behavior.

3   Application to Smart Card Programming

3.1   Smart Card Architectures

Smart cards are small, inexpensive embedded computers used as security tokens in several areas, such as credit cards and mobile phones. Traditional smart cards such as Eurocard-Mastercard-Visa credit cards behave very much like a small file system, with access control on directories and files, and determination of principals via PIN codes.

The newer Java Card architecture [10] offers a model closer to an applet-enabled Web browser, with several applications running in the same memory space, and post-issuance downloading of new applications. The applications are executed by a virtual machine that is a subset of the JVM. The security of this architecture relies heavily on the type safety of this JVM variant. For access control, the Java security manager based on stack inspection is replaced by a simpler "firewall" that associates owners to Java objects and prevents an application from accessing directly an object owned by another application. Inter-application communications are restricted to invocation of interface methods on objects explicitly declared as "shared".

Formal methods are being systematically applied to many aspects of the Java Card architecture [19]: formal specifications of the virtual machine, applet loading, the firewall, the APIs, and specific applications; and machine proofs of safety properties such as type safety and non-interference. As for program analyses, several approaches to on-card bytecode verification have been proposed [26,14]. Static analyses of firewall access control are described in [9]. Chugunov *et al.* [11] describe a more general framework for verifying safety properties of Java Card applets by model checking.

3.2 Hardware Attacks

The software-based security techniques presented in section 2 all assume that the programs execute on reliable, secured hardware: the best software access control will not prevent information leaks if the attacker can simply steal the hard disk containing the confidential data. In practice, hardware security is often ensured by putting the computers in secured premises (locked doors, armed guards).

For smart cards and similar embedded devices, this is not possible: the hardware is physically in the hands of the potential attackers. By construction, a smart card cannot be pulled apart as easily as a PC: smart card hardware is designed to be tamper proof to some extent. Yet, the small size and cost of a smart card does not allow extensive tamper proofing of the kind used for hardware security modules [39]. Thus, a determined attacker equipped with a good microelectronics laboratory can mount a variety of physical attacks on a smart card [23]:

– Non-intrusive observation: perform precise timings of operations; measure power consumption or electromagnetic emissions as a function of time.
– Intrusive observation: expose the chip and implant micro-electrodes on some data paths.
– Temporary perturbation: introduce "glitches" in the power supply or the external clock signal; "flash" the chip with high-energy particles.
– Permanent modification: destroy connections and transistors within the chip.

These attacks can defeat the security of the software in several ways. Power analysis can reveal the sequencing of instructions performed, thus reveal secret data such as the private keys in naive implementation of public-key cryptography [22]. Perturbations or modifications can prevent some instructions of the program from executing normally: for instance, a taken conditional branch can be skipped, thus deactivating a security check. Variables and registers can also be set to incorrect values, causing for instance a loop intended to send a communication buffer on the serial port to send a complete memory dump instead.

3.3 Software Countermeasures

The obvious countermeasure to these attacks is to harden the smart card hardware [24]. It is a little known fact that the programs running on smart cards can also be written in ways that complicate hardware attacks. This is surprising, because in general it is nearly impossible for a program to protect itself from execution on malicious hardware. (Some cryptographic techniques such as those described in [29] address this issue in the context of boolean circuits, but have not been demonstrated to be practical.)

The key to making smart card software more resistant is to notice that hardware attacks cannot change the behavior of the hardware arbitrarily. Permanent modifications are precise but irreversible, thus can be detected from within the program by running frequent self tests, and storing data in a redundant fashion (checksums). Temporary perturbations, on the other hand, are reversible but imprecise: they may cause all the memory to read as all zeroes or all ones for a few milliseconds, but cannot set a particular memory location to a particular value. Thus, their impact can be minimized by data redundancy, and also by control redundancy. For instance, a critical loop can be double-counted, with one counter that increases and another that decreases to zero; execution is aborted if the sum of the two counters is not the expected constant.

Finally, hardware attacks can be made much harder by program randomization. Randomizing data (as in the "blinding" technique for RSA [22]) renders information gained by power analysis meaningless. Randomizing control (e.g. calling independent subroutines in a random order, or choosing randomly between different implementations of the same function) makes it difficult to perform a perturbation at a given point in the program execution.

Software hardening techniques such as the ones outlined above are currently applied by hand on the source code, and often require assembly programming to get sufficient control on the execution. It is interesting to speculate how modern programming techniques could be used to alleviate this burden. The hardening code could possibly be separated from the main, algorithmic code using aspect-oriented programming [21]. Perhaps some of the hardening techniques are systematic enough to be performed transparently by a compiler, or by a virtual machine interpreter in the case of Java Card. Finally, reasoning about software hardening techniques could require a probabilistic semantics that reflects some of the time-precision characteristics of likely hardware attacks.

References

1. Martín Abadi. Secrecy by typing in security protocols. *Journal of the ACM*, 46(5):749–786, 1999.
2. Martín Abadi, Anindya Banerjee, Nevin Heintze, and Jon G. Riecke. A core calculus of dependency. In *26th symposium Principles of Programming Languages*, pages 147–160. ACM Press, 1999.
3. Martín Abadi and Bruno Blanchet. Secrecy types for asymmetric communication. In Furio Honsell and Marino Miculan, editors, *Proceedings of the 4th International Conference on Foundations of Software Science and Computation Structures*, volume 2030 of *Lecture Notes in Computer Science*, pages 25–41. Springer-Verlag, 2001.
4. Martín Abadi and Andrew D. Gordon. A calculus for cryptographic protocols: The Spi calculus. *Information and Computation*, 148(1):1–70, 1999.
5. Ross Anderson. *Security Engineering*. John Wiley & Sons, 2001.

6. Ross Anderson and Roger Needham. Programming Satan's computer. In *Computer Science Today: Recent Trends and Developments*, number 1000 in Lecture Notes in Computer Science, pages 426–441. Springer-Verlag, 1995.
7. Frédéric Besson, Thomas de Grenier de Latour, and Thomas Jensen. Secure calling contexts for stack inspection. In *Principles and Practice of Declarative Programming (PPDP 2002)*, pages 76–87. ACM Press, 2002.
8. Luca Cardelli. Type systems. In Allen B. Tucker, editor, *The Computer Science and Engineering Handbook*. CRC Press, 1997.
9. Denis Caromel, Ludovic Henrio, and Bernard Serpette. Context inference for static analysis of java card object sharing. In *Proceedings e-Smart 2001*, volume 2140 of *Lecture Notes in Computer Science*. Springer-Verlag, 2001.
10. Zhiqun Chen. *Java Card Technology for Smart Cards: Architecture and Programmer's Guide*. The Java Series. Addison-Wesley, 2000.
11. Gennady Chugunov, Lars Åke Fredlund, and Dilian Gurov. Model checking multi-applet Java Card applications. In *Smart Card Research and Advanced Applications Conference (CARDIS'02)*, 2002.
12. Thomas Colcombet and Pascal Fradet. Enforcing trace properties by program transformation. In *27th symposium Principles of Programming Languages*, pages 54–66. ACM Press, 2000.
13. Karl Crary and Joseph C. Vanderwaart. An expressive, scalable type theory for certified code. In *International Conference on Functional Programming 2002*. ACM Press, 2002.
14. Damien Deville and Gilles Grimaud. Building an "impossible" verifier on a Java Card. In *USENIX Workshop on Industrial Experiences with Systems Software (WIESS'02)*, 2002.
15. U. Erlingsson and Fred B. Schneider. IRM enforcement of Java stack inspection. In *Symposium on Security and Privacy*. IEEE Computer Society Press, 2000.
16. Morrie Gasser. *Building a secure computer system*. Van Nostrand Reinhold Co., 1988.
17. Li Gong. *Inside Java 2 platform security: architecture, API design, and implementation*. The Java Series. Addison-Wesley, 1999.
18. James A. Gosling. Java intermediate bytecodes. In *Proc. ACM SIGPLAN Workshop on Intermediate Representations*, pages 111–118. ACM, 1995.
19. Pieter H. Hartel and Luc A. V. Moreau. Formalizing the safety of Java, the Java virtual machine and Java Card. *ACM Computing Surveys*, 33(4):517–558, 2001.
20. Nevin Heintze and Jon G. Riecke. The SLam calculus: programming with secrecy and integrity. In *25th symposium Principles of Programming Languages*, pages 365–377. ACM Press, 1998.
21. Gregor Kiczales, John Lamping, Anurag Mendhekar, Chris Maeda, Cristina Videira Lopes, Jean-Marc Loingtier, and John Irwin. Aspect-oriented programming. In *European Conference on Object-Oriented Programming (ECOOP'97)*, number 1241 in Lecture Notes in Computer Science. Springer-Verlag, 1997.
22. Paul C. Kocher. Timing attacks on implementations of Diffie-Hellman, RSA, DSS, and other systems. In *Proceedings Crypto '96*, number 1109 in Lecture Notes in Computer Science, pages 104–113. Springer-Verlag, 1996.
23. Markus Kuhn. Tamper resistance - a cautionary note. In *USENIX Workshop on Electronic Commerce proceedings*, pages 1–11, 1996.
24. Markus Kuhn. Design principles for tamper-resistant smartcard processors. In *USENIX Workshop on Smartcard Technology proceedings*, 1999.

25. Xavier Leroy. Java bytecode verification: an overview. In G. Berry, H. Comon, and A. Finkel, editors, *Computer Aided Verification, CAV 2001*, volume 2102 of *Lecture Notes in Computer Science*, pages 265–285. Springer-Verlag, 2001.

26. Xavier Leroy. Bytecode verification for Java smart card. *Software Practice & Experience*, 32:319–340, 2002.

27. Xavier Leroy and François Rouaix. Security properties of typed applets. In J. Vitek and C. Jensen, editors, *Secure Internet Programming – Security issues for Mobile and Distributed Objects*, volume 1603 of *Lecture Notes in Computer Science*, pages 147–182. Springer-Verlag, 1999.

28. Tim Lindholm and Frank Yellin. *The Java Virtual Machine Specification*. The Java Series. Addison-Wesley, 1999. Second edition.

29. Sergio Loureiro, Laurent Bussard, and Yves Roudier. Extending tamper-proof hardware security to untrusted execution environments. In *USENIX Smart Card Research and Advanced Application Conference (CARDIS'02)*, 2002.

30. Greg Morrisett, Karl Crary, Neal Glew, and David Walker. Stack-based typed assembly language. *Journal of Functional Programming*, 12(1):43–88, 2002.

31. Greg Morrisett, David Walker, Karl Crary, and Neal Glew. From System F to typed assembly language. *ACM Transactions on Programming Languages and Systems*, 21(3):528–569, 1999.

32. George C. Necula. Proof-carrying code. In *24th symposium Principles of Programming Languages*, pages 106–119. ACM Press, 1997.

33. George C. Necula and Peter Lee. Safe, untrusted agents using proof-carrying code. In Giovanni Vigna, editor, *Mobile Agents and Security*, volume 1419 of *Lecture Notes in Computer Science*, pages 61–91. Springer-Verlag, 1997.

34. François Pottier and Sylvain Conchon. Information flow inference for free. In *International Conference on Functional Programming 2000*, pages 46–57. ACM Press, 2000.

35. François Pottier and Vincent Simonet. Information flow inference for ML. In *29th symposium Principles of Programming Languages*, pages 319–330. ACM Press, 2002.

36. François Pottier, Christian Skalka, and Scott Smith. A systematic approach to static access control. In David Sands, editor, *Proceedings of the 10th European Symposium on Programming (ESOP'01)*, volume 2028 of *Lecture Notes in Computer Science*, pages 30–45. Springer-Verlag, 2001.

37. Fred B. Schneider. Enforceable security policies. *ACM Transactions on Information and System Security*, 2(4), 2000.

38. Zhong Shao, Bratin Saha, Valery Trifonov, and Nikolaos Papaspyrou. A type system for certified binaries. In *29th symposium Principles of Programming Languages*, pages 217–232. ACM Press, 2002.

39. Sean W. Smith and Steve Weingart. Building a high-performance, programmable secure coprocessor. Technical Report RC 21102, IBM Research, 1998.

40. Peter Thiemann. Enforcing security properties by type specialization. In *European Symposium on Programming 2001*, volume 2028 of *Lecture Notes in Computer Science*. Springer-Verlag, 2001.

41. Dennis Volpano and Geoffrey Smith. A type-based approach to program security. In *Proceedings of TAPSOFT'97, Colloquium on Formal Approaches in Software Engineering*, volume 1214 of *Lecture Notes in Computer Science*, pages 607–621. Springer-Verlag, 1997.

42. Dennis Volpano, Geoffrey Smith, and Cynthia Irvine. A sound type system for secure flow analysis. *Journal of Computer Security*, 4(3):1–21, 1996.

43. Robert Wahbe, Steven Lucco, Thomas E. Anderson, and Susan L. Graham. Efficient software-based fault isolation. *ACM SIGOPS Operating Systems Review*, 27(5):203–216, 1993.
44. David Walker. A type system for expressive security policies. In *27th symposium Principles of Programming Languages*, pages 254–267. ACM Press, 2000.
45. Dan S. Wallach, Edward W. Felten, and Andrew W. Appel. The security architecture formerly known as stack inspection: A security mechanism for language-based systems. *ACM Transactions on Software Engineering and Methodology*, 9(4), 2000.
46. Hongwei Xi and Robert Harper. A dependently typed assembly language. In *International Conference on Functional Programming '01*, pages 169–180. ACM Press, 2001.
47. Hongwei Xi and Frank Pfenning. Eliminating array bound checking through dependent types. In *Programming Language Design and Implementation 1998*, pages 249–257. ACM Press, 1998.

What Makes a Cryptographic Protocol Secure? The Evolution of Requirements Specification in Formal Cryptographic Protocol Analysis

Catherine Meadows

Naval Research Laboratory
Center for High Assurance Computer Systems
Washington, DC 20375
meadows@itd.nrl.navy.mil

Abstract. Much attention has been paid to the design of languages for the specification of cryptographic protocols. However, the ability to specify their desired behavior correctly is also important; indeed many perceived protocol flaws arise out of a misunderstanding of the protocol's requirements. In this talk we give a brief survey of the history of requirements specification in formal analysis of cryptographic protocols. We outline the main approaches and describe some of the open issues.

1   Introduction

It has often been pointed out, that, although it is difficult to get cryptographic protocols right, what is really difficult is not the design of the protocol itself, but of the requirements. Many problems with security protocols arise, not because the protocol as designed did not satisfy its requirements, but because the requirements were not well understood in the first place.

Not surprisingly, the realization of this fact has lead to a considerable amount of research in security requirements for cryptographic protocols. However, most of this literature is scattered, and unlike the topic of cryptographic protocol analysis in general, there is little existing survey work providing roadmaps to readers interested in learning more about the topic. In this paper we attempt to remedy this deficiency by providing a brief history and survey of the work that has been done in this area, and outlining what we consider to be some of the open problems.

Any scheme for expressing requirements should satisfy three properties:

1. It should be expressive enough to specify properties of interest.
2. It should be unambiguous, and preferably compatible with with some system for formal analysis.
3. It should be easy to read and write.

It will helpful to keep these three properties in mind as we proceed through our survey.

P. Degano (Ed.): ESOP 2003, LNCS 2618, pp. 10–21, 2003.

The paper is organized as follows. We begin in the next section by describing some of the early approaches to specifying cryptographic protocol requirements, including that of Burrows, Abadi, and Needham. In the third section, we describe some of the main current approaches to requirements in terms of a spectrum from extensional to intensional requirements. In the fourth section and fifth sections, we discuss two emerging areas of research: graphical languages for specifying cryptographc protocol requirements, and the expression of quantitative requirements. In the final section, we sum up what we believe to be some of the open problems, and conclude the paper.

2   Early Work in Cryptographic Protocol Requirements

Most of the existing approaches to applying formal methods to cryptographic protocol analysis stem ultimately from that of Dolev and Yao [9], who developed for the first formalization of the intruder model that is commonly used today. However, since Dolev and Yao's work and its immediate successors was mainly focussed on theoretical results about the complexity of cryptographic protocol analysis, only one type of requirement was considered, and that was the simplest: that some term or set of terms designated as secret should not be learned by the intruder. Some of the earlier work on automated cryptographic protocol analysis, such as the first versions of the Interrogator [24], also restricted itself to this limited definition of secrecy. Others, such as the earlier versions of the NRL Protocol Analyzer[20], allowed the user to specify security in terms of the unreachability of insecure states, in which it was possible to specify such a state in terms of words known by the intruder and the values of local state variables of the principles. However, the user was not given any further assistance in constructing requirments.

Probably the first formal cryptographic protocol analysis system to provide a real mechanism for constructing formal requirments was the belief logic of Burrows, Abadi, and Needham [5].

BAN logic does not address secrecy at all. Rather it confines itself to questions of authentication. Questions that BAN logic can be used to decide have to do with beliefs the participating principals could derive about origin and use of information such as:

1. Where does the information come from?
2. What is the information intended for?
3. Is the information new, or is it a replay?
4. Who else has these beliefs about the information?

One uses BAN logic by attempting to see which of these beliefs can be derived from an idealization of the protocol. The BAN logic does not dictate which beliefs a protocol should be able to satisfy; rather it is up to the protocol analyst to decide what beliefs a protocol should guarantee, and to determine it those beliefs can be derived from the protocol. Thus, one might require that Alice believe that K is a good key for communicating for Bob, and that Bob believe that K is a good key for communicating with Alice, but one might or might not want to require that Alice believe that Bob believes that K is a good key for communicating with Alice, and vice versa. Thus BAN logic provides what it probably the first formal system for specifying cryptographic protocol requirements.

3   Safety Requirements for Cryptographic Protocols: Secrecy and Correspondence

In the early to mid-90's the approach to cryptographic protocol verification tended towards the application of general-purpose tools such as model-checkers and theorem provers. With this came the need to develop means for specifying the properties one was attempting to prove. Since, in general, researchers were now reasoning directly about messages passed in a protocol, rather than about beliefs that were developed as a result of receiving those messages, it now made sense to develop requirements in terms of messages sent and received rather than beliefs derived.

As is the case for requirements in general, requirements for cryptographic protocols tend to fall into two categories, extensional and intensional. Extensional systems provide a small set of generic requirements that can be defined independently of the details of any particular protocol. Intensional systems provide languages and techniques that can be used to specify requirements for specific protocols in terms of the protocols themselves. This concept was first discussed in detail in the context of cryptographic protocols by Roscoe in [27]. He noted that the earlier work in cryptographic protocol requirements, such as BAN, leaned to the extensional side, and he showed how one might specify intensional protocol requirements in CSP.

Requirements for cryptographic protocols also fall into two classes that are related to the properties that such protocols are intended to enforce: secrecy and correspondence. Secrecy requirements describe who should have access to data. Correspondence requirements describe dependencies between events that occur in a protocol, and are usually used to express authentication properties. These two types of requirements later turned out to be more closely related than one might think (both Syverson and Meadows [32] and Schneider [28] define secrecy requirements as a type of correspondence requirement), but for the moment we shall treat them as separate.

Of course, not all requirements can be characterized in terms of secrecy and correspondence. In particular, they are both safety properties, so any non-safety requirements (such as fairness and its relatives, which are relevant for many electronic commerce protocols) will not fall into either of these two categories. However, secrecy and correspondence cover most requirements relevant to authentication and key exchange, and thus make a good starting point.

At first, correspondence requirements appeared to be the most subtle and complex; thus the earlier work tended to concentrate on these. Moreover, the emphasis was on extensional requirements and the ability to characterize a general notion of correspondence in a single definition. Probably the first work in this area was that of Bird et al [4]. In the introduction to their paper, they describe an error-free history of a protocol runs between two prinicpals A and B to be one in which all executions viewed by both parties match exactly one-to-one. This is idea is refined by Diffie, van Oorschot and Wiener in [8] to the idea of *matching protocol runs*, which says that at the time Alice completes a protocol the other party's record of the run matches Alice's. This notion was further refined and formalized by Bellare and Rogaway in [3] to the notion of *matching conversations*, which developed the idea in terms of a complexity-theoretic framework.

Such general of notions of correspondence can be very useful, but they do have a drawback. They can be used to determine whether or not information was distributed correctly, but they can not be used to determine whether or not all information that should have been authenticated was included in the run.

To see what we mean, we consider the attack found by Lowe [18] on the Station-to-Station protocol of [8]. The protocol is defined as follows:

1. $A \to B \ : \ x^{N_A}$
2. $B \to A \ : \ x^{N_B}, E_K(S_B(x^{N_A}, x^{N_B}))$
   where K is the Diffie-Hellman key generated by A and B.
3. $A \to B \ : \ , E_K(S_A(x^{N_B}, x^{N_A}))$

Lowe's attack runs as follows:

1. $A \to B \ : \ x^{N_A}$
   An intruder I intercepts this message and forwards it to B, as if it came from C.
2. $B \to I_C \ : \ x^{N_B}, E_K(S_B(x^{N_B}, x^{N_B}))$
   The intruder forwards this message to A.

Thus, at the end of A's run, A believes that it shares a key with B. B, however, thinks that C is trying to establish a connection with it, and it will reject A's final message when it receives it, because it is expecting confirmation from C, not A. On the other hand, the protocol does satisfy the matching protocol runs definition of security, since A's picture of the authenticated portions of the messages is the same as B's. Indeed, this is the protocol used to illustrate the concept by Diffie, van Oorschot, and Wiener in [8].

Lowe's attack, of course, does not mean the Station-to-Station protocol is insecure. (Indeed, this very feature of that protocol is seen as a desirable property in the latest version of IKEv2, the proposed replacement to the Internet Key Exchange protocol [17]). All it does is show that, if the name of the intended recipient is not included in the responder's message, a definition of security that is specified in terms of conditions on correspondence between messages will not catch lack of agreement on information that is never sent.

Lowe's solution to this problem in [18] was to strengthen the matching protocol runs requirement to include the condition that when A completes a protocol run with B, then not only should the two protocol runs match, but B should believe that he has been running the protocol with A. In a later paper, [19],

he developed this idea further, developing a hierarchy of authentication requirements which gave conditions of varying degrees of strictness on the conclusions
a principal A could draw about B's view of the protocol after completing the
protocol with B. These were then formalized using the process algebra CSP.

The least restrictive requirement Lowe gave was liveness, which simply requires that, when A completes a run of the protocol, apparently with B, then
B has also been running the protocol. Moving further up the hierarchy, we require A and B to agree on messages sent as well as identities (this requirement
correspondes roughly to matching protocol runs), to agree on the roles they are
playing, to agree on the values of specific data items, and so forth.

We see now that we are moving away from extensional requirements that can
be specified independently of the protocol, and more to intensional requirements.
If principals need to agree on specific data items, we need to specify what these
data items are, and where they occur in the protocol. The next step would be
to specify the conditions on events that occur in protocols. Indeed, it should
be possible to specify the types of requirements we are interested in using the
temporal logics that are generally used to provide correctness specifications for
model checkers.

This is the sort of reasoning that lay behind Syverson and Meadows' development of a requirements language for the NRL Protocol Analyzer [32], which
eventually became known as the NRL Protocol Analyzer Temporal Requirements Language (NPATRL). The idea is to develop a simple temporal language
that can be used to specify the type of requirements that are commonly used
in authentication and key distribution protocols. The atomic components of the
language correspond to events in the protocol (e.g. the sending and receiving
of messages, or the intruder's learning a term). Besides the usual logical connectives, it contains only one temporal operator, $\diamondsuit$, or "happened previously."
The use of this single logical operator reflects the fact that most correspondence
requirements can be expressed in terms of events that must have or must have
not occurred before some other events.

Although NPATRL is a very simple language, we have found it useful for
specifying some widely varying types of cryptographic protocols. These include
key distribution and key agreement protocols [30,31], complex electronic commerce protocols such as SET [22], and, most recently, group key distribution
protocols [23].

One interesting result of our experience is that we have found NPATRL increasingly useful for specifying complex secrecy requirements as well as complex
authentication requirements. Early requirements for secrecy simply designated
some information, such as keys, as secret, and all that needed to be guaranteed was that these keys would not be available to an intruder. However, more
recently, requirements such as perfect forward secrecy put other conditions on
an intruder learning a term. Perfect forward secrecy requires that, if a master
key is compromised, then an intruder can only learn a session key after the
compromise, not before. Such a requirement is straightfoward to specify using a
temporal language.

Of course, temporal logics are not necessary in order to specify these types of requirements. Other formalisms will work as well. For example, Schneider [28] defines authentication in terms of the messages that must precede a given message, and secrecy in terms of another correspondence requirement, that the intruder should not learn data unless that data was explicitly sent to the intruder. Both of these are formalized in CSP.

Another approach to requirements, taken by Focardi et al. [12], allows one to specify requirements of varying degree of generality. They make use of notions derived from noninterference. Their notion of correctness, Generalized Nondeducibility on Composition, or $GNDC$, is defined as follows.

We let P be a process representing a cryptographic protocol operating in the absence of an intruder. Let $(P||X)$ denote the composition of P with an intruder X. Let α denote a function from processes to processes where $\alpha(P)$ is a process describing the "correct" behavior of P. Let $\approx$ denote a preorder. Let C denote the set of channels between honest principals, and let $Q\,C$ denote the restriction of a process Q to C. Then a process satisfies $GNDC_{\approx}^{\alpha}$, if, for all intruders X

$$(P||X)\backslash C \approx \alpha(P)$$

In the case of that α is the identity function and $\sim$ is trace equivalence, the property becomes NDC, or Nondeducibility on Composition, which requires that the traces produced by the process in composition with an intruder be the same as the traces produced by the process in the absence of the intruder. This can be thought of as an information-flow property in which the intruder and P play the apart of High and Low, respectively, corresponding to the standard multilevel application of noninterference for multilevel security [14]. NDC, since it requires that a process behave in the presence of an intruder exactly at it would behave in the absence, is more stringent than any of the other requirements that have been discussed in this section. As a matter of fact, we can consider it the most stringent definition possible, closely akin to the fail-stop definition of protocol security of Gong and Syverson[13]. Moreover, $GNDC$ provides a framework that allows one to specify less restrictive requirements such as the various forms of correspondence discussed earlier, and the types of requirements that would be defined in a temporal language such as NPATRL. Thus $GNDC$ can be thought of as providing a general framework for requirements, including requirements that go beyond the usual notions of correspondence, such as liveness.

Another technique that deserves mention is the notion of using type theory to specify security requirements and evaluate the correctness of protocols [1, 15]. Here components making up a protocol, such as data, channels, etc. are assigned different types, such as secret or public. Rules are also developed for deriving types from the results of applying operations, such as encryption, on data. Security violations can be defined in terms of typing violations, such as a piece of data type public appearing on a channel of type public. Most of this work has been applied to the type-checking of secrecy properties, but Gordon and Jeffrey [15,16] have developed ways of applying it to correspondence properties, specifically one-to-one (each event of a certain type should be preceded by one and only one event of a certain other type) and one-to-many (each event of a certain type should be preceded by at least one event of a certain type). Since the types are supplied as part of the protocol specification, this application of type theory gives a nice way of incorporating a requirements specification as an annotation on the protocol.

4   Graphical Requirements Languages

Languages and frameworks such as NPATRL and $GNDC$ allow us increasing flexibility and expressiveness for specifying requirements. But, the ability to specify more complex and subtle requirements also has a cost; the requirements become more difficult to comprehend and write. In this section we discuss two graphical approaches to increasing the ease of handling such specifications that make use of some of the common features of cryptographic protocols and their requirements.

The first of these is known as *Strand Space Pictures* [10]. Strand spaces [11] are a well-known and popular model for cryptographic protocol analysis, in which the actions of principals are modeled in terms of graphs. A *strand* represents a principal executing a role in a protocol. The sending and receiving of messages is represented by positive and negative nodes. Nodes that represent one event immediately preceding another on a strand are connected by double arrows. A *bundle* is a collection of strands, in which positive send nodes can be connected to negative receive nodes via a single arrow if the message sent matches the message received. This model facilitates the graphical representation of protocols, and [10] actually describes a number of ways in which the graphical features of strand spaces could be used, but the one of most interest to us is the way in which they can be used to represent requirements. Using strand space representation of protocols, it is possible to represent correspondence requirements in terms of relative placement of strands. Thus, if we want to specify a correspondence requirement which requires that if certain messages are accepted, then other messages were sent previously, we can represent sending and receipt of the messages we are interested in by portions of strands, and we can use the placement of the strands (so that earlier nodes appear above later ones) to indicate which events we want to occur before others.

The strand space pictures methodology, was never, as far as we know, developed into a full-fledged procedure with well-defined ways for representing major classes of requirements. However, in [10] the authors give several examples which show how some standard requirements such as freshness or agreement properties could be represented in this framework.

It is also possible to use strand spaces to provide a very convenient way of expressing a limited type of correspondence. Strands can be parameterized by the name of the principal executing the strand and the data it sends and receives. Thus, in the Station-to-Station protocol the initiator's strand would be parameterized by Init$[A, B, X, Y, K]$, while the responder's would be parameterized by Resp$[B, A, X, Y, K]$, where X and Y are the initiator's and responder's Diffie-Hellman components, respectively, and K is the key derived from the Diffie-Hellman exchange. Earlier, we described how Lowe showed that after A completed the Station-to-Station protocol, A and B would agree on B's identity and on the Diffie-Hellman components and key, but not A's identity. We could express that fact as a requirement that, after an initiator A finishes executing the protocol, apparently with a responder B, if the initiator's strand is $Init[A, B, X, Y, K]$, then the responder's strand is $Resp[*, A, X, Y, K]$, where * denotes a wild card. Unlike the strand space pictures, this notation cannot express conditions on the relative times of occurrence of events from two different strands. However, since many requirements have to do not so much with agreement on placement of events as with agreement on data such as keys, this notation has been useful for in a number of different cases. It would be interesting to see how far it could be extended and still retain its compactness and readability.

A somewhat different approach has been taken by Cervesato and Meadows [7] in the development of a graphical representation of the NPATRL language. This representation was based on the fact that queries in the NRL Protocol Analyzer, for which NPATRL was designed, are couched in terms of events that should or should not precede some specified event. Such a way of formatting queries has an obvious connection to fault trees. A fault tree is a graphical means of representing failure modes in safety-critical systems. The root of the tree represents the failure with which the system designer is concerned, and the branches represent the conditions under which the fault can occur. The main difference between NPA queries and fault trees is that in NPA queries the relationship is one of precedence, while in fault trees it is one of causality. Otherwise the structure is very similar. Moreover, the graphical representation makes it easier to understand the relationships between the various events. For this reason, we found it very helpful, in particular, to represent the GDOI requirements, especially the more complex ones, in terms of fault trees. In [7] a fault tree semantics for the subset of NPATRL requirements accepted by the NPA is developed, and some sample requirements are shown.

5   Quantitative and Probabilistic Requirements

So far, with few exceptions, the requirements we have looked at have dealt with safety requirements for discrete systems. This fits well when we want to analyze authentication and key distribution protocols that follow the Dolev-Yao model, where the cryptosystem is a black box, and principals communicate via a medium controlled by a hostile intruder who can read, alter, and intercept all traffic. But, since the correctness of a protocol depends on the correctness of the cryptoalgorithm that uses as well as the way it uses those algorithms, it would be useful to have correctness criteria that took the properties of the cryptoalgorithms into account.

Prior to and concurrent with the explosion of formal methods approaches to cryptographic protocol analysis, there has been a parallel effort in developing correctness criteria for cryptoalgorithms and cryptographic protocols based on complexity-theoretic approaches. Indeed, the work of Bellare and Rogaway cited earlier was developed in such a context. What has been lacking however, has been a means of integrating such a complexity-theoretic approach with the logical systems that we have been considering in this paper. However, some work in this area is beginning to appear, such as the work of Abadi and Rogaway [2], which considers a complexity-theory based model as a semantics for a logical system, although it restricts itself to secrecy requirements, and the work of Mitchell et al [25], which develops a notion of bisimulation that takes into account complexity-theoretic and probabilistic considerations.

The use of cryptography is not the only place where quantitative requirements become relevant. For example, many anonymity protocols, are intended to provide a statistical notion of security. An intruder may have a nontrivial chance of guessing the identity of a sender or receiver of traffic, but we do not want that chance to exceed a certain threshold. Protocols intended to protect against denial of service attacks may need to limit the the amount of resources expended by a responder in the early steps of the protocol. Recently, researchers have begun to investigate ways of applying formal methods to the analysis of protocols that must satisfy quantitative requirements. Examples include the work of Meadows on a model for the analysis of protocols resistance to denial of service [21] where requirements are specified in terms of a comparison between resources expended by a responder versus resources expended by an initiator; the work of Buttyán and Hubaux [6] on rational exchange protocols, in which a protocol is modeled as a game in which all principals are assigned payoffs, and an exchange protocol is deemed rational if the strategies available to all participants form a Nash equilibrium; and the work of Shmatikov on anonymity protocols and contract signing, in which the protocols and their requirements are modeled in terms of Markov chains [29,26], making them amenable to analysis by probabilistic model checkers.

6   Conclusion

We have given a brief survey of research in expressing cryptographic protocol requirements. We believe that it this point we have a good handle on the specification of the standard secrecy and correspondence requirements of security protocols. It appears possible to derive techniques that are compatible with just about any type of formal system, and we have a vast range of requirement specification styles, from one end of the extensional-intensional spectrum to the other.

There are of course a number of areas in which work on cryptographic protocol requirements needs to be extended. One is in making the requirements language user-friendly. Security protocols, and thus their requirements, can be complex; even more so when one must consider operation in partial failure modes such as compromise of temporary session keys. Thus it makes sense to concentrate on ways of making requirements languages easier to use, even when the requirements are complex. In this paper we discussed some of the work on graphic requirements languages that attempts to address this problem.

Another area in which work is just starting is in extending cryptographic requirements specifications beyond secrecy and correspondence. These would apply to protocols whose goals go beyond those of key distribution and authentication that have traditionally been handled in this area. One area of particular interest here is quantitative requirements. We have pointed out some areas in which the ability to understand a protocol's behavior from a quantitative point of view appears to be crucial. In this case, not only requirements need to be developed, but formal models for specifying the protocols that must satisfy the requirements. We have described some of the work in this area as well.

There are some other areas which could also use more exploring. For example, many electronic commerce protocols must satisfy various types of non-safety requirements. Is it possible to develop ways of characterizing and specifying these requirements in ways that are particularly relevant to security protocols, as has been done for the safety properties of secrecy and correspondence? Another area of research has to do with interoperability. Increasingly, many protocols will rely upon other protocols to supply some of their security services. What is the best way to specify services needed by one protocol in terms of requirements upon another? We hope to see research in these and other emerging areas in the near future.

References

1. M. Abadi. Secrecy by typing in security protocols. *Journal of the ACM*, 46(5):749–786, September 1999.
2. M. Abadi and P. Rogaway. Reconciling two views of cryptography (the computational soundness of formal encryption). *Journal of Cryptology*, to appear.
3. M. Bellare and P. Rogaway. Entity authentication and key distribution. In *Advances in Cryptology – CRYPTO '93*. Springer-Verlag, 1993.
4. R. Bird, I. Gopal, A. Herzberg, P. Janson, S. Kutten, R. Molva, and M. Yung. Systematic design of two-party authentication protocols. In *Advances in Cryptology – Proceedings of CRYPTO 91*. Springer-Verlag, 1991.
5. Michael Burrows, Martín Abadi, and Roger Needham. A Logic of Authentication. *ACM Transactions in Computer Systems*, 8(1):18–36, February 1990.
6. L. Buttyán and J.-P. Hubaux. Rational exchange – a formal model based on game theory. In *2nd International Workshop on Electronic Commerce (WELCOM'01)*, 16–17 November 2001.
7. I. Cervesato and C. Meadows. A fault-tree representation of NPATRL security requirements. submitted for publication, 2003.
8. Whitfield Diffie, Paul C. van Oorschot, and Michael J. Wiener. Authentication and Authenticated Key Exchanges. *Designs, Codes, and Cryptography*, 2:107–125, 1992.
9. D. Dolev and A. Yao. On the Security of Public Key Protocols. *IEEE Transactions on Information Theory*, 29(2):198–208, March 1983.
10. F. J. Thayer Fábrega, J. Herzog, and J. Guttman. Strand space pictures. In *Proceedings of the Workshop on Formal Methods and Security Protocols*, 1998. available at http://www.cs.bell-labs.com/who/nch/fmsp/program.html.

11. F. Javier Thayer Fábrega, Jonathan C. Herzog, and Joshua D. Guttman. Strand spaces: Why is a security protocol correct? In *Proceedings of the 1998 IEEE Symposium on Security and Privacy*, pages 160–171. IEEE Computer Society Press, May 1998.

12. R. Focardi, R. Gorrieri, and F. Martinelli. Non interference for the analysis of cryptographic protocols. In U. Montanari, editor, *27th International Colloquium on Automata, Languages and Programming (ICALP'00)*. Springer Verlag: LNCS 1583, July 2000.

13. Li Gong and Paul Syverson. Fail-stop protocols: An approach to designing secure protocols. In R. K. Iyer, M. Morganti, Fuchs W. K, and V. Gligor, editors, *Dependable Computing for Critical Applications 5*, pages 79–100. IEEE Computer Society, 1998.

14. J. Goquen and J. Meseguer. Security policy and security models. In *Proceedings of the 1982 Symposium on Security and Privacy*, pages 11–20. IEEE Computer Society Press, 1982.

15. A. Gordon and A. Jeffrey. Authenticity by typing in security protocols. In *Proceedings of the 14th IEEE Computer Security Foundations Workshop*. IEEE Computer Society Press, June 2001.

16. A. Gordon and A. Jeffrey. Typing one-to-one and one-to-many correspondences in security protocols. In *International Software Security Symposium (ISSS 2002)*. Springer LNCS, 2003.

17. Paul Hoffman. Features of proposed successors to IKE. Internet Draft draft-ietf-ipsec-soi-features-01.txt, May 31 2002. available at `http://ietf.org/internet-drafts/draft-ietf-ipsec-soi-features-01.txt`.

18. G. Lowe. Some new attacks on security protocols. In *Proceedings of the 9th IEEE Computer Security Foundations Workshop*, pages 162–169. IEEE Computer Society Press, 1996.

19. G. Lowe. A hierarchy of authentication specifications. In *Proceedings of the 10th IEEE Computer Security Foundations Workshop*, pages 31–43. IEEE Computer Society Press, 1997.

20. C. Meadows. Applying Formal Methods to the Analysis of a Key Management Protocol. *Journal of Computer Security*, 1:5–53, 1992.

21. C. Meadows. A cost-based framework for analysis of denial of service in networks. *Journal of Computer Security*, 2001.

22. C. Meadows and P. Syverson. A formal specification of requirements for payment in the SET protocol. In *Proceedings of Financial Cryptography '98*. Springer-Verlag LLNCS, 1998.

23. C. Meadows, P. Syverson, and I. Cervesato. Formalizing GDOI group key management requirements in NPATRL. In *Proceedings of the ACM Conference on Computer and Communications Security*. ACM, November 2001.

24. J. K. Millen, S. C. Clark, and S. B. Freedman. The Interrogator: Protocol Security Analysis. *IEEE Transactions on Software Engineering*, SE-13(2), 1987.

25. J.C. Mitchell, A. Ramanathan, A. Scedrov, and V. Teague. A probabilistic polynomial-time calculus for analysis of cryptographic protocols (preliminary report). *Electronic Notes in Theoretical Computer Science*, 45, 2001.

26. G. Norman and V. Shmatikov. Analysis of probabilistic contract signing. In *BCS-FACS Formal Aspects of Security (FASec '02)*, 2002.

27. A. W. Roscoe. Intensional specification of security protocols. In *Proceedings of the 9th IEEE Computer Security Foundations Workshop*, pages 28–38. IEEE Computer Society Press, June 10–12 1996.

28. S. Schneider. Security properties and CSP. In *IEEE Computer Society Symposium on Security and Privacy*. IEEE Computer Society Press, 1996.
29. V. Shmatikov. Probabilistic analysis of anonymity. In *Proceedings of the 15th Computer Security Foundations Workshop*. IEEE Computer Society Press, June 2002.
30. P. Syverson and C. Meadows. Formal requirements for key distribution protocols. In *Proceedings of Eurocrypt '94*. Springer-Verlag, 1994.
31. P. Syverson and C. Meadows. A formal language for cryptographic protocol requirements. *Designs, Codes, and Cryptography*, 7(1/2):27–59, 1996.
32. Paul Syverson and Catherine Meadows. A Logical Language for Specifying Cryptographic Protocol Requirements. In *Proceedings of the 1993 IEEE Computer Society Symposium on Research in Security and Privacy*, pages 165–177. IEEE Computer Society Press, Los Alamitos, California, 1993.

A Tail-Recursive Semantics for Stack Inspections

John Clements and Matthias Felleisen

Northeastern University
Boston, Massachusetts

Abstract. Security folklore holds that a security mechanism based on stack inspection is incompatible with a global tail call optimization policy. An implementation of such a language may have to allocate memory for a source-code tail call, and a program that uses only tail calls (and no other memory-allocating construct) may nevertheless exhaust the available memory. In this paper, we prove this widely held belief wrong. We exhibit an abstract machine for a language with security stack inspection whose space consumption function is equivalent to that of the canonical tail call optimizing abstract machine. Our machine is surprisingly simple and suggests that tail-calls are as easy to implement in a security setting as they are in a conventional one.

1 Stacks, Security, and Tail Calls

Over the last ten years, programming language implementors have spent significant effort on security issues. This effort takes many forms; one is the implementation of a strategy known as stack inspection [17]. It starts from the premise that trusted components may authorize potentially insecure actions for the dynamic extent of some 'grant' expression, provided that all intermediate calls are made by and to trusted code.

In its conventional implementation, stack inspection is incompatible with a traditional language semantics, because it clashes with the well-established idea of modeling function calls with a β or β_v reduction [13]. A β reduction replaces a function's application with the body of that function, with the function's parameters replaced by the application's arguments. In a language with stack inspection, a β or β_v reduction disposes of information that is necessary to evaluate the security primitives.

For this reason, Fournet and Gordon [7] model function calls with a nonstandard β-reduction. To be more precise, β does not hold as an equation for source terms. Abstraction bodies are wrapped with context-building primitives. Unfortunately, this formalization prohibits a transformation of this semantics into a tail-call optimizing (TCO) implementation. Fournet and Gordon recognize this fact and state that "[S]tack inspection profoundly affects the semantics of all programs. In particular, it invalidates [. . .] tail call optimizations." [7]

This understanding of the stack inspection protocol also pervades the implementation of existing run-time systems. The Java design team, for example, chose not to provide a TCO implementation in part because of the perceived

P. Degano (Ed.): ESOP 2003, LNCS 2618, pp. 22–37, 2003.
© Springer-Verlag Berlin Heidelberg 2003

incompatibility between tail call optimizations and stack inspection.[1] The .NET effort at Microsoft provides a runtime system that is properly TCO—except in the presence of security primitives, which disable it. Microsoft's documentation [12] states that "[t]he current frame cannot be discarded when control is transferred from untrusted code to trusted code, since this would jeopardize code identity security."

Wallach et al. [18] suggest an alternate security model that accommodates TCO implementations. They add an argument to each function call that represents the security context as a statement in their belief logic. Statements in this belief logic can be unraveled to determine whether an operation is permitted. Unfortunately, this transformation is global; it cannot be applied in isolation to a single untrusted component, but requires the rewriting of all procedures in all system libraries. They also fail to provide a formal language semantics that allows a Fournet-Gordon style validation of their claims.

Our security model exploits a novel mechanism for lightweight stack inspection [6]. We demonstrate the equivalence between our model and Fournet & Gordon's, and prove our claims of TCO. More precisely, our abstract implementation can transform *all* tail calls in the source program into instructions that do not consume any stack (or store) space. Moreover, the transformation that adds security annotations to the untrusted code is local.

We proceed as follows. First, we derive a CESK machine from Fournet & Gordon's semantics. Second, we develop a different, but extensionally equivalent CESK machine that uses a variant of Flatt's lightweight stack inspection mechanism [6]. Third, we show that our machine uses strictly less space than the machine derived from Fournet and Gordon's semantics and that our machine uses as much space as Clinger's canonical tail-call optimizing CESK machine [4].

The paper consists of nine sections. The second section introduces the λ_{sec} language: its syntax, semantics, and security mechanisms. The third section shows how a pair of tail calls between system and applet code can allocate an unbounded amount of space. In the fourth section, we derive an extensionally equivalent CESK machine from Fournet and Gordon's semantics; in the fifth section, we modify this machine so that it implements all tail calls in a properly optimized fashion. The sixth section provides a precise analysis of the space consumption of these machines and shows that our new machine is indeed tail-call optimizing. In the seventh section, we discuss the compatibility of our model of λ_{sec} with Fournet and Gordon's, using their theory of contextual equivalence. The last two sections place our work into context.

2   The λ_{sec} Language

Fournet and Gordon use as their starting point the λ_{sec}-calculus [14,16], a simple model of a programming language with security annotations. They present two languages: a source language, in which programs are written, and a target language, which includes an additional form for security annotations. A trusted

---

[1] Private communication between Guy Steele and second author at POPL 1996

annotator performs the translation from the source to the target, annotating each λ-expression with the appropriate permissions.

In this security model, all code is statically annotated with a given set of permissions, chosen from a fixed set $\mathcal{P}$. A program fragment that has permissions R may choose to enable some or all of these permissions. The set of enabled permissions at any point during execution is determined by taking the intersection of the permissions enabled for the caller and the set of permissions contained in the callee's label. That is, a permission is considered enabled only if two conditions are met: first, it must have been legally and explicitly enabled by some calling procedure, and second, all intervening stack frames must have been annotated with this permission.

The source language (M_s) adds three expressions to the basic call-by-value λ-calculus. The test expression checks to see whether a given set of permissions is currently enabled, and branches based on that decision. The grant expression enables a privilege, provided that the context endows it with those permissions. Finally, the fail expression causes the program to halt immediately, signaling a security failure. Our particular source language also changes the traditional presentation of the λ-calculus by adding an explicit name to each abstraction so that we get concise definitions of recursive procedures.

Syntax

$$M, N = x \mid M\ N \mid \lambda_f x.M \mid \text{grant } R \text{ in } M$$
$$\mid \text{test } R \text{ then } M \text{ else } N \mid \text{fail} \mid \underline{R[M]}$$
$$x \in \text{Identifiers}$$
$$R \subseteq \mathcal{P}$$
$$V \in \text{Values} = x \mid \lambda_f x.M$$

The target language (M) adds a framing expression to this source language (underlined in the grammar). A frame specifies the permissions of a component in the source text. To ensure that these framing expressions are present as the program is evaluated, we translate source components into target components by annotating the result with the source-appropriate permissions. In our case, components are λ-expressions. The annotator below performs this annotation, and simultaneously ensures that a grant expression refers only to those permissions to which it is entitled by its source location.[2]

Annotator $\mathcal{A} : 2^{\mathcal{P}} \to M_s \to M$

$$\mathcal{A}R[\![x]\!] = x$$
$$\mathcal{A}R[\![\lambda_f x.M]\!] = \lambda_f x.R[\mathcal{A}R[\![M]\!]]$$
$$\mathcal{A}R[\![M\ N]\!] = \mathcal{A}R[\![M]\!]\ \mathcal{A}R[\![N]\!]$$
$$\mathcal{A}R[\![\text{grant } S \text{ in } M]\!] = \text{grant } S \cap R \text{ in } \mathcal{A}R[\![M]\!]$$
$$\mathcal{A}R[\![\text{test } S \text{ then } M \text{ else } N]\!] = \text{test } S \text{ then } \mathcal{A}R[\![M]\!] \text{ else } \mathcal{A}R[\![N]\!]$$
$$\mathcal{A}R[\![\text{fail}]\!] = \text{fail}$$

---

[2] Fournet and Gordon present a semantics in which this check is performed at runtime. Section 7 discusses the differences between the two languages in more detail.

The annotator $\mathcal{A}$ consumes two arguments: the set of permissions appropriate for the source and the source code; it produces a target expression. It commutes with all expression constructors except for λ and grant. For a λ expression, it adds a frame expression wrapping the body. For a grant expression, it replaces the permissions S that the expression specifies with the intersection $S \cap R$. So, if a component containing the expression grant $\{a, b\}$ in E were annotated with the permissions $\{b, c\}$, the resulting expression would read grant $\{b\}$ in E' (where E' represents the recursive annotation of E).

We adapt Fournet & Gordon's semantics to our variant of λ_{sec} mutatis mutandis. Evaluation of programs is specified using a reduction semantics based on evaluation contexts. In such a semantics, every expression is divided into an evaluation context containing a single hole (denoted by $\bullet$), and a redex. An evaluation context is composed with a redex by replacing the context's hole with the redex. The choice of evaluation contexts determines where evaluation can occur, and typically the evaluation contexts are chosen to enforce deterministic evaluation; that is, each expression has a unique decomposition into context and redex. Reduction rules in such a semantics take the form "$E[f] \mapsto E[g]$," where f is a redex, g is its contractum, and E is the context (which may be observable, as for instance in the test rule).

Contexts

$$E = \bullet \mid E\ M \mid V\ E \mid \text{grant}\ R\ \text{in}\ E \mid R[E]$$

Reduction Rules

$$E[\lambda_f x.M\ V] \mapsto E[[\lambda_f x.M/f][V/x]M]$$
$$E[R[V]] \mapsto E[V]$$
$$E[\text{grant}\ R\ \text{in}\ V] \mapsto E[V]$$
$$E[\text{test}\ R\ \text{then}\ M\ \text{else}\ N] \mapsto \begin{cases} E[M] & \text{if } \mathcal{OK}[R][E] \\ E[N] & \text{otherwise} \end{cases}$$
$$E[\text{fail}] \mapsto \text{fail}$$

where

$$\mathcal{OK}[\emptyset][E] = \textit{true}$$
$$\mathcal{OK}[R][\bullet] = \textit{true}$$
$$\mathcal{OK}[R][E[\bullet\ M]] = \mathcal{OK}[R][E]$$
$$\mathcal{OK}[R][E[V\ \bullet]] = \mathcal{OK}[R][E]$$
$$\mathcal{OK}[R][E[S[\bullet]]] = R \subseteq S \wedge \mathcal{OK}[R][E]$$
$$\mathcal{OK}[R][E[\text{grant}\ S\ \text{in}\ \bullet]] = \mathcal{OK}[R - S][E]$$

This semantics is an extension of a standard call-by-value reduction semantics. The hole and the two application contexts are standard and enforce left-to-right evaluation of arguments. The reduction rule for applications is also standard. The added contexts and reduction rules for frame and grant expressions are interesting in that they are largely transparent; evaluation may proceed inside of either form, and each one disappears when its expression is a value. These expressions affect the evaluation only when a test expression occurs as a redex. In this case, the result of the reduction depends on the $\mathcal{OK}$ predicate, which is applied to the current context and the desired permissions.

The $\mathcal{OK}$ predicate recurs over the continuation from the inside out, succeeding either when the permissions remaining to check are empty or when the context is exhausted. The $\mathcal{OK}$ predicate commutes with both kinds of application context. In the case of a frame annotation, the desired permissions must occur in the frame, and the predicate must succeed recursively. Finally, a grant expression removes all permissions it grants from the set of those that need to be checked. The stack inspection protocol is, at heart, a lightweight form of continuation manipulation [3].

In Fournet and Gordon's framework, a program consists of a set of components, each one a closed λ-expression with its own set of permissions.

Definition 1 (Components). $A \in \text{Components} = \langle \lambda_f x.M_s, R \rangle$

Finally, the Eval function determines the meaning of a source program. A program consists of a list of components. Evaluation is performed by annotating each λ-expression with the permissions of its component, and combining all such expressions into a single application. This application uses the traditional abbreviation of a curried application as a single one.

Definition 2 (Eval).

$$\text{Eval}(\langle \lambda_f x.M_{u0}, R_0 \rangle \ldots) = V \text{ if } (\mathcal{A}R_0[\![\lambda_f x.M_{u0}]\!] \ldots) \overset{*}{\mapsto} V$$

Since the first component is applied to the rest, it is presumed to represent the runtime system, or at least a linker. Eval is undefined for programs that diverge or enter a stuck state.

3   Tail-Call Optimization

Modern functional programming languages avoid looping constructs in favor of recursion. Doing so keeps the language smaller and simplifies its implementation. Furthermore, it empowers programmers to match functions and data structures, which makes programs more comprehensible than random mixtures of loops and function calls. Even modern object-oriented programmers have recognized this fact, as indicated by the inclusion of tail-call instructions in Microsoft's CLR [2] and the promotion of traversal strategies such as the interpreter, composite, or visitor patterns [8].

Of course, if function calls were implemented naïvely, this strategy would introduce an unacceptably large overhead on iterative computations. Each iteration would consume a stack frame and long loops would quickly run out of space. As Guy Steele pointed out in the late 1970's, however, language designers can have efficiency and a small language if they translate so-called tail calls into instruction sequences that do not consume any space [9]. Typically, such function calls turn into plain jumps, and hence, the translation of a tail-recursive function equals the translation of a looping construct. Using this reasoning, the language definitions for Scheme require that correct implementations must optimize all tail-calls and thereby "support an unbounded number of active tail calls" [11].

At first glance, tail-call optimization seems inherently incompatible with stack inspection. To see this, consider a mutually recursive loop between applet and library code.

Abbreviations

$$\text{UserFn} \stackrel{\Delta}{=} \lambda_{user}\, sys.sys\ user$$

$$\text{SystemFn} \stackrel{\Delta}{=} \lambda_{sys}\, user.user\ sys$$

$$\mathcal{AR}_{\mathsf{A}}[\![\text{UserFn}]\!] = \lambda_{user}\, sys.R_{\mathsf{A}}[sys\ user]$$

$$\mathcal{AR}_{\mathsf{S}}[\![\text{SystemFn}]\!] = \lambda_{sys}\, user.R_{\mathsf{S}}[user\ sys]$$

Reduction (w/ Annotations)

$$\mathcal{AR}_{\mathsf{A}}[\![\text{UserFn}]\!]\ \mathcal{AR}_{\mathsf{S}}[\![\text{SystemFn}]\!]$$
$$\mapsto R_{\mathsf{A}}[\mathcal{AR}_{\mathsf{S}}[\![\text{SystemFn}]\!]\ \mathcal{AR}_{\mathsf{A}}[\![\text{UserFn}]\!]]$$
$$\mapsto R_{\mathsf{A}}[R_{\mathsf{S}}[\mathcal{AR}_{\mathsf{A}}[\![\text{UserFn}]\!]\ \mathcal{AR}_{\mathsf{S}}[\![\text{SystemFn}]\!]]]$$
$$\mapsto R_{\mathsf{A}}[R_{\mathsf{S}}[R_{\mathsf{A}}[\mathcal{AR}_{\mathsf{S}}[\![\text{SystemFn}]\!]\ \mathcal{AR}_{\mathsf{A}}[\![\text{UserFn}]\!]]]]$$
$$\mapsto R_{\mathsf{A}}[R_{\mathsf{S}}[R_{\mathsf{A}}[R_{\mathsf{S}}[\mathcal{AR}_{\mathsf{A}}[\![\text{UserFn}]\!]\ \mathcal{AR}_{\mathsf{S}}[\![\text{SystemFn}]\!]]]]]$$
$$\cdots$$

Reduction (w/o Annotations)

$$\text{UserFn SystemFn}$$
$$\mapsto \text{SystemFn UserFn}$$
$$\mapsto \text{UserFn SystemFn}$$
$$\mapsto \text{SystemFn UserFn}$$
$$\mapsto \text{UserFn SystemFn}$$
$$\cdots$$

This program consists of two copies of a mutually recursive loop function, one a 'user' component and one a 'system' component. Each takes the other as an argument, and then calls it, passing itself as the sole argument. To simplify the presentation of the looping functions, we introduce abbreviations for the user and system procedures.

This program is a toy example, but it represents the core of many interactions between user and system code. For instance, any co-routine-style interaction between producer and consumer exhibits this behavior—unfortunately, programmers are forced to avoid this powerful and natural style in Java precisely because of the lack of tail-call optimization. Perhaps the most common examples of this kind of interaction occur in OO-style traversals of data structures, such as the above-mentioned patterns.

The first reduction sequence illustrates the steps taken by λ_{sec} in evaluating the given program, where the two procedures are annotated with their permissions. In this example, the context quickly grows without bound. A functional programmer would expect to see a sequence more like the second one. This series is also a reduction sequence in λ_{sec}, but one which is obtained by evaluating the program's pure source.

As Fournet and Gordon point out in their paper, all is not lost. They introduce an additional reduction into their abstract machine that explicitly removes a frame before performing a call. Unfortunately, as they point out, indiscriminate application of this rule changes the semantics. Thus, they impose strict conditions that the machine must check before it can apply the rule. The rule and its side conditions clarify that an improved compiler can turn *some* tail calls into jumps, but Fournet and Gordon state that many tail calls cannot be optimized.

4   An Abstract Machine for λ_{sec}

Following Clinger's work on defining tail-optimized languages via space complexity classes [4], we reformulate the λ_{sec} semantics as a CESK machine [5]. We can then measure the space consumed by machine configurations, programs, and machines. Furthermore, we can determine whether the space consumption function of an implementation is in the same complexity class as Clinger's machine.

4.1   The fg Machine

We begin with a direct translation of λ_{sec}'s semantics into a CESK machine, which we call "frame-generating" or fg (see figure 1). A CESK machine has four registers: the control string, the environment, the store, and the continuation. The control string indicates which program instruction is being reduced. In conventional machines, this is called the program counter. The environment binds variable names to values, much like the current stack frame of an assembly language machine. The store, like a heap, contains shared values.[3] Finally, the continuation represents the instruction's control context; it is analogous to the stack.

The derivation of a CESK machine from a reduction semantics is straightforward [5]. In particular, the proof of equivalence of the two models is a refinement of Felleisen and Flatt's proof, which proceeds by a series of transformations from a simple reduction semantics to a register machine. At each step, we must strengthen the induction hypothesis by adding a claim about the value of the $\mathcal{OK}$ predicate when applied to the current context.

The new Eval function is abstracted over the machine under consideration. In particular, the definition of Eval_x for a machine x depends both on the transition function, $\mapsto_x$, and on the empty context, empty_x.

In order to ensure that Eval and Eval_{fg} are indeed the same function, the Eval_x function must employ a "load" function $\mathcal{L}$ at the beginning of an execution that coerces the target program to a valid machine configuration, and an "unload" function $\mathcal{U}$ at the end, which recursively substitutes values bound in the environment for the variables that represent them.

---

[3] The store in our model is necessitated by Clinger's model of tail call optimization; a machine with no store can grow without bound due to copying.

The FG Machine

$$C_{\text{fg}} = \langle M, \rho, \sigma, \kappa \rangle \mid \langle V, \rho, \sigma, \kappa \rangle \mid \langle V, \sigma \rangle \mid \text{fail}$$

$$\kappa = \langle \rangle \mid \langle \text{push} : M, \rho, \kappa \rangle \mid \langle \text{call} : V, \kappa \rangle \mid \langle \text{frame} : R, \kappa \rangle \mid \langle \text{grant} : R, \kappa \rangle$$

$$V \in \text{Values} = \langle \text{closure} : M, \rho \rangle$$

$$\rho \in \text{Identifiers} \rightarrow_f \text{Locations}$$

$$\alpha, \beta \in \text{Locations}$$

$$\sigma \in \text{Locations} \rightarrow_f \text{Values}$$

$$\text{empty}_{\text{fg}} = \langle \rangle$$

$$\langle \lambda_f x.M, \rho, \sigma, \kappa \rangle \mapsto_{\text{fg}} \langle \langle \text{closure} : \lambda_f x.M, \rho \rangle, \rho, \sigma, \kappa \rangle$$

$$\langle x, \rho, \sigma, \kappa \rangle \mapsto_{\text{fg}} \langle \sigma(\rho(x)), \rho, \sigma, \kappa \rangle$$

$$\langle M\ N, \rho, \sigma, \kappa \rangle \mapsto_{\text{fg}} \langle M, \rho, \sigma, \langle \text{push} : N, \rho, \kappa \rangle \rangle$$

$$\langle R[M], \rho, \sigma, \kappa \rangle \mapsto_{\text{fg}} \langle M, \rho, \sigma, \langle \text{frame} : R, \kappa \rangle \rangle$$

$$\langle \text{grant } R \text{ in } M, \rho, \sigma, \kappa \rangle \mapsto_{\text{fg}} \langle M, \rho, \sigma, \langle \text{grant} : R, \kappa \rangle \rangle$$

$$\langle \text{test } R \text{ then } M \text{ else } N, \rho, \sigma, \kappa \rangle \mapsto_{\text{fg}} \begin{cases} \langle M, \rho, \sigma, \kappa \rangle \text{ if } \mathcal{OK}_{\text{fg}}[\![R]\!][\![\kappa]\!] \\ \langle N, \rho, \sigma, \kappa \rangle \text{ otherwise} \end{cases}$$

$$\langle \text{fail}, \rho, \sigma, \kappa \rangle \mapsto_{\text{fg}} \text{fail}$$

$$\langle V, \rho, \sigma, \langle \rangle \rangle \mapsto_{\text{fg}} \langle V, \sigma \rangle$$

$$\langle V, \rho, \sigma, \langle \text{push} : M, \rho', \kappa \rangle \rangle \mapsto_{\text{fg}} \langle M, \rho', \sigma, \langle \text{call} : V, \kappa \rangle \rangle$$

$$\langle V, \rho, \sigma, \langle \text{call} : V', \kappa \rangle \rangle \mapsto_{\text{fg}} \langle M, \rho'[f \mapsto \beta][x \mapsto \alpha], \sigma[\alpha \mapsto V][\beta \mapsto V'], \kappa \rangle$$
$$\text{if } V' = \langle \text{closure} : \lambda_f x.M, \rho' \rangle \text{ and } \alpha, \beta \notin \text{dom}(\sigma)$$

$$\langle V, \rho, \sigma, \langle \text{frame} : R, \kappa \rangle \rangle \mapsto_{\text{fg}} \langle V, \rho, \sigma, \kappa \rangle$$

$$\langle V, \rho, \sigma, \langle \text{grant} : R, \kappa \rangle \rangle \mapsto_{\text{fg}} \langle V, \rho, \sigma, \kappa \rangle$$

$$\langle V, \rho, \sigma[\beta, \ldots \mapsto V', \ldots], \kappa \rangle \mapsto_{\text{fg}} \langle V, \rho, \sigma, \kappa \rangle$$
$$\text{if } \{\beta, \ldots\} \text{ is nonempty and}$$
$$\beta, \ldots \text{ do not occur in } V, \rho, \sigma, \text{ or } \kappa$$

where

$$\mathcal{OK}_{\text{fg}}[\![\emptyset]\!][\![\kappa]\!] = \text{true}$$

$$\mathcal{OK}_{\text{fg}}[\![R]\!][\![\langle \rangle]\!] = \text{true}$$

$$\mathcal{OK}_{\text{fg}}[\![R]\!][\![\langle \text{push} : M, \rho, \kappa \rangle]\!] = \mathcal{OK}_{\text{fg}}[\![R]\!][\![\kappa]\!]$$

$$\mathcal{OK}_{\text{fg}}[\![R]\!][\![\langle \text{call} : V, \kappa \rangle]\!] = \mathcal{OK}_{\text{fg}}[\![R]\!][\![\kappa]\!]$$

$$\mathcal{OK}_{\text{fg}}[\![R]\!][\![\langle \text{frame} : R', \kappa \rangle]\!] = \begin{cases} \mathcal{OK}_{\text{fg}}[\![R]\!][\![\kappa]\!] \text{ if } R \subseteq R' \\ \text{false otherwise} \end{cases}$$

$$\mathcal{OK}_{\text{fg}}[\![R]\!][\![\langle \text{grant} : R', \kappa \rangle]\!] = \mathcal{OK}_{\text{fg}}[\![R - R']\!][\![\kappa]\!]$$

Fig. 1.

Definition 3 (Eval$_x$).

$$\text{Eval}_x(A, \ldots) = \mathcal{U}(V, \sigma) \text{ if } \mathcal{L}_x(A, \ldots) \overset{*}{\mapsto}_x \langle V, \sigma \rangle$$

where

$$\mathcal{L}_x(\langle \lambda_f x.M_{u0}, R_0 \rangle, \ldots) = \langle (\mathcal{A}R_0[\![\lambda_f x.M_{u0}]\!] \ \ldots), \emptyset, \emptyset, \text{empty}_x \rangle$$

and

$$\mathcal{U}(\langle \text{closure} : M, \{\langle x_1, \alpha_1 \rangle, \ldots, \langle x_n, \alpha_n \rangle\}\rangle, \sigma) =$$
$$[\mathcal{U}(\sigma(\alpha_1))/x_1] \ldots [\mathcal{U}(\sigma(\alpha_n))/x_n]M$$

Theorem 1 (Machine Fidelity). *For all* $(\langle M_0, R_0 \rangle, \ldots)$,

$$\mathrm{Eval}_{\mathrm{fg}}(\langle M_0, R_0 \rangle, \ldots) = V \; \textit{iff} \; \mathrm{Eval}(\langle M_0, R_0 \rangle, \ldots) = V$$

The proof proceeds by induction on the length of a reduction sequence.

4.2   The fg Machine Is Not Tail-Call-Optimizing

To see that this implementation of the λ_{sec} language is not TCO, we show the reduction sequence in the fg machine for the program from section 3, and validate that the space taken by the configuration is growing without bound.

$$\mathrm{UserClo} \triangleq \langle \mathrm{closure} : \lambda_{user}\,sys.\mathcal{AR}_\mathsf{A}[\![\mathrm{UserFn}]\!], \emptyset \rangle$$
$$\mathrm{SystemClo} \triangleq \langle \mathrm{closure} : \lambda_{sys}\,user.\mathcal{AR}_\mathsf{S}[\![\mathrm{SystemFn}]\!], \emptyset \rangle$$
$$\rho_0 \triangleq [sys \mapsto \alpha,\, user \mapsto \beta]$$
$$\sigma_0 \triangleq [\alpha \mapsto \mathrm{SystemClo}, \beta \mapsto \mathrm{UserClo}]$$

$\langle \mathcal{AR}_\mathsf{A}[\![\mathrm{UserFn}]\!]\ \mathcal{AR}_\mathsf{S}[\![\mathrm{SystemFn}]\!], \emptyset, \emptyset, \langle\rangle \rangle$

$\mapsto_{\mathrm{fg}} \langle \mathcal{AR}_\mathsf{A}[\![\mathrm{UserFn}]\!], \emptyset, \emptyset, \langle \mathrm{push} : \mathcal{AR}_\mathsf{S}[\![\mathrm{SystemFn}]\!], \emptyset, \langle\rangle\rangle \rangle$

$\mapsto_{\mathrm{fg}} \langle \mathrm{UserClo}, \emptyset, \emptyset, \langle \mathrm{push} : \mathcal{AR}_\mathsf{S}[\![\mathrm{SystemFn}]\!], \emptyset, \langle\rangle\rangle \rangle$

$\mapsto_{\mathrm{fg}} \langle \mathcal{AR}_\mathsf{S}[\![\mathrm{SystemFn}]\!], \emptyset, \emptyset, \langle \mathrm{call} : \mathrm{UserClo}, \langle\rangle\rangle \rangle$

$\mapsto_{\mathrm{fg}} \langle \mathrm{SystemClo}, \emptyset, \emptyset, \langle \mathrm{call} : \mathrm{UserClo}, \langle\rangle\rangle \rangle$

$\mapsto_{\mathrm{fg}} \langle R_\mathsf{A}[sys\ user], \rho_0, \sigma_0, \langle\rangle \rangle$

$\mapsto_{\mathrm{fg}} \langle sys\ user, \rho_0, \sigma_0, \langle \mathrm{frame} : R_\mathsf{A}, \langle\rangle\rangle \rangle$

$\mapsto_{\mathrm{fg}} \langle sys, \rho_0, \sigma_0, \langle \mathrm{push} : user, \rho_0, \langle \mathrm{frame} : R_\mathsf{A}, \langle\rangle\rangle\rangle \rangle$

$\mapsto_{\mathrm{fg}} \langle \mathrm{SystemClo}, \rho_0, \sigma_0, \langle \mathrm{push} : user, \rho_0, \langle \mathrm{frame} : R_\mathsf{A}, \langle\rangle\rangle\rangle \rangle$

$\mapsto_{\mathrm{fg}} \langle user, \rho_0, \sigma_0, \langle \mathrm{call} : \mathrm{SystemClo}, \langle \mathrm{frame} : R_\mathsf{A}, \langle\rangle\rangle\rangle \rangle$

$\mapsto_{\mathrm{fg}} \langle \mathrm{UserClo}, \rho_0, \sigma_0, \langle \mathrm{call} : \mathrm{SystemClo}, \langle \mathrm{frame} : R_\mathsf{A}, \langle\rangle\rangle\rangle \rangle$

$\overset{2}{\mapsto}_{\mathrm{fg}} \langle R_\mathsf{S}[user\ sys], \rho_0, \sigma_0, \langle \mathrm{frame} : R_\mathsf{A}, \langle\rangle\rangle \rangle$

$\mapsto_{\mathrm{fg}} \langle user\ sys, \rho_0, \sigma_0, \langle \mathrm{frame} : R_\mathsf{S}, \langle \mathrm{frame} : R_\mathsf{A}, \langle\rangle\rangle\rangle \rangle$

$\mapsto_{\mathrm{fg}} \langle user, \rho_0, \sigma_0, \langle \mathrm{push} : sys, \rho_0, \langle \mathrm{frame} : R_\mathsf{S}, \langle \mathrm{frame} : R_\mathsf{A}, \langle\rangle\rangle\rangle\rangle \rangle$

$\mapsto_{\mathrm{fg}} \langle \mathrm{UserClo}, \rho_0, \sigma_0, \langle \mathrm{push} : sys, \rho_0, \langle \mathrm{frame} : R_\mathsf{S}, \langle \mathrm{frame} : R_\mathsf{A}, \langle\rangle\rangle\rangle\rangle \rangle$

$\mapsto_{\mathrm{fg}} \langle sys, \rho_0, \sigma_0, \langle \mathrm{call} : \mathrm{UserClo}, \langle \mathrm{frame} : R_\mathsf{S}, \langle \mathrm{frame} : R_\mathsf{A}, \langle\rangle\rangle\rangle\rangle \rangle$

$\mapsto_{\mathrm{fg}} \langle \mathrm{SystemClo}, \rho_0, \sigma_0, \langle \mathrm{call} : \mathrm{UserClo}, \langle \mathrm{frame} : R_\mathsf{S}, \langle \mathrm{frame} : R_\mathsf{A}, \langle\rangle\rangle\rangle\rangle \rangle$

$\overset{7}{\mapsto}_{\mathrm{fg}} \langle \mathrm{UserClo}, \rho_0, \sigma_0, \langle \mathrm{call} : \mathrm{SystemClo}, \langle \mathrm{frame} : R_\mathsf{A}, \langle \mathrm{frame} : R_\mathsf{S}, \langle \mathrm{frame} : R_\mathsf{A}, \langle\rangle\rangle\rangle\rangle\rangle \rangle$

$\overset{7}{\mapsto}_{\mathrm{fg}} \langle \mathrm{SystemClo}, \rho_0, \sigma_0,$

$\qquad \langle \mathrm{call} : \mathrm{UserClo}, \langle \mathrm{frame} : R_\mathsf{S}, \langle \mathrm{frame} : R_\mathsf{A}, \langle \mathrm{frame} : R_\mathsf{S}, \langle \mathrm{frame} : R_\mathsf{A}, \langle\rangle\rangle\rangle\rangle\rangle\rangle \rangle$

---

5   An Alternative Implementation

5.1   How Security Inspections Really Work

A close look at λ_{sec} shows that frame and grant contexts affect the computation only when they are observed by a test expression. That is, a program with no test expressions may be simplified by removing all frame and grant expressions without changing its meaning. Furthermore, the observations possible with the test expression are limited by the $\mathcal{OK}$ function.

In particular, any sequence of frame and grant expressions may be collapsed into a canonical table that provides a partial map from the set of permissions to one of two conditions: 'no', indicating that the permission is not granted by the sequence, and 'grant', indicating that the permission is granted (and legally so) by some grant frame in the sequence.

To derive update rules for this table, we consider evaluation of the $\mathcal{OK}$ function as the recognition of a context-free grammar over the alphabet of frame and grant expressions. We start by simplifying the model to one with a single permission. Then each frame is either empty or contains the desired permission. Likewise, there is only one possible grant. All other continuation frames are irrelevant. So a full evaluation context can be seen as an arbitrary string in the alphabet $\Sigma = \{y, n, g\}$, where y and n represent frames that contain or are missing the given permission, and g represents a grant. Assume the ordering of the letters in the word places the outermost frames at the left end of the string.

With the grammar in place, the $\mathcal{OK}_{\text{fg}}$ predicate can easily be interpreted as a finite-state machine that recognizes the regular expression $\Sigma^* g y^*$; that is, a string ending with a grant followed by any number of y's. The resulting FSA has just two states, one accepting and one non-accepting. A g always transitions to the accepting state, and a n always transitions to the non-accepting state. A y causes a (trivial) transition to the current state.

This last observation leads us to a further simplification. Since the presence of the character y does not affect the decision of the FSA, we may ignore the continuation frames that generate them, and consider only the grant frames and those security frames that do not include the desired permission. The regular expression indicating the success of $\mathcal{OK}_{\text{fg}}$ becomes simply $\Sigma^* g$.

Now consider the reduction semantics again. Although a context represents a long string, we cannot reduce all permission information in a context to a single state in our machine, because the context also contains expressions waiting to be evaluated. In other words, there are many prefixes of this "permission word" that evaluation depends on. Whenever a sequence of frame and grant expressions occurs without interruption, however, it is safe to collapse it, and it is easy to see how to do so. A substring ending in a g results in an accepting state, a substring ending in an n results in a non-accepting state, and the empty substring does not alter the decision. To extend this to the whole language, we must expand our single-permission state to a full table of permissions.

This reasoning also provides an intuitive understanding for the componential nature of our annotation scheme. Consider the evaluation of a program containing both annotated and unannotated components. Since this computation ignores security frames indicating the presence of a given permission, code that has not been annotated at all is equivalent to code that has been granted all permissions. This means that system libraries need not be recompiled to take advantage of such a scheme.

The CM Machine
$$m \in \mathcal{P} \to_f \{\text{grant}, \text{no}\}$$
$$\text{configurations} : C_{\text{cm}} = \langle M, \rho, \sigma, \kappa \rangle \mid \langle V, \rho, \sigma, \kappa \rangle \mid \langle V, \sigma \rangle \mid \text{fail}$$
$$\kappa = \langle \text{empty} : m \rangle \mid \langle \text{push} : M, \rho, \kappa, m \rangle \mid \langle \text{call} : V, \kappa, m \rangle$$
$$V \in \text{Values} = \langle \text{closure} : M, \rho \rangle$$
$$\rho \in \text{Identifiers} \to_f \text{Locations}$$
$$\alpha, \beta \in \text{Locations}$$
$$\sigma \in \text{Locations} \to_f \text{Values}$$
$$\text{empty}_{\text{cm}} = \langle \text{empty} : \emptyset \rangle$$

$$\langle \lambda_f x.M, \rho, \sigma, \kappa \rangle \mapsto_{\text{cm}} \langle \langle \text{closure} : \lambda_f x.M, \rho \rangle, \rho, \sigma, \kappa \rangle$$
$$\langle x, \rho, \sigma, \kappa \rangle \mapsto_{\text{cm}} \langle \sigma(\rho(x)), \rho, \sigma, \kappa \rangle$$
$$\langle M\ N, \rho, \sigma, \kappa \rangle \mapsto_{\text{cm}} \langle M, \rho, \sigma, \langle \text{push} : N, \rho, \kappa, \emptyset \rangle \rangle$$
$$\langle R[M], \rho, \sigma, \kappa \rangle \mapsto_{\text{cm}} \langle M, \rho, \sigma, \kappa[\overline{R} \mapsto \text{no}] \rangle$$
$$\langle \text{grant } R \text{ in } M, \rho, \sigma, \kappa \rangle \mapsto_{\text{cm}} \langle M, \rho, \sigma, \kappa[R \mapsto \text{grant}] \rangle$$
$$\langle \text{test } R \text{ then } M \text{ else } N, \rho, \sigma, \kappa \rangle \mapsto_{\text{cm}} \begin{cases} \langle M, \rho, \sigma, \kappa \rangle & \text{if } \mathcal{OK}_{\text{cm}}[\![R]\!][\![\kappa]\!] \\ \langle N, \rho, \sigma, \kappa \rangle & \text{otherwise} \end{cases}$$
$$\langle \text{fail}, \rho, \sigma, \kappa \rangle \mapsto_{\text{cm}} \text{fail}$$

$$\langle V, \rho, \sigma, \langle \text{empty} : m \rangle \rangle \mapsto_{\text{cm}} \langle V, \sigma \rangle$$
$$\langle V, \rho, \sigma, \langle \text{push} : M, \rho', \kappa, m \rangle \rangle \mapsto_{\text{cm}} \langle M, \rho', \sigma, \langle \text{call} : V, \kappa, \emptyset \rangle \rangle$$
$$\langle V, \rho, \sigma, \langle \text{call} : V', \kappa, m \rangle \rangle \mapsto_{\text{cm}} \langle M, \rho'[f \mapsto \beta][x \mapsto \alpha], \sigma[\alpha \mapsto V][\beta \mapsto V'], \kappa \rangle$$
$$\text{if } V' = \langle \text{closure} : \lambda_f x.M, \rho' \rangle \text{ and } \alpha, \beta \notin \text{dom}(\sigma)$$

$$\langle V, \rho, \sigma[\beta, \ldots \mapsto V, \ldots], \kappa \rangle \mapsto_{\text{cm}} \langle V, \rho, \sigma, \kappa \rangle$$
$$\text{if } \{\beta, \ldots\} \text{ is nonempty and}$$
$$\beta, \ldots \text{ do not occur in } V, \rho, \sigma, \text{ or } \kappa$$

where
$$\langle \ldots, m \rangle [R \mapsto c] = \langle \ldots, m[R \mapsto c] \rangle \text{ (pointwise extension)}$$

and
$$\mathcal{OK}_{\text{cm}}[\![\emptyset]\!][\![\kappa]\!] = \text{true}$$
$$\mathcal{OK}_{\text{cm}}[\![R]\!][\![\langle \text{empty} : m \rangle]\!] = (R \cap m^{-1}(\text{no}) = \emptyset)$$
$$\left.\begin{array}{l} \mathcal{OK}_{\text{cm}}[\![R]\!][\![\langle \text{push} : M, \rho, \kappa, m \rangle]\!] \\ \mathcal{OK}_{\text{cm}}[\![R]\!][\![\langle \text{call} : V, \kappa, m \rangle]\!] \end{array}\right\} = (R \cap m^{-1}(\text{no}) = \emptyset) \wedge \mathcal{OK}_{\text{cm}}[\![R - m^{-1}(\text{grant})]\!][\![\kappa]\!]$$

Fig. 2.

5.2   The cm Machine

In the cm (continuation-marks) machine, each continuation frame contains a table of permissions, called a *mark*. The evaluation steps for frame and grant expressions update the table in the enclosing continuation, rather than increasing the length of the continuation itself. The $\mathcal{OK}_{\text{cm}}$ predicate now inspects these marks, rather than the frame and grant elements of the continuation. Otherwise, the cm machine is the same as the fg machine (figure 2).

The Eval_{cm} function is an instance of Eval_x. That is, Eval_{cm} is the same as Eval_{fg}, except that it uses $\mapsto_{cm}$ as its transition function and empty_{cm} as its empty continuation.

The two machines produce the same results.

Theorem 2 (Machine Equivalence). *For all* $(\langle M_0, R_0 \rangle, \ldots)$,

$$\text{Eval}_{fg}(\langle M_0, R_0 \rangle, \ldots) = V \text{ iff } \text{Eval}_{cm}(\langle M_0, R_0 \rangle, \ldots) = V$$

To prove this theorem, we must show that if the fg machine terminates, the cm machine terminates with the same value, and that if the fg machine does not terminate in a final state, then the cm machine also fails to terminate.

For the purposes of the proof, we will assume that no garbage collection steps are taken, because garbage collection cannot affect the result of the evaluation.

Lemma 1 (No Garbage Collection). *For every evaluation sequence in either the fg or cm machine, removing every garbage-collection step produces another legal sequence, and no divergent computation is made finite by such a removal.*

To compare the machines, we introduce the function $\mathcal{T}$.

$$\mathcal{T}\langle M, \rho, \sigma, \kappa \rangle = \langle M, \rho, \sigma, \mathcal{T}(\kappa) \rangle$$
$$\mathcal{T}\langle V, \rho, \sigma, \kappa \rangle = \langle V, \rho, \sigma, \mathcal{T}(\kappa) \rangle$$
$$\mathcal{T}\langle V, \sigma \rangle = \langle V, \sigma \rangle$$
$$\mathcal{T}(\text{fail}) = \text{fail}$$
$$\mathcal{T}\langle\rangle = \langle \text{empty} : \emptyset \rangle$$
$$\mathcal{T}\langle \text{push} : M, \rho, \kappa \rangle = \langle \text{push} : M, \rho, \mathcal{T}(\kappa), \emptyset \rangle$$
$$\mathcal{T}\langle \text{call} : V, \kappa \rangle = \langle \text{call} : V, \mathcal{T}(\kappa), \emptyset \rangle$$
$$\mathcal{T}\langle \text{frame} : R, \kappa \rangle = \mathcal{T}(\kappa)[\overline{R} \mapsto \text{no}]$$
$$\mathcal{T}\langle \text{grant} : R, \kappa \rangle = \mathcal{T}(\kappa)[R \mapsto \text{grant}]$$

The function $\mathcal{T}$ maps configurations of the fg machine to configurations of the cm machine. A step in the fg machine corresponds to either no steps or one step in the cm machine.

Lemma 2 (Simulation). *Given a configuration C_{cm}, with $C_{cm} = \mathcal{T}(C_{fg})$, one of the following holds:*

1. C_{fg} *is either* fail *or* $\langle V, \sigma \rangle$
2. C_{fg} *and* C_{cm} *are both stuck.*
3. $C_{fg} \mapsto_{fg} C'_{fg}$ *and* $\mathcal{T}(C'_{fg}) = C_{cm}$
4. $C_{fg} \mapsto_{fg} C'_{fg}$ *and* $C_{cm} \mapsto_{cm} \mathcal{T}(C'_{fg})$

The proof is a case analysis on the four cases and the configurations of the machine. The fg machine takes extra steps only when "popping" frame and grant continuations after reducing their arguments to values.

The cm machine can always represent a sequence of frame and grant expressions with a single mark. The sequence of steps below illustrates this for the divergent mutually-recursive computation shown in section 3.

$$R_{\mathsf{S}} \overset{\Delta}{=} \{b, c\}$$
$$R_{\mathsf{A}} \overset{\Delta}{=} \{a, b\}$$

$\langle \mathcal{A}R_{\mathsf{A}}[\![\mathrm{UserFn}]\!] \; \mathcal{A}R_{\mathsf{S}}[\![\mathrm{SystemFn}]\!], \emptyset, \emptyset, \langle \mathrm{empty} : \emptyset \rangle \rangle$

$\mapsto_{\mathsf{cm}} \langle \mathcal{A}R_{\mathsf{A}}[\![\mathrm{UserFn}]\!], \emptyset, \emptyset, \langle \mathrm{push} : \mathcal{A}R_{\mathsf{S}}[\![\mathrm{SystemFn}]\!], \emptyset, \langle \mathrm{empty} : \emptyset \rangle, \emptyset \rangle \rangle$

$\mapsto_{\mathsf{cm}} \langle \mathrm{UserClo}, \emptyset, \emptyset, \langle \mathrm{push} : \mathcal{A}R_{\mathsf{S}}[\![\mathrm{SystemFn}]\!], \emptyset, \langle \mathrm{empty} : \emptyset \rangle, \emptyset \rangle \rangle$

$\mapsto_{\mathsf{cm}} \langle \mathcal{A}R_{\mathsf{S}}[\![\mathrm{SystemFn}]\!], \emptyset, \emptyset, \langle \mathrm{call} : \mathrm{UserClo}, \langle \mathrm{empty} : \emptyset \rangle, \emptyset \rangle \rangle$

$\mapsto_{\mathsf{cm}} \langle \mathrm{SystemClo}, \emptyset, \emptyset, \langle \mathrm{call} : \mathrm{UserClo}, \langle \mathrm{empty} : \emptyset \rangle, \emptyset \rangle \rangle$

$\mapsto_{\mathsf{cm}} \langle R_{\mathsf{A}}[sys \; user], \rho_0, \sigma_0, \langle \mathrm{empty} : \emptyset \rangle \rangle$

$\mapsto_{\mathsf{cm}} \langle sys \; user, \rho_0, \sigma_0, \langle \mathrm{empty} : [\{c\} \mapsto \mathrm{no}] \rangle \rangle$

$\mapsto_{\mathsf{cm}} \langle sys, \rho_0, \sigma_0, \langle \mathrm{push} : user, \rho_0, \langle \mathrm{empty} : [\{c\} \mapsto \mathrm{no}] \rangle \rangle \rangle$

$\mapsto_{\mathsf{cm}} \langle \mathrm{SystemClo}, \rho_0, \sigma_0, \langle \mathrm{push} : user, \rho_0, \langle \mathrm{empty} : [\{c\} \mapsto \mathrm{no}] \rangle, \emptyset \rangle \rangle$

$\mapsto_{\mathsf{cm}} \langle user, \rho_0, \sigma_0, \langle \mathrm{call} : \mathrm{SystemClo}, \langle \mathrm{empty} : [\{c\} \mapsto \mathrm{no}] \rangle, \emptyset \rangle \rangle$

$\mapsto_{\mathsf{cm}} \langle \mathrm{UserClo}, \rho_0, \sigma_0, \langle \mathrm{call} : \mathrm{SystemClo}, \langle \mathrm{empty} : [\{c\} \mapsto \mathrm{no}] \rangle, \emptyset \rangle \rangle$

$\overset{2}{\mapsto}_{\mathsf{cm}} \langle R_{\mathsf{S}}[user \; sys], \rho_0, \sigma_0, \langle \mathrm{empty} : [\{c\} \mapsto \mathrm{no}] \rangle \rangle$

$\mapsto_{\mathsf{cm}} \langle user \; sys, \rho_0, \sigma_0, \langle \mathrm{empty} : [\{a, c\} \mapsto \mathrm{no}] \rangle \rangle$

$\mapsto_{\mathsf{cm}} \langle user, \rho_0, \sigma_0, \langle \mathrm{push} : sys, \rho_0, \langle \mathrm{empty} : [\{a, c\} \mapsto \mathrm{no}] \rangle \rangle \rangle$

$\mapsto_{\mathsf{cm}} \langle \mathrm{UserClo}, \rho_0, \sigma_0, \langle \mathrm{push} : sys, \rho_0, \langle \mathrm{empty} : [\{a, c\} \mapsto \mathrm{no}] \rangle, \emptyset \rangle \rangle$

$\mapsto_{\mathsf{cm}} \langle sys, \rho_0, \sigma_0, \langle \mathrm{call} : \mathrm{UserClo}, \langle \mathrm{empty} : [\{a, c\} \mapsto \mathrm{no}] \rangle, \emptyset \rangle \rangle$

$\mapsto_{\mathsf{cm}} \langle \mathrm{SystemClo}, \rho_0, \sigma_0, \langle \mathrm{call} : \mathrm{UserClo}, \langle \mathrm{empty} : [\{a, c\} \mapsto \mathrm{no}] \rangle, \emptyset \rangle \rangle$

$\overset{7}{\mapsto}_{\mathsf{cm}} \langle \mathrm{UserClo}, \rho_0, \sigma_0, \langle \mathrm{call} : \mathrm{SystemClo}, \langle \mathrm{empty} : [\{a, c\} \mapsto \mathrm{no}] \rangle, \emptyset \rangle \rangle$

$\overset{7}{\mapsto}_{\mathsf{cm}} \langle \mathrm{SystemClo}, \rho_0, \sigma_0, \langle \mathrm{call} : \mathrm{UserClo}, \langle \mathrm{empty} : [\{a, c\} \mapsto \mathrm{no}] \rangle, \emptyset \rangle \rangle$

6   Space Consumption

In order to apply Clinger's analytic framework of TCO [4], we must extend his configuration-measuring function to handle security frames (in the case of the fg machine) and marks (in the case of the cm machine). Fortunately, we can use the same function for configurations of both machines. Applying the function to the configurations assumed by the fg and cm machines during the evaluation of a program yields space functions S_{fg} and S_{cm}, mapping programs to the maximum space consumed during the evaluations on their respective machines.

With this extension, we can define space complexity classes $O(S_{\mathsf{fg}})$ and $O(S_{\mathsf{cm}})$ as the sets of space functions that are asymptotically similar to S_{fg} and S_{cm}. We can demonstrate the inclusion of $O(S_{\mathsf{cm}})$ in $O(S_{\mathsf{fg}})$ by mapping configurations of the cm machine onto configurations of the fg machine and showing a worst-case growth of no more than the number of permissions $|\mathcal{P}|$, and the non-inclusion of $O(S_{\mathsf{fg}})$ in $O(S_{\mathsf{cm}})$ by choosing a program (like the example shown earlier) that grows without bound in the fg machine but has a finite bound in the cm machine.

To directly show that the cm machine is TCO, we must define TCO for this language. We define an oracular machine that makes the right security decisions with no information whatsoever, and then show that the cm machine's space use is asymptotically bounded by the complexity class $O(S_o)$ induced by the oracle's space function S_o.

Theorem 3 (Space Complexity). $O(S_o) = O(S_{cm}) \subset O(S_{fg})$

7 A Note on TCO in Fournet and Gordon

Our reduction semantics differs from that presented by Fournet & Gordon [7]. In particular, our semantics omits runtime checks for grant expressions against their source permissions. While we have justified this omission with a static check (section 5.2), it is important to understand that our evaluator differs from Fournet & Gordon's on programs that do not satisfy this predicate.

The difference in the evaluators induces a further difference in the respective contextual equivalence theories. In Fournet & Gordon's theory, the equation

$$\emptyset[\text{ grant } \emptyset \text{ in test } R \text{ then } e \text{ else } f] \equiv \emptyset[\text{ grant } R \text{ in test } R \text{ then } e \text{ else } f]$$

holds. The two expressions are contextually equivalent because the permissions enabled by the grant are dynamically reduced to the empty set at runtime. In our system, though, this runtime check is omitted and the two expressions therefore produce different results.

Although this difference might suggest that the results of this paper do not apply to the semantics of Fournet & Gordon, this is not the case. To make this point, we sketch an optimization path using their theory of contextual equivalence that reduces any program to one that contains at most two frame expressions and one grant expression for each ordinary expression. This guarantees that the amount of security information in the program is linear in the size of the ordinary program.

Consider an expression containing an arbitrarily long (nested) sequence of frame and grant expressions wrapped around a single ordinary expression e. Using Fournet & Gordon's contextual equivalence theory, it can be reduced to at most two frame expressions wrapped around at most one grant expression wrapped around e. Informally, this optimization path consists of three specific optimizations, using four laws from the theory [7, pp. 311–312].

Selected Equations
   (Frame Frame Frame) : $R_1[R_2[R_3[e]]] = (R_1 \cap R_2)[R_3[e]]$
         (Grant Grant) : $\text{grant } R_1 \text{ in grant } R_2 \text{ in } e = \text{grant } R_1 \cup R_2 \text{ in } e$
         (Frame Grant) : $R_1[\text{grant } R_2 \text{ in } e] = R_1[\text{grant } R_1 \cap R_2 \text{ in } e]$
   (Frame Grant Frame) : $R_1 \supseteq R_2 \Rightarrow R_1[\text{grant } R_2 \text{ in } R_3[e]] = R_1[R_3[\text{grant } R_2 \text{ in } e]]$

The first reduces a sequence of three or more frame expressions to two frame expressions. The second reduces two or more grant expressions to a single grant expression. The third moves a frame outward past a grant. We conjecture that these optimizations yield a provably TCO machine semantics that is a direct modification of Fournet & Gordon's reduction semantics.

8   Related Work

This paper is directly inspired by the POPL presentation of a semantics for stack inspection by Fournet & Gordon [7], and by our earlier research on an algebraic stepper for DrScheme [3]. In this work, we produced a portable and provably correct algebraic stepper, based on a novel, lightweight stack inspection mechanism. Using a primitive function, a program can place continuation marks on the stack and inquire about existing marks. If a function places two marks on the stack, the run-time environment replaces the first with the second. Hence, the manipulation of continuation marks automatically preserves tail-call optimizations. The key difference between our earlier work and this paper is that continuation marks for security permissions contain negative rather than positive information. Once we understood this, we could derive the rest of the ideas here in a straightforward manner.

The initial presentation of stack inspection is due to Wallach et al. [17,18]. They provide informal specifications and multiple implementations for this security architecture. Our paper aims to bridge the gap between this implementation work and the equational reasoning of Fournet & Gordon.

Several others [1,15] have considered the problem of adding tail calls to the JVM, which does support stack inspection. However, none of these specifically addressed stack inspection or security, and all of them made the simplifying assumption that TCO was only possible between procedures of the same component; that is, none of them considered calls between user and library code.

Karjoth [10] presents a semantics for access control in Java 2; his model presents rules for the maintenance of access control information, but leaves the rules for the evaluation of the language itself unspecified. Because he includes rules for matching 'call' and 'return' expressions, his system cannot be the foundation for a TCO implementation.

9   Conclusions

Our paper invalidates the widely held belief among programming language researchers that a global tail-call optimization policy is incompatible with stack inspection for security policies. We develop an alternative implementation of stack inspection; we prove that it preserves the observable behavior of all programs; and we show that its notion of tail call is consistent with Clinger's mathematical notion of tail-call optimization. It is our belief that translating our ideas into a compiler or a virtual machine imposes no additional cost on the implementation of any other construct. Finally, we expect that such an implementation will perform as well or better than a conventional stack inspection implementation.

Acknowledgments. We are grateful to C. Fournet and J. Marshall for their comments, and to M. Flatt for the design and implementation of continuation marks.

References

[1] Nick Benton, Andrew Kennedy, and George Russell. Compiling standard ML to Java bytecodes. In *ACM SIGPLAN International Conference on Functional Programming*, pages 129–140, 1998.

[2] Don Box. *Essential .NET, Volume I: The Common Language Runtime*. Addison-Wesley, To Appear.

[3] John Clements, Matthew Flatt, and Matthias Felleisen. Modeling an algebraic stepper. *Lecture Notes in Computer Science*, 2028:320–334, 2001.

[4] William D. Clinger. Proper tail recursion and space efficiency. In *ACM SIGPLAN Conference on Programming Language Design and Implementation*, pages 174–185, 1998.

[5] Matthias Felleisen and Matthew Flatt. Programming languages and their calculi. Unpublished Manuscript. Online at
<http://www.ccs.neu.edu/home/matthias/3810-w02/mono.ps.gz>, 1989–2002.

[6] Matthew Flatt. PLT MzScheme: Language manual. Online at
<http://www.plt-scheme.org>, 1995–2002.

[7] Cedric Fournet and Andrew D. Gordon. Stack inspection: theory and variants. In *Symposium on Principles of Programming Languages*, pages 307–318, 2002.

[8] Erich Gamma, Richard Helm, Ralph Johnson, and John Vlissides. *Design Patterns*. Addison-Wesley, 1995.

[9] Guy Lewis Steele Jr. Debunking the "expensive procedure call" myth. In *ACM Conference*, pages 153–162, 1977.

[10] Günter Karjoth. An operational semantics of Java 2 access control. In *The Computer Security Foundations Workshop*, pages 224–232, 2000.

[11] Richard Kelsey, William D. Clinger, and Jonathan Rees. Revised[5] report on the algorithmic language scheme. *SIGPLAN Notices*, 33(9):26–76, 1998.

[12] Microsoft. Common language runtime SDK documentation. Online at
http://www.microsoft.com. Part of .NET SDK documentation, 2002.

[13] Gordon D. Plotkin. Call-by-name, call-by-value and the λ-calculus. *Theoretical Computer Science*, pages 125–159, 1975.

[14] F. Pottier, Christian Skalka, and Scott Smith. A systematic approach to static access control. *Lecture Notes in Computer Science*, 2028:30–45, 2001.

[15] Michel Schinz and Martin Odersky. Tail call elimination on the Java virtual machine. In *SIGPLAN BABEL Workshop on Multi-Language Infrastructure and Interoperability*, pages 155–168, 2001.

[16] Christian Skalka and Scott Smith. Static enforcement of security with types. *ACM SIGPLAN Notices*, 35(9):34–45, 2000.

[17] Dan Wallach, Dirk Balfanz, Drew Dean, and Ed Felten. Extensible security architectures for Java. In *The 16th Symposium on Operating Systems Principles*, pages 116–128, october 1997.

[18] Dan Wallach, Edward Felten, and Andrew Appel. The security architecture formerly known as stack inspection: A security mechanism for language-based systems. *ACM Transactions on Software Engineering and Methodology*, 9(4):341–378, October 2000.

Flexible Models for Dynamic Linking

Sophia Drossopoulou[1], Giovanni Lagorio[2], and Susan Eisenbach[1] *

[1] Department of Computing at Imperial College
[2] DISI at the University of Genova

Abstract. Dynamic linking supports flexible code deployment: partially linked code links further code on the fly, as needed; and thus, end-users receive updates automatically. On the down side, each program run may link different versions of the same code, possibly causing subtle errors which mystify end-users.

Dynamic linking in Java and C# are similar: The same linking phases are involved, soundness is based on similar ideas, and executions which do not throw linking errors give the same result. They are, however, not identical: the linking phases are combined differently, and take place in a different order.

We develop a non-deterministic model, which includes the behaviour of Java and C#. The non-determinism allows us to describe the design space, to distill the similarities between the two languages, and to use one proof of soundness for both. We also prove that all execution strategies are equivalent in the sense that all terminating executions which do not involve a link error, give the same result.

1   Introduction

Dynamic linking supports flexible code deployment and update: instead of fully linking code before execution, further code is linked on the fly, as needed. Thus, the *newest* version of any imported code is always linked, and the most recent updates are automatically available to users. Dynamic linking was incorporated into operating systems, *e.g.*, Multics, Unix, and Windows, enabling applications to share code, thus saving disk and memory usage. Recently, Java and C# incorporated dynamic linking into the language.

One question connected to dynamic linking is the choice of components to be linked, when there are more than one with the same name. DLLs and .NET offer sophisticated systems of versioning, side-by-side components, registries, *etc*. Difficulties in managing DLLs led to the term "DLL Hell" [19]. The .NET architecture, with assemblies carrying versioning information claims to have solved this problem [20]. Java, on the other hand, links the first class with given name found in the classpath, and any more sophisticated scheme can be implemented through custom class loaders [17].

Another question connected to dynamic linking is the type safety guarantees given *after* choosing components. Breaking type safety jeopardizes the integrity of memory, and ultimately security [7,18]. DLLs do not attempt to guarantee type safety: type errors may occur and go undetected, or throw exceptions of an unrelated nature in unrelated parts of the code. Conversely, in Java and C# if the components linked turn out to be "incompatible", link related exceptions are thrown, describing the nature of the problem.

---

* Work partly supported by DART, EU project IST-2001-33477

P. Degano (Ed.): ESOP 2003, LNCS 2618, pp. 38–53, 2003.
© Springer-Verlag Berlin Heidelberg 2003

Thus, although Java and C# do not guarantee choice of compatible components, they guarantee type safety and give error messages that signal the source of the problem.

Our study is concerned with how Java and C# guarantee type safety. Java and C# dynamic linking are similar: The same linking phases are involved, *i.e.,* loading, verification, offset calculation, and layout determination. Soundness is based on similar ideas: *i.e.,* consistency of the layout and virtual tables, verifying intermediate code, and checking before calculating offsets. Executions which do not throw linking errors give the same result. However, Java and C# dynamic linking are not identical: The linking phases have different granularity, are combined differently and take place in a different order. Linking errors may be detected at different times in Java and C# executions.

We develop a non-deterministic model, to describe the behaviour of both Java and C#. We prove soundness, and that all executions that do not throw link errors give the same results. Our model is concerned with the interplay of the phases rather than with the particular phases themselves. It is at a higher level than the Java bytecode or the .NET IL. It abstracts from Java multiple loaders and .NET assemblies, and describes the verifier as a type checker, disregarding type inference and data flow analysis issues. It models intermediate code as being interpreted, disregarding the difference between JVM bytecode interpretation, and .NET IL code jit-compilation. It represents dynamic linking *not* necessarily as it *is*, but as it is *perceived* by the source language programmer.

Section 2 introduces Java and C# dynamic linking with an example. Section 3 describes the model. Section 4 states properties, soundness, and equivalence. Section 5 concludes. At `www.disi.unige.it/person/LagorioG/dart/papers/DLE02-long.ps` there is a longer version containing more examples, lemmas, and detail.

2 Introduction to the Dynamic Linking Phases

In the presence of dynamic linking, execution can be understood in terms of;

- evaluation, which is not affected by dynamic linking
- loading, which reads classes from the environment
- verification, which checks type-safety of the code
- laying out, which determines object layout and method tables,
- offset calculation, which replaces references to fields and methods through the corresponding offsets.

These phases apply to different units of granularity: Loading and laying out apply to classes, whilst verification applies to method bodies, and offset calculation applies to individual member access expressions.

Phases depend on each other: A class can only be laid out after it has been loaded. The offset of a member from a class may only be calculated after that class has been laid out. When verification requires some class to extend a further class it will load the two classes – although [21] suggest a lazier approach of posting constraints instead.

The phases are organized slightly differently in Java than in C#: In Java, offset calculation takes place per instruction, and only before the particular member is accessed, whereas in C#, offset calculation takes place per method, and is combined with verification, to give jit-compilation. In Java, all methods of a class are verified together, whereas in C# methods are jit-compiled only before execution. The example from table 2 illustrates these points in both Java and C#, (details `www-dse.doc.ic.ac.uk/~sue/`

Table 1. Execution of the program example – with verification

Java	C#	output
	calc. offset for main	

verify Food
↪ verify main
   ↪check Meal ≤ Meal
   ↪check Penne ≤ Penne
	jit main
	   ↪ check Meal ≤ Meal
	     ↪load Meal
	   ↪ lay out Meal
	   ↪ check Penne ≤ Penne
	     ↪load Penne; Pasta
	       ↪LoadErr if ¬ Cls
	   ↪ lay out Penne
	     ↪lay out Pasta
	   ↪ calc. offset for eat (Penne)	

calc. offset for main		
execute main	execute main	
		—1—

lay out   Meal
verify Meal
↪   verify eat (Penne)
   ↪   check Penne ≤ Pasta
     ↪load Penne; Pasta
       ↪LoadErr if ¬ Cls
       ↪VerifErr, if ¬ Sub
↪ verify chew (Pasta)		

create a new Meal object	create a new Meal object	
		—2—
verify Penne ↪ ... ↪verify Pasta ↪ ...		
create a new Penne object	create a new Penne object	
		—3—

calc. offset for eat (Penne)	jit eat (Penne)
	   ↪check Penne ≤ Pasta
	     ↪VerifErr, if ¬ Sub
	   ↪calc. offset for chew (Pasta)	

execute eat (Penne)	execute eat (Penne)	

calc. offset for chew (Pasta)	jit chew (Pasta)
	   ↪calc. offset for int cal from Pasta
	     ↪NoFieldErr, if ¬ Fld	

execute chew (Pasta)	execute chew (Pasta)	
		0
		—4—
execute eat (Penne)	execute eat (Penne)	
execute chew (Pasta)	execute chew (Pasta)	
calc. offset for int cal from Pasta ↪NoFieldErr, if ¬ Fld		
		100

Table 2. Example program

class Meal {
    void eat (Penne p){ chew (p); }
    void chew (Pasta p) {
       if (p ==**null**) print (0);
       else print (p.cal);   }
}
	class Food {
	    public static void main (**String[]** args) {
	       print ("— 1 —"); Meal m = **new** Meal ();
	       print ("— 2 —"); Penne p = **new** Penne ();
	       print ("— 3 —"); m.eat (**null**);
	       print ("— 4 —"); m.eat (p); }
	}

foodexample.html) and consists of classes Meal and Food, compiled in an environment containing compiled versions of Pasta and Penne:

   class Pasta { **int** cal = 100; }   **class** Penne **extends** Pasta { }

These classes satisfy the following three requirements:

   Cls: Classes Pasta and Penne are present
   Sub: Penne is a subclass of Pasta
   Fld: Pasta contains a field cal of type **int**

which are required by main in Food, *e.g.,* Sub guarantees successful verification of the eat method body, and Fld guarantees successful field access. If Cls, Sub and Fld hold, execution will be successful, and Java and C# will give the same output.

However, the versions of Pasta and Penne available at runtime might differ from those above: Pasta or Penne may not be available, *i.e.,* ¬ Cls. Penne may not be a subtype of Pasta. *i.e.,* ¬ Sub. Pasta may not contain a field **int** cal, *i.e.,* ¬ Fld.

These situations will lead to linking errors, detected by the corresponding linking phases. Because these take place at different times in Java and C#, the errors will be reported at different times. This is shown in table 1. The third column contains the output, *e.g.,* — 1 —. The first and second column contain the linking phases as they occur in Java or in C#, with their dependencies indicated through the ↪ symbol, *e.g.,* in Java, verification of class Meal requires verification of method eat, which in its turn checks that Pasta ≤ Pasta, and Penne ≤ Penne.

The table shows execution both when Cls, Sub, and Fld hold, and when they do not. Thus, if Cls, Sub, and Fld hold, the two executions will print the same output. However:

Verification is "lazier" in C#: Thus, ¬ Sub would cause a linking error after —1— in Java, and after —3— in C#. Java verification checks all methods of that class, whereas C# verifies each method when jit-compiling it before its first call.

Offset calculation is "lazier" in Java: Thus, ¬ Fld would cause a linking error after —3— in C#, and after —4— in Java. References to fields (or methods) are resolved in Java only when the field is actually accessed during execution, whereas in C# references are resolved when the method containing the reference is jit-compiled.

Subtypes are "optimistic" in Java. Thus, ¬ Cls could cause a linking error before —1— in C#, but only after —1— in Java. Checking that a class is a subclass of itself causes loading of the class in C#, but does not in Java.

3   The Model

The appendix lists all the judgments and terms of this model, and their place of definition. All mappings are partial; $dom(f)$, $rng(f)$ denote the domain and range of function f respectively, and ϵ denotes the undefined value.

3.1 Outline of the model. Programs, P (see fig. 1), describe code in all its forms, *i.e.,* the "raw" classes as loaded, the method bodies before and after verification/jit-compilation, and the class layout. Ps map identifiers to classes, and addresses to method bodies. Classes contain their superclass names, and they are either "raw", containing the signatures of fields and methods, and method bodies; or, they are "laid out", containing layout tables which map field and method signatures to offsets and virtual method tables which map offsets to addresses. Global contexts, W, represent the context from which "raw" classes may be loaded.

Heaps, H, map addresses to objects. Expressions, e, allow for method call, field access and assignment. Execution reads classes from a global context W, and modifies heaps, expressions, and programs. Therefore, it has the form: $P, H, e \leadsto_W P', H', e'$.

Loading, verification and laying out of classes can be understood as enriching the information in the program, represented through the judgement $W \vdash P' \leq P$. Loading is represented through an extension of P using the contents of W. The layout tables are required to extend those of the superclass. Verification and jit-compilation is represented through modification of method bodies indicating that they have been verified, and possible substitutions of symbolic references by offsets.

Offset calculation has the format $e \leadsto_P e'$, meaning that symbolic references in e are replaced by offsets in e', according to the layout tables in P.

Verification/jit-compilation is represented through: $P, e \leadsto_{W,E} P', e', t$ which means that e is verified/jit-compiled into expression e' and has type t. The program P may need to be extended to P', using information from W. The typing needs a typing environment E. Verification may need to check subtypes: $P, t', t \leadsto_W P'$ means that t' was established as a subtype of t, and in the process, P was extended to P'.

The model is highly non-deterministic, supporting the description of both languages:

Verification is "lazier" in C#. The model requires methods to have been verified/jit-compiled before being called (fourth rule in fig. 3), thus allowing the C# lazy approach. However, verification is part of program extension (fifth rule in fig. 2), and program extension may take place at any time during execution (first rule in fig. 3), thus allowing the Java approach too. Of course, it also allows further behaviour, *e.g.,* where only some methods are verified/jit-compiled, or where classes are verified upon loading.

Offset calculation is "lazier" in Java. The model combines verification and jit-compilation into one judgment, $P, e \leadsto_{W,E} P', e', t$, which requires offset calculation for its subexpressions (third to fifth rules in fig. 5). This describes C# jit-compilation. Offset calculation may also leave the expression unmodified (last rule in fig. 4), and that describes Java verification. Offset calculation may also take place during execution (last rule in fig. 3), and the operational semantics for member access requires the offset to have been calculated (fourth and fifth rules in fig. 3). This describes Java offset calculation. The model allows many more executions, *e.g.,* offsets may be calculated even if not required, or *only some* of the symbolic references are replaced.

Programs
$$P \in Prg = (ClassId \rightarrow (ClassRaw \uplus ClassLaidOut))$$
$$\times (\mathbb{N} \rightarrow Body) \qquad \text{programs}$$

$ClassRaw$	$= ClassId \times \Delta^F \times \Delta^M$	
$\delta^F \in \Delta^F$	$= FieldId \rightarrow Typ$	field descriptions
$\delta^M \in \Delta^M$	$= MethId \times Typ \times Typ \rightarrow Exp$	method descriptions

$ClassLaidOut$	$= ClassId \times \mathcal{T}^F \times \mathcal{T}^M \times \mathcal{T}^C$	
$\tau^F \in \mathcal{T}^F$	$= FieldId \times Typ \rightarrow \mathbb{N}^+$	field layout tables
$\tau^M \in \mathcal{T}^M$	$= MethId \times Typ \times Typ \rightarrow \mathbb{N}$	method layout tables
$\tau^C \in \mathcal{T}^C$	$= \mathbb{N} \rightarrow \mathbb{N}$	code tables

$$Body = (Typ \times Typ \times Exp) \qquad \text{meth. body before jit/verif.}$$
$$\uplus \; Exp \qquad \text{meth. body after jit/verif.}$$

Global contexts
$$W \in ClassId \rightarrow ClassRaw$$

Expressions
$e, e' \in Exp ::=$	$\textbf{new } c \mid$	instance creation
	$\iota \mid$	address
	$y \mid$	parameter
	$e\; ma(e') \mid$	method invocation
	$e\; fa = e' \mid$	field assignment
	$e\; fa \mid$	field access
	$\texttt{this} \mid$	this reference
	$\texttt{nllPExc} \mid$	null-pointer exception
	$\texttt{lnkExc}$	linking related exception
$t, t' \in Typ ::=$	c	type (class name)
$ma \in Ann^M ::=$	$.m[c, t, t'] \mid$	unresolved method annotation
	$[\kappa]$	resolved method annotation
$fa \in Ann^F ::=$	$.f[c, t] \mid$	unresolved field annotation
	$[\kappa]$	resolved field annotation
$a \in Ann ::=$	$fa \mid$	field annotation
	ma	method annotation

$c \in ClassId$	$= Id$	class identifiers
$f \in FieldId$	$= Id$	field identifiers
$m \in MethId$	$= Id$	method identifiers
$\iota \in \mathbb{N}$		addresses
$\kappa \in \mathbb{N}$		offsets

Subtypes

$$\frac{P(c_1)\downarrow_1 = c_2}{P \vdash c_1 \leq c_1} \qquad \frac{P \vdash c_1 \leq c_2 \quad P \vdash c_2 \leq c_3}{P \vdash c_1 \leq c_3}$$
$$P \vdash c_1 \leq c_2$$

Fig. 1. Expressions, programs, subtypes

$$\frac{}{W \vdash P \leq P}$$

$$\frac{W \vdash P' \leq P''}{W \vdash P'' \leq P}$$
$$\frac{W \vdash P'' \leq P}{W \vdash P' \leq P}$$

$$\frac{\begin{array}{l} P = c = P' \\ P(c) = \epsilon \\ P'(c) = W(c) = \langle c_s, \_, \_ \rangle \\ P(c_s) \neq \epsilon \end{array}}{W \vdash P' \leq P}$$

$$\frac{\begin{array}{l} P = c = P' \\ P(c) = \langle c_s, \delta^F, \delta^M \rangle, \ P'(c) = \langle c_s, \tau^F, \tau^M, \tau^C \rangle \\ P(c_s) = \langle \_, \tau_s^F, \tau_s^M, \tau_s^C \rangle \\ \tau^F \text{ injective, } dom(\tau^F) = \{ \langle f, t \rangle \mid \delta^F(f) = t \} \\ rng(\tau^F) \cap FdOffs(P, c_s) = \emptyset \\ \tau^M \leq \tau_s^M \text{ wrt } dom(\delta^M), \ \ \tau^C \preceq \tau_s^C \text{ wrt } \tau^M(dom(\delta^M)) \\ \delta^M(m, t, t') = e \implies \exists \iota : \\ \tau^C(\tau^M(m, t, t')) = \iota, P(\iota) = \epsilon, \ P'(\iota) = (t, t', e) \end{array}}{W \vdash P' \leq P}$$

$$\frac{\begin{array}{l} P = \iota = P' \\ P(\iota) = \langle t_r, t_p, e \rangle, \ \ P'(\iota) = e' \\ \exists c \in dom(P') : \\ \quad P(c') = \langle \_, \_, \_, \tau_1^C \rangle, \ \iota \in rng(\tau_1^C) \implies P \vdash c' \leq c \\ \quad P', e \leadsto_{W, \{this \mapsto c, y \mapsto t_p\}} P', e', t \\ \quad P' \vdash t \leq t_r \end{array}}{W \vdash P' \leq P}$$

Fig. 2. Program extension

Subtypes are "optimistic" in Java. The model considers any class identifier a subtype of itself (last rule in fig. 5); thus reflecting Java. However, subtype checking may extend a program during verification (penultimate rule in fig. 5), thus reflecting C#.

Timing of link-related actions. The model allows loading, jit-compilation, verification, and offset calculation to take place at any time (first rule in fig. 3), even if not needed. It allows linking exceptions (not null pointer exceptions) at any time (second rule in fig. 3), even if not necessary, and does not distinguish the reason. This does not reflect practical implementations but simplifies the model considerably.

3.2 Programs reflect the internal representation of code. They are described in figure 1. They map identifiers to raw (*ClassRaw*) or to laid out classes (*ClassLaidOut*), and addresses to method bodies. Raw classes correspond to *.class or *.dll files. They consist of the superclass name, the field descriptions ($\delta^F \in \Delta^F$) consisting of field identifiers and types, and method descriptions ($\delta^M \in \Delta^M$) consisting of method identifier, argument type, return type and method body. Laid out classes consist of a field layout table ($\tau^F \in \mathcal{T}^F$), which determines the offset for a field with given identifier and type, the method layout table ($\tau^M \in \mathcal{T}^M$), which maps method signatures to offsets, and the virtual table ($\tau^C \in \mathcal{T}^C$), which maps offsets to addresses of method bodies.

Method bodies which have not been checked consist of a signature and expression, *Typ* × *Typ* × *Exp*. Bodies which have been checked consist of an expression, *Exp*.

3.3 Expressions. The syntax is given in figure 1. It describes classes, subclasses, methods and fields for an imperative language.

$$\frac{W \vdash P' \leq P}{P, H, e \leadsto_W P', H, e} \qquad \frac{}{P, H, e \leadsto_W P, H, \mathtt{lnkExc}}$$

$$\frac{FdOffs(P, c) = \{\kappa_1, \ldots, \kappa_n\}, \quad \iota \text{ free in } H}{P, H, \mathtt{new}\ c \leadsto_W P, H[\iota \mapsto c, \iota+\kappa_1 \mapsto 0, \ldots \iota+\kappa_n \mapsto 0], \iota}$$

$$\frac{\begin{array}{l} H(\iota) = c \\ P(c) = \langle -,-,-,\tau^C\rangle \\ P(\tau^C(\kappa)) = e \end{array}}{P, H, \iota[\kappa](\iota') \leadsto_W P, H, e[\iota/\mathtt{this}, \iota'/\mathtt{y}]} \qquad \frac{\iota \neq 0}{\begin{array}{l} P, H, \iota[\kappa] \leadsto_W P, H, H(\iota+\kappa) \\ P, H, \iota[\kappa] = \iota' \leadsto_W P, H[\iota+\kappa \mapsto \iota'], \iota' \end{array}}$$

$$\frac{P, H, e \leadsto_W P', H', e'}{P, H, \ulcorner e \urcorner^{exe} \leadsto_W P', H', \ulcorner e' \urcorner^{exe}}$$

$$\frac{}{\begin{array}{l} P, H, 0[\kappa] \leadsto_W P, H, \mathtt{nllPExc} \\ P, H, 0[\kappa] = \iota \leadsto_W P, H, \mathtt{nllPExc} \\ P, H, 0[\kappa](\iota) \leadsto_W P, H, \mathtt{nllPExc} \end{array}} \qquad \frac{z = \mathtt{nllPExc}, \text{ or } z = \mathtt{lnkExc}}{P, H, \ulcorner z \urcorner^{exe} \leadsto_W P', H', z}$$

$$\frac{a \leadsto_P a'}{P, H, \ulcorner a \urcorner^{off} \leadsto_W P, H, \ulcorner a' \urcorner^{off}}$$

Fig. 3. Execution.

We use an augmented high level language, near to source code. The augmentations are memory offsets, and type annotations, used to disambiguate fields or methods with the same name. For example, the expression p.cal [Pasta,int] denotes the field called cal of p, of type int, and declared in class Pasta. This symbolic reference will be replaced during offset calculation; *e.g.*, if int cal has offset 3 in class Pasta then the expression will be rewritten to p[3].

Values are addresses, natural numbers denoted by ι, ι' *etc*; the null pointer is 0. When a field is accessed or a method is called on 0, the nllPExc exception is raised. Also, lnkExc stands for, and does not distinguish between, any link related exception, *i.e.*, verification errors, class not found, class circularities, absence of fields and methods.

3.4 Execution modifies the current program, expression and heap, and has the form

$$P, H, e \leadsto_W P', H', e'$$

expressing that the global context W may be used for program extension. It is defined through small step semantics in figure 3.

Heaps, H, map addresses to objects, which are memory blocks consisting of class identifier, and values for the fields. Values are object addresses, or 0. Heaps have form:

$$H : \mathbb{N}^+ \to \mathbb{N} \uplus \mathit{ClassId}.$$

If $H(\iota) = c \in \mathit{ClassId}$ then ι points to an object of class c. The fields of that object are stored at some offset, κ, from ι. An address ι is fresh in H iff $\forall \kappa : H(\iota+\kappa) = \epsilon$.

The following heap, H_0, contains a Penne object at 2, and a Food object at 4:

$H_0(2)$ = Penne start Penne object $H_0(3)$ = 55 field int cal from Pasta
$H_0(4)$ = Food   start Food object $H_0(\iota)$ = ϵ for all other ι 's

Thus, as in [4], heaps are modelled at a lower level than in verifier studies [24,10, 21], where objects are indivisible entities, and where there are no address calculations. Our lower level model enables the description of the potential damage when executing unverified code.

3.5 Program Extension. We define mapping extensions ($g' \leq g$ wrt A, $g' \preceq g$ wrt A), and program equality up to class or address ($P =c= P'$, $P =\iota= P'$):

Definition 1 *For injective mappings g, g', set A, and for P, P', and ι, and c :*

- $g' \leq g$ *wrt* A, *iff* $dom(g') = dom(g) \cup A$, *and* $\forall y \in dom(g) : g'(y) = g(y)$.
- $g' \preceq g$ *wrt* A, *iff* $dom(g') = dom(g) \cup A$, *and* $\forall y \in dom(g) \setminus A : g'(y) = g(y)$.
- $P =\iota= P'$ *iff* $\forall c : P(c) = P'(c)$, *and* $\forall \iota' \in dom(P) \setminus \{\iota\} : P(\iota') = P'(\iota')$.
- $P =c= P'$ *iff* $\forall c' \neq c : P(c') = P'(c')$, *and* $\forall \iota \in dom(P) : P(\iota) = P'(\iota)$.

A program P' extends another program P, if P' contains more information (through loading of classes), or more refined information (through verification, jit-compilation or layout calculation) than P. This relationship has the format

$$W \vdash P' \leq P$$

c.f. figure 2, and is defined in the global context of a W which expresses the environment (possibly a file system) from which classes are loaded.

In more detail, $W \vdash P' \leq P$ if: 1) P' is in the reflexive, transitive closure of the relation. 2) P' and P are identical up to c, a raw class read from W whose superclass (c_s) is already in P. 3) P' and P are identical up to class c, and a) the field layout of c extends that of c_s and fields introduced by c get fresh offsets, b) the method layout of c extends that of c_s, c) all methods in c which override (have the same signature as) methods in c_s are mapped to new addresses. 4) P' and P are identical up to address ι, and $P(\iota')$ contains the verified/jit-compiled version of the method at $P(\iota)$.

The first rule of figure 3 says that programs may be extended at any time. The second rule allows linking exceptions to be thrown at any time. This is, of course, highly non-deterministic, and does not prohibit linking phases or errors even if unnecessary.

3.6 Evaluation is not directly affected by dynamic linking. It is described by the third through eighth rule in figure 3.

Creation of a new object, new c, allocates fresh addresses for the fields of c at the corresponding offsets, initializing them with **0**. The auxiliary function which collects the field offsets from all superclasses:

$$FdOffs(P, c) = \bigcup_{P \vdash c \leq c'} rng(P(c') \downarrow_2)$$

Method call, $\iota[\kappa](\iota')$, looks up the method body e in the dynamic class of the receiver ι, using the offset κ, and executes that body after replacing this by the actual receiver ι, and the parameter y by the argument ι'. Therefore, evaluation only applies to expressions which do *not* contain this, or y. The format of the call $\iota[\kappa](\iota')$

$$\frac{P(c) = \langle \_, \tau^F, \_, \_ \rangle \quad \tau^F(f, t) = \kappa}{.f[c, t] \leadsto_P [\kappa]} \qquad \frac{P(c) = \langle \_, \_, \tau^M, \_ \rangle \quad \tau^M(m, t_r, t_p) = \kappa}{.m[c, t_r, t_p] \leadsto_P [\kappa]} \qquad \frac{}{a \leadsto_P a}$$

Fig. 4. Offset calculation.

(rather than $\iota.m[c, t_r, t_p](\iota'))$ means that the offset has been calculated. The requirement $P(c) = \langle \_, \_, \_, \tau^C \rangle$ (rather than $P(c) = \langle \_, \_, \_ \rangle$) means that the class c has been laid out. The requirement that $P(\tau^C(\kappa)) = e$ (rather than $P(\tau^C(\kappa)) = \langle \_, \_, \_ \rangle$) means that the particular method has been verified/jit-compiled.

Field lookup retrieves the contents of the heap at the given offset, whereas field assignment updates the heap at the given offset, as in the fifth rule. Method call and field access for **0** throw a nllPExc, as described in the sixth rule of the figure.

Execution is propagated to its context, as described in the seventh rule. Both link related, and unrelated exceptions (*i.e.*, z) are propagated out of their contexts, as described in the eighth rule. Execution contexts allow a succinct description of propagation:

$$\sqsubset \cdot \sqsupset^{exe} ::= \sqsubset \cdot \sqsupset^{exe} ma(e) \mid \iota \, ma(\sqsubset \cdot \sqsupset^{exe}) \mid$$
$$\sqsubset \cdot \sqsupset^{exe} fa = e \mid \iota \, fa = \sqsubset \cdot \sqsupset^{exe} \mid \sqsubset \cdot \sqsupset^{exe} fa$$

3.7 Offset Calculation replaces a symbolic reference through an offset, and has format

$$a \leadsto_P a'$$

where a represents a field or method annotation. Figure 4 says that for fields, we look up the name of the field and its type in the class, whilst for methods we look up the name, argument type and result type in the class. The last rule allows a to be left unmodified.

The last rule in 3 allows offset calculation to happen during execution, as in Java. For this, we have defined appropriate notion of offset calculation contexts as

$$\sqsubset \cdot \sqsupset^{off} ::= e \sqsubset \cdot \sqsupset^{off} \mid e \sqsubset \cdot \sqsupset^{off} = e \mid e \sqsubset \cdot \sqsupset^{off}(e)$$

Offset calculation also happens during jit-compilation, (figure 5) thus modelling C#. Combining this with the rule that leaves offsets unmodified we model Java verification which does not calculate the offsets.

3.8 Verification and Jit-Compilation. We describe the similarities between Java verification and C# jit-compilation through verification/jit-compilation, in fig. 5:

$$P, e \leadsto_{W,E} P', e', t$$

which transforms expression e to e', type checks e to type t, and possibly extends the program P to P'. The process takes place in an environment E which maps this and the parameter y to types, *i.e.*, $E : \{ \text{this}, \text{y} \} \to Typ$, and in the global context W.

The parameter y and the receiver this have the type given in the environment E. Verification/jit-compilation of an object creation expression requires c to be a class, and gives it type c. The value **0** has any class type c.

Method call requires the receiver and argument to be well-typed, and to be of subtypes of c and t_p, the receiver and argument types stored in the symbolic method annotation

$$\frac{}{\substack{P, \text{this} \leadsto_{W,E} P, \text{this}, E(\text{this}) \\ P, \text{y} \leadsto_{W,E} P, \text{y}, E(\text{y})}}$$

$$\frac{P, c, c \leadsto_W P'}{\substack{P, \text{new } c \leadsto_{W,E} P', \text{new } c, c \\ P, 0 \leadsto_{W,E} P', 0, c}}$$

$$\frac{\begin{array}{l} P, e_1 \leadsto_{W,E} P_1, e_1', t_1 \\ P_1, e_2 \leadsto_{W,E} P_2, e_2', t_2 \\ P_2, t_1, c \leadsto_W P_3 \\ P_3, t_2, t_f \leadsto_W P' \\ .f[c, t_f] \leadsto_{P'} fa \end{array}}{P, e_1.f[c, t_f] = e_2 \leadsto_{W,E} P', e_1' fa = e_2', t_f}$$

$$\frac{\begin{array}{l} P, e \leadsto_{W,E} P_1, e', t_e \\ P_1, t_e, c \leadsto_W P' \\ .f[c, t_f] \leadsto_{P'} fa \end{array}}{P, e.f[c, t_f] \leadsto_{W,E} P', e' fa, t_f}$$

$$\frac{\begin{array}{l} P, e_1 \leadsto_{W,E} P_1, e_1', t_1 \\ P_1, e_2 \leadsto_{W,E} P_2, e_2', t_2 \\ P_2, t_1, c \leadsto_W P_3 \\ P_3, t_2, t_p \leadsto_W P' \\ .m[c, t_r, t_p] \leadsto_{P'} ma \end{array}}{P, e_1.m[c, t_r, t_p](e_2) \leadsto_{W,E} P', e_1' ma(e_2'), t_r}$$

$$\frac{\begin{array}{l} W \vdash P'' \leq P \\ P'', e \leadsto_{W,E} P', e', t \end{array}}{P, e \leadsto_{W,E} P', e', t}$$

$$\frac{\begin{array}{l} W \vdash P' \leq P \\ P' \vdash t' \leq t \end{array}}{P, t', t \leadsto_W P'}$$

$$\frac{}{P, t, t \leadsto_W P}$$

Fig. 5. Verification and Jit-compilation.

$.m[c, t_r, t_p]$. The method call has type t_r, the result type of the annotation. The symbolic annotation may be replaced by an offset, thus modeling C# jit-compilation. Offset calculation also allows for the identity, thus modeling Java verification. Similar explanations apply to the rules which access fields.

Finally, verification may require classes to be loaded, and the offset calculation may require layout information about some classes. This is described through the sixth rule, which allows extension of the program at any time.

Verification/jit-compilation may need to check that a type is a subtype of another type, and while doing so may need to load further classes, as in judgment:

$$P, t_1, t_2 \leadsto_W P'$$

also given in figure 5. Notice, that this judgment allows any identifier to be a subtype of itself even if not loaded - this follows the "optimistic" Java approach.

4   Soundness and Equivalence of Strategies

The judgment $\vdash P$ defined in fig. 6 guarantees that program P is well formed, *i.e.*, that 1) the class Object is defined and has itself as a superclass, 2) all superclasses are present, and the subclass relationship is acyclic except for Object, 3) for any laid out class c with superclass c_s the fields and methods have distinct offsets, the methods defined in c_s have the same offsets in c, and 3) all the methods defined in c_s have the same offsets

$$P(\texttt{Object}) = \langle \texttt{Object}, \_, \_, \_\rangle$$
$$P \vdash c \leq c' \quad \Longrightarrow \quad c' \in dom(P) \ \text{ and } \ P \vdash c' \leq c \Longrightarrow c' = c$$

$$P(c) = \langle c', \tau^F, \tau^M, \tau^C\rangle \Longrightarrow
\begin{cases}
c = c' \Longrightarrow c = \texttt{Object} \\
\tau^F, \tau^M, \tau^C \text{ injective} \\
rng(\tau^M) = dom(\tau^C), \ rng(\tau^C) \subseteq dom(P{\downarrow}_2) \\
P \vdash c \leq c_s, c \neq c_s \Longrightarrow
\begin{cases}
P(c_s) = \langle \_, \tau_s^F, \tau_s^M, \_\rangle \\
rng(\tau_s^F) \cap rng(\tau^F) = \emptyset \\
\tau^M \leq \tau_s^M \text{ wrt some set}
\end{cases}
\end{cases}$$

$$\iota \in rng(P(c'){\downarrow}_4) \cap rng(P(c''){\downarrow}_4) \Longrightarrow
\begin{cases}
\exists c : \\
P \vdash c' \leq c, \ P \vdash c'' \leq c, \ \iota \in rng(P(c){\downarrow}_4) \\
\iota \in rng(P(c'''){\downarrow}_4) \Longrightarrow P \vdash c''' \leq c \\
P(\iota) = e \Longrightarrow
\begin{cases}
\exists e_0, \tau^M, \tau^C, m, t_r, t_p : \\
P, e_0 \leadsto_{\emptyset, \{\texttt{this} \mapsto c, y \mapsto t_p\}} P, e, t \\
P \vdash t \leq t_r \\
P(c) = \langle \_, \_, \tau^M, \tau^C\rangle \\
\tau^C(\tau^M(m, t_r, t_p)) = \iota
\end{cases}
\end{cases}$$

$$\vdash P$$

Fig. 6. Well-formed programs

$$\frac{\begin{array}{c} P \vdash c' \leq c \\ H(\iota) = c' \end{array}}{P, H \vdash \iota \triangleleft c} \qquad \frac{}{P, H \vdash \mathbf{0} \triangleleft c} \qquad \frac{\begin{array}{c} H(\iota) = c \\ P(c) = \langle \_, \tau^F, \_, \_\rangle \\ \forall \kappa : TypeOfFd(P, c, \kappa) = t \Longrightarrow P, H \vdash \iota + \kappa \triangleleft t \\ 1 \leq \kappa \leq max(FdOffs(P, c)) \Longrightarrow H(\iota + \kappa) \notin ClassId \end{array}}{P, H \vdash \iota}$$

$$\frac{H(\iota) \in ClassId \Longrightarrow P, H \vdash \iota}{P \vdash H}$$

Fig. 7. Conformance

in c, and 4) all method bodies which are considered as already verified/jit-compiled, *i.e.*, for which $P(\iota) = e$, can be verified/jit compiled, albeit without program extension, and therefore in the empty global context, $\emptyset$.

Figure 7 defines conformance. The judgment $P, H \vdash \iota$ expresses that the object stored at ι conforms to its class, c, as stored in $H(\iota)$. For all fields of c, the object must contain appropriate values at the corresponding offsets, and no other object may be stored between its fields. The judgment $P \vdash H$ requires all objects to conform to their class, and (implicitly) that the class of any objects stored in H is defined in P. Notice, that $\mathbf{0}$ conforms to any class, allowing fields initialized to $\mathbf{0}$, to belong even to a class that has not been loaded yet.

Types for runtime expressions are given by judgment $P, H \vdash e : t$, from fig. 8, with rules similar to those for verification/jit-compilation, with the difference that heaps *are* taken into account (to give types to addresses), environments are *not* taken into account (runtime expressions do not contain this, or y), and the program is *not* extended.

Runtime expressions containing field access offsets are typed using:

$$TypeOfFd(P, c, \kappa) = t \text{ if } P(c'){\downarrow}_2 (\_, t) = \kappa \text{ for } P \vdash c \leq c', \quad \epsilon \text{ otherwise}$$

$$\frac{}{P, H \vdash 0 : c} \qquad \frac{P, H \vdash \iota \quad P \vdash c \leq c' \quad H(\iota) = c}{P, H \vdash \iota : c'} \qquad \frac{P, H \vdash e : c' \quad P \vdash c' \leq c}{P, H \vdash e.f[c, t] : t} \qquad \frac{P, H \vdash e : c \quad TypeOfFd(P, c, \kappa) = t}{P, H \vdash e[\kappa] : t}$$

$$\frac{}{P, H \vdash \text{new } c : c}$$

$$\frac{P, H \vdash e\,fa : t \quad P, H \vdash e' : t' \quad P \vdash t' \leq t}{P, H \vdash e\,fa = e' : t} \qquad \frac{P, H \vdash e_1 : c_1 \quad P, H \vdash e_2 : t_2 \quad P \vdash c_1 \leq c \quad P \vdash t_2 \leq t_p}{P, H \vdash e_1.m[c, t_r, t_p](e_2) : t_r} \qquad \frac{P, H \vdash e_1 : c_1 \quad P, H \vdash e_2 : t_2 \quad P \vdash t_2 \leq t_p \quad P(c_1) = \langle \_, \_, \tau^M, \_ \rangle \quad \tau^M(\langle \ldots, t_r, t_p \rangle) = \kappa}{P, H \vdash e_1[\kappa](e_2) : t_r}$$

Fig. 8. Types of runtime expressions.

The above, and the inverse layout function for runtime types of method calls, are well-defined in well formed programs, because layout functions are injective.

In the longer version we prove that verification/jit-compilation and execution extend programs. Subtyping, conformance of heap, runtime types, verification of expressions, or well-formedness of program, established in a program P are preserved in an extending program P'. Therefore, execution of *any* expression preserves well-formedness of programs. Finally, a verified expression preserves its runtime type, when the receiver and argument have been replaced by addresses of appropriate class.

In theorem 1 we prove subject reduction which guarantees that the heap H' preserves conformance, uninitialized parts of the store are never dereferenced, and the expression preserves its type. In theorem 2 we prove that nondeterminism does *not* affect the result of evaluations which do not throw link related exceptions, provided we operate in the same global context W.

Theorem 1 *If* $P \vdash H$, *and* $\vdash P$, *and* $P, H \vdash e : t$, *and* $P, H, e \leadsto_W P', H', e'$ *then*

$P' \vdash H'$, *and*

if e' *does not contain an exception, then* $\quad \exists\, t' : \quad P', H' \vdash e' : t', \quad P' \vdash t' \leq t$.

Theorem 2 *For* e, P, P', P'', H, H', H'', ι, *and* $\nu, \nu' \in \mathbb{N} \cup \{\text{nllPExc}\}$, *if:*

$$P, H, e \leadsto^*_W P', H', \nu, \quad \text{and} \quad P, H, e \leadsto^*_W P'', H'', \nu',$$

then:

$$\nu = \nu', H' = H'' \text{ up to renaming of addresses.}$$

Theorem 2 does *not* apply for intermediate results, nor if ν were a link related exception – counterexamples apeared in section 2.

5   Conclusions, Related Work, and Further Work

Dynamic linking is a relatively new, very powerful language feature with complex semantics, which needs to be well understood. Our model is simple, especially considering the complexity of the feature, and compared to an earlier model for Java [4].

We have achieved simplicity through many iterations, and through the choice of appropriate abstractions: 1) we do not distinguish the causes of link related exceptions, 2) we allow link-related exceptions to be thrown at *any* time of execution, even when there exist other, legal evaluations, 3) we do not prescribe at which point of execution the program will be extended, and so allow "unnecessary" loading, verification or jit-compilations, 4) we combine in the concept of "program" loaded, verified, and laid out code, 5) we represent programs through mapping rather than texts or data structures. Most of these abstractions were introduced primarily to allow the model to serve for both Java and for C#, and had the agreeable effect of significant simplification.

Non-determinism seems to have been in the the Java designers' minds: the specification [17], sect. 12.1.1 requires resolution errors to be thrown only when linking actions related to the error are required. Through non-determinism we distilled the main ingredients of dynamic linking in both languages, and their dependencies. We prove type soundness, thus obtaining type soundness both for the Java and the C# strategies, and showed that different strategies within the model do not differ widely.

Extensive literature is devoted to the Java verifier [24,11]. Dynamic loading in Java is formalized in [14], while problems with security in the presence of multiple loaders are reported in [23], a solution presented in [16], which is found flawed and improved upon in [21]. Type safety for a substantial subset of the .NET IL is proven in [12].

The semantics of linking is studied in [2]. Module interconnection languages, and mixins [1,8,6] give explicit control of program composition at source code level.

Dynamic linking gave rise to the concept of binary compatible changes, [9], and [17], sect. 13, *i.e.*, changes which do not introduce more linking errors than the original code; the concept is explored in [5]. Tools that load most recent binary compatible versions of code were developed for Java [22] and C# [15]. Current JVMs go even further, and support replacing a class by a class of the same signature, as a "fix-and-continue" feature [3]. Dynamic software updates [13] support type safe dynamic reloading of code whose type may have changed, while the system is running.

Further work includes a better understanding of binary compatible library developments, extension of the model to allow verification also posting constraints, as suggested in [21], or to allow field lookup based on superclass's tables as in some of JVMs, incorporation of C# assemblies and modules, extensions of the model so as to avoid unnecessary linking steps, and "concretization" of the model so as to obtain Java or C# behaviour.

Acknowledgements. We are indebted to Vladimir Jurisic, Davide Ancona, Elena Zucca, Christopher Anderson, and Mark Skipper for suggestions and feedback.

References

1. Davide Ancona and Elena Zucca. A calculus of module systems. *Journal Functional Programming*, 12(3):91–132, 2002.
2. Luca Cardelli. Program Fragments, Linking, and Modularization. In *POPL'97 Proceedings*, January 1997.
3. Mikhail Dimitriev. Hotspot Technology Application for Advanced Profiling. In *ECOOP USE Workhop*, June 2002.

4. Sophia Drossopoulou. An Abstract model of Java dynamic Linking and Loading. In Robert Harper, editor, *Types in Compilation, Third International Workshop, Revised Selected Papers*. Springer, 2001.

5. Sophia Drossopoulou, Susan Eisenbach, and David Wragg. A Fragment Calculus - towards a model of Separate Compilation, Linking and Binary Compatibility. In *LICS Proceedings*, 1999.

6. Dominic Duggan. Sharing in Typed Module Assembly Language. In *Preliminary Proceedings of the Third Workshop on Types in Compilation (TIC 2000)*. Carnegie Mellon, CMU-CS-00-161, 2000.

7. G. Fenton and E. Felton. *Securing Java Getting Down to Business with Mobile Code*. John Wiley and Sons, 1999.

8. Kathleen Fisher, John Reppy, and Jon Riecke. A Calculus for Compiling and Linking Classes. In *ESOP Proceedings*, March 2000.

9. Ira Forman, Michael Conner, Scott Danforth, and Larry Raper. Release-to-Release Binary Compatibility in SOM. In *OOPSLA Proceedings*, October 1995.

10. Stephen N. Freund and J. C. Mitchell. A Formal Framework for the Java Bytecode Language and Verifier. In *OOPSLA Proceeedings*, November 1999.

11. Stephen N. Freund and J. C. Mitchell. A Type System for Object Initialization in the Java Bytecode Language. In *OOPSLA Proceeedings*, October 1998.

12. Andrew Gordon and Don Syme. Typing a multi-language intermediate code. In *Principles of programming Languages 2001*, pages 248–260. ACM Press, 2001.

13. Michael Hicks, Jonathan T. Moore, and Scott Nettles. Dynamic Software Updating. In *Programming Language Design and Implementation*. ACM, 2001.

14. Thomas Jensen, Daniel Le Metyayer, and Tommy Thorn. A Formalization of Visibility and Dynamic Loading in Java. In *IEEE ICCL*, 1998.

15. V. Jurisic. Deja-vu.NET: A Framework for Evolution of Component Based Systems. http://www.doc.ic.ac.uk/~ajf/Teaching/Projects/DistProjects.html, June 2002.

16. Sheng Liang and Gilad Bracha. Dynamic Class Loading in the Java^{TM} Virtual Machine. In *OOPSLA Proceedings*, October 1998.

17. Tim Lindholm and Frank Yellin. *The Java Virtual Machine*. Addison-Wesley, 1999.

18. Type Safety and Security. In *MSDN Magazine*, 2001.

19. M. Pietrek. Avoiding DLL Hell: Introducing Application Metadata in the Microsoft .NET Framework. In *MSDN Magazine*, msdn.microsoft.com/, October 2000.

20. S. Pratschner. Simplifying Deployment and Solving DLL Hell with the .NET Framework. msdn.microsoft.com/, November 2001.

21. Zhenyu Qian, Allen Goldberg, and Alessandro Coglio. A Formal Specification of Java^{TM} Class Loading. In *OOPSLA'2000*, November 2000.

22. C. Sadler S. Eisenbach and S. Shaikh. Evolution of Distributed Java Programs. In *IEEE Working Conf on Component Deployment*, June 2002.

23. Vijay Saraswat. Java is not type-safe. Technical report, AT&T Rresearch, 1997. http://www.research. att.comp/~vj/bug.html.

24. Raymie Stata and Martin Abadi. A Type System For Java Bytecode Subroutines. In *POPL'98 Proceedings*, January 1998.

A Overview of Terms and Judgments of This Paper

e	expressions	fig. 1
t	types	fig. 1
ι	addresses	fig. 1
κ	offsets	fig. 1
nllPExc	the null-pointer exception	fig. 1
lnkExc	link-related exception, *e.g.,* verification, load err. *etc*	fig. 1
fa, ma, a	field, method, or any annotation	fig. 1
δ^F	field descriptions	fig. 1
δ^M	method descriptions	fig. 1
τ^F	field layout tables	fig. 1
τ^M	method layout tables	fig. 1
τ^C	code tables	fig. 1
H	heaps	sec. 3
E	environment giving types to receiver and argument	sec. 3
$\llbracket \cdot \rrbracket^{exe}$	execution context	sect. 3
$\llbracket \cdot \rrbracket^{off}$	offset calculation context	sect. 3
$P, H, e \rightsquigarrow_W P', H', e'$	execution in global context W	fig 3
$a \rightsquigarrow_P a'$	offset calculation	fig. 4
$P, e \rightsquigarrow_{W,E} P', e', t$	verification or jit-compilation	fig. 5
$P, t', t \rightsquigarrow_W P'$	t' is a subtype of t, while extending program P to P'	fig. 5
$W \vdash P' \leq P$	program P' extends program P in global context W	fig. 2
$P \vdash t' \leq t$	in program P the type t' is a subtype of t	fig. 1
$\vdash P$	well formed program	fig. 6
$P \vdash H$	well formed heap H for the program P	fig. 7
$P, H \vdash e : t$	runtime expression e has type t in the context of P and H	fig. 8
$P, H \vdash \iota \lhd c$	ι conforms class c, or subclass	fig. 7
$g' \leq g$ wrt A	mapping g' injectively extends g into set A, preserving $dom(g)$	def. 1
$g' \preceq g$ wrt A	mapping g' injectively extends g into set A, preserving $dom(g) \setminus A$	def. 1
$P =_\iota= P'$	P and P' agree up to address ι	def. 1
$P =_c= P'$	P and P' agree up to class c	def. 1
$FdOffs(P, c)$	the set of all offsets allocated for the fields of c in P	page 46
$TypeOfFd(P, c, \kappa)$	the type of the field contained at the offset κ of c in P	page 49

Correction of Functional Logic Programs[*]

Maria Alpuente[1], Demis Ballis[2], Francisco J. Correa[3], and Moreno Falaschi[2]

[1] DSIC, Universidad Politécnica de Valencia, Camino de Vera s/n, Apdo. 22012, 46071 Valencia, Spain. `alpuente@dsic.upv.es`.
[2] Dip. Matematica e Informatica, Via delle Scienze 206, 33100 Udine, Italy. `{demis,falaschi}@dimi.uniud.it`.
[3] DIS, U. EAFIT, Cra. 49 N. 7 Sur 50, 3300 Medellín, Colombia. `fcorrea@eafit.edu.co`.

Abstract. We propose a new methodology for synthesizing correct functional logic programs. We aim to create an integrated development environment in which it is possible to debug a program and correct it automatically. We start from a declarative diagnoser that we have developed previously which allows us to identify wrong program rules w.r.t. an intended specification. Then a bug-correction, program synthesis methodology tries to correct the erroneous components of the wrong code. We propose a hybrid, top-down (unfolding–based) as well as bottom-up (induction–based), approach for the automatic correction of functional logic programs which is driven by a set of evidence examples which are automatically produced as an outcome by the diagnoser. The resulting program is proven to be correct and complete w.r.t. the considered example sets. Finally, we also provide a prototypical implementation which we use for an experimental evaluation of our system.

1 Introduction

The main motivation for this work is to provide a methodology for developing advanced debugging and correction tools for functional logic languages. Functional logic programming is now a mature paradigm and as such there exist modern environments which assist in the design, development and debugging of integrated programs. However, there is no theoretical foundation for integrating debugging and synthesis into a single unified framework. We believe that such an integration can be quite productive and hence develop useful techniques and new results for the process of automatically synthesizing correct programs.

In a previous work [6], a generic diagnosis method w.r.t. computed answers which generalizes the ideas of [11] to the diagnosis of functional logic programs has been proposed. The method works for eager (*call–by–value*) as well as for lazy (*call–by–name*) integrated languages. Given the intended specification $\mathcal{I}$ of a program $\mathcal{R}$, we can check the correctness of $\mathcal{R}$ w.r.t. $\mathcal{I}$ by a single step

---

[*] This work has been partially supported by CICYT under grant TIC2001-2705-C03-01, by Acción Integrada Hispano-Italiana HI2000-0161 and by Generalitat Valenciana under grant GV01-424.

P. Degano (Ed.): ESOP 2003, LNCS 2618, pp. 54–68, 2003.

of a (continuous) immediate consequence operator which we associate to our programs. This specification $\mathcal{I}$ may be partial or complete, and can be expressed in several ways: for instance, by (another) functional logic program [6,2], by an assertion language [10] or by equation sets (in the case when it is finite). Our methodology is based on abstract interpretation: we construct *over* and *under* specifications $\mathcal{I}^+$ and $\mathcal{I}^-$ to correctly over- (resp. under-) approximate the intended semantics $\mathcal{I}$. We then use these two sets respectively for the functions in the premises and the consequences of the immediate consequence operator, and by a simple static test we can determine whether some of the clauses are wrong. The debugging system B uggy[3] is an experimental implementation of the method which allows the user to specify the (concrete) semantics by means of a functional logic program. In [2], we also presented a preliminary correction algorithm based on the deductive synthesis methodology known as *example-guided unfolding* [8]. This methodology uses unfolding in order to discriminate positive from negative examples (resp. uncovered and incorrect equations) which are essentially obtained as an outcome by the diagnoser.

However, this pure deductive learner cannot be applied when the original wrong program is overspecialized (that is, it does not cover all the (positive) examples chosen to describe the pursued behavior). In this paper, we develop a new program corrector based on, and integrated with, the declarative debugger of [6,2], which integrates top–down as well as bottom–up synthesis techniques. The resulting method is conceptually cleaner than more elaborated, purely deductive or inductive learning procedures, and combines the advantages of both styles. Furthermore, our method is parametric w.r.t. the chosen bottom-up learner. As an instance of such parameter, we consider for the bottom-up part of the algorithm the functional logic inductive framework of [17,20]. Informally, our correction procedure works as follows. Starting from an overly general program (that is, a program which covers all positive examples as well as some negative ones), the top–down algorithm unfolds the program until a set of rules which only occur in the refutation of the negative examples is identified, and then they are removed from the program. When the original wrong program does not initially cover all positive examples, we first invoke the bottom–up procedure, which "generalizes" the program as to fulfil the applicability conditions. After introducing the new method we prove its correctness and completeness w.r.t. the considered example sets. Finally we present a prototypical implementation of our system and the relative benchmarks. The following example illustrates our method.

Example 1. Let us consider the program:

$$\mathcal{R} = \{ od(\mathbf{0}) \to true, od(\mathbf{s}(\mathbf{X})) \to od(X), z(0) \to \mathbf{1}, z(s(X)) \to z(X) \}$$

which is wrong w.r.t. the following specification of the intended semantics (mistakes in $\mathcal{R}$ are marked in bold):

$$\mathcal{I} = \{\ ev(0) \to true, ev(s(s(X))) \to ev(X),$$
$$od(s(X)) \to true \Leftarrow ev(X) = true, z(X) \to 0\ \}.$$

By running the diagnosis system Buggy, we are able to isolate the wrong rules of $\mathcal{R}$ w.r.t. the given specification. By exploiting the debugger outcome as described later, the following positive and negative example sets are automatically produced (the user is allowed to fix the cardinality of the example sets by tuning some system parameters):

$$E^+ = \{od(s^3(0)) = true, od(s(0)) = true, z(s^2(0)) = 0, z(s(0)) = 0, z(0) = 0\,\}$$
$$E^- = \{od(s^2(0)) = true, od(0) = true, z(0) = 1, z(s(0)) = 1, z(s^2(0)) = 1\,\}.$$

We observe that unfolding the rule $r \equiv od(s(X)) \to od(X)$ w.r.t. $\mathcal{R}$ results in replacing r by two new rules $r_1 \equiv od(s(0)) \to true$ and $r_2 \equiv od(s^2(X)) \to od(X)$. Now, by getting rid of rule $od(0) \to true$, we obtain a new recursive definition for function od covering the positive examples while no negative example can be proven, which corrects the bug on function od.

However, note that this approach cannot be used for correcting function z: unfolding the rules defining z does not contribute to demonstrate the positive examples since the original program is overspecialized and unfolding can only specialize it further. Nevertheless, by generalizing function z as in the bottom-up inductive framework of [20], we get the new rule $z(X) \to 0$. Now, by eliminating rule $z(0) \to 1$, which does not contribute to any positive example, we obtain the final outcome

$$\mathcal{R}^c = \{od(s(0)) \to true, od(s(s(X))) \to od(X), z(X) \to 0, z(s(X)) \to z(X)\,\}$$

which is correct w.r.t. the computed example sets.

The rest of the paper is organized as follows. Section 2 summarizes some preliminary definitions and notations. Section 3 recalls the framework for the declarative debugging of functional logic programs defined in [2]. In Section 4, we present the basic, top-down automatic correction procedure. Section 5 integrates this algorithm with a bottom-up inductive learner which allows us to apply the correction methodology when the original program is overly specialized. In Section 6, we present an experimental evaluation of the method on a set of benchmarks. Section 7 discusses some related work and concludes. Proofs of all technical results can be found in [1].

2   Preliminaries

Let us briefly recall some known results about rewrite systems [7,22] and functional logic programming (see [19,21] for extensive surveys). For simplicity, definitions are given in the one-sorted case. The extension to many–sorted signatures is straightforward, see [27]. Throughout this paper, V will denote a countably infinite set of variables and Σ denotes a set of function symbols, or *signature*, each of which has a fixed associated arity. $\tau(\Sigma \cup V)$ and $\tau(\Sigma)$ denote the nonground word (or term) algebra and the word algebra built on $\Sigma \cup V$ and Σ, respectively. $\tau(\Sigma)$ is usually called the *Herbrand universe* $(\mathcal{H}_\Sigma)$ over Σ and it will be denoted by $\mathcal{H}$. $\mathcal{B}$ denotes the *Herbrand base*, namely the set of all ground equations which can be built with the elements of $\mathcal{H}$. A *equation* $s = t$ is a pair of terms $s, t \in \tau(\Sigma \cup V)$. Terms are viewed as labelled trees in the usual way. Term *positions* are represented by sequences of natural numbers, where Λ denotes the empty sequence. $O(t)$ denotes the set of positions of a term t, while $\overline{O}(t)$ is the set of nonvariable positions of t. $t_{|u}$ is the subterm at the position u of t. $t[r]_u$ is the term t with the subterm at the position u replaced with r. These notions extend to sequences of equations in a natural way. By $Var(s)$ we denote the set of variables occurring in the syntactic object s, while $[s]$ denotes the set of ground instances of s. Identity of syntactic objects is denoted by $\equiv$. A *substitution* is a mapping from the set of variables V to the set $\tau(\Sigma \cup V)$. Given a set of equations E, $mgu(E)$ denotes the *most general unifier* of E [25].

A *conditional term rewriting system* (CTRS for short) is a pair $(\Sigma, \mathcal{R})$, where $\mathcal{R}$ is a finite set of reduction (or rewrite) rule schemes of the form $(\lambda \to \rho \Leftarrow C)$, $\lambda, \rho \in \tau(\Sigma \cup V)$, $\lambda \notin V$ and $Var(\rho) \subseteq Var(\lambda)$. The condition C is a (possibly empty) sequence $e_1, \ldots, e_n$, $n \geq 0$, of equations. We will often write just $\mathcal{R}$ instead of $(\Sigma, \mathcal{R})$. If a rewrite rule has no condition, we write $\lambda \to \rho$. A goal $\Leftarrow g$ is a rewrite rule with no head, and we simply denote it by g.

For CTRS $\mathcal{R}$, $r \ll \mathcal{R}$ denotes that r is a new variant of a rule in $\mathcal{R}$ such that r contains only *fresh* variables, i.e. contains no variable previously met during computation (standardized apart). Given a CTRS $\langle \Sigma, \mathcal{R} \rangle$, we assume that the signature Σ is partitioned into two disjoint sets $\Sigma = \mathcal{C} \uplus \mathcal{D}$, where $\mathcal{D} = \{f \mid (f(\tilde{t}) \to r \Leftarrow C) \in \mathcal{R}\}$ and $\mathcal{C} = \Sigma \setminus \mathcal{D}$. Symbols in $\mathcal{C}$ are called *constructors* and symbols in $\mathcal{D}$ are called *defined functions*. The elements of $\tau(\mathcal{C} \cup V)$ are *constructor* terms. A pattern is a term $f(l_1, \ldots, l_n)$ such that $f \in \mathcal{D}$ and $l_1, \ldots, l_n$ are constructor terms. A term s is a *normal form*, if there is no term t with $s \to_{\mathcal{R}} t$, where $\to_{\mathcal{R}}$ denotes the (conditional) rewriting relation. We omit the subscript $\mathcal{R}$ when no confusion can arise. In the remainder of this paper, a *(functional logic) program* is a finite CTRS. The program $\mathcal{R}$ is said to be canonical if the binary one-step rewriting relation $\to_{\mathcal{R}}$ defined by $\mathcal{R}$ is noetherian and confluent [22]. A *successful conditional rewriting sequence* (also called *proof*) for a goal g in $\mathcal{R}$ (extended with the rules for the equality) is a sequence $\mathcal{D} : g \equiv g_1 \to g_2 \to \ldots \to true$.

The standard operational semantics of functional logic programs is based on narrowing [15,29], a combination of unification for parameter passing and reduction as evaluation mechanism which subsumes rewriting and SLD-resolution. Essentially, narrowing consists of the instantiation of goal variables, followed by a reduction step on the instantiated goal. Narrowing is complete in the sense of functional programming (computation of normal forms) as well as logic programming (computation of answers). Due to the huge search space of unrestricted narrowing, steadily improved strategies have been proposed. A *narrowing strategy* (or *position constraint*) φ is any well-defined criterion that obtains a smaller search space by permitting narrowing to reduce only some chosen positions. We denote by $\leadsto_\varphi$ the narrowing relation with strategy φ (see [19] for a survey on narrowing strategies.) $\mathbb{R}_\varphi$ denotes the class of CTRSs which satisfy the conditions for the completeness of the strategy φ. For instance, needed narrowing is known to be an optimal narrowing strategy for inductively sequential programs, a class of TRS's following the constructor discipline with discriminating left-hand side, that is, typical functional programs. For the completeness of "lazy strategies" such as needed narrowing, the strict equality $\approx$ is considered, which is only defined on finite and completely determined data structures, and gives to equality the weak meaning of identity of finite objects (e.g., see [26]). Hence, we also assume that equations in g and C have the form $s = t$ (where $=$ denotes the standard equality) whenever we consider "eager strategies" such as innermost conditional narrowing ($\varphi = inn$), whereas the equations have the form $s \approx t$ when we consider needed narrowing ($\varphi = needed$).

2.1   Denotation of a Functional Logic Program

In order to formulate a semantics modeling computed answers, the usual Herbrand base has to be extended to the set of all (possibly) non-ground equations modulo variance [14]. $\mathcal{H}_V$ denotes the *V-Herbrand universe* which allows variables in its elements, and is defined as $\tau(\Sigma \cup V)/_{\cong}$, where $\cong$ is the equivalence relation induced by preorder $\leq$ of "relative generality" between terms. For the sake of simplicity, the elements of $\mathcal{H}_V$ have the same representation as the elements of $\tau(\Sigma \cup V)$ and are also called terms. $\mathcal{B}_V$ denotes the *V-Herbrand base*, namely, the set of all equations $s = t$ modulo variance, where $s, t \in \mathcal{H}_V$. Note that the standard Herbrand base $\mathcal{B}$ is equal to $[\mathcal{B}_V]$.

In non-strict languages, if the compositional character of meaning has to be preserved in presence of infinite data structures and partial functions, then non-normalizable terms, which may occur as subterms within normalizable expressions, also have to be assigned a denotation. Following [18,26], we introduce a fresh constant symbol $\perp$ into Σ to represent the value of expressions which would otherwise be undefined.

In the following we recall two useful semantics for functional logic programs (we refer to [6] for details).

Operational Semantics. The operational success set semantics $\mathcal{O}_\varphi^{ca}(\mathcal{R})$ of a program $\mathcal{R}$ w.r.t. narrowing strategy φ is defined by considering the answers computed for "most general calls":

$$\mathcal{O}_\varphi^{ca}(\mathcal{R}) = \Im_\mathcal{R}^\varphi \cup \{(f(x_1,\ldots,x_n) = x_{n+1})\theta \mid (f(x_1,\ldots,x_n) =_\varphi x_{n+1}) \overset{\theta}{\rightsquigarrow}_\varphi^*$$

$\top$ s.t. $f/n \in \mathcal{D}$, x_{n+1} and x_i are distinct variables, for $i = 1,\ldots,n$ }, where $\Im_\mathcal{R}^\varphi$ denotes the set of identical equations $c(x_1,\ldots,x_n) =_\varphi c(x_1,\ldots,x_n)$, c/n constructor symbol in $\mathcal{R}$.

Fixpoint Semantics. The (bottom-up) fixpoint semantics $\mathcal{F}_\varphi^{ca}(\mathcal{R})$, modeling computed answers w.r.t. a narrowing strategy φ, is defined as the least fixpoint $\mathcal{F}_\varphi^{ca}(\mathcal{R}) = T_\mathcal{R}^\varphi \uparrow \omega$ of a parametric immediate consequence operator $T_\mathcal{R}^\varphi : 2^{\mathcal{B}_V} \to 2^{\mathcal{B}_V}$ which generalizes the ground immediate consequences operator in [21] in order to model computed answers.

The relationship between the operational and fixpoint semantics is established by the following theorem.

Theorem 1. *[2]* $\mathcal{O}_\varphi^{ca}(\mathcal{R}) = \mathcal{F}_\varphi(\mathcal{R}) \setminus inprogress(\mathcal{F}_\varphi(\mathcal{R}))$, *where, for equation set S, $inprogress(S) = \{\lambda = \rho \in S \mid \bot$ occurs in ρ or ρ contains a defined function symbol of $\Sigma\}$.*

For the sake of clarity, let us summarize the relation among the two different program denotations $\mathcal{F}_\varphi(\mathcal{R})$ and $\mathcal{O}_\varphi^{ca}(\mathcal{R})$ introduced above. The compositional, fixpoint semantics $\mathcal{F}_\varphi(\mathcal{R})$ which models successful as well as partial (nonterminating as well as intermediate computations, i.e. those equations $f(\bar{t}) = s$ where s "has not reached its value") is obtained by computing the least fixpoint of the immediate consequences operator $T_\mathcal{R}^\varphi$. On the other hand, the operational success set semantics $\mathcal{O}_\varphi^{ca}(\mathcal{R})$ only catches successful derivations, that is, it models the computed answers observable.

3 Diagnosis of Declarative Programs

First we recall some basic definitions on the declarative diagnosis [11].

Definition 1. *Let $\mathcal{I}_{ca}$ be the specification of the intended success set semantics for $\mathcal{R}$. An* incorrectness symptom *is an equation e such that $e \in \mathcal{O}_\varphi^{ca}(\mathcal{R})$ and $e \notin \mathcal{I}_{ca}$. An* incompleteness symptom *is an equation e such that $e \in \mathcal{I}_{ca}$ and $e \notin \mathcal{O}_\varphi^{ca}(\mathcal{R})$.*

In case of errors, in order to determine the faulty rules, we make use of the following definitions. We need to consider a fixpoint intended semantics $\mathcal{I}_\mathcal{F}$, that models both successful and "in progress" computations. The relation between $\mathcal{I}_\mathcal{F}$ and the intended operational meaning is given by $\mathcal{I}_{ca} = \mathcal{I}_\mathcal{F} \setminus inprogress(\mathcal{I}_\mathcal{F})$.

Definition 2. *Let $\mathcal{I}_\mathcal{F}$ be the specification of the intended fixpoint semantics for $\mathcal{R}$. If there exists an equation $e \in T_{\{r\}}^\varphi(\mathcal{I}_\mathcal{F})$ and $e \notin \mathcal{I}_\mathcal{F}$, then the rule $r \in \mathcal{R}$ is* incorrect *on e. We also say that e is incorrect. Reciprocally, the equation e is* uncovered *if $e \in \mathcal{I}_\mathcal{F}$ and $e \notin T_\mathcal{R}^\varphi(\mathcal{I}_\mathcal{F})$.*

Since program denotations generally consist of an infinite number of equations, the above conditions for correctness and completeness of a program w.r.t. to a given specification cannot be effectively computed. In [2], an abstract diagnosis methodology based on the abstract interpretation theory [12] was proposed. Abstract diagnosis is a correct approximation of the diagnosis technique presented so far where the semantic domains and operators are replaced by abstract ones. First, we build a suitable abstract immediate consequences operator $(T_\mathcal{R}^{\sharp\varphi})$, which uses an abstraction of the program rules where all infinite computations have been removed and is also parametric w.r.t. the narrowing strategy. The approximation is done by using a loop-checker which replaces the calls which are (risky to be) responsible for the infinite derivations by a fresh irreducible symbol $\sharp$. The fixpoint of $T_\mathcal{R}^{\sharp\varphi}$ correctly approximates the fixpoint semantics of $\mathcal{R}$ and can be computed finitely. The abstract diagnosis process is performed w.r.t. two abstract (finite) semantics $\mathcal{I}^-$ and $\mathcal{I}^+$ which under- and over-approximate the intended semantics $\mathcal{I}$.

4   Correction Method

In this section, we present an inductive learning methodology which is able to repair a functional logic program containing buggy rules. The correction problem can be stated as follows. Let $\mathcal{R}$ be a program, $\mathcal{I}$ the intended specification, $\mathcal{R}' \subseteq \mathcal{R}$ a set of incorrect rules w.r.t. $\mathcal{I}$, and $E = E^+ \cup E^-$ two disjoint (ground) example sets which model the pursued (not pursued) computational behaviour. We denote by $\mathcal{R} \vdash E$ the fact that the (ground) equation set E can be reduced to $true$ by using the rules of $\mathcal{R}$. Then, we want to determine a set of rules $\mathcal{X}$ such that $\mathcal{R}^c = (\mathcal{R} \setminus \mathcal{R}') \cup \mathcal{X}$, $\mathcal{R}^c \vdash E^+$ and $\mathcal{R}^c \nvdash E^-$. Program $\mathcal{R}^c$ will be called $correct$ program (w.r.t. E^+ and E^-). We will call $\mathcal{R}^- = \mathcal{R} \setminus \mathcal{R}'$ the $diminished$ program. We note that $\mathcal{R} \vdash E$ can be checked, even in the case that $\mathcal{R}$ is not terminating, by using the "normalization via μ–normalization" method of [23] to compute, by levels, the 'maximal contexts' of the lhs's of the examples, and then comparing them with the ground constructor term in the corresponding rhs. By this technique, normal forms can be obtained by successively computing μ-normal forms and shifting computations to maximal non-replacing subterms when a μ-normal form has been obtained. The conditions for the completeness of this technique (csr–conditions) essentially amount to the termination of "context–sensitive rewriting" (csr) [24], which is much easier than the termination of rewriting. A csr practical tool for proving termination of csr is available at http://www.dsic.upv.es/users/elp/slucas/muterm.

The automatic search for a new rule in an induction process can be performed either bottom-up (i.e. from an overly specific rule to a more general) or top-down (i.e. from an overly general rule to a more specific). There are some reasons to prefer the top-down or $backward$ $reasoning$ process to the bottom–up or $forward$ $reasoning$ process [13]. On the one hand, it eliminates the need for navigating through all possible logical consequences of the program. On the other hand, it integrates inductive reasoning with the deductive process, so that the derived program is guaranteed to be correct. Unfortunately, it is known that the deductive process alone (i.e. unfolding) does not generally suffice for coming up with the corrected program, and inductive generalization techniques are necessary [13,28]. In [20,17], a bottom-up framework for synthesizing correct functional logic programs (w.r.t. the ground success set, Herbrand semantics) is presented which induces program rules from sets of equations which are respectively incorrect and correct w.r.t. the pursued program. Their methodology, however, is not particularly tailored for $theory$ $revision$, and we need to adapt it since the uncontrolled application of the method would produce much speculation in our framework, which we want to avoid. Therefore, we follow a hybrid, top-down as well as bottom-up approach, which is able to infer program corrections that are hard, if not at all impossible, to obtain with a simple deductive learner.

4.1   Automatic Generation of Positive and Negative Example Sets

Let us present a simple method for automatically generating the example sets which exploits the debugger outcome so that the user does not need to provide error symptoms, evidences or other kind of information which would require a good knowledge of the program semantics that she probably lacks.

Consider the diminished program $\mathcal{R}^-$. Due to the absence of faulty rules in $\mathcal{R}^-$, $\mathcal{R}^-$ is already partially correct; however $\mathcal{R}^-$ might be incomplete, as there can be equations which are covered in $\mathcal{I}$, but not in $\mathcal{R}^-$.

By applying the diagnosis method presented in Section 3, we are able to find out the sets of *uncovered* and *incorrect* equations w.r.t. an abstraction of the intended semantics, respectively E_1 and E_2. Considering equations in E_1 seems a sensible way for yielding *positive* examples (missing proofs which should be achieved by $\mathcal{R}$). On the other hand, set E_2 contains equations modeling erroneous behaviours, thus we can take them as *negative* examples.

Since E_1 and E_2 might contain non-ground equations, we find it useful to instantiate (a subset of) them in order to get ground positive/negative example sets E^+ and E^-. This allows us to perform some standard optimizations based on term rewriting which are very satisfactory in practice. On the other hand, since program $\mathcal{R}$ and specification $\mathcal{I}$ might use different auxiliary functions, we only consider ground examples of the form $l = d$ where l is a pattern and d is a constructor term. In this way, the inductive process becomes independent from the extra functions contained in $\mathcal{I}$, since we start synthesizing directly from data structures d. In order to achieve this, we normalize the term in the rhs of (the instantiated) examples. Finally, we disregard those examples which, after normalization, do not have a constructor term at the rhs.

4.2   Specialization Operators

Roughly speaking, *unfolding* a program $\mathcal{R}$ w.r.t. a rule r delivers to a new specialized version of $\mathcal{R}$ in which the rule r is replaced by new rules obtained from r by performing a narrowing step on the rhs or the conditional part of r.

Definition 3 (unfolding). *Let $\mathcal{R}$ be a CTRS and $r \equiv (\lambda \to \rho \Leftarrow C) \ll \mathcal{R}$ be a rule. Let $\{g \overset{\theta_i}{\leadsto}_\varphi (C_i', \rho_i' = y)\}_{i=1}^n$ be the set of all one-step narrowing derivations with strategy φ that perform an effective narrowing step for the goal $g \equiv (C, \rho = y)$ in $\mathcal{R}$. Then, $Unf_{\mathcal{R}}^\varphi(r) = \{(\lambda\theta_i \to \rho_i' \Leftarrow C_i')|i = 1 \ldots n\}$ (that is, the derived goal $(C_i', \rho_i' = y)$ is different from g.*

Definition 4 (Unfolding operator). *Let $\mathcal{R}$ be a CTRS, $r \equiv \lambda \to \rho \Leftarrow C$ be a rule in $\mathcal{R}$. The Rule Unfolding operator $\mathsf{U}_r^\varphi(\mathcal{R})$ on $\mathcal{R}$ w.r.t. r is defined by $\mathsf{U}_r^\varphi(\mathcal{R}) = \mathcal{R} \setminus \{r\} \cup Unf_{\mathcal{R}}^\varphi(r)$.*

As it has been proven in [4,5], for $\varphi = inn, needed$, unfolding using strategy φ preserves the semantics (even for the observable of computed answers) in $\mathbb{R}_\varphi$ programs. When needed narrowing is considered, completeness is only guaranteed under the condition that expressions in the rule are not unfolded beyond their head normal form [5]. On the other hand, the absence of narrowable positions in the rule to be unfolded yields no specialization of r. We just get the removal of r from $\mathcal{R}$. Therefore, we use the following notion of "unfoldable rule".

Definition 5. *Let $\mathcal{R}$ be a CTRS, r be a rule in $\mathcal{R}$. The rule r is* unfoldable *w.r.t.*
$\mathcal{R}$ *if* $\mathsf{U}_r^\varphi(\mathcal{R}) \neq \mathcal{R} \setminus \{r\}$. *If* $\varphi = needed$, *we also require that r is not unfolded beyond its head normal form.*

For the sake of simplicity, in the following we omit φ whenever this does not compromise readability. The *unfolding succession* $\mathcal{S}(\mathcal{R}) \equiv \mathcal{R}_0, \mathcal{R}_1, \ldots$ of program $\mathcal{R}$ is defined as follows: $\mathcal{R}_0 = \mathcal{R}$, $\mathcal{R}_{i+1} = \mathsf{U}_r(\mathcal{R}_i)$ where $r \in \mathcal{R}_i$ is unfoldable.

4.3   Top-Down Correction Algorithm

Following [9], the algorithm below works in two phases: the *unfolding phase* and the *deletion phase*. Roughly speaking, we first perform unfolding upon (arbitrarily selected) unfoldable rules, until we get a specialized version of the program $\mathcal{R}$ where no negative example can be proven by applying only rules used in proofs of positive examples. The following definition is auxiliary.

Definition 6. *Given $\mathcal{D} : g \equiv g_1 \xrightarrow{r_1} g_2 \xrightarrow{r_2} \ldots \xrightarrow{r_n} g_n$, the sequence $\langle r_1, r_2, \ldots, r_n \rangle$ is called the* rewriting rule sequence *of $\mathcal{D}$. The set $\mathsf{OR}(\mathcal{D}) = \{r_1, r_2, \ldots, r_n\}$ is called the set of* occurring rules *of $\mathcal{D}$.*

Given an equation e, let $\mathcal{D}_\mathcal{R}^\varphi(e)$ denote the successful rewrite sequence which proves e in program $\mathcal{R}$ (if it exists) by using a normalizing rewriting strategy for the class $\mathbb{R}_\varphi$. The key idea of the algorithm is thus applying unfolding until we get a specialized program $\mathcal{R}_i$ satisfying that, for each $e^- \in E^-$ there exists a rule $r \in \mathsf{OR}(\mathcal{D}_{\mathcal{R}_i}^\varphi(e^-))$ such that, for each example $e^+ \in E^+$, $r \notin \mathsf{OR}(\mathcal{D}_{\mathcal{R}_i}^\varphi(e^+))$. Now, since the rules which only contribute to the proof of negative examples are useless, in the subsequent phase we just remove these rules from the specialized program $\mathcal{R}_i$. By *discriminable rule* of $\mathcal{R}_i$ we mean an unfoldable rule of $\mathcal{R}_i$ which occurs in the proof of, at least, one positive and one negative example.

Algorithm *TD-Corrector$(\mathcal{R}, \mathcal{I})$*
$(E^+, E^-) = \text{GenerateExampleSets}(\mathcal{R}, \mathcal{I})$
if $\mathcal{R} \nvdash E^+$ **then** halt
{Unfolding phase}
let $i = 0$; $\mathcal{R}_0 = \mathcal{R}$
while $\exists e^- \in E^-$ s.t. $\forall r(r \in \mathsf{OR}(\mathcal{D}_{\mathcal{R}_i}(e^-)) \Rightarrow \exists e^+ \in E^+$ s.t. $r \in \mathsf{OR}(\mathcal{D}_{\mathcal{R}_i}(e^+)))$ **do**
$\quad\quad$ **select** a discriminable rule $r \in \mathsf{OR}(\mathcal{D}_{\mathcal{R}_i}(e^-))$ of $\mathcal{R}_i$
$\quad\quad\quad$ **let** $\mathcal{R}_{i+1} = \mathsf{U}_r(\mathcal{R}_i)$; $i = i + 1$
end while
{Deletion phase}
for each $e^- \in E^-$ **do**
$\quad\quad$ **let** $\mathcal{R}_{i+1} = \mathcal{R}_i \setminus \{r\}$, where $r \in \mathsf{OR}(\mathcal{D}_{\mathcal{R}_i}(e^-)) \wedge \forall e^+ \in E^+ \ r \notin \mathsf{OR}(\mathcal{D}_{\mathcal{R}_i}(e^+))$
$\quad\quad$ **let** $i = i + 1$
end for
let $\mathcal{R}^c = \mathcal{R}_i$

Example 2. Consider again the program $\mathcal{R}$ and specification $\mathcal{I}$ of example 1, with the example sets for learning function *od*. Since the rewriting proof for the negative example $od(s^2(0)) = true \in E^-$ uses the rule $od(s(X)) \rightarrow od(X)$ (either with $\varphi = inn$ or $\varphi = needed$), which is also used in the proofs of positive examples, we enter the main loop. By unfolding $od(s(X)) \rightarrow od(X)$ we get $\mathcal{R}_1 = \{od(0) \rightarrow true, od(s(0)) \rightarrow true, od(s^2(X)) \rightarrow od(X)\}$. Now we enter the deletion phase which purifies $\mathcal{R}_1$ by removing the rule $od(0) \rightarrow true$ that only occurs in the proof of a negative example, thus producing the expected correction shown in Section 1.

Example 2 allows us to clarify the differences between the preliminary correction algorithm in [2] and the one in this paper. The algorithm in [2] was based on unfolding the rules which incorrectly cover the negative examples. In our example, this could result in trying to unfold the rule $od(0) \rightarrow true$, which is fruitless, whereas the new correction procedure does consider any discriminable rule for unfolding, which is generally needed in order to achieve the desired correction.

We prove the correctness of the top-down correction algorithm in two steps: first we show that, provided that $\mathcal{R}$ covers E^+, the unfolding phase produces a specialized version $\mathcal{R}'$ of $\mathcal{R}$ (still covering E^+) such that, for each negative example, there is a rule occurring in the corresponding proof which is not used in the proof of any of the positive examples. Next, we demonstrate that the deletion phase yields a corrected version of $\mathcal{R}$ covering E^+ and not covering E^-.

The following proposition states our first result: by a suitable finite number of applications of the unfolding operator to a program in $\mathbb{R}_\varphi$, we get a specialized version such that, in any successful rewriting derivation of a negative example, there occurs a rule that is not applied in any successful rewriting derivation for the positive examples under the same strategy. A condition is necessary for proving this result: no negative/positive couple of the considered examples can have the same rewriting rule sequence, as shown in the following counterexample.

Example 3. Consider the program $\mathcal{R} = \{f(X) \rightarrow g(X), g(X) \rightarrow 0\}$ with example sets $E^+ = \{f(a) = 0\}$, $E^- = \{f(b) = 0\}$. Then $f(a) = 0$ and $f(b) = 0$ are proven by using the same rewriting rule sequence (using any of the considered rewriting strategies). By applying the top–down algorithm, we unfold rule $f(X) \rightarrow g(X)$, which produces the outcome $\mathcal{R}_1 = \{f(X) \rightarrow 0, g(X) \rightarrow 0\}$ which cannot be purified (by using the rule deletion operator) as removing rule $f(X) \rightarrow 0$ in order to get rid of E^- would cause losing E^+.

Proposition 1. *Let φ be a normalizing rewriting strategy for $\mathbb{R}_\varphi$ and $\mathcal{R}$ be a program in $\mathbb{R}_\varphi$. Let E^+ (resp. E^-) be a set of positive (resp. negative) examples. If there are no $e^+ \in E^+$ and $e^- \in E^-$ which can be proven in $\mathcal{R}$ by using the same rules sequence, then, for each unfolding succession $\mathcal{S}(\mathcal{R})$, there exists k such that $\forall e^- \in E^- \exists r \in OR(\mathcal{D}_{\mathcal{R}_k}(e^-))$ s.t. r is not discriminable*

We note that Proposition 1 holds for every unfolding succession of the original program; this implies that the rule to be unfolded at each unfolding step can be arbitrarily selected, provided that it is discriminable. Moreover, the termination of the unfolding phase is granted by the finite number k of applications of the unfolding operator that we need to obtain specialization $\mathcal{R}_k$.

After the unfolding phase, the refutation of every negative example contains a rule from $\mathcal{R}_k$ not occurring in the proof of any positive example, thus we can safely remove this rule without jeopardizing completeness. The deletion phase purifies $\mathcal{R}_k$ and yields correctness w.r.t. both positive and negative examples.

Theorem 2 (Correctness). *Let $\mathcal{R} \in \mathbb{R}_\varphi$ which satisfies the csr conditions, E^+ and E^- be two sets of examples such that $\mathcal{R} \vdash E^+$. If the rewriting rule sequences for $e^+ \in E^+$ and $e^- \in E^-$ are different, then the TD-Corrector algorithm yields a correct specialization of $\mathcal{R}$ w.r.t. E^+ and E^-.*

As in other approaches for example-guided program correction, the above result does not generally imply that a correction for the wrong program $\mathcal{R}$ w.r.t. the intended semantics is obtained as the outcome of the top-down correction algorithm (that is, a program $\mathcal{R}$ with the same semantics of $\mathcal{I}$, up to the extra auxiliary function symbols which might appear in $\mathcal{I}$), under the conditions required for the correctness of the algorithm, but it might happen that the output program is only correct w.r.t. E^+ and E^-. Therefore, derived programs would be newly diagnosed for correctness at the end.

5   Improving the Algorithm

In the following, we propose a bottom-up correction methodology which we smoothly combine with the deductive one in order to correct programs which do not fulfil the applicability condition (over–generality). Therefore, the methodology just consists of applying a bottom-up pre–processing to "generalize" the initial wrong program, before proceeding to the top-down correction.

5.1   Bottom-up Generation of Overly General (Wrong) Programs

We propose a methodology which is based on extending the original program with new rules, so that the entire set E^+ succeeds w.r.t. the generalized program, and hence the top-down corrector can be effectively applied.

Our generalization method is based on a simplified version of the bottom-up technique for the inductive learning of functional logic programs developed by Ferri, Hernández and Ramírez [17] which is able to produce an intensional description (expressed by a functional logic program) of a set of ground examples. The algorithm is also able to introduce functions, defined as a background theory, in the inferred intensional description (see [17,20] for details). In the following we recall the definitions of *restricted generalization* and *inverse narrowing* which are the heart of the bottom-up procedure of [17,20]. The former allows to generalize program rules, the latter is needed to introduce defined symbols in the right hand sides of the synthesized rules.

Definition 7 (Generalization operator). *The rule $r' \equiv (s' \to t' \Leftarrow C')$ is a restricted generalization of $r \equiv (s \to t \Leftarrow C)$ if there exists a substitution θ such* *that (i)* $\theta(r') \equiv r$; *(ii)* $Var(t') \subseteq Var(s')$. *The generalization operator* $\mathsf{RG}(r)$ *is defined as follows:* $\mathsf{RG}(r) = \{r'|r'$ *is a restricted generalization of* $r\}$.

Definition 8 (Inverse narrowing operator). *The rule* $r \equiv s \to t \Leftarrow C$ *reversely narrows into* $r' \equiv s \to t' \Leftarrow C'$ *(in symbols* $r \overset{u,r'',\theta}{\leftsquigarrow} r'$) *iff there exist a position* $u \in O(t)$ *and a rule* $r'' \equiv \lambda \to \rho \Leftarrow C''$ *such that (i)* $\theta = mgu(t_{|u}, \rho)$; *(ii)* $t' = (t[\lambda]_u)\theta$; *(iii)* $C' = (C'', C)\theta$.
The inverse narrowing *operator* $\mathsf{INV}(r, r'')$ *is given by:*

$$\mathsf{INV}(r, r'') = \{r' \mid r \overset{u,r'',\theta}{\leftsquigarrow} r' \text{ and extra-variables in the rhs of } r'$$
$$\text{are instantiated to variables in the rhs of } r\}.$$

The extra instantiation of variables in the rhs of the derived rules is necessary, since inverse narrowing considers the rules oriented reversely and hence extra-variables might be introduced in the synthesized rules, which is not allowed.

The following definitions are helpful for discerning the overspecialized program rules. $Def_{\mathcal{R}}(f)$ is the set of rules in $\mathcal{R}$ needed to define a function f. This might be computed by constructing a functional dependency graph of the program $\mathcal{R}$ and by statically analyzing it. Given a set E of positive examples, $Res_f(E)$ denotes the restriction of E to the set of f-rooted examples (that is, examples of the form $f(\bar{t}) = d$). We say that a function definition $Def_{\mathcal{R}}(f)$ is *overspecialized* w.r.t. the set of positive examples E^+, if there exists $e \in Res_f(E^+)$ which is not covered by $Def_{\mathcal{R}}(f)$. An incorrect rule belonging to an overspecialized function definition is called *overspecialized* rule.

The generalization algorithm in its initial phase discovers all function definitions which are overspecialized, by computing the subset of f-examples not provable in $\mathcal{R}$ (and hence not provable by the corresponding function definition). Then, overspecialized rules are deleted from $\mathcal{R}$. Now, applying generalization and inverse narrowing operators, starting from the positive examples, we try to reconstruct the missing part of the code, that is, we synthesize a functional logic program $\mathcal{A}$ such that $\mathcal{R} \cup \mathcal{A} \setminus \{r \in \mathcal{R} \mid r$ is overspecialized$\}$ allows us to derive the entire E^+. At the end, we get an overly general hypothesis to which the top-down corrector can be applied for repairing (incorrectness) bugs on the derived overly general faulty rules.

The bottom-up synthesis algorithm firstly generates a set P_H (Program Hypothesis set) which consists of unary programs associated with the restricted generalizations of E^+, that is, $P_H = \{\{r\} \mid r \in \mathsf{RG}(s \to t), s = t \in E^+\}$. Then it enters a loop in which, by means of INV and RG operators, new programs in P_H are produced. The algorithm leaves the loop when an "optimal" solution, which covers E^+ entirely, has been found in P_H, or a maximal number of iterations is reached. In the latter case no solution might be found.

Due to the huge search space which this method involves, some heuristics must be implemented to guide the search. Following [20], *Minimum Description Length*[1] (MDL) and *Covering Factor*[2] criteria could be taken into consideration,

---

[1] $length(e) = 1 + n_v/2 + n_f$, where n_v and n_f are the number of variables and functors in the rhs of e.

[2] $CovF(E) = card(\{e \in E \mid \mathcal{R} \vdash e\})/card(E)$.

so that inverse narrowing steps are only performed among the best programs and equations w.r.t. these criteria. Moreover, by means of MDL and Covering Factor, only the most concise programs are selected during the induction process. The notion of *Optimality* w.r.t. programs and equations could be defined as a linear combination of these two criteria. For a full discussion see [20]. A detailed description of the algorithm can be retrieved in [1]. Let us consider an example, in which we only pinpoint the relevant outcomes for the sake of clarity.

Example 4. Consider the following (wrong) program and the specification

$$\mathcal{R} = \{\ playdice(X) \rightarrow double(winface(X)), dd(0) \rightarrow 0, \mathbf{dd(s(X))} \rightarrow \mathbf{dd(X)}),$$
$$\mathbf{winface(s(X))} \rightarrow \mathbf{s(winface(X))}, \mathbf{winface(0)} \rightarrow \mathbf{0}\ \}$$

$$\mathcal{I} = \{\ playdice(X) \rightarrow dd(winface(X)), dd(X) \rightarrow sum(X, X),$$
$$sum(X, 0) \rightarrow X, sum(X, s(Y)) \rightarrow s(sum(X, Y)),$$
$$winface(s(0)) \rightarrow s(0), winface(s(s(0))) \rightarrow s(s(0))\ \}.$$

Program rules marked in boldface are signalled as incorrect by the diagnosis system. The example generation procedure described in Section 4.1 produces:

$$E^+ = \{\ playdice(s^2(0)) = s^4(0), playdice(s(0)) = s^2(0), dd(s^4(0)) = s^8(0),$$
$$dd(s^3(0)) = s^6(0), dd(s^2(0)) = s^4(0), dd(s(0)) = s^2(0)$$
$$dd(0) = 0, winface(s^2(0)) = s^2(0), winface(s(0)) = s(0)\ \}.$$

The analysis for *dd* and *winface* determines that *dd* is overspecialized. The generalization algorithm removes the rule $dd(s(X)) \rightarrow dd(X)$. Note that rule $dd(s(0)) \rightarrow s^2(0)$ inversely narrows to rule $r_{dd} \equiv dd(s(0)) \rightarrow s^2(dd(0))$ by using rule $dd(0) \rightarrow 0$. The following restricted generalizations of rule r_{dd} are computed: $dd(s(0)) \rightarrow s^2(dd(0)), \quad dd(s(X)) \rightarrow s^2(dd(0)), \quad dd(s(X)) \rightarrow s^2(dd(X))$. Now, when the third rule is added to the background knowledge, all the examples in E^+ are covered. Thus, the following overly general definition, which feeds the top-down corrector in order to repair the remaining errors, is delivered

$$\mathcal{R} = \{\ playdice(X) \rightarrow dd(winface(X)), dd(0) \rightarrow 0, dd(s(X)) \rightarrow s(s(dd(X)))),$$
$$\mathbf{winface(s(X))} \rightarrow \mathbf{s(winface(X))}, \mathbf{winface(0)} \rightarrow \mathbf{0}\ \}.$$

6   Automated Correction System

A prototypical implementation of our methodology and a full experimental evaluation are available at http://www.dsic.upv.es/users/elp/soft.html. We have improved the preliminary debugging system B uggy by adding the new features. The current implementation, called N obug, is now able to compute sets of positive and negative examples by using the methodology described in Section 4.1. Besides, we have developed a full implementation of the top-down correction method based on example-guided unfolding for the leftmost-innermost narrowing strategy. We are currently implementing the lazy version of the algorithm. The bottom-up synthesis method has not been integrated into the N obug system yet. Hence, in order to compute our benchmarks also for initially over-specialized programs, we used the inductive functional logic system F L IP [16].

We have performed some tests by means of our top-down corrector and the bottom-up learner F L IP, in order to repair overly general as well as overspecialized functional logic programs. We have taken into account programs on several domains: naturals, lists and finite domains. In order to systematize the generation of the benchmarks, we have slightly modified correct programs in order to obtain wrong program mutations. We were able to successfully repair incorrect mutations, achieving, in many cases, a correction both w.r.t. the example sets and the intended program semantics.

7 Conclusions

In this paper we have proposed a new methodology for synthesizing (partially) correct functional logic programs which complements the diagnosis method we developed previously in [6,2]. Our methodology is based on the combination, in a single framework, of a diagnoser [6,2] which identifies those parts of the code containing errors, together with a program learner which, once the bug has been located in the program, tries to repair it starting from evidence examples (uncovered as well as incorrect equations) which are essentially obtained as an outcome of the diagnoser. We follow a hybrid, *deductive* (top-down) as well as *inductive* (bottom-up) approach, which is able to infer program corrections that are hard to obtain with a simple (pure deductive or inductive) program learner. We plan to generalize the framework to other paradigms as future work.

Finally, we want to emphasize that this framework supersedes the preliminary approach of [2]. In [2], recursive definitions were sometimes impossible to repair, and no automated correction is provided for overspecialized programs either, whereas the new methodology in this paper overcomes both drawbacks.

References

1. M. Alpuente, D. Ballis, F. J. Correa, and M. Falaschi. Correction of Functional Logic Programs. Technical report, DSIC-II/23/02, UPV, 2002. Available at URL: http://www.dsic.upv.es/users/elp/papers.html.
2. M. Alpuente, F. J. Correa, and M. Falaschi. Debugging Scheme of Functional Logic Programs. In *Proc. of WFLP'01*, vol. 64 of *ENTCS*, 2002.
3. M. Alpuente, F. J. Correa, M. Falaschi, and S. Marson. The Debugging System buggy. Technical report, UPV, 2001. Available at URL: http://www.dsic.upv.es/users/elp/soft.html.
4. M. Alpuente, M. Falaschi, G. Moreno, and G. Vidal. Safe folding/unfolding with conditional narrowing. In *Proc. ALP'97*, pp. 1–15. Springer LNCS 1298, 1997.
5. M. Alpuente, M. Falaschi, G. Moreno, and G. Vidal. A Transformation System for Lazy Functional Logic Programs. In *Proc. of FLOPS'99*, pp. 147–162. Springer LNCS 1722, 1999.
6. M. Alpuente, F. Correa, and M. Falaschi. Declarative Debugging of Funtional Logic Programs. In *Proc. of WRS'01*, vol. 57 of *ENTCS*, 2001.

7. F. Baader and T. Nipkow. *Term Rewriting and All That*. Cambridge University Press, 1998.
8. H. Bostrom and P. Idestam-Alquist. Induction of Logic Programs by Example–guided Unfolding. *Journal of Logic Programming*, 40:159–183, 1999.
9. Henrik Bostrom. Specialization of recursive predicates. In *European Conference on Machine Learning*, pp. 92–106, 1995.
10. M. Comini, R. Gori, and G. Levi. Assertion based Inductive Verification Methods for Logic Programs. In *Proc. of MFCSIT'00*, vol. 40 of *ENTCS*, 2001.
11. M. Comini, G. Levi, and G. Vitiello. Declarative Diagnosis Revisited. In *Proc. of ILP'95*, pp. 275–287. The MIT Press, 1995.
12. P. Cousot and R. Cousot. Abstract Interpretation: A Unified Lattice Model for Static Analysis of Programs by Construction or Approximation of Fixpoints. In *Proc. of POPL'77*, pp. 238–252, 1977.
13. N. Dershowitz and U. Reddy. Deductive and Inductive Synthesis of Equational Programs. *Journal of Symbolic Computation*, 15:467–494, 1993.
14. M. Falaschi, G. Levi, M. Martelli, and C. Palamidessi. Declarative Modeling of the Operational Behavior of Logic Languages. *TCS*, 69(3):289–318, 1989.
15. M. Fay. First Order Unification in an Equational Theory. In *Proc of 4th Int'l Conf. on Automated Deduction*, pp. 161–167, 1979.
16. C. Ferri, J. Hernández, and M.J. Ramírez. The FLIP System Homepage. 2000. Available at http://www.dsic.upv.es/users/elp/soft.ht ml.
17. C. Ferri, J. Hernández, and M.J. Ramírez. Incremental Learning of Functional Logic Programs. In *Proc. FLOPS'01*, pp. 233–247. LNCS 2024, 2001.
18. E. Giovannetti, G. Levi, C. Moiso, and C. Palamidessi. Kernel Leaf: A Logic plus Functional Language. *JCSS*, 42:363–377, 1991.
19. M. Hanus. The Integration of Functions into Logic Programming: From Theory to Practice. *Journal of Logic Programming*, 19&20:583–628, 1994.
20. J. Hernández and M.J. Ramírez. Inverse Narrowing for the Induction of Functional Logic Programs. In *Proc. of APPIA–GULP–PRODE '98*, pp. 379–393, 1998.
21. S. Hölldobler. *Foundations of Equational Logic Programming*. LNAI 353, 1989.
22. J.W. Klop. Term Rewriting Systems. In *Handbook of Logic in Computer Science*, vol. I, pp. 1–112. Oxford University Press, 1992.
23. S. Lucas. Context-Sensitive Rewriting Strategies. *Information and Computation*, 178(1):294–343, 2002.
24. S. Lucas. Termination of Canonical Context-Sensitive Rewriting. In *Proc. RTA'02*, pp. 296–310. Springer LNCS 2378, 2002.
25. M.J. Maher. Equivalences of Logic Programs. In *Foundations of Deductive Databases and Logic Programming*, pp. 627–658. Morgan Kaufmann, 1988.
26. J.J. Moreno-Navarro and M. Rodríguez-Artalejo. Logic Programming with Functions and Predicates: The language Babel. *JLP*, 12(3):191–224, 1992.
27. P. Padawitz. *Computing in Horn Clause Theories*, vol. 16 of *EATCS Monographs on Theoretical Computer Science*. Springer-Verlag, Berlin, 1988.
28. A. Pettorossi and M. Proietti. Transformation of Logic Programs. In *Handbook of Logic in Artificial Intelligence*, vol. 5, pp. 697–787. Oxford University Press, 1998.
29. U.S. Reddy. Narrowing as the Operational Semantics of Functional Languages. In *Proc. of Second IEEE Int'l Symp. on Logic Programming*, pp. 138–151, 1985.

Approximate Pruning in Tabled Logic Programming

Luís F. Castro and David S. Warren

Computer Science Dept
SUNY at Stony Brook
Fax: +1 (631) 632-8334
{luis,warren}@cs.stonybrook.edu*

Abstract. Pruning provides an important tool for control of non-determinism in Prolog systems. Current Tabled Prolog systems improve Prolog's evaluation strategy in several ways, but lack satisfactory support for pruning operations. In this paper we present an extension to the evaluation mechanism of Tabled Prolog to support pruning. This extension builds on the concept of demand to select tables to prune. In particular, we concentrate on systems based on SLG resolution. A **once** operator is described, which approximates demand-based pruning, providing for an efficient implementation in the XSB system.

1 Introduction

Prolog is a programming language in which the programmer uses Horn clauses to specify a computation. Prolog uses a backward chaining, goal-directed, demand-driven evaluation strategy that can give it an advantage over forward chaining systems in that it tries to derive only subgoals that are relevant to the main query goal. So it evaluates only those predicates which are necessary to derive the goal. However, its strategy does allow it to derive the same (necessary) subgoal many times, leading, for example, to unnecessary exponential behavior when recognizing some context-free languages.

Tabled Prolog [14] improves on Prolog in that, in addition to deriving only what is necessary for the goal, it will derive such subgoals only once, using a table to short-circuit multiple recomputations of the same subgoal. So Tabled Prolog tries to compute only what is necessary to the goal at hand, and for what it does compute, it computes it only once. For example, this allows Tabled Prolog to be polynomial when recognizing any context-free language.

So it might seem that Tabled Prolog does the minimal amount of computation possible. (Of course, this is without "foreknowledge" of which nondeterministic choices would lead to a proof.) However, even Tabled Prolog still does computation that can easily be seen to be unnecessary.

Consider Prolog and its evaluation of a goal `:- p` applied to the following propositional program:

---

* This work has been partially supported by NSF grant EIA-9705998.

```
:- table_all.
p :- q,t.                q :- r.
p.                       q :- s.
r.                       s :- ...
```

Note that Prolog will evaluate all of s before eventually failing back to succeed through the second clause for p. (The first clause must fail since t, having no facts or rules, cannot succeed.) But note that it can be easily determined that s need not be evaluated. Once q succeeds (here due to r succeeding), there is no need to try any other clause that might lead to q succeeding again. For a ground goal, once it succeeds, there is no reason to search further for other proofs of that goal. That work is clearly unnecessary for proving (or failing to prove) the main goal.

Prolog provides a way for the programmer to control the computation so that the unnecessary evaluation of s in our example is not done. This can be accomplished by adding a cut (!) after the call to r at the end of the first clause for q. Alternatively, if we want to constrain somewhat how cuts are used, we could wrap the call to q with a once operator. These operators would prune the computation tree so that s would never be tried.

Thus we see that Prolog provides pruning operators that allow the programmer to eliminate this kind of unnecessary computation. But in Tabled Prolog there are no such pruning operators. And this is not just an oversight. In the presence of multiple tables and multiple demands on the same table, knowing when a table is not demanded is complex. In Prolog every computation is "on behalf of" a single chain of requesting goals, so if that chain is broken, all the computations along that chain can safely be deleted. However with Tabled Prolog, a single computation that fills a table is working "on behalf of" all users of that table. So a single user of the table may decide it no longer needs that table, but there may be other users still depending on the computation that fills it. Therefore a pruning operator in Tabled Prolog requires a more complex analysis of subgoal dependencies.

In this paper we present an extension to the evaluation mechanism of Tabled Prolog to support pruning. This extension builds on the concept of demand [9] to select tables to prune. In particular, we concentrate on systems based on SLG resolution [2].

Use of general demand for pruning requires an expensive reachability analysis on the evaluation graph. In order to avoid this, we present an approximate solution that is sound, and preserves the semantics of demand-based pruning.

1.1 Related Work

Implementation of pruning operators on systems where the evaluation strategy differs from that of standard Prolog present a set of interesting challenges, which have been the subject of previous study.

One area where this subject has seen a significant amount of work is that of parallel implementations of Prolog [6,1]. In that case, the usual goal is to maintain a semantics that is as close to Prolog as possible. This involves, among other requirements, the synchronization of tasks when pruning is present.

In the context of Tabled Prolog, the first attempt at providing a pruning operator, to the best of our knowledge, is presented in [10]. There, an implementation of the cut operator for SLG_0 is defined and shown to preserve Prolog semantics for *green* cuts [7].

Recently, a new approach has been proposed by Guo and Gupta in [5]. This work presents an implementation of cut for an alternative Tabled Prolog evaluation strategy called DRA [4]. This operator is defined in terms of the fixed operational semantics of DRA, which is based on recomputation of so-called *looping alternatives*. The main difference of our work is that we attempt to create a pruning operator with a semantics that is not dependent on the specific operational semantics of a given implementation.

2   Demand-Based Pruning

SLG resolution [2] is traditionally modeled as a forest of trees. Each tree corresponds to a unique call pattern (parameter instantiation) of a tabled predicate encountered during evaluation. Trees are expanded by performing *clause resolution* against the clauses of the program definitions of the table predicates. Each resolution step is represented by a node in a tree. Other calls to tabled predicates are represented by nodes of a special kind, called *consumer nodes*. Each node is represented in the form of a Prolog rule, where the head carries the substitutions performed on the variables of the subgoal, and the body represents the current continuation as a list of goals to be resolved.

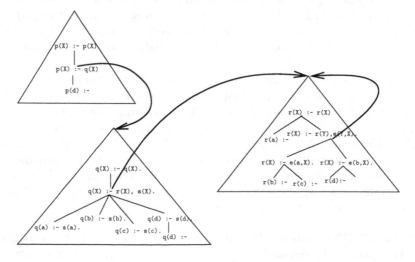

Fig. 1. Snapshot of an SLG evaluation

Figure 1 represents a possible state of the system during evaluation of the query :- p(X). against the program of Listing 1. Each tree is represented by a triangle inclosing a derivation tree. Edges between trees represent the dependence relation between consumer nodes and trees. In the remainder of the paper, we will abstract away the details of derivation trees, and concentrate on the trees in the system and the dependence relation among them, depicted in the form of edges.

```
:- table p/1, q/1, r/1.          e(a,b).
p(X) :- q(X).                     e(a,c).
q(X) :- r(X), s(X).              e(b,d).
r(a).                            e(c,d).
r(X) :- r(Y), e(Y,X).
s(d).
```

Listing 1: Reachability

In fact, the dependence relation defines a multi-graph, where nodes are the trees in the system, and there is an edge for each consumer node, connecting the *consuming* tree to its *supplier*. We call this graph the *Demand Graph*, since it denotes a relation of demand and supply between tables. A demand graph is a weak approximation of the notion of *Relevance* defined in [11].

Definition 1 (Demand Graph) *Given a snapshot of an SLG system, a Demand Graph $\mathcal{D}_G(N, E, Q_N)$ is a directed multi-graph where N is a set of nodes, each representing a tree in the SLG system, and E is the set of edges, representing the dependencies between trees. Q_N is the node representing the tree for the query being evaluated.*

This multi-graph expands as evaluation progresses and new trees and consumer nodes are created. In fact, in the absence of pruning operators, the graph only grows monotonically, until evaluation of the query is completed. Pruning introduces a non-monotonic component to the evaluation when undemanded trees are deleted.

The desired semantics of once(P) states that P should succeed at most once. In other words, as soon as the first successful derivation for P is found, the associated consumer node should be marked such that the goal once(P) does not succeed again. If P contains variables, only one possible binding for each variable is returned. Assuming that P is a tabled predicate, applying the once operator on P essentially amounts to removing an edge from the demand graph of the system when P succeeds. Clearly, this removal may affect the connectivity of the graph, rendering some trees unreachable from the query tree. This state is captured by the concept of *Demand* on trees.

Definition 2 (Demand on Trees) *Given a demand graph $\mathcal{D}_G(N, E, Q_N)$, a node T_1 is said to be demanded if there is a path in $\mathcal{D}_G$, from the query node Q_N to T_1. Similarly, if no such path exists, we say that T_1 is undemanded.*

For performance reasons, undemanded trees should not be scheduled for further evaluation, since there is no indication that other answers for them will be needed to evaluate the current query. Therefore, our algorithm eagerly detects undemanded trees when pruning occurs, and removes them from the set of active trees.

Listing 2 shows pseudo-Prolog code for a demand-based once operator. We assume that nodes are created in a stack-like structure, so that get_next_node_ref returns a reference to the next node to be created. A meta-call starts evaluation of the subgoal P, creating a new node, which is referred to by R. After the meta-call returns, remove_demand disconnects the consumer node referred to by R from the tree that supplies it. A reference to the query table is then obtained, and reachability from the query is computed. undemand_trees removes all trees in the system that are not demanded from the scheduling set.

```
once(P) :-                                undemand_trees(G) :-
        get_next_node_ref(R),                     table(T),
        call(P),                                  ( not member(G,T)
        remove_demand(R),                         ->  undemand_table(T)
        query(Q),                                 ;   true
        reachable(Q,Reach),                       ),
        undemand_trees(Reach).                    fail.
                                          undemand_trees(_).
```

Listing 2: once implementation in Prolog

While it represents our desired semantics, an actual implementation of the algorithm in Listing 2 would present a few drawbacks. First, an expensive traversal of the demanded trees has to be performed each time pruning takes place. Also, a *resumption* mechanism is necessary, in order to re-impose demand on previously undemanded trees for which new consumers are created.

Another point to notice is that it may be advantageous, from the point of view of memory management, to actually remove undemanded trees. In that case, if new calls to undemanded trees are created, these trees will have to be recomputed. On the other hand, if trees are never collected, memory usage may be problematic.

We next define a safe approximation of a demand-based once operator, which attempts to delete trees when demand on them is released.

3   Approximate Pruning

We have argued, in the previous section, that implementing a pruning operation based on exact demand is hard, requiring a full reachability analysis over the evaluation graph. In this section we present an approximation of this operation aimed at preserving our desired semantics, while decreasing the implementation costs of pruning. In the following, we describe the intuitions behind our approximation, before presenting the pruning algorithm.

One issue related to pruning in Tabled Prolog systems is whether unde-manded trees should be frozen, or completely deleted. Freezing trees allows for possible future calls to benefit from results already computed, and restart eval-uation from that point on, if necessary. On the other hand, if these trees are never called again, deleting them is a more memory-efficient solution. The prob-lem constitutes a tradeoff between evaluation time, which is minimized if trees are frozen, and memory usage, minimized when trees are deleted.

The pruning operator presented here deletes trees whenever possible. When undemanded trees are deleted, recomputation may become an issue, possibly altering termination characteristics of programs. Even so, we believe there are many applications where keeping undemanded trees may turn out to consume excessive amounts of resources and adversely affect system performance. Another advantage of this approach is its simplicity. Supporting resumption of trees, besides requiring extra bookkeeping, impacts the scheduling mechanism in a non-trivial way. On the other hand, it may improve long-running computations significantly, when trees are reused, and thus recomputations avoided.

A full demand-based pruning operation, as presented in the previous section, is able to select individual trees which become undemanded when a given edge is removed due to pruning. The algorithm we describe next uses an approximation to decide which trees to delete. The application of a pruning operation induces a *scope*. Intuitively, the scope consists of all those trees that have been created during the evaluation of the goal being pruned.

The notion of scope captures all those trees which could potentially be deleted from the system as a result of this application of pruning. The fact that a table is in the scope of a pruning operation does not directly mean that it can be deleted, since it can still be demanded. Instead of selecting which trees continue to be demanded, and which do not, our approximation decides whether to delete in the level of a scope. When all trees in a scope are undemanded, then they are all deleted. Otherwise, all trees in the scope are maintained in the system. However, instead of freezing these trees, they are maintained as active, and new (possibly unnecessary) answers for these trees may be computed. While this may cause superfluous work to be done, the semantics is guaranteed by removing the connection between the specific subgoal being pruned and the table that supplies answers to it.

In order to support this approximate pruning algorithm based on this notion of scope, we augment our evaluation model with timestamps that impose an ordering in events. Based on this extended model, the notion of scope is defined in terms of reachability over generator edges. Finally, the approximate pruning algorithm is presented and discussed.

3.1   Timestamped Forest of Trees

First we augment the concept of demand graph by introducing timestamps on its edges and trees. We assume a global counter of events is available, which is incremented each time a new edge is created. When an edge is created, it is tagged with the current value of the event counter. Also, trees are timestamped with the value of the event counter at the time they are created. When no pruning takes place, each tree has the same timestamp as its oldest incoming edge. In fact, this edge has a special significance, and is called the *Generator edge* for that tree.

Definition 3 (Generator edge) *An edge is said to be the* Generator *edge of a tree T_i if its destination is T_i, and its timestamp coincides with that of T_i.*

We denote the timestamp of an edge e (tree t) as $timestamp(e)$ $(timestamp(t))$. The source (destination) of an edge is defined in terms of the timestamp of the tree it points from (to).

Definition 4 (Edge properties) *Given an edge e, from tree T_s to tree T_d, we define:*

$$source(e) = timestamp(T_s)$$
$$dest(e) = timestamp(T_d)$$

Figure 2 shows the timestamps in the system depicted in Figure 1. Notice that the *query tree* has always a timestamp of 0.

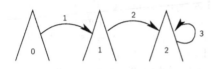

Fig. 2. Timestamps

The main characteristic of approximate pruning is that trees are only considered for removal when their corresponding generator edges are also removed. Removal of a non-generator edge never causes a tree to be removed. Therefore, in order to decide which trees can be removed, we have to consider only those trees which are reachable via generator edges.

The *scope* of a given application of **once** on a subgoal is, intuitively, the set of trees that may potentially be undemanded after the generator edge for the subgoal is removed. The scope is defined in terms of reachability over generator edges. We first define the *Generator-Restricted Demand Graph* as a restriction on the edges of a demand graph, such that only generator edges are included.

Definition 5 (Generator-Restricted Demand Graph) *Given a demand multi-graph $\mathcal{D}_G(N, E, Q_N)$, we define its induced generator-restricted demand graph as the graph $\mathcal{D}_G^{\mathcal{G}}(N, E', Q_N)$, where E' is defined by $E' = \{e \in E \mid e\ timestamp(e) = dest(e)\}$.*

Generator-reachability is defined as reachability over the generator-restricted graph entailed by a given demand graph.

Definition 6 (Generator-reachability) *Given a demand graph $\mathcal{D}_G(N, E, Q_N)$, and an edge $e \in E$, we define Generator-reachability as the set of edges reachable from e in the Generator-restricted graph induced by $\mathcal{D}_G$.*

$$reach_{\mathcal{G}}(e, \mathcal{D}_G(N, E, Q_N)) = \{e' \in E \mid e' \in reach(e, \mathcal{D}_G^{\mathcal{G}})\}$$

Finally, we define the scope of a pruning operation as the set of trees that are Generator-reachable from the edge being removed.

Definition 7 (Scope) *Given a demand graph* $\mathcal{D}_G(N, E, Q_N)$ *and an edge* $e \in E$ *that is the direct subject of a* **once** *operation, we define the scope of the* **once** *operation as*

$$scope(e, \mathcal{D}_G) = \{e' \in reach_G(e, \mathcal{D}_G)\}$$

Our algorithm is based on the principle that a pruning operation can only remove trees which appear in its scope. But the fact that a given tree t appears in a scope does not imply that it is not demanded. It may happen that there are other edges, in the demand graph, connecting nodes outside the scope to t, thus creating an alternate path from the query tree to t, which does not use the edge being removed. This alternative source of demand is called *external demand*. For example, consider the situation if Figure 3, where edge number 2 is being pruned.

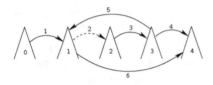

Fig. 3. External Demand

The scope, in this case, consists of trees with timestamps 2, 3 and 4. But edge number 6 imposes an external demand on tree 4, so that this tree cannot be deleted. In this case, approximate pruning removes edge 2, but does not delete any trees, since there is external demand on the scope.

In order to detect whether a given scope has external demand, we need to inspect all edges coming into trees in the scope. If the source of any of these edges is a tree that is not in this scope, then there is external demand. Otherwise, the scope is undemanded.

Definition 8 (External demand on a scope) *Given a demand graph* $\mathcal{D}_G(N, E, Q_N)$ *and an edge* $e \in E$ *that is the direct subject of a* **once** *operation, we define that the scope of this pruning operation is* externally demanded *as:*

$$external\_demand(e, \mathcal{D}_G(N, E, Q_N)) \iff \exists e' \in E \mid source(e') \notin scope(e, \mathcal{D}_G) \land$$
$$dest(e') \in scope(e, \mathcal{D}_G)$$

3.2 Approximate Pruning Algorithm

The algorithm for approximate pruning implementing the **once** operator is presented in Listing 3. It performs a meta-call on the subgoal being pruned, and releases demand on it after the meta-call succeeds. The algorithm is presented in a high-level Prolog form, and assumes the existence of the following builtin predicates, which form an interface for inspecting and manipulating the internally represented current demand graph.

edge(Source,Dest,Timestamp). A set of facts that describe the edges of the demand graph;

`timestamp(Timestamp)`. A builtin predicate that returns the current value of the timestamp counter;

`delete_edge(Timestamp)`. Removes the edge given by `Timestamp` from the graph;

`delete_tree(Timestamp)`. Removes the tree with timestamp `Timestamp`, and all edges outgoing from it.

```
once(SubGoal) :-
   timestamp(Timestamp),
   call(SubGoal),
   delete_edge(Timestamp),
   (  generator(Timestamp)
   -> (  demanded_scope(Timestamp)
      -> true
      ;  delete_scope(Timestamp)
      )
   ; true
   ).

generator(Timestamp) :-
      edge(_,Timestamp,Timestamp).

demanded_scope(Timestamp) :-
      edge(Source, Dest, Time),
      Time > Timestamp,
      not gen_reach(Source),
      gen_reach(Dest).
```

```
:- table gen_reach/2.
gen_reach(Timestamp,Tree) :-
      edge(Timestamp, Tree, Tree).
gen_reach(Timestamp,Tree) :-
      gen_reach(Timestamp,Tree1),
      edge(Tree1,Tree,Tree).

delete_scope(Timestamp) :-
      gen_reach(Timestamp,Tree),
      delete_tree(Tree),
      fail.
delete_scope(_).
```

Listing 3: Pseudo-code for optimized version of once

The predicate once receives as argument a subgoal to be resolved. It starts by recording the current timestamp, which is the timestamp of the next edge to be created. The subgoal is called using Prolog's meta-call builtin. Upon return of the meta-call, the edge corresponding to the subgoal is deleted, thus enforcing the desired semantics.

Further optimization is performed by deleting the tables created during computation of the subgoal, whenever possible. The general algorithm presented in Section 2 performs reachability from the query tree in order to select, individually, which trees are undemanded and can be deleted. In this optimized algorithm, tree removal is decided in terms of the scope of the once operation. That is, if there is external demand on any tree in the scope, then no trees are removed; otherwise, all trees in the scope are deleted.

This is performed by first checking whether the edge of the subgoal is a generator edge. In that case, demanded_scope checks whether any tree in the scope of the subgoal has external demand. If so, nothing is done, otherwise delete_scope removes all trees in the scope from the system. Both **demanded_scope** and **delete_scope** are defined in terms of **gen_reach**, which implements generator-reachability.

4   Implementation

We present an implementation of approximate pruning in the XSB Prolog[13] system. XSB is based on the SLG-WAM[8] abstract machine, a specialization of the original WAM[16]. We first provide a basic description of how XSB implements the SLG-WAM architecture, followed by a presentation of how the demand graph model is represented in the implementation.

4.1   SLG-WAM Architecture

Data areas in XSB are organized into four main stacks. The **Heap** maintains long-lived structures and variables. The **Local** stack maintains the environments for clause-local variables, much like activation records in imperative languages. The **Control** and **Trail** stacks store information required to perform backtracking.

Non-deterministic search in Prolog is implemented by backtracking. Each time a choice is encountered during execution, a *choice-point* is laid down in the **Control** stack. This stack works as a last-in-first-out source of alternatives. That is, when backtracking is necessary, the topmost choice-point in the **Control** stack is used. When a choicepoint is exhausted it can be discarded, and then its predecessor is taken as the next source of alternatives.

SLG evaluation may require that a computation be suspended and other alternatives be executed, before it may be resumed. Suspended computations are represented by portions of the stacks in the system. It is left to the implementation to decide how these stack sections are to be maintained. Typically, these are either protected and kept in the stacks, as in the original formulation of the SLG-WAM[12], or copied to an outside area, as in CHAT [3]. In the remainder of this paper we assume a shared stack management as in the original SLG-WAM. Notice that, in order to recreate the context of a suspended computation, the system may need to redo bindings undone by backtracking while this computation was suspended. Thus, the **Trail** is augmented to keep the values that conditional variables are bound to [15], so that the engine can run the trail not just backwards, but also forwards, rebinding variables needed to reconstruct an earlier context.

The central data-structure for table management is the *Subgoal Frame*. Each subgoal frame contains information about a variant call encountered during evaluation. Subgoal frames maintain references to the associated generator choice-point for the call and for the answers already generated. Also, each subgoal frame maintains a list of all consumer choicepoints which consume from its associated table.

4.2   Mapping the Demand Graph onto XSB

Table management and scheduling are essentially controlled by two data-structures in XSB. Subgoal frames centralize status information about trees in the system, and maintain references to all answers already found for the tree. Choicepoints represent internal nodes, and are classified into three main kinds. Prolog choicepoints are used to maintain unexplored choices in non-tabled predicate definitions. A generator choicepoint is created when the first call to a tabled predicate is encountered, and consumer choicepoints are laid down for calls to already-seen subgoals.

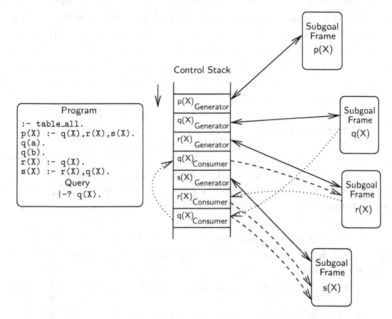

Fig. 4. XSB structures and their relationship

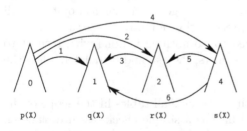

Fig. 5. Dependency Graph

As noted in Section 2, we are interested in those tree nodes which generate dependencies between trees. In XSB, these are represented by the consumer and generator choicepoints. Generator choicepoints have a dual role in XSB. Besides indicating that results from a given table T_d are demanded from the callee table T_s, they also serve the purpose of performing clause resolution to generate answers for T_d.

Figure 4 shows an example of these structures during evaluation of a query, and their relationship. The corresponding dependency graph is shown in Figure 5. Generator choicepoints are linked to their corresponding subgoal frames, and vice-versa. All consumers of a given table are chained together, and this chain is anchored in the subgoal frame of the table. This chain is called the *consumer chain* of the table.

Summarizing, edges are represented by the choicepoints in the stack. Generator edges correspond to generator choicepoints, which are distinguished in the system. Trees are mapped to Subgoal frames, and their auxiliary structures, which are not presented here. We now examine how the operations necessary to implement our algorithm can be efficiently realized, and describe the changes to the standard SLG-WAM data structures necessary to support these operations.

edge. The `edge` relation connects consuming trees to their suppliers. This relation is realized by consumer and generator choicepoints, and the timestamps for these edges are implicitly represented by the memory addresses of these choicepoints. Choicepoints already maintain references to the tables they are supplying, as shown in Figure 4 by the dashed arrows. Tables are connected to the consumers it supplies (dotted arrows). In order to provide fast access to the tree a given consumer is consuming from, we have augmented the SLG-WAM structure by creating a new chain that effectively transforms dotted arrows in Figure 4 into double arrows.

delete_edge. This function is responsible for ensuring that no more answers will be returned to a given choicepoint representing a tabled call. If the choicepoint is a consumer choicepoint, we simply delete it by removing it from the chain of choicepoints considered for scheduling. Generator choicepoints, as observed earlier, are responsible both for returning answers to a tabled call via its forward continuation, and for generating answers to a table, through its backwards continuation. When `delete_edge` is applied to a generator choicepoint, it modifies its forward continuation to a failure, so that no answers will be returned to the tabled call, even though it remains able to generate answers to the table.

delete_tree. Given the timestamp of a table, which in SLG-WAM is represented by the address of its generator choicepoint, `delete_tree` deletes its data structures and execution context. The Subgoal frame and all answers already computed for the table are deleted, as well as its generator choicepoint, and all consumers that supply this table. A precondition for `delete_edge` is that no demand exists on the table it is applied to, so nothing is done with respect to consumers of this table. If there are consumers, they should be deleted when the tables they are supplying are deleted.

gen_reach. This predicate is used both to traverse all tables in the scope of the operation (as in `demanded_scope`) and also as a simple check, as in `demanded`. `gen_reach` is realized in the implementation by performing a reachability analysis in the beginning of the algorithm, marking all choicepoints which are reachable, and thus in the scope of pruning. This provides for an easy, constant-time check for whether a given choicepoint is in the scope. Traversal of choicepoints in the scope is performed, when necessary, by a linear scan of the top of the choicepoint stack, skipping those choicepoints not marked.

demanded_scope. This predicate essentially collects all edges younger than the timestamp at entry of once, whose source is not in its scope. The key to implement this function is to realize that, since timestamps are implicitly represented by the address of choicepoints, a simple traversal of the top of the Control stack (back to the point where once started evaluation), selecting unmarked choicepoints, obtains all such edges. If any of these choicepoints consumes from a table in the scope of once, it means that the scope has external demand, and the predicate succeeds. This information is obtained by following the links from consumers to tables they supply (dashed lines in Figure 4.)

5 Experimental Results

In this section, we present some quantitative data that suggests that approximate pruning, with table deletion, can significantly impact execution times of programs.

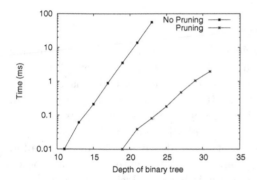

Fig. 6. Performance comparison for the stalemate game

In order to illustrate these possible gains, we benchmark a version of the classical Stalemate game depicted in Listing 4 in the form of the predicate win. Given a directed graph, this game states that a node is a winner if there is an edge connecting this node to a non-winner node. Nodes which have no possible moves are, by default, winner nodes. The goal is to determine if a given node is a winner node. It is important, in general, that the win predicate be tabled, so that the evaluation terminates in the presence of cycles in the input graph.

```
:- table win/0.                          test(Depth) :-
win(X) :-                                       create_bin_tree(Depth),
        move(X,Y),                              cputime(T1),
        tnot(win(Y)).                           win(0),
                                                cputime(T2),
                                                Time is T2 - T1,
                                                write(time(win(Depth),Time)).
```

Listing 4: The Stalemate win/not-win game

It is clear that it is uninteresting to collect alternative proofs for the winning status of a given node. This can be easily obtained by ensuring that negation builtins like XSB's tnot fail early when the first counter-proof is found. Currently, `tnot` does not perform pruning when it fails, so unnecessary computation is performed.

We have adapted the `tnot` operator to take advantage of approximate pruning, and compared execution times using the `test` predicate of Listing 4. The test dynamically creates full binary trees with variable depth. Figure 6 shows results obtained for tests run both with and without the modified `tnot` builtin. It is clear that, even though pruning does not change the exponential nature of this problem, it significantly lowers the slope of the curve[1]. Besides time, memory performance is important for this benchmark. In fact, we were unable to run the non-pruning version of the benchmark for trees of depth larger than 23 on a machine with 2Gb of memory.

Another important point when introducing new functionality is to measure the impact the added machinery imposes when the functionality is not being used. We have benchmarked a set of non-pruning benchmarks on XSB with and without support for our pruning operator. The maximum overhead observed was about 3%.

6 Summary

The backward chaining evaluation model of Prolog computes only those subgoals that are needed in order to resolve a given query. Pruning allows for a finer control of determinism, which can be used to further extend this concept of performing only demanded computations. It can be used by the Prolog engine itself, in order to improve its evaluation strategy, and also by the programmer, so that she can annotate programs with control information.

Tabled Prolog builds on the concept of demand-driven evaluation by allowing each relevant goal to be evaluated only once. But there are no satisfactory pruning operators in Tabled Prolog, since it is hard to decide which tables are demanded in the presence of suspension and resumption of subgoals.

We have presented an abstraction of SLG evaluation where the SLG forest of trees is represented by a directed graph, and demand is defined in terms of reachability from a query node. This allowed us to define a demand-based `once` pruning operator.

Full demand-based pruning is costly, so we presented sound approximate pruning in the form of a safe `once` operator. Approximate pruning uses a notion of the scope of the `once` operation as the basic unit for which demand is determined and implemented. This allows for an efficient pruning mechanism, which has been implemented in the XSB system.

One question when performing pruning on tabled systems is whether undemanded tables should be deleted, or whether they should be kept in a scratch area, so that future calls could use their results, and re-impose demand on them. Approximate pruning takes the approach of deleting undemanded tables, given that their scope is currently undemanded. This has the advantage of early memory reclamation, but may have adverse effects on the termination characteristics

---

[1] Notice that the y axis of the graph is plotted in a logarithmic scale.

of a program. We intend to study the alternative of maintaining undemanded trees, and supporting the re-imposition of demand on them. We believe each approach will prove effective in different situations.

References

1. K. A. M. Ali. A method for implementing cut in parallel execution of Prolog. In *ICSLP'87*.
2. W. Chen and D. S. Warren. Tabled Evaluation with Delaying for General Logic Programs. *Journal of the ACM*, 43(1):20–74, January 1996.
3. B. Demoen and K. Sagonas. CHAT: the Copy-Hybrid Approach to Tabling. In *PADL'99*, 1999.
4. H.-F. Guo and G. Gupta. A simple scheme for implementing tabled logic programming systems based on dynamic reordering of alternatives. In *ICLP'01*, pages 181–196, 2001.
5. H.-F. Guo and G. Gupta. Cuts in tabled logic programming. In B. Demoen, editor, *CICLOPS'02*, 2002.
6. G. Gupta and V. Santos Costa. Cuts and side-effects in and-or parallel prolog. *Journal of Logic Programming*, 27(1):45–71, 1996.
7. R. O'Keefe. *The Craft of Prolog*. MIT, 1990.
8. K. Sagonas and T. Swift. An abstract machine for tabled execution of fixed-order stratified logic programs. *TOPLAS*, 20(3):586–635, May 1998.
9. T. Swift. A new formulation of tabled resolution with delay. In *Recent Advances in Artificial Intelligence*.
10. T. Swift. *Efficient Evaluation of Normal Logic Programs*. PhD thesis, SUNY at Stony Brook, 1994.
11. T. Swift. A new formulation of tabled resolution with delay. In *EPIA'99*, 1999.
12. T. Swift and D. S. Warren. An abstract machine for SLG resolution: definite programs. In *SLP'94*, pages 633–654, 1994.
13. *The XSB Programmer's Manual: version 2.5, vols. 1 and 2*, 2002. http://xsb.sourceforge.net/.
14. D. S. Warren. Programming in tabled prolog – DRAFT. Available from http://www.cs.stonybrook.edu/~warren.
15. D. S. Warren. Efficient Prolog memory management for flexible control. In *ILPS'84*, pages 198–202, 1984.
16. D.H.D. Warren. An abstract Prolog instruction set. Technical Report 309, SRI, 1983.

Goal-Independent Suspension Analysis for Logic Programs with Dynamic Scheduling

Samir Genaim* and Andy King

[1] Ben-Gurion University of the Negev, PoB 653, Beer-Sheva, 84105 Israel.
[2] University of Kent, Canterbury, CT2 7NF, UK.

Abstract. A goal-independent suspension analysis is presented that infers a class of goals for which a logic program with delays can be executed without suspension. The crucial point is that the analysis does not verify that an (abstract) goal does not lead to suspension but rather it infers (abstract) goals which do not lead to suspension.

1 Introduction

A logic program can be considered as consisting of a logic component and a control component [15]. Although the meaning of the program is largely defined by its logical specification, choosing the right control is crucial in obtaining a correct and efficient program. In recent years, one of the most popular ways of defining control is by suspension mechanisms which delay the selection of a sub-goal until some condition is satisfied [2]. Delays have proved to be invaluable for handling negation, delaying non-linear constraints, enforcing termination, improving search and modelling concurrency. However, reasoning about logic programs with delays is notoriously difficult and one reoccurring problem for the programmer is that of determining whether a given program and goal can reduce to a state which possesses a sub-goal that suspends indefinitely. A number of abstract interpretation schemes [3,5,8] have therefore been proposed for verifying that a program and goal cannot suspend in this fashion. These analyses essentially simulate the operational semantics tracing the execution of the program with collections of abstract states, and are thus said to be goal-*dependent*. This paper presents a suspension analysis that is performed in a goal-*independent* way. Specifically, rather than verifying that a *particular* goal will not lead to a suspension, the analysis infers a *class* of goals that will not lead to suspension. This new approach has the computational advantage that the programmer need not rerun the analysis for different (abstract) queries.

The analysis also tackles suspension analysis from another new perspective – it verifies whether a logic program with delays can be scheduled with a *local* selection rule [20]. Under local selection, the selected atom is completely resolved, that is, those atoms it directly and indirectly introduces are also resolved, before any other atom is selected. Leftmost selection is one example of

---

* New address: Universita' degli Studi di Verona, 37134 Verona, Italy.

P. Degano (Ed.): ESOP 2003, LNCS 2618, pp. 84–98, 2003.

local selection. Knowledge about suspension within the context of local selection is useful within it own right [8,14] but it turns out that local selection also fits elegantly with backward reasoning. Moreover, any program that can be shown to be suspension-free under local selection is clearly suspension-free with a more general selection rule (though the converse does not follow). Our analysis draws together a number of strands in program analysis and therefore, for clarity, we summarise our contribution:

- The analysis performs goal-independent suspension analysis.
- The analysis, though technical, reduces to two simple bottom-up fixpoint computations – a lfp and a gfp – which, like the backward analysis of [13], makes it simple to implement. The rôle of the lfp is simply to calculate success patterns that are used within the gfp calculation to model the way the sub-goals of a compound goal can bind variables.
- The analysis is straightforward like the simple but successful suspension framework of Debray *et al* [8] that infers suspension-freeness under leftmost selection. The analysis in this paper additionally considers *all* local selection rules and therefore strikes a good balance between tractability and precision.
- The analysis is unique in that it exploits the property that Heyting closed domains [11] possess a pseudo-complement for two effects. First, the pseudo-complement which enables information flow to be reversed to obtain a goal-independent analysis (this idea is not new [13]). Second, pseudo-complement is used to model synchronisation. The crucial correctness result exploits a (reordering) relationship between monotonic and positive Boolean functions and Boolean implication.

The paper is structured as follows: Section 2 presents an example that illustrates the ideas behind the analysis. Section 3 introduces the necessary preliminaries. Section 4 details local selection. Section 5 explains the rôle of Boolean functions in analysis. Section 6 details the analysis itself and Section 7 presents an experimental evaluation. Section 8 reviews related work and Section 9 concludes.

2   Worked Example

Consider the Prolog program listed in the left-hand column of Figure 1. Declaratively, the program defines the relation that the second argument (a list) is an in-order traversal of the first argument (a tree). Operationally, the declaration :- block app(-,?,-) delays (blocks) app goals until their arguments are sufficiently instantiated. The dashes in the first and third argument positions specify that a call to app is to be delayed until either its first or third argument are bound to non-variable terms. Thus app goals can be executed in one of two modes. The problem is to compute input modes which are sufficient to guarantee that any inorder query which satisfies the modes will not lead to a suspension under local selection. This problem can be solved with backward analysis. Backward analysis infers requirements on the input which ensure that certain properties hold at (later) program points [13]. The analysis reduces to three steps: a program abstraction step; least fixpoint (lfp) and a greatest fixpoint (gfp) computation.

inorder(nil,[]).	inorder(T, I) :-	inorder(T, I) :-
inorder(tree(L,V,R),I) :-	true :	true : T ∧ I : true
app(LI,[V|RI],I),	T = nil, I = [] : true.	inorder(T, I) :-
inorder(L,LI),	inorder(T, I) :-	true :
inorder(R,RI).	true :	T ↔ (L ∧ V ∧ R),
	T = tree(L,V,R),	A ↔ (V ∧ RI) :
:- block app(-, ?, -).	A = [V|RI] :	app(LI,A,I),
app([], X, X).	app(LI,A,I),	inorder(L,LI),
app([X|Xs], Ys, [X|Zs]) :-	inorder(L,LI),	inorder(R,RI).
app(Xs,Ys,Zs).	inorder(R,RI).	
		app(L, Ys, A) :-
		L ∨ A :
	app(L, Ys, A) :-	L ∧ (A ↔ Ys) : true.
	nonvar(L) ∨ nonvar(A):	app(L, Ys, A) :-
	L = [], A = Ys : true.	L ∨ A :
	app(L, Ys, A) :-	L ↔ (X ∧ Xs),
	nonvar(L) ∨ nonvar(A):	A ↔ (X ∧ Zs) :
	L = [X|Xs], A = [X|Zs] :	app(Xs,Ys,Zs).
	app(Xs,Ys,Zs).	

Fig. 1. inorder program in Prolog, in ccp and as a *Pos* abstraction

2.1 Program Abstraction

Abstraction in turn reduces to two transformations: one from a Prolog with delay program to a concurrent constraint programming (ccp) program and another from the ccp program to a *Pos* abstraction. The Prolog program is re-written to a ccp program to make blocking requirements explicit in the program as ask constraints. More exactly, a clause of a ccp program takes the form h :- c' : c'' : g where h is an atom, g is a conjunction of body atoms and c' and c'' are the ask and tell constraints. The asks are guards that inspect the store and specify synchronisation behaviour whereas the tells are single-assignment writes that update the store. Empty conjunctions of atoms are denoted by true. The nonvar(x) constraint states the requirement that x is bound to a non-variable term. The second transform abstracts the ask and tell constraints with Boolean functions which capture instantiation dependencies. The ask constraints are abstracted from below whereas the tell constraints are abstracted from above. More exactly, an ask abstraction is stronger than the ask constraint – whenever the abstraction holds then the ask constraint is satisfied; whereas an tell abstraction is weaker than the tell constraint – whenever the tell constraint holds then so does its abstraction. For example, the function L ∨ A describes states where either L or A is ground [1] which, in turn, ensure that the ask constraint nonvar(L) ∨ nonvar(A) holds. On the other hand, once the tell A = [V|RI] holds, then the grounding behaviour of the state (and all subsequent states) is described by A ↔ (V ∧ RI).

2.2 Least Fixpoint Calculation

The second step of the analysis approximates the success patterns of the ccp program (and thus the Prolog with delays program) by computing a lfp of the abstract *Pos* program. A success pattern is an atom with distinct variables for arguments paired with a *Pos* formula over those variables. A success pattern summarises the behaviour of an atom by describing the bindings it can make. The lfp of the *Pos* program can be computed T_P-style [10] in a finite number of iterates. Each iterate is a set of success patterns: at most one pair for each predicate in the program. This gives the following lfp:

$$F = \left\{ \begin{array}{l} \langle \mathrm{inorder}(x_1, x_2), x_1 \leftrightarrow x_2 \rangle \\ \langle \mathrm{app}(x_1, x_2, x_3), (x_1 \wedge x_2) \leftrightarrow x_3 \rangle \end{array} \right\}$$

Observe that F faithfully describes the grounding behaviour of inorder and app.

2.3   Greatest Fixpoint Calculation

A gfp is computed to characterise the safe call patterns of the program. A call pattern has the same form as a success pattern. Iteration commences with

$$D_0 = \left\{ \begin{array}{l} \langle \mathrm{inorder}(x_1, x_2), true \rangle \\ \langle \mathrm{app}(x_1, x_2, x_3), true \rangle \end{array} \right\}$$

and incrementally strengthens the call pattern formulae until they are safe, that is, they describe queries which are guaranteed not to violate the ask constraints. The iterate D_{i+1} is computed by putting $D_{i+1} = D_i$ and then revising D_{i+1} by considering each $p(\boldsymbol{x})$:- $d : f : p_1(\boldsymbol{x}_1), \ldots, p_n(\boldsymbol{x}_n)$ in the abstract program and calculating a (monotonic) formula that describes input modes (if any) under which the atoms in the clause can be scheduled without suspension under local selection. A monotonic formula over set of variables X is any formula of the form $\bigvee_{i=1}^{n}(\wedge Y_i)$ where $Y_i \subseteq X$ [7]. Let d_i denote a monotonic formula that describes the call pattern requirement for $p_i(\boldsymbol{x}_i)$ in D_i and let f_i denote the success pattern formula for $p_i(\boldsymbol{x}_i)$ in the lfp (that is not necessarily monotonic). A new call pattern for $p(\boldsymbol{x})$ is computed using the following algorithm:

- Calculate $e = \wedge_{i=1}^{n}(d_i \rightarrow f_i)$ that describes the grounding behaviour of the compound goal $p_1(\boldsymbol{x}_1), \ldots, p_n(\boldsymbol{x}_n)$. The intuition is that $p_i(\boldsymbol{x}_i)$ can be described by $d_i \rightarrow f_i$ since if the input requirements hold (d_i) then $p_i(\boldsymbol{x}_i)$ can be executed without suspension, hence the output must also hold (f_i).
- Compute $e' = \wedge_{i=1}^{n} d_i$ which describes a groundness property sufficient for scheduling all of the goals in the compound goal without suspension. Then $e \rightarrow e'$ describes a grounding property which, if satisfied, when the compound goal is called ensures the goal can be scheduled by local selection without suspension (this relies on an unusual reordering property of monotonic functions that is explained in Section 5.3).
- Calculate $g = d \wedge (f \rightarrow (e \rightarrow e'))$ that describes a grounding property which is strong enough to ensure that both the ask is satisfied and the body atoms can be scheduled by local selection without suspension.
- Eliminate those variables not present in $p(\boldsymbol{x})$, Y say, by computing $g' = \forall_Y(g)$ where $\forall_{\{y_1 \ldots y_n\}}(g) = \forall_{y_1}(\ldots \forall_{y_n}(g))$. A single variable can be

eliminated by $\forall_x(f) = f'$ if $f' \in Pos$ otherwise $\forall_x(f) = 0$ where $f' = f[x \mapsto 0] \wedge f[x \mapsto 1]$. Hence $\forall_x(f)$ entails f and g' entails g, so that a safe calling mode for this particular clause is then given by g'.

- Compute a monotonic function g'' that entails g'. Since g'' is stronger than g' it follows that g'' is sufficient for scheduling the compound goal by local selection without suspension. The function g' needs to be approximated by a monotonic function since the $e \rightarrow e'$ step relies on d_i being monotonic.
- Replace the pattern $\langle p(\boldsymbol{x}), g''' \rangle$ in D_{i+1} with $\langle p(\boldsymbol{x}), g'' \wedge g''' \rangle$.

This procedure generates the following D_i sequence:

$$D_1 = \left\{ \begin{matrix} \langle \text{inorder}(x_1, x_2), true \rangle \\ \langle \text{app}(x_1, x_2, x_3), x_1 \vee x_3 \rangle \end{matrix} \right\} \qquad D_2 = \left\{ \begin{matrix} \langle \text{inorder}(x_1, x_2), x_1 \vee x_2 \rangle \\ \langle \text{app}(x_1, x_2, x_3), x_1 \vee x_3 \rangle \end{matrix} \right\}$$

The gfp is reached and checked in three iterations. The result asserts that a local selection rule exists for which inorder will not suspend if either its first or second arguments are ground. Indeed, observe that if the first argument is ground then body atoms of the second inorder clause can be scheduled as follows inorder(L,LI), then inorder(R,RI), and then app(LI,A,I) whereas if the second argument is ground, then the reverse ordering is sufficient for non-suspension.

3   Preliminaries

Let $\wp^+(S)$ (S^*) denote the set of multisets (sequences) whose elements are drawn from S. Let ϵ denote the empty sequence, let . denote sequence concatenation and let $\|s\|$ denote the length of a sequence s. If s is a sequence, let $\Pi(s)$ denote the set of permutations of s. Let $[l, u] = \{n \in \mathbb{Z} \mid l \leq n \leq u\}$. Transitive closure of a binary relation ϱ is denoted $\varrho^\star$.

3.1   Terms, Substitutions, and Equations

Let $Term$ denote the set of (possibly infinite) terms over an alphabet of functor symbols $Func$ and a (denumerable) universe of variables Var where $Func \cap Var = \emptyset$. Let $var(t)$ denote the set of variables occurring in the term t.

A substitution is a (total) map $\theta : Var \rightarrow Term$ such that $dom(\theta) = \{u \in Var \mid \theta(u) \neq u\}$ is finite. Let $rng(\theta) = \cup\{var(\theta(u)) \mid u \in dom(\theta)\}$ and let $var(\theta) = dom(\theta) \cup rng(\theta)$. A substitution θ is idempotent iff $\theta \circ \theta = \theta$, or equivalently, iff $dom(\theta) \cap rng(\theta) = \emptyset$. Let Sub denote the set of idempotent substitutions and let id denote the empty substitution. Let $\theta(t)$ denote the term obtained by simultaneously replacing each occurrence of a variable $x \in dom(\theta)$ in t with $\theta(x)$. An equation e is a pair $(s = t)$ where $s, t \in Term$. A finite set of equations is denoted E and Eqn denotes the set of finite sets of equations. Also define $\theta(E) = \{\theta(s) = \theta(t) \mid (s = t) \in E\}$. The map eqn : $Sub \rightarrow Eqn$ is defined eqn$(\theta) = \{x = \theta(x) \mid x \in dom(\theta)\}$. Composition $\theta \circ \psi$ of two substitutions is defined so that $(\theta \circ \psi)(u) = \theta(\psi(u))$ for all $u \in V$. Composition induces the (more general than) relation $\leq$ defined by $\theta \leq \psi$ iff there exists $\delta \in Sub$ such that $\psi = \delta \circ \theta$ which, in turn, defines the equivalence relation (variance) $\theta \approx \psi$ iff $\theta \leq \psi$ and $\psi \leq \theta$. Let Ren denote the set of invertible substitutions (renamings).

3.2   Most General Unifiers

The set of unifiers of E is defined by: $unify(E) = \{\theta \in Sub \mid \forall (s = t) \in E.\theta(s) = \theta(t)\}$. The set of most general unifiers (mgus) and the set of idempotent mgus (imgus) are defined: $mgu(E) = \{\theta \in unify(E) \mid \forall \psi \in unify(E).\theta \leq \psi\}$ and $imgu(E) = \{\theta \in mgu(E) \mid dom(\theta) \cap rng(\theta) = \emptyset\}$. Note that $imgu(E) \neq \emptyset$ iff $mgu(E) \neq \emptyset$ [16].

3.3   Logic Programs

Let Pred denote a (finite) set of predicate symbols, let $Atom$ denote the set of (flat) atoms over Pred with distinct arguments drawn from Var, and let $Goal = \wp^*(Atom)$. A logic program P (with dynamic scheduling assertions) is a finite set of clauses w of the form $w = h :- D : E : b$ where $h \in Atom$, $D \in \wp(Eqn)$ (the ask is a set of equations), $E \in Eqn$ (the tell is a single equation) and $b \in Goal$. An operational semantics (that ignores each D and therefore synchronisation) is defined in terms of the standard transition system:

Definition 1 (standard transition system). Given a logic program P, $\leadsto_P \subseteq (Goal \times Sub)^2$ is the least relation such that: $s = \langle g, \theta \rangle \leadsto_P \langle b.g', \delta \circ \theta \rangle$ if

  – there exists $p(\boldsymbol{x}) \in g$
  – and there exists $\rho \in Ren$ and $w \in \rho(P)$ such that $var(w) \cap var(s) = \emptyset$ and $w = p(\boldsymbol{y}) :- D : E : b$
  – and $\delta \in imgu(\{\theta(\boldsymbol{x}) = \boldsymbol{y}\} \cup E)$ and $g' = g \setminus \{p(\boldsymbol{x})\}$

Note that . denotes concatenation. The operational semantics is the transitive closure of the relation on (atomic) goals, that is, $\mathcal{O}(P) = \{\theta(p(\boldsymbol{x})) \mid \langle p(\boldsymbol{x}), id \rangle \leadsto_P^* \langle \epsilon, \theta \rangle\}$. The following lemmas are useful in establishing the main result, theorem 1, and follow from the switching lemma [17, lemma 9.1].

Lemma 1. Let $\langle a.g, \theta \rangle \leadsto_P^i \langle \epsilon, \theta' \rangle$. Then $\langle a, \theta \rangle \leadsto_P^j \langle \epsilon, \psi \rangle$ and $\langle g, \psi \rangle \leadsto_P^k \langle \epsilon, \psi' \rangle$ where $i = j + k$ and $\theta' \approx \psi'$.

Lemma 2. Suppose $\langle g_1, \theta_1 \rangle \leadsto_P^* \langle g_2, \theta_2 \rangle$ and $\theta_1 \approx \psi_1$. Then $\langle g_1, \psi_1 \rangle \leadsto_P^* \langle g_2, \psi_2 \rangle$ where $\theta_2 \approx \psi_2$.

A fixpoint semantics of P (that again ignores synchronisation) can be defined in terms of an immediate consequences operator $\mathcal{F}_P$. Let $Base = \{\theta(a) \mid a \in Atom \wedge \theta \in Sub\}$ and $Int = \{I \subseteq Base \mid \forall a \in I.\forall \theta \in Sub.\theta(a) \in I\}$. Then $\langle Int, \subseteq, \cup, \cap, Base, \emptyset \rangle$ is a complete lattice.

Definition 2. Given a logic program P, the operator $\mathcal{F}_P : Int \to Int$ is defined:

$$\mathcal{F}_P(I) = \left\{ \theta(h) \,\middle|\, \begin{array}{l} h :- D : E : a_1, \ldots, a_m \in P \wedge \\ \theta \in unify(E) \wedge \theta(a_i) \in I \end{array} \right\}$$

The operator $\mathcal{F}_P$ is continuous and hence the fixpoint semantics for a program P can be defined as $\mathcal{F}(P) = lfp(\mathcal{F}_P)$. The relationship between the operational and fixpoint semantics is stated below.

Theorem 1 (Partial correctness). $\mathcal{O}(P) \subseteq \mathcal{F}(P)$.

Although the fixpoint semantics is only partially correct – it does not consider synchronisation – it still provides a useful foundation for analysis since any safe (superset) abstraction of $\mathcal{F}(P)$ is also a safe approximation of $\mathcal{O}(P)$.

4   Local Selection

This section formalises the analysis problem, and in particular local selection, by introducing an operational semantics for logic programs which combines delay with local selection. A transition system is defined in terms of an augmented notion of state, that is, $State = \{susp\} \cup Goal \times Sub \cup Goal \times Goal \times Sub$.

Definition 3 (transition system for local selection with delay). Given a logic program P, $\twoheadrightarrow_P \subseteq State^2$ is the least relation such that:

- $s = \langle p(\boldsymbol{x}).g, \theta \rangle \twoheadrightarrow_P \langle b, g', \delta \circ \theta \rangle$ if
  - there exists $\rho \in Ren$ and $w \in \rho(P)$ such that $var(w) \cap var(s) = \emptyset$ and $w = p(\boldsymbol{y}) :- D : E : b$
  - and there exists $E' \in D$ and $\mu \in unify(E')$ such that $\mu(p(\boldsymbol{y})) = \theta(p(\boldsymbol{x}))$
  - and $\delta \in imgu(\{\theta(\boldsymbol{x}) = \boldsymbol{y}\} \cup E)$ and $g' = g \setminus \{p(\boldsymbol{x})\}$;
- $s = \langle p(\boldsymbol{y}).g, \theta \rangle \twoheadrightarrow_P susp$ if
  - there exists $\rho \in Ren$ and $w \in \rho(P)$ such that $var(w) \cap var(s) = \emptyset$ and $w = p(\boldsymbol{y}) :- D : E : b$
  - and $\mu(p(\boldsymbol{y})) \neq \theta(p(\boldsymbol{x}))$ for all $E' \in D$ and for all $\mu \in unify(E')$;
- $\langle b, g, \theta \rangle \twoheadrightarrow_P \langle b'.g, \theta \rangle$ if $b' \in \Pi(b)$.

Recall that . is concatenation and $\Pi(b)$ is the set of goals obtained by permuting of the sequence of body atoms b. These permuted body atoms ensure that the transition system considers each local selection rule rather than a particular local selection rule. The analysis problem can now be stated precisely: it is to infer a sub-class of states of the form $s = \langle p(\boldsymbol{x}), \theta \rangle$ such that if $s \leadsto_P^* \langle \epsilon, \psi \rangle$ then $s \twoheadrightarrow_P^* \langle \epsilon, \chi \rangle$ where $\psi \approx \chi$. Put another way, if the standard transition system produces a computed answer then a local selection rule exists that will produce a variant of that answer. The problem is non-trivial because local selection can bar derivations from occurring that arise in the standard transition system. The following proposition is an immediate consequence of this.

Proposition 1. $\mathcal{O}(P) \supseteq \{\theta(p(\boldsymbol{x})) \mid \langle p(\boldsymbol{x}), id \rangle \twoheadrightarrow_P^* \langle \epsilon, \theta \rangle\}$.

5   Boolean Functions

This section reviews Boolean functions and their rôle in analysis, before moving to introduce new properties of Boolean functions that are particularly pertinent to suspension analysis. A Boolean function is a function $f : Bool^n \to Bool$ where $n \geq 0$ and $Bool = \{0, 1\}$. A Boolean function can be represented by a propositional formula over $X \subseteq Var$ where $|X| = n$. The set of propositional formulae over X is denoted by $Bool_X$. Boolean functions and propositional formulae are used interchangeably without worrying about the distinction. The convention of identifying a truth assignment with the set of variables M that it maps to 1 is also followed. Specifically, a map $\psi_X(M) : \wp(X) \to Bool_X$ is introduced defined by: $\psi_X(M) = (\wedge M) \wedge \neg(\vee(X \setminus M))$. Henceforth suppose X is finite.

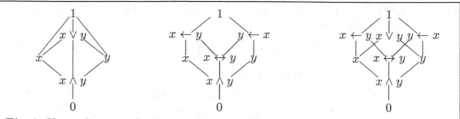

Fig. 2. Hasse diagrams for Mon_X, Def_X and Pos_X for the dyadic case $X = \{x, y\}$

Definition 4. The map $model_X : Bool_X \to \wp(\wp(X))$ is defined by: $model_X(f) = \{M \subseteq X \mid \psi_X(M) \models f\}$.

Example 1. If $X = \{x, y\}$, then the function $\{\langle 1, 1 \rangle \mapsto 1, \langle 1, 0 \rangle \mapsto 0, \langle 0, 1 \rangle \mapsto 0, \langle 0, 0 \rangle \mapsto 0\}$ can be represented by the formula $x \wedge y$. Moreover, $model_X(x \wedge y) = \{\{x, y\}\}$, $model_X(x \vee y) = \{\{x\}, \{y\}, \{x, y\}\}$, $model_X(false) = \emptyset$ and $model_X(true) = \wp(\wp(X)) = \{\emptyset, \{x\}, \{y\}, \{x, y\}\}$.

5.1   Classes of Boolean Functions

The suspension analysis is formulated with three classes of Boolean function.

Definition 5. A Boolean function f is positive iff $X \in model_X(f)$; f is definite iff $M \cap M' \in model_X(f)$ for all $M, M' \in model_X(f)$; f is monotonic iff $M' \in model_X(f)$ whenever $M \in model_X(f)$ and $M \subseteq M' \subseteq X$.

Let Pos_X denote the set of positive Boolean functions (augmented with 0); Def_X denote the set of positive functions over X that are definite (augmented with 0); and Mon_X denote the set of monotonic Boolean functions over X (that includes 0). Observe $Mon_X \subseteq Pos_X$ and $Def_X \subseteq Pos_X$. One useful representational property of Def_X is that if $f \in Def_X$ and $f \neq 0$, then $f = \wedge_{i=1}^{m}(y_i \leftarrow \wedge Y_i)$ for some $y_i \in X$ and $Y_i \subseteq X$ [7]. Moreover, if $f \in Mon_X$ and $f \neq 0$, then $f = \vee_{i=1}^{m}(\wedge Y_i)$ where $Y_i \subseteq X$ [6, Proposition 2.1]

The 4-tuple $\langle Pos_X, \models, \wedge, \vee \rangle$ is a finite lattice and Mon_X is a sub-lattice (whereas Def_X is not a sub-lattice as witnessed by the join of x and y in Figure 2). Existential quantification for Pos_X is defined by Schröder elimination, that is, $\exists x.f = f[x \mapsto 1] \vee f[x \mapsto 0]$. Universal projection is defined $\forall_x(f) = f'$ if $f' \in Pos_X$ otherwise $\forall_x(f) = 0$ where $f' = f[x \mapsto 0] \wedge f[x \mapsto 1]$. Note that $\exists x.(\exists y.f) = \exists y.(\exists x.f)$ and $\forall x.(\forall y.f) = \forall y.(\forall x.f)$ for all $x, y \in X$. Thus let $\exists\{y_1, \ldots, y_n\}.f = f_{n+1}$ where $f_1 = f$ and $f_{i+1} = \exists y_i.f_i$ and define $\forall\{y_1, \ldots, y_n\}.f$ analogously. Finally let $\overline{\exists}Y.f = \exists(X \backslash Y).f$ and $\overline{\forall}Y.f = \forall(X \backslash Y).f$.

5.2   Abstracting the Fixpoint Semantics Using Boolean Functions

Boolean functions are used to describe (grounding) properties of the program. The construction is to formalise the connection between functions and data (syntactic equations) and then extend it to semantic objects such as interpretations.

Definition 6. The abstraction $\alpha^{Pos} : \wp(Eqn) \rightarrow Pos$ and concretisation $\gamma^{Pos} : Pos \rightarrow \wp(Eqn)$ maps are defined:

$$\alpha^{Pos}(D) = \vee\{\alpha^{Def}(\theta) \mid \theta \in imgu(E) \wedge E \in D\} \quad \gamma^{Pos}(f) = \{E \mid \alpha^{Pos}(\{E\}) \models f\}$$

where $\alpha^{Def}(\theta) = \wedge\{x \leftrightarrow var(t) \mid x \mapsto t \in \theta\}$.

The lifting of α^{Pos} and γ^{Pos} to interpretations is engineered so as to simplify the statement of the gfp operator, though it also suffices for defining the lfp operator. The construction starts with $Base^{Pos} = \{\langle a, f \rangle \mid a \in Atom \wedge f \in Pos_{var(a)}\}$. To order these pairs, let $\boldsymbol{x} \leftrightarrow \boldsymbol{y} = \wedge_{i=1}^n(x_i \leftrightarrow y_i)$ where $\boldsymbol{x} = \langle x_1, \ldots, x_n \rangle$ and $\boldsymbol{y} = \langle y_1, \ldots, y_n \rangle$. The entailment order on Pos can be extended to $b_1, b_2 \in Base^{Pos}$ where $b_i = \langle p(\boldsymbol{x}_i), f_i \rangle$, $var(\boldsymbol{x}) \cap var(\boldsymbol{x}_i) = \emptyset$ and $f_i' = \exists var(\boldsymbol{x}_i).((\boldsymbol{x} \leftrightarrow \boldsymbol{x}_i) \wedge f_i)$ by defining $b_1 \models b_2$ iff $f_1' \models f_2'$. Observe that $\langle Base^{Pos}, \models \rangle$ is a pre-order since $\models$ is not reflexive. Equivalence on $Base^{Pos}$ is thus defined $b_1 \equiv b_2$ iff $b_1 \models b_2$ and $b_2 \models b_1$. Let $I_1, I_2 \subseteq Base^{Pos}/\equiv$. Then entailment lifts to $\wp(Base^{Pos}/\equiv)$ by $I_1 \models I_2$ iff for all $[b_1]_\equiv \in I_1$ there exists $[b_2]_\equiv \in I_2$ such that $b_1 \models b_2$.

Let Int^{Pos} denote the set of subsets I of $Base^{Pos}/\equiv$ such that there exists a *unique* $[\langle p(\boldsymbol{x}), f \rangle]_\equiv \in I$ for each $p \in Pred$. Since $Int^{Pos} \subseteq \wp(Base^{Pos}/\equiv)$, Int^{Pos} is also ordered by $\models$. Note, however, that $\models$ is the point-wise ordering on Int^{Pos} and that the lattice $\langle Int^{Pos}, \models, \vee, \wedge \rangle$ is equipped with simple $\vee$ and $\wedge$ operations. Specifically $\vee_{j \in J} I_j = \{[\langle p(\boldsymbol{x}), \vee_{j \in J} f_j \rangle]_\equiv \mid [\langle p(\boldsymbol{x}), f_j \rangle]_\equiv \in I_j\}$ and $\wedge_{j \in J} I_j$ is analogously defined. The following definition extends α^{Pos} and γ^{Pos} to interpretations and thereby completes the domain construction.

Definition 7. The concretisation map $\gamma^{Pos} : Int^{Pos} \rightarrow Int$ is defined:

$$\gamma^{Pos}(J) = \{\theta(a) \mid [\langle a, f \rangle]_\equiv \in J \wedge eqn(\theta) \in \gamma^{Pos}(f)\}$$

whereas $\alpha^{Pos} : Int \rightarrow Int^{Pos}$ is defined: $\alpha^{Pos}(I) = \wedge\{J \in Int^{Pos} \mid I \subseteq \gamma^{Pos}(J)\}$. An operator that abstracts the standard fixpoint operator $\mathcal{F}_P$ is given below.

Definition 8. Given a logic program P, the fixpoint operator $\mathcal{F}_P^{Pos} : Int^{Pos} \rightarrow Int^{Pos}$ is defined by: $\mathcal{F}_P^{Pos}(I) = \wedge\{J \in Int^{Pos} \mid K \models J\}$ where

$$K = \left\{ [\langle h, f \rangle]_\equiv \;\middle|\; \begin{array}{l} h :- D : E : a_1, \ldots, a_m \in P \quad \wedge \\ [\langle a_i, f_i \rangle]_\equiv \in I \qquad\qquad\quad \wedge \\ f = \bar{\exists} var(h).(\alpha^{Pos}(\{E\}) \wedge \wedge_{i=1}^m f_i) \end{array} \right\}$$

The operator $\mathcal{F}_P^{Pos}$ is continuous, hence an abstract fixpoint semantics is defined $\mathcal{F}^{Pos}(P) = \text{lfp}(\mathcal{F}_P)$. The following correctness result is (almost) standard.

Theorem 2. $\mathcal{F}(P) \subseteq \gamma^{Pos}(\mathcal{F}^{Pos}(P))$.

5.3   Monotonic Boolean Functions

One idea behind the analysis is to use implication to encode synchronisation. The intuition is that if d_i expresses the required input and f_i the generated output for $p_i(\boldsymbol{x}_i)$, then $d_i \rightarrow f_i$ represents the behaviour of $p_i(\boldsymbol{x}_i)$. One subtlety is that $\wedge_{i=1}^n(d_i \rightarrow f_i)$ does not always correctly describe the behaviour of a compound goal $p_1(\boldsymbol{x}_1), \ldots, p_n(\boldsymbol{x}_n)$ if $d_i \notin Mon_X$. This is illustrated below.

Example 2. Consider the compound goal $p_1(x, y, z), p_2(x, y, z)$ for a two clause program $p_1(x, y, z) :\!-D : z = c : true$ and $p_2(x, y, z) :\!-\text{nonvar}(x) : y = b : true$ where D is a (bizarre) ask constraint that is satisfied if y is ground whenever x is ground. Thus if $d_1 = (x \rightarrow y)$ and $d_2 = x$ hold then D and $\text{nonvar}(x)$ are satisfied whereas $z = c$ and $y = b$ ensure that $f_1 = z$ and $f_2 = y$ hold. Neither $p_1(x, y, z)$ can be scheduled before $p_2(x, y, z)$ or vice versa to bind z, yet $\wedge_{i=1}^2 (d_i \rightarrow f_i) \models z$. The problem stems from the implication in d_1. Ensuring that $d_i \in Mon_X$ avoids this problem as is formally asserted below.

Proposition 2. Let $f, f_i \in Def_X$ and $d_i \in Mon_X$ for all $i \in [1, m]$ and suppose $f \models (\wedge_{i=1}^m (d_i \rightarrow f_i)) \rightarrow (\wedge_{i=1}^m d_i)$. Then an injective map $\pi : [1, m] \rightarrow [1, m]$ exists such that $f \wedge \wedge_{j=1}^{j<i} f_{\pi(j)} \models d_{\pi(i)}$ for all $i \in [1, m]$.

The force of the result is that it states that the compound goal can be reordered as $p_{\pi(1)}(\boldsymbol{x}_{\pi(1)}), \ldots, p_{\pi(n)}(\boldsymbol{x}_{\pi(n)})$ so that the input requirement of goal $p_{\pi(i)}(\boldsymbol{x}_{\pi(i)})$ $(d_{\pi(i)})$ is satisfied by an initial binding (f) combined with those bindings output by the previous goals $(\wedge_{j=1}^{j<i} f_{\pi(j)})$. The following definitions explain how to (minimally) strengthen a positive function so as to obtain a monotonic function. The specification for this operation is captured in $\downarrow$.

Definition 9. The map $\downarrow: Pos_X \rightarrow Mon_X$ is defined $\downarrow f = \vee\{f' \in Mon_X \mid f' \models f\}$.

The operation $\downarrow$ arises during analysis and to construct a method for computing $\downarrow$, let $\rho : X \rightarrow X'$ be a bijective map where $X' \subseteq Var$ and $X \cap X' = \emptyset$. The proposition explains how $\circlearrowleft$ can be iteratively applied to finitely compute $\downarrow$.

Definition 10. The map $\circlearrowleft: Pos_X \rightarrow Pos_X$ is defined $\circlearrowleft f = \forall X'.f'$ where $f' = (\wedge_{i=1}^n x_i \rightarrow \rho(x_i)) \rightarrow \rho(f)$.

Proposition 3. Let $f \in Pos_X$. Then $\downarrow f = \wedge_{i \geq 1} f_i$ where $f_i \in Pos_X$ is the decreasing chain given by: $f_1 = f$ and $f_{i+1} = \circlearrowleft f_i$.

Example 3. Consider computing $\downarrow f$ where $X = \{x, y\}$ and $f = (x \rightarrow y)$. Suppose $\rho(x) = x'$ and $\rho(y) = y'$. Then $f' = ((x \rightarrow x') \wedge (y \rightarrow y')) \rightarrow (x' \rightarrow y')$, $f'[x' \mapsto 1] = (y \rightarrow y') \rightarrow y' = y \vee y'$ and $f'[x' \mapsto 0] = 1$ so that $\forall x'.f' = y \vee y'$. Put $f'' = y \vee y'$. Then $f''[y' \mapsto 1] = 1$ and $f''[y' \mapsto 0] = y$ so that $\circlearrowleft f = \forall y'.\forall x'.f' = \forall y'.f'' = y$. In fact $\circlearrowleft y = y$ so that $\downarrow f = y$. Observe that $y \models f$.

6   Suspension Analysis

This section draws together the previous sections to define the suspension analysis in terms of a backward fixpoint operator. To construct this operator, and specifically model asks, it is necessary to introduce a map $\alpha_{low}^{Pos} : \wp(Eqn) \rightarrow Pos$ that returns a lower approximation to a set of equations D. Recall that α^{Pos} yields an upper approximation in that if $E \in D$, then $\alpha^{Pos}(\{E\})$ entails $\alpha^{Pos}(D)$. Conversely α_{low}^{Pos}, which is defined below, delivers a lower approximation with the property that if $\alpha^{Pos}(\{E\})$ entails $\alpha_{low}^{Pos}(D)$, then $E \in D$.

Definition 11. The (lower) abstraction map $\alpha_{low}^{Pos} : \wp(Eqn) \to Pos$ is defined by: $\alpha_{low}^{Pos}(D) = \vee\{f \in Pos \mid \gamma^{Pos}(f) \subseteq D\}$.

Example 4. Let nonvar(x) and ground(y) denote the equation sets $\{E \in Eqn \mid \theta \in imgu(E) \wedge \theta(x) \notin Var\}$ and $\{E \in Eqn \mid \theta \in imgu(E) \wedge var(\theta(y)) = \emptyset\}$. Then $\alpha_{low}^{Pos}(Eqn) = 1$, $\alpha_{low}^{Pos}(\text{nonvar}(x)) = x$, $\alpha_{low}^{Pos}(\text{nonvar}(x) \cup \text{ground}(y)) = x \vee y$ and $\alpha_{low}^{Pos}(\{x = f(a)\}) = \alpha_{low}^{Pos}(\{x = y\}) = 0$.

Suspension analysis can now be formalised with an abstract fixpoint operator:

Definition 12. Given a logic program P, the operator $\mathcal{B}_P : Int^{Pos} \to Int^{Pos}$ is defined: $\mathcal{B}_P(I) = \vee\{J \in Int^{Pos} \mid \forall[b_1]_\equiv \in K.\exists[b_2]_\equiv \in J.b_2 \models b_1\}$ where

$$
K = \left\{ [\langle h, d'' \rangle]_\equiv \;\middle|\; \begin{array}{r l}
 & h :\!-D : E : a_1, \ldots, a_m \in P \qquad \wedge \\
 & [\langle a_i, f_i \rangle]_\equiv \in \mathcal{F}^{Pos}(P) \;\wedge\; [\langle a_i, d_i \rangle]_\equiv \in I \quad \wedge \\
 d = & \alpha_{low}^{Pos}(D) \;\wedge\; e = \alpha^{Pos}(\{E\}) \qquad \wedge \\
 d' = & (\wedge_{i=1}^m (d_i \to f_i)) \to (\wedge_{i=1}^m d_i) \qquad \wedge \\
 d'' = & \downarrow(\bar{\forall}var(h).(d \wedge (e \to d')))
\end{array} \right\}
$$

Recall that $\wedge_{i=1}^m(d_i \to f_i)$ captures the grounding behaviour of the goal $a_1, \ldots, a_m$ whereas $\wedge_{i=1}^m d_i$ describes a state with variables sufficiently bound to enable each a_i to be scheduled with local selection without suspension. The function d' is a grounding property that, if satisfied when $a_1, \ldots, a_m$ is called, guarantees that $a_1, \ldots, a_m$ can be reordered so that each a_i can be scheduled by local selection without suspension. The function d'' is monotonic, defined only over those variables in h, and is sufficient to ensure that both the ask is satisfied and that $a_1, \ldots, a_m$ can be scheduled by local selection without suspension. If P contains a predicate p defined over n clauses, then $\{[p(\boldsymbol{x}, f_i)]_\equiv\}_{i=1}^n \subseteq K$ so in general $K \notin Int^{Pos}$. However, $\mathcal{B}_P(I)$ contains a *unique* element $[p(\boldsymbol{x}, f)]_\equiv$ such that $f = \wedge_{i=1}^n f_i$. In effect, related elements of K are merged with meet.

$\mathcal{B}_P$ is co-continuous and since Int^{Pos} is a finite lattice, it follows that gfp$(\mathcal{B}_P)$ exists. The value of gfp$(\mathcal{B}_P)$ is explained by the following theorem (or rather its corollary). It states that gfp$(\mathcal{B}_P)$ characterises a set of initial states for which if the standard transition system leads to a computed answer (in k steps) then local selection with delay leads to a variant of that computed answer (in k steps).

Theorem 3. *Suppose* $\theta(p(\boldsymbol{x})) \in \gamma^{Pos}(\mathcal{B}_P^k(\top))$, $s_1 = \langle p(\boldsymbol{x}), \theta \rangle$, $s_1 \leadsto_P^k \langle \epsilon, \psi \rangle$. *Then* $s_1 \to_P^k \langle \epsilon, \chi \rangle$ *where* $\psi \approx \chi$.

Corollary 1. *Suppose* $\theta(p(\boldsymbol{x})) \in \gamma^{Pos}(\text{gfp}(\mathcal{B}_P))$, $s_1 = \langle p(\boldsymbol{x}), \theta \rangle$, $s_1 \leadsto_P^k \langle \epsilon, \psi \rangle$. *Then* $s_1 \to_P^k \langle \epsilon, \chi \rangle$ *where* $\psi \approx \chi$.

To emphasise the significance of gfp$(\mathcal{B}_P)$, the abstract backward semantics for P is defined $\mathcal{B}(P) = \text{gfp}(\mathcal{B}_P)$. Co-continuity enables $\mathcal{B}(P)$ to be computed by *lower* Kleene iteration, that is, as the limit of $\top$, $\mathcal{B}_P(\top)$, $\mathcal{B}_P^2(\top)$, ... where $\top = \{[\langle p(\boldsymbol{x}), 1 \rangle]_\equiv \mid p \in Pred\}$. The example illustrates how to handle builtins.

Example 5. Consider the temperature conversion program in the left column of Fig. 3 which converts Celsius to Fahrenheit and vice versa. The block declaration equates to the equation set $D = (\text{nonvar}(X) \cap \text{nonvar}(Y)) \cup (\text{nonvar}(X) \cap$

---

cf(C, F) :- mul(C, 1.8, S), add(S, 32, F).

:- block add(-, -, ?), add(-, ?, -), add(?, -, -).
add(X, Y, Z) :- ground(X+Y), Z is X+Y.
add(X, Y, Z) :- ground(Z-X), Y is Z-X.
add(X, Y, Z) :- ground(Z-Y), X is Z-Y.

:- block mul(-, -, ?), mul(-, ?, -), mul(?, -, -).
mul(X, Y, Z) :- ground(X*Y), Z is X*Y.
mul(X, Y, Z) :- ground(Z/X), Y is Z/X.
mul(X, Y, Z) :- ground(Z/Y), X is Z/Y.

cf(C, F) :- true : T1 ∧ T2 :
    mul(C, T1, S), add(S, T2, F).

add(X, Y, Z) :- f : T ↔ (X ∧ Y) :
    ground(T), is(Z, T).
add(X, Y, Z) :- f : T ↔ (X ∧ Z) :
    ground(T), is(Y, T).
add(X, Y, Z) :- f : T ↔ (Y ∧ Z) :
    ground(T), is(X, T).

mul(X, Y, Z) :- ...

ground(X) :- true : X : true.
is(X, Y) :- true : X ∧ Y : true.

Fig. 3. conv program in Prolog and in *Pos* where $f = (X \wedge Y) \vee (X \wedge Z) \vee (Y \wedge Z)$

---

nonvar(Z)) $\cup$ (nonvar(Y) $\cap$ nonvar(Z)) and $\alpha_{low}^{Pos}(D) = f$ (see Fig. 3). Note how the builtins ground and is are modelled in the abstract version of conv listed in the right column. For brevity, let $\mathbf{y} = \langle x_1, x_2 \rangle$ and $\mathbf{z} = \langle x_1, x_2, x_3 \rangle$. Then

$$\mathcal{F}^{Pos}(conv) = \left\{ \begin{array}{c} [\langle cf(\mathbf{y}), x_1 \wedge x_2 \rangle]_\equiv \\ [\langle add(\mathbf{z}), x_1 \wedge x_2 \wedge x_3 \rangle]_\equiv \\ [\langle mul(\mathbf{z}), x_1 \wedge x_2 \wedge x_3 \rangle]_\equiv \\ [\langle ground(x_1), x_1 \rangle]_\equiv \\ [\langle is(\mathbf{y}), x_1 \wedge x_2 \rangle]_\equiv \end{array} \right\} \quad K = \left\{ \begin{array}{c} [\langle cf(\mathbf{y}), 1 \rangle]_\equiv \\ [\langle add(\mathbf{z}), f \rangle]_\equiv \\ [\langle mul(\mathbf{z}), f \rangle]_\equiv \\ [\langle ground(x_1), 1 \rangle]_\equiv \\ [\langle is(\mathbf{y}), 1 \rangle]_\equiv \end{array} \right\}$$

where $f = (x_1 \wedge x_2) \vee (x_1 \wedge x_3) \vee (x_2 \wedge x_3)$. Hence $\mathcal{B}_{conv}(\top) = K$. Then $\mathcal{B}_{conv}^2(\top)$ differs from $\mathcal{B}_{conv}(\top)$ only in $[\langle cf(\mathbf{y}), x_1 \vee x_2 \rangle]_\equiv$. In fact $\mathcal{B}(conv) = \mathcal{B}_{conv}^2(\top)$.

7 Experimental Evaluation

To assess the value of the analysis it has been implemented in SICStus Prolog using the BDD package of Armstrong and Schachte [1]. The implementation consists of two meta-interpreters – one for each fixpoint. Each abstract clause $h :- d : f : b_1, \ldots, b_n$ is represented as two facts: my_clause($h, [id_f, b_1, \ldots, b_n]$) and assertion($h, id_d$) where id_f and id_d are identifiers for the BDDs of f and d. Facts of the form fact(gr,$p(\mathbf{x}), id_f$) and fact(ba,$p(\mathbf{x}), id_g$) are added and removed from the database to record the status of the lfp and then the gfp. Both fixpoint engines are realised as semi-naive meta-interpreters.

The analyser has been applied to a number of programs: bestpath, entails, fact, hamming, inorder, isotrees, pascal, mm, hanoi, msort, qsort, queens, sieve, most of which derive from the Super Monaco benchmark suite. All programs were analysed in less than 1 second on a 500MHZ, 512MB Pentium III running RedHat Linux 7.2 with Kernel 2.4.7-10. The Super Monaco programs are coded in kl1 –

an early ccp language – and therefore for analysis these programs were manually translated into SICStus Prolog with blocks. It was for these programs that the analysis occasionally produced unexpected results (modes) and close inspection revealed errors in the hand translation. Some errors were straightforward (`block` declarations of the wrong arity) and other were subtle, but none came to light in the testing, presumably because of the particular interleaving adopted by the SICStus scheduler. These results suggest that the analysis has a rôle in bug detection. The analysis also inferred non-trivial modes for all predicates except for 6 mutually recursive predicates in bestpath for which false was returned. It is not yet clear whether a local selection rule exists for these predicates that avoids suspension – the synchronisation is subtle and may even be buggy. What is clear, however, is that local selection is sufficient to infer useful modes for the vast majority of the predicates that were analysed. An experimental analyser can be found at `http://www.cs.bgu.ac.il/cgi-bin/genaim/susweb.cgi` and the benchmarks are available from the home page of the second author.

8   Related Work

One of the most closely related works comes surprisingly from the compiling control literature and in particular the problem of *generating* a local selection rule under which a program universally terminates [12]. The technique of [12] builds on the termination inference method of [19] which infers initial modes for a query that, if satisfied, ensure that a logic program left-terminates. The chief advance in [12] over [19] is that it additionally infers how goals can be statically reordered so as to improve termination behaviour. This is performed by augmenting each clause with body atoms $a_1, \ldots, a_n$ with $n(n-1)/2$ Boolean variables $b_{i,j}$ with the interpretation that $b_{i,j} = 1$ if a_i precedes a_j in the reordered goal and $b_{i,j} = 0$ otherwise. The analysis of [19] is then adapted to include consistency constraints among the $b_{i,j}$, for instance, $b_{j,k} \wedge \neg b_{i,k} \Rightarrow \neg b_{i,j}$. In addition, the $b_{i,j}$ are used to determine whether the post-conditions of a_i contribute to the pre-conditions of a_j. Although motivated differently and realised differently (in terms of the Boolean μ-calculus) this work also uses Boolean functions to finesse the problem of enumerating the goal reorderings. This work complements our own since termination is a related but orthogonal requirement to non-suspension.

King and Lu [13] show how to apply backward analysis to the problem of figuring how to query a logic program with fixed selection rule. The analysis traces control-flow of the program (backward) right-to-left to infer the modes in which a predicate must be called under the leftmost selection rule. Although this analysis can be reinterpreted as a suspension analysis it cannot reason about local selection accurately since it only considers leftmost selection.

The early work of [5] presents an and-or tree framework that applies local reexecution to simulate the dataflow under different interleavings. A more direct approach is to abstract each state in the transition system with an abstract state to obtain an abstract transition system [3]. Finiteness is enforced through a widening known as star-abstraction [3]. This approach achieves a degree of conceptual simplicity though the abstract states themselves can be unwieldy. The work of [8] is unusual in that it attempts to detect suspension-freeness for goals under leftmost selection. Although this approach only considers one local selection rule, it is surprising effective because of the way data often flows left-to-right. A particularly elegant approach to suspension analysis follows from a confluence semantics that approximates the standard semantics in the sense that suspension implies suspension in the confluent semantics [4]. The crucial point is that because of confluence, an analysis based on the confluence semantics need only consider one scheduling rule. None of these analyses, however, can infer initial queries that guarantee non-suspension – all check for non-suspension. Other works have proposed generic abstract interpretation frameworks for dynamic scheduling [9,18] but none of these are for goal-independent analysis.

9 Concluding Discussion

This paper has shown how suspension analysis can be tackled for a new perspective – that of goal-independence. It shows how an analysis for non-suspension under local selection can be formulated as two simple bottom-up fixpoint computations. The analysis strikes a good balance between tractability and precision. It avoids the complexity of goal interleaving by exploiting reordering properties of monotonic and positive Boolean functions.

For reasons of presentation, the analysis proposed in this paper has been specified for logic programs. To further simplify the presentation, the analysis was formulated in terms of simple groundness dependencies. The first constraint can be relaxed by following a standard constraint formulation [10]. The second can be relaxed by lifting the analysis to rigidity (type) dependencies using term extractor maps [3,10]. Another direction for future work will be to generalise the analysis to other abstract domains that possess a pseudo-complement.

Acknowledgements. EU working group 23677 and EPSRC grant GR/MO8769 funded Samir Genaim while he visited the University of Kent. We thank Jacob Howe, Fred Mesnard and Ulf Nilsson for their valuable comments, and Bart Massey and Evan Tick for the Super Monaco benchmarks.

References

1. T. Armstrong, K. Marriott, P. Schachte, and H. Søndergaard. Two classes of Boolean functions for dependency analysis. *Science of Computer Programming*, 31(1):3–45, 1998.
2. M. Carlsson. Freeze, Indexing, and Other Implementation Issues in the WAM. In *International Conference on Logic Programming*, pages 40–58. MIT Press, 1987.
3. M. Codish, M. Falaschi, and K. Marriott. Suspension Analyses for Concurrent Logic Programs. *Transactions on Programming Languages and Systems*, 16(3):649–686, 1994.

4. M. Codish, M. Falaschi, K. Marriott, and W. H. Winsborough. A Confluent Semantic Basis for the Analysis of Concurrent Constraint Logic Programs. *The Journal of Logic Programming*, 30(1):53–81, 1997.
5. C. Codognet, P. Codognet, and M. Corsini. Abstract Interpretation for Concurrent Logic Languages. In *North American Conference on Logic Programming*, pages 215–232. MIT Press, 1990.
6. A. Cortesi, G. Filé, and W. H. Winsborough. Optimal Groundness Analysis Using Propositional Logic. *The Journal of Logic Programming*, 27(2):137–167, 1996.
7. P. Dart. On Derived Dependencies and Connected Databases. *The Journal of Logic Programming*, 11(1–2):163–188, 1991.
8. S. Debray, D. Gudeman, and P. Bigot. Detection and Optimization of Suspension-free Logic Programs. *Journal of Logic Programming*, 29(1–3):171–194, 1992.
9. M. García de la Banda, K. Marriott, and P. J. Stuckey. Efficient Analysis of Logic Programs with Dynamic Scheduling. In *International Symposium on Logic Programming*, pages 417–431. MIT Press, 1995.
10. R. Giacobazzi, S. Debray, and G. Levi. Generalized Semantics and Abstract Interpretation for Constraint Logic Programs. *The Journal of Logic Programming*, 25(3):191–248, 1995.
11. R. Giacobazzi and F. Scozzari. A Logical Model for Relational Abstract Domains. *Transactions on Programming Languages and Systems*, 20(5):1067–1109, 1998.
12. S. Hoarau and F. Mesnard. Inferring and Compiling Termination for Constraint Logic Programs. In *Logic-based Program Synthesis and Transformation*, volume 1559 of *Lecture Notes in Computer Science*, pages 240–254. Springer-Verlag, 1999.
13. A. King and L. Lu. A Backward Analysis for Constraint Logic Programs. *Theory and Practice of Logic Programming*, 2(4–5):517–547, 2002.
14. A. King and P. Soper. Schedule Analysis of Concurrent Logic Programs. In *Joint International Conference and Symposium on Logic Programming*, pages 478–492. MIT Press, 1992.
15. R. Kowalski. Algorithm = Logic + Control. *Communications of the ACM*, 22(7):424–436, 1979.
16. J.-L. Lassez, M. Maher, and K. Marriott. Unification Revisited. In *Foundations of Deductive Databases and Logic Programming*. Morgan Kaufmann, 1988.
17. J. W. Lloyd. *Foundations of Logic Programming*. Springer-Verlag, 1993.
18. K. Marriott, M. García de la Banda, and M. Hermenegildo. Analyzing Logic Programs with Dynamic Scheduling. In *Principles of Programming Languages*, pages 240–254. ACM Press, 1994.
19. F. Mesnard. Inferring Left-terminating Classes of Queries for Constraint Logic Programs by means of Approximations. In *Joint International Conference and Symposium on Logic Programming*, pages 7–21. MIT Press, 1996.
20. L. Vielle. Recursive Query Processing: The Power of Logic. *Theoretical Computer Science*, 69(1):1–53, 1989.

Security Properties: Two Agents Are Sufficient

Hubert Comon-Lundh and Véronique Cortier*

Laboratoire Spécification et Vérification, CNRS, INRIA
Ecole Normale Supérieure de Cachan,
{comon,cortier}@lsv.ens-cachan.fr

Abstract. We consider arbitrary cryptographic protocols and security properties. We show that it is always sufficient to consider a bounded number of agents b (actually $b = 2$ in most of the cases): if there is an attack involving n agents, then there is an attack involving at most b agents.

1 Introduction

The task of automatically verifying cryptographic protocols has now been undertaken by several research groups, because of its relevance to secure internet transactions. Let us cite for instance (this is far from being exhaustive): CAPSL [13], CASRUL/Datac [19], casper/FDR [26].

Though cryptographic protocols are often described in a concise way (see e.g. [7]), the verification problem is difficult for two reasons:

1. The number of agents potentially using the protocol is unbounded, as well as the number of protocol sessions.
2. The size of messages which can be forged by an intruder is also unbounded.

And, in fact, even for simple properties such as secrecy and for subclasses of protocols, the verification problem is undecidable (see e.g. [15,14,9,2]).

The verification tools have either to assume stronger properties on the protocols (e.g. [20,10,27,2]) or to consider a bounded number of sessions (hence a bounded number of agents) only [3,25,16,22], in which case the security problem becomes co-NP-complete [25]. Yet another solution is to consider an upper approximation of the set of execution sequences, in such a way that, when no attack is found on this upper approximation, then there is no attack on the protocol. This is typically the approach of [6,5].

In this paper, we consider a simple reduction, which works for any protocols and security properties typically considered for automated verification. We show that it is always sufficient to consider a bounded number of agents b (actually $b = 2$; we will discuss this point later): if there is an attack involving n agents, then there is an attack involving at most b agents. Such a result is useful for automatic tools: we may forget the universal quantifications on agents ids and

---

* Partially supported by INRIA project SECSI and RNTL project EVA.

P. Degano (Ed.): ESOP 2003, LNCS 2618, pp. 99–113, 2003.
© Springer-Verlag Berlin Heidelberg 2003

consider finitely many (4 most of the time) instances of the protocol roles, without loosing information. This proves actually that the instanciation techniques in [19] are complete. This also provides completeness results for abstraction used in [6,23]. Of course, the verification problem will remain undecidable, because we cannot faithfully give a bound on the number of sessions. Still, approximation techniques such as [5,6] can be simplified and when considering a bounded number of sessions we may assume w.l.o.g. that only these b agents are involved. This reduction result also provides with a decision result for cryptographic protocols against a passive intruder.

Our result extends and clarifies a side result of [18]. Indeed, J. Heather and S. Schneider chow that one may consider only four agents (three honest, one dishonest) using implicitly that an agent may talk to herself. We prove actually that in J. Heather and S. Schneider case, only two agents are sufficient. In addition, our reduction result holds for more general security properties and also holds when an agent is disallowed to speak with herself.

The proof of our result is not difficult, once the protocol and its properties are expressed as Horn clauses: given an attack against a security property, we simply project every honest identity on one single honest identity and every dishonest identity on one single dishonest identity. Actually, the result can be stated for a class of Horn clauses, which encompasses protocols descriptions. Everybody has her (his) favorite model. We do not argue that the Horn clause model is better than others. It is simply more convenient for our proof and we claim that most other models can be reduced to this one, hence our reduction also applies to other models of cryptographic protocols. In order to support this claim, we provide (in [11]) with a reduction of the Millen-Rueß model [21] to Horn clauses. We hope that this will provide with enough evidence that the reduction result works for other models as well. (It is not possible to show in detail all reductions from other models to Horn clauses).

Our paper is organized as follows. We introduce our model in section 2. A more detailed definition can be found in [11]. In section 3.1 we prove that, if there is an attack involving n agents, then there is an attack involving at most 2 agents, besides the constant agents which might be used in the protocol description. In other words, we show that we have to consider only instances of the roles in a two-element sets. This result assumes however that the same agent may play different roles in a given protocol session: "an agent may talk to herself". Most of the models do not discard this ability. However, it may be considered as more realistic that an agent cannot play several roles in the same session. Some models [24,20] explicitly disallow this possibility. That is why we consider in section 3.2 models in which an agent cannot talk with herself. We prove in this case that, if there is an attack involving n agents, then there is an attack involving at most $k + 1$ agents where k is the number of roles in the protocol.

2   The Model

We define a trace model by means of Horn clauses, in which terms are messages. A similar representation can also be found in [5] for instance. The important feature is that we only use Horn clauses, which contain at least one positive literal. Hence there is a least Herbrand model $\mathcal{H}$, which is the intended trace semantics: the possible traces are the member of $T_\mathcal{H}$, the interpretation of the unary predicate T in $\mathcal{H}$.

Clauses come in two parts: the first part is protocol independent and the second part is protocol specific. It is a bit lengthy to describe the two parts in details: we will only show here examples and the less standard constructions. The reader is referred to [11] for more details.

2.1   Messages and Traces

The set of messages is the set of (ground) terms built over a set of function symbols $\mathcal{F}$ and basic sorts: Num, Agent, Ha, Da, Message, Event, Trace. $\mathcal{F}$ contains the following function symbols:

$$
\begin{array}{llrl}
0: & \to \mathsf{Num} & n_i: & \mathsf{Agent}^{k_i}, \mathsf{Num} \to \mathsf{Message} \\
s: & \mathsf{Num} \to \mathsf{Num} & st: & \mathsf{Agent}, \mathsf{Num}, \mathsf{Message} \to \mathsf{Event} \\
h: & \to \mathsf{Ha} & \bot: & \to \mathsf{Trace} \\
d: & \to \mathsf{Da} & [\_,\_]\cdot\_: & \mathsf{Event}, \mathsf{Num}, \mathsf{Trace} \to \mathsf{Trace} \\
s_h: & \mathsf{Ha} \to \mathsf{Ha} & srv_i: & \to \mathsf{Agent} \\
s_d: & \mathsf{Da} \to \mathsf{Da} & &
\end{array}
$$

Terms of sort Agent are called *agents*. All other symbols, including the classical cryptographic primitives for building keys, encryption and pairs take messages as arguments and return a message. This set of cryptographic primitives is denoted by:

$$\mathcal{F}_{\mathsf{msg}} = \{<\_,\_>, \{\_\}\_, \mathsf{pub}(\_), \mathsf{prv}(\_), \mathsf{shr}(\_)\}.$$

In addition, we may have e.g. hash function symbols.

We also assume that every agent is a message and every message is an event; we have the subsort relations Agent $\leq$ Message $\leq$ Event, Ha $\leq$ Agent and Da $\leq$ Agent. Let us comment a little bit:

- Num is only used for internal representations of session numbers, nonces... It is important to provide with one representation since we will consider Herbrand models. However, such a representation is irrelevant in what follows. In particular, neither the intruder nor the agents have access to this representation.
- There are two non-standard sorts Da, Ha. The terms of these sorts are respectively $s_d^k(d)$ and $s_h^k(h)$ and are intended to represent compromised and honest agents respectively. Again, this is for internal representation only. Of course, this distinction is never used in the protocol description. It is however

necessary in the protocol property definition: typically, we want to state that a secret *shared by honest agents* remains unknown to the intruder, hence we need a way to express that an agent is honest.

- srv_i are intended to be server names.
- n_i is a collection of function symbols, which are used to represent nonces (randomly generated data): n_i is intended to take as arguments some agent ids (who generates the nonce and who are supposed to receive the nonce) and a session number. i is intended to be the protocol step. Note that we may also consider a single symbol n with an additionnal argument i. Then $n_i(\_)$ is simply a notation for $n(i, \_)$.
- st is intended to represent the local state of an agent. Events will consist of either sending a message or increasing a local memory. Traces are sequences of pairs of an event and a session number.
- We do not assume any a priori typing of messages (there is no a priori way to distinguish between a nonce and a pair for instance), though any such policy could be specified at the protocol description level.

By abuse of notation, we will sometimes write e.g. 2 instead of $s(s(0))$, $< x, y, z >$ instead of $< x, < y, z >>$, or $\{x, y\}_z$ instead of $\{< x, y >\}_z$.

We will sometimes use unary predicate symbols instead of sort names in order to explicitly state the sort of a variable. For instance, we may write $\mathsf{Agent}(x)$, expressing that x is of sort Agent (other authors use the notation $x : \mathsf{Agent}$). Such unary predicate symbols can only be used with variable arguments.

2.2   Protocol Independent Clauses

We sketch here and in the following section how to design a set of Horn clauses defining valid traces. We also show in [11] that this is a reasonable definition since other models can be reduced to this one.

We use a binary predicate symbol I to describe the intruder knowledge. I takes two arguments: a message m and a trace t; $I(m, t)$ means that message m is known to the intruder after executing t. Some typical clauses defining I are displayed on figure 1. There are other clauses for e.g. (un)pairing.

Protocol independent clauses will also contain the definition of some auxiliary predicates, which will be described when needed as well as the clause $T(\bot)$, which states that the empty trace is a trace. How to continue a trace is protocol-dependent.

2.3   Protocol Dependent Clauses

We sketch here how to define the set of valid traces T on the Yahalom protocol. In this section, a, b will stand for variables of sort Agent, x, y, z for variables of sort $\mathsf{Message}$, s, t and e for variables of sort respectively Num, Trace and Event.

$$\mathsf{Agent}(x) \Rightarrow I(x,t) \qquad \text{The intruder knows all agents ids.}$$

$$\mathsf{Da}(x) \Rightarrow I(\mathsf{prv}(x),t) \qquad \text{The intruder knows all keys of compromised agents.}$$

$$I(x,t) \Rightarrow I(\mathsf{pub}(x),t) \qquad \text{The intruder knows all public keys.}$$

$$I(x,t), I(y,t) \Rightarrow I(\{x\}_y,t) \qquad \text{The intruder can encrypt a known message with a known key.}$$

$$I(\{x\}_{\mathsf{shr}(y)},t), I(\mathsf{shr}(y),t) \Rightarrow I(x,t) \qquad \text{The intruder can retrieve the clear text of a message encrypted with a known symmetric key.}$$

$$T([x,s]\cdot t) \Rightarrow I(x,[x,s]\cdot t) \qquad \text{All messages sent through the network are available to the intruder.}$$

$$I(x,t) \Rightarrow I(x,y\cdot t) \qquad \text{The intruder remembers a message whatever is added to the trace.}$$

Fig. 1. Some of the clauses defining I

$$A \to B : A, N_a$$
$$B \to S : B, \{A, N_a, N_b\}_{\mathsf{shr}(B)}$$
$$S \to A : \{B, K_{ab}, N_a, N_b\}_{\mathsf{shr}(A)}, \{A, K_{ab}\}_{\mathsf{shr}(B)}$$
$$A \to B : \{A, K_{ab}\}_{\mathsf{shr}(B)}, \{N_b\}_{K_{ab}}$$

We first state that, at any point, we may start a new session of the protocol assigning roles to any of the agents. This is expressed by:

$$\mathsf{Fresh}(t,s), T(t) \Rightarrow T(\ [st(a,1,< a,b,srv >),s]$$
$$\cdot [st(b,1,< b,srv >),s]$$
$$\cdot [st(srv,1,srv),s] \cdot t)$$

Fresh is an auxiliary predicate (defined in figure 2), which holds when the number s is larger than any number occurring in t. Then the trace t can be extended accordingly.

Now, if a has started session s, and if she has not already sent the first message of this session, she can do it, hence extending the trace, and moving to stage 2 for this session:

$$\left.\begin{array}{r} T(t), \\ \mathsf{In}([st(a,1,< a,b,srv >),s],t), \\ \mathsf{NotPlayed}(a,2,s,t) \end{array}\right\} \Rightarrow \begin{array}{l} T(\ [< a,n_1(a,s) >,s] \\ \cdot [st(a,2,< a,b,srv,n_1(a,b,s) >),s] \\ \cdot t) \end{array}$$

This uses the auxiliary predicates In and NotPlayed which are intended to be respectively the membership test on traces and a test that this step has not already been completed for the same session (see figure 2 for complete definitions).

Definition of Sup:
$$\mathsf{Num}(x) \Rightarrow \mathsf{Sup}(s(x), 0)$$
$$\mathsf{Sup}(x, y) \Rightarrow \mathsf{Sup}(s(x), s(y))$$

Definition of Fresh:
$$\Rightarrow \mathsf{Fresh}(\bot, s)$$
$$\mathsf{Fresh}(t, s), \mathsf{Sup}(s, s') \Rightarrow \mathsf{Fresh}([e, s'] \cdot t, s)$$

Definition of In:
$$\mathsf{Trace}([e, s] \cdot t) \Rightarrow \mathsf{In}([e, s], [e, s] \cdot t)$$
$$\mathsf{In}(x, t) \Rightarrow \mathsf{In}(x, [e, s] \cdot t)$$

Definition of NotPlayed:
$$\Rightarrow \mathsf{NotPlayed}(a, i, s, \bot)$$
$$\mathsf{NotPlayed}(a, i, s, t), \mathsf{Sup}(s, s') \Rightarrow \mathsf{NotPlayed}(a, i, s, [e, s'] \cdot t)$$
$$\mathsf{NotPlayed}(a, i, s, t), \mathsf{Sup}(s', s) \Rightarrow \mathsf{NotPlayed}(a, i, s, [e, s'] \cdot t)$$
$$\mathsf{NotPlayed}(a, i, s, t), \mathsf{Sup}(i, j) \Rightarrow \mathsf{NotPlayed}(a, i, s, [st(a, j, m), s] \cdot t)$$

Fig. 2. Definitions of the auxiliary predicates

Finally, let us describe how the last step of the protocol is translated: we require a to have completed the first step and assume that she receives a message of the expected form. This message may be forged by the intruder: we do not include receive events in the trace since messages that are possibly received are identical to messages that can be forged by the intruder.

$$\left. \begin{array}{r} T(t), \\ \mathsf{In}([u_1, s], t), \\ \mathsf{NotPlayed}(a, 3, s, t), \\ I(< \{b, x, n_1(a, b, s), y\}_{\mathsf{shr}(a)}, z >, t) \end{array} \right\} \Rightarrow T([< z, \{y\}_x >, s] \cdot [u_2, s] \cdot t)$$

where $u_1 = st(a, 2, < a, b, srv, n_1(a,b,s) >)$ and $u_2 = st(a, 3, < a, b, srv, n_1(a,b,s), x >)$.

2.4   The Model

Now, we assume defined the sets of Horn clauses $\mathcal{C}_I, \mathcal{C}_D$ for the protocol independent clauses and the protocol dependent clauses. For a protocol P, we let $\mathcal{C}_P$ be $\mathcal{C}_I \cup \mathcal{C}_D$. We assume that $\mathcal{C}_P$ does not contain negative clauses (i.e. we only specify what is possible). Then $\mathcal{C}_P$ has a least Herbrand model $\mathcal{H}_P$.

Definition 1. *A valid trace for the protocol P is a member of the interpretation of T in $\mathcal{H}_P$.*

2.5   Attacks

Let ϕ be the security property that we want to check. We assume that ϕ can be expressed as a clause using the primitives described in previous sections. This is not a strong restriction since, at least the trace properties can be expressed in this way (and possibly other properties which relate different traces), as shown by the following examples.

Example 1. We can express that $u(x, y, s)$ (or $u(x, y)$ if we want to express the secrecy of a constant data) is a (long term) secret shared by x and y by:

$$(\forall t, x, y, s).\neg T(t) \vee \neg \mathsf{Ha}(x) \vee \neg \mathsf{Ha}(y) \vee \neg I(u(x, y, s), t)$$

which means that, in any trace t, if x and y are honest agents, then $u(x, y, s)$ is unknown to the intruder.

Example 2. We can express that $u(x, y, s)$ is a short term secret. I does not know $u(x, y, s)$ as long as session s is not completed:

$$(\forall t, x, y, s).\neg T(t) \vee \neg \mathsf{Ha}(x) \vee \neg \mathsf{Ha}(y) \vee \neg I(u(x, y, s), t) \vee \neg \mathsf{NotPlayed}(x, 3, s, t).$$

If we assume that the last message of the protocol is sent by x then we express here that, in any trace t, if x and y are honest agents, then $u(x, y, s)$ is unknown to the intruder unless the session is already completed.

Example 3. We can express an authentication property: if x receives the message $m(x, y, s)$, then it has been sent previously by y: $(\forall t, x, y, s)$

$$\neg T(t) \vee \neg \mathsf{Ha}(x) \vee \neg \mathsf{Ha}(y) \vee \neg I(m(x, y, s), t) \vee \mathsf{In}([st(y, m(x, y, s)), s], t).$$

Definition 2. *A protocol P satisfies a property ϕ iff $\mathcal{H}_P \models \phi$.*

Dually, there is an attack when $\mathcal{H}_P \not\models \phi$. In such a case (by compactness), there is a finite subset $\mathcal{H}_0$ of $\mathcal{H}_P$ such that $\mathcal{H}_0 \not\models \phi$:

Definition 3. *An attack on P for ϕ is a finite subset $\mathcal{H}_0$ of $\mathcal{H}_P$ such that $\mathcal{H}_0 \not\models \phi$. $\mathcal{H}_0$ is an attack with n agents if there are at most n distinct terms of sorts Agent in $\mathcal{H}_0$.*

For instance, if the property ϕ is a "trace property", $\mathcal{H}_0$ may contain a single predicate $T(t)$ where t is a finite trace which violates the property.

2.6   Relevance of the Model

The model we present here is actually an extension of the Millen-Rueß model [21, 12] (hereafter referred to as the MR model), expressed in Horn clauses. The MR model is itself inspired from Paulson's model [24] and from the strand spaces [28]. Formally, we proved in [11] that for each protocol of the MR model, we can associate a finite set of Horn clauses $\mathcal{C}_P$ and a finite set of purely negative clauses Φ_P such that P is insecure if and only if there is an attack on $\mathcal{C}_P$ for some $\phi \in \Phi_P$.

3 Reduction to a Fixed Number of Agents

3.1 From n Agents to 2 Agents

We show that if there is an attack with n agents, then an attack with 2 agents can be constructed: given an attack using n agents, we project every honest identity on one single honest identity and every dishonest identity on one dishonest identity. Then we obtain a valid attack using only two agents. This projection uses the fact that our model allows an agent to speak to herself, which is the case of most of the models for cryptographic protocols [21,28,17,5,14,3]. However, a similar result holds even if an agent is disallowed to speak to herself (see subsection 3.2). We also consider here purely negative properties, which easily encompasses secrecy, but does not encompass authentication in a natural way. We will discuss this in section 3.3.

We emphasize that our result holds for all models of protocols which do not make use of our internal representation of agents ids. More precisely:

Definition 4. *A set of clauses $\mathcal{C}$ is* admissible *if it does not use the symbols s_h, s_d. A clause is said* purely negative *if it only contains negative literals.*

The clauses which were proposed in the previous sections are admissible. Furthermore, any protocol specification can not use our particular representation of names, hence it is always represented as an admissible set of clauses.

Theorem 1. *Let $\mathcal{C}_P$ be an admissible set of clauses. Let ϕ be a purely negative admissible clause. If there is an attack of P for ϕ, using n agents, then there is an attack using (at most) two agents.*

Proof. We first introduce some notations. Let $\mathcal{M}$ be the set of messages, $\mathcal{T}$ be the set of all positive ground literals, and Σ_g be the set of mappings from variables to ground terms, which are compatible with the sort constraints.

Given a Horn clause $c = B_1(\boldsymbol{x}), ..., B_n(\boldsymbol{x}) \Rightarrow A(\boldsymbol{x})$ where $B_1(\boldsymbol{x}), \dots, B_n(\boldsymbol{x})$, $A(\boldsymbol{x})$ are positive literals whose free variables are contained in $\boldsymbol{x}$, and a subset $\mathcal{S}$ of $\mathcal{T}$, we define $c(\mathcal{S})$ as follows:

$$c(\mathcal{S}) \overset{\text{def}}{=} \{A(\boldsymbol{x})\sigma \mid \sigma \in \Sigma_g, \forall i, B_i(\boldsymbol{x})\sigma \in \mathcal{S}\}.$$

Then, the immediate consequence relation $F_{\mathcal{C}}$ is the mapping from $2^{\mathcal{T}}$ to $2^{\mathcal{T}}$ defined by:

$$F_{\mathcal{C}}(\mathcal{S}) \overset{\text{def}}{=} \mathcal{S} \cup \bigcup_{c \in \mathcal{C}} c(\mathcal{S}).$$

For simplicity, we will write F_P for the mapping $F_{\mathcal{C}_P}$.

It is well-known that the set of positive literals $\mathcal{H}_P^+$ of the least Herbrand model $\mathcal{H}_P$ is the least fixed point of F_P:

$$\mathcal{H}_P^+ = \bigcup_{k=1}^{+\infty} F_P^k(\emptyset)$$

For every $L \in \mathcal{H}_0$ there is a minimal index n_L such that $L \in F_P^{n_L}(\emptyset)$.

We define now the projection function: we map every honest agent to h and every dishonest agent to d : for every literal L, let $\overline{L}$ be the literal L in which every maximal subterm of sort Ha is replaced with h and every maximal subterm of sort Da is replaced with d:

$$\overline{f(t_1,\dots,t_n)} \stackrel{\text{def}}{=} f(\overline{t_1},\dots,\overline{t_n}) \text{ If } f \notin \{s_h, s_d\}$$
$$\overline{s_h(t)} \stackrel{\text{def}}{=} h$$
$$\overline{s_d(t)} \stackrel{\text{def}}{=} d$$

Our proof relies on the following lemma which ensures that if a positive literal is in $\mathcal{H}_P$ then its projection is also in $\mathcal{H}_P$.

Lemma 1. *Let L be a positive literal of $\mathcal{H}_P$, then $\overline{L}$ is in $\mathcal{H}_P$.*

This is prove by induction on n_L. If $n_L = 0$, there is no literal such that $n_L = 0$ thus there is nothing to prove.

Suppose the property true for $n_l \leq n$ and consider a positive literal L of $\mathcal{H}_P$ such that $n_L = n+1$. There exists a clause c_L and positive literals $L_1,\dots,L_k \in \mathcal{H}_P^+$ such that $L \in c_L(\{L_1,\dots,L_k\})$ with $n_{L_i} \leq n$ for all $1 \leq i \leq k$. By induction hypothesis, $\overline{L_1},\dots,\overline{L_k} \in \mathcal{H}_P^+$. In addition, c_L is on the form $B_1(\boldsymbol{x}),\dots,B_k(\boldsymbol{x}) \Rightarrow A(\boldsymbol{x}) \mid C$ with $L = A(\boldsymbol{x})\sigma$, $L_i = B_1(\boldsymbol{x})\sigma$ for some $\sigma \in \Sigma_g$. Since c_L is an admissible clause, it does not contains the symbols s_h and s_d thus $\overline{L} = A(\boldsymbol{x})\overline{\sigma}$ and $\overline{L_i} = B_1(\boldsymbol{x})\overline{\sigma}$. Hence $\overline{L} \in c_L(\{\overline{L_1},\dots\overline{L_k}\})$ and $\overline{L} \in \mathcal{H}_P^+$.

We are now ready to complete the proof. Assume that $\mathcal{H}_0$ is a finite subset of $\mathcal{H}_P$ such that $\mathcal{H}_0 \not\models \phi$. Since ϕ is assumed to be purely negative, we may assume w.l.o.g. that $\mathcal{H}_0$ only contains positive literals.

Let $\mathcal{H}_1 = \{\overline{L} \mid L \in \mathcal{H}_0\}$. The set $\mathcal{H}_1$ is still finite and, by lemma 1, $\mathcal{H}_1 \subset \mathcal{H}_P$. Let us show that $\mathcal{H}_1 \not\models \phi$. Let $\phi\sigma$ an instance of ϕ falsified by $\mathcal{H}_0$. Then $\overline{\phi\sigma}$ is falsified by $\mathcal{H}_1$. Since ϕ is an admissible clause $\overline{\phi\sigma} = \phi\overline{\sigma}$, thus $\mathcal{H}_1 \not\models \phi$. $\qquad\square$

Actually, this theorem does not hold when ϕ may contain positive literals.

Example 4. Let $\mathcal{C}_P$ be:
$$\begin{cases} \mathsf{Da}(x) \Rightarrow A(x,y) \\ \mathsf{Da}(y) \Rightarrow A(x,y) \\ \qquad\quad \Rightarrow A(x,x) \end{cases}$$

and ϕ be $A(x,y)$. $\neg A(h, s_h(h))$ is an attack and there is no attack with a single honest agent.

We will consider in section 3.3 an extension of theorem 1 for formulas containing positive literals.

3.2   Disallowing an Agent to Speak with Herself

In the last section we used the ability for an agent to speak with herself, which was not explicitly ruled out by the specification. There are however examples in which the existence of an attack relies on this ability:

Example 5. Consider the following "toy" example where an agent A sends a secret to an agent B:

$$A \to B : \{A, B, N_a\}_{\mathsf{pub}(B)}, \{secret\}_{\{A,A,N_a\}_{\mathsf{pub}(B)}}.$$

B is able to build the compound key $\{A, A, N_a\}_{\mathsf{pub}(B)}$ and gets the secret. One can show that N_a will remain unknown to the intruder, thus $\{A, A, N_a\}_{\mathsf{pub}(B)}$ is unknown to the intruder unless $A = B$. Thus this protocol is flawed only if an honest agent sends a secret to herself.

We are now considering explicitly disallowing such self-conversations between honest agents. Still, a dishonest agent is enabled to speak with himself, which actually does not bring any new information to the intruder (see remark 1 below). For, we add a predicate symbol Distinct defined by the set of clauses:

$$C_{\neq} \overset{\mathrm{def}}{=} \begin{cases} \mathsf{Distinct}(x, y), \mathsf{Ha}(x), \mathsf{Ha}(y) \Rightarrow \mathsf{Distinct}(s_h(x), s_h(y)) \\ \mathsf{Ha}(x) \Rightarrow \mathsf{Distinct}(h, s_h(x)) \\ \mathsf{Ha}(x), \mathsf{Da}(y) \Rightarrow \mathsf{Distinct}(x, y) \\ \mathsf{Distinct}(x, y) \Rightarrow \mathsf{Distinct}(y, x) \\ \mathsf{Da}(x), \mathsf{Da}(y) \Rightarrow \mathsf{Distinct}(x, y) \end{cases}$$

The least Herbrand model of Distinct consists of pairs $(s_h^k(h), s_d^m(d))$, $(s_d^m(d), s_h^k(h))$, $(s_d^m(d), s_d^k(d))$ and $(s_h^i(h), s_h^j(h))$ with $i \neq j$.

We redefine the notion of an admissible clause and we introduce the definition of protocol clauses:

Definition 5. *A clause ϕ is* admissible *if*

- *ϕ does not contain the symbols s_h, s_d,*
- *Distinct occurs only negatively in ϕ.*

We can specify that the sender a is distinct from the (expected) receiver b with admissible clauses: it suffices to add negative literals $\mathsf{Distinct}(a, b)$. Note however that such a property is not expressible in e.g. the Millen-Rueß model. The protocol model $\mathcal{H}_P$ is now the least Herbrand model of $C_{\neq} \cup C_P$. All other definitions are unchanged.

Remark 1. If we want to specify that an agent is not allowed to speak with herself, even for dishonest agents, we can introduce a predicate Distinct whose semantic is exactly the pairs of distinct agents. In this case, an *admissible* clause should also verify that Distinct occurs at most once, which is sufficient to express that an agent is not allowed to speak to herself. In addition, the protocol has to verify that the correspondence between two compromised agents does not increase the intruder knowledge, which is the case of all "real" protocols ([7]). This leads to a specification which can be reduced to the above one.

Our reduction result will now depend on the security property under consideration: if the property ϕ uses k distinct agents variables then if there is an attack, there is an attack with (at most) $k + 1$ agents.

Theorem 2. *Assume C_P is an admissible set of clauses, which does not contain any variable of sort Ha and ϕ is a purely negative admissible clause. If there is an attack on P for ϕ using n agents, then there is an attack on P for ϕ using at most $k+1$ agents, where k is the number of variables of sort Ha occurring in ϕ.*

Note that disallowing variables of sort Ha in C_P is not a real restriction. Indeed, the specification of the protocol itself (C_D) should not distinguish between honest and dishonest agents, while the specification of the intruder power (C_I) should not give specific knowledge depending on honest agent: either data (depending on agents) are known for all agents (like agent ids) or data are known only for compromised agents (like private keys).

Proof. We keep the notations of the proof of theorem 1. Again, we consider a subset $\mathcal{H}_0$ of $\mathcal{H}_P$ which falsifies ϕ. As before, since ϕ is purely negative, we may assume that $\mathcal{H}_0$ does not contain any negative literal.

Now, we let θ be an instance of ϕ which is falsified by $\mathcal{H}_0$. If $x_1, \ldots x_k$ are the variables of sort Ha in ϕ, we let $s_h^{m_1}(h), \ldots, s_h^{m_p}(h)$ be the set $\{x_1\theta, \ldots, x_k\theta\}$ with $m_1 < \ldots < m_p$ ($p \leq k$). Next, we define the projection function as follows:

$$\begin{cases} \overline{f(t_1, \ldots, t_n)} \stackrel{\text{def}}{=} f(\overline{t_1}, \ldots, \overline{t_n}) & \text{If } f(t_1, \ldots, t_n) \text{ is not of sort Ha or Da} \\ \overline{s_h^{m_i}(h)} \stackrel{\text{def}}{=} s_h^{i-1}(h) & \text{For } i = 1, \ldots, p \\ \overline{t} \stackrel{\text{def}}{=} d & \text{Otherwise} \end{cases}$$

Again, we let $\mathcal{H}_1 = \{\overline{L} \mid L \in \mathcal{H}_0\}$ and we are going to prove that $\mathcal{H}_1 \subseteq \mathcal{H}_P$ and $\mathcal{H}_1$ falsifies $\phi\overline{\theta}$. This will conclude the proof since $\mathcal{H}_1$ will be an attack with $p+1$ agents: $d, h, s_h(h), \ldots, s_h^{p-1}(h), p \leq k$.

Actually, with the following lemma, the proof that $\mathcal{H}_1 \subseteq \mathcal{H}_P$ is very much the same as in theorem 1:

Lemma 2. *If* $\text{Distinct}(u_1, u_2) \in F_P^n(\emptyset)$, *then* $\overline{\text{Distinct}(u_1, u_2)} \in F_P^n(\emptyset)$.

Proof of lemma 2:

We may assume $n > 0$. Let $t_i = x_i\theta$. Then there are three possible situations (let us recall that Distinct only occurs positively in $C_{\neq}$):

- if $u_1, u_2 \notin \{t_1, \ldots, t_k\}$, then using that the least Herbrand model of Distinct consists of pairs $(s^k(h), s^m(d))$, $(s^m(d), s^k(h))$, $(s^m(d), s^k(d))$ and $(s^i(h), s^j(h))$ with $i \neq j$, we have that $\overline{\text{Distinct}(u_1, u_2)} = \text{Distinct}(d, d) \in F_P(\emptyset)$;
- if $u_1 \in \{t_1, \ldots, t_k\}$ and $u_2 \notin \{t_1, \ldots, t_k\}$ (or the converse), then $\overline{\text{Distinct}(u_1, u_2)} = \text{Distinct}(s_h^j(h), d)$ (or $\text{Distinct}(d, s_h^j(h))$), which also belongs to $F_P(\emptyset)$;
- if $u_1, u_2 \in \{t_1, \ldots, t_k\}$: $u_1 = s_h^{m_i}(h)$, $u_2 = s_h^{m_j}(h)$ with $i \neq j$, then $\overline{\text{Distinct}(u_1, u_2)} = \text{Distinct}(s_h^i(h), s_h^j(h)) \in F_P^{|j-i|}(\emptyset)$. In this last case, $|j-i| \leq |m_j - m_i|$ by construction, hence the result.

End of the proof of lemma 2.

As in theorem 1, we can now prove by induction on n_L that for any literal $L \in \mathcal{H}_P$, $\overline{L} \in \mathcal{H}_P$: Distinct literals are handled by lemma 2. We also need here that there is no variable of sort Ha in the clauses, in order to ensure the well-sortedness of $\overline{\sigma}$ (since, now, for some terms $t : \text{Ha}$, $\overline{t}$ is no longer of sort Ha). $\qquad \square$

Note that the bound $k + 1$ can be reached for some protocols P and some properties ϕ.

Example 6. Let $k \geq 2$. Consider the following protocol, inspired from the Needham-Schroeder public key protocol. $a_1, \ldots, a_k$ are variables of sort Agent. Let $u = < a_1, \ldots, a_k >$.

Initialization

$$\mathsf{Fresh}(t, s), T(t) \Rightarrow T([st(a_1, 1, u), s] \cdot [st(a_2, 1, a_2), s] \cdots [st(a_k, 1, a_k), s] \cdot t)$$

First message: $A_1 \to A_2 : \{A_1, A_2, \ldots, A_k, N_{A_1}\}_{\mathsf{pub}(A_2)}$, $A_i \neq A_j$, for $i \neq j$.

$$\left.\begin{array}{l} T(t), \mathsf{Distinct}(a_i, a_j) \quad i \neq j \\ \mathsf{In}([st(a_1, 1, u), s], t), \\ \mathsf{NotPlayed}(a_1, 2, s, t) \end{array}\right\} \Rightarrow \begin{array}{l} T(\ [\{u, n_1(a_1, \ldots, a_k, s)\}_{\mathsf{pub}(a_2)}, s] \\ \cdot[st(a_1, 2, < u, n_1(a_1, \ldots, a_k, s) >), s] \\ \cdot t) \end{array}$$

Second message: $A_2 \to A_1 : \{N_{A_1}, N_{A_2}\}_{\mathsf{pub}(A_1)}$

$$\left.\begin{array}{l} T(t), \mathsf{Distinct}(a_i, a_j) \quad i \neq j \\ I(\{u, x\}_{\mathsf{pub}(a_2)}, t) \\ \mathsf{In}([st(a_2, 1, a_2), s], t), \\ \mathsf{NotPlayed}(a_2, 2, s, t) \end{array}\right\} \Rightarrow \begin{array}{l} T(\ [\{x, n_2(a_1, \ldots, a_k, s)\}_{\mathsf{pub}(a_1)}, s] \\ \cdot[st(a_2, 2, < u, n_2(a_1, \ldots, a_k, s) >), s] \\ \cdot t) \end{array}$$

Third message: $A_1 \to A_2 : \{N_{A_2}\}_{\mathsf{pub}(A_2)}$

$$\left.\begin{array}{l} T(t), I(\{n_1(a_1, \ldots, a_k, s), y\}_{\mathsf{pub}(a_1)}, t) \\ \mathsf{In}([st(a_1, 2, < u, n >), s], t), \\ \mathsf{NotPlayed}(a_2, 3, s, t) \end{array}\right\} \Rightarrow \begin{array}{l} T(\ [\{y\}_{\mathsf{pub}(a_1)}, s] \\ \cdot[st(a_1, 3, < u, n, y >), s] \\ \cdot t) \end{array}$$

where $n = n_1(a_1, \ldots, a_k, s)$.

We could also add some other rules to make the roles of $a_3, \ldots, a_k$ less fictitious. We consider the property:

$$\phi = \neg \mathsf{Ha}(x_1) \vee \ldots \vee \neg \mathsf{Ha}(x_k) \vee \neg I(n_2(x_1, \ldots, x_k, s), t).$$

Then, following the Lowe attack, there is an attack on ϕ, using $k+1$ agent ids. Let us sketch why every attack on ϕ uses at least $k+1$ agent ids. Assume there is an attack, then there exist $t, s, a_1, \ldots, a_k$ such that $I(n_2(a_1, \ldots, a_k, s), t) \in \mathcal{H}_P$ where $\mathcal{H}_P$ is the least Herbrand model and $a_1, \ldots, a_k$ are honest agents. Since a_2 produces $n_2(a_1, \ldots, a_k, s)$ only if $\mathsf{Distinct}(a_i, a_j)$ for $i \neq j$ holds and since $a_1, \ldots, a_k$ are honest agents, we have that $a_1, \ldots, a_k$ are distinct. In addition, if no dishonest identity is used, then the intruder cannot decrypt any message thus he can not obtain $n_2(a_1, \ldots, a_k, s)$. Consequently, at least one compromised identity has been used, thus at least $k+1$ identities have been used for the attack.

3.3   Extensions

Theorems 1 and 2 assume that ϕ is purely negative which is necessary according to Example 4.

We have seen in section 2.5 that such a restriction to negative properties is not a problem for secrecy. On the other hand, authentication is naturally expressed as

$$\neg T(t) \vee \neg \mathsf{Ha}(x) \vee \neg \mathsf{Ha}(y) \vee \neg I(m(x,y,s),t) \vee \mathsf{In}([st(x,m(x,y,s)),s],t)$$

which involves a positive literal. However, it is still possible to handle such properties. Let us extend the definition of admissible properties to a class which encompasses authentication and secrecy properties.

Definition 6. *A security property ϕ is* admissible *if ϕ is of the form*

$$C \vee \mathsf{In}(u_1, t_1) \vee \cdots \vee \mathsf{In}(u_n, t_n),$$

where C is a purely negative clause, the t_i's are variables of sort Trace *and the u_i's are terms with variables of sort* Num *or* Ha. *In addition ϕ must still verify that:*

- *it does not contain the symbols s_h, s_d,*
- *if a ground subterm of some u_i is of sort* Agent *then it is of sort* Ha.

Then we can reduce such a case to the purely negative case and we get:

Theorem 3. *Assume that $\mathcal{C}_P$ is an admissible set of clauses, which does not contain any variable of sort* Ha, *ϕ is an admissible security property, then if there is an attack on P for ϕ using n agents, there is an attack on P for ϕ using at most $k + 1$ agents, where k is the number of variables of sort* Ha *occurring in ϕ.*

For instance, 3 agents are sufficient if we consider the above-specified authentication property.

Proof sketch:
For every positive literal $L = \mathsf{In}(u_i, t_i)$ occurring in ϕ, we construct a set of Horn clauses C_L defining a predicate $\widetilde{L}$ and such that:

- the least Herbrand model $\mathcal{H}_{P,\phi}$ of $\mathcal{C}_P \cup \mathcal{C}_{\neq} \cup \bigcup_L C_L$ contains $\mathcal{H}_P$;
- for every (well sorted) ground substitution σ, $\mathcal{H}_P \not\models L\sigma$ iff $\mathcal{H}_{P,\phi} \models \widetilde{L}\sigma$;
- the new set of clauses $\mathcal{C}_P \cup \bigcup_L C_L$ is admissible.

We first construct C_L using the complementation techniques, which yields a definition of the predicates negations (see e.g. [4,8]). Let $x_1^i, \ldots, x_n^i$ be the variables of u_i. The set of clauses C_L is defined by:

$$\Rightarrow \widetilde{L}(x_1^i, \ldots, x_n^i, \perp)$$
$$\widetilde{L}(x_1^i, \ldots, x_n^i, t), \mathsf{Diff}(u_i, y) \Rightarrow \widetilde{L}(x_1^i, \ldots, x_n^i, y \cdot t)$$

These clauses satisfy the above two first conditions. However, they make use of a predicate symbol Diff, whose semantics is the set of pairs of distinct terms, and the definition of Diff is not admissible. Then, we remove clauses defining Diff which are not admissible, and replace negative literals $\neg \mathsf{Diff}(x,y)$ where x, y are of sort Agent with $\neg \mathsf{Distinct}(x, y)$. The resulting clauses satisfy the three above conditions since the semantics for the new definition of Diff, restricted to instanciations of pairs (u_i, y), is still a set of pairs of distinct terms.   □

4 Conclusions

We have shown that it is possible to restrict the number of agents without loss of generality: security properties which fail in an unbounded network, also fail in a small limited network. This does not assume any property of the protocols.

To prove a security property for some protocol P, it is therefore sufficient to consider finitely many instances of the roles of P, typically 2^n where n is the number of roles in P (or $(k+1)^n$ if we don't allow an agent to be both the sender and the receiver of a message). These numbers are small since $n = 2$ for most protocols (sometimes $n = 3$). They can be further lowered since sessions only involving dishonest agents are not relevant.

This reduction result also provides with a decision result if we assume a passive attacker, i.e. an attacker who may only analyze the messages sent on the net but who cannot forge and send new messages. Indeed, in the presence of such an attacker (or eavesdropper), we can also assume that an agent cannot confuse messages from different sessions: it suffices to label the messages by a session nonce and the rule number (which is often the case for implemented protocols). Thus there is no need to consider interleaving of sessions. In addition, given a set of messages S and a message m, deciding whether the intruder may deduce m from S is in PTIME (side result of [1]). Since our reduction result ensures that only a finite number of agents have to be considered, we conclude that secrecy is decidable in $\mathsf{EXP}(n) \times \mathsf{PTIME}$ where n is the number of roles of the protocol.

Acknowledgments. We would to thank Michael Périn and anonymous referees for their helpful comments.

References

1. D. M. Allester. Automatic recognition of tractability in inference relations. In *Journal of the ACM 40(2)*, pages 284–303, April 1993.
2. R. Amadio and W. Charatonik. On name generation and set-based analysis in the dolev-yao model. In *Proc. CONCUR 02*. Springer-Verlag, 2002.
3. R. Amadio and D. Lugiez. On the reachability problem in cryptographic protocols. In *Proc. CONCUR, vol. 1877 of Lecture Notes in Computer Science*, pages 380-394, 2000.
4. R. Barbuti, P. Mancarella, D. Pedreshi, and F. Turini. A transformation approach to negation in logic programming. *Journal of Logic Programming*, 8:201–228, 1990.
5. B. Blanchet. An efficient cryptographic protocol verifier based on prolog rules. In *CSFW: Proceedings of 14th Computer Security Foundations Workshop*. IEEE Computer Society Press, 2001.
6. L. Bozga, Y. Lakhnech, and M. Périn. Pattern-based abstraction for verifying secrecy in protocols. In *Tools and Agorithms for the Construction and Analysis of Sytems (TACAS'03), to appear*, 2003.
7. J. Clark and J. Jacob. A survey of authentication protocol literature: Version, 1997.
8. H. Comon. Disunification: a survey. In J.-L. Lassez and G. Plotkin, editors, *Computational Logic: Essays in Honor of Alan Robinson*. MIT Press, 1991.
9. H. Comon and V. Cortier. Tree automata with one memory, set constraints and cryptographic protocols. Technical Report LSV-01-13, LSV, 2001.

10. H. Comon, V. Cortier, and J. Mitchell. Tree automata with memory, set constraints and ping pong protocols. In *Proc. ICALP 2001*, 2001.
11. H. Comon-Lundh and V. Cortier. Security properties: two agents are sufficient. In *Research Report LSV-02-10, Lab. Specification and Verification, ENS de Cachan, Cachan, France*, August 2002.
12. V. Cortier, J. Millen, and H. Rueß. Proving secrecy is easy enough. In *14th IEEE Computer Security Foundations Workshop*, pages 97–108. IEEE Computer Society, 2001.
13. G. Denker, J. Millen, and H. Rueß. The capsl integrated protocol environment. Technical Report SRI-CSL-2000-02, SRI International, Oct. 2000.
14. N. Durgin, P. Lincoln, J. Mitchell, and A. Scedrov. Undecidability of bounded security protocols. In *Proc. of Workshop on Formal Methods and Security Protocols, Trento, 1999.*, 1999.
15. S. Even and O. Goldreich. On the security of multi-party ping-pong protocols. In *Proc. IEEE Symp. on Foundations of Computer Science*, 1983.
16. M. Fiore and M. Abadi. Computing symbolic models for verifying cryptographic protocols. In *Proc.14th IEEE Computer Security Foundations Workshop*, Cape Breton, Nova Scotia, June 2001.
17. J. Heather, G. Lowe, and S. Schneider. How to prevent type flaw attacks on security protocols. In *CSFW: Proc. 13th IEEE Computer Security Foundations Workshop*. IEEE Computer Society Press, 2000.
18. J. Heather and S. Schneider. Towards automatic verification of authentication protocols on an unbounded network. In *Proceedings of the 13th Computer Security Foundations Workshop (CSFW'00)*, pages 132–143, Cambridge, England, 2000. IEEE Computer Society Press.
19. F. Jacquemard, M. Rusinowitch, and L. Vigneron. Compiling and verifying cryptographic protocols. In *Proc. Logic Programming and Automated Reasoning*, volume 1955 of *Lecture Notes in Computer Science*, 2000. See also the CASRUL page `http://www.loria.fr/equipes/cassis/softwares/casrul/`.
20. G. Lowe. Towards a completeness result for model checking of security protocols. *Journal of Computer Security*, 7(2–3):89–146, 1999.
21. J. Millen and H. Rueß. Protocol-independent secrecy. In *RSP: 21th IEEE Computer Society Symposium on Research in Security and Privacy*, 2000.
22. J. Millen and V. Shmatikov. Constraint solving for bounded-process cryptographic protocol analysis. In *Proc. 8th ACM Conference on Computer and Communications Security*, 2001.
23. L. Paulson. Mechanized proofs for a recursive authentication protocol. In *Proceedings of the 10th Computer Security Foundations Workshop*, pages 84–95. IEEE Computer Society Press, 1997.
24. L. Paulson. The inductive approach to verifying cryptographic protocols. *Journal of Computer Security*, 6(1):85–128, 1998.
25. M. Rusinowitch and M. Turuani. Protocol insecurity with finite number of sessions is NP-complete. In *14th IEEE Computer Security Foundations Workshop*, 2001.
26. P. Ryan, S. Schneider, M. Goldsmith, G. Lowe, and A. Roscoe. *The modelling and analysis of security protocols: the CSP approach*. Addison-Wesley, 2000.
27. S. D. Stoller. A bound on attacks on payment protocols. In *Proc. 16th Annual IEEE Symposium on Logic in Computer Science (LICS)*, pages 61–70. IEEE Computer Society Press, June 2001.
28. J. Thayer, J. Herzog, and J. Guttman. Strand spaces: proving security protocols correct. In *Journal of Computer Security, Vol. 7*, pages 191–230. IEEE Computer Society, 1999.

A Simple Language for Real Time Cryptographic Protocol Analysis⋆

Roberto Gorrieri[1], Enrico Locatelli[1], and Fabio Martinelli[2]

[1] Dipartimento di Scienze dell'Informazione, Università di Bologna, Italy.
{gorrieri,locatelli}@cs.unibo.it
[2] Istituto di Informatica e Telematica C.N.R., Pisa, Italy.
Fabio.Martinelli@iit.cnr.it

Abstract. A real-time process algebra, enhanced with specific constructs for handling cryptographic primitives, is proposed to model cryptographic protocols in a simple way. We show that some security properties, such as authentication and secrecy, can be re-formulated in this timed setting. Moreover, we show that they can be seen as suitable instances of a general information flow-like scheme, called $tGNDC$, parametric w.r.t. the observational semantics of interest. We show that, when considering timed trace semantics, there exists a most powerful hostile environment (or enemy) that can try to compromise the protocol. Moreover, we hint some compositionality results.

1 Introduction

In the last years there has been an increasing interest in the formal analysis of cryptographic protocols, as they have become the basic building blocks for many distributed services, such as home banking or electronic commerce. These analyzes have been very successful in many cases, uncovering subtle inaccuracies in many specifications of cryptographic protocols. However, such analyzes are usually restricted to very high abstractions of the real protocols, where concrete information about the timing of events are usually omitted (with the relevant exceptions of [2,16]).

Our starting point is the work on $CryptoSPA$ [7,9], which is an extension of SPA [4] (a CCS-like process algebra with actions belonging to two different levels of confidentiality), with some new constructs for handling cryptographic primitives. On such a language a general schema for the definition of security properties, called $GNDC$, has been proposed [9]. It is based on the idea of checking the system against all the possible hostile environments. The general schema has the following form:

$$P \text{ satisfies } S^{\alpha}_{\lhd} \text{ iff } \forall X \in Env : P||X \lhd \alpha(P)$$

where the general property $S^{\alpha}_{\lhd}$ requires that the system P satisfies (via the behavioral pre-order $\lhd$) a specification $\alpha(P)$ when composed in parallel with any possible hostile

---

⋆ Work partially supported by MURST Progetto "Metodi Formali per la Sicurezza" (MEFISTO); IST-FET project "Design Environments for Global ApplicationS (DEGAS)"; Microsoft Research Europe; by CNR project "Tecniche e Strumenti Software per l'analisi della sicurezza delle comunicazioni in applicazioni telematiche di interesse economico e sociale" and by a CSP grant for the project "SeTAPS II".

P. Degano (Ed.): ESOP 2003, LNCS 2618, pp. 114–128, 2003.

environment (or enemy) X. The problem of the universal quantification is overcome when it is possible to show that there exists the "most powerful" enemy; hence, one check against the most powerful enemy is as discriminating as an infinity of different checks against all the possible enemies. This lucky case occurs when the behavioral pre-order $\lhd$ is a pre-congruence, e.g., for trace semantics.

The main goal of this paper is to show that the real-time information flow theory developed for $tSPA$ (a real-time extension of SPA reported in [8]), can be extended to $CryptoSPA$, yielding $timedCryptoSPA$ ($tCryptoSPA$ for short). The main results from such an effort are the following:

- A language for describing cryptographic protocols, where information about the concrete timing of events is necessary, e.g., because of the presence of timeouts or time-stamps.
- A general scheme, called $tGNDC$, for describing uniformly the many security properties in a real-time setting; we will present three instances of such a general scheme, namely *timed authentication, timed integrity* and *timed secrecy*.
- Some specific results for the security properties based on semantics that are pre-congruences, such as the existence of a (real-time) most general enemy.

Moreover, we will hint some initial compositionality results, i.e., we will show some conditions under which secure real-time protocols can be safely composed.

The paper is organized as follows: in Section 2 we define the $tCryptoSPA$ syntax, operational and behavioral semantics. In Section 3 we define the general schema $tGNDC$, hence the notion of hostile environment (or enemy) and we present some general results, such as the existence of a real-time most general enemy. In Section 4 we present some security properties, namely $tNDC$, *timed authentication, timed integrity* and *timed secrecy*. Section 5 reports some initial results about conditions for safe composition of real-time security protocols. Finally in Section 6 we give some concluding remarks and comparison with related literature.

2   The Model

In this section we present the model we will use for the specification of cryptographic protocols and security properties. It is a real-time extension of the *Cryptographic Security Process Algebra* ($CryptoSPA$ for short) proposed in [9,7], which is in turn an extension of *Security Process Algebra* (SPA for short) proposed in [4] where processes are explicitly given the possibility of manipulating messages. In $CryptoSPA$ it is possible to express qualitative ordering among events, while quantitative timing aspects cannot be expressed. Thus, we extend $CryptoSPA$ with operators that permit to express the elapsing of time.

2.1   The Language Syntax

We call the language *Timed Cryptographic Security Process Algebra* ($tCryptoSPA$ for short). Its syntax is based on the following elements:

- A set Ch of channels, partitioned into a set I of input channels (ranged over by c) and a set O of output channels (ranged over by $\bar{c}$, the output corresponding to the input c);

- A set $\mathcal{M}$ of messages;
- A set Var of variables, raged over by x;
- A set $Const$ of constants, ranged over by A.

The set $\mathcal{L}$ of tCryptoSPA terms (or processes) is defined as follows:

$$P ::= \mathbf{0}|\ c(x).P\ |\ \overline{c}e.P\ |\ \tau.P\ |\ tick.P\ |\ P + P\ |\ P||P\ |\ P\backslash L\ |$$

$$A(e_1, \dots, e_n)\ |\ [\langle e_1, \dots, e_r \rangle \vdash_{rule} x]P\ |\ \iota(P)$$

where $e, e', e_1, \dots, e_r$ are messages or variables and L is a set of channels. Both the operators $c(x).P$ and $[\langle e_1 \dots e_r \rangle \vdash_{rule} x]P$ bind the variable x in P.

Besides the standard (value-passing) CCS operators [15], we have an additional prefix action $tick$, used to model time elapsing, a delay operator $\iota(P)$, used to make lazy the initial actions of P, and the operator $[\langle m_1 \dots m_r \rangle \vdash_{rule} x]P$ introduced in order to model message handling and cryptography. Informally, process $[\langle m_1 \dots m_r \rangle \vdash_{rule} x]P$ tries to deduce a piece of information z from the tuple of messages $\langle m_1 \dots m_r \rangle$ through one application of rule $\vdash_{rule}$; if it succeeds, then it behaves like $P[z/x]$, otherwise it is stuck. See the next subsection for a more detailed explanation of derivation rules.

The time model we use is known as the *fictitious clock* approach of, e.g., [17]. A global clock is supposed to be updated whenever all the processes agree on this, by globally synchronizing on action $tick$. All the other actions are assumed to take no time. This is reasonable if we choose a time unit such that the actual time of an action is negligible w.r.t. the time unit. Hence, the computation proceeds in lock-steps: between the two global synchronizations on action $tick$ (that represent the elapsing of one time unit), all the processes proceed asynchronously by performing durationless actions.

Let $Def : Const \longrightarrow \mathcal{L}$ be a set of defining equations of the form $A(x_1, \dots, x_n) \stackrel{def}{=} P$, where P may contain no free variables except $x_1, \dots, x_n$, which must be distinct. Constants permit us to define recursive processes, but we have to be a bit careful in using them. A term P is *closed* w.r.t. Def if all the constants occurring in P are defined in Def (and, recursively, for their defining terms). A term P is *guarded* w.r.t. Def if all the constants occurring in P (and, recursively, for their defining terms) occur in a prefix context [15].

The set $Act = \{c(m) \mid c \in I\} \cup \{\overline{c}m \mid \overline{c} \in O\} \cup \{\tau\} \cup \{tick\}$ of actions (τ is the internal, invisible action, $tick$ is the special action used to model time elapsing), ranged over by a (with abuse of notation); we let l range over $Act\backslash\{tick\}$. We call $\mathcal{P}$ the set of all the $tCryptoSPA$ *closed* terms (i.e., with no free variables), that are closed and guarded w.r.t. Def. We define $sort(P)$ to be the set of all the channels syntactically occurring in the term P. Moreover, for the sake of readability, we always omit the termination $\mathbf{0}$ at the end of process specifications, e.g., we write a in place of $a.\mathbf{0}$.

We give an informal overview of $tCryptoSPA$ operators:

- $\mathbf{0}$ is a process that does nothing;
- $c(x).P$ represents the process that can get an input m on channel c behaving like P where all the occurrences of x are replaced by m (written $P[m/x]$);
- $\overline{c}m.P$ is the process that can send m on channel c, then behaving like P;
- $\tau.P$ is the process that executes the invisible action τ and then behaves like P;
- $tick.P$ is a process willing to let one time unit pass and then behaving as P;

- $P_1 + P_2$ *(choice)* represents the nondeterministic choice between the two processes P_1 and P_2; time passes when both P_1 and P_2 are able to perform a *tick* action – and in such a case by performing *tick* a configuration where both the derivatives of the summands can still be chosen is reached – or when only one of the two can perform *tick* – and in such a case the other summand is discarded; moreover, τ prefixed summands have priority over *tick* prefixed summands.
- $P_1 \| P_2$ *(parallel)* is the parallel composition of processes that can proceed in an asynchronous way but they must synchronize on complementary actions to make a communication, represented by a τ. Both components must agree on performing a *tick* action, and this can be done even if a communication is possible;
- $P \backslash L$ is the process that cannot send and receive messages on channels in L, for all the other channels it behaves exactly like P;
- $A(m_1, \dots, m_n)$ behaves like the respective defining term P where all the variables $x_1, \dots, x_n$ are replaced by the messages $m_1, \dots, m_n$;
- $[\langle m_1, \dots, m_r \rangle \vdash_{rule} x]P$ is the process used to model message handling and cryptography. The process $[\langle m_1, \dots, m_r \rangle \vdash_{rule} x]P$ tries to deduce an information z from the tuple of messages $\langle m_1, \dots, m_r \rangle$ through the application of rule $\vdash_{rule}$; if it succeeds then it behaves like $P[z/x]$, otherwise it is stuck. The set of rules that can be applied is defined through an inference system (e.g., see Figure 1);
- $\iota(P)$ *(idling)* allows process P to wait indefinitely. At every instant of time, if process P performs an action l, then the whole system proceeds in this state, while dropping the idling operator.

2.2   The Operational Semantics of tCryptoSPA

In order to model message handling and cryptography we use a set of inference rules. Note that $tCryptoSPA$ syntax, its semantics and the results obtained are completely parametric with respect to the inference system used. We present in Figure 1 the same inference system of [9]. This inference system can combine two messages obtaining a pair (rule $\vdash_{pair}$); it can extract one message from a pair (rules $\vdash_{fst}$ and $\vdash_{snd}$); it can encrypt a message m with a key k obtaining $\{m\}_k$ and finally decrypt a message of the form $\{m\}_k$ only if it has the same key k (rules $\vdash_{enc}$ and $\vdash_{dec}$). In this framework, cryptography is completely reliable, i.e., that a crypted message can be deciphered only by knowing the suitable decryption key.

In a similar way, the inference system can contain rules for handling the basic arithmetic operations and boolean relations among numbers, so that the value-passing CCS **if then else** construct can be obtained via the $\vdash_{rule}$ operator.

Example 1. We do not explictly define equality check among messages in the syntax. However, this can be implemented through the usage of the inference construct. E.g., consider rule $equal \overset{def}{=} \dfrac{x \quad x}{Equal(x,x)}$. Then $[m = m']A$ (with the expected semantics) may be equivalently expressed as $[m \quad m' \vdash_{equal} y]A$ where y does not occur in A. Similarly, we can define inequalities, e.g., $\leq$, among natural numbers.

We consider a function $\mathcal{D}$, from finite sets of messages to sets of messages, such that $\mathcal{D}(\phi)$ is the set of messages that can be deduced from ϕ by using the inference rules. We assume that $\mathcal{D}$ is decidable.

$$\frac{m \quad m'}{(m,m')}(\vdash_{pair}) \qquad \frac{(m,m')}{m}(\vdash_{fst}) \qquad \frac{(m,m')}{m'}(\vdash_{snd})$$

$$\frac{m \quad k}{\{m\}_k}(\vdash_{enc}) \qquad \frac{\{m\}_k \quad k}{m}(\vdash_{dec})$$

Fig. 1. An example inference system for shared key cryptography.

The operational semantics of a $tCryptoSPA$ term is described by means of the *labelled transition system* (*lts*, for short) $\langle \mathcal{P}, Act, \{\xrightarrow{a}\}_{a\in Act}\rangle$, where $\{\xrightarrow{a}\}_{a\in Act}$ is the least relation between $tCryptoSPA$ processes induced by the axioms and inference rules of Figure 2. Such a relation is well-defined even if negative premises occur in a rule for the idling operator and in one rule for $+$, because the relation is *strictly stratifiable* [12].

Note that $tCryptoSPA$ is *tick-deterministic* i.e., the time elapsing never moves a process to two different states. The proof of the following proposition can be easily given by inspecting the operational rules. In particular, the first two rules of the idling operator and the rules for nondeterministic choice are the key rules enforcing time determinacy.

Proposition 1. *For every tCryptoSPA process P we have:*

If $P \xrightarrow{tick} P'$ *and* $P \xrightarrow{tick} P''$ *then* $P' = P''$.

Example 2. In $tCryptoSPA$ there are processes, such as $\mathbf{0}$, that do not allow time to proceed; hence, as rule $\|_3$ for parallel composition forces a global synchronisation on *tick* actions, the effect of composing a process P with $\mathbf{0}$ is to prevent P from letting time pass. In other words, $\mathbf{0}$ acts as a time annihilator for its parallel context. On the contrary, $\iota(\mathbf{0})$ is process that, even if functionally terminated, let time to proceed indefinitely. Hence, $\iota(\mathbf{0})$ acts as a neutral element for parallel composition.

Example 3. Consider a process $P = \iota(a)\|\iota(\overline{a})$ that can perform any sequence (possibly empty) of *tick* actions followed by a τ. It is worth-observing that, contrary to $tSPA$ [8], we do not assume maximal communication progress, i.e., τ's do not have priority over *tick* actions or, equivalently, a process cannot idle if it can perform a τ. Hence in $tSPA$ process P can perform only the sequence τ.

Example 4. We can easily model timeout constructs in $tCryptoSPA$.
Assume $n_1 \leq n_2$ and define a process

$$Time\_out(n_1, n_2, A, B) = tick^{n_1}.\iota(A) + tick^{n_2}.\tau.B$$

By looking at the rules for choice and idling, we see that $Time\_out(n_1, n_2, A, B)$ first performs a sequence of n_1 *tick* actions; then, the system may perform other $n_2 - n_1$ *tick* actions, unless A resolves the choice by performing an action; instead if A does nothing, after n_2 units of time, through the execution of action τ, the process is forced to act as B. Note that rule $+_3$ is responsible for preventing the selection of process A at timeout expiration. This semantics for the $+$ operator is different from the one in $tSPA$ (a *tick* action can be performed *only if* both summands can do so) and is motivated by the need of a more flexible way of programming the choice between different components.

$$(input)\frac{m \in \mathcal{M}}{c(x).P \xrightarrow{c(m)} P[m/x]} \qquad (output)\frac{}{\overline{c}m.P \xrightarrow{\overline{c}m} P}$$

$$(internal)\frac{}{\tau.P \xrightarrow{\tau} P} \qquad (tick)\frac{}{tick.P \xrightarrow{tick} P}$$

$$(\|_1)\frac{P_1 \xrightarrow{l} P_1'}{P_1\|P_2 \xrightarrow{l} P_1'\|P_2} \qquad (\|_2)\frac{P_1 \xrightarrow{c(x)} P_1' \quad P_2 \xrightarrow{\overline{c}m} P_2'}{P_1\|P_2 \xrightarrow{\tau} P_1'\|P_2'}$$

$$(\|_3)\frac{P_1 \xrightarrow{tick} P_1' \quad P_2 \xrightarrow{tick} P_2'}{P_1\|P_2 \xrightarrow{tick} P_1'\|P_2'} \qquad (\backslash L)\frac{P \xrightarrow{c(m)} P' \quad c \notin L}{P\backslash L \xrightarrow{c(m)} P'\backslash L}$$

$$(+_1)\frac{P_1 \xrightarrow{l} P_1'}{P_1 + P_2 \xrightarrow{l} P_1'} \qquad (+_2)\frac{P_1 \xrightarrow{tick} P_1' \quad P_2 \xrightarrow{tick} P_2'}{P_1 + P_2 \xrightarrow{tick} P_1' + P_2'}$$

$$(+_3)\frac{P_1 \xrightarrow{tick} P_1' \quad P_2 \xrightarrow{tick}\!\!\!\!\!/ \quad P_2 \xrightarrow{}\!\!\!\!/}{P_1 + P_2 \xrightarrow{tick} P_1'}$$

$$(Def)\frac{P[m_1/x_1,\ldots,m_n/x_n] \xrightarrow{a} P' \quad A(x_1,\ldots,x_n) \overset{def}{=} P}{A(m_1,\ldots,m_n) \xrightarrow{a} P'}$$

$$(\mathcal{D})\frac{\langle m_1,\ldots,m_r\rangle \vdash_{rule} m \quad P[m/x] \xrightarrow{a} P'}{[\langle m_1,\ldots,m_r\rangle \vdash_{rule} x]P \xrightarrow{a} P'}$$

$$(\mathcal{I}_1)\frac{P \xrightarrow{tick}\!\!\!\!/}{\iota(P) \xrightarrow{tick} \iota(P)} \qquad (\mathcal{I}_2)\frac{P \xrightarrow{tick} P'}{\iota(P) \xrightarrow{tick} \iota(P')} \qquad (\mathcal{I}_3)\frac{P \xrightarrow{l} P'}{\iota(P) \xrightarrow{l} P'}$$

Fig. 2. Structured Operational Semantics for tCryptoSPA (symmetric rules for $+_1, +_3, \|_1, \|_2$ and $\backslash L$ are omitted)

3 A General Schema for the Definition of Timed Security Properties

In this section we propose a general schema for the definition of timed security properties. We call it *Timed Generalized NDC* (*tGNDC* for short), since it is a real-time generalization of *Generalized NDC* (*GNDC* for short) [9], which is in turn a generalization of *Non Deducibility on Compositions* (*NDC* for short) [4]. The main idea is the following: a system P is $tGNDC_\lhd^\alpha$ iff for every hostile environment (or enemy) X the composition of the system P with X satisfies the timed specification $\alpha(P)$. Essentially $tGNDC_\lhd^\alpha$ guarantees that the timed property α is satisfied, with respect to the $\lhd$ timed behavioral relation, even when the system is composed with any possible enemy.

This section is organized as follows. We first define timed trace semantics as the behavioral semantics of interest. Then, we discuss the issue of hostile environments, showing that it is necessary to restrict their initial knowledge. Finally, we present the *tGNDC* schema and some general results on it, some of which are independent of the chosen behavioral notion.

3.1 Behavioural Semantics

Here we define the semantic pre-order and equivalence we will use to formalize security properties, *timed trace* pre-order and equivalence, the timed version of the classic untimed semantics.

The expression $P \stackrel{a}{\Rightarrow} P'$ is a shorthand for $P(\stackrel{\tau}{\longrightarrow})^* P_1 \stackrel{a}{\longrightarrow} P_2 (\stackrel{\tau}{\longrightarrow})^* P'$ where $(\stackrel{\tau}{\longrightarrow})^*$ denotes a (possibly empty) sequence of transitions labeled τ. Let $\gamma = a_1, \ldots, a_n \in (Act\backslash\{\tau\})^*$ be a sequence of actions; then $P \stackrel{\gamma}{\Rightarrow} P'$ iff there exist $P_1, \ldots, P_{n-1} \in \mathcal{P}$ such that $P \stackrel{a_1}{\Rightarrow} P_1 \stackrel{a_2}{\Rightarrow}, \ldots, P_{n-1} \stackrel{a_n}{\Rightarrow} P'$.

Definition 1. *For any $P \in \mathcal{P}$ the set $T(P)$ of timed traces associated with P is defined as follows $T(P) = \{\gamma \in (Act\backslash\{\tau\})^* \mid \exists P'.P \stackrel{\gamma}{\Rightarrow} P'\}$. The timed trace pre-order, denoted by $\leq_{ttrace}$, is defined as follows: $P \leq_{ttrace} Q$ iff $T(P) \subseteq T(Q)$. P and Q are timed trace equivalent, denoted by $P =_{ttrace} Q$, if $T(P) = T(Q)$.*

As an example, it is easy to see that $T(P(K_{ab})) = \{\epsilon, tick, tick\ tick, tick\ tick\ tick\}$, where ϵ denotes the empty sequence.

3.2 Hostile Environments

Here we characterize the notion of admissible hostile environments similarly to what done in [9] for the untimed setting. Such a characterization is necessary to analyze protocols where some information is assumed to be secret, as in cryptographic protocols. A hostile environment, or *enemy*, is a process which tries to attack a protocol by stealing and faking information which is transmitted on *public* channels, say C. Such an agent is modeled as a generic process X which can communicate only through channels in C, imposing some constraints on the initial data that are known by the enemy and requiring that such a protocol is *weakly time alive*, i.e., the agent may always perform $tick$ eventually. Otherwise X could prevent time from elapsing when composed in parallel with some system, since in a compound system time can pass iff all components let it pass. So the enemy could block the time flow and we want to avoid this unrealistic case. Let $Der(P)$ be the set of all derivatives of P, i.e., all the P's reachable from P through a sequence of actions in Act.

Definition 2. *A process P is directly weakly time alive iff $P \stackrel{tick}{\Longrightarrow} P'$. P is weakly time alive iff for all $P' \in Der(P)$, we have P' is directly weakly time alive.*

Now, let $ID(P)$ be the set of messages that appear in P (see [5] for a formal definition) and $\phi \subseteq \mathcal{M}$ be the initial knowledge we would like to give to the enemies, i.e., the public information such as the names of the entities and the public keys, plus some possible private data of the enemies (e.g., their private key or nonces). For some enemy X, we want that all the messages in $ID(X)$ are deducible from ϕ. We thus define the set $t\mathcal{E}_C^{\phi_I}$ of timed hostile processes as:

$$t\mathcal{E}_C^\phi = \{X \in \mathcal{P} \mid sort(X) \subseteq C \text{ and } ID(X) \subseteq \mathcal{D}(\phi) \text{ and } X \text{ is weakly time alive}\}$$

3.3 The $tGNDC$ Schema

In this section we formally define the $tGNDC_{\trianglelefteq}^\alpha$ family of properties. We will use $A||_C B$ as a shortcut for $(A||B)\backslash C$. The proposed family of security properties is as follows.

Definition 3. *P is $tGNDC^{\alpha}_{\lhd}$ iff $\forall X \in t\mathcal{E}^{\phi_I}_C$: $(P||_C X) \lhd \alpha(P)$ where $\lhd \in \mathcal{P} \times \mathcal{P}$ is a pre-order, C is a set of channels and $\alpha : \mathcal{P} \mapsto \mathcal{P}$ is a function between processes defining the property specification for P as the process $\alpha(P)$.*

We propose a sufficient criterion for a static characterization (i.e., not involving the universal quantification $\forall$) of $tGNDC^{\alpha}_{\lhd}$ properties. We will say that $\lhd$ is a *pre-congruence* w.r.t. $||_C$ if it is a pre-order and for every $P, Q, Q' \in \mathcal{P}$ if $Q \lhd Q'$ then $P||_C Q \lhd P||_C Q'$. Thus it is easy to prove the following:

Proposition 2. *If $\lhd$ is a pre-congruence w.r.t. $||_C$ and if there exist a process $Top \in t\mathcal{E}^{\phi_I}_C$ such that for every process $X \in t\mathcal{E}^{\phi_I}_C$ we have $X \lhd Top$, then $\forall \alpha$:*

$$P \in tGNDC^{\alpha}_{\lhd} \quad \text{iff} \quad (P||_C Top) \lhd \alpha(P)$$

In particular if the hypotheses of the proposition above hold it is sufficient to check that $\alpha(P)$ is satisfied when P is composed with the most general hostile environment Top. This permits to make only one single check, in order to prove that a property holds whatever attacker we choose. We also have the following corollary for the congruence induced by $\lhd$:

Corollary 1. *Let $\lhd$ be a pre-congruence w.r.t. $||_C$ and let $\equiv = \lhd \cap \lhd^{-1}$. If there exist two processes $Bot, Top \in t\mathcal{E}^{\phi_I}_C$ such that for every process $X \in t\mathcal{E}^{\phi_I}_C$ we have $Bot \lhd X \lhd Top$ then*

$$P \in tGNDC^{\alpha}_{\equiv} \quad \text{iff} \quad (P||_C Bot) \equiv (P||_C Top) \equiv \alpha(P)$$

Given these very general results, we show that they are instanciable in the model we presented so far. Indeed, this is the case, at least for the trace pre-order $\leq_{ttrace}$, which is a pre-congruence.

Proposition 3. *Timed trace pre-order is a pre-congruence w.r.t. $||_C$.*

Note that in the $tSPA$ model, timed trace pre-order is not a pre-congruence, since the semantic rules enforce the so called *maximal communication progress*, i.e., when a communication is possible it must start immediately, and it is not possible to perform a *tick* [8].

Now we single out the minimal element Bot and the maximum element Top in $t\mathcal{E}^{\phi_I}_C$ w.r.t. $\leq_{ttrace}$. As for Bot it is clear that the minimum set of traces is generated by the weakly time alive process that does nothing, that is generated by process $\iota(\mathbf{0})$. As a matter of fact, $(P||\iota(\mathbf{0})) =_{ttrace} P$ for timed trace equivalence and most other equivalences. We thus define the Top element using a family of processes $Top^{C,\phi}_{ttrace}$ each representing an instance of the enemy with knowledge ϕ:

$$Top^{C,\phi}_{ttrace} = \sum_{c \in C} \iota(c(x).Top^{C,\phi \cup \{x\}}_{ttrace}) + \sum_{c \in C, m \in \mathcal{D}(\phi) \cap \mathcal{M}} \iota(\bar{c}m.Top^{C,\phi}_{ttrace})$$

The initial element of the family is Top^{C,ϕ_I}_{ttrace} as ϕ_I is the initial knowledge of the enemy. This may accept any input message to be bound to the variable x which is then added to the knowledge set that becomes $\phi_I \cup \{x\}$, and may output only messages that can pass on the channel c and that are deducible from the current knowledge set ϕ via the deduction function $\mathcal{D}$. Furthermore it can let time pass. Note that τ summands are not considered, as inessential for trace pre-order. As done in [9] we prove the following:

Proposition 4. *If $X \in t\mathcal{E}^{\phi}_C$ then $X \leq_{ttrace} Top^{C,\phi}_{ttrace}$.*

4   Some Timed Security Properties

In this section we show how to redefine four timed security properties as suitable instances of the $tGNDC^\alpha_\lhd$ schema, by suitably defining function α. As for the behavioral semantics $\lhd$, we will always consider the timed trace semantics. The four properties we consider are:

- The timed version of Non Deducibility on Compositions [4], which has been proposed to study information flow security; we will show that $tNDC$ is the strongest property in the $tGNDC^\alpha_\lhd$family, under some mild assumptions.
- A timed notion of authentication, called *timed agreement* (see also [14]), according to which agreement must be reached within a certain deadline, otherwise authentication does not hold.
- A timed notion of secrecy, we call *timed secrecy*, according to which a message is secret only within a time interval and after the deadline it can become a public piece of information.
- A timed notion of integrity, called *timed integrity*, which simply requires a correct delivery of messages within a certain amount of time.

4.1   Timed Non Deducibility on Compositions

We start with $tNDC$ since $tGNDC^\alpha_\lhd$is a generalization of such a property. Its underlying idea is that the system behavior must be invariant w.r.t. the composition with every hostile environment. Indeed, there is no possibility of establishing a communication (i.e. sending information). In the $CryptoSPA$ untimed setting the NDC [1] idea can thus be defined as follows:

Definition 4. $P \in NDC$ *if and only if* $\forall X \in \mathcal{E}^{\phi_I}_C$, *we have* $(P||_C X) =_{trace} P \backslash C$.

where $=_{trace}$ is trace pre-order and the only difference with the definition given in SPA is that the knowledge of process X is bounded by ϕ_I. Now we present *timed NDC* ($tNDC$, for short) ([8]) which is the natural extension of NDC to a timed setting.

Definition 5. $P \in tNDC$ *if and only if* $\forall X \in t\mathcal{E}^{\phi_I}_C$ *we have* $(P||_C X) =_{ttrace} P \backslash C$.

where the difference is that we use the timed hostile environment and timed trace pre-order. Note that $tNDC$ corresponds to $tGNDC^{P \backslash C}_{=_{ttrace}}$. It is also possible to apply Corollary 1 obtaining the following static characterization.

Proposition 5. $P \in tNDC$ *if and only if* $(P||_C Top^{C,\phi_I}_{ttrace}) =_{ttrace} P \backslash C$.

Now we suggest that $tNDC$ is the most restrictive $\alpha(P)$ hence inducing the strongest property for timed trace semantics. The most restrictive $\alpha(P)$ should return an *encapsulation* of protocol P, i.e., a version of P which is completely isolated from the environment, corresponding to the execution of P in a perfectly secure network where only the honest parties are present. In our process algebra setting, this corresponds to the *restriction* of all public channels in C along which protocol messages are sent.

Note that for every process P we have $(P||\iota(\mathbf{0})) \backslash C =_{ttrace} P \backslash C$. This means that P restricted on C is equivalent to the protocol in composition with the enemy that

---

[1] As for $tGNDC^\alpha_\lhd$, also NDC and $tNDC$ are implicitly parametric w.r.t. the set C of public channels and the set ϕ_I of initial knowledge. We usually omit these parameters when clear from the context.

does nothing. Note also that, by definition, $\iota(\mathbf{0}) \in t\mathcal{E}_C^\phi$ for every ϕ. So it is very natural to consider α functions and processes P such that $P \setminus C \leq_{ttrace} \alpha(P)$. This simply means that the protocol P is correct (as it satisfies its specification $\alpha(P)$) at least when it is not under attack. This condition can be somehow seen as a reasonable criterion for any *good* protocol: it must be correct at least when it is not under attack! Under this mild assumption, it is clear that $P \in tNDC$ implies $P \in tGNDC^\alpha_{\leq_{ttrace}}$.

Another way to avoid universal quantification over all the admissible enemies is to show the equivalence between $tNDC$ and *Timed Strong Nondeterministic Non-Interference* ($tSNNI$, for short); such equivalence result holds in the untimed case [4], but that does not hold for $tSPA$ [8] because of the maximal communication assumption of that language.

A *CryptoSPA* process is $SNNI_C^\phi$ if $P\setminus C$, where all actions in C are forbidden, behaves like the system P where all the actions in C are *hidden* (i.e., transformed into internal τ actions). To express this second system we need to introduce first the *hiding* operator $P/^\phi C$:

$$\frac{P \xrightarrow{a} P'}{P/^\phi C \xrightarrow{a} P'/^\phi C}(a \notin C \cup \overline{C}) \quad \frac{P \xrightarrow{\overline{c}m} P' \quad c \in C \cup \overline{C}}{P/^\phi C \xrightarrow{\tau} P'/^{\phi \cup \{m\}} C}$$

$$\frac{P \xrightarrow{c(m)} P' \quad c \in C \cup \overline{C} \quad m \in \mathcal{D}(\phi)}{P/^\phi C \xrightarrow{\tau} P'/^\phi C}$$

Now we are ready to define the property *timed* $SNNI_C^\phi$ as follows.

Definition 6. *A process is* $tSNNI_C^\phi$ *if* $P\setminus C =_{ttrace} P/^\phi C$.

It is rather intuitive that $P/^\phi C$ can be seen as $P||_C Top$, where Top is the top element of the trace pre-order for $CryptoSPA$. Hence, such a static characterization can be seen as a corollary of the existence of a top element in the trace pre-order (together with the fact that trace pre-order is a pre-congruence).

Proposition 6. *For every* $P \in \mathcal{P}$ *we have that* $(P||_C Top_{ttrace}^{C,\phi}) =_{ttrace} P/^\phi C$.

Proposition 7. $P \in tNDC_C^\phi$ *iff* $P \in tSNNI_C^\phi$.

4.2 Timed Agreement

We now present the *Timed Agreement* Property [14]:

> "A protocol guarantees *Timed Agreement* between a responder B and an initiator A on a set of data items ds if, whenever B (acting as responder) completes a run of the protocol, apparently with initiator A, then A has previously been running the protocol, apparently with B, in the last n *ticks* (where n is a prefixed timeout value) and the two agents agreed on the data values corresponding to all the variables in ds, and each such a run of B corresponds to a unique run of A."

As done in [9] for the non real-time version of *Agreement*, what we do is to have for each party an action representing the running of a protocol and another one representing the completion of it. We consider an action $commit\_res(B, A, d)$ representing a correct termination of B as a responder, convinced to communicate with A that agrees on data d. On the other hand we have an action $running\_ini(A, B, d)$ that represents the fact that A is running the protocol as initiator, apparently with B, with data d. If we specify these two actions in the protocol, the *Timed Agreement* property requires that when B executes $commit\_res(B, A, d)$ then A has previously executed $running\_ini(A, B, d)$ and at most n *tick* actions, where n is the prefixed timeout value, occurred between these actions. We assume that the actions representing the running and the commit are correctly specified in the protocol. We can see them as output actions over two particular channels $running\_ini$ and $commit\_res$. We assume that d can assume values in a set D. Let $NotObs(P) = sort(P) \backslash (C \cup \{running\_ini, commit\_res\})$ be the set of channels in P that are not public and are different from $running\_ini$ and $commit\_res$, i.e., that will not be observed. Function $\alpha_{tAgree}^{t(n)}$ can be thus defined as follows:

$$P'(x, y) = \sum_{d \in D, i \in 0..n} \iota(\overline{running\_ini}(x, y, d).tick_1..tick_i.\overline{commit\_res}(y, x, d).\iota(\mathbf{0}))$$
$$P'' = \sum_{c \in NotObs(P)} \iota(c(x).P'') + \sum_{c \in NotObs(P), m \in \mathcal{M}} \iota(\overline{c}m.P'')$$
$$\alpha_{tAgree}^{t(n)}(P) = P'' \| P'(A, B)$$

Note that P'' is essentially the process that executes every possible action over channels in $sort(P)$ which are not in C and are different from $running\_ini$ and $commit\_res$, or let time pass. Given P, $\alpha_{tAgree}^{t(n)}(P)$ represents the most general system which satisfies the *Timed Agreement* property and has the same sort of P. In fact in $\alpha_{tAgree}^{t(n)}(P)$ action $\overline{running\_ini}(x, y, d)$ always precedes $\overline{commit\_res}(y, x, d)$ for every datum d, and every combination of the other actions of P can be executed. Finally the number of $tick$ actions is at most n. In order to analyze more than one session, it suffices to consider an extended α which has several processes P' in parallel.

We want that even in the presence of a hostile process, P does not execute traces that are not in $\alpha_{tAgree}^{t(n)}(P)$. So we can give the following definition:

Definition 7. *P satisfies Timed Agreement* iff P is $tGNDC_{\leq_{ttrace}}^{\alpha_{tAgree}^{t(n)}(P)}$, i.e.,

$$\forall X \in t\mathcal{E}_C^{\phi_I} \; : \; (P \|_C X) \leq_{ttrace} \alpha_{tAgree}^{t(n)}(P)$$

4.3 Timed Secrecy

We now present the *Timed Secrecy* Property:

> "A protocol guarantees to an initiator A the property of *Timed Secrecy* on a set of data items ds within a time n if, whenever a data item in ds becomes public, at least n ticks passed since A started the protocol"

As done for *Timed Agreement*, what we do is to have an action representing the running of a protocol and another one representing that a secret is revealed. We consider an action $running\_ini(A, d)$ that represents the fact that A is running the protocol as initiator, with data d. On the other hand we have an action $\overline{public}(d)$ representing that data item d is made public. If we specify these two actions in the protocol, the *Timed Secrecy* property requires that when someone executes $\overline{public}(d)$ then A has executed $running\_ini(A, d)$ and at least n tick actions, where n is the prefixed timeout value, occurred between them. We assume that the actions representing the running and the publication are correctly specified in the protocol. We can see the first as an output action over a particular channel $running\_ini$. The second action, following the approach of [6] is performed by a particular process called *Key Expired Notifier* (KEN, for short) that reads from a public channel c not used in the protocol and performs the output of what it has read on the channel $\overline{public}$, i.e. $KEN = c(x).\overline{public}(x)$.

Let $NotObs(P) = sort(P)\backslash(C \cup \{c, running\_ini, public\})$ be the set of channels in P that are not public and are different from $running\_ini$ and $public$, i.e., that will not be observed. We assume that d can take values in a set of secret values D. Function $\alpha_{tSec}^{t(n)}$ can be thus defined as follows:

$$P'(x) = \sum_{d \in D} \iota(\overline{running\_ini}(x,d).tick_1 \ldots tick_n.(\iota(\overline{public}(d).\iota(\mathbf{0})) + \iota(\tau.\iota(\mathbf{0}))))$$
$$P'' = \sum_{c \in NotObs(P)} \iota(c(x).P'') + \sum_{c \in NotObs(P), m \in \mathcal{M}} \iota(\overline{c}m.P'')$$
$$\alpha_{tSec}^{t(n)}(P) = P''||P'(A)$$

Given P, $\alpha_{tSec}^{t(n)}(P)$ represents the most general system which satisfies the *Timed Secrecy* property and has the same sort of P. In fact in $\alpha_{tSec}^{t(n)}(P)$ action $\overline{public}(d)$ is always executed at least n $ticks$ after $\overline{running\_ini}(x,d)$ for every datum d, and every combination of the other actions of P can be executed. In order to analyze more than one session, it suffices to consider an extended α which has several processes P' in parallel.

We want that, even in the presence of a hostile process, P does not execute traces that are not in $\alpha_{tSec}^{t(n)}(P)$. So we can give the following definition:

Definition 8. *P satisfies Timed Secrecy iff P is* $tGNDC_{\leq_{ttrace}}^{\alpha_{tSec}^{t(n)}(P)}$, *i.e.*,

$$\forall X \in t\mathcal{E}_C^{\phi_I} \ : \ (P||_C X) \leq_{ttrace} \alpha_{tSec}^{t(n)}(P)$$

4.4 Timed Integrity

We now present the *Timed Integrity* Property:

"A protocol guarantees to the user B the property of *Timed Integrity* on a set of data items ds within a time n if B only accepts data items in ds and this may only happen in at most n ticks since the beginning of the protocol"

For instance, imagine that you would like to receive your favorite newspaper each day before noon. This may be expressed as an integrity property rather than an authenticity one, since you are not actually interested in the sender but simply on the data (the newspaper). Consider a channel out used for expressing the reception of a message and let $NotObs(P) = sort(P)\backslash(C \cup \{out\})$ be the set of channels in P that are not public and d ranging over a set of data D. Then, *Timed Integrity* may be formally specified as follows:

$$P'(y,n) = ||_{d \in D} tick_1. \ldots .tick_n.\tau.\iota(\mathbf{0}) + \iota(\overline{out}(y,d).\iota(\mathbf{0}))$$
$$P'' = \sum_{c \in NotObs(P)} \iota(c(x).P'') + \sum_{c \in NotObs(P), m \in \mathcal{M}} \iota(\overline{c}m.P'')$$
$$\alpha_{tInt}^{t(n)}(P) = P''||P'(B,n)$$

5   Compositionality Results

In this section we illustrate some compositional proof rules for establishing that a system enjoys a $tGNDC$ property, in particular $tSNNI_C^\phi$. However, remember that, as it is equivalent to $tNDC$, this property implies all the other ones based on trace semantics, that are the most frequently used in security analysis.

Within the SPA theory, $SNNI$ is compositional, i.e. if $P, Q \in SNNI$ then $(P||Q) \in SNNI$. Unfortunately, the same does not hold when considering enemies with limited knowledge, as for $tSNNI_C^\phi$. For instance, consider the processes:

$$P = \overline{c_1}m_1.c_2(x)[x = m_2].\overline{c_3}m_2 \qquad Q = \overline{c_1}m_2.c_2(x)[x = m_1].\overline{c_3}m_1$$

Now, assuming $C = \{c_1, c_2\}$ and $\phi = \emptyset$, we have that $P, Q \in tSNNI_C^\phi$. However, $P||Q \notin tSNNI^\phi$. As a matter of fact, $(P||Q)\backslash C$ is equivalent to $\mathbf{0}$, while $(P||Q)/^\phi C$ may perform both $\overline{c_3}m_1$ and $\overline{c_3}m_2$.

However, if we strengthen the assumptions we can get a compositional rule for establishing that a process belongs to $tSNNI_C^\phi$. The *stability* assumption we make is that the process cannot increment its knowledge.

Definition 9. *We say that a process P is stable w.r.t. ϕ, whenever if $P/^\phi C \Longrightarrow P'/^{\phi'} C$ then $\mathcal{D}(\phi) = \mathcal{D}(\phi')$.*

Thus, the following proposition holds.

Proposition 8. *Assume that $P, Q \in tSNNI_C^\phi$ and that P, Q are stable w.r.t. ϕ. Then $(P||Q) \in tSNNI_C^\phi$ and $P||Q$ is stable w.r.t. ϕ.*

We have another compositionality principle for the $tGNDC_{\leq_{ttrace}}^\alpha$ schema, again under the assumption that the involved processes are stable.

Proposition 9. *Given the set of initial knowledge ϕ and the set of public channels C, assume $P_i \in tGNDC_{\leq_{ttrace}}^{\alpha_i(P_i)}$, with $i = 1, 2$, and P_1, P_2 are stable w.r.t. ϕ. It follows that $(P_1||P_2) \in tGNDC_{\leq_{ttrace}}^{\alpha_1(P_1)||\alpha_2(P_2)}$ and $P_1||P_2$ is stable w.r.t. ϕ.*

One may wonder if the stability condition is too restrictive. As a matter of fact (see [11]), the above compositional proof principles can be successfully applied for checking integrity in stream signature protocols, as the ones in [10,3].

6   Conclusions

We have shown how to extend the $GNDC$ schema to a real time setting while preserving the properties of the untimed schema. In particular, we have shown the existence of a "most powerful" timed enemy, at least for the timed trace semantics. We have also shown how to express uniformly in this general schema some timed security properties, such as timed Non Deducibility on Compositions, (one definition of) timed authentication, timed secrecy and also timed integrity. We have also introduced a compositional proof principle that allows us to compose safely two real-time security protocols, preserving the security properties they enjoy.

Related literature on real-time security include the prominent papers [16,2]. The former paper presents tock-CSP – a real-time language similar to tSPA – that is used to specify real-time crytpographic protocols. The main differences consists of a different treatment of timed operators, in the absence of a mechanism for handling cryptoprimitives, in the lack of a uniform schema, and in the absence of compositionality results. The latter paper [2] is mainly concerned with the model checking of the interesting case study of TESLA, a protocol for stream broadcasting over the internet. The main focus is on showing that it is possible to give a finite model for the unbounded supply of fresh cryptographic keys used during the protocol. The so-called *security condition* of the protocol is similar to timed agreement.

Compositional proof techniques for reasoning about cryptographic protocols in an untimed setting may be found in [1,13]. In [1], a compositional proof system for an environment-sensitive bisimulation has been developed. One main difference from ours, is that we consider a weak notion of observation where the internal actions are not visible. This permits us to have more abstract specifications. (As a matter of fact, the authors of [1] leave as future work the treatment of such a form of weak equivalence.) In [13], the authors develop the concept of disjoint encryption and, under this hypothesis, are able to perform compositional reasoning both for secrecy and authentication properties. While on the one hand, their approach seems to deal better with authentication properties than ours, on the other one it seems that there are situations where stability holds while disjoint encryption does not. (A deeper comparison deserves more time and space and is left as future work.)

Future work will be also devoted to study other security properties in a timed setting, such as non repudiation, for which apparently there is the need for using semantics more discriminating than timed trace semantics.

Acknowledgments. We would like to thank the anonymous referees for their helpful comments for the preparation of the final version of this paper.

References

1. M. Boreale and D. Gorla. on Compositional Reasoning in the Spi-calculus In proc. of FOS-SACS'02, LNCS 2303, 2002.
2. P. Broadfoot and G. Lowe. Analysing a Stream Authentication Protocol using Model Checking In Procs. ESORICS'02, LNCS, Springer, 2002.
3. N. De Francesco and M. Petrocchi. Authenticity in a Reliable Protocol for Mobile Computing. Accepted at 18th ACM Symposium on Applied Computing (SAC03). U.S., March 2003.
4. R. Focardi and R. Gorrieri. A classification of security properties. *Journal of Computer Security*, 3(1):5–33, 1995.
5. R. Focardi, R. Gorrieri and F. Martinelli. A comparison of three authentication properties. To appear on Theoretical Computer Science.
6. R. Focardi, R. Gorrieri and F. Martinelli. Secrecy in Security Protocols as Non Interference. *Electronic Notes in Theoretical Computer Science*, 32. (2000)
7. R. Focardi, R. Gorrieri and F. Martinelli. Non-interference for the analysis of cryptographic protocols. In Procs. *Int.l Colloquium on Automata, Languages and Programming* (ICALP'00), LNCS 1853, 354–372, Springer, 2000.
8. R. Focardi, R. Gorrieri and F. Martinelli. Real-time Information Flow Analysis *Journal of Selected Areas of Communications*, IEEE Press, 2002, to appear.

9. R. Focardi and F. Martinelli. A uniform approach for the definition of security properties. In *Proceedings of World Congress on Formal Methods (FM'99)*, pages 794–813. Springer, LNCS 1708, 1999.

10. R. Gennaro and P. Rohatgi. How to Sign Digital Streams. Information and Computation 165(1), pp.100–116 (2001).

11. R. Gorrieri, F. Martinelli, M. Petrocchi and A. Vaccarelli. Using compositional reasoning and Non-interference for verifying integrity in digital stream protocols. Technical Report IIT, 2003. Submitted for publication.

12. J.F. Groote. Transition system specifications with negative premises. *Theoretical Computer Science*, 118:263–299, 1993.

13. J. Guttman and F.J. Thayer. Protocol Independence through Disjoint Encryption. In Proc. CSFW'00. IEEE Press, 2000.

14. G. Lowe. A Hiearchy of Autentication Specifications. In Proc. CSFW'97, pp. 31–43, IEEE Press.

15. R. Milner. Communication and Concurrency. Prentice Hall, 1989.

16. S. Schneider. Analysing Time-Dependent Security Properties in CSP using PVS. In Procs. ESORICS, LNCS 1895, 2000.

17. I. Ulidowski and S. Yuen. Extending process languages with time. In *Proceedings of AMAST*, LNCS 1349, pages 524–538, 1997.

Rule Formats for Non Interference[*]

Simone Tini

Dipartimento di Scienze CC.FF.MM., Università dell'Insubria, Via Valleggio 11,
I-22100, Como, Italy
simone.tini@uninsubria.it

Abstract. We present the *SBSNNI rule format*. We prove that any
Process Algebra construct whose SOS-style semantics is defined by SOS
transition rules respecting such a format, preserves the well known non
interference properties Persistent BNDC, SBSNNI, and SBNDC.

1   Introduction

One of the problems in computer security is the necessity to guarantee that only
legitimate users can access some kind of information. To face this problem, one
should take into account that malicious users could attempt to access information
not only directly, but also indirectly through so called *covert channels*.

In *multilevel systems* [4], users are bound to several levels of security, and
it must be guaranteed that users at any level cannot *interfere* with users at
lower levels and cause different status of the system in which they operate to be
perceived. This means that *information flow* from high levels to lower levels must
be prevented. A drastic solution to this kind of problems is to avoid at all these
possible interferences. A lot of *non interference* definitions have been proposed
in the literature since [11], for several formal models of interaction between users.
In most of these papers, for simplicity multilevel systems are represented by two
level systems: Users are bound either to a *high level* of security, or to a *low level*
of security. In [6,7,8,16,3,15] some of the non interference definitions given in the
literature have been translated into the context of *Process Algebras*.

The most successful non interference definition in [6,7,8] is called
Bisimulation-based Non Deducibility on Compositions (BNDC, for short). Intuitively, a system enforces BNDC if, by interacting with any possible high level
user, the system always appears the same to low level users. Among the other
non interference definitions in [6,7,8], we mention *Strong Bisimulation Strong
Non-deterministic Non Interference* (SBSNNI, for short), which is stronger than
BNDC, and *Strong BNDC* (SBNDC, for short), which, in turn, is stronger than
SBSNNI. The mentioned properties are studied for systems specified by using
the language of *Security Process Algebra* (SPA, for short), which is an extension
of CCS [13] tailored to deal with two level systems. BNDC has been a successful
non interference definition for systems lying in static contexts. In [9] it has been

---

[*] Research partially supported by Progetto Cofinanziato "Metodi Formali per la Sicurezza e il Tempo" (Mefisto)

P. Degano (Ed.): ESOP 2003, LNCS 2618, pp. 129–143, 2003.
© Springer-Verlag Berlin Heidelberg 2003

shown that BNDC is too weak for systems running into a dynamic environment that can be reconfigured at run-time, or, equivalently, for systems that can migrate on the web during their computation. For this reason, the more restrictive non interference definition of *Persistent BNDC* (P_BNDC, for short) has been introduced. Intuitively, a system enforces P_BNDC if every state that can be reached by the system during its computation enforces BNDC. This means that even if the environment changes during the execution of the system, the security of the system is not compromised. P_BNDC is equivalent to SBSNNI, meaning that any system enforces P_BNDC if and only if it enforces SBSNNI (see [9]).

All the mentioned non interference properties are not, in general, *compositional*, meaning that there are constructs of SPA that do not preserve them. This is a critical issue, since one is not guaranteed that by putting a secure system into a SPA context, the obtained system is, in turn, secure. Another consequence of non compositionality is that the non interference properties cannot be checked compositionally with respect to the syntactic structure of systems [8,12].

In the present paper we argue that the non compositionality of the non interference properties depends on general *semantic properties* of SPA constructs. This implies that other Process Algebras having constructs with the same semantic properties suffer of the same problem. This is a typical situation in Process Algebras: A big amount of results depend on general semantic properties of the language constructs and do not depend on the particular language that is considered. An interesting challenge is to develop a meta theory for Process Algebras to study which semantic properties the constructs must have to preserve non interference properties. To this purpose, we recall that since the pioneering work [17], the concept of *rule format* has played a major rôle to develop meta theories for Process Algebras endowed with a *Structural Operational Semantics* [14] (SOS, for short). A rule format consists of a set of restrictions on the syntax of the SOS transition rules admitted. In particular, several rule formats have been proposed for ensuring that a given behavioral preorder (resp. equivalence) notion over processes is a precongruence (resp. congruence) (see [2] for a survey). Now, in the present paper we present the *SBSNNI rule format*, and we prove that any Process Algebra construct preserves both SBSNNI (and, therefore, P_BNDC) and SBNDC, provided that the operational semantics of such a construct is given by SOS transition rules respecting the SBSNNI format.

In Section 2 we recall SPA and the various non interference properties. In Section 3 we define our rule format. In Section 4 we prove that all constraints on SOS transition rules are needed. In Section 5 we prove that the format is correct for SBSNNI and SBNDC. Finally, in Section 6 we draw some conclusions.

2   Security Process Algebra

The *Security Process Algebra* (SPA) [6] models systems where the set *Act* of the actions that can be performed by each (sub)system is partitioned into a set of *visible input actions*, ranged over by $a, a_1, \ldots$, a set of *visible output actions*, ranged over by $\overline{a}, \overline{a_1}, \ldots$, and the *invisible action* τ, which models an internal computation step that cannot be observed outside the system. A *complementation function* $(\text{-}) : Act \rightarrow Act$ is defined over actions such that $\overline{\overline{a}} = a$, for each $a \in Act \setminus \{\tau\}$, and $\overline{\tau} = \tau$. The intuition is that actions a and $\overline{a}$ performed by two processes running in parallel can synchronize, thus producing action τ.

To reflect two different levels of security, the set of (input and output) visible actions is partitioned into the set H of *high actions*, ranged over by $h, h_1, \ldots,$ $\overline{h}, \overline{h_1}, \ldots$, and the set L of *low actions*, ranged over by $l, l_1, \ldots, \overline{l}, \overline{l_1}, \ldots$. Both sets H and L are closed under complementation.

The abstract syntax of SPA is given by the grammar below:

$$E ::= 0 \mid \mu \cdot E \mid E_1 + E_2 \mid E_1 | E_2 \mid E \setminus A \mid E[f]$$

where $E, E_1, \ldots$ are SPA process variables, μ is an action in Act, A is a set of actions in $Act \setminus \{\tau\}$ closed w.r.t. complementation, and $f : Act \rightarrow Act$ is a relabeling function over actions such that $f(\tau) = \tau$.

Process 0 does nothing. Process $\mu \cdot E$ performs action μ and then behaves as E. Process $E_1 + E_2$ can choose nondeterministically to behave like either E_1 or E_2. Process $E_1 | E_2$ is the parallel composition of E_1 and E_2, which interleave and can synchronize on complementary actions, thus producing action τ. Process $E \setminus A$ behaves as E, but it cannot perform actions in A. Finally, process $E[f]$ behaves as the process E where all actions are relabeled by function f. The SOS style semantics of SPA is given by the SOS transition rules in Table 1.

Table 1. The SOS transition rules for SPA

$$\frac{}{\mu \cdot E \xrightarrow{\mu} E} \qquad \frac{E_1 \xrightarrow{\mu} E_1'}{E_1 + E_2 \xrightarrow{\mu} E_1'} \qquad \frac{E_2 \xrightarrow{\mu} E_2'}{E_1 + E_2 \xrightarrow{\mu} E_2'}$$

$$\frac{E_1 \xrightarrow{\mu} E_1'}{E_1 | E_2 \xrightarrow{\mu} E_1' | E_2} \qquad \frac{E_2 \xrightarrow{\mu} E_2'}{E_1 | E_2 \xrightarrow{\mu} E_1 | E_2'} \qquad \frac{E_1 \xrightarrow{\mu} E_1' \ E_2 \xrightarrow{\overline{\mu}} E_2'}{E_1 | E_2 \xrightarrow{\tau} E_1' | E_2'} \ \mu \neq \tau$$

$$\frac{E \xrightarrow{\mu} E'}{E \setminus A \xrightarrow{\mu} E' \setminus A} \ \mu \notin A \qquad \frac{E \xrightarrow{\mu} E'}{E[f] \xrightarrow{f(\mu)} E'[f]}$$

As in [8], for any set of actions $A \subseteq Act$, we denote with E/A the process $E[f]$ such that $f(\mu) \equiv \begin{cases} \tau & \text{if } \mu \in A \\ \mu & \text{otherwise.} \end{cases}$

Moreover, we denote with $\mathcal{E}$ the set of all processes.

Let us recall the notion of weak bisimulation [13] over SPA processes. We need before some more notation.

Let $E \xRightarrow{\hat{\mu}} E'$ be either a shorthand for $E(\xrightarrow{\tau})^* E_1 \xrightarrow{\mu} E_2(\xrightarrow{\tau})^* E'$, if $\mu \in Act \setminus \{\tau\}$, or a shorthand for $E(\xrightarrow{\tau})^* E'$, if $\mu = \tau$. (As usual $(\xrightarrow{\tau})^*$ denotes a possibly empty sequence of τ transitions.)

Let $E \Longrightarrow E'$ denote that E' is *reachable* from E, i.e. either $E \xRightarrow{\hat{\tau}} E'$, or there is a sequence $\mu_1 \ldots \mu_n \in Act^*$ such that $E \xRightarrow{\hat{\mu_1}} \ldots \xRightarrow{\hat{\mu_n}} E'$.

Definition 1. *A relation $R \subseteq \mathcal{E} \times \mathcal{E}$ is a* weak bisimulation *if $(E, F) \in R$ implies, for all $\mu \in Act$,*

- *whenever $E \overset{\mu}{\longrightarrow} E'$ for some process E', then there is a process F' such that $F \overset{\hat{\mu}}{\Longrightarrow} F'$ and $(E', F') \in R$*
- *whenever $F \overset{\mu}{\longrightarrow} F'$ for some process F', then there is a process E' such that $E \overset{\hat{\mu}}{\Longrightarrow} E'$ and $(E', F') \in R$.*

Two SPA processes E, F are weakly bisimilar, *written $E \approx F$, iff there is a weak bisimulation containing the pair (E, F).*

Let us recall the notion of BNDC [6,7,8]. Let $\mathcal{E}_H$ denote the set of all SPA processes in $\mathcal{E}$ having only actions in $H \cup \{\tau\}$.

Definition 2. *A process E enforces the property of* Bisimulation-based Non Deducibility on Compositions, *written E is BNDC, iff*

$$\text{for each process } F \in \mathcal{E}_H, \text{ it holds that } (E|F) \setminus H \approx E/H$$

As explained in [6,7,8], E/H is what a low level observer can see of E, i.e. the part of E with which such an observer can synchronize. So, E is BNDC if, for each high level process F, a low level observer cannot distinguish E from $(E|F) \setminus H$, i.e. what the low level observer can see of E is not modified by composing any high level process F in parallel with E and by forcing synchronization on high actions between E and F.

In [9] it is shown that BNDC guarantees non interference only in static contexts. To guarantee non interference in completely dynamic hostile environments, the property of Persistent BNDC has been defined.

Definition 3. *A process E enforces the property of* Persistent BNDC, *written E is P_BNDC, iff*

$$\text{for each process } E' \in \mathcal{E}, E \Longrightarrow E' \text{ implies that } E' \text{ is BNDC}$$

P_BNDC requires that each state that is reachable from E is BNDC.

We recall also the property SBSNNI [6,7,8], which is equivalent to P_BNDC and does not require universal quantification over high level processes.

Definition 4. *A process E enforces the property of* Strong Bisimulation Strong Non-deterministic Non Interference, *written E is SBSNNI, iff*

$$\text{for each process } E' \in \mathcal{E}, E \Longrightarrow E' \text{ implies that } E' \setminus H \approx E'/H$$

Finally, we recall the property SBNDC [6,7,8].

Definition 5. *A process E enforces the property of* Strong BNDC, *written E is SBNDC, iff*

$$\text{for processes } E', E'' \in \mathcal{E}, E \Longrightarrow E' \overset{h}{\longrightarrow} E'' \text{ implies that } E' \setminus H \approx E'' \setminus H$$

SBNDC requires that before and after each high action, the system appears to be the same, for a low level perspective.

The following results on non interference properties were proved in [6,9].

Proposition 1. *If a process is SBNDC then it is SBSNNI. A process is SBSNNI if and only if it is P_BNDC. If a process is SBSNNI then it is BNDC.*

Both SBSNNI and SBNDC are preserved by operators "|" and "\" (see [6]). Unfortunately, they are not preserved by operator "+", as it is shown below.

Example 1. Let $E \equiv h_1 \cdot l_1 \cdot 0 + l_1 \cdot 0$ and $F \equiv h_2 \cdot l_2 \cdot 0 + l_2 \cdot 0$. Both processes E and F are SBSNNI and SBNDC. Intuitively, in both processes, the high action guards a low action that can be performed also without performing the high action. The process $E + F$ is neither SBSNNI nor SBNDC. Intuitively, by performing the high action h_1, $E + F$ reaches a state in which it has no choice and it can perform only action l_1. Analogously, by performing the high action h_2, $E + F$ reaches a state in which it has no choice and it can perform only action l_2. Now, without performing any high action, $E + F$ is in a state in which it can choose between performing l_1 or l_2. So, such a state cannot be simulated by the two states reached by performing h_1 or h_2. Formally, the process E' reachable from E that violates conditions of Def. 4 is E itself. The processes E' and E'' that violate conditions of Def. 5 are E and the process reachable through h_1 (or that reachable through h_2), respectively.

3   The Format SBSNNI

In this section we present the format SBSNNI.

Let us return to Example 1. The reason for which process $E + F$ is neither SBSNNI nor SBNDC is that the high action h_1 of E forces $E + F$ to discard F (and, symmetrically, the high action h_2 of F forces $E + F$ to discard E).

We note that a quite similar reason implies another well know problem of operator $+$, i.e. that it does not preserve weak bisimulation (see [13]). In fact, notwithstanding $\tau \cdot a \cdot 0 \approx a \cdot 0$, it holds that $\tau \cdot a \cdot 0 + b \cdot 0 \not\approx a \cdot 0 + b \cdot 0$. Here the problem is that action τ of $\tau \cdot a \cdot 0 + b \cdot 0$ forces $\tau \cdot a \cdot 0 + b \cdot 0$ to discard $b \cdot 0$. To preserve weak bisimulation, operator $+$ must be *patient*, meaning that, given any process $E + F$, the performance of some action τ by E (resp. F) should not imply discarding F (resp. E). To this purpose, as it has been observed in [5,18, 10], SOS transition rules of Table 1 for operator $+$ must require that μ is not action τ, and, moreover, *patient rules* for operator $+$ must be added as below:

$$\frac{E \xrightarrow{\tau} E'}{E + F \xrightarrow{\tau} E' + F} \qquad\qquad \frac{F \xrightarrow{\tau} F'}{E + F \xrightarrow{\tau} E + F'}$$

In order to preserve SBSNNI and SBNDC, operator $+$ must have rules for high actions similar to the patient rules above.

Before introducing our format, we recall that, in general, the abstract syntax of a process algebra is given by a *signature* Σ, i.e. a set of *function* symbols with their *arities*. The algebra of (open) *terms* freely constructed over a set of variables Var (ranged over by $E, F, \ldots$) by applying function symbols in Σ is ranged over by t, s, r. Terms that do not contain variables are called *closed terms*, or *processes*, and are ranged over by p, q. A SOS *transition rule* (with only positive premises and without predicates) ρ has the form $\frac{H}{\alpha}$, where:

- H is a collection of *premises* of the form $t \xrightarrow{\mu} t'$
- α is a *conclusion* of the form $s \xrightarrow{\mu_1} s'$, where term s is called the *source* of ρ, term s' is called the *target* of ρ, and μ_1 is called the *action* of ρ.

Definition 6. *A Process Algebra having operator "·" of CCS and defined by SOS transition rules is SBSNNI if:*

1. *For each high action $h \in H$, the following transition rule is admitted:*

$$\overline{h \cdot E \xrightarrow{h} E}$$

2. *Transition rules ρ of the following form are admitted:*

$$\frac{\{E_i \xrightarrow{l_i} F_i \mid i \in I(\rho)\}}{f(E_1, \ldots, E_n) \xrightarrow{\mu} t}, \ \ where:$$

   - $I(\rho) \subseteq \{1, \ldots, n\}$
   - $l_i \in L$ *for each* $i \in I(\rho)$, *and* $\mu \in L \cup \{\tau\}$
   - $E_1, F_1, \ldots, E_n, F_n$ *are the only variables occurring in ρ, and no variable E_i with $i \in I(\rho)$ occurs in the target t*
   - *no subterm $h \cdot s$ appears in t, for any $h \in H$.*

3. *Transition rules ρ of the following form are admitted:*

$$\frac{\{E_i \xrightarrow{h_i} F_i \mid i \in I(\rho)\}}{f(E_1, \ldots, E_n) \xrightarrow{\mu} f(F'_1, \ldots, F'_n)}, \ \ where:$$

   - $I(\rho) \subseteq \{1, \ldots, n\}$ *and* $I(\rho) \neq \emptyset$
   - $h_i \in H$ *for each* $i \in I(\rho)$, *and* $\mu \in H \cup \{\tau\}$
   - *for each* $i \in \{1, \ldots, n\}$, $F'_i \equiv \begin{cases} F_i & if\ i \in I(\rho) \\ E_i & otherwise. \end{cases}$

4. *For all transition rules ρ, and all $i \in I(\rho)$, there is a* patient transition rule

$$\frac{E_i \xrightarrow{\tau} F_i}{f(E_1, \ldots, E_n) \xrightarrow{\tau} f(E_1, \ldots, E_{i-1}, F_i, E_{i+1}, \ldots, E_n)}$$

   and, moreover, for each action $h \in H$, there is a H-patient transition rule

$$\frac{E_i \xrightarrow{h} F_i}{f(E_1, \ldots, E_n) \xrightarrow{h} f(E_1, \ldots, E_{i-1}, F_i, E_{i+1}, \ldots, E_n)}$$

5. *No further transition rule is admitted.*

Notice that, on one hand, clause 1 above implies that high prefixing cannot preserve SBSNNI and SBNDC. On the other hand, clause 1 is reasonable and is needed to let processes perform high actions. So, we require that all operators except "·" preserve SBSNNI and SBNDC.

SPA becomes SBSNNI if we modify Table 1 as follows:

- in the transition rules for operator "+" we require that $\mu \notin H \cup \{\tau\}$, and we add the patience and H-patience transition rules for "+"
- in the transition rule for $E[f]$ we require that $f(h) \in H \cup \{\tau\}$, for each $h \in H$, and that $f(l) \in L \cup \{\tau\}$, for each $l \in L$, and we add the H-patience transition rules for $E[f]$
- in the transition rule for "\" we require that $A \subseteq L$
- no modification for transition rules for operators "·" and "|" is needed.

Let SPA' be SPA with these modifications. One could ask whether Def. 2 is well defined for SPA', since it considers process $(E|F) \setminus H$ and the operator \ of SPA' admits process $G \setminus A$ only if $A \subseteq L$. We have two (independent) explanations that this is not a contradiction. The first explanation is that the classic \ used in Def. 2 is defined outside the format, and Def. 2 is valid also for languages in which the classic \ is not defined. The idea is that, also for these languages, Def. 2 simply says that E is BNDC iff "what a low lever observer sees of E is not modified by composing any high level process F in parallel with E and by forcing synchronization on high actions between E and F", even if forcing synchronization on high actions is not admitted inside E. Here, classic \ is simply a tool that is used to discover whether there is some information flow in systems (that are specified without such a tool). The second explanation is that we could consider SPA' with the classic operator \ and require that all operators except \ and, obviously, · preserve non interference properties.

In the following, let us denote with $\oplus$ the operator + with patience and H-patience transition rules, and with + the classic operator defined in Table 1.

We conclude by observing that the formats in the literature that are closer to our format are *simply WB format* [5] and *de Simone format* [17]. Our format is more restrictive than simply WB format since simply WB does not distinguish between high and low actions and, therefore, it does not impose H-patience rules. As de Simone format, our format admits neither premises of the form $E \not\xrightarrow{\mu}$ (*negative premises*), nor variables appearing both in the left hand side of a premise and in the right hand side of another premise (*look ahead*), nor variables appearing in the left hand side of two premises (*double testing*), nor variables appearing both in the left hand side of a premise and in the target. Moreover, on one side, our format imposes H-patient rules, which are not considered by de Simone format, since it does not distinguish between high and low actions. On the other side, de Simone format does not admit variables to appear more than once in the target of transition rules, which is allowed by our format.

4   Necessity of Restrictions

In this section we show that all constraints of the SBSNNI format are needed. The necessity for having H-patience transition rules follows by Example 1.

First of all we show that SBSNNI format cannot admit transition rules where either high actions appear in premises and the action of the rule is low, or low actions appear in premises and the action of the rule is high.

Example 2. Let $p \equiv l_1 \cdot l_2 \cdot 0$. Process p is trivially SBSNNI and SBNDC. Let f be the function whose semantics is described by the following transition rules

$$\frac{E \xrightarrow{l_1} E'}{f(E) \xrightarrow{h} f(E')} \qquad \frac{E \xrightarrow{l_2} E'}{f(E) \xrightarrow{l_2} f(E')}$$

and by the patience and H-patience transition rules. Process $f(p)$ is isomorphic to $h \cdot l_2 \cdot 0$ and is neither SBSNNI nor SBNDC, since action h guards action l_2.

Let $p \equiv h_1 \cdot 0$ and $q \equiv h_2 \cdot 0$. Processes p and q are SBSNNI and SBNDC. Let f be the function whose semantics is described by the following transition rule

$$\frac{E \xrightarrow{h_1} E' \quad F \xrightarrow{h_2} F'}{f(E, F) \xrightarrow{l} f(E', F')}$$

and by the patience and H-patience transition rules. Process $f(p, q)$ is isomorphic to $h_1 \cdot h_2 \cdot 0 + h_2 \cdot h_1 \cdot 0 + l \cdot 0$, and it is neither SBSNNI nor SBNDC. In fact both actions h_1 and h_2 guard subprocesses that cannot perform the low action l, which can be performed in the initial state.

We show now that negative premises cannot be admitted in SBSNNI format.

Example 3. Let $p \equiv h \cdot l_1 \cdot \tau \cdot l_2 \cdot 0 \oplus l_1 \cdot l_2 \cdot 0$. Process p is isomorphic to $h \cdot (l_1 \cdot \tau \cdot l_2 \cdot 0 + l_1 \cdot l_2 \cdot 0) + l_1 \cdot l_2 \cdot 0$. It can be proved that p is SBSNNI and SBNDC. Intuitively, the reason is that the subprocess $l_1 \cdot \tau \cdot l_2 \cdot 0 + l_1 \cdot l_2 \cdot 0$ that is guarded by h is weakly bisimilar to the subprocess $l_1 \cdot l_2 \cdot 0$ that is not guarded by h. Let f, g be the functions whose semantics is described by the rules

$$\frac{E \xrightarrow{l_1} E'}{f(E) \xrightarrow{l_1} g(E')} \qquad \frac{E \xrightarrow{l_2} E'}{g(E) \xrightarrow{l_2} E'} \qquad \frac{E \xarrownot{l_2}}{g(E) \xrightarrow{l_3} 0}$$

and by the patience and H-patience transition rules. Process $f(p)$ is neither SBSNNI nor SBNDC. In fact, $f(p)$ can perform l_3 only in the branch guarded by h. So, process E' violating conditions of Def. 4 is $f(p)$, and processes E' and E'' violating conditions of Def. 5 are $f(p)$ and that reachable from $f(p)$ through h. Note that the subprocess $l_1 \cdot \tau \cdot l_2 \cdot 0 + l_1 \cdot l_2 \cdot 0$ in p that is guarded by h is weakly bisimilar to the subprocess $l_1 \cdot l_2 \cdot 0$ that is not guarded by h since $\approx$ does not distinguish $l_1 \cdot \tau \cdot l_2 \cdot 0$ and $l_1 \cdot l_2 \cdot 0$. On the contrary, $f(l_1 \cdot \tau \cdot l_2 \cdot 0 + l_1 \cdot l_2 \cdot 0)$ and $f(l_1 \cdot l_2 \cdot 0)$ are not weakly bisimilar. In fact, the former process can perform l_1 and reach $g(\tau \cdot l_2 \cdot 0)$, whereas if the latter process performs l_1, it can reach only $g(l_2 \cdot 0)$. So, $\tau \cdot l_2 \cdot 0$ cannot perform l_2, and, therefore, $g(\tau \cdot l_2 \cdot 0)$ can perform l_3, whereas $l_2 \cdot 0$ can perform l_2, and, therefore, $g(l_2 \cdot 0)$ cannot perform l_3.

We show now that double testing cannot be admitted in SBSNNI format.

Example 4. Let $q \equiv ((l_1 \cdot l_3 \cdot 0 \oplus l_2 \cdot l_4 \cdot 0) \mid (\overline{l_1} \cdot 0 \oplus \overline{l_2} \cdot 0)) \setminus \{l_1, l_2, \overline{l_1}, \overline{l_2}\}$. Process q is isomorphic to $\tau \cdot l_3 \cdot 0 + \tau \cdot l_4 \cdot 0$. Let $p \equiv ((h \cdot (l_3 \cdot 0 \oplus l_4 \cdot 0) \oplus l \cdot q) \mid \overline{l}) \setminus \{l, \overline{l}\}$. Process p is isomorphic to $h \cdot (l_3 \cdot 0 + l_4 \cdot 0 + \tau \cdot (\tau \cdot l_3 \cdot 0 + \tau \cdot l_4 \cdot 0)) + \tau \cdot (\tau \cdot l_3 \cdot 0 + \tau \cdot l_4 \cdot 0)$. It can be proved that p is SBSNNI and SBNDC. The reason is that the subprocess

$l_3 \cdot 0 + l_4 \cdot 0 + \tau \cdot (\tau \cdot l_3 \cdot 0 + \tau \cdot l_4 \cdot 0)$ that is guarded by h is weakly bisimilar to the subprocess $\tau \cdot (\tau \cdot l_3 \cdot 0 + \tau \cdot l_4 \cdot 0)$ that is not guarded by h. Let f be the function whose semantics is described by the following transition rule

$$\frac{E \xrightarrow{l_3} E' \quad E \xrightarrow{l_4} E''}{f(E) \xrightarrow{l_5} 0}$$

and by patience and H-patience rules. Process $f(p)$ is neither SBSNNI nor SB-NDC, since it can perform l_5 only in the branch guarded by h. As seen above, the subprocess $l_3 \cdot 0 + l_4 \cdot 0 + \tau \cdot (\tau \cdot l_3 \cdot 0 + \tau \cdot l_4 \cdot 0)$ in p guarded by h is weakly bisimilar to the subprocess $\tau \cdot (\tau \cdot l_3 \cdot 0 + \tau \cdot l_4 \cdot 0)$ that is not guarded by h. On the contrary, $f(l_3 \cdot 0 + l_4 \cdot 0 + \tau \cdot (\tau \cdot l_3 \cdot 0 + \tau \cdot l_4 \cdot 0))$ and $f(\tau \cdot (\tau \cdot l_3 \cdot 0 + \tau \cdot l_4 \cdot 0))$ are not weakly bisimilar. In fact, since $l_3 \cdot 0 + l_4 \cdot 0 + \tau \cdot (\tau \cdot l_3 \cdot 0 + \tau \cdot l_4 \cdot 0)$ can perform both l_3 and l_4, the former process performs l_5, whereas no subprocess reachable by $\tau \cdot (\tau \cdot l_3 \cdot 0 + \tau \cdot l_4 \cdot 0)$ can perform both l_3 and l_4 and, therefore, the latter process cannot perform l_5.

We show now that look ahead cannot be admitted in SBSNNI format.

Example 5. Let $p \equiv h \cdot l_1 \cdot l_2 \cdot 0 \oplus l_1 \cdot \tau \cdot l_2 \cdot 0$. Process p is isomorphic to $h \cdot (l_1 \cdot l_2 \cdot 0 + l_1 \cdot \tau \cdot l_2 \cdot 0) + l_1 \cdot \tau \cdot l_2 \cdot 0$ and is SBSNNI and SBNDC. Intuitively, the reason is that the subprocess $l_1 \cdot l_2 \cdot 0 + l_1 \cdot \tau \cdot l_2 \cdot 0$ guarded by h is weakly bisimilar to the subprocess $l_1 \cdot \tau \cdot l_2 \cdot 0$ not guarded by h. Let f be the function whose semantics is described by the following transition rule

$$\frac{E \xrightarrow{l_1} E' \quad E' \xrightarrow{l_2} E''}{f(E) \xrightarrow{l_3} 0} \qquad \frac{E \xrightarrow{l} E'}{f(E) \xrightarrow{l} E'} \text{ for any } l \in L$$

and by patience and H-patience rules. The process $f(p)$ is neither SBSNNI nor SBNDC. In fact, $f(p)$ can perform l_3 only in the branch guarded by h. Note that the subprocess $l_1 \cdot l_2 \cdot 0 + l_1 \cdot \tau \cdot l_2 \cdot 0$ in p that is guarded by h is weakly bisimilar to the subprocess $l_1 \cdot \tau \cdot l_2 \cdot 0$ that is not guarded by h since $\approx$ does not distinguish between $l_1 \cdot l_2 \cdot 0$ and $l_1 \cdot \tau \cdot l_2 \cdot 0$. On the contrary, $f(l_1 \cdot l_2 \cdot 0 + l_1 \cdot \tau \cdot l_2 \cdot 0)$ and $f(l_1 \cdot \tau \cdot l_2 \cdot 0)$ are not weakly bisimilar. In fact, since $l_1 \cdot l_2 \cdot 0$ can perform action l_1 followed by l_2, the former process can perform l_3, whereas actions l_1 and l_2 in $l_1 \cdot \tau \cdot l_2 \cdot 0$ are separated by τ and, therefore, $f(l_1 \cdot \tau \cdot l_2 \cdot 0)$ cannot perform l_3.

Finally, we show that in SBSNNI format variables appearing in left hand side of premises cannot appear in the target of the transition rule.

Example 6. Let p be the SBSNNI and SBNDC process of Example 4. Let f be the function whose semantics is described by the following transition rule

$$\frac{E \xrightarrow{l} E'}{f(E) \xrightarrow{l} f(E)} \text{ for any } l \in L$$

and by patience and H-patience rules. The process $f(p)$ is neither SBSNNI nor SBNDC, since it can perform infinite sequences of actions l_3 and l_4 only in the branch guarded by h. As we have seen in Ex. 4, the subprocess $l_3 \cdot 0 +$

$l_4 \cdot 0 + \tau \cdot (\tau \cdot l_3 \cdot 0 + \tau \cdot l_4 \cdot 0)$ in p guarded by h is weakly bisimilar to the subprocess $\tau \cdot (\tau \cdot l_3 \cdot 0 + \tau \cdot l_4 \cdot 0)$ that is not guarded by h. On the contrary, $f(l_3 \cdot 0 + l_4 \cdot 0 + \tau \cdot (\tau \cdot l_3 \cdot 0 + \tau \cdot l_4 \cdot 0))$ and $f(\tau \cdot (\tau \cdot l_3 \cdot 0 + \tau \cdot l_4 \cdot 0))$ are not weakly bisimilar. In fact, since $l_3 \cdot 0 + l_4 \cdot 0 + \tau \cdot (\tau \cdot l_3 \cdot 0 + \tau \cdot l_4 \cdot 0)$ can perform l_3 and l_4, the former process can perform l_3 and l_4 and can remain in the same state, i.e. it can perform an infinite sequence with both l_3 and l_4, whereas no subprocess reachable by $\tau \cdot (\tau \cdot l_3 \cdot 0 + \tau \cdot l_4 \cdot 0)$ can perform both l_3 and l_4 and, therefore, the latter process cannot perform an infinite sequence with both l_3 and l_4.

5   The Soundness of SBSNNI Format

In this section we prove that SBSNNI operators except high prefixing preserve SBSNNI and SBNDC. Since at first glance it could seem that SBSNNI and SB-NDC coincide under the assumption of patience and H-patience rules, we show that this is not the case, thus requiring a proof for each of the two properties.

Example 7. For process $p \equiv h \cdot l \cdot 0$ and the function f such that

$$\frac{E \xrightarrow{\mu} E'}{f(E) \xrightarrow{\mu} f(E')} \text{ for any } \mu \in Act \qquad \frac{E \xrightarrow{h} E'}{f(E) \xrightarrow{\tau} f(E')} \qquad \frac{E \xrightarrow{h} E'}{f(E) \xrightarrow{l} f(E')},$$

$f(p)$ is isomorphic to $\tau \cdot l \cdot 0 + l \cdot l \cdot 0 + h \cdot l \cdot 0$ and it is SBSNNI but not SBNDC.

As usual, a context $C(t_1, \ldots, t_n)$ is a term where terms $t_1, \ldots, t_n$ can appear. For context $C(E_1, \ldots, E_n)$ and terms $s_1, \ldots, s_n$, $C[s_1, \ldots, s_n \setminus E_1, \ldots, E_n]$ is the term obtained by replacing in $C(E_1, \ldots, E_n)$ each variable E_i with s_i.

The second sentence of the theorem below implies that SBSNNI is preserved by operators defined by SBSNNI format.

Theorem 1. *Let R be the set of pairs*

$$(C[r_1, \ldots, r_k \setminus E_1, \ldots, E_k] \setminus H, C[r'_1, \ldots, r'_k \setminus E_1, \ldots, E_k]/H)$$

where $C(E_1, \ldots, E_k)$ is a context that does not contain any term $h \cdot s$ with $h \in H$, and, for each $1 \le i \le k$, r_i, r'_i are SBSNNI and $r_i \setminus H \approx r'_i/H$. It holds that:

- *The set R is a weak bisimulation.*
- *Terms $C[r_1, \ldots, r_k \setminus E_1, \ldots, E_k]$ and $C[r'_1, \ldots, r'_k \setminus E_1, \ldots, E_k]$ are SBSNNI.*

Proof. For readability, in this proof we write $E \overset{A}{\Longrightarrow} E'$, with $A \subseteq Act$, to denote that there is a sequence $E \overset{\hat{\mu}_1}{\Longrightarrow} \ldots \overset{\hat{\mu}_n}{\Longrightarrow} E'$ with $\mu_1, \ldots, \mu_n \in A$.

We prove by induction over the syntactic structure of context $C(E_1, \ldots, E_k)$ the first sentence of the thesis. The second sentence follows from the first one. In fact, each process $\hat{r}$ reachable from $C[r_1, \ldots, r_k \setminus E_1, \ldots, E_k]$ has the form $C'[\hat{r}_1, \ldots, \hat{r}_k \setminus E_1, \ldots, E_k]$, for some context $C'(E_1, \ldots, E_k)$ that does not contain any subterm $h \cdot q$ with $h \in H$ and for some terms $\hat{r}_1, \ldots, \hat{r}_k$ that are reachable from $r_1, \ldots, r_k$, respectively (this fact can be immediately proved by induction over the number of transitions needed to reach $\hat{r}$). Now, since $\hat{r}_i$ is reachable from r_i and since r_i is SBSNNI, it holds that also $\hat{r}_i$ is SBSNNI, and, therefore, $\hat{r}_i \setminus H \approx$

$\hat{r}_i/H$. So, we can consider the first sentence of the thesis and we can instantiate, for each $1 \le i \le k$, r_i and r'_i with the same SBSNNI term $\hat{r}_i$, thus obtaining that $\hat{r} \setminus H \equiv C'[\hat{r}_1, \ldots, \hat{r}_k \setminus E_1, \ldots, E_k] \setminus H \approx C'[\hat{r}_1, \ldots, \hat{r}_k \setminus E_1, \ldots, E_k]/H \equiv \hat{r}/H$. So, since each term $\hat{r}$ reachable from $C[r_1, \ldots, r_k \setminus E_1, \ldots, E_k]$ satisfies $\hat{r} \setminus H \approx \hat{r}/H$, it holds that $C[r_1, \ldots, r_k \setminus E_1, \ldots, E_k]$ is SBSNNI. Analogously, we can prove that $C[r'_1, \ldots, r'_k \setminus E_1, \ldots, E_k]$ is SBSNNI.

So, let us prove by induction the first sentence of the thesis.

The base case $C(E_1, \ldots, E_n) \equiv c$ for a constant c is immediate, since clauses of SBSNNI format imply that each process reachable from c is a constant and that constants cannot perform high actions, thus ensuring that $c \setminus H \approx c/H$.

Also the base case $C(E_1, \ldots, E_k) \equiv E_i$ is immediate, since $E_i[r_1, \ldots, r_k \setminus E_1, \ldots, E_k] \equiv r_i$, $E_i[r'_1, \ldots, r'_k \setminus E_1, \ldots, E_k] \equiv r'_i$, and $r_i \setminus H \approx r'_i/H$ by the hypothesis.

As regards the inductive step, we assume the thesis for $C_1(E_1, \ldots, E_k)$, ..., $C_n(E_1, \ldots, E_k)$, and we prove it for $f(C_1(E_1, \ldots, E_k), \ldots, C_n(E_1, \ldots, E_k))$. To this purpose, for each $1 \le i \le n$, let us denote with t_i the term $C_i[r_1, \ldots, r_k \setminus E_1, \ldots, E_k]$, and with s_i the term $C_i[r'_1, \ldots, r'_k \setminus E_1, \ldots, E_k]$. We must prove that $f(t_1, \ldots, t_n) \setminus H \approx f(s_1, \ldots, s_n)/H$ follows from $t_i \setminus H \approx s_i/H$, for $1 \le i \le n$.

It suffices to prove the following properties:

1. $f(t_1, \ldots, t_n) \setminus H \xrightarrow{\mu} t$ implies $f(s_1, \ldots, s_n)/H \xrightarrow{\hat{\mu}} s$, for some term s such that $(t, s) \in R$

2. $f(s_1, \ldots, s_n)/H \xrightarrow{\mu} s$ implies $f(t_1, \ldots, t_n) \setminus H \xRightarrow{\hat{\mu}} t$, for some term t such that $(t, s) \in R$.

We should prove both properties, since the proofs are not perfectly symmetric, but for lack of space we prove only the first.

Let us assume that $f(t_1, \ldots, t_n) \setminus H \xrightarrow{\mu} t$. We have one of the following three cases:

1. Transition $f(t_1, \ldots, t_n) \setminus H \xrightarrow{\mu} t$ is inferred by means of the following proof:

$$\frac{\dfrac{\{t_i \xrightarrow{l_i} t'_i \mid i \in I(\rho)\}}{f(t_1, \ldots, t_n) \xrightarrow{\mu} G(\hat{t}_1, \ldots, \hat{t}_n)}}{f(t_1, \ldots, t_n) \setminus H \xrightarrow{\mu} G(\hat{t}_1, \ldots, \hat{t}_n) \setminus H}$$

where $l_i \in L$ for each $i \in I(\rho)$, $\mu \in L \cup \{\tau\}$, $t \equiv G(\hat{t}_1, \ldots, \hat{t}_n) \setminus H$ and $\hat{t}_i \equiv \begin{cases} t'_i & \text{if } i \in I(\rho) \\ t_i & \text{otherwise.} \end{cases}$ For each index $i \in I(\rho)$, $t_i \xrightarrow{l_i} t'_i$ with $l_i \in L$ implies $t_i \setminus H \xrightarrow{l_i} t'_i \setminus H$, which, in turn, implies that there is a term s'_i such that $s_i/H \xRightarrow{\hat{l}_i} s'_i/H$ and $t'_i \setminus H \approx s'_i/H$. Therefore, there are terms s''_i and s'''_i such that $s_i \xRightarrow{H \cup \{\tau\}} s''_i \xrightarrow{l_i} s'''_i \xRightarrow{H \cup \{\tau\}} s'_i$. Now, by patience and H-patience rules we obtain that

$$\frac{\{s_i \stackrel{H\cup\{\tau\}}{\Longrightarrow} s_i'' \mid i \in I(\rho)\}}{f(s_1,\ldots,s_n) \stackrel{H\cup\{\tau\}}{\Longrightarrow} f(\hat{s}_1'',\ldots,\hat{s}_n'')}}{f(s_1,\ldots,s_n)/H \stackrel{\hat{\tau}}{\Longrightarrow} f(\hat{s}_1'',\ldots,\hat{s}_n'')/H}$$

where $\hat{s}_i'' \equiv \begin{cases} s_i'' & \text{if } i \in I(\rho) \\ s_i & \text{otherwise.} \end{cases}$ Now, it holds that

$$\frac{\{s_i'' \stackrel{l_i}{\longrightarrow} s_i''' \mid i \in I(\rho)\}}{f(\hat{s}_1'',\ldots,\hat{s}_n'') \stackrel{\mu}{\longrightarrow} G(\hat{s}_1''',\ldots,\hat{s}_n''')}}{f(\hat{s}_1'',\ldots,\hat{s}_n'')/H \stackrel{\mu}{\longrightarrow} G(\hat{s}_1''',\ldots,\hat{s}_n''')/H}$$

where $\hat{s}_i''' \equiv \begin{cases} s_i''' & \text{if } i \in I(\rho) \\ s_i & \text{otherwise.} \end{cases}$ Finally, by patience and H-patience rules we obtain

$$\frac{\{s_i''' \stackrel{H\cup\{\tau\}}{\Longrightarrow} s_i' \mid i \in I(\rho)\}}{G(\hat{s}_1''',\ldots,\hat{s}_n''') \stackrel{H\cup\{\tau\}}{\Longrightarrow} G(\hat{s}_1',\ldots,\hat{s}_n')}}{G(\hat{s}_1''',\ldots,\hat{s}_n''')/H \stackrel{\hat{\tau}}{\Longrightarrow} G(\hat{s}_1',\ldots,\hat{s}_n')/H}$$

where $\hat{s}_i' \equiv \begin{cases} s_i' & \text{if } i \in I(\rho) \\ s_i & \text{otherwise.} \end{cases}$ Summarizing, it holds that $f(s_1,\ldots,s_n)/H \stackrel{\hat{\mu}}{\Longrightarrow}$ $G(\hat{s}_1',\ldots,\hat{s}_n')/H$. The term $G(\hat{s}_1',\ldots,\hat{s}_n')/H$ is the term s we were looking for. In fact, $(G(\hat{t}_1,\ldots,\hat{t}_n)\setminus H, G(\hat{s}_1',\ldots,\hat{s}_n')/H)$ is a pair in R, since, for each $1 \le i \le n$, $\hat{t}_i$ and $\hat{s}_i'$ are reachable from t_i and s_i, respectively, and are SBSNNI, and since, for each $i \in I(\rho)$, it holds that $\hat{t}_i \setminus H \equiv t_i' \setminus H \approx s_i'/H \equiv \hat{s}_i'/H$, and, for each $i \notin I(\rho)$, it holds that $\hat{t}_i \setminus H \equiv t_i \setminus H \approx s_i/H \equiv \hat{s}_i'/H$.

2. Transition $f(t_1,\ldots,t_n)\setminus H \stackrel{\mu}{\longrightarrow} t$ is inferred by means of the following proof:

$$\frac{\{t_i \stackrel{h_i}{\longrightarrow} t_i' \mid i \in I(\rho)\}}{f(t_1,\ldots,t_n) \stackrel{\tau}{\longrightarrow} f(\hat{t}_1,\ldots,\hat{t}_n)}}{f(t_1,\ldots,t_n)\setminus H \stackrel{\tau}{\longrightarrow} f(\hat{t}_1,\ldots,\hat{t}_n)\setminus H}$$

where $h_i \in H$ for each $i \in I(\rho)$, $\mu = \tau$, $t \equiv f(\hat{t}_1,\ldots,\hat{t}_n)\setminus H$, and $\hat{t}_i \equiv \begin{cases} t_i' & \text{if } i \in I(\rho) \\ t_i & \text{otherwise.} \end{cases}$ For each $i \in I(\rho)$, $t_i \stackrel{h_i}{\longrightarrow} t_i'$ with $h_i \in H$ implies $t_i/H \stackrel{\tau}{\longrightarrow}$ t_i'/H. Since t_i is SBSNNI, this last fact implies that $t_i \setminus H \stackrel{\hat{\tau}}{\Longrightarrow} t_i'' \setminus H$ for some term t_i'' such that $t_i'' \setminus H \approx t_i'/H$. It follows that there is a term s_i' such that $s_i/H \stackrel{\hat{\tau}}{\Longrightarrow} s_i'/H$ and $t_i'' \setminus H \approx s_i'/H$. Now, $s_i/H \stackrel{\hat{\tau}}{\Longrightarrow} s_i'/H$ is due to a sequence of transitions $s_i \stackrel{H\cup\{\tau\}}{\Longrightarrow} s_i'$. By patience and H-patience rules we obtain that

$$\frac{\{s_i \stackrel{H\cup\{\tau\}}{\Longrightarrow} s_i' \mid i \in I(\rho)\}}{f(s_1,\ldots,s_n) \stackrel{H\cup\{\tau\}}{\Longrightarrow} f(\hat{s}_1,\ldots,\hat{s}_n)}}{f(s_1,\ldots,s_n)/H \stackrel{\hat{\tau}}{\Longrightarrow} f(\hat{s}_1,\ldots,\hat{s}_n)/H}$$

where $\hat{s}_i \equiv \begin{cases} s'_i \text{ if } i \in I(\rho) \\ s_i \text{ otherwise.} \end{cases}$ Term $f(\hat{s}_1, \ldots, \hat{s}_n)/H$ is the term s we were looking for. In fact, $(f(\hat{t}_1, \ldots, \hat{t}_n) \setminus H, f(\hat{s}_1, \ldots, \hat{s}_n)/H)$ is a pair in R, since, for each $1 \leq i \leq n$, $\hat{t}_i$ and $\hat{s}_i$ are reachable from t_i and s_i, respectively, and are SBSNNI, and since, for each $i \in I(\rho)$, it holds that $\hat{t}_i \setminus H \equiv t'_i \setminus H \approx$ (since t'_i is reachable from t'_i and is SBSNNI) $t'_i/H \approx t''_i \setminus H \approx s'_i/H \equiv \hat{s}_i/H$, and, for each $i \notin I(\rho)$, it holds that $\hat{t}_i \setminus H \equiv t_i \setminus H \approx s_i/H \equiv \hat{s}_i/H$.

3. Transition $f(t_1, \ldots, t_n) \setminus H \xrightarrow{\mu} t$ is inferred by means of the following proof:

$$\frac{\dfrac{t_i \xrightarrow{\tau} t'_i}{f(t_1, \ldots, t_n) \xrightarrow{\tau} f(t_1, \ldots, t_{i-1}, t'_i, t_{i+1}, \ldots, t_n)}}{f(t_1, \ldots, t_n) \setminus H \xrightarrow{\tau} f(t_1, \ldots, t_{i-1}, t'_i, t_{i+1}, \ldots, t_n) \setminus H}$$

where $\mu = \tau$ and $t \equiv f(t_1, \ldots, t_{i-1}, t'_i, t_{i+1}, \ldots, t_n) \setminus H$. Since $t_i \xrightarrow{\tau} t'_i$, it holds that $t_i \setminus H \xrightarrow{\tau} t'_i \setminus H$, which implies that there is some term s'_i such that $s_i/H \xRightarrow{\hat{\tau}} s'_i/H$ and $t'_i \setminus H \approx s'_i/H$. The sequence of transitions $s_i/H \xRightarrow{\hat{\tau}} s'_i/H$ is inferred by a sequence $s_i \xRightarrow{H \cup \{\tau\}} s'_i$. By patience and H-patience rules we obtain

$$\frac{\dfrac{s_i \xRightarrow{H \cup \{\tau\}} s'_i}{f(s_1, \ldots, s_n) \xRightarrow{H \cup \{\tau\}} f(s_1, \ldots, s_{i-1}, s'_i, s_{i+1}, \ldots, s_n)}}{f(s_1, \ldots, s_n)/H \xRightarrow{\hat{\tau}} f(s_1, \ldots, s_{i-1}, s'_i, s_{i+1}, \ldots, s_n)/H}$$

The term $f(s_1, \ldots, s_{i-1}, s'_i, s_{i+1}, \ldots, s_n)/H$ is the term s we were looking for. In fact, the pair $(f(t_1, \ldots, t_{i-1}, t'_i, t_{i+1}, \ldots, t_n) \setminus H, f(s_1, \ldots, s_{i-1}, s'_i, s_{i+1}, \ldots, s_n)/H)$ is in R, since $t'_i \setminus H \approx s'_i/H$, t'_i and s'_i are reachable from t_i and s_i, respectively, and are SBSNNI, and, for each $j \neq i$, $t_j \setminus H \approx s_j/H$. □

The second sentence of the theorem below implies that SBNDC is preserved by operators defined by SBSNNI format.

Theorem 2. *Let R be the set of pairs*

$$(C[r_1, \ldots, r_k \setminus E_1, \ldots, E_k] \setminus H, C[r'_1, \ldots, r'_k \setminus E_1, \ldots, E_k] \setminus H)$$

where $C(E_1, \ldots, E_k)$ is a context that does not contain any term $h \cdot s$ with $h \in H$, and, for each $1 \leq i \leq k$, r_i, r'_i are SBNDC and $r_i \setminus H \approx r'_i \setminus H$. It holds that:

- *The set R is a weak bisimulation.*
- *Terms $C[r_1, \ldots, r_k \setminus E_1, \ldots, E_k]$, and $C[r'_1, \ldots, r'_k \setminus E_1, \ldots, E_k]$ are SBNDC.*

6 Conclusions

We have presented the SBSNNI format. It guarantees that all operators, except high prefixing, preserve SBSNNI and SBNDC [6,7,8], which are successful non interference properties for systems running into dynamic environments (systems migrating on the network). Compositionality of non interference properties is useful since by composing secure (according to the property chosen) processes, one obtains secure processes. Moreover, compositionality can be exploited also to check non interference inductively with respect to the structure of the system.

We have compared our format with those in the literature. We have shown by some examples that all the restrictions imposed by the format are needed.

Our next aim is to extend our results by proposing formats for other non interference properties. We shall consider BNDC [6,7,8], which is a successful property for systems running into static environments, and the properties defined in [3,15,16]. Finally, we aim to understand what addition to our format is needed to have compositionality also w.r.t. high prefixing. Our starting point is that it seems natural to think that if E is secure, then $h \cdot E + \tau \cdot E$ is also secure, i.e. that high prefixing could be admitted provided that a duplicate of its derivative can be reached also through a silent action.

References

1. L. Aceto and W.J. Fokkink, editors, Special issue on process algebra, Information Processing Letters, 80, 2001.
2. L. Aceto, W.J. Fokkink, and C. Verhoef, Structural operational semantics, in J.A. Bergstra, A. Ponse, and S.A. Smolka, editors, Handbook of Process Algebra, Elsevier, Amsterdam, 2001, 197–292.
3. P.G. Allen, A comparison of non interference and non deducibility using CSP, Proc. IEEE Computer Security Foundation Workshop, IEEE Computer Society Press, 1991, 43–54.
4. D. Bell and L.J. La Padula, Secure computer systems: Unified exposition and multics interpretation, Technical report ESD-TR-75-301, MITRE MTR-2997, 1976.
5. B. Bloom, Structural operational semantics for weak bisimulation, Theoretical Computer Science, 146, 1995, 25–68.
6. R. Focardi and R. Gorrieri, A classification of security properties for process algebras, Journal of Computer Security, 3, 1995, 5–33.
7. R. Focardi and R. Gorrieri, The compositional security checker: A tool for the verification of information flow security properties, IEEE Transactions on Software Engineering, 23, 1997, 550–571.
8. R. Focardi and R. Gorrieri, Classification of security properties (Part I: Information flow), Foundations of Security Analysis and Design, Tutorial Lectures, Lecture Notes in Computer Science, 2171, Springer, Berlin, 2001, 331–396.
9. R. Focardi and S. Rossi, Information flow security in dynamic contexts, Proc. IEEE Computer Security Foundation Workshop, IEEE Computer Society Press, 2002, 307–319.
10. W.J. Fokkink, Rooted branching bisimulation as a congruence, Journal of Computer and System Sciences, 60, 2000, 13–37.
11. J.A. Goguen and J. Meseguer, Security policy and security models, Proc. IEEE Symposium on Security and Privacy, IEEE Computer Society Press, 1982, 11–20.
12. F. Martinelli, Partial model checking and theorem proving for ensuring security properties, Proc. IEEE Computer Security Foundation Workshop, IEEE Computer Society Press, 1998, 44–52.

13. R. Milner, Communication and concurrency, Prentice-Hall, London, 1989.
14. G. Plotkin, A structural approach to operational semantics, Technical report DAIMI FN-19, University of Aarhus, Denmark, 1981.
15. A.W. Roscoe, J.C.P. Woodcock, and L. Wulf, Non interference through determinism, Proc. European Symposium on Research in Computer Security, Lecture Notes in Computer Science, 875, Springer, Berlin, 1994, 33–53.
16. P.Y.A. Ryan, A CSP formulation of non-interference, Proc. IEEE Computer Security Foundation Workshop, IEEE Computer Society Press, 1990.
17. R. De Simone, Higher level synchronization devices in SCCS-Meije, Theoretical Computer Science, 37, 1985, 245–267.
18. I. Ulidowski and I. Phillips, Formats of ordered SOS rules with silent actions, Proc. Theory and Practice of Software Development, Lecture Notes in Computer Science, 1214, Springer, Berlin, 1997, 297–308.

On the Secure Implementation of Security Protocols*

Pablo Giambiagi and Mads Dam

Swedish Institute of Computer Science
Box 1263, S-164 49 Kista, Sweden
{pablo,mfd}@sics.se

Abstract. We consider the problem of implementing a security protocol in such a manner that secrecy of sensitive data is not jeopardized. Implementation is assumed to take place in the context of an API that provides standard cryptography and communication services. Given a dependency specification, stating how API methods can produce and consume secret information, we propose an information flow property based on the idea of invariance under perturbation, relating observable changes in output to corresponding changes in input. Besides the information flow condition itself, the main contributions of the paper are results relating the admissibility property to a direct flow property in the special case of programs which branch on secrets only in cases permitted by the dependency rules. These results are used to derive an unwinding-like theorem, reducing a behavioral correctness check (strong bisimulation) to an invariant.

1 Introduction

We consider the problem of securely implementing a security protocol given an API providing standard services for cryptography, communication, key- and buffer management. In particular we are interested in the problem of confidentiality, that is, to show that a given protocol implementation which uses standard features for encryption, random number generation, input-output etc. does not leak confidential information provided to it, either because of malicious intent, or because of bugs.

Both problems are real. Malicious implementations (Trojans) can leak intercepted information using anything from simple direct transmission to, e.g., subliminal channels, power, or timing channels. Bugs can arise because of field values that are wrongly constructed, mistaken representations, nonces that are reused or generated in predictable ways, or misused random number generators, to give just a few examples.

Our work starts from the assumption that the protocol and the API is known. The task, then, is to ensure that confidential data is used at the correct times and in the correct way by API methods. The constraints must necessarily be quite rigid and detailed. For instance, a non-constant time API method which is made freely available to be applied to data containing secrets can immediately be used in conjunction with otherwise legitimate output to create a timing leak.

---

* This material is based upon work partially supported by the European Office of Aerospace Research and Development, Air Force Office of Scientific Research, Air Force Research Laboratory, under Contract No. F61775-01-C0006, and by the European IST project VerifiCard.

P. Degano (Ed.): ESOP 2003, LNCS 2618, pp. 144–158, 2003.

Our approach is to formulate a set of rules, which determine the required dependencies between those API method calls that produce and/or consume secrets. An example of such a dependency rule might be

$$\textbf{send}(v, \text{outchan}) \leftarrow k := \textbf{key}(\text{Bob}) \wedge m := \textbf{receive}(\text{inchan}) \wedge v := \text{enc}(m, k)$$

indicating that, if upon its last invocation of the **receive** method with argument inchan the protocol received m (and analogously for **key**, Bob, and k), then the next invocation of **send** with second parameter outchan must, as its first parameter, receive the encryption of m with key k.

A dependency specification determines an information flow property. The rules determine a required dependency relation between API calls. Assurance, then, must be given that no other flows involving secrets exist. Our approach to this is based on the notion of admissibility, introduced first in [4]. The idea is to extract from the dependency specification a set of system perturbation functions g which will allow a system s processing a secret v to act as if it is actually processing another value of that secret, v'. Then, confidentiality is tantamount to showing that system behaviour is invariant under perturbation, i.e. that

$$s[g] \sim s,$$

where $[g]$ is the system perturbation operator. One problem is that, provided this is licensed by the dependency rules, secrets actually become visible at the external interface. For this reason, the perturbation operator $[g]$ must be able to identify the appropriate cases where this applies, so that internal changes in the choice of secret can be undone.

The paper has two main contributions. First, we show how the idea can be realized in the context of a simple sequential imperative language, IMP0. Secondly we establish results which provide efficient (thought not yet fully automated) verification techniques, and give credence to the claim that admissibility is a good formalisation of confidentiality in this context. In particular, we show that, for the special case of programs which branch on secrets only in cases permitted by the dependency rules, admissibility can be reduced to a direct flow property (an invariant) which we call flow compatibility. Vice versa, we show that under some additional assumptions, flow compatibility can be reduced to admissibility.

This work clearly has strong links to previous work in the area of information flow theory and language-based security (cf. [8]). The idea of invariance under perturbation and logical relations underpins most work on secrecy and information flow theory, though not always very explicitly (cf. [3,5,11,9]). The main point, in contrast e.g. to work by Volpano [10] is that we make no attempt to address information flow of a cryptographic program in absolute terms, but are satisfied with controlling the use of cryptographic primitives according to some external protocol specification. This is obviously a much weaker analysis, but at the same time it reflects well, we believe, the situation faced by the practical protocol implementor.

The rest of the paper is structured as follows. In Section 2, we present IMP0 and introduce the main example used in the paper, a rudimentary credit card payment protocol. In Section 3 we introduce an annotated semantics, used in Section 4 to formalize the dependency rules. The notion of flow compatibility is presented in Section 5 to describe the direct information flow required by a protocol specification. In Section 6 the main

Table 1. IMP0: Syntax

Basic values (BVal)	$b ::= n \mid a \mid \textbf{true} \mid (b_1, \ldots, b_n)$
Values (Val)	$v ::= b \mid \textbf{xcpt}$
Functions (Fun)	$f ::= \text{pf} \mid h$
Expressions (Expr)	$e ::= v \mid x \mid (e_1, \ldots, e_n) \mid f\ e$
Commands (Com)	$c ::= \textbf{skip} \mid \textbf{throw} \mid x := e \mid c_0; c_1 \mid \textbf{if } e \textbf{ then } c_0 \textbf{ else } c_1 \mid$
	$\textbf{while } e \textbf{ do } c \textbf{ end} \mid \textbf{try } c_0 \textbf{ catch } c_1$

information flow condition, admissibility, is introduced. In Section 7 we state and prove the unwinding theorem, while in Section 8 we further investigate the relation between flow compatibility and admissibility. Finally Section 9 concludes with discussion and related work.

2 A Sequential Imperative Language

In this section we introduce IMP0, the language we use for protocol implementation. The intention is to formalise the basic functionality of simple protocol implementations in as uncontroversial a manner as possible.

Table 1 defines the syntax of IMP0, with variables $x \in \text{Var}$, including the anonymous variable _ , primitive function and procedure calls, and primitive data types including natural numbers ($n \in \text{Nat}$) and channels ($a \in \text{Chan}$). The set of primitive function symbols, ranged over by pf, includes the standard arithmetic and logical operators. Each primitive function is assumed to execute in constant time, regardless of its arguments. There are also non-primitive (or API) functions, ranged over by h, for encryption (**enc**), decryption (**dec**), extracting a key from a keystore (**key**), and receiving resp. sending a value on a channel (**receive** and **send**). To each (primitive or non-primitive) function symbol f is associated a binary relation $f \subseteq \text{Val} \times \text{Val}_\perp$ so that $\forall v \in \text{Val}. \exists v' \in \text{Val}_\perp. f(v, v')$ (i.e. functions may be non-deterministic, and may not terminate), and $f(\textbf{xcpt}, v)$ iff $v = \textbf{xcpt}$ (i.e. function invocations propagate exceptions from arguments to results). Moreover, primitive functions are assumed not to have local side effects. Communication effects are brought out using transition labels in the next section.

As a running example we use a greatly simplified version of the 1-Key-Protocol (1KP), a protocol for electronic payments [2]. This example is chosen because it is paradigmatic for many simple e-commerce applets which input a collection of data, some sensitive, some not, performs some cryptographic operations on the data, and then transmits the result on a public channel. In the full version of the paper [6] we use a simple declassifier as a second example.

2.1 A Simple Payment Protocol

The protocol involves three players: A Customer, a Merchant and an Acquirer (ACQ). The Customer possesses a credit card account (ACC) with which it places an order to the

Prog 1 :

   while true do

     ACQ := **receive** acq; ORDER := **receive** order; ACC := **receive** acc;

     try

       PKA := **key** ACQ;

       _ := **send**((ACQ, ORDER, **enc**((ORDER, ACC), PKA)), **lookup**(merchant))

     catch

       _ := **send**("error report", local)

   end

Fig. 1. Payment protocol – sample Customer implementation

Merchant. The Acquirer is a front-end to the existing credit card clearing/authorization network, that receives payments records from merchants and responds by either accepting or rejecting the request. The Customer is required to encrypt the order and account information with the Acquirer's public key before sending them to the Merchant.

Figure 1 shows what a simple implementation of the Customer's side of the payment protocol might look like in IMP0. In general, an implementation needs to deal with a lot more issues than what are explicitly addressed at the protocol specification level. These include: Initialisation and use of cryptographic services, where and how data is stored and addressed, communication services, and error handling. Further, in some applications the protocol implementation may well be bundled with the user interface, in which case a further set of issues arise.

It may be instructive to also show some of the means available to implementations wishing to violate confidentiality. For instance, a hostile implementation might embed account information in the ordering field by replacing line 5 of Figure 1 by

$$\_ := \mathbf{send}(((\mathrm{ACQ}, \mathbf{embed}(\mathrm{ORDER}, \mathrm{ACC}), \mathbf{enc}(\ldots)), \ldots), \ldots),$$

or it might try to replace good nonces or keys by bad ones, for instance by replacing the same line as before by

$$\_ := \mathbf{send}(((\ldots, \mathbf{enc}((\mathrm{ORDER}, \mathrm{ACC}), \mathrm{PK}_{\mathrm{MERCHANT}})), \ldots), \ldots).$$

There are many other simple ways of building covert channels, such as timing channels, for instance by introducing data-dependent delays, either explicitly, or by exploiting timing properties of library functions.

3   Annotated Semantics

The first challenge is to identify the direct flows and computations on critical data (typically: secrets, keys, nonces, or time stamps). Once this is accomplished, other techniques based on non-interference are brought to bear to handle the indirect flows. The direct flows are tracked using annotations. In particular, we need to identify:

Table 2. Annotated semantics, expressions

$$\sigma \vdash x \xrightarrow{\tau} \sigma(x) \qquad \frac{\sigma \vdash \epsilon \xrightarrow{\alpha} \epsilon'}{\sigma \vdash (\ldots, \epsilon, \ldots) \xrightarrow{\alpha} (\ldots, \epsilon', \ldots)} \qquad \frac{[\![w]\!] = \mathbf{xcpt}}{\sigma \vdash (\ldots, w, \ldots) \xrightarrow{\tau} w}$$

$$\frac{\sigma \vdash \epsilon \xrightarrow{\alpha} \epsilon'}{\sigma \vdash f\epsilon \xrightarrow{\alpha} f\epsilon'} \qquad \frac{\mathrm{pf}([\![w]\!], v)}{\sigma \vdash \mathrm{pf}\, w \xrightarrow{\tau} v : \mathrm{pf}\, w} \qquad \frac{h([\![w]\!], v)}{\sigma \vdash h\, w \xrightarrow{v := h\, w} v : h\, w}$$

1. The operations that cause critical values to enter the system (such as execution of **receive** a for some given value of a).
2. The operations that are applied to secrets, once they have been input.

To account for this we provide IMP0 with an annotated semantics. Annotations are intended to reveal how a value has been computed, from its point of entry into the system. For instance, the annotated value

$$347 : \mathbf{enc}(717 : \mathbf{receive}\, a,\ 101 : \mathbf{key}\, 533)$$

is intended to indicate that the value 347 was computed by applying the primitive function **enc** to the pair $(717, 101)$ for which the left hand component was computed by evaluating **receive** a, and so on.

Annotated expressions and values are obtained by changing the definition of expressions (resp. values) in Table 1:

Annotated basic values (aBVal)	β	$::= b \mid (\beta_1, \ldots, \beta_n) \mid b : \varphi$
Annotated values (aVal)	w	$::= \beta \mid \mathbf{xcpt} \mid \mathbf{xcpt} : \varphi$
Annotated expressions (aExp)	ϵ	$::= w \mid x \mid (\epsilon_1, \ldots, \epsilon_n) \mid f\epsilon$
Annotations (Ann)	φ	$::= fw$

Annotations are erased using the operation $[\![w]\!]$ which removes annotations in the obvious way.

Table 2 defines the small-step semantics for expression evaluation. The transition relation has the shape

$$\sigma \vdash \epsilon \xrightarrow{\alpha} \epsilon',$$

where α is an action of the form τ (internal computation step) or $v := fw$ (f is applied to the annotated value w resulting in the value v), and σ is an annotated store, a partial function $\sigma \in \mathrm{aStore} \triangleq [\mathrm{Var} \to \mathrm{aBVal}]$.

Annotations give only static information in the style "the value v' was computed by evaluating **key** v : **receive** acq", but not information concerning which actual invocations of the **key** and **receive** functions were involved. However, this information is vital to the subsequent information flow analysis, and so we introduce a notion of context to record the last value returned by some given annotated function call (i.e. annotation).

Definition 1 (Context). A *context* is a partial function $s : [\text{Ann} \rightarrow \text{Val}]$.

So, if s is a context then $s \, \varphi$ is the last value returned by the annotated function call φ. Contexts form part of program configurations in the annotated semantics:

Definition 2 (Annotated Configuration).
An *annotated configuration* is a triple $\langle c, \sigma, s \rangle$ where c is a command, $\sigma \in \text{aStore}$ and $s \in \text{Context}$.

The annotated command-level semantics, which derives transitions of the shape $\langle c, \sigma, s \rangle \xrightarrow{\alpha} \langle c', \sigma', s' \rangle$, is standard in its treatment of commands and stores. Concerning contexts, if α is the action $v := \varphi$, then s' is defined as $s[v/\varphi]$. Details are given in the full version of the paper [6].

4 Dependency Rules

Our approach to confidentiality is to ensure that the direct flows of information follow the protocol specification, and then use information flow analysis to protect against indirect flows. In this section we introduce dependency rules to formalize the permitted, direct flows.

Definition 3 (Dependency Specification). A *dependency specification* is a pair $P = \langle S, A \rangle$ where $S \subseteq \text{Ann}$ is a set of annotations, and A is a finite set of clauses of the form

$$f \, e \leftarrow x_1 := f_1 \, e_1 \wedge \ldots x_n := f_n \, e_n \wedge \psi \tag{1}$$

where none of the expressions $e, e_1, \ldots, e_n$ mention functions or exceptions, ψ is a boolean expression, and variables in e_i do not belong to $\{x_i, \ldots, x_n\}$.

The intention is that S represents a set of secret entry points (such as: **receive** acc), and that the rules in A represent the required data flow through the program.

A clause in the policy declares a function invocation $f \, e$ to be admissible if the conditions to the right of the arrow are satisfied. Conjuncts of the form $x_i := f_i \, e_i$ are satisfied if variable x_i matches the last input from annotation $f_i \, e_i$. The boolean expression ψ represents an extra condition that relates the values returned by the different function invocations. More precisely, let a context s be given. A *valid substitution* for clause (1) is an annotated store σ such that

1. $\sigma(x_i) = s(f_i \, (e_i \sigma)) : f_i \, (e_i \sigma)$ for all $i : 1 \leq i \leq n$,
2. for $x \neq x_i \, (\forall i : 1 \leq i \leq n)$, $\sigma(x)$ has not annotation in S,
3. $\text{eval}(\psi \sigma) = \text{true}$.

That is, boolean conditions are true, and the value bound to x_i is the last value returned by the annotated function call $f_i \, (e_i \sigma)$. By $e\sigma$ we mean the annotated expression (aExpr) that results from substituting $\sigma(x)$ for every variable x in e. Notice that the restrictions on e_i in Def. 3 guarantee that $e_i \sigma$ is an annotated value. The function eval just evaluates the annotated boolean expression $\psi \sigma$ in the expected way.

We can now determine whether a particular function invocation is admitted by the dependency specification.

Definition 4 (Admissible Invocation). Let α be an annotated action of the form $v :=$ $f\ w$. A dependency specification $P = \langle \mathcal{S}, \mathcal{A} \rangle$ *admits annotated action* α in context s iff either

1. no annotation in w belongs to $\mathcal{S}$ (that is, the output does not depend directly on any secret annotation), or
2. there is a clause $f\ e \leftarrow x_1 := f_1\ e_1 \wedge \ldots \wedge x_n := f_n\ e_n\ \wedge\ b$ in $\mathcal{A}$ and a valid substitution σ for this clause such that $e\sigma = w$.

If one of these conditions holds we write $P, s \vdash \alpha$ ok.

Observe that the concept of admissible action covers both those actions whose execution is required by the protocol specification, as well as those that do not (explicitly) involve any sensitive data. In particular, internal τ transitions are always admissible (i.e. $P, s \vdash \tau$ ok).

Example 1 (Dependency Specification for 1KP Clients).
In the simplified version of the 1KP protocol, the only piece of local information that the Customer should protect is her account number. Therefore, $\mathcal{S} = \{$**receive** acc$\}$. Neither the key (which is public), the acquirer's name, nor the order need to be protected. The set $\mathcal{A}$ contains the clauses:

$$\mathbf{enc}((y, z), k) \leftarrow x := \mathbf{receive}\ \mathrm{acq}\ \wedge\ z := \mathbf{receive}\ \mathrm{acc}\ \wedge\ k := \mathbf{key}\ x$$

$$\mathbf{send}(u, s) \leftarrow u := \mathbf{enc}((y, z), k)$$

The first clause expresses when an invocation of the encryption function is admissible. In this example, encryption is used just once in each protocol run, but in general this might not be so. Moreover, since invocation of the encryption function, as any other function with a non-constant execution time, could be used to create a timing leak, the dependency specification does need to say under which circumstances it may be invoked, apart from its usage in the main input-output flow.

Notice how the variables y and s are not bound to the right of the clauses, reflecting the fact that we do not put any requirement on the format of the order and neither its destination (since it is intended for transmission in the clear anyway), beyond the restriction that it should not be used to encode secret information.

Let now $P = \langle \mathcal{S}, \mathcal{A} \rangle$.

- Let $\alpha_1 = b_1 := \mathbf{receive}\ \mathrm{acq}$. Then $P, s \vdash \alpha_1$ ok for any s since no annotation in acq belongs to $\mathcal{S}$.
- Let $\alpha_4 = b_4 := \mathbf{enc}((b, b_2 : \mathbf{receive}\ \mathrm{acc}), b_3 : \mathbf{key}\ (b_1 : \mathbf{receive}\ \mathrm{acq}))$. Consider a context s where $s(\mathbf{receive}\ \mathrm{acq}) = b_1$, $s(\mathbf{receive}\ \mathrm{acc}) = b_2$ and $s(\mathbf{key}\ b_1 : \mathbf{receive}\ \mathrm{acq}) = b_3$. Then $P, s \vdash \alpha_4$ ok since we find the substitution σ mapping x to b_1, z to b_2, k to b_3 and y to b, validating the condition 4.2. If on the other hand e.g. $s(\mathbf{receive}\ \mathrm{acq}) = b_5 \neq b_1$ then the condition would be violated and α_4 would not be admissible in the context s.

As the example show, dependency specifications are very low-level objects. They are not really meant as external specifications of confidentiality requirements, but rather as intermediate representations of flow requirements, generated from some more user-friendly protocol specification once a specific runtime platform has been chosen.

5   Flow Compatibility

Dependency specifications determine, through Definition 4, when a function invocation is admissible. In this section we tie this to the transition semantics to obtain an account of the direct information flow required by a dependency specification.

Let the relation

$$\langle c, \sigma, s \rangle \Rightarrow \langle c', \sigma', s' \rangle$$

be the reflexive, transitive closure of the annotated transition relation, i.e. the smallest relation such that $\langle c, \sigma, s \rangle \Rightarrow \langle c', \sigma', s' \rangle$ holds iff either $c = c'$, $\sigma = \sigma'$ and $s = s'$ or else c_1, σ_1, s_1 exists such that $\langle c, \sigma, s \rangle \Rightarrow \langle c_1, \sigma_1, s_1 \rangle$ and $\langle c_1, \sigma_1, s_1 \rangle \xrightarrow{\alpha} \langle c', \sigma', s' \rangle$.

Definition 5. Let the dependency specification $P = \langle \mathcal{S}, \mathcal{A} \rangle$ be given. The command $c \in Com$ is *flow compatible with* P for initial store σ and initial context s, if whenever

$\langle c, \sigma, s \rangle \Rightarrow \langle c_1, \sigma_1, s_1 \rangle \xrightarrow{\alpha} \langle c_2, \sigma_2, s_2 \rangle$ then $P, s_1 \vdash \alpha$ ok.

Example 2 (Flow Compatibility for 1KP Client). The command **Prog 1** of Figure 1 is flow compatible with the 1KP client dependency specification of Example 1 above, for any initial store σ. This is seen by proving an invariant showing that whenever execution of **Prog 1** reaches one of the send statements of **Prog 1** then for suitable choices of v_1, v_2 and v_3,

$$s(\textbf{receive acq}) = v_1 = \sigma(\text{ACQ})$$
$$s(\textbf{receive acc}) = v_2 = \sigma((ACC))$$
$$s(\textbf{key } x) = v_3 = \sigma(\text{PKA})$$

If we attempt to use a subliminal channel by replacing line 5 (the first send statement) of **Prog 1** by a command such as

$\_ := \textbf{send}((\text{ACQ}, \textbf{embed}(\text{ACC}, \text{ORDER}), \textbf{enc}((\text{ORDER}, \text{ACC}), \text{PKA})),$
$$\textbf{lookup}(\text{MERCHANT})),$$

then flow compatibility is violated, as expected. On the other hand, the command obtained by adding after the first send statement of **Prog 1** the command

if ACC = "some fixed value v" **then send**("FOUND!", leak_channel) **else skip**

is flow compatible, also as expected, since the indirect leak will not be traced by the annotation regime.

6   Admissibility

If there is an admissible flow of information from some input, say **receive** acc, to some output, say, **send**$(\ldots, \textbf{enc}((\ldots, \text{acc}), \ldots), \ldots)$ then by perturbing the input, corresponding perturbations of the output should result, and only those. In this section we formalize this idea.

In the context of multilevel security it is by now quite well understood how to model absence of information flow (from Hi to Lo) as invariance of system behaviour under perturbation of secret inputs (c.f. [3,5,11,9], see also [1] for application of similar ideas in the context of protocol analysis). For instance, the intuition supporting Gorrieri and Focardi's Generalized Noninterference model is that there should be no observable difference (i.e. behaviour should be invariant) whether high-level inputs are blocked or allowed to proceed silently. So the perturbation of high-level inputs, in this case, is whether or not they take place at all.

Here the situation is somewhat different since the multilevel security model is not directly applicable: There is no meaningful way to define security levels reflecting the intended confidentiality policy, not even in the presence of a trusted downgrader. On the contrary, the task is to characterize the admissible flows from high to low in such a manner that no trust in the downgrader (i.e. the protocol implementation) will be required.

The idea is to map a dependency specification to a set of system perturbations. Each such function is a permutation on actions and configurations which will make a configuration containing a secret, say x, appear to the external world as if it actually contains another secret, say x'. If the behaviour of the original and the permuted configuration are the same, the external world will have no way of telling whether the secret is x or x'.

At the core of any configuration permutation there is a function permuting values (e.g. x and x'). This leads to the following definition:

Definition 6 (Value Permutation). A bijection g: aVal $\to$ aVal is a *value permutation* if it preserves the structure of annotated values:

1. $g(v) = v$,
2. $g(\beta_1, \ldots, \beta_n) = (g(\beta_1), \ldots, g(\beta_n))$, and
3. $g(v : f\ w) = v' : f\ g(w)$, for some suitable value v';

and it preserves the meaning of functions:

4. Suppose $g(v : f\ w) = v' : f\ w'$ and that there is at least a value u' s.t. $f([\![w']\!], u')$. Then $f([\![w']\!], v')$, whenever $f([\![w]\!], v)$ or $\nexists u \in$ Val. $f([\![w]\!], u)$.

We extend value permutations over transition labels and contexts. In the first case, let $g(\tau) \stackrel{\Delta}{=} \tau$ and $g(v := \varphi) \stackrel{\Delta}{=} v' := \varphi'$, where $g(v : \varphi) = v' : \varphi'$. For contexts, define

$$g(s)(f\ w) \stackrel{\Delta}{=} [\![g(v' : f\ g(w))]\!], \text{ where } v' = s(f\ g(w)).$$

The following lemma establishes the coherence of the above definitions. It states that the relation between contexts s and $g(s)$ is preserved after the execution of action $v := \varphi$, resp. $g(v := \varphi)$.

Lemma 1. *If $g(v : \varphi) = v' : \varphi'$ then $g(s[v/\varphi]) = g(s)[v'/\varphi']$.*

Not all value permutations are interesting for our purposes. In fact, we are only interested in those that permute secrets as dictated by a dependency specification.

Definition 7 (Secret Permuter). Assume given a dependency specification P. A *secret permuter for P* is a value permutation g satisfying the following conditions:

1. if $f\,w$ does not contain annotations in $\mathcal{S}$ then $g(v : f\,w) = v : f\,w$,
2. if $f\,w \in \mathcal{S}$ then $f\,g(w) \in \mathcal{S}$,
3. if $P, s \vdash \alpha$ ok then $P, g(s) \vdash g(\alpha)$ ok,
4. if $\exists s.\ P, s \vdash v := f\,w$ ok, then
   - $g(\mathbf{xcpt} : f\,w) = \mathbf{xcpt} : f\,g(w)$, and
   - $f[\![w]\!] \Uparrow$ iff $f[\![g\,w]\!] \Uparrow$, where $f\,v \Uparrow$ iff $\nexists v' \in \mathrm{Val}.f(v,v')$
5. $g = g^{-1}$.

As expected, a secret permuter affects only secret values. This is implied by the first condition in Definition 7. According to the second condition, permutations must also stay within the bounds imposed by set $\mathcal{S}$. Condition (7.3) implies that a secret permuter must respect the admissibility predicate so that actions α that are admissible in a context s will remain admissible once both the action and the context have been permuted. On the other hand, if a dependency specification admits a certain function call $f\,w$ (admissible invocation), then we assume that it also permits the observation of f's exceptional and terminating behaviour. Thus, if the execution of $f\,w$ raises an exception (resp. does not terminate), we should not consider those cases where $f\,g(w)$ does not raise an exception (resp. does terminate). This is reflected by condition (7.4).

Finally we impose the requirement that g be a period 2 permutation (7.5). This seems natural given the intuition that the role of g is to interchange values of secrets. Not only does this requirement help simplify several results, but we conjecture that its introduction in Def. 7 represents no loss of generality.

The following lemma and proposition further characterize the set of secret permuters associated to a dependency specification.

Lemma 2. *Let g be a secret permuter. Then*

1. *$g(g(\alpha)) = \alpha$, and*
2. *$g(g(s)) = s$.*

Proposition 1 (Composition of Secret Permuters). *Given a dependency specification, the set of secret permuters is closed under functional composition.*

Example 3 (Secret Permuter for the 1KP Example). Let g exchange values as follows:

$$212 : \mathbf{receive}\ \mathrm{acc} \leftrightarrow 417 : \mathbf{receive}\ \mathrm{acc}$$

$$\{b, 212\}_{b_3} : \mathbf{enc}((b, 212 : \mathbf{receive}\ \mathrm{acc}), b_3 : \mathbf{key}\ b_1 : \mathbf{receive}\ \mathrm{acq}) \leftrightarrow$$
$$\{b, 417\}_{b_3} : \mathbf{enc}((b, 417 : \mathbf{receive}\ \mathrm{acc}), b_3 : \mathbf{key}\ b_1 : \mathbf{receive}\ \mathrm{acq})$$

where $\{b\}_{b'}$ represents a value $v \in \mathrm{Val}$ such that $\mathbf{enc}((b, b'), v)$. On all other values, g acts in accordance with conditions in Defs. 6 and 7. Conditions (6.1)–(6.4) and (7.x, with $x \neq 3$) are easily validated. To verify condition (7.3) consider the action

$$\alpha = \{b, 212\}_{b_3} := \mathbf{enc}((\ldots, 212 : \mathbf{receive}\ \mathrm{acc}), \ldots).$$

If $P, s \vdash \alpha$ ok then $s(\mathbf{receive}\ \mathrm{acc}) = 212$, by Def. 4. To see that $P, g(s) \vdash g(\alpha)$ ok observe that

$$g(\alpha) = \{b, 417\}_{b_3} := \mathbf{enc}((\ldots, 417 : \mathbf{receive}\ \mathrm{acc}), \ldots)$$

and $g(s)(\mathbf{receive}\ \mathrm{acc}) = 417$ by the definition of $g(s)$, so we can indeed conclude that $P, g(s) \vdash g(\alpha)$ ok.

We have extended secret permuters over transition labels and contexts. Stores and commands can equally be permuted. The extension of a secret permuter g over a store is given by the equation $g(\sigma)(x) = g(\sigma(x))$. For a command c, define $g(c)$ to preserve the structure of the command, down to the level of single annotated values which are permuted according to g. For example, $g(\_ := \mathbf{enc}((b, b_2 : \mathbf{receive}\ \mathrm{acc}), PKA)) = \_ := \mathbf{enc}((b, g(b_2 : \mathbf{receive}\ \mathrm{acc})), PKA)$. Commands like these occur naturally during the course of expression evaluation, which is governed by a small-step semantics.

The idea now is to compare the behaviour of a given command on a given store and context with its behaviour where secrets are permuted internally and then restored to their original values at the external interface, i.e. at the level of actions. For this purpose we introduce a new construct at the command level, perturbation $c[g]$, somewhat reminiscent of the CCS relabelling operator, with the following transition semantics

$$
\frac{\langle c, \sigma, s \rangle \xrightarrow{\alpha} \langle c', \sigma', s' \rangle}{\langle c[g],\ \sigma,\ s \rangle \xrightarrow{[\![g(s, \alpha)]\!]} \langle c'[g], \sigma', s' \rangle} \tag{2}
$$

where $[\![v := f\ w]\!] = v := f\ [\![w]\!]$, and $g(s, \alpha)$ permutes α only if it is an admissible invocation (i.e. $g(s, \alpha) = g(\alpha)$, if $P, s \vdash \alpha$ ok; and $g(s, \alpha) = \alpha$, otherwise). So a perturbed command is executed by applying the secret permuter at the external interface, and forgetting annotations. The latter point is important since the annotations describe data flow properties internal to the command at hand; the externally observable behaviour should depend only on the functions invoked at the interface, and the values provided to these functions as arguments.

Notice the use of $g(s, \alpha)$ in (2). The effect of this condition is that actions are only affected by the permuter when they are "ok". Secret input actions are generally always "ok", and so in general cause the internal choice of secret to be permuted. Output actions that are not "ok", however, are not affected by $g(s, \alpha)$, and so in this case a mismatch between value input and output may arise.

Thus, if the behaviour of a command is supposed to be invariant under perturbation, the effect is that it must appear to the external world to behave the same whether or not a secret permuter is applied to the internal values. This is reflected in the following definition.

Definition 8 (Admissibility). A command $c \in Com$ is admissible for the store σ and context s, the dependency specification P, if for all secret permuters g for P:

$$
\langle c[I], \sigma, s \rangle \sim \langle g(c)[g], g(\sigma), g(s) \rangle \tag{3}
$$

where I is the identity secret permuter and $\sim$ is the standard Park-Milner strong bisimulation equivalence.

Observe that the effect of perturbing a command with the identity secret permuter is just to erase annotations at the interface, but keeping all values intact.

7 Local Verification Conditions

Applying the definition of admissibility out of the box can be quite cumbersome, since it is tantamount to searching for, and checking, a bisimulation relation. In case the control flow is not affected by the choice of secrets one may hope to be able to do better, since only data-related properties need to be checked. In this section we give such a local condition.

Definition 9 (Stability for Commands). Let a dependency specification P be given. Let $\preccurlyeq$ be the smallest reflexive and transitive relation over commands such that, for all commands c_0 and c_1, $c_0 \preccurlyeq c_0; c_1$ and $c_0 \preccurlyeq \mathbf{try}\ c_0\ \mathbf{catch}\ c_1$. The command $c \in Com$ is *stable* if for all $c' \preccurlyeq c$ and for all secret permuter g,

1. if $c' = \mathbf{if}\ \beta\ \mathbf{then}\ c_2\ \mathbf{else}\ c_3$, then $[\![\beta]\!] = [\![g(\beta)]\!]$,
2. if $c' = r[\epsilon]$ and w is a subterm of ϵ, then $[\![w]\!] = \mathbf{xcpt}$ iff $[\![g(w)]\!] = \mathbf{xcpt}$, and
3. if $c' = r[\epsilon]$ and $f\ w$ is a subterm of ϵ, then $f\ [\![w]\!] \Uparrow$ iff $f\ [\![g\ w]\!] \Uparrow$,

where $r[\cdot] ::= x := \cdot\ |\ \mathbf{if}\ \cdot\ \mathbf{then}\ c_0\ \mathbf{else}\ c_1$.

For stable commands we obtain strong properties concerning the way secret permuters can affect the state space.

Lemma 3. *Suppose that $c \in$ Com is stable w.r.t. dependency specification P. Then,*

$$\langle c, \sigma, s \rangle \xrightarrow{\alpha} \langle c', \sigma', s' \rangle \text{ iff } \langle g(c), g(\sigma), g(s) \rangle \xrightarrow{g(\alpha)} \langle g(c'), g(\sigma'), g(s') \rangle.$$

Definition 10 (Stability for Configurations). *Let a dependency specification be given. The configuration $\langle c,\ \sigma,\ s \rangle$ is stable if whenever $\langle c,\ \sigma,\ s \rangle \Rightarrow \langle c',\ \sigma',\ s' \rangle$, then c' is a stable command.*

Theorem 1. *If $c \in$ Com is flow compatible with dependency specification P for store σ and context s, and $\langle c,\ \sigma,\ s \rangle$ is stable, then c is admissible (for σ, s, P and $\sim$).*

Theorem 1 does not provide necessary conditions. In fact, there are admissible programs whose control flow *is* affected by the perturbations. However, the import of Theorem 1 is that, in order to verify Admissibility it is sufficient to check that the flow of control is not affected by the relabelling of secret inputs and of admissible outputs. Furthermore, it suffices to check this for a (smaller) subset of the reachable configurations.

To formalize this, consider a dependency specification P and an initial configuration $\langle c_0, \sigma_0, s_0 \rangle$. For each configuration $\langle c, \sigma, s \rangle$ define $g(\langle c, \sigma, s \rangle)$ as the configuration that results from applying g to all three components, i.e. $g(\langle c, \sigma, s \rangle) = \langle g(c), g(\sigma), g(s) \rangle$. Then assume the existence of a set of program configurations $\{\xi_i\}_{i \in \mathcal{I}}$ where $0 \in \mathcal{I} \subseteq \mathbb{N}$, which satisfies the three properties below:

P1) $\xi_0 = \langle c_0, \sigma_0, s_0 \rangle$,
P2) for all $i \in \mathcal{I}$, if $\xi_i = \langle c, \sigma, s \rangle$ then c is a stable command,
P3) for all $i \in \mathcal{I}$ and for all action α such that $\xi_i \xrightarrow{\alpha} q$, then
   - there is a $j \in \mathcal{I}$ and a secret permuter g for P such that $q = g(\xi_j)$, and
   - $P, s \vdash \alpha$ ok, if $\xi_i = \langle c, \sigma, s \rangle$.

Under these conditions, we can use Lemma 3 to prove the following

Theorem 2. *Consider a set $\{\xi_i\}_{i \in \mathcal{I}}$ satisfying conditions P1–P3 as above. Then, for each reachable configuration $\xi = \langle c, \sigma, s \rangle$,*

1. *there is an $i \in \mathcal{I}$ and a secret permuter g such that $\xi = g(\xi_i)$,*
2. *c is a stable command, and*
3. *if $\xi \xrightarrow{\alpha} q$ then $P, s \vdash \alpha$ ok.*

To conclude, notice that statements 2 and 3 in this theorem imply that $\langle c_0, \sigma_0, s_0 \rangle$ is admissible, by means of Theorem 1. In the full version of this paper [6], we show how to apply Theorem 2 to prove that **Prog 1** (Fig. 1) is admissible for all initial stores and contexts.

8   Admissibility vs. Flow Compatibility

In general, admissibility does not imply flow compatibility. At a first glance this may seem somewhat surprising. The point, however, is that flow compatibility provides a syntactical tracing of data flow, not a semantical one. Consider for instance the command

> SECRET := **receive** a_1 ;
> if SECRET $= 0$ then _ := **send**(SECRET, a_2) else _ := **send**$(0, a_2)$

in the context of a dependency specification $P = \langle \{\textbf{receive } a_1\}, \emptyset \rangle$.

This command is clearly admissible for P (for any store and context), but not flow compatible for quite obvious reasons. However, if the control flow does not permit branching on secrets, we can show that in fact flow compatibility is implied. For this purpose some additional assumptions need to be made concerning the domains and functions involved.

Clearly, if constant functions are allowed there are trivial examples of direct flows which violate flow compatibility without necessarily violating admissibility.

However, we are able to establish the following result as a partial converse to Theorem 1.

Lemma 4. *Suppose $\langle c_0, \sigma_0, s_0 \rangle$ is stable and admissible for dependency specification P. Then for all behaviours*

$$\langle c_0, \sigma_0, s_0 \rangle \Rightarrow \langle c_1, \sigma_1, s_1 \rangle \xrightarrow{v := f\,w} \langle c_2, \sigma_2, s_2 \rangle$$

of minimal length such that $P, s_1 \not\vdash v := f\,w$ ok, the set

$$\{[\![g(w)]\!] \mid g \text{ is a secret permuter}\}$$

is finite.

Thus, if we can guarantee infinite variability of the set in Lemma 4 (which we cannot in general), flow compatibility does indeed follow from admissibility and stability.

9   Discussion and Conclusions

We have studied and presented conditions under which an implementation is guaranteed to preserve the confidentiality properties of a protocol. We first determine, using annotations, the direct flow properties. If all direct dependencies are admitted by the policy, we use an extension of the admissibility condition introduced first in [4] to detect the presence of any other dependencies. If none are detected we conclude that the implementation preserves the confidentiality properties of the protocol.

As our main results we establish close relations between the direct and the indirect dependency analysis in the case of programs which mirror the "only-high-branching-on-secrets" condition familiar from type-based information flow analyses (cf. [11,9]). In fact, in our setting the condition is more precisely cast as "only-*permitted*-branching-on-secrets", since branching on secrets is admissible as long as its "observational content" is allowed by the dependency rules. The correspondence between the direct and the indirect dependency analysis provides an "unwinding theorem" which can be exploited to reduce a behavioral check (in our case: strong bisimulation equivalence) to an invariant.

One of the main goals of our work is to arrive at information flow analyses which can control dependencies in a secure way, rather than prevent them altogether, since this latter property prevents too many useful programs to be handled. Other attempts in this direction involve the modeling of observers as resource-bounded processes following well-established techniques in Cryptography (cf. [10]). The scope of approaches such as this remains very limited, however.

Intransitive noninterference [7] is a generalization of noninterference that admits downgrading through a trusted downgrader. Although it prevents direct downgrading (i.e. flows around the downgrader), it does not prevent Trojan Horses from exploiting legal downgrading channels to actively leak secret information. A solution is to resort to Robust Declassification [12], which provides criteria to determine whether a downgrader may be exploited by an attacker. Unfortunately, the observation powers of attackers are too strong in the presence of cryptographic functions, so that the approach cannot be applied without major changes to our examples.

One important property which our approach does not handle satisfactorily is nonce freshness. Our formalism has, as yet, no way (except by the introduction of artificial data dependencies) of introducing constraints such as "x was input after y", and thus we must at present resort to external means for this check.

One worry of more practical concern is the amount of detail needed to be provided by the dependency rules. It is quite possible that this problem can be managed in restricted contexts such as JavaCard. In general, though, it is not a priori clear how to ensure that the rules provide enough implementation freedom, nor that they are in fact correct. It may be that the rules can be produced automatically from abstract protocol and API specifications, or, alternatively, that they can be synthesized from the given implementation and then serve as input for a manual correctness check.

References

1. M. Abadi and A. D. Gordon. A Bisimulation Method for Cryptographic Protocols. *Nordic Journal of Computing*, 5(4):267–303, 1998.
2. M. Bellare, J. Garay, R. Hauser, A. Herzberg, H. Krawczyk, M. Steiner, G. Tsudik, and M. Waidner. iKP – a family of secure electronic payment protocols. In *First USENIX Workshop on Electronic Commerce*, May 1995.
3. E. S. Cohen. Information Transmission in Sequential Programs. In R. A. DeMillo, D. P. Dobkin, A. K. Jones, and R. J. Lipton, editors, *Foundations of Secure Computation*, pages 297–335. Academic Press, 1978.

4. M. Dam and P. Giambiagi. Confidentiality for Mobile Code: The case of a simple payment protocol. In *Proceedings of 13th IEEE Computer Security Foundations Workshop*, 2000.
5. R. Focardi and R. Gorrieri. A Classification of Security Properties for Process Algebras. *Journal of Computer Security*, 3(1):5–33, 1995.
6. P. Giambiagi and M. Dam. On the Secure Implementation of Security Protocols. Full version, available from `http://www.sics.se/fdt/publications/gd03-secImpl-full.pdf`, 2003.
7. A. W. Roscoe and M. H. Goldsmith. What is Intransitive Noninterference? In *Proceedings of 12th IEEE Computer Security Foundations Workshop*, 1999.
8. A. Sabelfeld and A. C. Myers. Language-Based Information-Flow Security. *IEEE Journal on Selected Areas in Communications*, 21(1), 2003.
9. A. Sabelfeld and D. Sands. A PER Model of Secure Information Flow in Sequential Programs. *Higher-Order and Symbolic Computation*, 14(1), 2001.
10. D. Volpano. Secure Introduction of One-Way Functions. In *Proceedings of 13th IEEE Computer Security Foundations Workshop*, 2000.
11. D. Volpano, G. Smith, and C. Irvine. A Sound Type System for Secure Flow Analysis. *Journal of Computer Security*, 4(3):167–187, 1996.
12. S. Zdancewic and A. Myers. Robust Declassification. In *Proceedings of 14th IEEE Computer Security Foundations Workshop*, 2001.

Handling Encryption in an Analysis for Secure Information Flow

Peeter Laud*

Tartu University and Cybernetica AS
peeter@cyber.ee

Abstract. This paper presents a program analysis for secure information flow. The analysis works on a simple imperative programming language containing a cryptographic primitive—encryption—as a possible operation. The analysis captures the intuitive qualities of the (lack of) information flow from a plaintext to its corresponding ciphertext. The analysis is proved correct with respect to a complexity-theoretical definition of the security of information flow. In contrast to the previous results, the analysis does not put any restrictions on the structure of the program, especially on the ways of how the program uses the encryption keys.

1 Introduction

Executing a program causes information about its inputs to flow to its outputs. If the inputs and outputs of a program are partitioned into public and secret ones then it is important to be sure that the program has *secure information flow* — no information about secret inputs flows to public outputs in a way that an adversary could make use of it.

If one wants to prove correct an analysis checking programs for secure information flow, one has to formalize when the public outputs of the program contain or do not contain information about secret inputs that is useful for an adversary. The usual formalization is *noninterference* [9] which states that the public outputs must not contain *any* information about the private inputs. In its variant for probabilistic systems [10], noninterference means that the probability of private inputs being equal to some value must be equal to the conditional probability of private inputs having that value, under the condition that the public outputs have a certain value.

Consider a program that takes two inputs — an encryption key k and a message M — and outputs $\mathcal{E}nc(k, M)$ — the encryption of M under key k. Obviously, $\mathcal{E}nc(k, M)$ contains information about M as it is in principle possible to find M from $\mathcal{E}nc(k, M)$. Hence, if M is secret and $\mathcal{E}nc(k, M)$ is public then the noninterference property does not hold. On the other hand, the security of $\mathcal{E}nc$ requires that an adversary, whose resources (computation time and space) have certain bounds, cannot derive anything about M from $\mathcal{E}nc(k, M)$. If we consider only such bounded adversaries then we could deem this program secure. The bounds on working time (and space) of the adversaries are lax

* Supported by Estonian Science Foundation grant #5279. Most of this work was done while the author was at the University of Saarland, Germany.

enough (probabilistic polynomial time) for all realistic adversaries to satisfy them. This example shows that for taking into account the effects of cryptographic primitives, we need a bit weaker definition of noninterference. We give that definition in this paper.

Having given that weaker definition, we obviously want to know which programs satisfy it and which ones do not. We use static program analysis to determine this. This analysis is the other contribution of this paper. The analysis also takes into account the intuitive qualities of the encryption operation.

The structure of this paper is the following. In Sec. 2 we describe some related work. Particularly, we describe our own earlier results [11] and explain what they were lacking. In Sec. 3 we explain what the security of an encryption scheme means. We also explain what the sameness means in cryptography. In Sec. 4 we introduce our programming language and give the definition of secure information flow. The information flow is deemed secure if certain two probability distributions, containing the inputs and outputs of the program, are "the same". In Sec. 5 we describe the structures that the analysis works on; these structures are abstractions of probability distributions over program states. Sec. 6 presents the analysis itself and also gives a small example of it in action. Sec. 7 says some words about the correctness proof. Finally, Sec. 8 concludes.

2   Related Work

Using program analysis for certification of secure information flow was pioneered by Denning and Denning [7,8]. They annotated the program statements with the information flow between the variables caused by that statement, and analyzed this flow. Volpano et al. [24] gave a definition of secure information flow and accompanying analysis without using any instrumentations.

Leino and Joshi [13] define a program to be secure if, no matter what its secret inputs are, the public outputs always look the same for the same non-secret inputs. "Looking the same" is not specified further, different security definitions can be obtained by plugging in different formalizations. The security definition that we are using can be seen as an instance of theirs.

Recently, some work has been done to define weaker notions of secure information flow which allow analyzing programs containing cryptographic primitives without losing the precision one intuitively assigns to these primitives. Volpano and Smith [23,22] have presented analyses of programs containing one-way functions as primitive operations. Unfortunately, one is quite restricted in using the one-way function if one wants to take advantage of the weakened security definition.

Another approach has been our own [11], analyzing programs containing encryption as a primitive operation, and having its own set of restrictions. The restriction was in the usage of encryption keys — their only allowed usage was as an encryption key. They were not allowed to occur in any other situations, for example in other expressions. Particularly, the encryption keys were not allowed to be plaintexts in encryptions. Such usage would have created dependencies (between values of different variables) that our abstraction could not keep track of.

There was also another restriction on programs. The equality and inequality of different variables storing encryption keys had to be known statically at each program point. Making the equality of keys depend on the inputs of the program again introduced dependencies that our abstraction could not keep track of.

There have also been attempts to precisely formalize and analyse cryptographic protocols. Instead of the usual assumption that cryptographic primitives are perfectly secure—they are modeled as functions for which only a very restricted set of formulas holds ([5,1] are among the most prominent examples), one attempts to take into account that the cryptographic primitives may be implemented by any algorithm satisfying some complex complexity-theoretical definition; dealing with those definitions is an issue that both the analyses for secure information flow and the analyses of cryptographic protocols must handle. Mitchell et al. [14,15,16] extended the spi-calculus [1] with (polynomial) bounds on message lengths and execution time, and developed a probabilistic semantics for this extension. This has allowed them to prove the protocols correct with respect to polynomially bounded adversaries, where the cryptographic primitives that the protocols employ are real ones. These proofs are entirely hand-crafted, though; there are no mechanical means (like program analysis) to derive them. Pfitzmann et al. [18,19, 20,4] have given a framework to faithfully abstract the cryptographic primitives, such that the proofs about protocols using these abstractions would also hold if the abstractions are replaced with the actual primitives. Abadi and Rogaway [3] have shown that the formal construction of messages from simpler ones by tupling and encryption is computationally justified—if two formal messages look the same (where "looking the same" is defined over the formal structure; it makes the contents of the encrypted submessages irrelevant), and if the encryption primitive satisfies certain requirements, then no polynomially bounded adversary can distinguish the actual representations of these messages as bit-strings. This work was later extended by Abadi and Jürjens [2]. They considered program traces instead of expressions.

3   Cryptography and Secure Encryption

Encryption plays a big part in our contribution, so let us formally explain what it is and what its security means. In the course of this explanation we also cover the notion of *indistinguishability* — the computational equivalent of sameness.

An *encryption scheme* is a triple of algorithms $(\mathcal{G}, \mathcal{E}, \mathcal{D})$. They all must have running times polynomial to the length of their arguments. The algorithm $\mathcal{G}$ is the *key-generation algorithm*. It is invoked to create new encryption keys. The algorithm $\mathcal{G}$ takes one argument — the *security parameter* $n \in \mathbb{N}$ (represented in unary, because of the comment about the running times of algorithms) which determines the security of the system — more concretely, it determines the length of the keys. Larger security parameter means longer keys. The *encryption algorithm* takes as its arguments the security parameter, a key returned by $\mathcal{G}(1^n)$ (actually, we could assume that the security parameter is contained in that key but this is the usual presentation), and a plaintext — a bit-string. It returns the corresponding ciphertext. The arguments and the return value of the *decryption algorithm* are similar, only the places of plaintext and ciphertext are reversed. The key generation algorithm is obviously probabilistic, the decryption algorithm is deterministic. The encryption algorithm may either be deterministic or probabilistic but for satisfying the security requirements stated below it has to be probabilistic. It is required that the decryption of an encryption of a bit-string is equal to that bit-string.

The security requirement we put on the encryption scheme is the same as Abadi and Rogaway [3] used. We want the encryption to conceal the identity of both plaintexts and encryption keys and we want it also to hide the length of the plaintexts. The precise definition follows.

Let $\mathcal{A}$ be a probabilistic polynomial-time (PPT) algorithm, let $n \in \mathbb{N}$ and $b \in \{0, 1\}$. Consider the following experiment $\mathbf{Exp}^{\mathcal{A}}(n)$:

1. Generate a random bit $b \in \{0, 1\}$ by tossing a fair coin.
2. Define two black boxes $\mathcal{O}_1$ and $\mathcal{O}_2$. A black box is something that can be queried with bit-strings, for each query the black box returns an answer — another bit-string. There are no other ways to find out the implementation details of a black box. The contents of the boxes $\mathcal{O}_1$ and $\mathcal{O}_2$ depends on the value of b:
   - If $b = 0$, then generate two keys k, k' by invoking $\mathcal{G}(1^n)$ twice. Let $\mathcal{O}_1$ be a box that, on input $x \in \{0, 1\}^*$, invokes $\mathcal{E}(1^n, k, x)$ and outputs its return value. Similarly, let $\mathcal{O}_2$ be a box that encrypts its inputs with the key k'.
   - If $b = 1$, then let $\mathbf{0} \in \{0, 1\}^*$ be a fixed (and known to all) bit-string. Generate a key k by invoking $\mathcal{G}(1^n)$. Let $\mathcal{O}_1$ be a box that, on input $x \in \{0, 1\}^*$, invokes $\mathcal{E}(1^n, k, \mathbf{0})$ and outputs its return value. Let $\mathcal{O}_2$ be identical to $\mathcal{O}_1$.
3. Invoke the algorithm $\mathcal{A}$, giving it 1^n as an argument, and also giving it (oracle) access to the black boxes $\mathcal{O}_1$ and $\mathcal{O}_2$. Let b^* be its output.
4. If $b = b^*$ then output true, else output false.

Consider the quantity $\mathbf{Adv}^{\mathcal{A}}(n) = 2 \cdot \Pr[\mathbf{Exp}^{\mathcal{A}}(n) = \text{true}] - 1$. Here the probability is taken over the choice of b, as well as over the random choices of $\mathcal{G}$ (while generating the key(s)), $\mathcal{E}$ (while invoking the oracles) and $\mathcal{A}$. The quantity $\mathbf{Adv}^{\mathcal{A}}$ (called the *advantage* of $\mathcal{A}$; it shows how much better $\mathcal{A}$ is in guessing b, compared to simple coin-tossing) is a function from $\mathbb{N}$ to $\mathbb{R}$. We say that the encryption scheme is *type-0 secure*[1], if $\mathbf{Adv}^{\mathcal{A}}$ is *negligible* for all PPT algorithms $\mathcal{A}$. A function $f : \mathbb{N} \to \mathbb{R}$ is negligible if its absolute value is asymptotically smaller than the reciprocal of any positive polynomial.

It is possible to construct type-0 secure encryption schemes (under standard assumptions). See [3] for details.

The security definition was an instance of demanding the *indistinguishability* of certain families (indexed by $n \in \mathbb{N}$) of probability distributions. In our case, we demanded the indistinguishability of the following families of distributions over pairs of black boxes:

$$\{|(\mathcal{E}(1^n, k, \cdot), \mathcal{E}(1^n, k', \cdot)) \ : \ k, k' \leftarrow \mathcal{G}(1^n)|\}_{n \in \mathbb{N}}$$

and

$$\{|(\mathcal{E}(1^n, k, \mathbf{0}), \mathcal{E}(1^n, k, \mathbf{0})) \ : \ k \leftarrow \mathcal{G}(1^n)|\}_{n \in \mathbb{N}} \ .$$

Here $x \leftarrow D$ denotes that the variable x is distributed according to the probability distribution D. The brackets $\{| \cdot |\}$ are used to construct new probability distributions.

---

[1] Alternative name of this property is: repetition-concealing, which-key concealing and message-length concealing

For defining the indistinguishability of two families of probability distributions D and D' we have to change the wording of the description of the experiment $\mathbf{Exp}^{\mathcal{A}}(n)$ a bit. Namely, let the 2nd and 3rd point be the following:

2. Generate a quantity x, according to one of the probability distributions D_n or D'_n. If $b = 0$ then use D_n, else use D'_n.
3. Invoke the algorithm $\mathcal{A}$, giving it 1^n as an argument, and also giving it access to x.

The meaning of the phrase "access to x" depends on the type of x. If x is a bit-string then it is simply given as an argument to $\mathcal{A}$. If x is a black box then $\mathcal{A}$ is given oracle access to it. If x is a tuple then $\mathcal{A}$ is given access to all components of the tuple. Again, we consider the advantage of $\mathcal{A}$ and demand its negligibility for all PPT algorithms. We let $D \approx D'$ denote that D and D' are indistinguishable.

Our definition of secure information flow is given through the notion of *[compu-tational] independence*, which is defined as follows. Let D be a family of probability distributions over some set of tuples. We assume that all tuples in that set have same arity and also same names of components. In the rest of this paper, the program state is represented as a tuple, its components are the values of the variables. If f is a tuple and X is a set of component names, then we let $f(X)$ denote the sub-tuple of f, consisting of only the components with names in X. Let X and Y be two sets of component names. We say that X and Y are independent (or that X is independent from Y) in the family of distributions D, if

$$\{(f(X), f(Y)) : f \leftarrow D\}_{n \in \mathbb{N}} \approx \{(f(X), f'(Y)) : f, f' \leftarrow D\}_{n \in \mathbb{N}} . \quad (1)$$

4 Syntax, Semantics, and Security Definition

The programs whose information flow we are studying are written in the following simple imperative programming language (the WHILE-language):

$$\mathsf{P} ::= x := o(x_1, \dots, x_k) \mid skip \mid \mathsf{P}_1; \mathsf{P}_2 \mid if\ b\ then\ \mathsf{P}_1\ else\ \mathsf{P}_2 \mid while\ b\ do\ \mathsf{P}' .$$

Here $x, x_1, \dots, x_k, b$ are variables from the set **Var** and o is an *operator* from the set **Op**. Each operator has a fixed arity. We assume that there are two special operators in the set **Op** — a binary operator $\mathcal{E}nc$ that denotes encryption, and a nullary operator $\mathcal{G}en$ that denotes the generation of new keys. Our analysis handles these two operators in a more optimistic way than others. Decryption is not handled differently from other operators, therefore it will not be mentioned any more.

Our security definition is given in terms of the inputs and outputs of the program, therefore it is natural to use denotational semantics. The denotational semantics $[\![\mathsf{P}]\!]$ of the program P maps the initial state of the program to the final state, i.e. its type is **State** $\to$ **State**$_\perp$. For imperative programs, the state is a function mapping the variables to their values (or alternatively, a tuple of values, indexed by variables) from the set **Val**. The extra element $\perp$ denotes non-termination. Note that the denotational semantics hides some aspects that may be observable in the real world — for example the running time of the program, the power consumption of the computer executing the program, the electromagnetic radiation emitted by that computer etc. Our security definition cannot take these aspects into account.

We mentioned that the encryption algorithm has to be probabilistic. If this is the case, then the semantics of programs also has to accommodate probabilism. The range of $[\![P]\!]$ therefore has to be $\mathcal{D}(\mathbf{State}_\perp)$. Here $\mathcal{D}(X)$ denotes the set of all probability distributions over the set X. Another detail that the semantics has to incorporate is the security parameter. For this we let $[\![P]\!]$ to be not just a single function from $\mathbf{State}$ to $\mathcal{D}(\mathbf{State}_\perp)$, but an entire family of functions (of the same type), indexed by $n \in \mathbb{N}$.

The rest of the definition of $[\![P]\!]_n$ is quite standard (see for example [17, Sec. 4.1]). First, we need semantics $[\![o]\!]_n$ for each operator $o \in \mathbf{Op}$. For a k-ary operator o, the semantics $[\![o]\!]_n$ is a function from $\mathbf{Val}^k$ to $\mathbf{Val}$. We demand that there exists a type-0 secure encryption scheme $(\mathcal{G}, \mathcal{E}, \mathcal{D})$, such that $[\![\mathcal{G}en]\!]_n = \mathcal{G}(1^n)$ and $[\![\mathcal{E}nc]\!]_n = \mathcal{E}(1^n, \cdot, \cdot)$. Now the semantics $[\![P]\!]_n$ is defined exactly as in Fig. 4.1 in [17] and we are not going to elaborate it here any more.

The model of security that we have in mind here is the following: There is a certain set of *private* variables $\mathbf{Var}_S \subseteq \mathbf{Var}$ whose initial values we want to keep secret. After the program P has run, the values of the variables in a certain set $\mathbf{Var}_P \subseteq \mathbf{Var}$ become *public*. The attacker tries to find out something about the initial values of secret variables. It can read the final values of public variables.

The possible inputs of the program P are somehow distributed. For the security parameter $n \in \mathbb{N}$, let their distribution be $D_n \in \mathcal{D}(\mathbf{State})$. The (structure of the) family of distributions D is assumed to be public knowledge.

We define security only for programs that run in (expected) polynomial time. We claim that this decision causes us no loss of generality. Namely, before the attacker obtains the final values of public variables, it is expected to wait for the program to finish its execution. If the program runs for too long time and the attacker keeps waiting then it cannot find out anything about the initial values of secret variables. Alternatively, at a certain moment the attacker may decide that the program is taking too long time to run and should be considered to be effectively nonterminating; the final state should be considered to be $\perp$. We "compose" the original program and the attacker's decision-making process about the running time of the program. The result is a program that runs in polynomial time. We could define the original program to be secure iff the composed program is. This composition amounts to running a clock parallel to the program (here "parallel to" means "interleaved with") and terminating after having run for a long enough time.

If the program runs in polynomial time then we no longer have to take the possible non-termination into account. Therefore the semantics of the program $[\![P]\!]$ transforms the initial family of probability distributions D to a final family of probability distributions $D' = [\![P]\!]_n(D_n)]_{n \in \mathbb{N}}$ (we have somewhat abused the notation here). Let us make one more assumption — that the program does not change the values of the private variables $\mathbf{Var}_S$. This assumption obviously is not a significant one — we can always add new variables to the program and use them instead of the ones in $\mathbf{Var}_S$. We now say that the program P (with inputs distributed according to D) has *secure information flow* if $\mathbf{Var}_S$ and $\mathbf{Var}_P$ are [computationally] independent in the family of distributions D'.

5 Abstract Domain

The domain of the analysis is an abstraction of the set $\mathcal{D}(\mathbf{State})^{\mathbb{N}}$ — the set of families of probability distributions over $\mathbf{State}$. The analysis then maps the abstraction of the initial family of distributions D to an abstraction of the final family of distributions D'. Note that we said "an abstraction", not "the abstraction" — the analysis is allowed to err to the safe side. The question of secure information flow is obviously incomputable therefore an always precise analysis cannot exist.

Let us introduce some notation first. Let $S \in \mathbf{State}$ and $x \in \mathbf{Var}$. Then $S(x)$ denotes the value of the variable x in the program state S. Additionally, we let $S([x]_\mathcal{E})$ denote a black box that encrypts its inputs, using $S(x)$ as the key. If we let $\widetilde{\mathbf{Var}}$ denote the set $\mathbf{Var} \cup \{[x]_\mathcal{E} \,:\, x \in \mathbf{Var}\}$ then we can assume that S is a tuple whose components are named with the elements of $\widetilde{\mathbf{Var}}$ — the state S contains all the values of program variables as well as all black boxes encrypting with these values.

The abstraction $A = \alpha(D)$ of a family of distributions D is a pair $(A_{\mathsf{indep}}, A_{\mathsf{key}})$ where $A_{\mathsf{indep}} \subseteq \mathcal{P}(\widetilde{\mathbf{Var}}) \times \mathcal{P}(\widetilde{\mathbf{Var}})$ (here $\mathcal{P}(X)$ denotes the power set of the set X) and $A_{\mathsf{key}} \subseteq \mathbf{Var}$ (so $A \in \mathcal{F}(\mathbf{Var}) = \mathcal{P}(\mathcal{P}(\widetilde{\mathbf{Var}}) \times \mathcal{P}(\widetilde{\mathbf{Var}})) \times \mathcal{P}(\mathbf{Var})$). Here the set A_{indep} contains all such pairs $(X, Y) \in \widetilde{\mathbf{Var}} \times \widetilde{\mathbf{Var}}$ where X and Y are independent in the family of distributions D. The set A_{key} contains all such variables $x \in \mathbf{Var}$ where the black box $S_n([x]_\mathcal{E})$, where S_n is distributed according to D_n, is indistinguishable from a "real" encrypting black box $\mathcal{E}(1^n, k, \cdot)$ where k is distributed according to $\mathcal{G}(1^n)$. "Erring to the safe side" while abstracting D means leaving out some elements from these two sets.

The introduction of the encrypting black boxes $[x]_\mathcal{E}$ allows us to track different "kinds of dependence". As an example, let x, k and l be variables and let D be such a family of distributions, that the value of k is distributed as an encryption key, the value of x is some ciphertext that has been created by encrypting something with the key k, and the value of l is obtained from the value of k through a simple (and reversible) arithmetic operation. Then neither $\{l\}$ nor $\{x\}$ are independent from $\{k\}$ in the family of distributions D (for detecting whether the value of x and the value of k come from the same state or from different states, try to decrypt the value of x with the value of k and consider, whether the result is a sensible plaintext). However, the dependence of l and k is of quite different quality than the dependence of x and k. Someone that knows (the value of) l can decrypt ciphertexts encrypted with k. Someone that knows only x surely cannot do that. Independence from $[k]_\mathcal{E}$ distinguishes l and x. The sets $\{x\}$ and $\{[k]_\mathcal{E}\}$ are independent in the family of distributions D. The sets $\{l\}$ and $\{[k]_\mathcal{E}\}$ are not.

The analysis takes the program text and an abstraction A of the initial family of distributions D. The description of this family of distributions must be found from the context where the program is used. This description should be precise enough, such that a reasonable abstraction A can be deduced from it. Describing D and finding A is, however, not the topic of this paper. In most of earlier papers, an implicit assumption has been made that all variables are independent of each other.

6 Analysis

The analysis $\mathbb{A}^{(\mathbf{Var})}[\![\mathsf{P}]\!]$ is defined inductively over the structure of program P. Here **Var** denotes the set of variables currently in consideration. We have introduced it because for computing the analysis of certain programs we may need to analyse their subprograms with respect to more variables. For analyzing the program *if b then* P_1 *else* P_2 we need to introduce an extra variable while analyzing P_1 and P_2. This extra variable is used to keep track of the dependencies of the initial value of the variable b.

Let P be an assignment $x := o(x_1, \ldots, x_k)$ and let $A \in \mathcal{F}(\mathbf{Var})$ be an abstract value. In this case $A' = \mathbb{A}^{(\mathbf{Var})}[\![\mathsf{P}]\!](A)$ is defined in the following way:

- The sets A'_{indep} and A'_{key} contain all the elements to satisfy the rules on Fig. 1.
- A'_{indep} is symmetric: if $(X, Y) \in A'_{\mathsf{indep}}$ then also $(Y, X) \in A'_{\mathsf{indep}}$.
- A'_{indep} is monotone: if $(X, Y) \in A'_{\mathsf{indep}}$ and $X' \subseteq X$ and $Y' \subseteq Y$ then also $(X', Y') \in A'_{\mathsf{indep}}$.
- A'_{indep} and A'_{key} are the smallest sets satisfying the above conditions.

Let us explain this definition a bit. The requirements of symmetry and monotonicity have been added to decrease the number of different cases that the rules must cover. It is obvious (from the definition of independence) that it is safe to state that A'_{indep} is symmetric. It is almost as obvious that monotonicity is also a safe requirement — if X' and Y' are not independent, i.e. there exists an algorithm that can distinguish the two distributions in (1) for X' and Y', then the same algorithm can also distinguish these two distributions for X and Y.

As next we will explain what is the basis of the rules in Fig. 1. The rule (2) says that if the program P does not change the values of certain variables (namely those in sets X and Y) then their independence before the execution of the program implies their independence after the execution. The rule (3), as well as its variants say that if a certain set of variables (the set Y) is independent from another one then everything that can be computed from the values of these variables is still independent of that other set.

The rule (4) makes use of the type-0 security of the encryption scheme. Consider, what do we need for the independence of X and $Y \cup \{x\}$ in the final family of distributions.

First, by monotonicity X and Y must be independent in the final family of distributions, and by the rule (2) also in the initial family. Obviously, the variable k must be an encryption key. And if we want the value of x to appear like a random bit-string, then everything else in our possession (the values of variables and encrypting black boxes in X and Y) must not help us in decrypting it. We also have to add the value of y to the things that do not help us in decrypting x because the security definition of the encryption scheme does not cover the case where something that is related to the encryption key is encrypted with it (Abadi and Rogaway [3, Sec. 4.2] explain this case in more detail). As we have explained in Sec. 5, this non-relatedness corresponds to the last antecedent in the rule (4).

The rule (5) states that a "real" encrypting black box (which $[x]_{\mathcal{E}}$ in this case is) is independent of itself. This is a simple consequence of the security definition of the encryption scheme. The rules (6) and (6') state that if some value is distributed as an encryption key before the execution then the same *value* is still distributed as an

$$P \text{ is } x := o(x_1, \ldots, x_k)$$
$$(X, Y) \in A_{\text{indep}}$$
$$\frac{x, [x]_\varepsilon \notin X \cup Y}{(X, Y) \in A'_{\text{indep}}} \tag{2}$$

$$P \text{ is } x := o(x_1, \ldots, x_k)$$
$$(X, Y) \in A_{\text{indep}}$$
$$x, [x]_\varepsilon \notin X \cup Y$$
$$\frac{x_1, \ldots, x_k \in Y}{(X, Y \cup \{x, [x]_\varepsilon\}) \in A'_{\text{indep}}} \tag{3}$$

$$P \text{ is } x := \mathcal{E}nc(k, y)$$
$$(X, Y) \in A_{\text{indep}}$$
$$x, [x]_\varepsilon \notin X \cup Y$$
$$\frac{y, [k]_\varepsilon \in Y}{(X, Y \cup \{x, [x]_\varepsilon\}) \in A'_{\text{indep}}} \tag{3'}$$

$$P \text{ is } x := y$$
$$(X, Y) \in A_{\text{indep}}$$
$$x, [x]_\varepsilon \notin X \cup Y$$
$$X' := X \cup \langle\!\langle y \in X \,?\, \{x\} : \emptyset \rangle\!\rangle \cup \langle\!\langle [y]_\varepsilon \in X \,?\, \{[x]_\varepsilon\} : \emptyset \rangle\!\rangle$$
$$\frac{Y' := Y \cup \langle\!\langle y \in Y \,?\, \{x\} : \emptyset \rangle\!\rangle \cup \langle\!\langle [y]_\varepsilon \in Y \,?\, \{[x]_\varepsilon\} : \emptyset \rangle\!\rangle}{(X', Y') \in A'_{\text{indep}}} \tag{3''}$$

$$P \text{ is } x := \mathcal{E}nc(k, y)$$
$$(X, Y) \in A_{\text{indep}}$$
$$x, [x]_\varepsilon \notin X \cup Y$$
$$k \in A_{\text{key}}$$
$$\frac{(\{[k]_\varepsilon\}, X \cup Y \cup \{y\}) \in A_{\text{indep}}}{(X, Y \cup \{x, [x]_\varepsilon\}) \in A'_{\text{indep}}} \tag{4}$$

$$P \text{ is } x := \mathcal{G}en()$$
$$(X, Y) \in A_{\text{indep}}$$
$$\frac{x \notin X \cup Y}{(X \cup \{[x]_\varepsilon\}, Y \cup \{[x]_\varepsilon\}) \in A'_{\text{indep}}} \tag{5}$$

$$P \text{ is } x := o(\ldots)$$
$$\frac{k \in A_{\text{key}} \setminus \{x\}}{k \in A'_{\text{key}}} \tag{6}$$

$$P \text{ is } x := y$$
$$\frac{y \in A_{\text{key}}}{x \in A'_{\text{key}}} \tag{6'}$$

$$\frac{P \text{ is } x := \mathcal{G}en()}{x \in A'_{\text{key}}} \tag{7}$$

Fig. 1. The analysis $A^{(\text{Var})}[\![P]\!]$ for assignments

encryption key afterwards. Last, the rule (7) states that the operation $\mathcal{G}en$ generates encryption keys.

Let us go on with the definition of $\mathbb{A}^{(\mathbf{Var})}[\![P]\!]$. The analysis $\mathbb{A}^{(\mathbf{Var})}[\![skip]\!]$ is the identity function over $\mathcal{F}(\mathbf{Var})$. Also, $\mathbb{A}^{(\mathbf{Var})}[\![P_1; P_2]\!]$ is the composition of $\mathbb{A}^{(\mathbf{Var})}[\![P_2]\!]$ and $\mathbb{A}^{(\mathbf{Var})}[\![P_1]\!]$. Consider now the program $if\ b\ then\ P_1\ else\ P_2$. Let $\mathbf{Var}_{\mathrm{asgn}} \subseteq \mathbf{Var}$ be the set of variables that are assigned to in at least one of the programs P_1 and P_2. Let N be a variable that is not an element of $\mathbf{Var}$ and let $\mathbf{Var}' = \mathbf{Var} \uplus \{N\}$. Given an abstract value $A \in \mathcal{F}(\mathbf{Var})$, representing the abstraction of the initial family of distributions, compute

$$A^{(1)} = \mathbb{A}^{(\mathbf{Var}')}[\![N := b; P_1]\!](A)$$
$$A^{(2)} = \mathbb{A}^{(\mathbf{Var}')}[\![N := b; P_2]\!](A)\ .$$

So, we have used the extra variable N to "save" the initial value of b. In the analyses of P_1 and P_2, the variable N appears where the initial value of b would have appeared.

The next step is to take the meet of the analyses of P_1 and P_2. The order on $\mathcal{F}(\mathbf{Var})$ is defined so that larger values are more precise and smaller values more conservative, therefore the meet of two values is the most precise value that is at least as conservative as any of them. Let $A'' \in \mathcal{F}(\mathbf{Var}')$ be such, that $A''_{\mathrm{indep}} = A^{(1)}_{\mathrm{indep}} \cap A^{(2)}_{\mathrm{indep}}$ and $A''_{\mathrm{key}} = A^{(1)}_{\mathrm{key}} \cap A^{(2)}_{\mathrm{key}}$. As the last step, we have to record the flow of information from N to the variables in $\mathbf{Var}_{\mathrm{asgn}}$. The analysis result $A' = \mathbb{A}^{(\mathbf{Var})}[\![if\ b\ then\ P_1\ else\ P_2]\!]$ is defined as follows:

- The sets A'_{indep} and A'_{key} contain all the elements to satisfy the rules on Fig. 2. Here $\widetilde{\mathbf{Var}_{\mathrm{asgn}}}$ denotes the set $\mathbf{Var}_{\mathrm{asgn}} \cup \{[x]\varepsilon\ :\ x \in \mathbf{Var}_{\mathrm{asgn}}\}$.
- A'_{indep} is symmetric and monotone.
- A'_{indep} and A'_{key} are the smallest sets satisfying the above conditions.

Some explanation is in order for the rules in Fig. 2, too. In the rule (8), the only entities that may have been modified in one of the branches are the encrypting black boxes $[x_1]\varepsilon, \ldots, [x_m]\varepsilon$. They are distributed in the same way at the ends of both branches — no matter what the branch was, they are "real" encrypting black boxes. As they also are independent of everything else (this is stated by the first group of antecedents and by the antecedent just above it), their values cannot give away which of the branches was taken. The second group of antecedents states that for having $[x_i]\varepsilon$ independent of itself after the if-statement, it also has to be independent of itself at the end of both branches.

The rule (9) says that if something is independent of N (the initial value of the guard variable b) and Y at the end of both branches then it is also independent of Y after the if-statement. This follows from the possibility to find the values of the variables and black boxes in Y after the if-statement, if we know their values at the end of both branches and we also know which branch was taken. The additional black boxes $[x_1]\varepsilon, \ldots, [x_m]\varepsilon$ that are in the other side of the pair of variables and encrypting black boxes, have to satisfy similar conditions as in the previous rule.

The rule (10) is the same as the rule (6). But if k may have been changed in the branches then its distribution as a key at the end of both branches does not necessarily

$$\frac{\begin{array}{c}(X,Y) \in A''_{\mathsf{indep}} \\ x_1,\dots,x_l,x_{l+1},\dots,x_m \in \mathbf{Var}_{\mathsf{asgn}} \\ (\{[x_1]_\varepsilon,\dots,[x_m]_\varepsilon\}, X \cup Y \cup \{N\}) \in A''_{\mathsf{indep}} \\ \left[\begin{array}{c}(\{[x_1]_\varepsilon\}, \{[x_2]_\varepsilon,\dots,[x_m]_\varepsilon\}) \in A''_{\mathsf{indep}} \\ (\{[x_2]_\varepsilon\}, \{[x_3]_\varepsilon,\dots,[x_m]_\varepsilon\}) \in A''_{\mathsf{indep}} \\ \cdots\cdots\cdots\cdots\cdots\cdots\cdots\cdots\cdots \\ (\{[x_{m-1}]_\varepsilon\}, \{[x_m]_\varepsilon\}) \in A''_{\mathsf{indep}} \end{array}\right] \\ \left[\begin{array}{c}(\{[x_{l+1}]_\varepsilon\}, \{[x_{l+1}]_\varepsilon\}) \in A''_{\mathsf{indep}} \\ \cdots\cdots\cdots\cdots\cdots\cdots\cdots\cdots\cdots \\ (\{[x_m]_\varepsilon\}, \{[x_m]_\varepsilon\}) \in A''_{\mathsf{indep}} \end{array}\right] \\ x_1,\dots,x_m \in A''_{\mathsf{key}} \\ (X \cup Y) \cap (\widetilde{\mathbf{Var}_{\mathsf{asgn}} \cup \{N\}}) = \emptyset \end{array}}{(X \cup \{[x_1]_\varepsilon,\dots,[x_m]_\varepsilon\}, Y \cup \{[x_{l+1}]_\varepsilon,\dots,[x_m]_\varepsilon\}) \in A'_{\mathsf{indep}}} \qquad (8)$$

$$\frac{\begin{array}{c}x_1,\dots,x_l,x_{l+1},\dots,x_m,y_1,\dots,y_r,y_{r+1},\dots,y_s \in \mathbf{Var}_{\mathsf{asgn}} \\ (X \cup \{[x_1]_\varepsilon,\dots,[x_m]_\varepsilon\}, \\ Y \cup \{N,[x_{l+1}]_\varepsilon,\dots,[x_m]_\varepsilon,y_1,[y_1]_\varepsilon,\dots,y_r,[y_r]_\varepsilon,[y_{r+1}]_\varepsilon,\dots,[y_s]_\varepsilon\}) \\ \in A''_{\mathsf{indep}} \\ (X, \{[x_1]_\varepsilon,\dots,[x_m]_\varepsilon\}) \in A''_{\mathsf{indep}} \\ \left[\begin{array}{c}(\{[x_1]_\varepsilon\}, \{[x_2]_\varepsilon,\dots,[x_m]_\varepsilon\}) \in A''_{\mathsf{indep}} \\ (\{[x_2]_\varepsilon\}, \{[x_3]_\varepsilon,\dots,[x_m]_\varepsilon\}) \in A''_{\mathsf{indep}} \\ \cdots\cdots\cdots\cdots\cdots\cdots\cdots\cdots\cdots \\ (\{[x_{m-1}]_\varepsilon\}, \{[x_m]_\varepsilon\}) \in A''_{\mathsf{indep}} \end{array}\right] \\ x_1,\dots,x_m \in A''_{\mathsf{key}} \\ (X \cup Y) \cap (\widetilde{\mathbf{Var}_{\mathsf{asgn}} \cup \{N\}}) = \emptyset \end{array}}{\begin{array}{c}(X \cup \{[x_1]_\varepsilon,\dots,[x_m]_\varepsilon\}, \\ Y \cup \{[x_{l+1}]_\varepsilon,\dots,[x_m]_\varepsilon,y_1,[y_1]_\varepsilon,\dots,y_r,[y_r]_\varepsilon,[y_{r+1}]_\varepsilon,\dots,[y_s]_\varepsilon\}) \\ \in A'_{\mathsf{indep}}\end{array}} \qquad (9)$$

$$\frac{k \in A''_{\mathsf{key}} \qquad k \notin \mathbf{Var}_{\mathsf{asgn}}}{k \in A'_{\mathsf{key}}} \qquad (10)$$

$$\frac{k \in \mathbf{Var}_{\mathsf{asgn}} \qquad k \in A''_{\mathsf{key}} \qquad (\{[k]_\varepsilon\}, \{N\}) \in A''_{\mathsf{indep}}}{k \in A'_{\mathsf{key}}} \qquad (11)$$

Fig. 2. Merging the branches together

guarantee its distribution as a key at the end of the *if*-statement. Namely, the value of k may have influenced, which of the branches was taken. But if the value of k has not influenced the chosen branch (i.e. k is independent of the initial value of the guard variable) then its distribution as a key at the end of both branches is sufficient for its distribution as a key at the end of the *if*-statement.

Consider now the program *while b do* P and let $A \in \mathcal{F}(\mathbf{Var})$. Let $A^{(0)} = A$ and

$$A^{(i)} = \mathbb{A}^{(\mathbf{Var})}[\![if \ b \ then \ P \ else \ skip]\!](A^{(i-1)}) \ .$$

Finally, the analysis value $\mathbb{A}^{(\mathbf{Var})}[\![while \ b \ do \ P]\!](A)$ is defined as the meet (i.e. componentwise intersection) of all $A^{(i)}$. It is computable because the sequence of abstract values $A^{(0)}, A^{(1)}, A^{(2)}, \ldots$ stabilizes at some point. Stabilization is caused by the finiteness of the lattice $\mathcal{F}(\mathbf{Var})$ and by the monotonicity of the analysis.

Let us give an example of the analysis in action. Consider the following program.

1: $k_1 := \mathcal{G}en()$
2: *if b then* $k_2 := k_1$ *else* $k_2 := \mathcal{G}en()$
3: $x_1 := \mathcal{E}nc(k_1, y_1)$
4: $x_2 := \mathcal{E}nc(k_2, y_2)$

With the help of the presented analysis, we can derive that $\{b\}$ is independent of $\{x_1, x_2\}$ at the end of the program (without making any assumptions about the initial distribution of values of variables). This program is a sequence of four statements (the second of which is an *if*-statement), let $A^{(0)}$ be the abstraction of the initial family of distributions and let $A^{(i)}$, where $1 \le i \le 4$ be the abstract value computed by the analysis after the i-th statement. We have

(A). $(\emptyset, \{b, y_1, y_2\}) \in A^{(0)}_{\text{indep}}$, because $\emptyset$ is independent of everything else.

(B). $(\emptyset, \{b, y_1, y_2\}) \in A^{(i)}_{\text{indep}}$, where $i \in \{1, \ldots, 4\}$, from 6 and rule (2).

We are not any more going to mention the use of rules (2), (6) and (10) below. Basically, if some pair of sets of variables or some variable belongs to a component of $A^{(i)}$, and if none of these variables are changed in the statements $i+1, \ldots, j$, then the same pair of sets of variables or the same variable also belongs to the same component of $A^{(j)}$.

(C). $(\{[k_1]\varepsilon\}, \{b, y_1, y_2, [k_1]\varepsilon\}) \in A^{(1)}_{\text{indep}}$ by 6 and rule (5).

(D). $k_1 \in A^{(1)}_{\text{key}}$ by rule (7).

As next we have to analyse the *if*-statement. Let N be a new variable and let $\mathbf{Var}' = \mathbf{Var} \cup \{N\}$. According to the description of the analysis, we have to compute

$$B^{(0)} = \mathbb{A}^{(\mathbf{Var}')}[\![N := b]\!](A^{(1)})$$

$$B^{\text{true}} = \mathbb{A}^{(\mathbf{Var}')}[\![k_2 := k_1]\!](B^{(0)}) \qquad B^{\text{false}} = \mathbb{A}^{(\mathbf{Var}')}[\![k_2 := \mathcal{G}en()]\!](B^{(0)})$$

$$A'' = B^{\text{true}} \wedge B^{\text{false}}$$

and $A^{(2)}$ from A'' by using the rules in Fig. 2. We have

(E). $(\{[k_1]\varepsilon\}, \{b, N, y_1, y_2, [k_1]\varepsilon\}) \in B^{(0)}_{\text{indep}}$ by 6 and rule (3).

(F). $(\{[k_2]\varepsilon\}, \{b, N, y_1, y_2, [k_1]\varepsilon\}) \in B^{\text{true}}_{\text{indep}}$ by 6 and rule (3").

(G). $k_2 \in B^{\text{true}}_{\text{key}}$ by 6 and rule (6').

(H). $(\{[k_2]\varepsilon\}, \{b, N, y_1, y_2, [k_1]\varepsilon\}) \in B^{\text{false}}_{\text{indep}}$ by 6, rule (5) and monotonicity.

(I). $k_2 \in B^{\text{false}}_{\text{key}}$ by rule (7).

(J). $(\{[k_2]\varepsilon\}, \{b, N, y_1, y_2, [k_1]\varepsilon\}) \in A''_{\text{indep}}$ by 6 and 6.

(K). $k_2 \in A''_{\text{key}}$ by 6 and 6.

(L). $(\{[k_2]\varepsilon\}, \{b, y_2\}) \in A^{(2)}_{\text{indep}}$ by 6, 6, 6 and rule (8).

(M). $(\{[k_2]\varepsilon, b, y_1, y_2\}, \{[k_1]\varepsilon\}) \in A^{(2)}_{\text{indep}}$ by 6, 6, 6 and rule (8).

(N). $k_2 \in A^{(2)}_{\text{key}}$ by 6, 6 and rule (11).

(O). $(\{b\}, \{x_1\}) \in A^{(3)}_{\text{indep}}$ by 6, 6, 6 and rule (4).

(P). $(\{[k_2]\varepsilon\}, \{b, x_1, y_2\}) \in A^{(3)}_{\text{indep}}$ by 6, 6, 6 and rule (4).

(Q). $(\{b\}, \{x_1, x_2\}) \in A^{(4)}_{\text{indep}}$ by 6, 6, 6 and rule (4).

The domain of the analysis — $\mathcal{F}(\mathbf{Var})$ — is quite large, therefore we may ask, whether the analysis can be implemented in a way that does not cause prohibitive running times. It turns out that it can indeed be implemented in such a way. The set $\mathcal{P}(\mathcal{P}(\widetilde{\mathbf{Var}}) \times \mathcal{P}(\widetilde{\mathbf{Var}}))$ is isomorphic to the set of formulas of propositional calculus, where the set of variables is $\widetilde{\mathbf{Var}} \uplus \widetilde{\mathbf{Var}}$. Indeed,

$$\mathcal{P}(\mathcal{P}(\widetilde{\mathbf{Var}}) \times \mathcal{P}(\widetilde{\mathbf{Var}})) \cong \mathcal{P}(\mathcal{P}(\widetilde{\mathbf{Var}} \uplus \widetilde{\mathbf{Var}})) \cong \{0,1\}^{\widetilde{\mathbf{Var}} \uplus \widetilde{\mathbf{Var}}} \to \{0,1\} \ .$$

These formulas can be implemented as binary decision diagrams (BDD). The analysis will then transform one BDD to another one. The rules on Fig. 1 and Fig. 2 are such, that these transformations can be efficiently implemented on BDD-s. We believe from our experimentation with the implementation that the size of the abstract domain will not be the cause of long running times — small programs like above example can be analyzed in split-second on a modern computer.

7 About the Proof of Correctness

The correctness of the analysis means that if the analysis says that two sets of variables are independent of each other at the end of the execution of the program, then it really is so.

Proving the rules in Fig. 1 and Fig. 2 correct is simple, it takes some elementary cryptography. However, these proofs alone are not enough for the correctness of the entire analysis. They are enough for the correctness of everything but the analysis of loops.

For using the standard results [6] about the approximation of fixed points (the semantics of loops is defined through a fix-point operation, the same holds for the analysis of loops), we need the continuity of the abstraction function α from $\mathcal{D}(\mathbf{State}_\perp)^{\mathbb{N}}$ to $\mathcal{F}(\mathbf{Var})$. However, as we show in [12, Sec. 3.3], there are no non-trivial (abstraction) functions α from $\mathcal{D}(\mathbf{State}_\perp)^{\mathbb{N}}$ with the following properties:

1. α is continuous;
2. if $D, \tilde{D} \in \mathcal{D}(\mathbf{State}_\perp)^{\mathbb{N}}$ are such that $D \approx \tilde{D}$, then $\alpha(D) = \alpha(\tilde{D})$.

The second requirement should come as something obvious, we want to abstract away everything that does not affect polynomial-time computations.

In [12, Sec. 3.3] we show that for all $D, \tilde{D} \in \mathcal{D}(\mathbf{State}_\perp)^{\mathbb{N}}$ there exist $D^{(i)}, \tilde{D}^{(i)} \in \mathcal{D}(\mathbf{State}_\perp)^{\mathbb{N}}$ (here $i \in \mathbb{N}$), such that the least upper bound of the family $\{D^{(i)}\}_{i\in\mathbb{N}}$ is

D, the least upper bound of the family $\{\tilde{D}^{(i)}\}_{i\in\mathbb{N}}$ is $\tilde{D}$, and $D^{(i)} \approx \tilde{D}^{(i)}$ holds for each $i \in \mathbb{N}$. Therefore $\alpha(D^{(i)}) = \alpha(\tilde{D}^{(i)})$ by the second condition on α and $\alpha(D) = \alpha(\tilde{D})$ by the first.

Our abstraction function α cannot therefore be continuous. We have devised an *ad hoc* proof of the correctness of the analysis. If D is the initial family of distributions, $A = \alpha(D)$ and $A' = \mathbb{A}^{(\mathbf{Var})}[\![\mathsf{P}]\!](A)$, then to show that $(X, Y) \in A'_{\mathsf{indep}}$ implies the independence of X and Y in the final distribution D', we first fix the security parameter n. Then we construct two "slices" of the program P, whose output distributions are the left and right distribution in (1), respectively. We then introduce a number of possible steps for transforming these slices. We show that

1. The first slice can be transformed to second in a number of steps polynomial in n. This sequence of steps can be efficiently constructed.
2. Each step has only a negligible effect on the output distribution.

This construction and transformation are described in [12, Chapter 4].

8   Conclusions

We have devised an analysis for secure information flow for programs containing encryptions. We believe that we have found the right abstractions this time, as the analysis puts no restrictions at all on the program structure. We do not even have the restriction that Abadi and Rogaway [3] had — we also allow *encryption cycles* — cases where encryption keys are encrypted with other keys, and where the relation "is encrypted with" is circular. This relation is defined by the program structure, therefore it is even a bit surprising that an analysis that does not keep track of the program structure is able to gracefully handle encryption cycles.

The main future direction for extending this work should be the inclusion of authentication primitives (signatures, MACs, etc.) and active adversaries. It may be hard to extend the full analysis, if we do not have convenient means for approximating fixed points, but we may try to devise the analysis for some kind of language that does not contain a looping construct. There exist simple intuitive formalisms (without a looping construct) for expressing cryptographic protocols, for example strand spaces [21].

Another extension would be the handling of other primitives for ensuring confidentiality. It should be quite easy to add public-key encryption to our language and analysis. In the analysis, the public keys would behave similarly to the encrypting black boxes — one can encrypt with them, but not decrypt.

References

1. M. Abadi and A. Gordon. A Calculus for Cryptographic Protocols: The Spi Calculus. *Information and Computation*, 148(1):1–70, Jan. 1999.
2. M. Abadi and J. Jürjens. Formal Eavesdropping and Its Computational Interpretation. In proc. of *TACS 2001* (LNCS 2215), pages 82–94.
3. M. Abadi and P. Rogaway. Reconciling Two Views of Cryptography (The Computational Soundness of Formal Encryption). In proc. of *International Conference IFIP TCS 2000* (LNCS 1872), pages 3–22.

4. M. Backes. *Cryptographically Sound Analysis of Security Protocols*. PhD thesis, Universität des Saarlandes, 2002.
5. M. Burrows, M. Abadi, and R. Needham. A Logic of Authentication. *ACM Transactions on Computer Systems*, 8(1):18–36, Feb. 1990.
6. P. Cousot. Constructive Design of a Hierarchy of Semantics of a Transition System by Abstract Interpretation. *Theoretical Computer Science* 277(1-2):47–103, Apr. 2002.
7. D. Denning. A Lattice Model of Secure Information Flow. *Communications of the ACM*, 19(5):236–243, 1976.
8. D. Denning and P. Denning. Certification of Programs for Secure Information Flow. *Communications of the ACM*, 20(7):504–513, 1977.
9. J. Goguen and J. Meseguer. Security Policies and Security Models. In proc. of *IEEE S&P 1982*, pages 11–20.
10. J. Gray III. Probabilistic Noninterference. In proc. of *IEEE S&P 1990*, pages 170–179.
11. P. Laud. Semantics and Program Analysis of Computationally Secure Information Flow. In proc. of *ESOP 2001* (LNCS 2028), pages 77–91.
12. P. Laud. *Computationally Secure Information Flow*. PhD thesis, Universität des Saarlandes, 2002.
13. K. Leino and R. Joshi. A Semantic Approach to Secure Information Flow. In proc. of *Matehematics of Program Construction '98* (LNCS 1422), pages 254–271.
14. P. Lincoln, J. Mitchell, M. Mitchell, and A. Scedrov. A Probabilistic Poly-Time Framework for Protocol Analysis. In proc. of *ACM CCS '98*, pages 112–121.
15. P. Lincoln, J. Mitchell, M. Mitchell, and A. Scedrov. Probabilistic Polynomial-Time Equivalence and Security Analysis. In proc. of the *World Congress on Formal Methods in the Development of Computing Systems '99* (LNCS 1708), pages 776–793.
16. J. Mitchell. Probabilistic Polynomial-Time Process Calculus and Security Protocol Analysis. In proc. of *ESOP 2001* (LNCS 2028), pages 23–29.
17. H. Nielson and F. Nielson. *Semantics with Applications: A Formal Introduction*. Wiley, 1992.
18. B. Pfitzmann, M. Schunter, and M. Waidner. Cryptographic Security of Reactive Systems. In proc. of *Workshop on Secure Architectures and Information Flow* (ENTCS 32), 2000.
19. B. Pfitzmann and M. Waidner. Composition and integrity preservation of secure reactive systems. In proc. of *ACM CCS 2000*, pages 245–254.
20. B. Pfitzmann and M. Waidner. A Model for Asynchronous Reactive Systems and its Application to Secure Message Transmission. In proc. of *IEEE S&P 2001*, pages 184–200.
21. F. Thayer, J. Herzog, and J. Guttman. Strand Spaces: Proving Security Protocols Correct. *Journal of Computer Security*, 7(2/3):191–230, 1999.
22. D. Volpano. Secure Introduction of One-way Functions. In proc. of *CSFW '00*, pages 246–254.
23. D. Volpano and G. Smith. Verifying Secrets and Relative Secrecy. In proc. of *POPL 2000*, pages 268–276.
24. D. Volpano, G. Smith, and C. Irvine. A Sound Type System for Secure Flow Analysis. *Journal of Computer Security*, 4(2,3):167–187, 1996.

Using Controller-Synthesis Techniques to Build Property-Enforcing Layers

Karine Altisen[1], Aurélie Clodic[2], Florence Maraninchi[1], and Eric Rutten[3]

[1] VERIMAG Centre Equation, 2 Av. de Vignate – F38610 GIERES
www-verimag.imag.fr – {Karine.Altisen,Florence.Maraninchi}@imag.fr
[2] LAAS-CNRS, 7 av. Colonel Roche – F-31077 TOULOUSE
www.laas.fr – Aurelie.Clodic@laas.fr
[3] INRIA Rhône-Alpes, MONTBONNOT – F-38334 ST ISMIER Cedex
www.inrialpes.fr – Eric.Rutten@inrialpes.fr

Abstract. In complex systems, like robot plants, applications are built on top of a set of components, or devices. Each of them has particular individual constraints, and there are also logical constraints on their interactions, related to e.g., mechanical characteristics or access to shared resources. Managing these constraints may be separated from the application, and performed by an intermediate layer.
We show how to build such property-enforcing layers, in a mixed imperative/declarative style: 1) the constraints intrinsic to one component are modeled by an automaton; the product of these automata is a first approximation of the set of constraints that should be respected; 2) the constraints that involve several components are expressed as temporal logic properties of this product; 3) we use general controller synthesis techniques and tools in order to combine the set of communicating parallel automata with the global constraint.

1 Introduction

Consider the programming of a small robot made of two devices: an elevator table and a rotating arm placed on it. The elevator has a motor than can be switched on and off, in either direction, and two sensors at its extreme positions. The rotating arm also has a motor with commands on and off, and a choice between two speeds. The requests for moving up or down, and rotating the arm, come from an application program in charge of performing some given sequence of tasks with the robot.

At a low level, independently of any particular application, the programming of the robot has to ensure safety properties related to the characteristics of the devices composing the robot, and the way they interact. These can concern the mechanics, or the access to shared resources. For instance, the motor of the elevator should be turned off when the elevator reaches one of its extreme positions. This type of local constraint can be specified independently of the behavior of the arm. Similarly, the arm motor should be turned off before a change of speeds can be performed.

P. Degano (Ed.): ESOP 2003, LNCS 2618, pp. 174–188, 2003.

We may also have to take into account some global constraints, concerning their interactions, like "the arm should not be turning at its highest speed while the elevator is moving up". There are several methods we can think of for ensuring such properties in the running application:

- The responsibility could be left to the application; the code ensuring the safety properties related to the mechanics of the robot has to be included in all application programs; it may be difficult to intertwine with the proper code of the application. Even if we can provide powerful static verification tools to check the properties before running the application on the actual robot, this solution should be avoided, because it makes writing the application very difficult.

- A solution that allows to separate the code of the application and the code that is in charge of ensuring the safety properties, is to introduce an *intermediate layer*. The application does not talk directly to the robot but to this *layer*, that may delay or reject its requests to the actuators of the robot. This layer is in charge of enforcing the safety properties, and may be reused with various applications. Using this architecture means that the application is aware of the fact that its requests may be postponed or canceled. This is where an acknowledge mechanism is needed.

In all cases, note that we cannot rely on *monitoring* techniques and dynamic checks, because we are mainly interested in embedded systems. These systems should not raise exceptions at runtime. Our aim is not to reject faulty programs, either statically or dynamically, but to help in designing them correctly.

In this paper we formalize the general intermediate layer approach, thereby allowing for the automatic generation of such *property-enforcing layers* from a mixed-style description of the properties: several automata for the individual properties of the devices, and temporal-logic formulas for the global properties. Controller synthesis techniques are used as a compilation technique here.

2   The Approach

Expressing Individual Constraints and Global Constraints. The individual constraints on the behavior of the devices can be conveniently modeled as simple reactive state machines with the sensors from the physical devices and requests from the application (**sensor**, **req**) as inputs and the commands to the actuators (**start**, **stop**) as outputs (see figure 1-a). Each automaton records significant states of the corresponding device, e.g., I for idle, and A for active. The automaton of figure 1-a enforces the following property: "a request is ignored if it happens while a previous request is being treated.". Note that we may think of various protocols between the application and the intermediate layer: it may be useful to send an acknowledgment (**ack**) on the transition that stops the motor, meaning: "the request has been executed". In particular, it is not sent when a request is ignored.

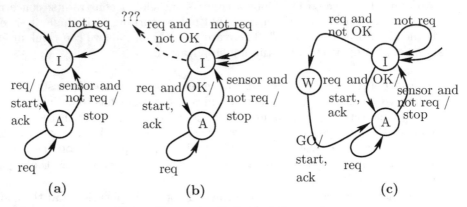

Fig. 1. Expressing Individual Constraints

The parallel composition of all the individual automata models all the *individual constraints*. In terms of these parallel automata, a *global property* like "the arm should not be turning at its highest speed while the elevator is moving up" means that one particular global state (or, perhaps, a *set* of global states) should be unreachable. More generally, we are interested in *safety* properties of the parallel composition (see [9] for the distinction between safety and liveness properties).

Mixing the two kinds of Constraints. Of course, if we start from a set of automata $A = A_1 || A_2 || ... || A_n$ that were designed in isolation, and impose a global safety property ϕ, it is very likely that A does not satisfy ϕ. For example, if the application requires that the arm motor be switched on, while the elevator is moving up, nothing can be done to avoid the faulty situation.

When global constraints appear, due to the joint use of several devices, the automaton describing one component has to be designed in a more flexible way. For instance, if obeying a request from the application immediately is forbidden by a global constraint, given the states of the other devices, the request has to be either rejected or delayed.

We choose to introduce an additional component (i.e. a *controller*), that knows about the global safety property to be ensured, and may constrain the individual automata about the transitions they take in order to ensure this property. Then, we re-design the individual automata in a more controllable way, allowing them to respond to events from the application, the physical device, *and* the controller. The transitions that were labeled by "**req**" are now labeled by "**req AND ok**", meaning that the request is taken into account only if the controller allows it (see Figure 1-b). But then, what happens when "**req AND NOT ok**"? The missing transition may be a loop, meaning that the request is simply canceled. In this case, the application is likely to apply a protocol that maintains the request as long as it is not taken into account.

Another solution is to memorize the request. Instead of responding directly to a request by the appropriate command to the physical device, the automaton enters a *waiting* state W, hence postponing the request until it can be obeyed without violating the global safety property. This gives the machine of Figure 1-c, where label "GO" corresponds to the controller releasing the waiting request.

We could model even more sophisticated behaviors. For instance, the application might cancel its requests; or several requests might be queued, etc.

Again, writing the controller by hand may be hard to do if there are a lot of individual devices and global properties. It can even be the case that such a controller does not exist.

The solution we propose is to let the general *controller synthesis* technique do the job for us. Instead of programming the controller and the communications between the machines by hand, we state this control objective in a very declarative way (as a logical formula on the set of states). Then we let the *controller synthesis* technique generate the controller that, put in parallel with the individual machines, will ensure the global property.

Summarizing the Method. Consider an application program A and a physical system under control, e.g., a robot R. The latter requires that a property ϕ be respected, i.e. $A||R \models \phi$. Our method is the following:

- First, design A with a software architecture that introduces an intermediate layer I_ϕ to ensure ϕ: $A = A'||I_\phi$. The problem becomes: $A'||I_\phi||R \models \phi$. A' is easier to write, and I_ϕ is reusable.
- I_ϕ includes properties that can be expressed for each component or device independently of the others, and also global constraints. ϕ is of the form $\phi_1 \wedge \phi_2 \ldots \wedge \phi_n \wedge \phi_{glob}$:
- For the individual constraints, propose a set of *automata* $A_1, A_2, \ldots A_n$ (like the ones presented in Figure 1), composable with a controller, i.e. able to respond to an application and to a controller, and corresponding to the properties $\phi_1, \phi_2, \ldots \phi_n$.
- For the global constraints ϕ_{glob}, express them as safety properties, and let the controller synthesis technique build the controller. This gives the *most permissive* controller, that has to be made deterministic since we want to use it as a program. We will use techniques from *optimal controller synthesis* [14] to reduce the non-determinism and to impose some kind of *progress*.

If a controller exists, the final picture is: $I_\phi = A_1||A_2|| \ldots ||A_n||C_{\phi_{glob}}$, and $A'||I_\phi||R \models \phi$, by construction, for all A'. If there exists no controller, it means that some of the automata have to be redesigned, introducing more "controllability" (e.g., OK and GO inputs, waiting states) so that the controller should be able to ensure the property.

The paper. Section 3 sets a formal framework in which our approach can be explained together with the main results of controller synthesis. An example taken from robotics is described in section 4, with a list of global constraints one may want to ensure for this kind of systems. Section 5 gives some quick hints on the implementation of the approach. Section 6 comments on the method. Section 7 reviews related work, and section 8 is the conclusion.

3   Framework

Our work uses general controller synthesis results (see [18]): we present them in a unified formal framework by using synchronous Mealy machines from synchronous languages (see, for instance, [11]), augmented with state *weights*. A presentation of controller synthesis with Mealy machines can also be found in [2], with similar motivations: Mealy machines give programs straightforwardly.

3.1   Synchronous Automata with Outputs and Weights

Definition 1 (Automaton). *An automaton $\mathcal{A}$ is the tuple $\mathcal{A} = (Q, s_{init}, \mathcal{I}, \mathcal{O}, \mathcal{T}, \mathcal{W})$ such that Q is the set of states, $s_{init} \in Q$ is the initial state, $\mathcal{I}$ and $\mathcal{O}$ are the sets of Boolean input and output variables respectively, $\mathcal{T} \subseteq Q \times Bool(\mathcal{I}) \times 2^{\mathcal{O}} \times Q$ is the set of transitions, and $\mathcal{W} : Q \longrightarrow \mathbb{N}$ is a function that labels states with natural weights. $Bool(\mathcal{I})$ denotes the set of Boolean formulas with variables in $\mathcal{I}$. For $t = (s, \ell, O, s') \in \mathcal{T}$, $s, s' \in Q$ are the source and target states, $\ell \in Bool(\mathcal{I})$ is the triggering condition of the transition, and $O \subseteq \mathcal{O}$ is the set of outputs emitted whenever the transition is triggered. We consider that the Boolean formulas used as input labels are conjunctions of literals and their negation. Disjunctions lead to several transitions between the same two states.*

Definition 2 (Reactivity and Determinism). *Let $\mathcal{A} = (Q, s_{init}, \mathcal{I}, \mathcal{O}, \mathcal{T}, \mathcal{W})$ be an automaton. $\mathcal{A}$ is reactive iff $\forall s \in Q, \bigvee_{(s,\ell,O,s') \in \mathcal{T}} \ell$. $\mathcal{A}$ is deterministic iff $\forall s \in Q, \forall t_i = (s, \ell_i, O_i, s_i) \in \mathcal{T}, i = 1, 2 . \ell_1 = \ell_2 \implies (O_1 = O_2) \wedge (s_1 = s_2)$.* [1]

Every automaton in this paper is reactive but is not necessarily deterministic. The automata of figure 1 are of this kind. However, in the concrete syntax, we often omit the transitions that are loops and do not emit anything. When the weights on states are omitted, they are 0.

The semantics of an automaton $\mathcal{A} = (Q, s_{init}, \mathcal{I}, \mathcal{O}, \mathcal{T}, \mathcal{W})$ is given in terms of input/output/state *traces*.

Definition 3 (Trace). *Let $\mathcal{A} = (Q, s_{init}, \mathcal{I}, \mathcal{O}, \mathcal{T}, \mathcal{W})$ be an automaton. A sequence of tuples $t = \{(v_i, O_i, s_i)\}_i$ where the v_i are valuations of the inputs, the O_i are subsets of outputs, and the s_i are states, is a trace of $\mathcal{A}$ iff*

$$\begin{cases} s_1 = s_{init} \\ \forall n \quad \exists (s_n, \ell, O_n, s_{n+1}) \in \mathcal{T} \text{ such that } \ell \text{ has value } \textbf{true} \text{ in } v_n . \end{cases}$$

In state s_i, upon reception of input valuation v_i, the automaton emits O_i and goes to s_{i+1}. We note $Trace(\mathcal{A})$ the set of all traces of $\mathcal{A}$.

Definition 4 (Trace with hidden inputs). *Let $\mathcal{A} = (Q, s_{init}, \mathcal{I}, \mathcal{O}, \mathcal{T}, \mathcal{W})$ be an automaton, and let $J \subseteq \mathcal{I}$ be a set of input variables to be hidden. A trace of $\mathcal{A}$ with hidden values J is a sequence of tuples $t_{\mathcal{I} \setminus J} = \{(v'_i, O_i, s_i)\}_i$ where*

---

[1] The equality $\ell_1 = \ell_2$ stands for syntactical equality since there is no disjunction in labels.

$\forall i \, . \, v'_i : \mathcal{I} \setminus J \longrightarrow \{\textit{true}, \textit{false}\}$, $O_i \subseteq \mathcal{O}$ and $s_i \in \mathcal{Q}$ such that there exists a trace $t = \{(v_i, O_i, s_i)\}_i \in \textit{Trace}(\mathcal{A})$ and $\forall i \, . \, \forall x \in \mathcal{I} \setminus J \, . \, v'_i(x) = v_i(x)$.

The trace with hidden inputs J built from a trace $t \in \textit{Trace}(\mathcal{A})$ is noted $t_{(\mathcal{I} \setminus J)}$ as above. And we note the set of all traces with hidden inputs J: $\textit{Trace}_{(\mathcal{I} \setminus J)}(\mathcal{A})$.

Definition 5 (Synchronous Product). *Let $\mathcal{A}_1 = (\mathcal{Q}_1, s_{init1}, \mathcal{I}_1, \mathcal{O}_1, \mathcal{T}_1, \mathcal{W}_1)$ and $\mathcal{A}_2 = (\mathcal{Q}_2, s_{init2}, \mathcal{I}_2, \mathcal{O}_2, \mathcal{T}_2, \mathcal{W}_2)$ be automata. The* synchronous product *of $\mathcal{A}_1$ and $\mathcal{A}_2$ is the automaton $\mathcal{A}_1 \| \mathcal{A}_2 = (\mathcal{Q}_1 \times \mathcal{Q}_2, (s_{init1} s_{init2}), \mathcal{I}_1 \cup \mathcal{I}_2, \mathcal{O}_1 \cup \mathcal{O}_2, \mathcal{T}, \mathcal{W})$ where $\mathcal{T}$ is defined by: $(s_1, \ell_1, O_1, s'_1) \in \mathcal{T}_1 \wedge (s_2, \ell_2, O_2, s'_2) \in \mathcal{T}_2 \Longleftrightarrow (s_1 s_2, \ell_1 \wedge \ell_2, O_1 \cup O_2, s'_1 s'_2) \in \mathcal{T}$; $\mathcal{W}$ is defined by: $\mathcal{W}(s_1 s_2) = \mathcal{W}_1(s_1) + \mathcal{W}_2(s_2)$ (more general composition of weights may be defined if needed).*

The synchronous product of automata is both commutative and associative, and it is easy to show that it preserves both determinism and reactivity.
Encapsulation makes variables local to some subprogram and enforces synchronization; the following definition is taken from ARGOS [11]. In general, the encapsulation operation does not preserve determinism nor reactivity. This is related to the so-called "causality" problem intrinsic to synchronous languages (see, for instance [3]). However, these problems can appear only if two parallel components communicate in both directions, in the same instant. We will use encapsulation only in simple cases for which this is not necessary.

Definition 6 (Encapsulation). *Let $\mathcal{A} = (\mathcal{Q}, s_{init}, \mathcal{I}, \mathcal{O}, \mathcal{T}, \mathcal{W})$ be an automaton and $\Gamma \subseteq \mathcal{I} \cup \mathcal{O}$ be a set of inputs and outputs of $\mathcal{A}$. The* encapsulation *of $\mathcal{A}$ w.r.t. Γ is the automaton $\mathcal{A} \setminus \Gamma = (\mathcal{Q}, s_{init}, \mathcal{I} \setminus \Gamma, \mathcal{O} \setminus \Gamma, \mathcal{T}', \mathcal{W})$ where $\mathcal{T}'$ is defined by: $(s, \ell, O, s') \in \mathcal{T} \wedge \ell^+ \cap \Gamma \subseteq O \wedge \ell^- \cap \Gamma \cap O = \emptyset \Longleftrightarrow (s, \exists \Gamma \, . \, \ell, O \setminus \Gamma, s') \in \mathcal{T}'$.*

ℓ^+ is the set of variables that appear as positive elements in the monomial ℓ (i.e. $\ell^+ = \{x \in \mathcal{I} \mid (x \wedge \ell) = \ell\}$). ℓ^- is the set of variables that appear as negative elements in the monomial l (i.e. $\ell^- = \{x \in \mathcal{I} \mid (\neg x \wedge \ell) = \ell\}$).

Example 1. In figure 2 two automata $\mathcal{A}$ and $\mathcal{B}$ are composed by a synchronous product, and then $\{b\}$ is encapsulated. The typical use of an encapsulation is to enforce the synchronization between two parallel components, by means of a variable which is an input on one side, and an output on the other side. In the product, this variable appears in both the triggering condition and the output set of transitions.

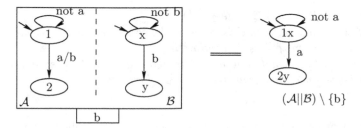

Fig. 2. An encapsulation example

Definition 7 (Temporal Properties of the Automata). *Let* $\mathcal{A} = (\mathcal{Q}, s_{init}, \mathcal{I}, \mathcal{O}, \mathcal{T}, \mathcal{W})$ *be an automaton, let* $S \subseteq \mathcal{Q}$ *be a set of states and let* $t = \{(v_i, O_i, s_i)\}_i \in Trace(\mathcal{A})$ *be a trace of* $\mathcal{A}$. *The properties* ϕ *we are interested in are the two CTL [7] formulas defined below.*

Invariance of S: $\phi = \forall\Box(S)$. *A trace* t *satisfies* $\Box(S)$ *(noted* $t \vDash \Box(S)$*) iff* $\forall i \, . \, s_i \in S$. *For automata:* $\mathcal{A} \vDash \forall\Box(S) \Longleftrightarrow \forall t \in Trace(\mathcal{A}) \, . \, t \vDash \Box(S)$.

Reachability of S: $\phi = \forall\Diamond(S)$. *A trace* t *satisfies* $\Diamond(S)$ *iff* $\exists s \in S \, . \, \exists i \, . \, s = s_i$. *For automata:* $\mathcal{A} \vDash \forall\Diamond(S) \Longleftrightarrow \forall t \in Trace(\mathcal{A}) \, . \, t \vDash \Diamond(S)$.

3.2   Controllers and Controller Synthesis

Controllers. Let $\mathcal{A} = (\mathcal{Q}, s_{init}, \mathcal{I}, \mathcal{O}, \mathcal{T}, \mathcal{W})$ be an automaton. We partition the set $\mathcal{I}$ of inputs into a set $\mathcal{I}_u$ of *uncontrollable* inputs (those coming from the application or from the physical devices, like req, sensor in figure 1) and a set $\mathcal{I}_c$ of *controllable* inputs (i.e. inputs coming from the controller, like OK, GO).

Definition 8 (Controller of an Automaton). *A controller of* $\mathcal{A}$ *is an automaton* $\mathcal{C} = (\mathcal{Q}, s_{init}, \mathcal{I}_u, \mathcal{O} \cup \mathcal{I}_c, \mathcal{T}', \mathcal{W}')$ *such that* $\exists t = (s, \ell_u \wedge \ell_c, O, s') \in \mathcal{T} \Longleftrightarrow \exists \gamma \subseteq \mathcal{I}_c \wedge \exists t' = (s, \ell_u, O \cup \gamma, s') \in \mathcal{T}'$, *where* ℓ_u *(resp.* ℓ_c*) is only written with variables in* $\mathcal{I}_u$ *(resp.* $\mathcal{I}_c$*) and* $\gamma \subseteq \mathcal{I}_c$ *at most contains the controllable inputs involved in* ℓ_c *(i.e.,* $\ell_u^+ \cup \ell_u^- \subseteq \mathcal{I}_u$, *and* $\gamma \subseteq \ell_c^+ \cup \ell_c^- \subseteq \mathcal{I}_c$*). Moreover* $\forall s \in \mathcal{Q} \, . \, \mathcal{W}'(s) = 0$.

Notice that one $t \in \mathcal{T}$ may define several $t' \in \mathcal{T}'$ as defined above. The controller $\mathcal{C}$ of an automaton $\mathcal{A}$ has the same structure (states and transitions). The controllable variables are *inputs* in $\mathcal{A}$, whereas they are *outputs* of the controller. This means that the role of the controller is to choose whether controllable variables should be emitted, depending on uncontrollable inputs and states.

The automaton $(\mathcal{A}||\mathcal{C}) \setminus \mathcal{I}_c$ represents the *controlled automaton of* $\mathcal{A}$ *by* $\mathcal{C}$: the interaction between the controller and its automaton is formalized by a synchronous product ($\mathcal{A}$ and $\mathcal{C}$ execute in parallel, communicating *via* $\mathcal{I}_c$ variables) and the $\mathcal{I}_c$ variables are kept as local variables (and so encapsulated).

Properties 1 *Let* $\mathcal{A} = (\mathcal{Q}, s_{init}, \mathcal{I}, \mathcal{O}, \mathcal{T}, \mathcal{W})$ *and let its input variables* $\mathcal{I}$ *be partitioned into the two subsets* $\mathcal{I}_c$ *and* $\mathcal{I}_u$. *Let* $\mathcal{C}$ *be a controller of* $\mathcal{A}$.

1. $Trace((\mathcal{A}||\mathcal{C}) \setminus \mathcal{I}_c) \subseteq Trace_{\mathcal{I}_u}(\mathcal{A})$.
2. *If* $\mathcal{A}$ *is reactive, then* $\mathcal{C}$ *is reactive, by construction. But* $\mathcal{C}$ *may not be deterministic even if* $\mathcal{A}$ *is deterministic.*
3. $(\mathcal{A}||\mathcal{C}) \setminus \mathcal{I}_c$ *is reactive and, if* $\mathcal{C}$ *is deterministic, then so is* $(\mathcal{A}||\mathcal{C}) \setminus \mathcal{I}_c$. *This holds because the encapsulation is used in a case for which causality problems do not occur.*

The first property means that every trace of the controlled automaton of $\mathcal{A}$ by $\mathcal{C}$ is also a trace of $\mathcal{A}$ with hidden variables $\mathcal{I}_c$: the controller restricts the execution of the automaton. 2 and 3 are specific to the way we build controllers. Reactivity and determinism are required if we want to obtain *programs* with this method.

Example 2. Let us observe figure 3. The right part of the figure depicts a controller $\mathcal{C}$: the set of controllable inputs is $\mathcal{I}_c = \{\text{OK}\}$, whereas req and stop are uncontrollable. The controller shown here enforces the fact that the task always has to wait before executing. This is done by deciding which of the controller transitions do emit OK, in such a way that the transition to wait remains, whereas the transition to EX disappears, in the product.

The controlled automaton $(\mathcal{A}\|\mathcal{C}) \setminus \mathcal{I}_c$ is shown in figure 4, where the synchronous product of the automaton $\mathcal{A}$ and of its controller $\mathcal{C}$ has been performed (left part), and where the encapsulation of the controllable input OK has been realized (right part).

In the transition from stopped to wait, OK appears as a negative element in the triggering condition of $\mathcal{A}$; the controller chooses not to emit it in the corresponding transition, hence the transition remains in the encapsulated product. Conversely, from stopped to execute, OK appears as a positive element in $\mathcal{A}$; since the controller does not emit it, the transition disappears in the encapsulated product.

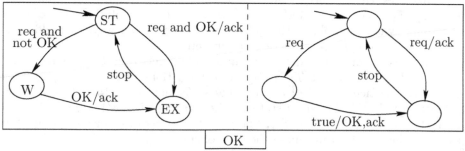

Fig. 3. An automaton and a controller for it

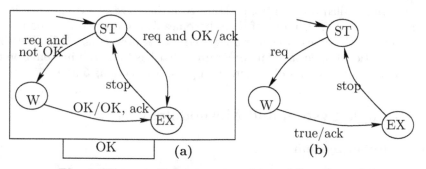

Fig. 4. The controlled automaton obtained from figure 3

Controller Synthesis Problem. Let $\mathcal{A} = (\mathcal{Q}, s_{\text{init}}, \mathcal{I}, \mathcal{O}, \mathcal{T}, \mathcal{W})$ be a *deterministic* and *reactive* automaton $\mathcal{I} = \mathcal{I}_c \cup \mathcal{I}_u$. Let ϕ be one of the two CTL properties on $\mathcal{A}$ given by definition 7.

Problem 1 (Controller Synthesis). The controller synthesis problem consists in finding a controller $\mathcal{C}$ of $\mathcal{A}$ such that the controlled automaton of $\mathcal{A}$ by $\mathcal{C}$, satisfies the property ϕ: $(\mathcal{A}\|\mathcal{C}) \setminus \mathcal{I}_c \vDash \phi$.

The problem may have several solutions but has a greatest solution, called the *most permissive* controller: if $\phi = \forall\square(S)$ (resp. $\phi = \forall\Diamond(S)$), the controller $\mathcal{C}$ is the most permissive iff if $\exists t \in Trace(\mathcal{A})$ such that $t \vDash \square(S)$ (resp. $t \vDash \Diamond(S)$) then $t_{(\mathcal{I}_u)} \in Trace((\mathcal{A}||\mathcal{C}) \setminus \mathcal{I}_c)$.

Reducing Non-determinism in the Controller. We are interested in deterministic controllers because our aim is to build a *program*.

Let $\mathcal{A} = (\mathcal{Q}, s_{\text{init}}, \mathcal{I}, \mathcal{O}, \mathcal{T}, \mathcal{W})$ be a deterministic and reactive automaton with $\mathcal{I} = \mathcal{I}_c \cup \mathcal{I}_u$. Let ϕ be one of the two CTL properties on $\mathcal{A}$ defined in definition 7. Let $\mathcal{C}$ be a solution of the controller synthesis given by $\mathcal{A}$ and ϕ.

We are looking for a controller $\mathcal{C}'$ which is a solution of the same controller synthesis problem, and which is more deterministic. First, we impose that $\mathcal{C}$ and $\mathcal{C}'$ have the same set of states and outputs but not necessarily the same set of transitions and inputs.

Second, we want to ensure the property $Trace_{\mathcal{I}_u}(\mathcal{C}') \subseteq Trace_{\mathcal{I}_u}(\mathcal{C})$ since it guarantees that: $Trace_{\mathcal{I}_u}((\mathcal{A}||\mathcal{C}') \setminus \mathcal{I}_c) \subseteq Trace_{\mathcal{I}_u}((\mathcal{A}||\mathcal{C}) \setminus \mathcal{I}_c)$ and then $(\mathcal{A} || \mathcal{C})\setminus \mathcal{I}_c \vDash \phi \implies (\mathcal{A}||\mathcal{C}') \setminus \mathcal{I}_c \vDash \phi$, i.e. if $\mathcal{C}$ is a solution of the above controller synthesis problem then also is $\mathcal{C}'$. We give two ways of building $\mathcal{C}'$ from $\mathcal{C}$: *static* or *dynamic* reduction of non-determinism.

Static reduction of non-determinism: $\mathcal{C}'$ only differs from $\mathcal{C}$ by its transition set, $\mathcal{T}_{\mathcal{C}'}$: $\mathcal{T}_{\mathcal{C}'} \subseteq \mathcal{T}_{\mathcal{C}}$, where $\mathcal{T}_{\mathcal{C}}$ is the set of transitions of $\mathcal{C}$. In this paper, we use a very particular case of this approach: $\mathcal{T}_{\mathcal{C}'}$ may be obtained from $\mathcal{T}_{\mathcal{C}}$ by a local optimization based on state weights: $\forall t = (s, \ell, O, s') \in \mathcal{T}_{\mathcal{C}'}$. $\mathcal{W}(s') = \min\{\mathcal{W}(s'') \mid \exists(s, \ell, O'', s'') \in \mathcal{T}_{\mathcal{C}}\}$. Notice that this operation may not completely suppress the non-determinism of the controller.

Dynamic reduction of non-determinism: $\mathcal{C}'$ differs from $\mathcal{C}$ by its set of inputs $\mathcal{I}_{\mathcal{C}'}$ such that $\mathcal{I}_u \subseteq \mathcal{I}_{\mathcal{C}'}$, and by its triggering conditions. The idea is to add special inputs called *oracles*: from a state S, if there are two transitions labeled by the same input ℓ, then one of them becomes $\ell . i$ and the other one becomes $\ell . \bar{i}$, where i is the oracle. In general we need several oracles (see [10]). We obtain a deterministic automaton (or a "program") that has to be run in a environment that decides on the values of the oracle inputs. See sections 5 and 6.

4   Example System and Methodology

4.1   A Robot System

We illustrate the proposed methodology with a case study [5] concerning a robot system: an automated mobile cleaning machine, designed by ROBOSOFT[2]. It can learn a mission, with trajectories to be followed, and starting and stopping of cleaning tools at pre-recorded points. It can play them back, using sensors like odometry, direction angle and laser sensors to follow the trajectories and detect beacons. One of the tools is a brush, mounted on an articulated arm, under the robot body, that can achieve vertical translation (in order to be in contact with the floor or not), horizontal translation (in order to reach corners), and rotation.

---

[2] www.robosoft.fr

The constraints are the following: 1) the brush should rotate only when on the floor, in low position, because otherwise, when in high position, it might damage the lower part of the mobile robot; 2) it can be moved laterally only when on the floor, and not rotating, for the same reason.

4.2   Modeling the Brush Individual Constraints

The brush individual constraints are modeled in terms of three automata, each one representing the activation of control laws for one degree of freedom of the brush: vertical movement, horizontal movement and rotation.

Vertical movement: the initial state **up** in Figure 5(a) represents the brush being in high position. Upon reception of a request from the application to move down, **r_down**, either the controller accepts it, in the absence of any conflict at global level, by **okV**, or not. If yes, then the **going_down** state is reached, with emission of the acknowledgement **start_down**. Otherwise, the request is memorized by going to state **wait_down**. The controller may then authorize the activation from state **wait_down** to state **going_down**, by **okV** with emission of **start_down**. When the uncontrollable event **sensor_down** occurs from the physical device, corresponding to the reaching of the low position, the state **down** is reached, with emission of **stopV**. Movement upwards follows a symmetrical scheme, also subject to controller authorization.

Horizontal movement: the automaton for horizontal movements follows exactly the same scheme as for vertical movement.

Rotation: the automaton for rotation follows a different scheme (figure 5(b)): there is no intermediate state going to the rotation state. State **imm** designates an immobile brush. A request for rotating, **r_rot**, is either accepted directly by **okR**, which leads into the **rotate** state, or not, which leads to the **wait_rot** state. Going back from rotation to immobility is done through a request **r_imm**, and follows the same scheme as before, with a waiting state **wait_imm** in case not authorized, and a deceleration state **going_imm**.

4.3   Safety Properties to Be Ensured by the Controller

We introduce a notation to define sets of global states in terms of local states. Let $\mathcal{A}_1, ..., \mathcal{A}_n$ be n automata. $(\mathcal{A}_i = (\mathcal{Q}_i, s_{\text{init } i}, \mathcal{I}_i, \mathcal{O}_i, \mathcal{T}_i, \mathcal{W}_i)$. Let $\mathcal{A} = \mathcal{A}_1 || \mathcal{A}_2 ... || \mathcal{A}_n = (\mathcal{Q}, s_{\text{init}}, \mathcal{I}, \mathcal{O}, \mathcal{T}, \mathcal{W})$. Let $s_i \in \mathcal{Q}_i$ be a state of automaton $\mathcal{A}_i$. We note $\underline{s_i}$ for all the states of $\mathcal{A}$ whose projection of $\mathcal{Q}_i$ is equal to s_i: $\underline{s_i} = \{s \in \mathcal{Q} \mid s = (s'_1, s'_2, ..., s'_n) . s'_i = s_i\}$ The set of global states excluding s_i is noted $\overline{s_i}$ for $\mathcal{Q} \setminus \underline{s_i}$. The set of global states excluding $S \subseteq \mathcal{Q}$ is noted $\overline{S}$.

Global states must be avoided where the properties mentioned in section 4.1 are violated. To define them, we identify states where:

- the brush turns, which can happen when in states **rotate**, **wait_imm** and **going_imm**, as a decelerating brush is still in motion. This is expressed by the set of states: $Rotating = \underline{rotate} \cup \underline{wait\_imm} \cup \underline{going\_imm}$;
- the brush arm is in low position, i.e. in state **down** and also **wait_up**: $Low = \underline{down} \cup \underline{wait\_up}$;

– the brush arm is moving laterally i.e., in states going_out and going_back:
Lateral = *going_out* ∪ *going_back* .

The set of safe states wrt properties described in section 4.1 is then given by:
$S = (\overline{Rotating} \cup Low) \cap (\overline{Lateral} \cup \overline{Rotating} \cap Low)$. Finally, we compute a
controller for the property $\forall\square(S)$.

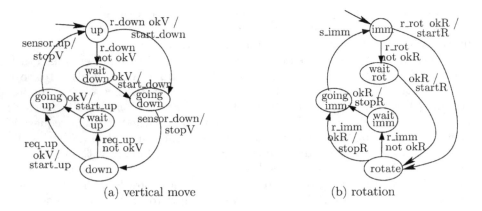

(a) vertical move   (b) rotation

Fig. 5. The brush control tasks.

4.4   Result of the Controller Synthesis Phase

The result is a non-deterministic controller (see section 3.2). In particular, the
choice remains between staying in a wait state and moving to the active state,
both being safe with respect to the property. This is the usual problem when
specifying a system by safety properties: a very simple way of respecting them is
to do nothing. Hence, some *progress* should be expressed and taken into account.

We propose to use the weights associated with states. The weight of the
waiting states is set to 1, and the weight of all other states is set to 0. The
static reduction of non-determinism produces a controller where, whenever there
are two transitions sourced in the same state, with the same inputs, only the
transitions that go to the states with minimal weight are kept.

In the example, this is sufficient for ensuring that at least one component
leaves its waiting state when it is possible. This does not yield a deterministic
automaton, as some global states might have the same weight due to the composition of local weights. Dynamic reduction of non-determinism can then be
used. In the framework of our case study, we worked in a context of interactive
simulation: the values for the oracles are given by the end-user.

5   Implementation

The current implementation of the method, which has been used for the example,
relies on the chain of Figure 6: the individual constraints are described using a

synchronous formalism called "mode-automata" [12]; Yann Rémond provided the compiler into z3z, the input format of the synthesis tool *Sigali*. The global properties and the weights are expressed into z3z by the means of *Sigali* macros. *Sigali* [13] is a tool that performs model-checking, controller synthesis for logical goals, and optimal controller synthesis.

The result of *Sigali* is a controller, in the form of an executable black-box. Y. Rémond and K. Altisen developed the tool *SigalSimu*, to simulate the behavior of the controlled system. This corresponds to a dynamic resolution of the non-determinism, where the human being plays the role of the oracle.

The next step will be to transform the interpretation chain into a *compilation* chain, producing the controlled system as an explicit automata that can then be compiled into C code (see below).

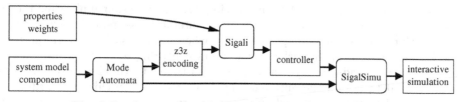

Fig. 6. Implementation of the approach: the tools involved.

6   Evaluation of the Method

Patterns for the individual constraints: The whole approach requires that the mechanical devices (or, more generally, the "resources" for which we build an application program) be modeled as small automata. We suggest that a set of reusable *patterns* — in the spirit of "design patterns" [8] — be designed for that purpose. It is likely to be specific of a domain.

Cost: The algorithms involved in controller synthesis techniques are expensive. If the whole intermediate layer had to be built as the result of a synthesis, starting from a declarative specification only, it could be too costly to be considered as a viable implementation technique. The reason why it is reasonable in our case is that part of the specification is already given as a set of automata. Controller synthesis is used only to further restrict the possible behaviors of the product.

Towards a compilation chain (non-determinism, progress and fairness): First, we want programs, so we have to determinize the controllers. Second, a specification S made of safety properties only, leads to trivial solutions that do not *progress*. Hence we have to *specify* progress properties, and to remove transitions in the controller obtained from S, so that only progressing behaviors remain. Third, what about *fairness*? Our example system is an instance of a *mutual exclusion* problem, and we defined *critical sections* as sets of states in each of the individual automata. In some sense, the effect of the controller-synthesis phase is to add the protocol between the components, so that mutual exclusion is respected. This is a typical case where a non-deterministic choice remains, for choosing the component to serve. Usually, a dynamic scheduler is used to ensure fairness between the concurrent processes willing to access the shared resource.

In our case, we would like to obtain a deterministic controller and to compile it into a single program. This can be done by 1) determinizing the controller with oracles (see section 3.2); 2) adding in parallel an automaton Or that sends the oracle values, and encapsulating the oracle variables. Or is responsible for the fairness of the whole system.

7   Related Work

Previous Work. In previous work [15,16], an approach is proposed for the modeling of robot control tasks, using simple pre-defined control patterns, and generic logical properties regarding their interactions. A teleoperation application is considered, as an illustration of a safety-critical interactive system. An extension of this work concerns multi-mode tasks [14], where each task has several activity modes or versions, distinguished by weights capturing quality (as in e.g., image processing) and cost (typically: execution time). Optimal control synthesis is then used to obtain the automatic control of mode switchings according to objectives of bounded time and maximal quality. The approach in this paper is a generalization of this more specialized work.

On "Property-Enforcing" techniques. A number of approaches has been proposed for enforcing properties of programs, but they mainly rely on dynamic checks. In [6], a program transformation technique is presented, allowing to equip programs with runtime checks in a minimal way. Temporal properties are taken into account, and abstract interpretation techniques are used in order to avoid the runtime checks whenever the property can be proven correct, statically. In the general case, the technique relies on runtime checks, anyway.

The approach described in [17] is a bit different because it does not rely on program transformation. The authors propose the notion of *security automaton*. Such a security automaton is an observer for a safety property, that can be run in parallel with the program (performing an on-the-fly synchronous product). When the automaton reaches an error state, the program is stopped.

On the use of Controller-Synthesis Techniques. In [4], the authors use controller synthesis techniques to help in designing component interfaces.

In their sense, an interface is a (possibly synchronous) black box that is specified by input and output conditions (input and output behaviors). Interfaces may be composed as far as they are compatible, i.e. as far as there exist some inputs for which the composition works. Compatibility is computed by a controller synthesis algorithm which finds the most permissive application (wrt input and output conditions) under which the composed interfaces may work.

The unusual thing here (regarding the use of controller synthesis) is that they constrain the application, i.e. the environment of the interfaces, in order to fit input and output conditions, whereas, in usual controller synthesis framework, we use it to make the system work whatever the application/environment does.

In [1], the authors use controller synthesis techniques to build real-time schedulers. A layered modeling methodology is also provided here. First, real-time processes are individually modeled by timed transition systems; then a synchronization layer is built ensuring functional properties; finally, a scheduler is computed by controller synthesis, ensuring the non functional properties of the layer.

8 Conclusion and Further Work

We presented a method that automates partially the development of *property-enforcing* layers, to be used between an application program and a set of resources for which safety properties are defined and should be respected by the global system (the application, plus the intermediate layer, plus the set of resources).

We illustrated the approach with a case-study where the set of resources is a robot. However, the method can be generalized to other kinds of applications.

The method relies on two ideas. First, the specification of the properties to be respected often comes in a mixed form: simple and "local" properties, typically those imposed by one mechanical device in isolation, are better given as simple automata; on the contrary, the interferences between the devices, and the situations that should be avoided, are better described in a declarative way, for instance with trace properties in a temporal logic. Second, mixing the two parts of the specification is not easy, and we show how to use very general controller-synthesis techniques to do so. The technique that enforces the safety part of the specification has to be complemented, in order to ensure some progress. We adapted the notion of optimal synthesis to obtain progress properties.

Further work has to be devoted to the notion of "*progress*" in layers that enforce safety properties. We encountered the problem and solved it only in a very particular case. The first questions are: what kind of progress properties do we need? How can they be expressed in terms of optimal synthesis goals?

We really believe that optimal control synthesis is the appropriate method because, in the contexts we are interested in, the "progress" properties are often related to a notion of "quality". The states in the individual automata might be labeled by weights related to CPU time, memory use, energy consumption, quality of service, etc. (additivity of weights in parallel components may not fit all the needs, of course). In these cases, progress means "improve the quality".

Acknowledgments. The authors would like to thank Hervé Marchand, the author of *Sigali*, and Yann Rémond, the author of mode-automata, for their work on the implementation.

References

1. K. Altisen, G. Gößler, and J. Sifakis. Scheduler modelling based on the controller synthesis paradigm. *Journal of Real-Time Systems*, 23(1), 2002.

2. S. Balemi. *Control of Discrete Event Systems: Theory and Application*. PhD thesis, Automatic Control Laboratory, Swiss Federal Institute of Technology (ETH), Zurich, Switzerland, May 1992.
3. G. Berry. The foundations of esterel. *Proof, Language and Interaction: Essays in Honour of Robin Milner*, 2000. Editors: G. Plotkin, C. Stirling and M. Tofte.
4. A. Chakrabarti, L. de Alfaro, T.A. Henzinger, and F.Y.C. Mang. Synchronous and bidirectional component interfaces. In *CAV 2002: 14th International Conference on Computer Aided Verification*, LNCS. Springer Verlag, 2002.
5. Aurélie Clodic. Tâches multi-modes et génération automatique de contrôleurs. Master thesis report, Institut National Polytechnique de Grenoble, June 2002. *(in French)*.
6. Thomas Colcombet and Pascal Fradet. Enforcing trace properties by program transformation. In *Proceedings of the 27th ACM SIGPLAN-SIGACT Symposium on Principles of Programming Languages (POPL-00)*. ACM Press, January 19–21 2000.
7. E.A. Emerson and E. Clarke. Design and synthesis of synchronization skeletons using branching-time temporal logic. In *Proc. Workshop on Logic of Programs*. LNCS 131, Springer Verlag, 1981.
8. Erich Gamma, Richard Helm, Ralph Johnson, and John Vlissides. *Design Patterns*. Addison Wesley, Reading, MA, 1995.
9. L. Lamport. Proving the correctness of multiprocess programs. *IEEE Transactions on Software Engineering*, SE-3(2):125–143, 1977.
10. F. Maraninchi and N. Halbwachs. Compositional semantics of non-deterministic synchronous languages. In *European Symposium On Programming*, Linkoping (Sweden), April 1996. Springer verlag, LNCS 1058.
11. F. Maraninchi and Y. Rémond. Argos: an automaton-based synchronous language. *Computer Languages*, (27):61–92, 2001.
12. F. Maraninchi and Y. Rémond. Mode-automata: a new domain-specific construct for the development of safe critical systems. *Science of Computer Programming*, to appear, 2002.
13. H. Marchand, P. Bournai, M. Le Borgne, and P. Le Guernic. Synthesis of discrete-event controllers based on the Signal environment. *Discrete Event Dynamical System: Theory and Applications*, 10(4), October 2000.
14. Hervé Marchand and Éric Rutten. Managing multi-mode tasks with time cost and quality levels using optimal discrete control synthesis. In *Proceedings of the 14th Euromicro Conference on Real-Time Systems, ECRTS'02*, 2002.
15. Eric Rutten. A framework for using discrete control synthesis in safe robotic programming and teleoperation. In *Proceedings of the IEEE International Conference on Robotics and Automation, ICRA'2001*, 2001.
16. Eric Rutten and Hervé Marchand. Task-level programming for control systems using discrete control synthesis. Research Report 4389, INRIA, February 2002.
17. Fred B. Schneider. Enforceable security policies. *ACM Transactions on Information and System Security*, 3(1):30–50, February 2000.
18. W. M. Wonham and P. J. Ramadge. On the supremal controllable sublanguage of a given language. *SIAM Journal on Control and Optimization*, 25(3):637–659, May 1987.

Automatic Software Model Checking Using CLP

Cormac Flanagan

Systems Research Center
Hewlett Packard Laboratories
flanagan@hpl.hp.com

Abstract. This paper proposes the use of constraint logic programming (CLP) to perform model checking of traditional, imperative programs. We present a semantics-preserving translation from an imperative language with heap-allocated mutable data structures and recursive procedures into CLP. The CLP formulation (1) provides a clean way to reason about the behavior and correctness of the original program, and (2) enables the use of existing CLP implementations to perform bounded software model checking, using a combination of symbolic reasoning and explicit path exploration.

1 Introduction

Ensuring the reliability of software systems is an important but challenging problem. Achieving reliability through testing alone is difficult, due to the test coverage problem. For finite state systems, model checking techniques that explore all paths have been extremely successful. However, verifying software systems is a much harder problem, because such systems are inherently infinite-state: many variables are (essentially) infinite-domain and the heap is of unbounded size.

A natural method for describing and reasoning about infinite-state systems is to use *constraints*. For example, the constraint $a[i] > y$ describes states in which the ith component of a is greater than y. The close connection between constraints and program semantics is illustrated by Dijkstra's weakest precondition translation [10]. This translation expresses the behavior of a code fragment that does not use iteration or recursion as a boolean combination of constraints. Fully automatic theorem provers, such as Simplify [9], provide an efficient means for reasoning about the validity of such combinations of constraints. These techniques provide the foundation of the extended static checkers ESC/Modula-3 [8] and ESC/Java [14].

Unfortunately, iterative and recursive constructs, such as while loops, for loops, and recursive procedure calls, cannot be directly translated into boolean combinations of constraints. Instead, extended static checkers rely on the programmer to supply loop invariants and procedure specifications to aid in this translation.[1] The need for invariants and specifications places a significant burden on programmer, and is perhaps the reason these checkers are not more widely used, even though they catch defects and improve software quality [14].

---

[1] Loops without invariants are handled in a manner that is unsound but still useful.

P. Degano (Ed.): ESOP 2003, LNCS 2618, pp. 189–203, 2003.

This paper presents a variant of the extended static checking approach that avoids the need for programmer-supplied invariants and specifications. Instead, we start with an unannotated program, which may include iterative and recursive constructs, and asserted correctness properties. We translate this program into in an extended logic called *constraint logic programming* (CLP) [19,21,20, 22]. Essentially, a constraint logic program consists of the sequence of rules, each of which defines a particular relation symbol as a boolean combination of constraints. Since constraints may refer to relation symbols, these rules can be self- and mutually-recursive. By expressing iterative and recursive constructs of the original imperative program as recursive CLP rules, we avoid the need for programmer-supplied invariants and specifications.

This paper presents a semantics-preserving translation into CLP from an imperative language that is infinite-state and that supports global and local variables, heap-allocated mutable data structures, and recursive procedure calls. We use this translation to illustrate the connection between imperative programs and CLP, between program executions and depth-first CLP derivations, between procedure behaviors and sets of ground atoms, and between erroneous program executions and satisfiable CLP queries.

Our translation enables the use of efficient CLP implementations, such as SICStus Prolog [27], to check correctness properties of software. This implementation performs a depth-first search for a satisfying assignment, using efficient constraints solvers to symbolically reason about boolean variables, linear arithmetic, and functional maps. This search strategy corresponds to *explicitly* exploring all program execution paths, but *symbolically* reasoning about data values. That is, instead of explicitly enumerating all possible values for an integer variable x, the CLP implementation symbolically reasons about the consistency of a collection of constraints or linear inequalities on x. This symbolic analysis provides greater coverage and more efficient checking.

The depth-first search strategy may diverge on software with infinitely long or infinitely many execution paths. To cope with such systems, we bound the depth of the CLP search, thus producing a bounded software model checker. Our translation also facilitates software model checking using other CLP implementation techniques, such as breadth-first search, tableaux methods, or subsumption, which may provide stronger termination and error detection properties.

The remainder of the paper proceeds as follows. The next section provides a review of CLP. Section 3 illustrates our CLP translation by applying it to an example program, and uses the CLP representation to detect defects in the program. Section 4 presents the imperative language that is the basis for our formal development, and section 5 translates this language into CLP. Section 6 uses the CLP representation for program checking and defect detection. Section 7 discusses related work, and we concluded in Section 8.

2 A Review of Constraint Logic Programming

In this section, we provide a brief review of the constraint logic programming paradigm [19,21,20,22]. A *term* t is either a variable or the application of a primitive function f to a sequence of terms. An *atom* $r(\vec{t})$ is the application of a user-defined relation r to a term sequence $\vec{t}$. A *primitive constraint* $p(\vec{t})$ is the application of a primitive predicate p to a term sequence. *Constraints* include primitive constraints and their negations, conjunction, disjunction, and atoms. A *rule* $r(\vec{t}) \leftarrow c$ is an (implicitly universally quantified) implication, and provides a definition of the relational symbol r. For example, the rule $r(x,y) \leftarrow x = y$ defines r as the identity relation.

Primitive functions include binary functions for addition and subtraction, nullary constants, and the `select` and `store` operations, which are explained in Section 5. Primitive predicates include equality, disequality, inequalities, and the nullary predicates *true* and *false*. We sometimes write binary function and predicate applications using infix instead of prefix notation.

CLP Syntax

(terms)	$t ::= x \mid f(\vec{t})$	*(variables)*	x, y, z
(atoms)	$a ::= r(\vec{t})$	*(constants)*	$k \in \{0, 1, 2, \ldots\}$
(constraints)	$c ::= p(\vec{t}) \mid \neg p(\vec{t})$	*(primitive fns)*	$f \in \{k, +, -, \mathtt{select}, \mathtt{store}\}$
	$\mid\ c \wedge c \mid c \vee c \mid a$	*(primitive preds)*	$p \in \{true, false, =, \neq, <, \ldots\}$
(rules)	$R ::= a \leftarrow c$	*(relation names)*	r

A CLP program $\vec{R}$ is a sequence of rules. These rules may be self- or mutually-recursive, and so the CLP program $\vec{R}$ may yield multiple models. We are only interested in the least model of $\vec{R}$ that is compatible with the intended interpretation $\mathcal{D}$ of the primitive functions and predicates. In particular, we are interested in the question of whether this least compatible model of $\vec{R}$ implies a particular *goal* or atom a, which we write as $lm(\vec{R}, \mathcal{D}) \models \tilde{\exists} a$, where $\tilde{\exists} a$ existentially quantifies over all free variables in a.

Much work on the implementation and optimization of CLP programs has focused on answering such queries efficiently. In the following section, we leverage this effort to check correctness properties of an example program, without the need for procedure specifications or loop invariants.

3 Overview

To illustrate our method, consider the example program shown in Figure 1, column 1. This program is a variant of the locking example used by the BLAST checker [18]. The procedures `lock` and `unlock` acquire and release the lock L, respectively, where $L = 1$ if the lock is held, and is zero otherwise. The correctness property we wish to check is that (1) the procedure `lock` is never called when the lock is already held, and (2) procedure `unlock` is never called unless the lock is already held. These correctness properties are expressed as assertions in the `lock` and `unlock` procedures. Hence, checking these properties reduces to

Program	Transfer relations	Error relations

`lock() {`
`    assert L = 0;`
`    L := 1;`
`}`
 	
`unlock() {`
`    assert L = 1;`
`    L := 0;`
`}`
 	
`main() {`
`    loop();`
`    unlock();`
`}`
 	
`loop() {`
`    lock();`
`    D := N;`
`    unl();`
`    if (N != D) {`
`        loop();`
`    } else {`
`        // skip`
`    }`
`}`
 	
`unl() {`
`    if (*) {`
`        unlock();`
`        // N++;`
`    } else {`
`        // skip`
`    }`
`}`
	$\mathbf{T}lock(L, N, D, L_1, N, D) \leftarrow$
	$\wedge\; L = 0$
	$\wedge\; L_1 = 1$
	
	$\mathbf{T}unlock(L, N, D, L_1, N, D) \leftarrow$
	$\wedge\; L = 1$
	$\wedge\; L_1 = 0$
	
	$\mathbf{T}main(L, N, D, L_2, N_2, D_2) \leftarrow$
	$\wedge\; \mathbf{T}loop(L, N, D, L_1, N_1, D_1)$
	$\wedge\; \mathbf{T}unlock(L_1, N_1, D_1, L_2, N_2, D_2)$
	
	$\mathbf{T}loop(L, N, D, L_4, N_4, D_4) \leftarrow$
	$\wedge\; \mathbf{T}lock(L, N, D, L_1, N_1, D_1)$
	$\wedge\; D_2 = N_1$
	$\wedge\; \mathbf{T}unl(L_1, N_1, D_2, L_3, N_3, D_3)$
	$\wedge \vee \wedge\; N_3 \neq D_3$
	$\qquad\wedge\; \mathbf{T}loop(L_3, N_3, D_3, L_4, N_4, D_4)$
	$\vee \wedge\; N_3 = D_3$
	$\qquad\wedge\; L_4 = L_3$
	$\qquad\wedge\; N_4 = N_3$
	$\qquad\wedge\; D_4 = D_3$
	
	$\mathbf{T}unl(L, N, D, L_1, N_1, D_1) \leftarrow$
	$\vee\; \mathbf{T}unlock(L, N, D, L_1, N_1, D_1)$
	$\vee \wedge\; L_1 = L$
	$\qquad\wedge\; N_1 = N$
	$\qquad\wedge\; D_1 = D$
		$\mathbf{E}lock(L, N, D) \leftarrow$
		$L \neq 0$
		
		$\mathbf{E}unlock(L, N, D) \leftarrow$
		$L \neq 1$
		
		$\mathbf{E}main(L, N, D) \leftarrow$
		$\vee\; \mathbf{E}loop(L, N, D)$
		$\vee \wedge\; \mathbf{T}loop(L, N, D, L_1, N_1, D_1)$
		$\qquad\wedge\; \mathbf{E}unlock(L_1, N_1, D_1)$
		
		$\mathbf{E}loop(L, N, D) \leftarrow$
		$\vee\; \mathbf{E}lock(L, N, D)$
		$\vee \wedge\; \mathbf{T}lock(L, N, D, L_1, N_1, D_1)$
		$\qquad\wedge\; D_2 = N_1$
		$\qquad\wedge \vee\; \mathbf{E}unl(L_1, N_1, D_2)$
		$\qquad\qquad\vee \wedge\; \mathbf{T}unl(L_1, N_1, D_2, L_3, N_3, D_3)$
		$\qquad\qquad\qquad\wedge\; N_3 \neq D_3$
		$\qquad\qquad\qquad\wedge\; \mathbf{E}loop(L_3, N_3, D_3)$
		
		$\mathbf{E}unl(L, N, D) \leftarrow$
		$\mathbf{E}unlock(L, N, D)$

Fig. 1. The example program and the corresponding error and transfer relations.

checking whether the example program *goes wrong* by violating either of these assertions.

The example contains three other routines, which manipulate two additional global variables, N and D. Thus, the state of the store is captured by the triple $\langle L, N, D \rangle$. The example uses the notation if (*) ... to express nondeterministic choice.

Our method translates each procedure m into two CLP relations:

1. the *error relation* $\mathbf{E}m(L, N, D)$, which describes states $\langle L, N, D \rangle$ from which the execution of m may go wrong by failing an assertion, and

2. the *transfer relation* $\mathbf{T}m(L, N, D, L', N', D')$, which, when m terminates normally, describes the relation between the pre-state $\langle L, N, D \rangle$ and post-state $\langle L', N', D' \rangle$ of m.

The transfer and error relations for the example program are shown in Figure 1, columns 2 and 3, respectively. The relation $\mathbf{E}$lock says that lock goes wrong if L is not initially 0, and $\mathbf{T}$lock says that lock terminates normally if L is initially 0, where $L = 1$ and N and D are unchanged the post-state. The relation $\mathbf{E}$main says that main goes wrong if either loop goes wrong, or loop terminates normally and unlock goes wrong in the post-state of loop. The other relation definitions are similarly intuitive. Automatically generating these definitions from the program source code is straightforward.

We use these relation definitions to check if an invocation of main may go wrong by asking the CLP query $\mathbf{E}$main(L, N, D). This query is satisfiable in the case where $L = 1$, indicating that the program may go wrong if the lock is held initially, and an inspection of the source code shows that this is indeed the case.

If we provide the additional precondition that the lock is not initially held, then the corresponding CLP query

$$L = 0 \wedge \mathbf{E}\text{main}(L, N, D)$$

is still satisfiable. An examination of the satisfying CLP derivation shows that it corresponds to the following execution trace: main calls loop, which calls lock, which returns to loop, which calls unl, which calls unlock, which returns to unl, which returns to loop, which returns to main, which calls unlock, which fails its assertion, since there are two calls to unlock without an intervening call to lock.

The reason for this bug is that the increment operation N++ in unl (which is present in the original BLAST example) is commented out. After uncommenting this increment operation, the modified transfer relation for unl is:

$$
\begin{aligned}
\mathbf{T}\text{unl}(L, N, D, L_1, N_2, D_1) \leftarrow \\
\vee \wedge \mathbf{T}\text{unlock}(L, N, D, L_1, N_1, D_1) \\
\wedge N_2 = N_1 + 1 \\
\vee \wedge L_1 = L \\
\wedge N_2 = N \\
\wedge D_1 = D
\end{aligned}
$$

The above CLP query is now unsatisfiable, indicating that the fixed example program does not go wrong and thus satisfies the desired correctness property.

4   The Source Language

This section presents the syntax and semantics of the imperative language that we use as the basis for our formal development.

4.1   Syntax

A program is a sequence of procedure definitions. Each procedure definition consists of a procedure name and a sequence of formal parameters, which are bound in the procedure body, and can be α-renamed in the usual fashion. The procedure body is an expression. Expressions include variable reference and assignment, `let`-expressions, application of primitive functions and user-defined procedures, conditionals, and assertions. To illustrate the handling of heap-allocated data structures, the language includes mutable pairs, and provides operations to create pairs and to access and update each field i of a pair, for $i = 1, 2$. Although our language does not include iterative constructs such as `while` or `for` loops, they can easily being encoded as tail-recursive procedures. In addition to local variables bound by `let`-expressions and parameter lists, programs may also manipulate the global variables $\vec{g}$. For simplicity, the language is untyped, although we syntactically distinguish boolean expressions, which are formed by the application of a primitive predicate to a sequence of arguments.

Programming Language Syntax

(*programs*) $P ::= \vec{D}$		(*procedure names*) m
(*definitions*) $D ::= m(\vec{x})\ \{e\}$		(*global variables*) $\vec{g}$
(*expressions*) $e ::= x \mid x := e \mid \mathtt{let}\ x = e\ \mathtt{in}\ e$		(*special variables*) $\vec{h} = h.h_1.h_2$
$\qquad \mid\ f(\vec{e}) \mid m(\vec{e}) \mid \mathtt{if}\ p(\vec{e})\ e\ e$		
$\qquad \mid\ \mathtt{assert}\ p(\vec{e}) \mid \langle e, e \rangle \mid e.i \mid e.i := e$		

Throughout this paper, we assume the original program and the desired correctness property have already been combined into an *instrumented program*, which includes `assert` statements that check that the desired correctness property is respected by the program. We say an execution of the instrumented program *goes wrong* if it fails an assertion because the original program fails the desired correctness property. The focus of this paper is to statically determine if the instrumented program can go wrong.

Notation. We use $\vec{X}$ to denote a sequence of entities, $\vec{X}.\vec{Y}$ denotes sequence concatenation, and ϵ is the empty sequence. We sometimes interpret sequences as sets, and vice-versa. If M is a (partial) map, then the map $M[X := Y]$ maps X to Y and is otherwise identical to M, and the map $M[-X]$ is undefined on X and is otherwise identical to M. The operations $M[\vec{X} := \vec{Y}]$ and $M[-\vec{X}]$ are defined analogously. We use $\vec{X} = \vec{Y}$ to abbreviate $X_1 = Y_1 \wedge \ldots \wedge X_n = Y_n$. We use $e_1 ; e_2$ to abbreviate $\mathtt{let}\ x = e_1\ \mathtt{in}\ e_2$, where x is not free in e_2.

4.2   Semantics

We formalize the meaning of programs using a "big step" operation semantics. A store σ is a partial mapping from variables to values. The set of values includes constants and maps. To represent pairs, the store σ maps three special variables,

$$\boxed{P \vdash e : \sigma \to \sigma', v \qquad P \vdash e : \sigma \ \mathbf{wr}}$$

$$\frac{}{P \vdash x : \sigma \to \sigma, \sigma(x)} \qquad \frac{P \vdash e : \sigma \ \mathbf{wr}}{P \vdash x := e : \sigma \ \mathbf{wr}} \qquad \frac{P \vdash e : \sigma \to \sigma', v}{P \vdash x := e : \sigma \to \sigma'[x := v], v}$$

$$\frac{P \vdash e_1 : \sigma \ \mathbf{wr}}{P \vdash \mathtt{let}\ x = e_1\ \mathtt{in}\ e_2 : \sigma \ \mathbf{wr}} \qquad \frac{P \vdash e_1 : \sigma \to \sigma', v_1 \qquad P \vdash e_2 : \sigma'[x := v_1] \ \mathbf{wr}}{P \vdash \mathtt{let}\ x = e_1\ \mathtt{in}\ e_2 : \sigma \ \mathbf{wr}}$$

$$\frac{P \vdash e_1 : \sigma \to \sigma', v_1 \qquad P \vdash e_2 : \sigma'[x := v_1] \to \sigma'', v_2}{P \vdash \mathtt{let}\ x = e_1\ \mathtt{in}\ e_2 : \sigma \to \sigma''[-x], v_2}$$

$$\frac{P \vdash \vec{e} : \sigma \ \mathbf{wr}}{P \vdash f(\vec{e}) : \sigma \ \mathbf{wr}} \qquad \frac{P \vdash \vec{e} : \sigma \to \sigma', \vec{v}}{P \vdash f(\vec{e}) : \sigma \to \sigma', \mathcal{M}_f(f, \vec{v})} \qquad \frac{P \vdash \vec{e} : \sigma \ \mathbf{wr}}{P \vdash m(\vec{e}) : \sigma \ \mathbf{wr}}$$

$$\frac{\begin{array}{c} P \vdash \vec{e} : \sigma \to \sigma', \vec{v} \\ m(\vec{x})\ \{e\} \in P \\ \vec{x} \cap dom(\sigma') = \emptyset \\ P \vdash e : \sigma'[\vec{x} := \vec{v}] \ \mathbf{wr} \end{array}}{P \vdash m(\vec{e}) : \sigma \ \mathbf{wr}} \qquad \frac{\begin{array}{c} P \vdash \vec{e} : \sigma \to \sigma', \vec{v} \\ m(\vec{x})\ \{e\} \in P \\ \vec{x} \cap dom(\sigma') = \emptyset \\ P \vdash e : \sigma'[\vec{x} := \vec{v}] \to \sigma'', v \end{array}}{P \vdash m(\vec{e}) : \sigma \to \sigma''[-\vec{x}], v} \qquad \frac{\begin{array}{c} P \vdash \vec{e} : \sigma \to \sigma', \vec{v} \\ \text{if } \mathcal{M}_p(p, \vec{v}) \text{ then } i = 1 \text{ else } i = 2 \\ P \vdash e_i : \sigma' \to \sigma'', v \end{array}}{P \vdash \mathtt{if}\ p(\vec{e})\ e_1\ e_2 : \sigma \to \sigma'', v}$$

$$\frac{P \vdash \vec{e} : \sigma \ \mathbf{wr}}{P \vdash \mathtt{if}\ p(\vec{e})\ e_1\ e_2 : \sigma \ \mathbf{wr}} \qquad \frac{\begin{array}{c} P \vdash \vec{e} : \sigma \to \sigma', \vec{v} \\ \text{if } \mathcal{M}_p(p, \vec{v}) \text{ then } i = 1 \text{ else } i = 2 \\ P \vdash e_i : \sigma' \ \mathbf{wr} \end{array}}{P \vdash \mathtt{if}\ p(\vec{e})\ e_1\ e_2 : \sigma \ \mathbf{wr}}$$

$$\frac{P \vdash \vec{e} : \sigma \ \mathbf{wr}}{P \vdash \mathtt{assert}\ p(\vec{e}) : \sigma \ \mathbf{wr}} \qquad \frac{P \vdash \vec{e} : \sigma \to \sigma', \vec{v} \qquad \mathcal{M}_p(p, \vec{v}) = false}{P \vdash \mathtt{assert}\ p(\vec{e}) : \sigma \ \mathbf{wr}} \qquad \frac{P \vdash \vec{e} : \sigma \to \sigma', \vec{v} \qquad \mathcal{M}_p(p, \vec{v}) = true}{P \vdash \mathtt{assert}\ p(\vec{e}) : \sigma \to \sigma, 0}$$

$$\frac{P \vdash e_1.e_2 : \sigma \ \mathbf{wr}}{P \vdash \langle e_1, e_2 \rangle : \sigma \ \mathbf{wr}} \qquad \frac{P \vdash e_1.e_2 : \sigma \to \sigma', v_1.v_2 \qquad \sigma'(h)(l) = 0 \qquad \sigma'' = \sigma'[h := \sigma'(h)[l := 1], h_i := \sigma'(h_i)[l := v_i]^{i \in 1,2}]}{P \vdash \langle e_1, e_2 \rangle : \sigma \to \sigma'', l}$$

$$\frac{P \vdash e : \sigma \ \mathbf{wr}}{P \vdash e.i : \sigma \ \mathbf{wr}} \qquad \frac{P \vdash e : \sigma \to \sigma', l}{P \vdash e.i : \sigma \to \sigma', \sigma(h_i)(l)}$$

$$\frac{P \vdash e_1.e_2 : \sigma \ \mathbf{wr}}{P \vdash e_1.i := e_2 : \sigma \ \mathbf{wr}} \qquad \frac{P \vdash e_1.e_2 : \sigma \to \sigma', v_1.v_2 \qquad \sigma'' = \sigma'[h_i := \sigma'(h_i)[v_1 := v_2]]}{P \vdash e_1.i := e_2 : \sigma \to \sigma'', v_2}$$

$$\boxed{P \vdash \vec{e} : \sigma \to \sigma', \vec{v} \qquad P \vdash \vec{e} : \sigma \ \mathbf{wr}}$$

$$\frac{}{P \vdash \epsilon : \sigma \to \sigma, \epsilon} \qquad \frac{P \vdash e : \sigma \ \mathbf{wr}}{P \vdash e.\vec{e} : \sigma \ \mathbf{wr}} \qquad \frac{P \vdash e : \sigma \to \sigma', v \qquad P \vdash \vec{e} : \sigma' \ \mathbf{wr}}{P \vdash e.\vec{e} : \sigma \ \mathbf{wr}} \qquad \frac{P \vdash e : \sigma \to \sigma', v \qquad P \vdash \vec{e} : \sigma' \to \sigma'', \vec{v}}{P \vdash e.\vec{e} : \sigma \to \sigma'', v.\vec{v}}$$

Fig. 2. Evaluation rules.

h, h_1, and h_2, to maps. The map $\sigma(h)$ describes which locations have been allocated, and $\sigma(h_1)$ and $\sigma(h_2)$ describe the components of allocated pairs. For any heap location l, if $\sigma(h)(l) = 0$ then the location l is not allocated, otherwise the components of the pair at location l are given by $\sigma(h_1)(l)$ and $\sigma(h_2)(l)$, respectively. This representation of pairs significantly simplifies the correspondence proof between imperative programs and constraint logic programs.

The judgment $P \vdash e : \sigma \rightarrow \sigma', v$ states that, when started from an initial store σ, the evaluation of expression e may terminate normally yielding a result value v and resulting store σ'. The judgment $P \vdash e : \sigma$ wr states that, when started from an initial store σ, the evaluation of expression e may go wrong by failing an assertion. Similarly, the judgments $P \vdash \vec{e} : \sigma \rightarrow \sigma', \vec{v}$ and $P \vdash \vec{e} : \sigma$ wr describes whether an expression sequence $\vec{e}$ terminates normally, yielding value sequence $\vec{v}$, or goes wrong, respectively. The rules defining these judgments are shown in Figure 2. These rules rely on the function $\mathcal{M}_f : FnSym \times Value^* \rightarrow Value$ and the relation $\mathcal{M}_p \subseteq PredSym \times Value^*$ to provide the meaning of primitive functions and predicates, respectively.

5   Translating Imperative Programs into CLP

We now describe the translation of imperative programs into CLP. At each step in the translation, the environment Γ maps each program variable x into a CLP term that provides a symbolic representation of the value of x. Given the initial environment Γ for an expression e, the judgment

$$\Gamma \vdash e \rightarrow w \,|\, n \cdot \Gamma' \cdot t$$

describes the behavior of e. The *wrong condition* w is a constraint describing initial states from which e may go wrong by failing an assertion. For example, the wrong condition of assert $x = 0$ is $\Gamma(x) \neq 0$, i.e., the assertion goes wrong if x is not initially 0. Similarly, the *normal condition* n describes the initial states from which e may terminate normally. In this case, the environment Γ' symbolically describes values of variables in the post-state, and the term t is a symbolic representation of the result of e. The judgment $\Gamma \vdash \vec{e} \rightarrow w \,|\, n \cdot \Gamma' \cdot \vec{t}$ behaves in a similar manner on expression sequences, which may go wrong or may terminate normally producing a value sequence represented by $\vec{t}$.

The rules defining these judgements are shown in Figure 3. The rule [EXP VAR] states that the variable access x never goes wrong and always terminate normally without changing the program state. The rule retrieves a symbolic representation $\Gamma(x)$ for the value of x from the environment. The rule [EXP ASSIGN] for an assignment $x := e$ determines a symbolic representation t for e, and updates the environment to record that t represents of the current value of x. The rule [EXP LET] states that let $x = e_1$ in e_2 goes wrong if either e_1 goes wrong or if e_1 terminates normally and e_2 goes wrong.

Some translation rules are more complicated. For example, the rule [EXP IF] for the conditional if $p(\vec{e})\ e_1\ e_2$ needs to merge the environments Γ'_i produced by the translation of e_i, for $i = 1, 2$. To accomplish this merge, the rule determines

$$\boxed{\Gamma \vdash e \rightarrow w \,|\, n \cdot \Gamma' \cdot t \qquad \Gamma \vdash \vec{e} \rightarrow w \,|\, n \cdot \Gamma' \cdot \vec{t}}$$

[EXP VAR]

$$\frac{}{\Gamma \vdash x \rightarrow false \,|\, true \cdot \Gamma \cdot \Gamma(x)}$$

[EXP ASSIGN]

$$\frac{\Gamma \vdash e \rightarrow w \,|\, n \cdot \Gamma' \cdot t}{\Gamma \vdash x := e \rightarrow w \,|\, n \cdot \Gamma'[x := t] \cdot t}$$

[EXP LET]

$$\frac{\Gamma \vdash e_1 \rightarrow w_1 \,|\, n_1 \cdot \Gamma_1 \cdot t_1 \qquad \Gamma_1[x := t_1] \vdash e_2 \rightarrow w_2 \,|\, n_2 \cdot \Gamma_2 \cdot t_2}{\Gamma \vdash \text{let } x = e_1 \text{ in } e_2 \rightarrow w_1 \vee (n_1 \wedge w_2) \,|\, n_1 \wedge n_2 \cdot \Gamma_2[-x] \cdot t_2}$$

[EXP FN]

$$\frac{\Gamma \vdash \vec{e} \rightarrow w \,|\, n \cdot \Gamma' \cdot \vec{t}}{\Gamma \vdash f(\vec{e}) \rightarrow w \,|\, n \cdot \Gamma' \cdot f(\vec{t})}$$

[EXP CALL]

$$\frac{\begin{array}{c} \Gamma \vdash \vec{e} \rightarrow w \,|\, n \cdot \Gamma' \cdot \vec{t} \\ z, \vec{g}', \vec{h}' \text{ fresh} \\ w' \equiv w \vee (n \wedge E_m(\vec{t}, \Gamma'(\vec{g}), \Gamma'(\vec{h}))) \\ n' \equiv n \wedge T_m(\vec{t}, \Gamma'(\vec{g}), \Gamma'(\vec{h}), \vec{g}', \vec{h}', z) \\ \Gamma'' \equiv \Gamma'[\vec{g} := \vec{g}', \vec{h} := \vec{h}'] \end{array}}{\Gamma \vdash m(\vec{e}) \rightarrow w' \,|\, n' \cdot \Gamma'' \cdot z}$$

[EXP IF]

$$\frac{\begin{array}{c} \Gamma \vdash \vec{e} \rightarrow w \,|\, n \cdot \Gamma' \cdot \vec{t} \qquad \Gamma' \vdash e_i \rightarrow w_i \,|\, n_i \cdot \Gamma_i' \cdot t_i \\ z \text{ fresh} \qquad \vec{y} = \{y \mid \Gamma_1'(y) \neq \Gamma_2'(y)\} \\ \Gamma''(x) = \begin{cases} \Gamma_1'(x) & \text{if } x \notin \vec{y} \\ \text{fresh var if } x \in \vec{y} \end{cases} \\ w' \equiv w \vee (n \wedge p(\vec{t}) \wedge w_1) \vee (n \wedge \neg p(\vec{t}) \wedge w_2) \\ n_1' \equiv n \wedge \ p(\vec{t}) \wedge n_1 \wedge z = t_1 \wedge \Gamma''(\vec{y}) = \Gamma_1'(\vec{y}) \\ n_2' \equiv n \wedge \neg p(\vec{t}) \wedge n_2 \wedge z = t_2 \wedge \Gamma''(\vec{y}) = \Gamma_2'(\vec{y}) \end{array}}{\Gamma \vdash \text{if } p(\vec{e}) \ e_1 \ e_2 \rightarrow w' \,|\, (n_1' \vee n_2') \cdot \Gamma'' \cdot z}$$

[EXP ASSERT]

$$\frac{\Gamma \vdash \vec{e} \rightarrow w \,|\, n \cdot \Gamma' \cdot \vec{t}}{\Gamma \vdash \text{assert } p(\vec{e}) \rightarrow w \vee (n \wedge \neg p(\vec{t})) \,|\, n \wedge p(\vec{t}) \cdot \Gamma' \cdot 0}$$

[EXP PAIR]

$$\frac{\begin{array}{c} \Gamma \vdash e_1.e_2 \rightarrow w \,|\, n \cdot \Gamma' \cdot t_1.t_2 \\ \Gamma'' \equiv \Gamma'[h_i := \text{store}(\Gamma'(h_i), l, t_i)^{i \in 1,2}, h := \text{store}(h, l, 1)] \\ l \text{ fresh} \qquad n' \equiv n \wedge \text{select}(\Gamma(h), l) = 0) \end{array}}{\Gamma \vdash \langle e_1, e_2 \rangle \rightarrow w \,|\, n' \cdot \Gamma'' \cdot l}$$

[EXP FIELD REF]

$$\frac{\Gamma \vdash e \rightarrow w \,|\, n \cdot \Gamma' \cdot t}{\Gamma \vdash e.i \rightarrow w \,|\, n \cdot \Gamma' \cdot \text{select}(\Gamma'(h_i), t)}$$

[EXP FIELD ASSIGN]

$$\frac{\Gamma \vdash e_1.e_2 \rightarrow w \,|\, n \cdot \Gamma' \cdot t_1.t_2 \qquad \Gamma'' \equiv \Gamma'[h_i := \text{store}(\Gamma'(h_i), t_1, t_2)]}{\Gamma \vdash e_1.i := e_2 \rightarrow w \,|\, n \cdot \Gamma'' \cdot t_2}$$

[EXPS NONE]

$$\frac{}{\Gamma_1 \vdash \epsilon \rightarrow false \,|\, true \cdot \Gamma \cdot \epsilon}$$

[EXPS SOME]

$$\frac{\Gamma \vdash e \rightarrow w \,|\, n \cdot \Gamma' \cdot t \qquad \Gamma' \vdash \vec{e} \rightarrow w' \,|\, n' \cdot \Gamma'' \cdot \vec{t}}{\Gamma \vdash e.\vec{e} \rightarrow w \vee (n \wedge w') \,|\, n \wedge n' \cdot \Gamma'' \cdot t.\vec{t}}$$

$$\boxed{\vdash D \rightarrow \vec{R} \qquad \vdash P \rightarrow \vec{R}}$$

[DEF]

$$\frac{\begin{array}{c} \Gamma \equiv [\vec{x} := \vec{x}, \vec{g} := \vec{g}, \vec{h} := \vec{h}] \\ \Gamma \vdash e \rightarrow w \,|\, n \cdot \Gamma' \cdot t \\ \vec{R} = \left\{ \begin{array}{l} E_m(\vec{x}, \vec{g}, \vec{h}) \leftarrow w \\ T_m(\vec{x}, \vec{g}, \vec{h}, \Gamma'(\vec{g}), \Gamma'(\vec{h}), t) \leftarrow n \end{array} \right\} \end{array}}{\vdash m(\vec{x}) \ \{e\} \rightarrow \vec{R}}$$

[DEFS]

$$\frac{P = D_1 \cdots \cdot D_n \qquad \vdash D_i \rightarrow \vec{R}_i}{\vdash P \rightarrow \vec{R}_1 \cdots \cdot \vec{R}_n}$$

Fig. 3. Translation rules.

the set $\vec{y}$ of variables assigned in either e_1 or e_2, and introduces an environment Γ'' that maps $\vec{y}$ to fresh variables. Then, having determined that the branch e_i of the conditional is executed, the rule asserts that the $\Gamma''(\vec{y}) = \Gamma_i'(\vec{y})$, thus recording that the representation of $\vec{y}$ in the resulting environment Γ'' come from the branch e_i. This translation of conditionals avoids the exponential blow-up of traditional VC generation algorithms [10], and is analogous to the compact VC generation algorithm of ESC/Java [16].

Our translation for pairs relies on the primitive functions $\mathtt{select}$ and $\mathtt{store}$, where $\mathtt{store}(a, i, v)$ extends a functional map a at index i with value v, and $\mathtt{select}(a, i)$ selects the element at index i from map a. These two functions satisfy the select-of-store axioms:

$$\mathtt{select}(\mathtt{store}(a, i, v), i) = v$$
$$i \neq j \Rightarrow \mathtt{select}(\mathtt{store}(a, i, v), j) = select(a, j)$$

To aid in the translation, the environment Γ maps the special variables h, h_1, h_2 into CLP terms that symbolically model of the current state of the heap. The rule [EXP PAIR] for the pair creation expression $\langle e_1, e_2 \rangle$ introduces a fresh variable l and asserts that $\mathtt{select}(\Gamma(h), l) = 0$, which means that the location l is not yet allocated. The rule then updates the environment (1) to map h to $\mathtt{store}(\Gamma(h), l, 1)$, indicating that location l is now allocated, and (2) to map each h_i to $\mathtt{store}(\Gamma(h_i), l, t_i)$, where the term t_i represents the value of e_i, for $i = 1, 2$. Thus, the rule records the contents of the pair in the new terms for h_1 and h_2. The rules for accessing and updating pairs operate in a similar manner.

The most novel aspect of our translation concerns its handling of procedure calls. Earlier approaches translated procedure calls using user-supplied specifications. However, since writing specifications for all procedures imposes a significant burden on the programmer, we use a different approach that leverages the ability to define relation symbols recursively in CLP.

We translate each procedure definition $m(\vec{x}) \{e\}$ into two rules. The first rule defines an *error relation* E_m that describes pre-states from which an invocation of m may go wrong; the second rule defines a *transfer relation* T_m that, in situations where m terminates normally, describes the pre-state/post-state relation of m. The arguments to the error relation E_m are the formal parameters $\vec{x}$, the global variables $\vec{g}$, plus the three special variables $\vec{h} = h.h_1.h_2$ that model the heap. The arguments to T_m are again the formal parameters $\vec{x}$, the globals $\vec{g}$, the special variables $\vec{h}$, followed by $\vec{g'}$, which represents the post-state of the global variables, followed by $\vec{h} = h'.h_1'.h_2'$, which represents the post heap state, followed by a term representing the return value of m. The rule [EXP CALL] for a procedure call $m(\vec{e})$ generates a wrong condition w' that uses E_m to express states from which the execution of $m(\vec{e})$ may go wrong, and generates a normal condition n' that uses T_m to describe how $m(\vec{e})$ may terminate normally.

5.1   Correctness of the Translation

Given an imperative program P, we translate it into error and transfer relations $\vec{R}$ according to the translation rule $\vdash P \rightarrow \vec{R}$. For any expression e, the judgement

$$\Gamma \vdash e \to w \mid n \cdot \Gamma' \cdot t$$

describes the behavior of that expression from any initial state σ that is compatible with Γ, *i.e.*, where $dom(\Gamma) \subseteq dom(\sigma)$ and $lm(\vec{R}, \mathcal{D}) \models \tilde{\exists}(\sigma = \Gamma)$. We use the notation $\sigma = \Gamma$ to abbreviate $\bigwedge_{x \in dom(\sigma)} \sigma(x) = \Gamma(x)$, where $\sigma(x)$ means the ground term representing the value $\sigma(x)$.

To determine if e goes wrong from σ (*i.e.*, $P \vdash e : \sigma \text{ wr}$), we check

$$lm(\vec{R}, \mathcal{D}) \models \tilde{\exists}(\sigma = \Gamma \wedge w) .$$

Similarly, to check if e terminates normally, yielding post-store σ' and result v, we check

$$lm(\vec{R}, \mathcal{D}) \models \tilde{\exists}(\sigma = \Gamma \wedge n \wedge \sigma' = \Gamma' \wedge v = t) .$$

Thus, to check if the program's initial procedure *main* goes wrong, we use the CLP query:

$$lm(\vec{R}, \mathcal{D}) \models \tilde{\exists} E_{main}(\vec{g}, \vec{h}) .$$

If this query is satisfiable, the CLP implementation returns a satisfying assignment for $\vec{g}$ and $\vec{h}$, describing the initial state of an erroneous execution. If the CLP implementation also returns a CLP derivation, then this derivation corresponds in a fairly direct manner to a trace of the erroneous execution.

6   Applications

We next consider the example program shown in Figure 4, which, for clarity, is presented using Java syntax. This class implements rational numbers, where a rational is represented as a pair of integers for the numerator and denominator. The class contains a constructor for creating rationals and a method `trunc` for converting a rational to an integer. The example also contains a test harness, which reads in two integers, `n` and `d`, ensures that `d` is not zero, creates a corresponding rational, and then repeatedly prints out the truncation of the rational.

We wish to check that a division-by-zero error never occurs. We express this correctness property as an assertion in the `trunc` method, and translate the instrumented program into CLP rules. The CLP query **Emain**() is satisfiable, indicating an error in the program. An investigation of a satisfying CLP derivation reveals the source of the error: the arguments are passed to the `Rational` constructor in the wrong order. Note that since both arguments are integers, Java's type system does not catch this error.

After fixing this bug, the query **Emain**() is now unsatisfiable, indicating that a division-by-zero error cannot occur. However, the CLP implementation that we use, SICStus Prolog [27], requires several seconds to answer this query, since its depth-first search strategy explicitly iterates through the loop in `main` 10,000 times.

To avoid this inefficiency, we are currently developing a CLP implementation optimized towards software model checking. This implementation uses lazy

```
class Rational {

    int num, den;

    Rational(int n, int d) {
        num = n;
        den = d;
    }

    int trunc() {
        assert den != 0;
        return num/den;
    }

}
```

```
public static void main(String[] a) {
    int n = readInt(), d = readInt();
    if( d == 0 ) {
        return;
    }
    Rational r = new Rational(d,n);
    for(int i=0; i<10000; i++) {
        print( r.trunc() );
    }
}
```

Fig. 4. The example program Rational.

predicate abstraction and counter-example driven abstraction refinement. Our prototype implementation determines the unsatisfiability of the Rational example in just two iterations. We are currently extending this implementation to handle more realistic benchmarks.

7   Related Work

This paper can be viewed as a synthesis of ideas from extended static checking [8,14] and model checking [5,24,3,23]. An extended static checker translates the given program into a combination of constraints over program variables, and uses sophisticated decision procedures to reason about the validity of these constraints, thus performing a precise, goal-directed analysis. However, the translation of (recursive) procedure calls requires programmer-supplied specifications. We build on top of the ESC approach, but avoid the need for procedure specifications by targeting the extended logic of CLP, in which we can express recursion directly.

The depth-first search of standard CLP implementations [27] corresponds to explicit path exploration, much like that performed by software model checkers, such as Bandera [11]. However, whereas Bandera relies on programmer-supplied abstractions to abstract (infinite-state) data variables, the CLP implementation reasons about data values using collections of constraints, thus providing a form of automatic data abstraction. The programmer-supplied abstractions of Bandera do provide stronger termination guarantees, but may yield false alarms.

The software checkers SLAM [1] and BLAST [18] use a combination of predicate abstraction [17] and automatic predicate inference to avoid false alarms and the need for programmer-supplied abstractions, though they may not terminate. These tools have been successfully applied to a number of device drivers. Both tools abstract the given imperative program to a finite-state boolean program, which is then model checked. This paper suggests that the well-studied logic of CLP may also provide a suitable foundation for the development of such tools.

Delzanno and Podelski [7] also explore the use of CLP for model checking. They focus on concurrent systems expressed in the guarded-command specification language proposed by Shankar [26], which does not provide explicit support for dynamic allocation or recursion. The performance of their CLP-based model checking approach is promising.

Bruening [2] has built a dynamic assertion checker based on state-space exploration for multithreaded Java programs. Stoller [28] provides a generalization of Bruening's method to allow model checking of programs with either message-passing or shared-memory communication. Both of these approaches operate on the concrete program without any abstraction. Yahav [30] describes a method to model check multithreaded Java programs using a 3-valued logic [25] to abstract the store.

Abstract interpretation [6] is a standard framework for developing and describing program analyses. It provides the semantics basis for the abstractions in the above model checking tools and it has been applied successfully in many applications, including rocket controllers [29].

Instead of avoiding the need for loop invariants and specifications, another approach is to infer such annotations automatically. The Houdini annotation inference system [15,13] re-uses ESC/Java as a subroutine in a generate-and-test approach to annotation inference. Daikon uses an empirical approach to find probable invariants [12].

Symbolic execution is the underlying technique of the successful bug-finding tool PREfix for C and C++ programs [4]. For each procedure in the given program, PREfix synthesizes a set of execution paths, called a *model*. Models are used to reason about calls, which makes the process somewhat modular, except that fixpoints of models are approximated iteratively for recursive and mutually recursive calls.

8   Conclusion

This paper explores the connection between two programming paradigms: the traditional imperative paradigm and the constraint logic programming paradigm. We have expressed the correctness of imperative programs in terms of CLP satisfiability, based on a novel, semantics-preserving translation from imperative programs to CLP programs. The resulting CLP programs provide a clean way to reason about the behavior and correctness of the original imperative program.

This connection has immediate practical applications: it enables us to use existing CLP implementations to check correctness properties of imperative programs. For depth-first CLP implementations, this approach yields an efficient method for bounded model checking of software, using a combination of symbolic reasoning for data values and explicit path exploration.

Finally, the logic of CLP is well-studied [19,21,20,22], and may provide optimizations and implementation techniques such as tableaux methods and subsumption [22], which offer the promise of complete model checking on certain classes of infinite-state programs. More experience on practical examples is certainly necessary, and may provide intuition and motivation to develop specialized CLP implementations optimized for software model checking.

References

1. T. Ball and S. K. Rajamani. Automatically validating temporal safety properties of interfaces. In M. B. Dwyer, editor, *Model Checking Software, 8th International SPIN Workshop*, volume 2057 of *Lecture Notes in Computer Science*, pages 103–122. Springer, May 2001.
2. D. Bruening. Systematic testing of multithreaded Java programs. Master's thesis, Massachusetts Institute of Technology, 1999.
3. J. R. Burch, E. M. Clarke, K. L. McMillan, D. L. Dill, and L. J. Hwang. Symbolic model checking: 10^{20} states and beyond. *Information and Computation*, 98(2):142–170, 1992.
4. W. R. Bush, J. D. Pincus, and D. J. Sielaff. A static analyzer for finding dynamic programming errors. *Software—Practice & Experience*, 30(7):775–802, June 2000.
5. E. M. Clarke and E. A. Emerson. Design and synthesis of synchronization skeletons using branching-time temporal logic. In *Workshop on Logic of Programs*, Lecture Notes in Computer Science, pages 52–71. Springer-Verlag, 1981.
6. P. Cousot and R. Cousot. Abstract interpretation: A unified lattice model for static analyses of programs by construction or approximation of fixpoints. In *Proceedings of the Symposium on the Principles of Programming Languages*, pages 238–252, 1977.
7. G. Delzanno and A. Podelski. Model checking in CLP. *Lecture Notes in Computer Science*, 1579:223–239, 1999.
8. D. L. Detlefs, K. R. M. Leino, G. Nelson, and J. B. Saxe. Extended static checking. Research Report 159, Compaq Systems Research Center, Dec. 1998.
9. D. L. Detlefs, G. Nelson, and J. B. Saxe. A theorem prover for program analysis. Manuscript in preparation, 2002.
10. E. W. Dijkstra. *A Discipline of Programming*. Prentice Hall, Englewood Cliffs, NJ, 1976.
11. M. Dwyer, J. Hatcliff, R. Joehanes, S. Laubach, C. Pasareanu, Robby, W. Visser, and H. Zheng. Tool-supported program abstraction for finite-state verification. In *Proceedings of the 23rd International Conference on Software Engineering*, 2001.
12. M. D. Ernst, A. Czeisler, W. G. Griswold, and D. Notkin. Quickly detecting relevant program invariants. In *Proceedings of the 22nd International Conference on Software Engineering (ICSE 2000), Limerick, Ireland*, June 2000.
13. C. Flanagan, R. Joshi, and K. R. M. Leino. Annotation inference for modular checkers. *Inf. Process. Lett.*, 77(2–4):97–108, Feb. 2001.
14. C. Flanagan, K. Leino, M. Lillibridge, G. Nelson, J. Saxe, and R. Stata. Extended static checking for Java. In *Proceedings of the Conference on Programming Language Design and Implementation*, pages 234–245, June 2002.
15. C. Flanagan and K. R. M. Leino. Houdini, an annotation assistant for ESC/Java. In J. N. Oliveira and P. Zave, editors, *FME 2001: Formal Methods for Increasing Software Productivity*, volume 2021 of *Lecture Notes in Computer Science*, pages 500–517. Springer, Mar. 2001.
16. C. Flanagan and J. B. Saxe. Avoiding exponential explosion: Generating compact verification conditions. In *Conference Record of the 28th Annual ACM Symposium on Principles of Programming Languages*, pages 193–205. ACM, Jan. 2001.

17. S. Graf and H. Saïdi. Construction of abstract state graphs via PVS. In O. Grumberg, editor, *Computer Aided Verification, 9th International Conference, CAV '97,* volume 1254 of *Lecture Notes in Computer Science,* pages 72–83. Springer, 1997.

18. T. A. Henzinger, R. Jhala, and R. Majumdar. Lazy abstraction. In *Proceedings of the 29th Symposium on Principles of Programming Languages,* January 2001.

19. J. Jaffar and J. L. Lassez. Constraint logic programming. In *Proceedings of ACM SIGPLAN Symposium on Principles of Programming Languages,* pages 111–119, Jan. 1987.

20. J. Jaffar and M. J. Maher. Constraint logic programming: A survey. *Journal of Logic Programming,* 19/20:503–581, 1994.

21. J. Jaffar, M. J. Maher, K. Marriott, and P. J. Stuckey. The semantics of constraint logic programs. *Journal of Logic Programming,* 37(1-3):1–46, 1998.

22. M. J. Maher. A logic programming view of CLP. In *International Conference on Logic Programming,* pages 737–753, 1993.

23. K. L. McMillan. *Symbolic Model Checking: An Approach to the State-Explosion Problem.* Kluwer Academic Publishers, 1993.

24. J.-P. Queille and J. Sifakis. Specification and verification of concurrent systems in CESAR. In M. Dezani-Ciancaglini and U. Montanari, editors, *Fifth International Symposium on Programming,* volume 137 of *Lecture Notes in Computer Science,* pages 337–351. Springer-Verlag, 1982.

25. M. Sagiv, T. Reps, and R. Wilhelm. Parametric shape analysis via 3-valued logic. In *Proceedings of the 26th Symposium on Principles of Programming Languages,* pages 105–118, 1999.

26. A. U. Shankar. An introduction to assertional reasoning for concurrent systems. *Computing Surveys,* 25(3):225–302, 1993.

27. SICStus Prolog. On the web at http://www.sics.se/sicstus/.

28. S. Stoller. Model-checking multi-threaded distributed Java programs. In *Proceedings of the 7th International SPIN Workshop on Model Checking and Software Verification,* Lecture Notes in Computer Science 1885, pages 224–244. Springer-Verlag, 2000.

29. M. Turin, A. Deutsch, and G. Gonthier. La vérification des programmes d'ariane. *Pour la Science,* 243:21–22, Jan. 1998. (In French).

30. E. Yahav. Verifying safety properties of concurrent Java programs using 3-valued logic. In *Proceedings of the 28th Symposium on Principles of Programming Languages,* pages 27–40, January 2001.

Verifying Temporal Heap Properties Specified via Evolution Logic [*]

Eran Yahav[1], Thomas Reps[2], Mooly Sagiv[1], and Reinhard Wilhelm[3]

[1] School of Comp. Sci., Tel-Aviv Univ., Tel-Aviv, Israel, {yahave,msagiv}@post.tau.ac.il
[2] Comp. Sci. Dept., Univ. of Wisconsin, Madison, WI 53706, USA, reps@cs.wisc.edu
[3] Informatik, Univ. des Saarlandes, Saarbrücken, Germany, wilhelm@cs.uni-sb.de

Abstract. This paper addresses the problem of establishing temporal properties of programs written in languages, such as Java, that make extensive use of the heap to allocate—and deallocate—new objects and threads. Establishing liveness properties is a particularly hard challenge. One of the crucial obstacles is that heap locations have no static names and the number of heap locations is unbounded. The paper presents a framework for the verification of Java-like programs. Unlike classical model checking, which uses propositional temporal logic, we use first-order temporal logic to specify temporal properties of heap evolutions; this logic allows domain changes to be expressed, which permits allocation and deallocation to be modelled naturally. The paper also presents an abstract-interpretation algorithm that automatically verifies temporal properties expressed using the logic.

1 Introduction

Modern programming languages, such as Java, make extensive use of the heap. The contents of the heap may evolve during program execution due to dynamic allocation and deallocation of objects. Moreover, in Java, threads are first-class objects that can be dynamically allocated. Statically reasoning about temporal properties of such programs is quite challenging, because there are no *a priori* bounds on the number of allocated objects, or restrictions on the way the heap may evolve. In particular, proving liveness properties of such programs, e.g., that a thread is eventually created in response to each request made to a web server, can be a quite difficult task.

The contributions of this paper can be summarized as follows:

1. We introduce a first-order modal (temporal) logic [9,8] that allows specifications of temporal properties of programs with dynamically evolving heaps to be stated in a natural manner.
2. We develop an abstract interpretation [4] for verifying that a program satisfies such a specification.
3. We implemented a prototype of the analysis using the TVLA system [11] and applied it to verify several temporal properties, including liveness properties of Java programs with evolving heaps.

[*] This research was supported by a grant from the Ministry of Science, Israel, a grant from the Academy of Science Israel, by the RTD project IST-1999-20527 "DAEDALUS" of the European FP5 programme, by ONR under contract N00014-01-1-0796, and by the A. von Humboldt Foundation.

P. Degano (Ed.): ESOP 2003, LNCS 2618, pp. 204–222, 2003.

We have used the framework to specify and verify the following:

Specify general heap-evolution properties: The framework has been used to specify in a general manner, various properties of heap evolution, such as properties of garbage-collection algorithms.

Verify termination of sequential heap-manipulating programs: Termination is shown by providing a ranking function based on the set of items reachable from a variable iterating over the linked data structure. In particular, we have verified termination of all example programs from [6].

Verify temporal properties of concurrent heap-manipulating programs: We have used the framework to verify temporal properties of concurrent heap-manipulating programs — in particular, liveness properties, such as the absence of starvation in programs using mutual exclusion, and response properties [13]. We have applied this analysis to programs with an unbounded number of threads.

Due to space limitations, the prototype implementation is only discussed in [17,20].

The remainder of this paper is organized as follows: Section 2 gives an overview of the verification method and contrasts it with previous work. Section 3 introduces trace semantics based on first-order modal logic, and discusses how to state trace properties using the language of evolution logic. Section 4 defines an implementation of trace semantics via first-order logic. Section 5 shows how abstract traces are used to conservatively represent sets of concrete traces. Section 6 summarizes related work. Finally, Section 7 concludes the paper.

2   Overview

2.1   A Temporal Logic Supporting Evolution

The specification language, *Evolution Temporal Logic* (ETL), is a first-order linear temporal logic that allows specifying properties of the way program execution causes dynamically allocated memory ("the heap") to evolve. It is natural to consider the concrete semantics of a program as the set of its execution traces [5,16], where each trace is an infinite sequence of *worlds*. First-order logical structures provide a natural representation of worlds with an unbounded number of objects: an individual of the structure's domain (universe) corresponds to an anonymous, unique store location, and predicates represent properties of store locations. Such a representation allows properties of the heap contents to be maintained while abstracting away any information about the actual physical locations in the store.

This gives rise to traces in which worlds along the trace may have different domains. Such traces can be seen as models of a first-order modal logic with a varying-domain semantics [8]. This could be equivalently, but less naturally, modelled using constant-domain semantics.

This framework generalizes other specification methods that address dynamic allocation and deallocation of objects and threads. In particular, its descriptive power goes beyond Propositional LTL and finite-state machines (e.g., [1]).

Program properties can be verified by showing that they hold for all traces. Technically, this can be done by evaluating their first-order modal-logic formulae against all traces. We use a variant of Lewis's counterpart theory [12] to cast modal models (and formula evaluation) in terms of classical predicate logic with transitive closure (FO^{TC}) [3].

Program verification using the above concrete semantics is clearly non-computable in general. We therefore represent potentially infinite sets of infinite concrete traces by one abstract trace. Infinite parts of the concrete traces are folded into cycles of the abstract traces. Termination of the abstract interpretation on an arbitrary program is guaranteed by bounding the size of the abstract trace. Two abstractions are employed: (i) representing multiple concrete worlds by a single abstract world, and (ii) creating cycles when an abstract world reoccurs in the trace.

Because of these abstractions, we may fail to show the correctness of certain programs, even though they are correct. Fortunately, we can use reduction arguments and progress monitors as employed in other program-verification techniques (e.g., [10]).

As in finite-state model checking (e.g., [16]), we let the specification formula affect the abstraction by making sure that abstract traces that fulfill the formula are distinguished from the ones that do not. However, our abstraction does not fold the history of the trace into a single state. This idea of using the specification to affect the precision of the analysis was not used in [15,18], which only handle safety properties.

2.2   Overview of the Verification Procedure

First, the property φ is specified in ETL. The formula is then translated in a straight-forward manner into an FO^{TC} logical formula, $(\varphi)^\dagger$, using a translation procedure described in Appendix A. An abstract-interpretation procedure is then applied to explore finite representations of the set of traces, using Kleene's 3-valued logic to conservatively interpret formulae. The abstract-interpretation procedure essentially computes a greatest fixed point over the set of traces, starting with an abstract trace that represents all possible infinite traces from an initial state, and gradually increasing the set of abstract traces and reducing the set of represented concrete traces. Finally, the formula $(\varphi)^\dagger$ is evaluated on all of the abstract traces in the fixed point. If $(\varphi)^\dagger$ is satisfied in all of them, then the original ETL formula φ must be satisfied by all (infinite) traces of the program. However, it may be the case that for some programs that satisfy the ETL specification, our analysis only yields "maybe".

2.3   Running Example

Consider a web server in which a new thread is dynamically allocated to handle each http request received. Each thread handles a single request, then terminates and is subject to garbage collection. Assume that worker threads compete for some exclusively shared resource, such as exclusive access to a data file. Figure 1 shows fragments of a Java program that implements such a naive web server.

A number of properties for the naive web-server implementation are shown in Tab. 1 as properties P1–P4. For now you may ignore the formulae in the third column; these will become clear as ETL syntax is introduced in Sec. 3.

Due to the unbounded arrival of requests to the web server, and the fact that a thread is dynamically created for each request, absence of starvation (P2) does not hold in the naive implementation. To guarantee absence of starvation, we introduce a scheduler

```
public class Worker implements Runnable {
 Request request;
 Resource resource; ...
 public void run() { ...
  synchronized(resource) {           lw₁
   resource.processRequest(request);  lwc
  }                                   lw₂
}}
```

Fig. 1. Java fragment for worker thread in a web server with no explicit scheduling.

thread into the web server. The web server now consists of a listener thread (as before) and a queue of worker threads managed by the scheduler thread. The listener thread receives an `http` request, creates a corresponding worker thread, and places the new thread on a scheduling queue. The scheduler thread picks up a worker thread from the queue and starts its execution (which is still a very naive implementation).

When using a web server with a scheduler, a number of additional properties of interest exist, labeled P5–P8 (for additional properties of interest see [17]). Figure 2 shows fragments of a web-server program in which threads use an explicit FIFO scheduler.

The ability of our framework to model explicit scheduling queues provides a mechanism for addressing issues of fairness in the presence of dynamic allocation of threads. (Further discussion of fairness is beyond the scope of this paper).

```
public class Scheduler               public class Listener
      implements Runnable {                implements Runnable {
 protected Queue schedQ;               protected Queue schedQ; ...
 protected Resource resource; ...      public void run() {
 public void run() {                     while(true) { ...
  while(true) { ...           ls₁         req=rqStream.readObject();   la₂
   synchronized(resource) {   ls₂         worker=
    while(resource.isAcquired())            new Thread(new Worker(req)); la₃
     resource.wait();         ls₃          schedQ.enqueue(worker);      la₄
    // may block until                  ... }
    // queue not empty                 }}
    worker=schedQ.dequeue();   ls₄     public class Worker
    worker.start();            ls₅           implements Runnable {
   }                                   Request req;
  }                                    Resource resource; ...
 }                                     public void run() {
}                                       synchronized(resource) { ... lw₁
                                         resource.processRequest(req); lwc
                                         resource.notifyAll();
                                        }                            lw₂
                                      }}
```

Fig. 2. Java code fragment for a web server with an explicit scheduler.

3   Trace Based Evolution Semantics

In this section, we define a trace-based semantic domain for programs that manipulate unbounded amounts of dynamically allocated storage. To allow specifying temporal properties of such programs, we employ first-order modal logic [8]. Various such logics have been defined, and in general they can be given a *constant-domain* semantics, in which the domain of all worlds is fixed, or a *varying-domain* semantics, in which the domains of worlds can vary and domains of different worlds can overlap. In the most

Table 1. Web server ETL specification using predicates of Tab. 2.

Pr.	Description	Formula
P1	mutual exclusion over the shared resource	$\Box \forall t_1, t_2 : thread.(t_1 \neq t_2)$ $\rightarrow \neg(at[lw_c](t_1) \wedge at[lw_c](t_2))$
P2	absence of starvation for worker threads	$\Box \forall t : thread.at[lw_1](t) \rightarrow \Diamond at[lw_c](t)$
P3	a thread only created when a request is received	$\Box(\forall t : thread. \neg \odot t) \vee$ $(\forall t : thread. \neg \odot t) \; \mathcal{U} \; (\exists v : request. \odot v)$
P4	each request is followed by thread creation	$\Box \exists v : request. \odot v \rightarrow \Diamond \exists t : thread. \odot t$
P5	mutual exclusion of listener and scheduler over scheduling queue	$\Box \forall t_1, t_2 : thread.(t_1 \neq t_2)$ $\rightarrow \neg(at[ls_2](t_1) \wedge at[la_3](t_2))$
P6	each created thread is eventually inserted into the scheduling queue	$\Box \forall t : thread. \odot t$ $\rightarrow \Diamond \exists q : queue.rval[head.next^*](q, t)$
P7	each scheduled worker thread was removed from the scheduling queue	$\Box \forall t : thread.at[lw_1](t)$ $\rightarrow \neg \exists q : queue.rval[head.next^*](q, t)$
P8	each worker thread waiting in the queue eventually leaves the queue	$\exists q : queue.\Box \forall t : thread.$ $(rval[head.next^*](q, t))$ $\rightarrow \Diamond \neg(rval[head.next^*](q, t))$

general setting, in both types of semantics an object can exist in more than a single world, and an equality relation is predefined to express global equality between individuals.

To model the semantics of languages such as Java, and to hide the implementation details of dynamic memory allocation, we use a semantics with varying domains. However, the semantics is deliberately restricted because of our intended application to program analysis. By design, our *evolution semantics* has a notion of equality in the presence of dynamic allocation and deallocation, without the need to update a predefined global-equality relation. Evolution semantics is adapted from Lewis's counterpart semantics [12]. In both evolution and counterpoint semantics, an individual *cannot* exist in more than a single world; each world has its own domain, and domains of different worlds are non-intersecting. Under this model, equality need only be defined within a single world's boundary; individuals of different worlds are unequal by definition. To relate individuals of different worlds, an evolution mapping is defined; however, unlike Lewis, we are interested in an evolution mapping that is reflexive, transitive, and symmetric, which models the fact that, during a computation, an allocated memory cell does not change its identity until deallocated. In Sec. 5.3, we show how to track statically, in the presence of abstraction, the equivalence relation induced by the evolution mapping.

As is often done, we add a skip action from the exit of the program to itself, so that all terminating traces are embedded in infinite traces. The semantics of the program is its set of infinite traces.

In the rest of this paper, we work with a fixed set of predicates (or vocabulary) $\mathcal{P} = \{eq, p_1, \ldots, p_k\}$. We denote by $\mathcal{P}^k$ the set of predicates from $\mathcal{P}$ with arity k.

Definition 1. *A **world** (program configuration) is represented via a first-order logical structure $W = \langle U_w, \iota_w \rangle$, where U_w is the domain (universe) of the structure, and ι_w is the interpretation function mapping predicates to their truth values; that is, for each $p \in \mathcal{P}^k$, $\iota_w(p) : U_w^k \rightarrow \{0, 1\}$, such that for all $u \in U_w$, $\iota_w(eq)(u, u) = 1$, and for all $u_1, u_2 \in U_w$ such that u_1 and u_2 are distinct individuals $\iota_w(eq)(u_1, u_2) = 0$.*

Definition 2. *A **trace** is an infinite sequence of worlds* $\pi_1 \xrightarrow{D_{\pi_1}, e_{\pi_1}, A_{\pi_2}} \pi_2 \xrightarrow{D_{\pi_2}, e_{\pi_2}, A_{\pi_3}}$
*..., where: (i) each world represents a global state of the program, π_1 is an initial state, and for each π_i, its successor world π_{i+1} is derived by applying a single program action to π_i; (ii) $D_{\pi_i} \subseteq U_{\pi_i}$ is the set of individuals deallocated at π_i, and $A_{\pi_{i+1}} \subseteq U_{\pi_{i+1}}$ is the set of individuals newly allocated at π_{i+1}; (iii) each pair of consecutive worlds π_i, π_{i+1} is related by a stepwise **evolution function**, a bijective renaming function $e_{\pi_i}: U_{\pi_i} \setminus D_{\pi_i} \to U_{\pi_{i+1}} \setminus A_{\pi_{i+1}}$.*

Extracting Trace Properties

To extract trace properties, we need a language that can relate information from different worlds in a trace. We define the language of evolution logic (ETL), which is a first-order linear temporal logic with transitive closure, as follows:

Definition 3. *[ETL Syntax] An **ETL formula** is defined by*

$$\varphi ::= 0 \mid 1 \mid p(v_1, \dots, v_n) \mid \odot v_1 \mid \oslash v_1 \mid \varphi_1 \vee \varphi_2 \mid \neg\varphi_1 \mid \exists v_1.\varphi_1 \mid (TC\ v_1, v_2 \colon \varphi_1)(v_3, v_4)$$
$$\mid \varphi_1\ \mathcal{U}\ \varphi_2 \mid \chi\varphi_1$$

where v_i are logical variables.

The set of free variables in a formula φ denoted by $FV(\varphi)$ is defined as usual. In a transitive closure formula, $FV((TC\ v_1, v_2 \colon \varphi_1)(v_3, v_4)) = (FV(\varphi_1) \setminus \{v_1, v_2\}) \cup \{v_3, v_4\}$.

The operators $\odot$ and $\oslash$ allow the specification to refer to the exact moments of birth and death (respectively) of an individual.[1]

Shorthand Formulae: For convenience, we also allow formulae to contain the shorthand notations $(v_1 = v_2) \triangleq eq(v_1, v_2)$, $(v_1 \neq v_2) \triangleq \neg eq(v_1, v_2)$, $\varphi_1 \wedge \varphi_2 \triangleq \neg(\neg\varphi_1 \vee \neg\varphi_2)$, $\varphi_1 \to \varphi_2 \triangleq \neg\varphi_1 \vee \varphi_2$, $\forall v.\varphi_1 \triangleq \neg(\exists v.\neg\varphi_1)$, $\Diamond\varphi_1 \triangleq 1 \mathcal{U} \varphi_1$, and $\Box\varphi_1 \triangleq \neg(1 \mathcal{U} \neg\varphi_1)$. We also use the shorthand $p^*(v_3, v_4)$ for $(TC\ v_1, v_2 \colon p(v_1, v_2))(v_3, v_4) \vee (v_3 = v_4)$, when p is a binary predicate.

In our examples, the predicates that record information about a single world include the predicates of Tab. 2, plus additional predicates defined in later sections. The set of predicates $\{at[lab](t) \colon lab \in Labels\}$ is parameterized by the set of program labels. Similarly, the set of predicates $\{rval[fld](o_1, o_2) \colon fld \in Fields\}$ is parameterized by the set of selector fields. We use the shorthand notation $rval[x.fld^*](v_1, v_2) \triangleq \exists v'.rval[x](v_1, v') \wedge rval[fld]^*(v', v_2)$. The transitive closure allows specifying properties relating to unbounded length of heap-allocated data structures (e.g., in $rval[fld]^*(v', v_2)$).

We use unary predicates, such as $thread(t)$, to represent type information. This could have been expressed using a many-sorted logic, but we decided to avoid this for expository purposes. Instead, for convenience we define the shorthands $\exists v \colon type.\varphi \triangleq \exists v.type(v) \wedge \varphi$ and $\forall v \colon type.\varphi \triangleq \forall v.type(v) \to \varphi$.

---

[1] These operators could be extended to handle allocation and deallocation of a (possibly unbounded) set of individuals.

Table 2. Predicates used to record information about a single world

Predicates	Intended Meaning
$thread(t)$	t is a thread
$\{at[lab](t) : lab \in Labels\}$	thread t is at label lab
$\{rval[fld](o_1, o_2) : fld \in Fields\}$	field fld of the object o_1 points to the object o_2
$heldBy(l, t)$	the lock l is held by the thread t
$blocked(t, l)$	the thread t is blocked on the lock l
$waiting(t, l)$	the thread t is waiting on the lock l

Example 1. Property P2 of Tab. 1 specifies the absence of starvation for worker threads (Fig. 1). The formula $\exists t: thread.\Diamond at[lw_c](t)$ states that some thread eventually enters the critical section. The formula $\Box \exists t: thread.\Diamond at[lw_c](t)$ expresses the fact that globally some thread eventually enters the critical section.

The property $\Box(\forall v. \odot v \rightarrow \Diamond \oslash v)$ states that globally, each individual that is allocated during program execution is eventually deallocated. Note that the universal quantifier quantifies over individuals of the world in which it is evaluated. This property is an instance of the commonly used "Response structure" [13,7], in which an allocation in a world has a deallocation response in some future world.

The properties

$$\forall t: thread.\Box(at[l_{lh}](t) \rightarrow \exists v.rval[i.next^*](t, v) \wedge \Diamond(at[l_{lh}](t) \wedge \neg rval[i.next^*](t, v)))$$
$$\forall t: thread.\Box(\forall v.at[l_{lh}](t) \wedge \neg rval[i.next^*](t, v) \rightarrow \Box \neg at[l_{lh}](t) \vee \neg rval[i.next^*](t, v))$$

establish a ranking function for linked data structures based on transitive reachability. These properties state that at the loop head l_{lh}, the set of individuals transitively reachable from program variable i decreases on each iteration of the loop. (Typically i is a pointer that traverses a linked data structure during the loop.) Note that these properties relate an unbounded number of individuals of one world to another.

The property $\Box(\forall v.\Diamond \Box \forall t: thread.\bigwedge_{\substack{x \in Var \\ fld \in Fields}} \neg rval[x.fld^*](t, v) \rightarrow \Diamond \oslash v)$ is a desired property of a garbage collector — that all non-reachable items are eventually collected.

Evolution Semantics. In the following definitions, $head(\pi)$ denotes the first world in a trace π, $tail(\pi)$ denotes the suffix of π without the first world, and π^i denotes the suffix of π starting at the i-th world. We also use $last(\tau)$ to denote the last world of a finite trace prefix τ.

Definition 4. *[Evolution mapping] Let τ be the finite prefix of length k of the trace π. We say that an individual $u \in U_{head(\tau)}$ **evolves into** an individual $u' \in U_{last(\tau)}$ in the trace π in k steps, and write $\pi \models_k u \rightsquigarrow u'$ when there is a sequence of individuals $u_1, \ldots, u_k$ such that $u_1 = u$ and $u_k = u'$ and for each two successive worlds in τ, $u_{i+1} = e_{\tau_i}(u_i)$.*

Definition 5. *[Assignment evolution] Let τ be the finite prefix of length k of the trace π. Given a formula φ and an assignment Z mapping free variables of φ to individuals* *of a domain $U_{head(\tau)}$, we say that $\pi \models_k Z \rightsquigarrow Z'$ (Z **evolves into** Z' in π in k steps) if for each free variable fv_i of φ, $\pi \models_k Z(fv_i) \rightsquigarrow Z'(fv_i)$, $Z(fv_i) \in U_{head(\tau)}$, and $Z'(fv_i) \in U_{last(\tau)}$.*

Definition 6. *[ETL evolution semantics] We define inductively when an ETL formula φ is satisfied over a trace π with an assignment Z (denoted by $\pi, Z \models \varphi$) as follows:*

- $\pi, Z \models \mathbf{1}$, and not $\pi, Z \models \mathbf{0}$.
- $\pi, Z \models p(v_1, \ldots, v_k)$ when $\iota_{head(\pi)}(p)(Z(v_1), \ldots, Z(v_k)) = 1$
- $\pi, Z \models \neg\varphi$ when not $\pi, Z \models \varphi$
- $\pi, Z \models \varphi \vee \psi$ when $\pi, Z \models \varphi$ or $\pi, Z \models \psi$
- $\pi, Z \models \exists v.\varphi(v)$ when there exists $u \in U_{head(\pi)}$ s.t. $\pi, Z[v \mapsto u] \models \varphi(v)$
- $\pi, Z \models (TC\, v_1, v_2 : \varphi)(v_3, v_4)$ when there exists $u_1, \ldots, u_{n+1} \in U_{head(\pi)}$, such that $Z(v_3) = u_1, Z(v_4) = u_{n+1}$, and for all $1 \leq i \leq n$, $\pi, Z[v_1 \mapsto u_i, v_2 \mapsto u_{i+1}] \models \varphi$.
- $\pi, Z \models \odot v$ when $Z(v) \in A_{head(tail(\pi))}$.
- $\pi, Z \models \oslash v$ when $Z(v) \in D_{head(\pi)}$.
- $\pi, Z \models \chi\varphi$ when there exists Z' such that $tail(\pi), Z' \models \varphi$ and $\pi \models_1 Z \rightsquigarrow Z'$.
- $\pi, Z \models \varphi\, \mathcal{U}\, \psi$ when there exists $k \geq 1$, Z', and Z'' s.t., $\pi^k, Z' \models \psi$ and $\pi \models_k Z \rightsquigarrow Z'$ and for all $1 \leq j < k$, $\pi^j, Z'' \models \varphi$ and $\pi \models_j Z \rightsquigarrow Z''$,

We write $\pi \models \varphi$ when $\pi, Z \models \varphi$ for every assignment Z.

It is worth noting that the first-order quantifiers in this definition only range over the individuals of a single world, yet the overall effect achieved by using the evolution mapping is the ability to reason about individuals of different worlds, and how they relate to each other. In essence, the assignment $Z[v \mapsto u]$ binds v to (the evolution of) an individual from the domain of the world over which the quantifier was evaluated (cf. the semantics of χ and $\mathcal{U}$).

The combination of first-order quantifiers and modal operators creates complications that do not occur in propositional temporal logics. In particular, the quantification domain of a quantifier may vary as the domain of underlying worlds varies. Verification of ETL properties therefore requires a mechanism for recording the domain related to each quantifier, and for relating members of quantification domains to individuals of future worlds. For ETL, this mechanism is provided by evolution-mappings, which relate individuals of a world to the individuals of its successor world. Transitively composing evolution-mappings captures the evolution of individuals along a trace.

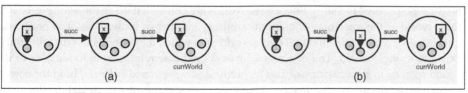

(a)   (b)

Fig. 3. Interaction of first-order quantifiers and temporal operators

Example 2. The formula $\exists v.\Box x(v)$ states that the pointer variable x remains constant throughout program execution, and points to an object that existed in the program's initial world. On the other hand, the formula $\Box \exists v.x(v)$ merely states that x never has the value null; however, x is allowed to point to different objects at different times in the program's execution, and in particular x can point to objects that did not exist in the initial world. Examples illustrating the two situations are shown in Fig. 3, where in (a) x points to the same object in all worlds, and in (b) it points to different objects in different worlds.

Definition 7. *We say that a program **satisfies** an ETL formula φ when all (infinite) traces of the program satisfy φ.*

The evolution semantics allows each world to have a different domain, thus conceptually representing a varying-domain semantics, which allows dynamic allocation and deallocation of objects and threads. In Section 4, we give a possible implementation of this semantics in terms of evolving first-order logical structures.

Separable Specifications. It is interesting to consider subclasses of ETL for which the verification problem is somewhat easier. Two such classes are: (i) *spatially separable specifications* — do not place requirements on the relationships between individuals of one world; this allows each individual to be considered separately, and the verification problem can be handled as a set of propositional verification problems; (ii) *temporally separable specifications* — do not relate individuals across worlds. Essentially, this corresponds to the extraction of propositional information from each world, and having temporal specifications over the extracted propositions. This class was addressed in [2, 19].

4   Expressing Trace Semantics Using First Order Logic

In this section, we use first-order logic to express a trace semantics; we encode temporal operators using standard first-order quantifiers. This allows us to automatically derive an abstract semantics in Section 5. This approach also extends to other kinds of temporal logic, such as the μ-calculus. Our initial experience is that we are able to demonstrate that some temporal properties, including liveness properties, hold for programs with dynamically allocated storage.

4.1   Representing Infinite Traces via First Order Structures

We encode a trace via an infinite first-order logical structure using the set of designated predicates specified in Tab. 3. Successive worlds are connected using the *succ* predicate. Each world of the trace may contain an arbitrary number of individuals. The predicate $exists(o, w)$ relates an individual o to a world w in which it exists. Each individual only exists in a single world. The $evolution(o_1, o_2)$ predicate relates an individual o_1 to its counterpart o_2 in a successor world. The predicates $isNew$ and $isFreed$ hold for newly created or deallocated individuals and are used to model the allocation and deallocation operators.

Definition 8. *A **concrete trace** is a trace encoded as an infinite first-order logical struc-ture $T = \langle U_T, \iota_T \rangle$, where U_T is the domain of the trace, and ι_T is the interpretation function mapping predicates to their truth value in the logical structure, i.e., for each $p \in \mathcal{P}^k$, $\iota_T(p) \colon U_T^k \to \{0,1\}$. To exclude structures that cannot represent valid traces, we impose certain integrity constraints [15]. For example, we require that each world has at most one successor (predecessor), and that equality (eq) is reflexive.*

Table 3. Trace predicates.

Predicate	Intended Meaning	Predicate	Intended Meaning
$world(w)$	w is a world	$exists(o, w)$	object o is in world w
$currWorld(w)$	w is the current world	$evolution(o_1, o_2)$	object o_1 evolves to o_2
$initialWorld(w)$	w is the initial world	$isNew(o)$	object o is new
$succ(w_1, w_2)$	w_2 is the successor of w_1	$isFreed(o)$	object o is freed

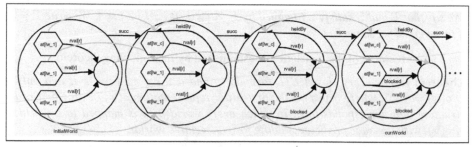

Fig. 4. A concrete trace $T_4^\natural$.

Example 3. Figure 4 shows four worlds of the trace $T_4^\natural$ where each world is depicted as a large node containing other nodes and worlds along the trace are related by successor edges. Information in a single world is represented by a first-order logical structure, which is shown as a directed graph. Each node of the graph corresponds to a heap-allocated object. Hexagon nodes correspond to thread objects, and small round nodes to other types of heap-allocated objects. Predicates holding for an object are shown inside the object node, and binary predicates are shown as edges. For brevity, we use the label $rval[r]$ to stand for $rval[resource]$. Grey edges, crossing world boundaries, are evolution edges, which relate objects of different worlds. Note that these are the only edges that cross world boundaries.

4.2   Exact Extraction of Trace Properties

Once traces are represented via first-order logical structures, trace properties can be extracted by evaluating formulae of first-order logic with transitive closure.

We translate a given ETL formula φ to an FO^{TC} formula $(\varphi)^\dagger$ by making the underlying trace structure explicit, and translating temporal operators to FO^{TC} claims over worlds of the trace. The translation procedure is straightforward, and given in Appendix A.

Example 4. The property $\exists t: thread.\Diamond at[lw_c](t)$ of Example 1 is translated to

$\exists w: world.\exists t: thread.initialWorld(w) \wedge exists(t, w) \wedge \exists w' \exists t': thread.succ^*(w, w') \wedge$
$exists(t', w') \wedge evolution^*(t, t') \wedge at[lw_c](t')$

which evaluates to 1 for the trace prefix of Fig. 4.

Definition 9. *The* **meaning** *of a formula φ over a concrete trace T, with respect to an assignment Z, denoted by $[\![\varphi]\!]_2^T(Z)$, yields a truth value in $\{0, 1\}$. The meaning of φ is defined inductively as follows:*

$$[\![l]\!]_2^T(Z) = l \text{ (where } l \in \{0, 1\})$$
$$[\![p(v_1, \ldots, v_k)]\!]_2^T(Z) = \iota^T(p)(Z(v_1), \ldots, Z(v_k))$$
$$[\![\varphi_1 \vee \varphi_2]\!]_2^T(Z) = \max([\![\varphi_1]\!]_2^T(Z), [\![\varphi_2]\!]_2^T(Z))$$
$$[\![\neg\varphi_1]\!]_2^T(Z) = 1 - [\![\varphi_1]\!]_2^T(Z)$$
$$[\![\exists v_1.\varphi_1]\!]_2^T(Z) = \max_{u \in U} [\![\varphi_1]\!]_2^T(Z[v_1 \mapsto u])$$
$$[\![(TC\ v_1, v_2 : \varphi_1)(v_3, v_4)]\!]_2^T(Z) =$$
$$\max_{\substack{n \geq 1, u_1, \ldots, u_{n+1} \in U, \\ Z(v_3) = u_1, Z(v_4) = u_{n+1}}} \min_{i=1}^{n} [\![\varphi_1]\!]_2^T(Z[v_1 \mapsto u_i, v_2 \mapsto u_{i+1}])$$

We say that T and Z **satisfy** *φ (denoted by $T, Z \models \varphi$) if $[\![\varphi]\!]_2^T(Z) = 1$. We write $T \models \varphi$ if for every Z we have $T, Z \models \varphi$.*

The correctness of the translation is established by the following theorem:

Theorem 1. *For every closed ETL formula φ and a trace π, $\pi \models \varphi$ if and only if $rep(\pi) \models (\varphi)^\dagger$, where $rep(\pi)$ is the first-order representation of π, i.e., the first-order structure that corresponds to π, in which every world in π is mapped to a world in $rep(\pi)$, with the succ predicate holding for consecutive worlds.*

4.3   Semantics of Actions

Informally, a program action ac consists of a *precondition* ac_{pre} under which the action is *enabled*, which is expressed as a logical formula, and a set of formulae for updating the values of predicates according to the effect of the action. An enabled action specifies that a possible next world in the trace is one in which the interpretations of every predicate p of arity k is determined by evaluating a formula $\varphi_p(v_1, v_2, \ldots, v_k)$, which may use $v_1, v_2, \ldots, v_k$ and all predicates in $\mathcal{P}$ (see [15]).

5   Exploring Finite Abstract Traces via Abstract Interpretation

In this section, we give an algorithm for conservatively determining the validity of a program with respect to an ETL property. A key difficulty in proving liveness properties is the fact that a liveness property might be violated only by an infinite trace. Therefore, our procedure for verifying liveness properties is a greatest fixed-point computation, which works down from an initial approximation that represents all infinite traces. In this section, we present our abstract-interpretation algorithm; procedure `explore` of Figure 8.

Our approach uses finite representations of infinite traces. Finite representations are obtained by abstraction to three-valued logical structures. The third logical value, 1/2, represents "unknown" and may result from abstraction. The abstract semantics conservatively models the effect of actions on abstract representations.

5.1   A Finite Representation of Infinite Traces

The first step in making the algorithm of Figure 8 feasible is to define a finite representation of sets of infinite traces. Technically, we use 3-valued logical structures to finitely represent sets of infinite traces.

Definition 10. *An **abstract trace** is a 3-valued first-order logical structure* $T = \langle U_T, \iota_T \rangle$*, where* U_T *is the domain of the abstract trace, and* ι_T *is the interpretation, mapping predicates to their truth values, i.e., for each* $p \in \mathcal{P}^k$*,* $\iota_T(p) \colon U_T^k \to \{0, 1, 1/2\}$*. We refer to the values 0 and 1 as **definite values**, and to 1/2 as a **non definite value**.*

An individual u *for which* $\iota_T(eq)(u, u) = 1/2$ *is called a **summary individual**;[2] a summary individual may represent more than one concrete individual.*

*The **meaning** of a formula* φ *over a 3-valued abstract trace* T*, with respect to an assignment* Z*, denoted by* $[\![\varphi]\!]_3^T(Z)$*, is defined exactly as in Def. 9, but interpreted over* $\{0, 1, 1/2\}$*.*

We say that a trace T *with an assignment* Z ***potentially satisfies*** *a formula* φ *when* $[\![\varphi]\!]_3^T(Z) \in \{1, 1/2\}$ *and denote this by* $T, Z \models_3 \varphi$*.*

We now define how concrete traces are represented by abstract traces. The idea is that each individual of a concrete trace is mapped by the abstraction into an individual of an abstract trace. The new two definitions permit an (abstract or concrete) trace to be related to a less-precise abstract trace. Abstraction is a special case of this in which the first trace is a concrete trace. First, the following definition imposes an order on truth values of the 3-valued logic:

Definition 11. *For* $l_1, l_2 \in \{0, 1, 1/2\}$*, we define the **information order** on truth values as follows:* $l_1 \sqsubseteq l_2$ *if* $l_1 = l_2$ *or* $l_2 = 1/2$*.*

The embedding ordering of abstract traces is then defined as follows:

Definition 12. *Let* $T = \langle U, \iota \rangle$ *and* $T' = \langle U', \iota' \rangle$ *be abstract traces encoded as first-order structures. A function* $f \colon T \to T'$ *such that* f *is surjective is said to **embed** T **into** T' if for each predicate* $p \in \mathcal{P}^k$*, and for each* $u_1, \dots, u_k \in U$*:*

$$\iota(p(u_1, u_2, \dots, u_k)) \sqsubseteq \iota'(p(f(u_1), f(u_2), \dots, f(u_k)))$$

We say that T' ***represents*** T *when there exists such an embedding* f*.*

One way of creating an embedding function f is by using *canonical abstraction*. Canonical abstraction maps individuals to an abstract individual based on the values of the individuals' unary predicates. All individuals having the same values for unary predicate symbols are mapped by f to the same abstract individual. We denote the canonical abstraction of a trace T by $t\_embed(T)$. Canonical abstraction guarantees that each abstract trace is no larger than some fixed size, known *a priori*.

Example 5. Figure 5 shows an abstract trace, with four abstract worlds, that represents the concrete trace of Fig. 4. An individual with double-line boundaries is a summary

---

[2] Note that for all $u \in U_T$, $\iota_T(eq)(u, u) = 1$ or $\iota_T(eq)(u, u) = 1/2$.

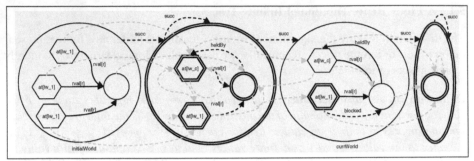

Fig. 5. An abstract trace T_4 that represents the concrete trace $T_4^\natural$.

individual representing possibly more than a single concrete individual. Similarly, the worlds with double-line boundaries are summary worlds that possibly represent more than a single world. Dashed edges are $1/2$ edges, that represent relations that may or may not hold. For example, a $1/2$ successor edge between two worlds represents the possible succession of worlds. The summary world following the initial world represents the two concrete worlds between the initial and the current world of $T_4^\natural$, which have the same values for their unary predicates. Similarly, the summary node labeled $at[lw_1]$ represents all thread individuals in these worlds that reside at label lw_1.

Note that this abstract trace also represents other concrete traces besides $T_4^\natural$, for example, concrete traces in which in the current world some threads are blocked on the lock and some are not blocked.

5.2 Abstract Interpretation

The abstract semantics represents abstract traces using 3-valued structures. Intuitively, applying an action to an abstract trace unravels the set of possible next successor worlds in the trace. That is, an abstract action elaborates an abstract trace by materializing a world w from the summary world at the tail of the trace; w becomes the definite successor of the current world $currWorld$, and w's (indefinite) successor is the summary world at the tail of the trace. $currWorld$ is then advanced to w, which often causes the former $currWorld$ to be merged with its predecessor. When a trace is extended, we evaluate the formula's precondition and its update formulae using 3-valued logic (as in Def. 10).

Example 6. Figures 5, 6, and 7 illustrate the application of the action that releases a lock. Figure 6 shows the materialization of the next successor world for the trace T_4 of Figure 5. In the successor world, the thread that was at label lw_c no longer holds the lock and has advanced to label lw_2. The $currWorld$ predicate is then advanced, and the former $currWorld$ is merged with its predecessor, resulting in the abstract trace shown in Figure 7.

The abstract-interpretation procedure `explore` is shown in Figure 8. It computes a greatest fixed point starting with the set $\{T_1^\top, T_2^\top\}$; these two abstract traces represent all possible concrete (infinite) traces that start at a given initial state. $T_1^\top$ and $T_2^\top$ each

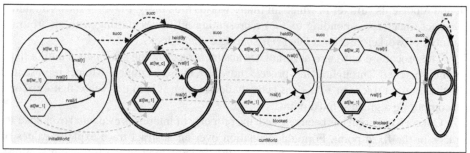

Fig. 6. An intermediate abstract trace, which represents the first stage of applying an action to T_4.

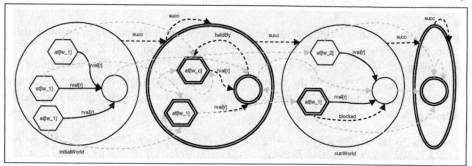

Fig. 7. The resulting abstract trace after applying an action over T_4 (after advancing $currWorld$).

have two worlds: an initial world that represents the initial program configuration connected by a 1/2-valued successor edge to a summary world that represents the unknown possible suffixes. The summary world w_{s1} of $T_1^\top$ has a summary individual u_{s1} related to it. The summary individual u_{s1} has 1/2 values for all of its predicates, including $exists(u_{s1}, w_{s1}) = 1/2$, meaning that future worlds of the trace do not necessarily contain any individuals. The summary world of $T_2^\top$ has no summary individual related to

```
explore() {
 Traces = {T_1^T, T_2^T}
 while changes occur {
  select and remove τ from Traces
  for each action ac enabled for τ
   Traces = Traces ⋃{ac(τ)}
 }
 for each τ ∈ Traces
  if τ ⊭_3 (φ)^† report possible error
}
```

Fig. 8. Computing the set of abstract traces and evaluating the property $(\varphi)^\dagger$.

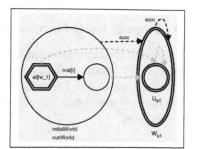

Fig. 9. An initial abstract trace $T_1^\top$.

it and represents suffixes in which all future worlds are empty. Figure 9 shows an initial abstract trace (corresponding to $T_1^\top$) representing all traces starting with an arbitrary number of worker threads at label lw_1 sharing a single lock.

The procedure `explore` accumulates abstract traces in the set $Traces$ until a fixed point is reached. Throughout this process, however, the set of concrete traces represented by the abstract traces in $Traces$ is actually decreasing. It is in this sense that `explore` is computing a greatest fixed point.

Once a fixed point has been reached, the property of interest is evaluated over abstract traces in the fixed point. Formula evaluation over an abstract trace exploits values of instrumentation predicates when possible (this is explained in the following section). This allows the use of recorded definite values, whereas re-evaluation might have yielded $1/2$.

We now show the soundness of the approach. We extend mappings on individuals to operate on assignments: If $f: U^T \to U^{T'}$ is a function and $Z: Var \to U^T$ is an assignment, $f \circ Z$ denotes the assignment $f \circ Z: Var \to U^{T'}$ such that $(f \circ Z)(v) = f(Z(v))$. One of the nice features of 3-valued logic is that the soundness of the analysis is established by the following theorem (which generalizes [15] for the infinite case):

Theorem 2. *[Embedding Theorem] Let $T = \langle U^T, \iota^T \rangle$ and $T' = \langle U^{T'}, \iota^{T'} \rangle$ be two traces encoded as first-order structures, and let $f: U^T \to U^{T'}$ be a function such that $T \sqsubseteq^f T'$. Then, for every formula φ and complete assignment Z for φ, $[\![\varphi]\!]_3^T (Z) \sqsubseteq [\![\varphi]\!]_3^{T'} (f \circ Z)$.*

The algorithm in Figure 8 must terminate. Furthermore, whenever it does not report an error, the program satisfies the original ETL formula φ.

It often happens that this approach to verifying temporal properties yields $1/2$, due to an overly conservative approximation. In the next section, we present machinery for refining the abstraction to allow successful verification in interesting cases.

Example 7. Space precludes us from showing a real application, such as the web server. Instead, we use an artificial example, which is also used in the next section. Figure 10 shows an abstract trace in which the property $\exists v. P(v) \, \mathcal{U} \, Q(v)$ holds for all the concrete traces represented by the abstract trace, but the formula $\exists v. P(v) \, \mathcal{U} \, Q(v)$ evaluates to $1/2$ because the successor and evolution edges have value $1/2$.

5.3   Property Guided Instrumentation

To refine the abstraction, we can maintain more precise information about the correctness of temporal formulae as traces are being constructed. This principle is referred to in [15] as the *Instrumentation Principle*. This work goes beyond what was mentioned there, by showing how one could actually obtain instrumentation predicates from the temporal specification.

Trace Instrumentation. The predicates in Tab. 4 are required for preserving properties of interest under abstraction. The instrumentation predicate $current(o)$ denotes that

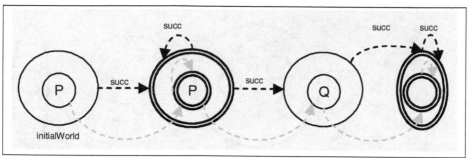

Fig. 10. $\exists v.P(v)\ \mathcal{U}\ Q(v)$ holds in all concrete traces that the abstract trace T_{10} represents, yet $\exists v.P(v)\ \mathcal{U}\ Q(v)$ evaluates to $1/2$ on T_{10} itself.

o is a member of the current world and should be distinguished from individuals of predecessor worlds. This predicate is required due to limitations of canonical embedding. The predicate $twe(o_1, o_2)$ records equality across worlds and is required due to the loss of information about concrete locations caused by abstraction.

Table 4. Trace instrumentation predicates.

Predicate	Intended Meaning	Formula
$twe(o_1,o_2)$	object o_1 is equal to object o_2 possibly across worlds	$(o_1 = o_2) \vee evolution^*(o_1, o_2)$ $\vee evolution^*(o_2, o_1)$
$current(o)$	object o is a member of current world	$\exists w: world(o, w) \wedge currWorld(w)$

Transworld Equality: In the evolution semantics, two individuals are considered to be different incarnations of the same individual when one may transitively evolve into the other. We refer to this notion of equality as *transworld equality* and introduce an instrumentation predicate $twe(v_1, v_2)$ to capture this notion.

Because the abstraction operates on traces (and not only single worlds), individuals of different worlds may be abstracted together. Transworld equality is crucial for distinguishing a summary node that represents different incarnations of the same individual in different worlds from a summary node that may represent a number of different individuals.

Transworld equality is illustrated in Fig. 11; the 1-valued twe self-loop to the summary thread-node at label lw_c records the fact that this summary node actually represents multiple incarnations of a single thread, and not a number of different threads.

Temporal Instrumentation. Given an ETL specification formula, we construct a corresponding set of instrumentation predicates for refining the abstraction of the trace according to the property of interest. The set of instrumentation predicates corresponds to the sub-formulae of the original specification.

Example 8. In Example 7, the property $\exists v.P(v)\ \mathcal{U}\ Q(v)$ evaluated to $1/2$ although it is satisfied by all concrete traces that T_{10} represents. We now add the temporal instrumentation predicates $I_p(v)$ and $I_q(v)$ to record the values of the temporal subformulae $P(v)$ and $Q(v)$. The predicates are updated according to their value in the previous worlds. Note the use of transworld equality instrumentation to more precisely record transitive

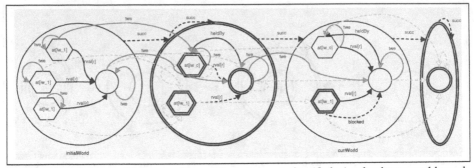

Fig. 11. Abstract trace with transworld equality instrumentation (Only 1-valued transworld equality edges are shown).

evolution of objects. In particular, this provides the information that the summary node of the second world is an abstraction of different incarnations of the same single object. This is shown in Fig. 12.

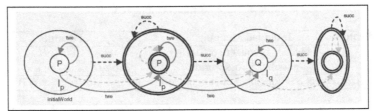

Fig. 12. In the abstract trace T_{12}, $\exists v. P(v) \, \mathcal{U} \, Q(v)$ evaluates to 1.

6 Related Work

The Bandera Specification Language (BSL) [2] allows writing specifications via common high-level patterns. In BSL, it is impossible to relate individuals of different worlds, and impossible to refer to the exact moments of allocation and deallocation of an object.

In [14], a special case of the abstraction from [18,19], named "counter abstraction", is used to abstract an infinite-state parametric system into a finite-state one. They use static abstraction, i.e., they have a preceding model-extraction phase. In contrast, in our work abstraction is applied dynamically on every step of state-space exploration, which enables us to handle dynamic allocation and deallocation of objects and threads.

In [19], we have used observing-propositions defined over a first-order configuration to extract a propositional Kripke structure from a first-order one. The extracted structure was then subject to PLTL model-checking techniques. This approach is rather limited, because individuals of different worlds could not be specifically related.

7 Conclusion

We believe this work provides a foundation for specifying and verifying properties of programs manipulating the heap with dynamic allocation and deallocation of objects and threads. In the future, we plan to develop more scalable approaches, and in particular abstract-interpretation algorithms that are tailored for ETL.

Acknowledgments. We would like to thank Patrick Cousot, Nissim Francez, and Amir Pnueli for helpful discussions and insightful comments. We would also like to thank the anonymous referees for providing useful comments on this paper.

References

1. E.M. Clarke, O. Grumberg, and D. Peled. *Model Checking*. MIT Press, 1999.
2. J. C. Corbett, M. B. Dwyer, J. Hatcliff, and Robby. A language framework for expressing checkable properties of dynamic software. In *SPIN*, 2000.
3. B. Courcelle. On the expression of graph properties in some fragments of monadic second-order logic. In N. Immerman and P.G. Kolaitis, editors, *Descriptive Complexity and Finite Models: Proceedings of a DIAMCS Workshop*, chapter 2, pages 33–57. American Mathematical Society, 1996.
4. P. Cousot and R. Cousot. Abstract interpretation: A unified lattice model for static analysis of programs by construction of approximation of fixed points. In *POPL*, 1977.
5. P. Cousot and R. Cousot. Temporal abstract interpretation. In *Proc. of 27th POPL*, pages 12–25, January 2000.
6. N. Dor, M. Rodeh, and M. Sagiv. Checking cleanness in linked lists. In *SAS*. Springer, 2000.
7. M. B. Dwyer, G. S. Avrunin, and J. C. Corbett. Patterns in property specifications for finite-state verification. In *Proc. of Int. Conf. on Software Engineering*, pages 411–421, May 1999.
8. M. Fitting and R.L. Mendelsohn. *First-Order Modal Logic*, volume 277 of *Synthese Library*. Kluwer Academic Publishers, Dordrecht, 1998.
9. G.E. Hughes and M.J. Creswel. *An Introduction to Modal Logic*. Methuen, London, 1982.
10. Y. Kesten, A. Pnueli, and M. Vardi. Verification by augmented abstraction: The automata-theoretic view. *JCSS: J. of Comp. Sys. Sci.*, 62, 2001.
11. T. Lev-Ami and M. Sagiv. TVLA: A framework for Kleene based static analysis. In *Static Analysis Symposium*. Springer, 2000.
12. D. Lewis. Counterpart theory and quantified modal logic. *Journal of Philosophy*, LXV(5):113–126, 1968.
13. Z. Manna and A. Pnueli. *Temporal Verification of Reactive Systems: Safety*. Springer, 1995.
14. A. Pnueli, J. Xu, and L. Zuck. Liveness with (0,1,infinity)-counter abstraction. CAV 2002.
15. M. Sagiv, T. Reps, and R. Wilhelm. Parametric shape analysis via 3-valued logic. *ACM Transactions on Programming Languages and Systems*, 24(3):217.
16. M.Y. Vardi and Pierre Wolper. Reasoning about infinite computations. *Information and Computation*, 115(1):1–37, 15 November 1994.
17. E. Yahav. http://www.cs.tau.ac.il/~yahave.
18. E. Yahav. Verifying safety properties of concurrent Java programs using 3-valued logic. In *Proc. of 27th POPL*, pages 27–40, March 2001.
19. E. Yahav, T. Reps, and M. Sagiv. LTL model checking for systems with unbounded number of dynamically created threads and objects. Technical Report TR-1424, CS Dept., Univ. of Wisconsin, Madison, WI, March 2001.
20. E. Yahav, T. Reps, M. Sagiv, and R. Wilhelm. Automatic verification of temporal properties of concurrent heap-manipulating programs using evolution logic. Technical Report 338/02, School of CS, Tel Aviv University, Israel, July 2002.

A   Translation of ETL to FO^{TC}

We say that a ETL sub-formula is temporally-bound if it appears under a temporal operator. Translations for temporally-bound and non-temporally-bound formulae are different, since non-temporally-bound formulae should be bound to the initial world of the trace.

Definition 13. *[ETL translation to FO^{TC}] We denote by $(\varphi)^{\dagger w}$ the bounded translation of a formula φ in a world w and by $(\varphi)^{\dagger}$ the non-bounded translation.*

- $(\varphi)^{\dagger} = \exists w \colon world.initialWorld(w) \wedge (\varphi)^{\dagger w}$
- *if φ is an atomic formula other than $\odot x$ and $\oslash x$ then $(\varphi)^{\dagger w} = \varphi$. If $\varphi = \odot x$ then $(\varphi)^{\dagger w} = isNew(x)$. If $\varphi = \oslash x$ then $(\varphi)^{\dagger w} = isFreed(x)$.*
- $(\varphi \wedge \psi)^{\dagger w} = (\varphi)^{\dagger w} \wedge (\psi)^{\dagger w}$, $(\varphi \vee \psi)^{\dagger w} = (\varphi)^{\dagger w} \vee (\psi)^{\dagger w}$, $(\neg\varphi)^{\dagger w} = \neg(\varphi)^{\dagger w}$
- $(\exists x\, \varphi)^{\dagger w} = \exists x.exists(w, x) \wedge (\varphi)^{\dagger w}$
- $((TC\ x_1, x_2 \colon \varphi)(x_3, x_4))^{\dagger w} = (TC\ \ x_1, x_2 \colon (\varphi)^{\dagger w} \wedge\ exists(w, x_1) \wedge exists(w, x_2))(x_3, x_4)$
- $(\varphi(x_1, \dots, x_n)\ \mathcal{U}\ \psi(y_1, \dots, y_k))^{\dagger w} =$

    $\exists w' \colon world.\exists y_1', \dots, y_k'.succ^*(w, w') \wedge (\psi(y_1', \dots, y_k'))^{\dagger w'}$
    $\wedge \bigwedge_{1 \leq i \leq k} evolution^*(y_i, y_i') \wedge \forall \tilde{w} \colon world.\exists x_1', \dots, x_n'.(succ^*(w, \tilde{w})$
    $\wedge\ succ^*(\tilde{w}, w') \rightarrow (\varphi(x_1', \dots, x_n'))^{\dagger \tilde{w}} \wedge \bigwedge_{1 \leq j \leq n} evolution^*(x_j, x_j'))$

- $(\chi\varphi(x_1, \dots, x_n))^{\dagger w} =$

    $\exists w' \colon world.\exists x_1', \dots, x_n'.succ(w, w')$
    $\wedge (\varphi(x_1', \dots, x_n'))^{\dagger w'} \wedge \bigwedge_{1 \leq j \leq n} evolution(x_j, x_j') \wedge exists(x_j', w')$

Note that x_i and y_i are not necessarily distinct. Simplified translations may be used for the $\diamond$ and $\square$ temporal operators.

Correctness of Data Representations Involving Heap Data Structures

Uday S. Reddy[1] and Hongseok Yang[2]

[1] School of Computer Science, University of Birmingham
[2] ROPAS, Korean Advanced Inst. of Science and Technology

Abstract. While the semantics of local variables in programming languages is by now well-understood, the semantics of pointer-addressed heap variables is still an outstanding issue. In particular, the commonly assumed relational reasoning principles for data representations have not been validated in a semantic model of heap variables. In this paper, we define a parametricity semantics for a Pascal-like language with pointers and heap variables which gives such reasoning principles. It is found that the correspondences between data representations are not simply relations between states, but more intricate correspondences that also need to keep track of visible locations whose pointers can be stored and leaked.

1 Introduction

Programming languages with dynamically allocated storage variables ("heap variables") date back to Algol W [27] and include the majority of languages in use today: imperative languages like C, Pascal and Ada, object-oriented languages ranging from Simula 67 to Java, and functional languages like Scheme, Standard ML, and variants of Haskell [6]. However, the semantic structure of these languages is not yet clear. In particular, the oft-used principles for data representation reasoning, involving invariants or simulation relations, have not been validated. While remarkable progress has been made in understanding local variables (cf. the collection [15]), none of this theory is directly applicable to heap variables because the shape of the heap storage dynamically varies.

A number of attacks have been made on the problem: Stark's thesis [25, 24], which deals with dynamic allocation but not pointers, and Ghica's and Levy's theses [4,5,7,8], which address the general semantic structure but not data representation reasoning. The recent paper of Banerjee and Naumann [2] is the first to address data representation correctness with heap variables and pointers. While their work is remarkably successful in dealing with a Java-like language with dynamically allocated objects, their treatment falls short of explicating the semantic structure of the language relying instead on a strong notion of "confinement" to simplify the problem.

In this paper, we define a parametricity semantics for a Pascal-like language with dynamically allocated variables, pointers, and call-by-value procedures. The validity of simulation-based reasoning principles follows from the structure of the

P. Degano (Ed.): ESOP 2003, LNCS 2618, pp. 223–237, 2003.

semantics (similar to Tennent's treatment in [26] for local variables). The type structure of the semantics makes explicit where information hiding is going on, while the formal parametricity conditions back up one's intuitions and allow one to produce formal proofs. We do not use any confinement conditions in our definitions. Where there is information leakage, our semantics explicates the breakdown of the data encapsulation, so that faulty conclusions are avoided.

Our treatment bears a close relationship with the ongoing work on separation logic for local reasoning about heap storage [22,11,28]. In particular, our relations are "local" in the same sense as the assertions of separation logic. We use the ideas of partial heaps and heap-splitting developed there to formulate the relations. We envisage that in future work, these connections with local reasoning will be further strengthened.

2   Motivation

Local variables get hidden in program contexts due to scope restrictions in the programming language. This gives rise to information hiding which is exploited in devising data representations. Since dynamically allocated heap variables can only be accessed through entry points given by local variables, the same scope restrictions also give rise to information hiding for heap data structures. In this section, we give an informal introduction to these information hiding aspects through a series of examples.

Example 1. Consider the following program block adapted from Meyer and Sieber [9]:

   { **local var** int x; x := 0; p(); **if** x = 0 **then diverge** }

Here, p is an arbitrary non-local procedure with no arguments, and diverge is a diverging command. The program block should be observationally equivalent to diverge for the following reason: The local variable x is not visible to the non-local procedure p. Hence, if x is 0 before the procedure call, it should be 0 after the procedure call too.

Next consider a similar program using pointer-addressed variables:[1]

   { x := **new** int; x↑ := 0; p(); **if** x↑ = 0 **then diverge** }

Here, x is a non-local variable (of type ↑int) that can store pointers to integer variables in the heap. The command x := **new** int allocates a new integer variable on the heap and sets x to point to this variable. Unlike in the local variable case, we cannot expect this program block to be equivalent to diverge. The reason is that the heap variable is accessible to p via the non-local variable x and p has the ability to modify it. There is no information hiding for the heap variable.

On the other hand, the following variant does implement information hiding:

   { **local var** (↑int) x; x := **new** int; x↑ := 0; p(); **if** x↑ = 0 **then diverge** }

---

[1] The notation for pointers is borrowed from Pascal. For any data type δ, $\uparrow\delta$ is the type of pointers to δ-typed variables. If p is a pointer, $p\uparrow$ denotes the variable that p points to. (In the syntax of C, $\uparrow\delta$ would be written as $\delta*$ and $p\uparrow$ as $*p$.)

Here, the pointer variable x is local. Since it is the only access point to the heap variable, the procedure p has no access to the heap variable. If x↑ is 0 before the procedure call, it should remain 0 after the procedure call. Hence, this block is equivalent to `diverge`.   □

We give an indication of how this form of selective information hiding can be modelled in the semantics. Using a possible world form of semantics as in [21,16, 13], we take worlds to be sets of typed locations (or equivalently record types) of the form $W = \{l_1 : \delta_1, \ldots, l_k : \delta_k\}$. We write $X <: W$ to mean that X is an extension of W with additional locations (or a "subtype" of W). All program terms are given meanings with reference to a possible world W denoting the set of locations available in a particular (dynamic) context of execution. Now, in a world W, the procedure p denotes a parametrically polymorphic function of type:

$$\llbracket p \rrbracket : \forall_{X <: W} \mathrm{St}(X) \to \mathrm{St}(X)$$

where $\mathrm{St}(X)$ means the set of states for the location world X. Here, X refers to the set of locations available when p may be called, which will include all the locations of W plus any additional locations allocated before the call. However, since p has been defined before these new locations are allocated, it should have no direct access to these new locations. The parametric interpretation of $\forall_{X <: W}$ captures information hiding for *all parts of X that are not accessible from W*. This is defined via relation-preservation for appropriate kinds of relations. The definition of these relations is the main technical contribution of this paper.

Corresponding to the subtyping $X <: W$, there is a relation-subtyping $S <: R$ that says that a relation S between potential instantiations of X is an extension of a relation R between potential instantiations of W. Intuitively the relation-subtyping $S <: R$ says that the S relation expects the contents of all W-accessible locations to be related by R and imposes new constraints for the other new locations that are inaccessible from W. The parametric interpretation of $\forall_{X <: W}$ implies that $\llbracket p \rrbracket$ must preserve all relations S that extend the identity relation I_W, i.e., preserve all additional conditions that can be stated for W-inaccessible locations. Using this intuition, we can explain how the three program blocks in Example 1 are treated. In each case, we choose W to be the set of all locations allocated before the entry of the program block:

- In the first program block with a local variable x, the extended relation S can impose the condition that the new location for x contains a specific value such as 0. Since the binding of p preserves all such relations, it follows that p cannot affect x.
- In the second program block, where the heap location is accessible via a *non-local* pointer variable x, recall that the extended relation S can impose additional conditions only for *W-inaccessible* locations. Since the new location is accessible from W before the procedure call to p, there is no requirement that p should preserve its value.
- In the third program block where the heap location is accessible via a *local* pointer variable x, both x and the heap location are inaccessible from W.

Hence the extended relation S can impose the additional condition $x\uparrow = 0$ and p must preserve it.

The second example, due to Peter O'Hearn, illustrates information leakage:

Example 2. Consider the program block that calls a non-local procedure h of type $\uparrow$int $\rightarrow$ **com**:

```
{ local var (↑int) x; x := new int;
  h(x); x↑ := 0; p(); if x↑ = 0 then diverge }
```

As in the previous example, x and x↑ are not directly visible to the non-local procedures. However, h is given as argument the pointer value of x. It has the ability to dereference x and modify x↑. It can also store the pointer x in a non-local variable. In other words, the access to the local data structure x↑ has been *leaked* and encapsulation is lost. It is not guaranteed that the later call to p will not affect x↑ because p can receive access to x↑ from h via a shared variable. This block is not equivalent to **diverge** in general.

If, however, h were to be passed x↑ as an argument, instead of the pointer value x, it would not have the ability to store x and information leakage would be avoided.[2]   □

To model information leakage, we split the relations mentioned previously into two parts: one part that relates *visible* heap locations, given by a partial bijection between the location sets $\rho : W \leftrightarrow W'$, and a second part that relates the contents of *hidden* locations, given by a relation R between partial states. A pair consisting of the two parts $(\rho, R) : W \leftrightarrow W'$ will be referred to as a "relational correspondence." Such a correspondence determines a relation between state sets expressed as $EQ_\rho * R$, where EQ_ρ means that the ρ-related locations have equal values (modulo ρ) and the $*$ connective, adapted from separation logic [22,11,28], means that the two parts of the relation access disjoint sets of locations. Now, a state transformation that preserves $EQ_\rho * R$ is allowed to look up and update ρ-related locations. It is also allowed to store pointers to ρ-related locations in other locations. However, it cannot store pointers to locations not related by ρ. The parametricity constraints imply that only the ρ-related locations can be leaked.

The information leakage in Example 2 is then explained as follows: The procedure call to h must preserve all relational correspondences $(\sigma, S) <: I_W$ that allow its argument x to be interpreted. Since the argument is a pointer to a heap location, the extended partial bijection σ must contain a pair (l, l), where l is the heap location that x points to. Hence h(x) can store pointers to l in W-accessible locations with the result that l itself becomes W-accessible. This has an effect for the later procedure call p(), which can modify any W-accessible location including l.

---

[2] Because of the subtle distinction between pointer values x and the pointed variables x↑, we prefer to work with an explicit pointer language like Pascal. Languages like Java, where pointers are treated implicitly, do not make this distinction and consequently lack the facility to control access. Surreptitious leakage is pervasive in the programs of such languages.

Both of our previous examples have to do with data abstraction, albeit in a veiled form. (The program blocks create local data structures which they attempt to hide from the client procedures in varying ways.) Our programming language also contains a class construct, previously studied in [18,19], providing a more direct form of data abstraction. The next example uses this to illustrate relational reasoning:

Example 3. Consider a list class implemented using linked lists in heap:

```
List = class : listsig
            local var (↑node) head; init head := nil; meth ...
       end
```

Here, `listsig` is the interface type of the `List` class and `node` is a recursively-defined storable data type: `node = int × ↑node`. We omit the details of the methods which include the usual operations for insertion, deletion and look-up.

To verify the correctness of such a class, one can prove its equivalence with another class that uses mathematical sequences as the internal representation:

```
List' = class : listsig
            local var (int*) s; init s := ⟨⟩; meth ...
        end
```

Here int* represents the set of integer sequences regarded as a data type, and the methods update the variable s to achieve the same effect as the methods in the concrete class. Intuitively, one reasons about the equivalence of the two classes by considering a relation between their states to the effect that the variable s in `List'` holds exactly the sequence of elements stored in the linked list starting at `head`, and showing that all the methods preserve this relation. Such a relation is formalized in our setting as follows.

The two representation worlds contain one location each, for the local variables of the classes: $W = \{l : \uparrow node\}$ and $W' = \{l' : int^*\}$. The partial bijection part of the correspondence is the empty relation $\emptyset : W \leftrightarrow W'$ because only visible locations need be included in the partial bijection but l and l' are not visible to the clients of the classes. The state relation part of the correspondence is a relation R defined as follows:

$$s\,[R]\,s' \iff \text{rep}(s, l, s'(l'))$$
$$\text{rep}(s, l, \alpha) \iff (s(l) = \text{nil} \wedge \alpha = \langle\rangle) \vee \exists n, k, \beta.(s(l) = (n, k) \wedge \alpha = \langle n\rangle \cdot \beta \wedge \text{rep}(s, k, \beta))$$

□

The important point to notice is that R is not simply a relation between St(W) and St(W'). In fact, the world W does not contain any locations that can be used for the nodes of the linked list. Rather R should be viewed as a relation that applies not only to the states for W and W' but also to *all their future extensions* with additional locations. This is one of the key technical issues that is addressed in the definitions to follow.

3 Definitions

Let δ range over a collection of data types. In particular, we assume that $\uparrow\delta$ is a data type for any data type δ.

Let $\mathrm{Loc} = \uplus_\delta \mathrm{Loc}_\delta$ be a countable set, countable for each δ, whose elements are regarded as names of "typed locations." A *location world* is a finite subset $W \subseteq_{\mathrm{fin}} \mathrm{Loc}$. It is also intuitive to think of a location world as a record type $[l_1 : \delta_1, \ldots, l_n : \delta_n]$. A *subtype* $X <: W$ is a superset $X \supseteq W$ of locations. In terms of records, X is a longer record type than W.

Fix a set of values $\mathrm{Val}(\delta)$ for each data type δ such that $\mathrm{Val}(\uparrow\delta) = \mathrm{Loc}_\delta \uplus \{\mathrm{nil}\}$.

We use the following technical notion of a "heap" (or a partial state with pointers) from the work on separation logic [11]. A *heap* is a pair $\langle L, s \rangle$ where $L \subseteq_{\mathrm{fin}} \mathrm{Loc}$ and $s : \prod_{l^\delta \in L} \mathrm{Val}(\delta)$ is a mapping of locations to values. We simply denote a heap $\langle L, s \rangle$ by s, and denote L by $\mathrm{dom}(s)$. If $s(l)$ is a data value involving another location l', l' may or may not be in $\mathrm{dom}(s)$. If $l' \notin \mathrm{dom}(s)$ then its occurrence in $s(l)$ is called a "dangling pointer." A heap with no dangling pointers is said to be *total*.

Whenever s_1 and s_2 are heaps with disjoint domains, $s_1 * s_2$ denotes their *join* with $\mathrm{dom}(s_1 * s_2) = \mathrm{dom}(s_1) \uplus \mathrm{dom}(s_2)$. Much use is made of this operation in the separation logic [11] and the Banerjee-Naumann work [2]. It will play a central role in our work as well.

A *state* for a world W is a heap s such that $\mathrm{dom}(s) = W$ and there are *no dangling pointers* in s. The set of states for a world W is denoted $\mathrm{St}(W)$.

Definition 1. A **renaming relation** is a triple $\rho = \langle W, W', \rho \rangle$ where

– W and W' are location worlds, and
– $\rho \subseteq W \times W'$ is a type-respecting relation that is single-valued and injective.

(That is, ρ is a type-respecting bijection between some subsets $L \subseteq W$ and $L' \subseteq W'$.) We refer to W as $\mathrm{dom}(\rho)$, W' as $\mathrm{cod}(\rho)$ and the relation as the "graph" of ρ.

If $X <: W$ and $X' <: W'$ are extended worlds and $\sigma = \langle X, X', \sigma \rangle$ and $\rho = \langle W, W', \rho \rangle$ are renaming relations, we say that σ is an *extension* of ρ and write $\sigma <: \rho$ if $\sigma \cap (W \times W') = \rho$. □

As mentioned in the context of Example 2, the purpose of renaming relations is to identify the visible locations. Since the pointers to such locations can be stored in other visible locations, we define the following notation. For $d, d' \in \mathrm{Val}(\delta)$, we say that d and d' are equivalent modulo ρ, and write $d \equiv_\rho d'$, if d and d' denote the same data value assuming that all ρ-related locations are deemed to be equal.

In the following definitions, we make crucial use of relations between *partial* heaps. Even though we are, in the end, interested in relations between total states, these relations will be defined using those on heaps.

– If ρ is a renaming relation, EQ_ρ relates heaps that have equal values in ρ-related locations (where $\rho \upharpoonright i$ denotes projection of i'th components):

$$s \, [EQ_\rho] \, s' \iff \mathrm{dom}(s) = \rho \upharpoonright 1 \wedge \mathrm{dom}(s') = \rho \upharpoonright 2 \wedge \forall (l, l') \in \rho. \, s(l) \equiv_\rho s'(l').$$

– The relation emp relates empty heaps: $s \, [\mathrm{emp}] \, s' \iff \mathrm{dom}(s) = \emptyset = \mathrm{dom}(s')$

– The relation $R * S$ puts together two relations R and S side by side:

$$s \: [R * S] \: s' \iff \exists s_1, s_2, s_1', s_2'. \: s = s_1 * s_2 \wedge s' = s_1' * s_2' \wedge s_1 \: [R] \: s_1' \wedge s_2 \: [S] \: s_2'$$

This is the binary version of the $*$ connective in separation logic [11] and is extremely powerful. Its power owes to the fact that we do not have to specify in advance which parts of the heaps R and S run between. In a manner of speaking, R and S are "untyped" relations even if $R * S$ may be a "typed" relation.

Definition 2. A **relational correspondence** between location worlds is a pair $(\rho, R) : W \leftrightarrow W'$ where

– ρ is a renaming relation between W and W' and
– R is a function mapping all extensions $\pi <: \rho$ to relations between heaps,

such that, whenever $\pi_2 <: \pi_1 <: \rho$, $R(\pi_1) \subseteq R(\pi_2)$.

The extension relation for correspondences is defined by $(\sigma, S) <: (\rho, R)$ if and only if (i) $\sigma <: \rho$, and (ii) for any $\pi <: \sigma$, there is a relation P such that $S(\pi) = R(\pi) * P$. □

This is the key definition of this paper. We explain it in detail. The intuition is that the state consists of

– *visible locations*, identified by ρ, which must allow look-up, update and storage, and
– *hidden locations*, related by $R(\pi)$, which contain representations for abstract data and, so, can only be modified by invariant-preserving operations.

The visible locations and the hidden locations are disjoint. The visible locations must have equal values in related states. The hidden locations, on the other hand, are related by some relation $R(\pi)$ that captures the data representation invariants. The relation $R(\pi)$ is parameterized by renamings π so that information about visible locations mentioned in π can be incorporated in its formulation. The condition $R(\pi_1) \subseteq R(\pi_2)$ means that related states continue to be related if the states are extended with additional visible locations. The intuition for the definition of $(\sigma, S) <: (\rho, R)$ is that S extends R by imposing additional conditions for new locations but does not alter R for the part of the heap that R deals with. This is the same intuition as that in [16,14] for local variables.

The identity correspondence for a world W is $I_W = (\iota_W, \mathrm{emp}_W) : W \leftrightarrow W$, where ι_W is the diagonal relation for W and emp_W maps every $\pi <: \iota_W$ to emp.

Fact 1. *Whenever* $X <: W$, $I_X <: I_W$.

Having defined relational correspondences, we must specify how these are used to relate states. Note that the relation $EQ_\rho * R(\rho)$ relates *heaps* (or partial states with arbitrary domains). The corresponding relation for states is obtained by restricting the heap relation to states:

$$\mathrm{St}(\rho, R) : \mathrm{St}(W) \leftrightarrow \mathrm{St}(W')$$
$$\mathrm{St}(\rho, R) = (EQ_\rho * R(\rho)) \cap (\mathrm{St}(W) \times \mathrm{St}(W'))$$

The idea is that in order to define a typed relation between states, we transit to the untyped world of partial heaps where we have the powerful $*$ connective available and coerce the results back to the typed world. Defining the required relations without the $*$ connective would be extremely awkward.

Fact 2. $\text{St}(I_W)$ *is the identity relation on* $\text{St}(W)$.

To make these definitions concrete, we give an example:

Example 4. Consider the list data structure from Example 3 but now adapted to contain pointers to integer cells instead of just integers. The type of nodes is given by $node = \uparrow\text{int} \times \uparrow node$. For the worlds $W = \{l : \uparrow node\}$ and $W' = \{l' : (\uparrow\text{int})^*\}$, we define a correspondence $(\emptyset, R)$ where the relation function $R(\pi)$ is defined by:

$$s\ [R(\pi)]\ s' \iff \text{rep}_\pi(s, l, s'(l'))$$
$$\text{rep}_\pi(s, l, \alpha) \iff (s(l)=\text{nil} \wedge \alpha=\langle\rangle) \vee$$
$$\exists n, n', k, \beta.(s(l)=(n, k) \wedge \alpha=\langle n'\rangle \cdot \beta \wedge (n, n') \in \pi \wedge \text{rep}_\pi(s, k, \beta))$$

Notice the use of π argument in relating the contents of the list cells. The corresponding definition for Example 3 would use a constant function $R(\pi)$ because no pointers are to be related.   □

Categorical Matters

We use the setting of reflexive graph categories [14,23,3] to explicate the categorical structure that we use.

Proposition 3. *There is a reflexive graph of categories* **World** *with the following data: worlds as vertices, extensions* $X <: W$ *as vertex morphisms, correspondences* $(\rho, R) : W \leftrightarrow W'$ *as edges and extensions* $(\sigma, S) <: (\rho, R)$ *as edge morphisms. The identity edges are the identity correspondences.*

Let **Set** denote the reflexive graph with sets and functions forming the vertex category and binary relations and relation-preserving squares forming the edge category. We will be working with the functor category $\textbf{Set}^{\textbf{World}^{\text{op}}}$ whose objects are reflexive graph-functors $\textbf{World}^{\text{op}} \to \textbf{Set}$ and morphisms are parametric natural transformations. (To deal with divergence and recursion, we must really use **Cpo** in place of **Set**. We omit the treatment of recursion in this version of the paper, but it can be treated the same way as in [14].)

Definitions of parametric limits $\forall_X F(X)$ and parametric colimits $\exists_X F(X)$ for arbitrary reflexive graph-functors F may be found in [3]. In our case, we will be using these with nonvariant functors $F : \textbf{World}^\circ \to \textbf{Set}$ (where $\textbf{World}^\circ$ is the discrete reflexive graph corresponding to **World** with only identity morphisms). We will also use parametric ends $\int_X F(X, X)$ for functors F of type $\textbf{World} \times \textbf{World}^{\text{op}} \to \textbf{Set}$. See below for explicit constructions for these limits, colimits and ends.

The notation $\forall_{X<:W} F(X)$ is used to denote the parametric limit of the functor $F \circ J^\circ : (\textbf{World}_{<:W})^\circ \to \textbf{Set}$ where $\textbf{World}_{<:W}$ is the reflexive subgraph of **World** with vertices $X <: W$ and edges $(\sigma, S) <: I_W$, and J is its inclusion in **World**. It is to be noted that the type expression $\forall_{X<:W} F(X)$ forms a contravariant functor $T(W)$. The notation $\exists_{X<:W} F(X)$ similarly refers to the parametric colimit of $F \circ J^\circ$ (covariantly in W) and $\int_{X<:W} F(X,X)$ refers to the parametric end of $F \circ (J \times J^{op})$ (contravariantly in W).

The functor category $\mathbf{Set}^{\mathbf{World}^{op}}$ is cartesian closed with products given pointwise and exponents $F \Rightarrow G$ given by $(F \Rightarrow G)(W) = \int_{X<:W} F(X) \to G(X)$ [14,3].

Explicit Constructions

For the benefit of the reader unfamiliar with parametric limits, we give direct definitions of these constructions (which may be seen to be special cases of the definitions in [3]).

Let F be a type operator that associates, to every world W, a set $F(W)$ and, to every correspondence $(\rho, R) : W \leftrightarrow W'$, a relation $F(\rho, R) : F(W) \leftrightarrow F(W')$ such that $F(I_W) = \Delta_{F(W)}$. Then,

- $\prod_X F(X)$ is the set of families of the form $\{p_X \in F(X)\}_X$ indexed by all worlds X. $\prod_{X<:W} F(X)$ is similar except that the families are indexed only by subtypes of W.
- $\forall_X F(X)$ is a subset of $\prod_X F(X)$ consisting of families satisfying the *parametricity* condition: for all correspondences $(\rho, R) : X \leftrightarrow X'$ between different worlds, the components p_X and $p_{X'}$ are related by $F(\rho, R)$.
- $\forall_{X<:W} F(X)$ is a subset of $\prod_{X<:W} F(X)$ with a parametricity condition that applies only to correspondences $(\rho, R) <: I_W$. We say that the families are parametric with respect to W.
- $\sum_X F(X)$ is the set of pairs of the form $\langle X, a \rangle$ where X is a world and $a \in F(X)$. Such pairs should be viewed as "implementations" of abstract data types, where X denotes the representation type and a is the collection of operations. The set $\sum_{X<:W} F(X)$ is similar except that the worlds X are restricted to subtypes of W.
- $\exists_X F(X)$ is the quotient of $\sum_X F(X)$ under a *behavioral equivalence* relation. First, if $\langle X, a \rangle$ and $\langle X', a' \rangle$ are pairs in $\sum_X F(X)$, a *simulation* relation between them is a correspondence $(\rho, R) : X \leftrightarrow X'$ such that a and a' are related by $F(\rho, R)$. Two pairs $\langle X, a \rangle$ and $\langle X', a' \rangle$ are behaviorally equivalent, written $\langle X, a \rangle \approx \langle X', a' \rangle$, if there is a sequence of pairs $\langle X, a \rangle, \langle X_1, a_1 \rangle, \ldots,$ $\langle X_{n-1}, a_{n-1} \rangle, \langle X', a' \rangle$ with simulation relations between successive pairs. The equivalence class of a pair $\langle X, a \rangle$ under the behavioral equivalence relation is denoted $\langle\!\langle X, a \rangle\!\rangle$. These equivalence classes denote true "abstract data types" [10,19].
- $\exists_{X<:W} F(X)$ is a quotient of $\sum_{X<:W} F(X)$ where the allowed simulations between pairs are restricted to correspondences $(\rho, R) <: I_W$. The induced behavioral equivalence relation with respect to W is denoted $\approx_W$ and the equivalence class of a pair $\langle X, a \rangle$ is denoted $\langle\!\langle X, a \rangle\!\rangle_W$. These equivalence classes should be viewed as "partially abstract" types whose representations X are hidden except for the knowledge that they form subtypes of W.

The intuitive reading of $\exists_{X<:W}\mathrm{St}(X)$ is that all the locations in X that are not accessible from W are hidden. This intuition can be clearly seen in the following "garbage collection" lemma:

Lemma 4. Let $\mathrm{GC}_W : \exists_{X<:W}\mathrm{St}(X) \to \exists_{X<:W}\mathrm{St}(X)$ be defined by

$$\mathrm{GC}_W(\langle\!| X, s\rangle\!|) = \langle\!| \mathrm{reach}_X(W, s), \, s \restriction \mathrm{reach}(W, s)\rangle\!|$$

where $\mathrm{reach}_X(W, s)$ is the subset of X consisting of all locations reachable from W in the heap s. Then GC_W is the identity function on $\exists_{X<:W}\mathrm{St}(X)$.

This result signifies that reachability of locations has been properly captured by the relational correspondences.

A *reflexive graph-functor* $F : \mathbf{World}^{\mathrm{op}} \to \mathbf{Set}$ is a type operator that also has an associated contravariant action on the morphisms of $\mathbf{World}$. That means that, for all subtypings $X <: W$, there are functions $F(X<:W) : F(W) \to F(X)$ preserving identity and composition. Moreover, if $(\sigma, S) <: (\rho, R)$ then the functions $F(X<:W)$ and $F(X'<:W')$ map $F(\rho, R)$-related arguments to $F(\sigma, S)$-related results.

We note two general cases of functors arising in our setting:

- The type expression $T(W) = \forall_{X<:W}F(X)$ forms a contravariant functor in W, independent of whether F is functorial. The morphism part $T(V<:W)$ sends $\{p_X\}_{X<:W}$ to $\{p_X\}_{X<:V}$. The relation action $T(\rho, R):T(W) \leftrightarrow T(W')$ is given by

$$\{p_X\}_{X<:W} \, [T(\rho, R)] \, \{p'_{X'}\}_{X'<:W'} \iff$$
$$\text{for all } (\sigma, S): X \leftrightarrow X' \text{ such that } (\sigma, S) <: (\rho, R), \; p_X \, [F(\sigma, S)] \, p'_{X'}$$

  We write this relation as $\forall_{(\sigma,S)<:(\rho,R)}F(\sigma, S)$.

- The type expression $T(W) = \exists_{X<:W}F(X)$ determines a covariant functor in W. If $V <: W$, we have the morphism part $T(V<:W) : T(V) \to T(W)$ which sends $\langle\!| X, a\rangle\!|_V$ to $\langle\!| X, a\rangle\!|_W$. Since any simulation relation with respect to V is also a simulation relation with respect to W, this function is well-defined. We use the notation $hide_{V<:W}$ to denote it. The relation action $T(\rho, R):T(W) \leftrightarrow T(W')$ is given by

$$\langle\!| X, a\rangle\!|_W \, [T(\rho, R)] \, \langle\!| X', a'\rangle\!|_{W'} \iff$$
$$\text{there exist } \langle Y, b\rangle \approx_W \langle X, a\rangle, \; \langle Y', b'\rangle \approx_{W'} \langle X', a'\rangle$$
$$\text{and } (\sigma, S) : Y \leftrightarrow Y' \text{ such that } (\sigma, S) <: (\rho, R) \text{ and } b \, [F(\sigma, S)] \, b'$$

  We write this relation as $\exists_{(\sigma,S)<:(\rho,R)}F(\sigma, S)$.

The $\forall$ quantifier uses relational parametricity to capture uniformity and information hiding. The categorical condition of natural transformation is an alternative condition for uniformity. In [17,3], it is argued that ideally naturality should be subsumed under parametricity. However, our relational correspondences for heap worlds are not rich enough to subsume naturality. So, for the present paper, we treat naturality separately. If F, $G : \mathbf{World}^{\mathrm{op}} \to \mathbf{Set}$ are functors, we use the notation $\forall_X F(X) \to G(X)$ to mean families of functions that are *parametric as well as natural* (which would be written more formally as $\int_X F(X) \to G(X)$ in the notation of [3].) Similarly, $\forall_{X<:W}F(X) \to G(X)$ denotes families that are parametric as well as natural in X with respect to W.

Table 1. Type syntax of terms

$$\frac{}{\Gamma, x : \nu \vdash x : \exp \nu} \qquad \frac{\Gamma \vdash C_1 : \mathbf{com} \quad \Gamma \vdash C_2 : \mathbf{com}}{\Gamma \vdash C_1 ; C_2 : \mathbf{com}} \qquad \frac{\Gamma, x : \mathbf{var}\, \delta \vdash C : \mathbf{com}}{\Gamma \vdash \{\mathbf{local\ var}\, \delta\, x; C\} : \mathbf{com}}$$

$$\frac{\Gamma \vdash V : \exp(\mathbf{var}\, \delta)}{\Gamma \vdash \mathbf{read}\ V : \exp \delta} \qquad \frac{\Gamma \vdash V : \exp(\mathbf{var}\, \delta) \quad \Gamma \vdash E : \exp \delta}{\Gamma \vdash V := E : \mathbf{com}} \qquad \frac{}{\Gamma \vdash \mathbf{skip} : \mathbf{com}}$$

$$\frac{\Gamma \vdash E : \exp(\delta_1 \times \cdots \delta_n)}{\Gamma \vdash E.i : \exp \delta_i} \qquad \frac{\Gamma \vdash V : \exp(\mathbf{var}(\delta_1 \times \cdots \times \delta_n)) \quad \Gamma \vdash E : \exp \delta_i}{\Gamma \vdash V.i := E : \mathbf{com}}$$

$$\frac{}{\Gamma \vdash \mathbf{nil} : \exp(\uparrow\delta)} \qquad \frac{\Gamma \vdash E : \exp(\uparrow\delta)}{\Gamma \vdash E\uparrow : \exp(\mathbf{var}\, \delta)} \qquad \frac{\Gamma \vdash V : \exp(\mathbf{var}(\uparrow\delta))}{\Gamma \vdash V := \mathbf{new}\ \delta : \mathbf{com}}$$

$$\frac{\Gamma, x : \nu \vdash M : \pi}{\Gamma \vdash \lambda x.\, M : \exp\ (\nu \to \pi)} \qquad \frac{\Gamma \vdash M : \exp(\nu \to \pi) \quad \Gamma \vdash N : \exp \nu}{\Gamma \vdash M(N) : \pi}$$

$$\frac{\Gamma, x : \mathbf{var}\, \delta \vdash A : \mathbf{com} \quad \Gamma, x : \mathbf{var}\, \delta \vdash M : \exp \nu}{\Gamma \vdash \mathbf{class} : \nu\ \mathbf{local\ var}\, \delta\, x\ \mathbf{init}\ A\ \mathbf{meth}\ M\ \mathbf{end} : \exp\ (\mathbf{cls}\ \nu)}$$

$$\frac{\Gamma \vdash K : \exp\ (\mathbf{cls}\ \nu) \quad \Gamma, x : \nu \vdash C : \mathbf{com}}{\Gamma \vdash \{\mathbf{local}\ K\ x; C\} : \mathbf{com}}$$

Notation. We use convenient notation borrowed from the polymorphic lambda calculus [20] to denote polymorphic families. A family $\{P(X)\}_{X<:W}$ is written as $\Lambda X{<:}W.\, P(X)$ and, if ϕ is such a family, then component selection ϕ_X is written as $\phi[X]$.

4   Semantics

We consider a Pascal-like language with types given by the following syntax:

$$\begin{aligned}
\text{(data types)} \quad & \delta ::= \mathbf{int} \mid \uparrow\delta \mid \delta_1 \times \cdots \times \delta_n \\
\text{(value types)} \quad & \nu ::= \delta \mid \mathbf{var}\, \delta \mid \nu_1 \times \cdots \times \nu_n \mid \nu \to \pi \mid \mathbf{cls}\ \nu \\
\text{(phrase types)} \quad & \pi ::= \exp \nu \mid \mathbf{com}
\end{aligned}$$

Data types identify storable values, and value types identify bindable values (or values that can be passed to procedures). Phrase types are the types of terms.

The term syntax for our language is given in Table 1. We use a sample of command forms. Other forms can be accommodated in a similar fashion. The notation for classes is borrowed from [18,19].

The types are interpreted as reflexive graph-functors $\mathbf{World}^{\mathrm{op}} \to \mathbf{Set}$. The interpretation comes in three parts: the set part $[\![\tau]\!]$ maps worlds to sets, the relation part $\langle\!\langle\tau\rangle\!\rangle$ maps correspondences $(\rho, R) : W \leftrightarrow W'$ to relations $[\![\tau]\!](W) \leftrightarrow [\![\tau]\!](W')$ and the morphism part gives, for every subtyping $X <: W$, a function $[\![\tau]\!](X{<:}W) : [\![\tau]\!](W) \to [\![\tau]\!](X)$ such that correspondences are preserved.

$$\begin{aligned}
[\![\mathbf{int}]\!](W) &= Int \\
[\![\uparrow\delta]\!](W) &= (\mathrm{Loc}_\delta \cap W) + \{\mathrm{nil}\} \\
[\![\mathbf{var}\, \delta]\!](W) &= [\![\delta \to \mathbf{com}]\!](W) \times [\![\exp \delta]\!](W) \\
[\![\nu_1 \times \cdots \times \nu_n]\!](W) &= [\![\nu_1]\!](W) \times \cdots \times [\![\nu_n]\!](W)
\end{aligned}$$

Table 2. Semantic combinators

$unit^\nu_W : [\![\nu]\!](W) \to [\![\mathbf{exp}\,\nu]\!](W)$

$unit_W\,d = \Lambda X{<:}W.\,\lambda s.\,d\uparrow^X_W$

$bind^{\nu,\pi}_W : [\![\mathbf{exp}\,\nu]\!](W) \times [\![\nu \to \pi]\!](W) \to [\![\pi]\!](W)$

$bind_W\,(e,f) = \Lambda X{<:}W.\,\lambda s.\,\text{let } d = e\,[X]\,s$
$\qquad\qquad\qquad\qquad \text{in if } d = \text{fault then fault else } f\,[X]\,d\,[X]\,s$

$bind^{\nu_1,\nu_2,\pi}_W : [\![\mathbf{exp}\,\nu_1]\!](W) \times [\![\mathbf{exp}\,\nu_2]\!](W) \times [\![\nu_1 \times \nu_2 \to \pi]\!](W) \to [\![\pi]\!](W)$

$bind_W\,(e_1,e_2,f) = \Lambda X{<:}W.\,\lambda s.\,\text{let } d_1 = e_1\,[X]\,s,\ d_2 = e_2\,[X]\,s$
$\qquad\qquad\qquad\qquad\qquad \text{in if } d_1 = \text{fault} \vee d_2 = \text{fault then fault}$
$\qquad\qquad\qquad\qquad\qquad\qquad \text{else } f\,[X]\,(d_1,d_2)\,[X]\,s$

$hide_{Y<:X} : [(\exists_{Z<:Y}\mathrm{St}(Z)) + \{\text{fault}\}] \to [(\exists_{Z<:X}\mathrm{St}(Z)) + \{\text{fault}\}]$

$hide_{Y<:X}\,r = \text{case } r \text{ of } \langle\!\langle Z,s\rangle\!\rangle_Y \Rightarrow \langle\!\langle Z,s\rangle\!\rangle_X \mid \text{fault} \Rightarrow \text{fault}$

$seq_W : [\![\mathbf{com}]\!](W) \times [\![\mathbf{com}]\!](W) \to [\![\mathbf{com}]\!](W)$

$seq_W\,(c,c') = \Lambda X{<:}W.\,\lambda s.\begin{cases}\text{fault} & \text{if } c\,[X]\,s = \text{fault}\\ hide_{Y<:X}\left(c'\,[Y]\,s'\right) & \text{if } c\,[X]\,s = \langle\!\langle Y,s'\rangle\!\rangle_X\end{cases}$

$[\![\nu \to \pi]\!](W) = \forall_{X<:W}[\![\nu]\!](X) \to [\![\pi]\!](X)$

$[\![\mathbf{cls}\,\nu]\!](W) = \forall_{X<:W}\exists_{Z<:X}[\![\mathbf{exp}\,\nu]\!](Z) \times [\mathrm{St}(X) \to \exists_{Y<:Z}\mathrm{St}(Y) + \{\text{fault}\}]$

$[\![\mathbf{exp}\,\nu]\!](W) = \forall_{X<:W}\mathrm{St}(X) \to [\![\nu]\!](X) + \{\text{fault}\}$

$[\![\mathbf{com}]\!](W) = \forall_{X<:W}\mathrm{St}(X) \to \exists_{Y<:X}\mathrm{St}(Y) + \{\text{fault}\}$

The position of the type quantifications $\forall$ and $\exists$ in the type interpretations has been recognized in earlier work [25,4,8]. Intuitively, a command defined for a world W should be prepared to accept additional locations (represented by X) in its input state, and it might itself allocate new locations during the execution (represented by Y). The parametricity interpretation of the type quantifiers means that the command does not have direct access to the extra locations in its input state and the successor commands will not have direct access to the locations allocated by the present command.

Variables are interpreted as pairs of "put" and "get" methods, as in Reynolds [21]. Indeed, if $l \in W$ is a δ-typed location, we can map it to a pair of methods $var^\delta_W(l) = (put^\delta_W(l), get^\delta_W(l))$ defined as follows:

$$put^\delta_W(l)\,[Y]\,k\,[Z]\,s = \langle\!\langle Z, s[l \to k]\rangle\!\rangle_Z, \text{ and } get^\delta_W(l)\,[Y]\,s = s(l).$$

The relation interpretation of types $\langle\!\langle\tau\rangle\!\rangle$ is straightforward: $\langle\!\langle\mathrm{int}\rangle\!\rangle(\rho,R) = \Delta_{Int}$, $\langle\!\langle\uparrow\delta\rangle\!\rangle(\rho,R) = \rho+\Delta_{\{nil\}}$ and, for all other cases, it follows from the structure of $[\![\tau]\!]$. For the morphism part, $[\![\mathrm{int}]\!](X{<:}W)$ is id_{Int}, $[\![\uparrow\delta]\!](X{<:}W)$ is the evident inclusion, and for all other cases, it follows from the structure of the types. We use the shorthand notation $a\uparrow^X_W$ for $[\![\tau]\!](X{<:}W)(a)$ when $a \in [\![\tau]\!](W)$.

The semantics of a term with typing $x_1{:}\nu_1, \ldots, x_n{:}\nu_n \vdash M : \pi$ is a parametric natural transformation of type $\forall_W [\![\nu_1]\!](W) \times \cdots \times [\![\nu_n]\!](W) \to [\![\pi]\!](W)$. (As usual values of the type $[\![\nu_1]\!](W) \times \cdots \times [\![\nu_n]\!](W)$ will be regarded as "environments" ranged over by the symbol η.)

We use the semantic combinators from Table 2. We also assume that there is a family of functions $newloc_\delta(X)$ that give, for each world X, a δ-typed location that is not in X.

$\llbracket x \rrbracket_W \eta = unit_W(\eta(x))$

$\llbracket \mathbf{skip} \rrbracket_W \eta = \Lambda X <: W. \lambda s. \langle\!\langle X, s \rangle\!\rangle_X$

$\llbracket C_1; C_2 \rrbracket_W \eta = seq_W(\llbracket C_1 \rrbracket_W \eta, \llbracket C_2 \rrbracket_W \eta)$

$\llbracket \{\mathbf{local\ var}\ \delta\ x; C\} \rrbracket_W \eta =$

$\qquad \Lambda X <: W. \lambda s.\, hide_{X^+ <: X}\left(\llbracket C \rrbracket_{X^+}\, (\eta \uparrow_W^{X^+} [x \to var_{X^+}^\delta(l)])\, [X^+]\, (s * [l \to \mathrm{init}_\delta]) \right)$

$\qquad\qquad\qquad$ where $l = newloc_\delta(X)$ and $X^+ = X \uplus \{l\}$

$\llbracket \mathbf{read}\ V \rrbracket_W \eta = bind_W\, (\llbracket V \rrbracket_W \eta,\ \Lambda X <: W. \lambda(p, g).\, g)$

$\llbracket V := E \rrbracket_W \eta = bind_W\, (\llbracket V \rrbracket_W \eta,\ \llbracket E \rrbracket_W \eta,\ \Lambda X <: W. \lambda((p, g), k).\, p[X]k)$

$\llbracket E\!\uparrow \rrbracket_W \eta = bind_W\, (\llbracket E \rrbracket_W \eta,\ deref_W^\delta)$

$\llbracket V := \mathbf{new}\ \delta \rrbracket_W \eta = bind_W\, (\llbracket V \rrbracket_W \eta,\ alloc_W^\delta)$

$\llbracket \lambda x.\, M \rrbracket_W \eta = unit_W(\Lambda X <: W. \lambda d.\, \llbracket M \rrbracket_X(\eta \uparrow_W^X [x \to d]))$

$\llbracket M(N) \rrbracket_W \eta = bind_W\, (\llbracket M \rrbracket_W \eta,\ \llbracket N \rrbracket_W \eta,\ \Lambda X <: W. \lambda(f, d).\, f[X](d))$

$\llbracket \mathbf{class} : \nu\ \mathbf{local\ var}\ \delta\ x\ \mathbf{init}\ A\ \mathbf{meth}\ M\ \mathbf{end} \rrbracket_W \eta =$

$\qquad unit_W(\Lambda X <: W. \langle\!\langle X^+, \llbracket M \rrbracket_{X^+} \eta^+, \lambda s.\, \llbracket A \rrbracket_{X^+}(\eta^+)(s * [l \to \mathrm{init}_\delta]) \rangle\!\rangle_X)$

$\qquad\qquad$ where $l = newloc_\delta(X)$, $X^+ = X \uplus \{l\}$, and $\eta^+ = \eta \uparrow_W^{X^+} [x \to var_{X^+}^\delta(l)]$

$\llbracket \{\mathbf{local}\ K\ x; C\} \rrbracket_W \eta =$

$$bind_W \left(\begin{array}{l} \llbracket K \rrbracket_W \eta, \end{array} \quad \begin{array}{l} \Lambda X <: W. \lambda k.\, \Lambda Y <: X. \lambda s. \\ \quad \text{let } \langle\!\langle Z, m, i \rangle\!\rangle_Y = k[Y] \\ \quad \text{in if } \langle\!\langle Z', s' \rangle\!\rangle_Z = i(s) \wedge m[Z']s' \neq \text{fault} \\ \quad \text{then } hide_{Z' <: Y}(\llbracket C \rrbracket_{Z'}(\eta \uparrow_W^{Z'}[x \to m[Z']s']) s') \\ \quad \text{else fault} \end{array} \right)$$

These definitions are expressed using operations $alloc_W^\delta \colon \llbracket \mathbf{var}(\uparrow\delta) \to \mathbf{com} \rrbracket(W)$ and $deref_W^\delta \colon \llbracket \uparrow\delta \to \mathbf{exp\,(var\ }\delta) \rrbracket(W)$:

$$alloc_W^\delta\, [X]\, (p, g)\, [Z]\, s = hide_{Z^+ <: Z}(p\, [Z^+]\, l\, [Z^+]\, (s * [l \to \mathrm{init}_\delta]))$$
$$\text{where } l = newloc^\delta(Z) \text{ and } Z^+ = Z \uplus \{l\}$$
$$deref_W^\delta\, [X]\, l\, [Z]\, s = \text{if } l \neq \text{nil then } var_Z^\delta(l) \text{ else fault}$$

5   Results

The most basic result to be proved about our semantics is that it satisfies an abstraction theorem. (Really, this is not a separate result from the semantic definition, but rather an integral part of checking that the semantics is well-defined.)

Theorem 5. *The meaning of every term* $\llbracket \Gamma \vdash M : \theta \rrbracket$ *is a parametric natural transformation of type* $\llbracket \Gamma \rrbracket \to \llbracket \theta \rrbracket$. *That is,*

1. *for all worlds* W *and all environments* $\eta \in \llbracket \Gamma \rrbracket(W)$, $\llbracket M \rrbracket_W \eta \in \llbracket \theta \rrbracket(W)$;
2. *for all* $(\rho, R) \colon W \leftrightarrow W'$, *and all related environments* $\eta[\langle\!\langle \Gamma \rangle\!\rangle(\rho, R)] \eta'$, $\llbracket M \rrbracket_W \eta\, [\langle\!\langle \theta \rangle\!\rangle(\rho, R)]\, \llbracket M \rrbracket_{W'} \eta'$; *and*
3. *for all extensions* $X <: W$ *and all* $\eta \in \llbracket \Gamma \rrbracket(W)$, $(\llbracket M \rrbracket_W \eta) \uparrow_W^X = \llbracket M \rrbracket_X(\eta \uparrow_W^X)$.

The abstraction theorem immediately implies the soundness of the simulation principle for data representation reasoning. Suppose $\{\langle\!\langle F(Y), m_Y, i_Y \rangle\!\rangle\}_Y$ and $\{\langle\!\langle F'(Y), m'_Y, i'_Y \rangle\!\rangle\}_Y$ are two *similar* implementations of a class, i.e., for any world Y, there is a simulation relation $(\sigma, S) : F(Y) \leftrightarrow F'(Y)$ such that $(\sigma, S) <: I_Y$ and $m_Y \ [\langle\!\langle \exp \nu \rangle\!\rangle (\sigma, S)] \ m'_Y$ and i_Y and i'_Y are related by $\mathrm{St}(I_Y) \to \exists_{(\tau, T) <:(\sigma, S)} \mathrm{St}(\tau, T) + \Delta_{\{\text{fault}\}}$. Then in any command term of the form $\Gamma, C : \mathbf{cls}\, \nu \vdash \{\mathbf{local} \quad C\, x;\, M\} : \mathbf{com}$, we get the same results independent of which implementation is used for C. This is because when $i_Y\, s = \langle\!\langle Z, s_1 \rangle\!\rangle_{F(Y)}$ and $i'_Y\, s = \langle\!\langle Z', s'_1 \rangle\!\rangle_{F'(Y)}$,

$$hide_{Z<:Y}\left([\![M]\!]_Z(\eta\!\uparrow_W^Z[x{\to}m[Z]s_1])[Z]s_1\right) =$$
$$hide_{Z'<:Y}\left([\![M]\!]_{Z'}(\eta\!\uparrow_W^{Z'}[x{\to}m'[Z']s'_1])[Z']s'_1\right)$$

for all $\eta \in [\![\Gamma]\!]_W$ and $Y <: W$, which follows from the abstraction theorem.

The separation logic for reasoning about heap data structures [22,11,28] contains an important rule called the "frame rule," which is central to the *local reasoning* methodology developed there. The frame rule is supported by the frame property of commands which says that if a command is safe in a given state, then the result of executing it in a larger state can be predicted based on an execution on the smaller state. This property is satisfied by our semantics. Say that a command $c \in [\![\mathbf{com}]\!](W)$ is *safe* for world $X <: W$ and state $s \in \mathrm{St}(X)$ if $c[X](s) \neq \text{fault}$.

Theorem 6. *Let $c \in [\![\mathbf{com}]\!](W)$ be safe for world $X <: W$ and state s. Then for all extended worlds $X \uplus Z$ and states $s * t \in \mathrm{St}(X \uplus Z)$,*

1. *c is safe for $X \uplus Z$ and $s * t$, and*
2. *there exist world $Y <: X$ and state $s' \in \mathrm{St}(Y)$ such that $Y \cap Z = \emptyset$, $c[X]\,s = \langle\!\langle Y, s' \rangle\!\rangle_X$, and $c[X \uplus Z]\,(s * t) = \langle\!\langle Y \uplus Z, s' * t \rangle\!\rangle_{X \uplus Z}$.*

We expect that this connection will pave the way for integrating the data representation reasoning studied here and the state-based reasoning developed with separation logic.

Acknowledgments. We have benefited from discussions with Peter O'Hearn and David Naumann. Yang was supported by Creative Research Initiatives of the Korean Ministry of Science and Technology.

References

1. ABRAMSKY, S., HONDA, K., AND MCCUSKER, G. A fully abstract game semantics for general references. In *LICS 1998* (1998), pp. 334–344.
2. BANERJEE, A., AND NAUMANN, D. A. Representation independence, confinement and access control. In *POPL 2002* (2002), ACM.
3. DUNPHY, B. P. *Parametricity as a Notion of Uniformity in Reflexive Graphs.* PhD thesis, University of Illinois, Dep. of Mathematics, 2002.
4. GHICA, D. R. Semantics of dynamic variables in Algol-like languages. Master's thesis, Queen's University, Kingston, Canada, Mar 1997. (available electronically from ftp://ftp.qucis.queensu.ca/pub/rdt).
5. GHICA, D. R. Parameters and linked structures in algol-like languages. In *Report of the Dagstuhl Seminar 98261: The Semantic Challenge of Object-oriented Programming* (1998), Schloss Dagstuhl.

6. LAUNCHBURY, J., AND PEYTON JONES, S. L. State in Haskell. *J. Lisp and Symbolic Comput. 8*, 4 (1995), 293–341.

7. LEVY, P. B. *Call-by-Push-Value*. PhD thesis, Queen Mary, University of London, March 2001.

8. LEVY, P. B. Possible world semantics for general storage in call-by-value. In *CSL 2002* (2002), pp. 232–246.

9. MEYER, A. R., AND SIEBER, K. Towards fully abstract semantics for local variables. In *Fifteenth Ann. ACM Symp. on Princ. of Program. Lang.* (1988), ACM, pp. 191–203. (Reprinted as Chapter 7 of [15]).

10. MITCHELL, J. C., AND PLOTKIN, G. D. Abstract types have existential types. *ACM Trans. Program. Lang. Syst. 10*, 3 (1988), 470–502.

11. O'HEARN, P., REYNOLDS, J., AND YANG, H. Local reasoning about programs that alter data structures. In *CSL 2001* (Berlin, 2001), L. Fribourg, Ed., vol. 2142 of *LNCS*, Springer-Verlag, pp. 1–19.

12. O'HEARN, P. W., AND REYNOLDS, J. C. From Algol to polymorphic linear lambda-calculus. *J. ACM 47*, 1 (2000), 167–223.

13. O'HEARN, P. W., AND TENNENT, R. D. Semantics of local variables. In *Applications of Categories in Computer Science*, M. P. Fourman, P. T. Johnstone, and A. M. Pitts, Eds. Cambridge Univ. Press, 1992, pp. 217–238.

14. O'HEARN, P. W., AND TENNENT, R. D. Parametricity and local variables. *J. ACM 42*, 3 (1995), 658–709. (Reprinted as Chapter 16 of [15]).

15. O'HEARN, P. W., AND TENNENT, R. D. *Algol-like Languages (Two volumes)*. Birkhäuser, Boston, 1997.

16. OLES, F. J. *A Category-Theoretic Approach to the Semantics of Programming Languages*. PhD thesis, Syracuse University, 1982.

17. REDDY, U. S. When parametricity implies naturality. Electronic manuscript, July 1997. URL http://www.cs.bham.ac.uk/~udr.

18. REDDY, U. S. Objects and classes in Algol-like languages. In *Fifth Intern. Workshop on Foundations of Object-oriented Languages* (Jan 1998), electronic proceedings at http://pauillac.inria.fr/~remy/fool/proceedings.html.

19. REDDY, U. S. Objects and classes in Algol-like languages. *Information and Computation 172* (2002), 63–97.

20. REYNOLDS, J. C. Towards a theory of type structure. In *Coll. sur la Programmation*, vol. 19 of *LNCS*. Springer-Verlag, 1974, pp. 408–425.

21. REYNOLDS, J. C. The essence of Algol. In *Algorithmic Languages*, J. W. de Bakker and J. C. van Vliet, Eds. North-Holland, 1981, pp. 345–372. (Reprinted as Chapter 3 of [15]).

22. REYNOLDS, J. C. Intuitionistic reasoning about shared mutable data structure. In *Millenial Perspectives in Computer Science*. Palgrave, 2000.

23. ROBINSON, E., AND ROSOLINI, G. Reflexive graphs and parametric polymorphism. In *Proceedings, Ninth Annual IEEE Symposium on Logic in Computer Science* (July 1994), IEEE Computer Society Press.

24. STARK, I. Names and higher-order functions. Technical Report 363, University of Cambridge Computer Laboratory, April 1995.

25. STARK, I. Categorical models for local names. *Lisp and Symbolic Computation 9*, 1 (Feb. 1996), 77–107.

26. TENNENT, R. D. Correctness of data representations in Algol-like languages. In *A Classical Mind: Essays in Honor of C. A. R. Hoare*, A. W. Roscoe, Ed. Prentice-Hall International, 1994, pp. 405–417.

27. WIRTH, N., AND HOARE, C. A. R. A contribution to the development of Algol. *Comm. ACM 9*, 6 (June 1966), 413–432.

28. YANG, H. Local reasoning for stateful programs. Tech. Rep. UIUCDCS-R-2001-2227, University of Illinois, Dep. of Computer Science, July 2001.

Modeling Web Interactions

Paul Graunke[1], Robert Bruce Findler[2], Shriram Krishnamurthi[3], and
Matthias Felleisen[1]

[1] Northeastern University
[2] University of Chicago
[3] Brown University

Abstract. Programmers confront a minefield when they design interactive Web
programs. Web interactions take place via Web browsers. With browsers, consumers can whimsically navigate among the various stages of a dialog and can
thus confuse the most sophisticated corporate Web sites. In turn, Web services can
fault in frustrating and inexplicable ways. The quickening transition from Web
scripts to Web services lends these problems immediacy.

To address this programming problem, we develop a foundational model of Web
interactions and use it to formally describe two classes of errors. The model suggests techniques for detecting both classes of errors. For one class we present
an incrementally checked record type system, which effectively eliminates these
errors. For the other class, we introduce a dynamic safety check, which catches
the mistakes relative to programmers' simple annotations.

1 Introduction

Over the past decade, the Web has become an interactive medium. Far more than half of
all Web transactions are interactive [4]. While this rapid growth suggests that Web page
developers and programmers have mastered the mechanics of interactive Web content,
consumers still encounter many, and sometimes costly, program errors as they utilize
these new services. In short, designing interactive Web programs poses interesting and
complex problems.

To understand these problems, let us briefly recall how Web programs work. When a
Web browser submits a request whose path points to a Web program, the server invokes
the program with the request via any of a number of protocols (CGI [16], Java servlets [6],
or Microsoft's ASP.NET [15]). It then waits for the program to terminate and turns the
program's output into a response that the browser can display. Put differently, each
individual Web program simply consumes an HTTP request and produces a Web page
in response. It is therefore appropriate to call such programs "scripts" considering that
they only read some inputs and write some output. This very simplicity, however, also
makes the design of multi-stage Web dialogs difficult.

First, multi-stage interactive Web programs consist of many scripts, each handling
one request. These scripts communicate with each other via external media, because the
participants in a dialog must remember earlier parts of a conversation. Not surprisingly,
forcing the scripts to communicate this way causes many problems, considering that
such communications rely on oft-unstated, and therefore easily violated, invariants.

P. Degano (Ed.): ESOP 2003, LNCS 2618, pp. 238–252, 2003.

Second, the use of a Web browser for the consumer's side of the dialog introduces even more complications. The primary purpose of a Web browser is to empower consumers to navigate among a web of hyperlinked nodes in a graph at will. A consumer naturally wants this same power to explore dialogs on the Web. For example, a consumer may wish to backtrack to an earlier stage in a dialog, clone a page with choices and explore different possibilities in parallel, bookmark an interaction and come back to it later, and so on. Hence, a programmer must be extremely careful about the invariants that govern the communication among the scripts that make up an interactive Web program. What appears to be invariant in a purely sequential dialog context may not be so in a dialog medium that allows whimsical navigation actions.

In this paper, we make three contributions to the problem of designing reliable interactive Web programs. First, we develop a simple but formal model of Web interactions. Using this model, we can explain the above problems concisely. Second, we develop a type system that solves one of these problems in a provable manner (relative to the model). Third, because not all the checks can be performed statically, we suggest run-time checks to supplement the type system.

2 A Sample Problem

Let us illustrate one of the Web programming problems with a commercial example. Figure 1 contains snapshots from an actual interaction with Orbitz,[1] which sells travel services from many vendors. It naturally invites comparison shopping. In particular, a customer may enter the origin and destination airports to look for some flights between cities, receive a list of flight choices, and then conduct the following actions:

1. Use the "open link in new window" option to study the details of a flight that leaves at 5:50pm. The consumer now has two browser windows open.
2. Switching back to the choices window, the consumer can inspect a different option, e.g., a flight leaving at 9:30am. Now the consumer can perform a side-by-side comparison of the options in two browser windows.
3. After comparing the flight details, the customer decides to take the first flight after all. The consumer switches back to the window with the 5:50pm flight. Using this window (form), the consumer submits the request for the 5:50pm flight.

At this point, the consumer expects the reservation system to respond with a page confirming the 5:50pm flight. Alarmingly, even though the page says a click on some link would reserve the 5:50pm flight, Orbitz instead chooses the 9:30am flight. A customer who doesn't pay close attention may end up reserving the wrong flight.

The Orbitz problem dramatically illustrates our case. Sadly, this is not an isolated error. Rather it exists in other services (such as hotel reservations) on the Orbitz site. Furthermore, as plain consumers, we have stumbled across this and related problems while using several vendor's sites, including Apple, Continental Airlines, Hertz car rentals, Microsoft, and Register.com. Clearly, an error that occurs repeatedly across organizations suggest not a one-time programming fault but rather a systemic problem. Hence, we believe that it is time to develop a foundational model. Before we do so, however, we review related attempts at overcoming such programming problems.

---

[1] The screenshots were produced on June 28, 2002, but the problems persist as of October 24.

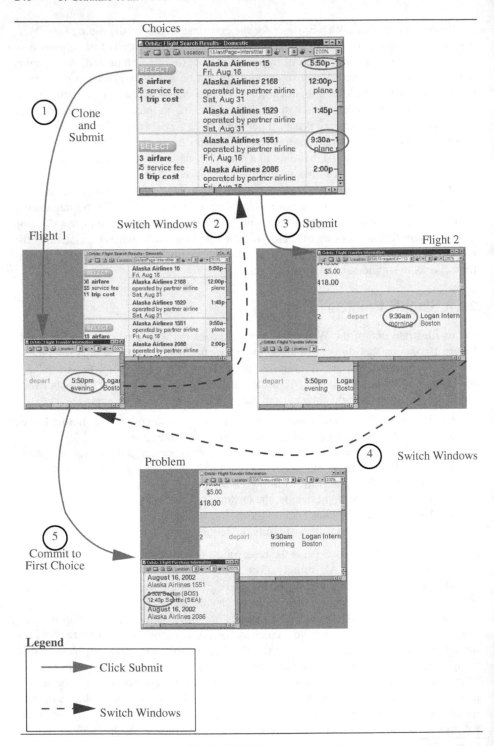

Fig. 1. Orbitz Interactions

3   Prior Work

The Bigwig project [2] (a descendant of Bell Lab's Mawl project [1]) provides a radical solution to the problem. The main purpose of the project is to provide a domain-specific language for composing interactive Web sessions. The language's runtime system enforces the (informal) model of a session as a pair of communicating threads [3]. For example, clicking on the back button takes the consumer back to the very beginning of the dialog. While such a runtime system prevents damage, it is also overly draconian, especially when compared to other approaches to dealing with Web dialogs.

John Hughes [14], Christian Queinnec [18], and Paul Graham [11] independently had the deep insight that a browser's navigation actions correspond to the use of first-class continuations in a program. In particular, they show that an interaction with the consumer corresponds to the manipulation of a continuation. If the underlying language and server support these manipulations, a program doesn't have to terminate to interact with a consumer but instead captures a continuation and suspends the evaluation. Every time a consumer submits a response, the computation resumes the proper continuation. Put differently, the communication among scripts is now internalized within one program and can thus be subjected to the safety mechanisms of the language.

Our prior work explored the implications of Queinnec's in two ways. First, we built a Web server that enables Web programs to interact directly with consumers [13]. Programming in this world eliminates many of the Web design problems in a natural manner. Second, after we realized that this solution doesn't apply to languages without such mechanisms, we explored the automatic generation of robust Web programs via functional compilation techniques [12]. While this idea works in principle, we recognized that a full-fledged implementation requires a re-engineered library system and runtime environment for the targeted language (say Perl).

Thiemann [21] started with Hughes's ideas and provides a monad-based library for constructing Web dialogs. In principle, his solution corresponds to our second approach; his monads take care of the "compilation" of Web scripts into a suitable continuation form. Working with Haskell, Thiemann can now use Haskell's type system to check the natural communication invariants between the various portions of a Web program. Haskell, however, is also a problem because Thiemann must accommodate effects (interactions with file systems, data bases, etc) in an unnatural manner. Specifically, for each interaction, his CGI scripts are re-executed from the beginning to the current point of interaction. Even though his monad-based approach avoids the re-execution of effects, it is indicative of the problems with Thiemann's approach. Like our second solution, Thiemann's approach won't easily apply to other languages.

4   Modeling the Web

To study the problems of designing interactive Web programs, we formulate a model with four characteristics. First, it consists of a single server and a single client, because we wish to study the problems of simple sequential Web dialogs. Second, it deals exclusively with dynamically generated Web pages, called forms, to mirror HTML's sub-language of requests. Third, the model allows the consumer to switch among Web pages arbitrarily; as we show later, this suffices to represent the "Orbitz problem" and similar errors. Finally, the model is abstracted over the programming language so that we can experiment with alternatives; here we use a λ calculus for forms and basic data.

Our model lacks several properties that are orthogonal to our goals. First, the model ignores client-side storage, a.k.a. "cookies," which primarily addresses customization and storage optimizations. Server-side storage suffices for our goals. Second, Web programmers must address concurrency via locking, possibly relying on a server that serializes each session's requests or relying on a database. Distributing the server software across multiple machines complicates concurrency further. Third, monitoring and restarting servers improves fault tolerance. The model neither addresses nor introduces any security concerns, so existing solutions for ensuring authentication and privacy apply [7, 9].

4.1 Server and Client

Figure 2 describes the components of our model. Each Web configuration (W) consists of a single server (S) and a single client (C). The server consists of storage (Σ) and a dispatcher (see figure 3). The latter contains a table (P) that associates URLS with programs and an evaluator that applies programs from the table to the submitted form. Programs are closed terms (M°) in a yet to be specified language.

$$
\begin{array}{llll}
W & = S \times C & \{\ ""\ ,\ "x",\ "why",\ "zee"\ \} & \subset String \\
S & = \Sigma \times P & \{\ x, y, z\ \} & \subset Id \\
P & = Url \mapsto M^\circ & \{\ www.drscheme.org,\ www.plt\text{-}scheme.org\ \} & \subset Url \\
M^\circ & = programs & & \\
C & = F \times \overrightarrow{F} & & \\
F & = (\textbf{form}\ Url\ \overrightarrow{(Id\ V_\flat)}) & & \\
V_\flat & = Int \mid String & &
\end{array}
$$

Fig. 2. The Web

The client consists of the current Web form and a set of all previously visited Web forms. The set of previously visited forms starts as a singleton set: the home page. It then grows as the consumer visits additional pages. The model assumes that the consumer can freely (non-deterministically) replace the current page with some previously visited page. Since the current page is always an element of all previously visited pages, the consumer can also return to this page. We claim that this model of a consumer represents all interesting browser navigation actions, including those not yet conceived by current browser implementors.

The model distills a Web page to a minimal representation. Every page is simply a form (F). It contains the URL to which the form is submitted and a set of form fields. A field names a value that the consumer may edit at will.

Figure 3 illustrates how the pieces of the model interact. The server and client may run on different machines, connected by a network. The client sends its current form

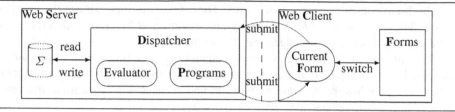

Fig. 3. The Web Picture

to the server. The server applies a program to the form and then produces a response, possibly accessing the store in the process. Finally, the response replaces the current form on the client and appears in the client's set of visited forms.

$$\texttt{fill-form} : W \longrightarrow W$$
$$\langle s, \langle (\textbf{form}\ u\ \overrightarrow{(k\ v_0)}),\ \overrightarrow{f}\rangle\rangle \hookrightarrow \langle s, \langle (\textbf{form}\ u\ \overrightarrow{(k\ v_1)}),\ \{(\textbf{form}\ u\ \overrightarrow{(k\ v_0)})\} \cup \overrightarrow{f}\rangle\rangle$$

$$\texttt{switch} : W \longrightarrow W$$
$$\langle s, \langle f_0,\ \overrightarrow{f}\rangle\rangle \hookrightarrow \langle s, \langle f_1,\ \overrightarrow{f}\rangle\rangle\ \textbf{where}\, f_1 \in \overrightarrow{f}$$

$$\texttt{submit} : W \longrightarrow W$$
$$\langle\langle \sigma_0,\ p\rangle,\ \langle f_0,\ \overrightarrow{f}\rangle\rangle \hookrightarrow \langle\langle \sigma_1,\ p\rangle,\ \langle f_1,\ \{f_1\} \cup \overrightarrow{f}\rangle\rangle$$
$$\textbf{where}\ \langle \sigma_1,\ f_1\rangle = d_p(\sigma_0, f_0)$$

Fig. 4. Transitions

To specify behavior, we use rewriting rules to relate Web configurations. Figure 4 contains rules that determine the behavior of the client and server as far as Web programs are concerned. The *fill-form* rule allows the client to edit the values of fields in the current form. The *switch* rule brings a different Web form to the foreground. In practice, this happens in a number of ways: switching active browser windows, revisiting a cached page[2] using the back or forward buttons, or selecting a bookmark. The *submit* rule dispatches on the current form's URL to run the program found in table p, resulting in a new current client form and updated server storage. The actual dispatching and the evaluation are specific to the chosen programming language, which we introduce next.

4.2 Functional Web Programming

Figure 5 specifies the WrForm programming language. WrForm extends the call-by-value λ-calculus with integers, strings, and Web forms, which are records with a reference to a program. The programming language connects to the Web model (figure 2) in three ways: the syntax for forms, the syntax for terms (M), and the dispatch function d_p.

---

[2] Returning to a non-cached page falls under the *submit* rule.

The **form** construct creates Web forms. The $M.Id$ construct extracts the value of a form field with the name Id. We specify the semantics of WrForm with a reduction semantics [8]. There are two reductions: β_v and **select**.

The bottom half of figure 5 specifies dispatching. It shows how d_p processes a submitted form $form_0$. First, it uses the URL in $form_0$ to extract a program from its table p. Second, it applies the program to the form and reduces this application to a value $form_1$. The store σ_0 remains the same.

Syntax	Semantics
$M = V$	$E \quad = [] \mid (E\ M) \mid (V\ E)$
$\quad \mid (M\ M)$	$\quad \mid (\textbf{form}\ url\ \overrightarrow{(id\ V)}\ (id\ E)\ \overrightarrow{(id\ M)})$
$\quad \mid Id$	$\quad \mid E.Id$
$\quad \mid (\textbf{form}\ Url\ \overrightarrow{(Id\ M)})$	
$\quad \mid M.Id$	$(\beta_v) \quad E[((\lambda\ (x)\ body)\ v)] \longrightarrow_v E[body[x\backslash v]]$
	$(\textbf{select})\ E[(\textbf{form}\ url\ \overrightarrow{(n_i\ v_i)}\ (n_j\ v_j)\ \overrightarrow{(n_k\ v_k)}).n_j] \longrightarrow_v E[v_i]$
$V = V_b \mid (\lambda\ (Id)\ M) \mid \text{F}$	

Language to Web Connection

$d_p : \Sigma \times F \longrightarrow \Sigma \times F$

$d_p(\sigma_0, (\textbf{form}\ url\ \overrightarrow{(id\ v)})) = \langle \sigma_0, form_1 \rangle$

where $prog = p(url)$ **and** $(prog\ (\textbf{form}\ url\ \overrightarrow{(id\ v)})) \longrightarrow_v^* form_1$

Fig. 5. Web Programming Language

4.3 Stateful Web Programming

Up to this point, scripts in our model can only communicate with each other through forms. In practice, however, Web scripts often communicate not only via forms but also through external storage (files, session objects). To model such stateful communications, we extend WrForm with **read** and **write** primitives. Figure 6 presents these language extensions. The two primitives empower programs to read flat values from and to write flat values to store locations. The reduction relation $\longrightarrow_{v\sigma}$ is the natural extension of the relation $\longrightarrow_v$. The extended relation relates pairs of terms and stores rather than just terms. Consequently the dispatcher starts a reduction with the invoked program and the current store. At the end it uses the modified store to form the next Web configuration. Thus, the server model remains sequential and does not include any concurrency.

5   Problems with the Web

Our model of Web interactions can represent some common Web programming problems concisely. The first problem is that a Web script expects a different kind of form than is delivered. We dub this problem the "(script) communication problem." The second

Syntax

$M = \cdots \mid (\textbf{read } Id) \mid (\textbf{write } Id\ M)$

Language to Web Connection

$\Sigma \sqsubseteq (Id \longrightarrow V_b)$

Semantics

$$\frac{e_0 \longrightarrow_v e_1}{\langle \sigma, e_0 \rangle \longrightarrow_{v\sigma} \langle \sigma, e_1 \rangle}$$

$\langle \sigma, E[(\textbf{write } id\ v)] \rangle \longrightarrow_{v\sigma} \langle \sigma[id\backslash v], E[v] \rangle$

$\langle \sigma, E[(\textbf{read } id)] \rangle \longrightarrow_{v\sigma} \langle \sigma, E[\sigma(id)] \rangle$

where $id \in dom(\sigma)$

$d_p(\sigma_0, (\textbf{form } url\ \overrightarrow{(id\ s)})) = \langle \sigma_1, form_1 \rangle$

where $prog = p(url)$

$\langle \sigma_0, (prog\ (\textbf{form } url\ \overrightarrow{(id\ s)}))) \rangle$

$\longrightarrow_{v\sigma}^* \langle \sigma_1, form_1 \rangle$

Fig. 6. Language Extensions for Storage

---

problem reveals a weakness of the hypertext transfer protocol. Due to the lack of an update method, information on client Web pages becomes obsolete and misleads the consumer. We dub this problem the "(HTTP) observer problem" indicating that the HTTP protocol does not permit a proper implementation of the Observer pattern [10].

5.1   The Communication Problem

Since standard Web programs must terminate to interact with a consumer, non-trivial interactive software consists of many small Web programs. If the software needs to interact N times with the client, it consists of $N + 1$ scripts, and all scripts must communicate properly with their successors.[3] Worse, since the client can arbitrarily resubmit pages, the programmer cannot assume anything about the scripts' execution sequence.

Even without the difficulties of unusual execution sequences, splitting Web programs into pieces can introduce errors. Consider the example in figure 7. The server's table contains two programs: *start.ss* and *next.ss*. The *start.ss* program prompts for the user's name and directs this information to *next.ss*. This second program attempts to verify some properties about the consumer. In doing so, it assumes that the input form contains both *name* and *phone* fields, and attempts to extract both. The attempt to extract the non-existent *phone* field results in a runtime error. The diagram illustrates the problem graphically. When programmers mistakenly encode such assumptions into the store—a mistake that is easily made with Java servlet and ASP.NET session objects—these safety errors concerning form field accesses become even more nefarious.

By now, programmers are well-aware of this problem and employ extensive dynamic testing to find these mistakes. In the next section, we present a type system that discovers such problems statically and still allows programmers to develop complex interactive Web programs in an incremental manner.

---

[3] A good programmer may recognize opportunities for aggregating some of the programs. It is also possible to use a "multiplexer" technique that merges all these scripts into one single file and uses a dispatcher to find the proper subroutine. The problems remain the same.

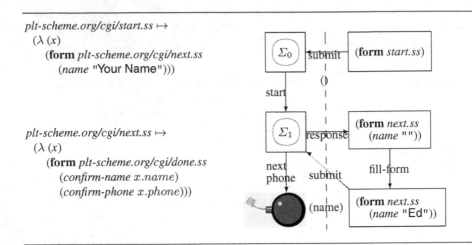

plt-scheme.org/cgi/start.ss ↦
  (λ (*x*)
    (**form** *plt-scheme.org/cgi/next.ss*
      (*name* "Your Name")))

plt-scheme.org/cgi/next.ss ↦
  (λ (*x*)
    (**form** *plt-scheme.org/cgi/done.ss*
      (*confirm-name x.name*)
      (*confirm-phone x.phone*)))

Fig. 7. Collaborating Programs

5.2 The Observer Problem

In a model-view-controller (MVC) architecture, each change to the model notifies all the views to update their display. Web programs do not enjoy this privilege, because HTTP does not provide for an update (or "push") method. Once a browser receives a page, it becomes outdated when the model changes on the server, which may be due to additional form submissions from the consumer.

The Observer problem is often, but not always, due to a confusion of environments and stores, or form and server-side storage. Clearly, a program that reserves flights needs both. Unfortunately, programmers who don't understand the difference may place information into the store when it really belongs in the Web form.

Figure 8 shows a reformulation of Orbitz's problem (see section 2) in WrForm. The first of these programs, *pick-flight*, asks the customer for a preferred flight time. The second program, *confirm-flight*, writes the selected flight time into external storage before asking the user to confirm the flight time. The third program, *receipt-flight*, reads the selected flight from storage and charges the customer for a ticket.

It is easy to see that the WrForm program models the problem in section 2. Submitting two requests for the *confirm-flight* program results in two pages displaying different flight times on the client, yet only one flight time resides in the server's external storage. Submitting the outdated form that no longer matches the storage produces the mistake.

6   Type Checking Communication

Trying to extract a field from a form fails in WrForm if the form does not contain the named field. To prevent such errors, languages often employ a type system (and/or safety checks). Our Web model shows, however, that straightforward type checking doesn't work, because programs consist of many separate scripts loosely connected via forms and storage. Checking all the scripts together is infeasible. Not only are these scripts

pick-flight ↦ (λ (*empty-form*) (**form** *confirm-flight* (*departure-time* "hh:mm")))

confirm-flight ↦ (λ (*first-form*)
                    (**write** *your-flight* *first-form.departure-time*)
                    (**form** *receipt-flight* (*confirm-time* (**read** *your-flight*))))

receipt-flight ↦ (λ (*confirmed-form*)
                    (*buy-flight* (**read** *your-flight*))
                    (**form** *next-action* (*itinerary* (**read** *your-flight*))))

Fig. 8. Stateful Web Programs

developed and deployed in an incremental manner, they may also reside on different Web servers and/or be written in different programming languages.

We, therefore, provide an incremental type system for Web applications. When the server receives a request for an unknown URL, it installs a program into its table to handle the request. Before installing the new program, the server type checks the program for "internal consistency." In addition, the server also derives constraints that this new program imposes on other Web programs. We refer to this second step as "external consistency" checking. If either step fails, the program is rejected, resulting in an error. In practice, a programmer may register several programs of one application and have them typed checked before they are deployed.

The type system for internal consistency checking heavily borrows from simply-typed λ-calculi with records [5,17,19]. Figure 9 defines the type system. In addition to the usual function type (⟶) and primitive types *Int* and *String*, the type language also includes types for Web forms. Similar to record types, **form** types contain the names and types of the form fields, which—according to their intended usage—must have flat (marshallable) types. We overload the type environment to map both variables and store locations to types. An initial type environment Γ_0 maps locations in the external storage to flat types.[4] Typed WrForm differs from WrForm only by requiring types for function arguments. That is, (λ (*x*) *M*) becomes (λ (*x* : *τ*) *M*) in typed WrForm.

The type system also serves as the basis for external consistency checking. As it traverses the program, it generates constraints on external programs. Each type judgment, as shown in figure 9, includes a set of constraints. A constraint *url* : (**form** $\overrightarrow{(id\ \tau_b)}$) insists that the program associated with *url* consumes Web forms of type (**form** $\overrightarrow{(id\ \tau_b)}$).

Most type rules in figure 9 handle constraints in a straightforward manner. Checking atomic expressions yields the empty set of constraints. Checking most expressions that contain subexpressions simply propagates the constraints from checking the subexpressions. The only expressions that generate constraints are **form** expressions.

The expression (**form** *url* $\overrightarrow{(id\ m)}$) constructs a **form** value, so its type is similar to a record type. This **form** expression also indirectly connects the program associated with *url* to the **form** the consumer will submit later. If the type-checker looked up

---

[4] The environment Γ_0 is fixed when beginning to check an individual program, but programmers may add extra locations for new programs.

Types	Type Judgments
$Type = Type \longrightarrow Type$ $\qquad \mid (\textbf{form } \overrightarrow{(Id\, Type_b)})$ $\qquad \mid Type_b$ $Type_b = String \mid Int$	$\Gamma \vdash M : Type, \Xi$ $where$ $\qquad \Xi = \{url : (\textbf{form } \overrightarrow{(id\, \tau)})\}$

Type Derivation Rules

$$\Gamma \vdash string : String, \{\} \qquad \dfrac{\Gamma \vdash m : (\textbf{form } \overrightarrow{(id_a\, \tau_{ba})}\, (id_x\, \tau_{bx})\, \overrightarrow{(id_b\, \tau_{bb})}), \xi}{\Gamma \vdash m.id_x : \tau_{bx}, \xi}$$

$$\Gamma \vdash n : Int, \{\}$$

$$\dfrac{\Gamma(x) = \tau}{\Gamma \vdash x : \tau, \{\}} \qquad \dfrac{\overrightarrow{\Gamma \vdash m : \tau_b, \xi_m}}{\Gamma \vdash (\textbf{form } url\, \overrightarrow{(id\, m)}) : (\textbf{form } \overrightarrow{(id\, \tau_b)}),}$$
$$\{url : (\textbf{form } \overrightarrow{(id\, \tau_b)})\} \cup \overrightarrow{\xi_m}$$

$$\dfrac{\Gamma, x : \tau_x \vdash m : \tau, \xi}{\Gamma \vdash (\lambda\, (x : \tau_x)\, m) : \tau_x \longrightarrow \tau, \xi}$$

$$\dfrac{\Gamma(l) = \tau_b}{\Gamma \vdash (\textbf{read } l) : \tau_b, \{\}}$$

$$\dfrac{\Gamma \vdash m_0 : \tau_x \longrightarrow \tau, \xi_0 \qquad \Gamma \vdash m_1 : \tau_x, \xi_1}{\Gamma \vdash (m_0\, m_1) : \tau, \xi_0 \cup \xi_1} \qquad \dfrac{\Gamma(l) = \tau_b \qquad \Gamma \vdash m : \tau_b, \xi}{\Gamma \vdash (\textbf{write } l\, m) : \tau_b, \xi}$$

Fig. 9. Internal Types for WrForm

the program associated with *url* immediately and compared the **form** type with the function's argument type, this would suffice. It would not, however, allow for independent development of connected Web programs. Instead, type checking the **form** expression generates the constraint *url* : (**form** $\overrightarrow{(id\, \tau_b)}$), which must be checked later.

Figure 10 extends the definition of the server state S with a set of constraints Ξ. The function *Install-program* adds a new program m to the server's table p at a given *url* if the program is okay. That is, the program must type check and the generated constraints must be consistent with the constraints already on the server. A set of constraints is consistent iff the set is a function from URLs to types.[5] The *Constrain* function ensures that the program m is well typed, and it extends the existing set of constraints ξ_0 to include constraints generated during type checking ξ_1.

With type annotations, type checking, constraint generation, and constraint checking in place, the system provides three levels of guarantees. The first theorem shows that individual Web scripts respond to appropriately typed requests without getting stuck.

Theorem 1. *For all m in M, τ in Type, and set of Constraints ξ, if $\Gamma_0 \vdash m : \tau, \xi$ then for some v in V, $m \longrightarrow_v^* v$.*

The second theorem shows that the server does not apply Web programs to forms of the wrong type, as long as the server starts in a good state. Before we can state the theorem, though, we need to explain what it means for a server state to be well-typed

---

[5] Relaxing this restriction could allow forms to contain extra, unanticipated fields.

Server Extension and Additional Functions

$S = \Sigma \times P \times \Xi$

Install-program : *URL M W* $\longrightarrow$ *W*

Install-program$(url, m, \langle\langle\sigma, p, \xi\rangle, c\rangle) = \langle\langle\sigma, p[url\backslash m], Constrain(\xi, url, m)\rangle, c\rangle$
when *Consistent*$(Constrain(\xi, url, m))$

Consistent : $\Xi \longrightarrow$ *boolean*

Consistent$(\xi) \equiv$
$\quad (url : (\textbf{form } \overrightarrow{(id_0\ \tau_0)})) \in \xi \wedge$
$\quad (url : (\textbf{form } \overrightarrow{(id_1\ \tau_1)})) \in \xi \Longrightarrow$
$\quad \overrightarrow{(id_0\ \tau_0)} = \overrightarrow{(id_1\ \tau_1)}$

Constrain : Ξ *url M* $\longrightarrow \Xi$
Constrain$(\xi_0, url, m) =$
$\quad \xi_0 \cup \xi_1 \cup \{url : (\textbf{form } \overrightarrow{(id_{in}\ \tau_{in})})\}$
$\quad$ *where*
$\quad\quad \Gamma_0 \vdash m : (\textbf{form } \overrightarrow{(id_{in}\ \tau_{in})})$
$\quad\quad\quad \longrightarrow (\textbf{form } \overrightarrow{(id_{out}\ \tau_{out})}), \xi_1$

Fig. 10. Constraint Checking

and for a submitted form to be well-typed. A server is well typed when all the programs
have function types that map forms to forms and when all the constraints are consistent:

server-typechecks$(\langle\sigma, p, \xi\rangle)$ iff *Consistent*(ξ) and for each *url* in *dom*(p),
$\quad \Gamma_0 \vdash p(url) : (\textbf{form } \overrightarrow{(id_1\ \tau_{b1})}) \longrightarrow (\textbf{form } \overrightarrow{(id_2\ \tau_{b2})}), \xi_{url}$ and
$\quad \xi_{url} \in \xi$ and *url* : $(\textbf{form } \overrightarrow{(id\ \tau_{b1})}) \in \xi$

A form is well typed with respect to a server if it refers to a program on the server that
accepts that type of form.

form-typechecks$(\langle\sigma, p, \xi\rangle, (\textbf{form } url\ \overrightarrow{(id\ v_b)}))$ iff
$\quad$ there are types $\overrightarrow{\tau_b}$ such that $\Gamma_0 \vdash v_b : \tau_b, \{\}$ and *url* : $(\textbf{form } \overrightarrow{(id\ \tau_b)})$ is in ξ

Theorem 2. *If server-typechecks(s_0) and form-typechecks(s_0, f_0) then for some*
$\langle s_1, \langle f_1, \overrightarrow{f}\rangle\rangle, \langle s_0, \langle f_0, \overrightarrow{f}\rangle\rangle \hookrightarrow_{submit} \langle s_1, \langle f_1, \overrightarrow{f}\rangle\rangle.$

If the server's set of constraints is closed, the resulting configuration also guarantees
the success of the next submission.

Theorem 3. *If* $\langle\langle\sigma, p, \xi\rangle, \langle f_0, \overrightarrow{f}\rangle\rangle \hookrightarrow_{submit} \langle s_1, \langle f_1, \overrightarrow{f}\rangle\rangle,$
server-typecheck$(\langle\sigma, p, \xi\rangle)$, form-typechecks$(\langle\sigma, p, \xi\rangle, f_0)$,
and for each constraint url : $(\textbf{form } \overrightarrow{(id\ \tau)})$ *in* ξ, *url is in dom(p) then*
server-typecheck(s_1) and form-typechecks(s_1, f_1).

Alternative Web Programming Languages. It is not necessary to instantiate our model
with a functional programming language. Instead, we could have used a language such
as<bigwig>, which is the canonical imperative while-loop language over a basic data
type of Web documents [20]. Furthermore, the<bigwig> language already provides an
internal type system that derives and checks information about Web documents. Its type
system is stronger than ours, allowing programmers to use complex mechanisms for
composing Web documents.

The<bigwig> project and our analysis differ with respect to the ultimate goal. First,
our primary goal is to accommodate the existing Web browser mechanisms. In contrast,
<bigwig>'s runtime system disables the back button. Second, we wish to accommodate

an open world, where scripts in ASP.NET, Perl, or Python can collaborate. Our theorems show how type checks in the language and in the server can accommodate just this kind of openness. The <bigwig> project does not provide a model and therefore does not provide a foundation for investigating Web interactions in general.

Separating constraints on collaborating programs from the type checking of individual programs lends the system flexibility. For WrForm, the set of forms produced could more easily be computed by examining the program's return type. For other languages the local type checking and the constraint generation may be less connected. Extending our constraint checking to dynamically typed languages requires a type inference system capable of determining the types of all possible forms a program might produce.

7   Notifying Outdated Observers

When a script creates a form, it reflects the server's current state. Due to HTTP's shortcomings, a form can lose currency with the server's state. Submitting such a form may, from the consumer's perspective, result in incomprehensible or erroneous behavior.

One way to avoid such errors is to reload pages periodically. Since pages are generated with scripts, reloading implies re-executing scripts. Of course, the re-execution must avoid a duplication of effects on the state of the server, which is precisely what Thiemann's work enables [21]. Unfortunately, this solution doesn't work in general for a number of reasons, some of which were discussed in the section on prior work.[6]

An alternative and general method is to modify the server so that it detects when a submitted form does not reflect the server state. Roughly speaking, this corresponds to the execution of a safety check like the one for array indexing or list destructuring. If the "up-to-date" test fails, the server informs the consumer of the situation, which prevents the erroneous computation from causing further damage. Again, in analogy to safety checks, the server signals an exception and thus informs the consumer at the earliest opportunity that something went wrong. We believe that this approach is general, because it is independent of the scripting language, and that dynamic checking is the appropriate compromise, because these kinds of situations depend on dynamic configurations rather than statically predictable properties.

To check on the datedness of a submitted form, the server must perform some additional bookkeeping. Specifically, determining if something is outdated requires a notion of time, and therefore the server must keep track of time. For us, time is the number of processed submissions. The external storage changes so that it maps locations not only to flat values but also to a timestamp for the last **write**: $\Sigma \sqsubseteq Id \longrightarrow Time \times V_\flat$.

In addition, the server maintains a *carrier* set of all storage locations read or written during the execution of a script. When it sends each page to the consumer, the server adds the current time stamp and this set of locations as an extra hidden field on the page.

With this additional bookkeeping, the server can now check whether each request is up-to-date. When a request arrives, the server extracts both the carrier set and the page

---

[6] A WASH-CGI program with the problem demonstrated in figure 1, built using WASH-CGI-1.0 downloaded on October 8, 2002, compiled without complaint using GHC-5.02.2 and "reserved" the wrong flight when run. Unfortunately, the program is too long to include in (the margin of) this paper.

creation time. If any of the timestamps attached to the locations in the carrier set are out of date, then the submitted form may be inconsistent with the current server storage:

> A *form* with carrier set CS and time stamp T submitted to a server with current state σ is **out of date** if and only if any of the locations in CS have a time stamp in σ that is larger than T.

Clearly, a naïve use of this test produces many false positives. For example, a script may use and modify the server state to compute a page counter, a set of advertisements, or other information irrelevant to the consumer. If a form is out of date only for "irrelevant" storage locations, the consumer should clearly not receive a warning. We therefore allow programs to specify whether reading or writing a location in the server state is a relevant or irrelevant action from the consumer's perspective. Assuming that language implementors make this change, the Web server can reduce the carrier set that it collects during a script execution and the number of warnings it issues.

8   Conclusion

Our paper introduces a formal model of sequential interactive Web programs. We use the model to describe classes of errors that occur when consumers interact with programs using the natural capabilities of Web browsers. The analysis pinpoints two classes of problems with scripting languages and servers.

To remedy the situation, languages used for scripting should come with type checkers that compute the shape of expected forms on the input side and the shape of forms that the scripts may produce. These languages should also allow scripts to specify which actions on the server's state are relevant for the consumer. Furthermore, servers should be modified to integrate the type information from the scripts. In particular, servers should only submit forms to a script if the form is well-typed and up-to-date.

In short, the formal model helps us to understand what the problems are and which components of the Web should change to avoid such interactions. We have implemented a first prototype of our results and hope to report on experiments with the improved server and servlet language in the near future.

References

1. Atkins, D. L., T. Ball, G. Bruns and K. C. Cox. Mawl: A domain-specific language for form-based services. *Software Engineering*, 25(3):334–346, 1999.
2. Brabrand, C., A. Møller, A. Sandholm and M. Schwartzbach. A language for developing interactive Web services, 1999. Unpublished manuscript.
3. Brabrand, C., A. Møller, A. Sandholm and M. I. Schwartzbach. A runtime system for interactive Web services. In *Journal of Computer Networks*, pages 1391–1401, 1999.
4. BrightPlanet. DeepWeb.
   http://www.completeplanet.com/Tutorials/DeepWeb/.
5. Cardelli, L. Type systems. In *Handbook of Computer Science and Engineering*. CRC Press, 1996.
6. Coward, D. Java servlet specification version 2.3, October 2000.
   http://java.sun.com/products/servlet/.

7. Dierks, T. and C. Allen. The transport layer security protocol, January 1999.
    `http://www.ietf.org/rfc/rfc2246.txt`.
8. Felleisen, M. and R. Hieb. The revised report on the syntactic theories of sequential control
    and state. *Theoretical Computer Science*, 102:235–271, 1992. Original version in: Technical
    Report 89-100, Rice University, June 1989.
9. Freier, A. O., P. Karlton and P. C. Kocher. Secure socket layer 3.0, November 1996. IETF
    Draft `http://wp.netscape.com/eng/ssl3/ssl-toc.html`.
10. Gamma, E., R. Helm, R. Johnson and J. Vlissides. *Design Patterns, Elements of Reusable
    Object-Oriented Software*. Addison-Wesley, 1994.
11. Graham, P. Beating the averages. `http://www.paulgraham.com/avg.html`.
12. Graunke, P., R. B. Findler, S. Krishnamurthi and M. Felleisen. Automatically restructuring
    programs for the Web. In *IEEE International Conference on Automated Software Engineering*,
    pages 211–222, 2001.
13. Graunke, P., S. Krishnamurthi, S. van der Hoeven and M. Felleisen. Programming the Web
    with high-level programming languages. In *European Symposium on Programming*, pages
    122–136, 2001.
14. Hughes, J. Generalising monads to arrows. *Science of Computer Programming*, 37(1–3):67–
    111, May 2000.
15. Microsoft Corporation. `http://www.microsoft.com/net/`.
16. NCSA. The Common Gateway Interface. `http://hoohoo.ncsa.uiuc.edu/cgi/`.
17. Pierce, B. C. *Types and Programming Languages*. MIT Press, 2002.
18. Queinnec, C. The influence of browsers on evaluators or, continuations to program Web
    servers. In *ACM SIGPLAN International Conference on Functional Programming*, pages
    23–33, 2000.
19. Rémy, D. Typechecking records and variants in a natural extension of ML. In *ACM Symposium
    on Principles of Programming Languages*, pages 77–88, 1989.
20. Sandholm, A. and M. I. Schwartzbach. A type system for dynamic Web documents. In
    Symposium on Principles of Programming Languages, pages 290–301, 2000.
21. Thiemann, P. WASH/CGI: Server-side Web scripting with sessions and typed, compositional
    forms. In *Practical Applications of Declarative Languages*, pages 192–208, 2002.

Type Inference for a Distributed π-Calculus*

Cédric Lhoussaine

University of Sussex, Brighton, UK
clh23@cogs.susx.ac.uk

Abstract. We study the type inference problem for a distributed π-calculus with explicit notions of *locality* and *migration*. Location types involve names that may be bound in terms. This requires some accurate new treatments. We define a notion of *principal typing*. We provide a formal description of sound and complete type inference algorithm.

1 Introduction

In wide area distributed systems, such as the Internet, sensitive administrative domains have to be protected against malicious agents, and tools are required for the analysis of security properties. In this paper we focus on this topic using Hennessy and Riely's distributed π-calculus Dπ [6]. It is based on the polyadic asynchronous π-calculus, involving explicit and simple notions of *locality* and *migration*. The distribution is one dimensional: in contrast with Djoin [5] or Mobile Ambients [4], locations do not contain sub-locations (as in π_ℓ [1]). As in Mobile Ambients, communication is purely local: only co-located processes can communicate. Mobility is *weak* in the sense that we migrate code instead of computations (as it is the case in Mobile Ambients and Djoin). Thus, this calculus provides a simple but powerful framework to model fundamental features of distributed computations.

In [6] a type system is proposed for Dπ. It does not only deal with arity mismatch of communications as sorts do for the polyadic π-calculus. It also investigates an important issue of distributed systems: the *controlled access to system resources*. There, a resource is represented by a communication channel bound to a particular location. Hence, a *location type* is the set of channels available to a process at a location. It is of the form:

$$\{a_1 : \gamma_1, \ldots, a_n : \gamma_n\}$$

where each a_i is a channel name and γ_i a *channel type*. Locations can be sent through channels that have a type $Ch(\psi)$ where ψ is a location type. For instance, a process knowing of a location ℓ with type $\{a : \gamma, b : \gamma'\}$ has permission to use channels a and b at ℓ and only these. In [2], this type system is required to guarantee the *message deliverability* property.

---

* Research supported by "MyThs: Models and Types for Security in Mobile Distributed Systems", EU FET-GC IST-2001-32617.

Even though it checks crucial properties, this type system assumes that all agents are well-typed. However, in networks such as the Internet, only few locations may be statically typed, and a dynamic type checking is necessary for agents coming from untyped or unknown locations. A fundamental question arises: does a type checking algorithm exist ?

We design a type inference algorithm *à la* ML for Dπ with undecorated terms (à la Curry). Usually, such an algorithm proceeds in two steps:

- given a term S and its *initial typing context* Γ (associating a type variable to each location name of S), generate type constraints involving type variables;
- produce a substitution μ of type variables for types solving the constraints.

If the algorithm succeeds, then the application of the substitution to the initial context $\mu\Gamma$ is a valid typing context for S. Otherwise, S is not typable. Despite this simple scheme, we have to face two major difficulties described below together with the solutions worked out in this paper.

Principal typing. Basically, a principal typing is a typing context which represents all possible types by ground instantiation of type variables. Unfortunately, this definition is not suitable here because our type system involves *subtyping* on location types.

Indeed, consider the term $\bar{a}\ell \mid a(k).P$ that sends the location name ℓ over the channel a and binds k to ℓ in P, and suppose that a has type $Ch(\{b\colon \gamma, c\colon \gamma'\})$. Then P is allowed to use *at most* b and c at the received location, that is k has a type $\psi \subseteq \{b\colon \gamma, c\colon \gamma'\}$. And, all location names sent through a, must have a type that declares *at least* b and c, that is ℓ has a type $\psi' \supseteq \{b\colon \gamma, c\colon \gamma'\}$. We see that the types of ℓ and k are related to the one of a, and all valid typings for that term have to satisfy this relation.

Therefore, we define a principal typing for a term S as a pair $(\Gamma; \mathcal{A})$ where Γ is a typing context involving type variables and $\mathcal{A}$ is a set of subtyping constraints. And an instance $\mu\Gamma$ is a valid typing for S if and only if μ satisfies $\mathcal{A}$. Thus, our algorithm generates not only equations of types but also inequations.

Dependant types. The second and most important difficulty comes from the fact that location types are so-called *dependant* types: they involve names that may be bound in terms. For instance, consider the term $Q = a(b).(\nu\ell)\,P$ that receives a name b, creates a location ℓ, and triggers P. Here b is bound to $(\nu\ell)\,P$, and ℓ may be given a type $\{b\colon \gamma\}$. If we create the location ℓ before the reception as in $R = (\nu\ell)\,a(b).P$, then ℓ cannot have a type where b occurs. Otherwise typing would not be preserved by α-equivalence of terms. However, the type inference algorithm cannot find a type for ℓ before the exploration of P where there is not anymore difference between the creation of ℓ before the reception of b and the reverse. Thus, a naive algorithm may assign types to untypable terms!

Our solution introduces a novel notion of *binding relation* that, intuitively, keeps track of the order in which channels are bound. It relates channel names and type variables such that if (a, α), is in the relation, then it is forbidden to substitute type variable α by a type in which name a occurs. In the first step

$$u, v \ldots ::= a \mid \ell \mid a@\ell \qquad\qquad\qquad\qquad\qquad values$$

$$P, Q, R \ldots ::= \mathbf{0} \mid \bar{a}u \mid a(u).P \mid (P \mid Q) \mid (\nu u)\, P \mid \mathrm{go}\,\ell.P \mid {!P} \qquad processes$$

$$S, T, \ldots ::= \mathbf{0} \mid \ell\llbracket P \rrbracket \mid (S \mid T) \mid (\nu a@\ell)\, S \mid (\nu\ell)\, S \qquad networks$$

Fig. 1. Syntax of terms

of the algorithm, this relation is updated each time a bound channel is met. For instance, consider R above, and suppose that ℓ is given a type variable α. When the algorithm treats the reception, it updates the binding relation by associating b to each current type variable. In particular, the pair (b, α) is added to the binding relation, thus preventing ℓ to be assigned a type where b occurs. In Q, ℓ is given a fresh type variable α when the creation is met, i.e. after the reception of b. Hence, α is not associated to b and may be substituted by $\{b : \gamma\}$.

We give a sound and complete type inference algorithm that produces a principal typing. We express our algorithm in the form of a rewriting system, which allows for neat formal proofs that can be found in [8].

Related works. Our calculus is actually a variant of the one in [6]: the latter uses a synchronous communication and an explicit typing (terms involve types). However, we could easily treat synchronous and decorated terms. For instance, consider the term $Q = (\nu a : \tau)\, P$. Applied to $(\nu a)\, P$, either our algorithm fails and Q is not typable. Or it succeeds and produces a type σ for a. And Q is typable if and only if τ is an instance of σ. Our location types are very similar to record types of [13,10,11,7]. However, using techniques developed in these papers, the use of a binding relation requires some accurate new treatments. To our knowledge, the type inference algorithm presented in this paper is the first one dealing with these kind of dependant types.

2   A Calculus with Localities

In this section we introduce our distributed calculus, we give the operational semantics and the syntax of types. For the sake of simplicity, this calculus is presented in its monadic version. Apart from that, it is the usual asynchronous π-calculus with some primitives for spatial distribution and migration of processes organised as a two-levels model: the processes (or thread) one and the network (or configuration) one. As in [6] communication is local, that is we cannot directly send a message from a location ℓ to a remote process at location k: we must migrate the message to k, and then we can communicate.

In order to state the syntax, we consider a denumerable set $\mathcal{N}$ of (*simple*) *names* which is assumed to be partitioned into two sets: the channel names $\mathcal{N}_{chan} = \{a, b, \ldots\}$ and the location names $\mathcal{N}_{loc} = \{\ell, k, \ldots\}$. The objects of communications may be *compound* that is a channel name a together with a location name ℓ denoted by $a@\ell$ and meaning "the channel a (to be) used at location ℓ". We can also abstract and restrict location names. The grammar of terms is given in figure 1. We denote by $U, V \dots$ a process or a network, $fn(U)$ (resp. $bn(U), nm(U)$) the set free (resp. bound, all) names occurring in U.

Before describing types, we briefly present the operational semantics in the "chemical style" of BERRY and BOUDOL [3]. To this aim, we define the *structural equivalence* as the least equivalence satisfying the commutative monoid laws for parallel composition, containing the α-equivalence and satisfying the following:

$$((\nu u)\, U \mid V) \equiv (\nu u)\, (U \mid V) \quad \text{if } subj(u) \notin fn(V)$$

$$\ell[\![(\nu u)\, P]\!] \equiv (\nu u @ \ell)\, \ell[\![P]\!] \quad \text{if } subj(u) \neq \ell$$

$$!P \equiv (P \mid !P) \qquad \ell[\![P \mid Q]\!] \equiv \ell[\![P]\!] \mid \ell[\![Q]\!] \qquad U \equiv V \Rightarrow \mathbf{E}[U] \equiv \mathbf{E}[V]$$

where

$$u@\ell = \begin{cases} a@\ell & \text{if } u = a \\ u & \text{otherwise} \end{cases} \qquad subj(u) = \begin{cases} a & \text{if } u = a \text{ or } u = a@\ell \\ \ell & \text{if } u = \ell \end{cases}$$

and $\mathbf{E}$ is any *evaluation context*, defined by: $\mathbf{E} ::= \bullet \mid (\mathbf{E} \mid U) \mid (\nu u)\, \mathbf{E} \mid \ell[\![\mathbf{E}]\!]$

As usual, in an evaluation context $\bullet$ stands for a "hole" and $\mathbf{E}[U]$ denotes the substitution of the hole for the term U in $\mathbf{E}$ providing that the resulting term is valid. The reduction is built upon two laws, that is the standard communication one plus a *law of movement* for migration:

$$(\bar{a}v \mid a(u).P) \rightarrow [v/u]P \qquad \ell[\![\text{go}\, k.P]\!] \rightarrow k[\![P]\!]$$

up to structural equivalence and under evaluation context.

3   The Type System

Let $\mathcal{V} = \{\alpha, \beta, \dots\}$ be a denumerable set of type variables partitioned into three sets: the set of *general type variables* $(t, t', \dots)$, the set of *channel type variables* $(h, h', \dots)$, and the set of location type variables (or *row variables*) ranged over by $\rho_L, \rho'_L, \dots$ where $L \in \mathcal{P}_{fin}(\mathcal{N}_{chan})$. Types are based on the following grammar:

$$\begin{array}{lll} \tau, \sigma, \dots ::= \psi \mid \gamma \mid \gamma @ \psi \mid t & & \textit{types} \\ \gamma, \delta, \dots ::= Ch(\tau) \mid h & & \textit{channel types} \\ \psi, \phi, \dots ::= \{a : \gamma, \psi\} \mid \{\} \mid \rho_L & & \textit{location types} \end{array}$$

We denote by $var(\tau)$ the set of the type variables occurring in τ. We denote by $\tau, \gamma, \psi, \dots$ the ground types that is the types τ such that $var(\tau) = \emptyset$. We will often note $\{a_1 : \gamma_1, \dots, a_n : \gamma_n, \psi\}$ for $\{a_1 : \gamma_1, \{\dots, \{a_n : \gamma_n, \psi\}\}\dots\}$. Typing a location name means: "recording the names and types of channels on which a communication is possible inside the location". That is, a location type is a record of channel names together with their types: this a *dependant type* since it contains terms, viz. channel names. Extension of location type is achieved by means of a row variable that may be substituted with a location type. A location type that ends with a row variable is called an *extensible location type*. In the latter, the row variable is obtained by means of the partial function ρvar (e.g. $\rho var(\{a : \gamma, \rho_L\}) = \rho_L$). We also denote the set of names typed in a

$$\frac{}{k:\psi \vdash_\ell k:\psi} \qquad \frac{}{\ell:\{a:\gamma\} \vdash_\ell a:\gamma} \qquad \frac{}{\ell:\{a:\gamma,\psi\} \vdash_k a@\ell:\gamma@\psi} \qquad \frac{\Gamma \vdash_\ell u:\tau}{\Gamma,\Delta \vdash_\ell^W u:\tau}$$

Fig. 2. Type system for names

$$\frac{\Gamma,\Delta \vdash_\ell P \quad , \quad \Delta \vdash_\ell u:\tau}{\ell:\{a:Ch(\tau)\},\Gamma \vdash_\ell a(u).P} \qquad \frac{\ell:\{a:\gamma\},\Gamma \vdash_\ell P}{\Gamma \vdash_\ell (\nu a)P} \qquad \frac{k:\{a:\gamma\},\Gamma \vdash_\ell P}{\Gamma \vdash_\ell (\nu a@k)P} \qquad \frac{k:\psi,\Gamma \vdash_\ell P}{\Gamma \vdash_\ell (\nu k)P}$$

$$\frac{\Gamma \vdash_\ell^W u:\tau}{\ell:\{a:Ch(\tau)\},\Gamma \vdash_\ell \bar{a}u} \qquad \frac{\Gamma \vdash_\ell P \quad , \quad \Gamma \vdash_\ell Q}{\Gamma \vdash_\ell P \mid Q} \qquad \frac{\Gamma \vdash_k P}{\Gamma \vdash_\ell \mathsf{go}\,k.P} \qquad \frac{\Gamma \vdash_\ell P}{\Gamma \vdash_\ell !P} \qquad \frac{}{\Gamma \vdash_\ell \mathbf{0}}$$

Fig. 3. Type system for processes

$$\frac{}{\Gamma \vdash \mathbf{0}} \qquad \frac{\Gamma \vdash_\ell P}{\Gamma \vdash \ell[\![P]\!]} \qquad \frac{\Gamma \vdash S \quad , \quad \Gamma \vdash T}{\Gamma \vdash S \mid T} \qquad \frac{\ell:\{a:\gamma\},\Gamma \vdash S}{\Gamma \vdash (\nu a@\ell)\,S} \qquad \frac{\ell:\psi,\Gamma \vdash S}{\Gamma \vdash (\nu\ell)\,S}$$

Fig. 4. Type system for networks

location type ψ by $dom(\psi)$ (e.g. $dom(\{a:\gamma,b:\delta,\psi\}) = \{a,b\}$). As for record types in $\{a_1 : \gamma_1,\ldots,a_n : \gamma_n,\rho_L\}$ the names $a_1,\ldots,a_n$ have to be distinct, an assumption we will take throughout the paper. In order to preserve this property by instantiation, the row variable of a type ψ is equipped with a subscript, that is a set of names which is meant to contain at least $dom(\psi)$. Intuitively, the subscript L of a row variable ρ_L allows one to substitute it for a location type defining channels that do not occur in L, thus avoiding duplicated assignments. However, in the section 4 we show that with dependant types this is not sufficient.

The type of a compound name $a@\ell$ is a "located channel type" $\gamma@\psi$ meaning: "a has the type γ at a remote location with a type *at least* ψ". These types are *existential* because $\gamma@\psi$ should be read as $\exists a.\{a:\gamma,\psi\}$. We assume that in $a(u).P$ we have $u \neq a$, and in $\{a_1 : \gamma_1,\ldots,a_n : \gamma_n,\rho_L\}$ we have $\rho_L \notin var(\gamma_1,\ldots,\gamma_n)$.

The type system is given in figures 2 to 4. We give a formal definition of well-formed types in the next section. The type system deals with sequents of the form $\Gamma \vdash_\ell P$, for checking that the process P, placed at the current location ℓ, conforms to the typing assumption Γ, and similarly $\Gamma \vdash S$ for systems. We have two kinds of sequents for names: $\Gamma \vdash_\ell^W u:\tau$ to type names *with weakening* of hypotheses and sequents $\Gamma \vdash_\ell u:\tau$ *without weakening*. The latter are used to type formal parameters in input.

A typing context Γ is a mapping from a finite subset $dom(\Gamma)$ of $\mathcal{N}_{loc}$ into the set of ground location types. We use of a partial operation of union Δ,Γ of typing contexts, defined as follows:

$$(\Delta, \Gamma)(x) = \begin{cases} \Delta(\ell) & \text{if } \ell \in dom(\Delta) - dom(\Gamma) \\ \phi \sqcap \psi & \text{if } \Delta(\ell) = \phi \ \& \ \Gamma(\ell) = \psi \\ \Gamma(\ell) & \text{if } \ell \in dom(\Gamma) - dom(\Delta) \end{cases}$$

where $\psi \sqcap \phi$ denotes the union of ψ and ϕ, which is only defined if ψ and ϕ assign the same types to the names they share. As usual, we assume that bound names are renamed such that no collision with other bound or free names arises.

We comment the rules and note some elementary properties. In the rules for names without weakening the conclusion determines the context. Namely, if $\Gamma \vdash_\ell u : \tau$ and $\Delta \vdash_\ell u : \tau$ then $\Gamma = \Delta$. The rule for output involves a form of subtyping for localities: for instance, the judgement

$$\ell : \{b : \gamma, c : \delta\}, \ k : \{a : Ch(\{b : \gamma\})\} \vdash_k \bar{a}\ell$$

is valid, even though the type of ℓ given by the context is more generous than the one carried by the channel a. As usual, to type the body of an input the context is enriched with the information necessary for the typing the formal parameters. There are three cases for typing a name generation $(\nu u) P$ and the rules follow the same pattern as these for typing names. To type a migrating process $go\,\ell.P$, one must type P at locality ℓ, while the resulting current locality is immaterial.

The main result concerning this type system is the subject reduction property: if $\Gamma \vdash S$ and $S \to T$, then $\Gamma \vdash T$. The proof can be found in [8].

4   Managing the Dependant Types

In this section, we define and motivate the notions of *principal typing* and *binding relations*. Our type inference algorithm consists, as usual, of two steps:

1. from a term and an initial typing context, generate type schemes constraints,
2. then we search the most general solution to the constraints such that its application to the initial typing context provides a principal typing. This is so-called *constraint unification*.

Let us begin with substitutions. A substitution $(\mu, \lambda, \ldots)$ is a finite mapping from type variables to types. For $\mu = [\tau_1/\alpha_1, \ldots, \tau_n/\alpha_n]$ we denote by $dom(\mu)$ the set $\{\alpha_1, \ldots, \alpha_n\}$ and by $vrang(\mu)$ the set $\bigcup_{i \in \{1 \ldots n\}} var(\tau_i)$. We consider idempotent substitutions, in particular we have $dom(\mu) \cap vrang(\mu) = \emptyset$. Outside its domain a substitution is intended to be the identity. They are trivially extended to homomorphisms on types and other objects (as contexts, subtyping assertions, etc.). We note $\lambda\mu$ the composition of λ and μ, and $\emptyset$ the empty substitution.

Principal Typing. Usually, by principal typing for a term U, we mean a context involving type schemes (denoted by $\Gamma, \Delta, \ldots$ and called *context schemes*) and whose all ground instantiations are valid typing contexts for U. However, this definition is too permissive because such a principal typing could involve invalid instantiations as the following example emphasises.

Example 4.1. Consider $S = \ell[\![\overline{a}\ell \mid \overline{b}c]\!]$ where c has some type γ. Then ℓ has type

$$\{a: Ch(\psi), b: Ch(\gamma), c: \gamma\}$$

where ψ can be either $\{b: Ch(\gamma), c: \gamma\}$, $\{b: Ch(\gamma)\}$, $\{c: \gamma\}$ or $\{\}$. One might expect the context scheme $\mathbf{\Gamma} = \ell: \{a: Ch(\rho'_\emptyset), b: Ch(\gamma), c: \gamma, \rho_{\{a,b,c\}}\}$ to be a most general typing for ℓ. Obviously this is not case since, for instance, the application of the substitution $[\{b: Ch(Ch(\gamma))\}/\rho'_\emptyset]$ does not give a valid type for ℓ. This happens because b is used as a channel of type $Ch(Ch(\gamma))$ whereas a actually sends ℓ where b has the type $Ch(\gamma)$. □

We introduce a relation $\psi <: \phi$ on location types (similar to the one of [6]) that can be understood as $\phi \subseteq \psi$, seeing location types as sets. More formally,

Definition 4.1. *We define the relation* $<:$ *on location types as follows:*

$$\psi <: \{\} \qquad \psi <: \rho_L \qquad \psi <: \phi \Rightarrow \{a: \tau, \psi\} <: \{a: \tau, \phi\}$$

This relation defines subtyping *assertions. The subtyping assertions of the form* $\psi <: \rho_L$ *are called* atomic. *Moreover, we write* $\psi \equiv \phi$ *if* $\psi <: \phi$ *and* $\phi <: \psi$. [1]

We can observe subtyping in receptions and emissions of location names. For instance, if P in $a(\ell).P$ uses channels $a_1, \ldots, a_n$ at location ℓ then a must have a type $Ch(\psi)$ where ψ assigns *at least* a type to each a_i. Therefore, in P, ℓ has a type ϕ such that $\psi <: \phi$. Symmetrically, when emitting k on a, k must have a type ϕ' that assigns to each a_i the same type as ψ does; that is $\phi' <: \psi$.

Example 4.2. Let us consider the term $S = \ell[\![\overline{a}k \mid a(\ell').\text{go } \ell'.\overline{b}d]\!] \mid k[\![\overline{c}d]\!]$ where d has some type γ. After the input of k on a, S migrates to k a message on b. Then any location transmitted on a has to define at least a channel b with type $Ch(\gamma)$. Then, S can be associated with the following context scheme:

$$\ell: \{a: Ch(\{b: Ch(\gamma), \rho_{\{b\}}\}), \rho'_{\{a\}}\}, k: \{b: Ch(\gamma), c: Ch(\gamma), \rho''_{\{b,c\}}\}$$

a may also have the type $Ch(\{b: Ch(\gamma), c: Ch(\gamma)\})$ that can be obtained by the ground substitution $[\{c: Ch(\gamma)\}/\rho_{\{b\}}]$. Not all substitutions of $\rho_{\{b\}}$ give valid typings for a (as for instance $[\{c: Ch(Ch(\gamma))\}/\rho_{\{b\}}]$). However, whether or not a substitution gives valid types for S is easily decidable: any substitution μ that preserves the atomic subtyping assertion $\{c: Ch(\gamma), \rho''_{\{b,c\}}\} <: \rho_{\{b\}}$ (that is such that $\mu\{c: Ch(\gamma), \rho''_{\{b,c\}}\} <: \mu\rho_{\{b\}}$ is still valid), preserves the typing of S. This leads to the following definition of principle typing. □

Definition 4.2. *Let* $\mathcal{A}$ *be a set of atomic subtyping assertions, we say that* $\mathbf{\Gamma}; \mathcal{A}$ *is a* principal typing *for S if 1) for all ground substitution λ that preserves $\mathcal{A}$, we have $\lambda\mathbf{\Gamma} \vdash S$, 2) for all Δ such that $\Delta \vdash S$, there exists a ground substitution λ that preserves $\mathcal{A}$ such that $\Delta =_{dom(\mathbf{\Gamma})} \lambda\mathbf{\Gamma}$ and $\lambda\mathbf{\Gamma} \vdash S$.*

Binding relations. In order to keep the names of a location type distinct, as in [11], a row variable of a type ψ is equipped with a subscript. It is a set of names which is meant to contain at least $dom(\psi)$. In this case ψ is said *well-formed*. Substitutions have to satisfy the following requirements: (i) if $\mu\rho_L = \psi$, then

---

[1] We assume that this should not be confused with structural equivalence. Intuitively, $\psi \equiv \phi$ means that ψ and ϕ are identical modulo their row variables.

$dom(\psi) \cap L = \emptyset$, (ii) and if $\rho var(\psi) = \rho'_L$, then $L \subseteq L'$. Condition (i) forbids the substitution of a row variable with a type that contains a label belonging to the subscript. However, in presence of dependant types, those subscripts are not anymore sufficient. Indeed, the names occuring in location types belongs to the same syntactic category of the names that may be bound in the terms. Moreover, the latter are not supposed to occur in the principal typing produced for it. However, the algorithm "deconstructs" the term, and names that were initially bound appear later free. For instance, associating the context scheme $\ell : \rho_\emptyset, k : \rho'_\emptyset$ to the network $S = \ell[\![a(b).go\, k.\overline{b}c]\!]$, after two deconstructions the term $go\, k.\overline{b}c$ appears in which b is free and supposed by known at k. So, we may substitute $\rho'_\emptyset$ with a location type that assigns a type to b. However, S is not typable since it tries to use the name b local to ℓ at a remote location k. To amend this, we could declare that if the generated substitution has bound names in its range, then it is not a valid one, and conclude that the term is not typable. However, this would be too strong. Indeed, consider the term

$$T = \ell[\![d(b).(\nu a)\, Q]\!] \quad \text{where} \quad Q = (\overline{a}\ell \mid a(k).go\, k.\overline{b}c)$$

that waits at location ℓ for a channel b, then it creates a channel a carrying the location ℓ. Since b and c are used by a process spawned at a location received along a, a must have *at least* the type $Ch(\{b: Ch(\gamma), c: \gamma\})$. A bound name ($b$) appears in the type of a. However, this is not at variance with the fact that bound names do not appear in the typing context of a term because T is actually typable with the context $\ell : \{d: Ch(Ch(\gamma))\}$ in which the type of a does not appear. But in the type inference we have to compute all the types and produce a substitution that may contains bound names in its range. Therefore, we generalise the notion of subscripts of row variables to all type variables in a stronger form. Intuitively, we associate to each variable α, a set L representing the names not compatibles with α. That is, substitution are not allowed to map α into a type containing elements from L. Contrary to the row variables, those generalised subscripts have to be dynamically updated along the type inference. We formalised this notion by means of finite relations of $\mathcal{N}_{chan} \times \mathcal{V}$.

Definition 4.3. *A* binding relation *$\mathcal{B}$ is a finite subset of $\mathcal{N}_{chan} \times \mathcal{V}$. We note $\mathcal{B}(\alpha)$ the set $\{a \mid (a, \alpha) \in \mathcal{B}\}$ and $im(\mathcal{B})$ the set $\{a \mid \exists \alpha.(a, \alpha) \in \mathcal{B}\}$.*

Binding relations appears as subscripts of row variables: $\{a: \gamma, b: \delta, \rho_{\{b\}}\}$ can be considered well-formed with respect to the binding relation $\mathcal{B} = \{(a, \rho_{\{b\}})\}$. Indeed, a substitution that respects $\mathcal{B}$ never substitutes $\rho_{\{b\}}$ by a type containing a and therefore never duplicates its typing. However, we must keep the subscripts of the row variables because the binding relations are stronger constraints. For instance, we want to be able to extend $\{b: \gamma, \alpha\}$ with $\{a: Ch(\{b: \gamma\})\}$. This would be allowed by subscripts (that is if $\alpha = \rho_{\{b\}}$), but not by binding relations (that is if $\alpha = \rho_\emptyset$ and $\mathcal{B}(\rho_\emptyset) = \{b\}$) because subscripts are only concerned with the domains of location types, while binding relations are concerned with the types (in this sense binding relations are stronger). The consequence is that the well-formedness of types depends on binding relations. We say that ψ is well-formed with respect to $\mathcal{B}$ if the names of $dom(\psi)$ are all distinct, and, if ψ is

$$\frac{}{t :: \mathcal{B}} \qquad \frac{}{h :: \mathcal{B}} \qquad \frac{\tau :: \mathcal{B}}{Ch(\tau) :: \mathcal{B}} \qquad \frac{\gamma :: \mathcal{B} \quad , \quad \psi :: (L, \mathcal{B})}{\gamma @ \psi :: \mathcal{B}}$$

$$\frac{\psi :: (L, \mathcal{B})}{\psi :: \mathcal{B}} \qquad \frac{}{\{\} :: (L, \mathcal{B})} \qquad \frac{\gamma :: \mathcal{B} \quad , \quad \psi :: (L \uplus \{a\}, \mathcal{B})}{\{a : \gamma, \psi\} :: (L, \mathcal{B})} \qquad \frac{L' = L \cup \mathcal{B}(\rho_L)}{\rho_L :: (L', \mathcal{B})}$$

Fig. 5. Well-formedness of types with respect to a binding relation

extensible with row variable ρ_L, then $dom(\psi) \subseteq L \cup \mathcal{B}(\rho_L)$. More formally, a type τ is well-formed with respect to $\mathcal{B}$ if there exists a proof of the judgement $\tau :: \mathcal{B}$ in the inference system given in figure 5 where L is finite set of names.

Definition 4.4. *We say that a substitution μ respects a binding relation $\mathcal{B}$ if*

1. $\forall \alpha \in dom(\mu), nm(\mu\alpha) \cap \mathcal{B}(\alpha) = \emptyset$ and $\mu\alpha :: \mathcal{B}$,
2. $\forall \rho_L \in dom(\mu), dom(\mu\rho_L) \cap L = \emptyset$, and if $\rho var(\mu\rho_L) = \rho'_{L'}$, then $\mathcal{B}(\rho_L) \subseteq \mathcal{B}(\rho'_{L'})$ and $L \subseteq L' \cup \mathcal{B}(\rho'_{L'})$.

The first point of this definition simply says that μ assigns types to variables according to what the binding relation allows, and that those types are still well-formed. The second point is a generalisation of the requirements (i) and (ii) given above to guarantee that substitution preserves the well-formedness.

Lemma 4.1. *1. if $\tau :: \mathcal{B}$ and μ respects $\mathcal{B}$, then $\mu\tau :: \mathcal{B}$,*
 2. if $\mathcal{B} \subseteq \mathcal{B}'$ and $\tau :: \mathcal{B}$ then $\tau :: \mathcal{B}'$.

Unfortunately, the composition of two substitutions that respect $\mathcal{B}$ does not necessarily respect $\mathcal{B}$. For instance, $\mu = [\rho_\emptyset / t]$ and $\lambda = [\{a : \gamma, \rho'_{\{a\}}\} / \rho_\emptyset]$ respect $\mathcal{B} = \{(a, t)\}$. However, the composition $\lambda\mu = [\{a : \gamma, \rho'_{\{a\}}\} / \rho_\emptyset, \{a : \gamma, \rho'_{\{a\}}\} / t]$ does not respect $\mathcal{B}$, because $a \in nm(\lambda\mu t)$ whereas $a \in \mathcal{B}(t)$.

Definition 4.5. *$\mathcal{B}$ is μ-closed if $\forall \alpha \in dom(\mu), \forall \beta \in dom(\mu\alpha).\mathcal{B}(\alpha) \subseteq \mathcal{B}(\beta)$.*

Lemma 4.2. *Let μ be a substitution that respects $\mathcal{B}$ and $\mathcal{B}$ be μ-closed, then for all substitution λ that respects $\mathcal{B}$, $\lambda\mu$ respects $\mathcal{B}$.*

It is easy, from a binding relation to construct an another one that is μ-closed.

Definition 4.6. *We define the μ-closure of $\mathcal{B}$ as the following binding relation:*

$$\mathcal{B} \cup \bigcup_{\alpha \in dom(\mu)} \bigcup_{\beta \in var(\mu\alpha)} \mathcal{B}(\alpha) \times \{\beta\}$$

The reader can easily check that if μ respects $\mathcal{B}$, then μ still respects its μ-closure.

5 Solving Type Constraints

In this section we give an algorithm solving type constraints in terms of a rewriting system. The usual unification problem is: given equations between types, does there exist a substitution for type variables that equates types ? As for unification of record types, all type equality is supposed to be modulo the equation E:

$$\{a: h, \{b: h', \rho_L\}\} =_E \{b: h', \{a: h, \rho_L\}\}$$

That is, the ordering of the fields of location types doesn't matter. For instance, $\{a: \gamma, b: \gamma', \rho_{\{a,b\}}\}$ and $\{b: \gamma', a: \gamma, \rho_{\{a,b\}}\}$ define the same location type.

Definition 5.1. *A* typing constraint *is a set $\mathcal{E}$ of equations between type schemes $\{\tau_1 \doteq \sigma_1, \ldots, \tau_n \doteq \sigma_n\}$. A* subtyping constraint *is a set $\mathcal{I}$ of inequations between location types $\{\psi_1 < \phi_1, \ldots, \psi_n < \phi_n\}$. We say that μ is a* solution *of $\mathcal{E}$ (resp. $\mathcal{I}$) if $\mu\tau_i = \mu\sigma_i$ (resp. $\mu\psi_i <: \mu\phi_i$) for all $1 \le i \le n$. We note $\mathcal{E} :: \mathcal{B}$ if $\tau_i :: \mathcal{B}$ and $\sigma_i :: \mathcal{B}$ for all $1 \le i \le n$ and similarly for $\mathcal{I} :: \mathcal{B}$. We write $\psi \doteq \phi$ for $\psi < \phi \wedge \phi < \psi$.*

We write $\mu =_{\mathcal{X}} \lambda$ where $\mathcal{X}$ is a set of type variables if $\mu\alpha = \lambda\alpha$ for all $\alpha \in \mathcal{X}$.

Definition 5.2. *μ is* more general on *$\mathcal{X}$ than λ if and only if there exists a substitution μ' such that $\lambda =_{\mathcal{X}} \mu'\mu$. In this case we write $\mu \le_{\mathcal{X}} \lambda$.*

Definition 5.3. *A* constraint *is a tuple $(\mathcal{E}, \mathcal{I})_{\mathcal{B}}$ such that $\mathcal{E} :: \mathcal{B}$ and $\mathcal{I} :: \mathcal{B}$. A substitution μ is a* principal solution *of $(\mathcal{E}, \mathcal{I})_{\mathcal{B}}$ on $\mathcal{X}$, if for all ground solution λ of $\mathcal{E}$ and $\mathcal{I}$ that respects $\mathcal{B}$, we have $\mu \le_{\mathcal{X}} \lambda$.*

In figure 6 we define a reduction relation $\rightsquigarrow$ on tuples $(\mathcal{E}, \mathcal{I}, \mu)_{\mathcal{B}}^{\mathcal{X}}$. We make use of the abbreviation $\psi \triangleleft \rho_L$ for $[\rho_L/\rho\text{var}(\psi)]\psi$. The idea is that starting from $(\mathcal{E}, \mathcal{I}, \emptyset)_{\mathcal{B}}^{\mathcal{X}}$ – that is a constraint $(\mathcal{E}, \mathcal{I})_{\mathcal{B}}$, a set of type variables $\mathcal{X}$ containing those occuring in $\mathcal{E}$ and $\mathcal{I}$ and the empty substitution – we apply the reduction relation until we reach either a configuration $(\emptyset, \mathcal{A}, \mu)_{\mathcal{B}}^{\mathcal{Y}}$ where μ is a principal solution of $(\mathcal{E}, \mathcal{I})_{\mathcal{B}}$ on $\mathcal{X}$, or the failure configuration $\bot$ if $\mathcal{E}$ and $\mathcal{I}$ have no common solution. This relation almost consists of the decompositions of pairs of types until one of these is a type variable. Then (rule $(elim)$), the current substitution μ is composed with the substitution of the type variable for the other type (the latter being also applied to the remaining constraint) provided that it respects the current binding relation. The condition $\alpha \notin \text{var}(\tau)$ ensures that there is no remaining occurrence of the eliminated variable in the resulting constraint, thus avoiding infinite reductions. If this condition fails, the occurs check rule (oc) leads to the failure configuration. The rule $(triv)$ removes trivial equations. The rules $(chan)$ and (at) simply decompose types. Rule (loc_2) unifies location types with disjoint domains: it extends each location by means of an appropriate substitution of their row variables.

Rules (st_1) and (st_2) are used to solve subtyping inequations. The first one asserts that $\{a: \gamma, \psi\} < \{a: \delta, \phi\}$ has a solution if we can unify γ with δ and if $\psi < \phi$ has a solution. Rule (st_2) applies on $\psi < \phi$ when the channels defined in ϕ are not in ψ. We then extend ψ with the channels typed in ϕ with respect to the current binding relation.

Definition 5.4. *We say that $(\mathcal{E}, \mathcal{I}, \mu)_{\mathcal{B}}^{\mathcal{X}}$ is a* well-formed configuration *if $\text{dom}(\mu) \cap \text{var}(\mathcal{E}, \mathcal{I}) = \emptyset$, $\text{var}(\mathcal{E}, \mathcal{I}, \mu) \subseteq \mathcal{X}$, μ respects $\mathcal{B}$ that is μ-closed, $\mathcal{E} :: \mathcal{B}$ and $\mathcal{I} :: \mathcal{B}$.*

This definition gives some invariants for the reduction relation of unification.

Lemma 5.1. *The property of well-formed configuration is preserved by $\rightsquigarrow$.*

The following lemma states the *preservation of solutions* by the reductions.

$(triv)$ $\qquad (\{\alpha \doteq \alpha\} \cup \mathcal{E}, \mathcal{I}, \mu)_\mathcal{B}^\mathcal{X} \rightsquigarrow (\mathcal{E}, \mathcal{I}, \mu)_\mathcal{B}^\mathcal{X}$

$(elim)$ $\qquad (\{\alpha \doteq \tau\} \cup \mathcal{E}, \mathcal{I}, \mu)_\mathcal{B}^\mathcal{X} \rightsquigarrow ([\tau/\alpha]\mathcal{E}, [\tau/\alpha]\mathcal{I}, [\tau/\alpha]\mu)_{\mathcal{B}'}^\mathcal{X}$

$(chan)$ $\qquad (\{Ch(\tau) \doteq Ch(\sigma)\} \cup \mathcal{E}, \mathcal{I}, \mu)_\mathcal{B}^\mathcal{X} \rightsquigarrow (\{\tau \doteq \sigma\} \cup \mathcal{E}, \mathcal{I}, \mu)_\mathcal{B}^\mathcal{X}$

(at) $\qquad (\{\gamma@\psi \doteq \delta@\phi\} \cup \mathcal{E}, \mathcal{I}, \mu)_\mathcal{B}^\mathcal{X} \rightsquigarrow (\{\gamma \doteq \delta, \psi \doteq \phi\} \cup \mathcal{E}, \mathcal{I}, \mu)_\mathcal{B}^\mathcal{X}$

(loc_1) $\qquad (\{\{a : \gamma, \psi\} \doteq \{a : \delta, \phi\}\} \cup \mathcal{E}, \mathcal{I}, \mu)_\mathcal{B}^\mathcal{X} \rightsquigarrow (\{\gamma \doteq \delta\} \cup \{\psi \doteq \phi\} \cup \mathcal{E}, \mathcal{I}, \mu)_\mathcal{B}^\mathcal{X}$

(loc_2) $\qquad (\{\psi \doteq \phi\} \cup \mathcal{E}, \mathcal{I}, \mu)_\mathcal{B}^\mathcal{X} \rightsquigarrow (\lambda\mathcal{E}, \lambda\mathcal{I}, \lambda\mu)_{\mathcal{B}'}^\mathcal{Y}$

$(clash)$ $\qquad (\{\sigma \doteq \tau\} \cup \mathcal{E}, \mathcal{I}, \mu)_\mathcal{B}^\mathcal{X} \rightsquigarrow \perp$

(oc) $\qquad (\{\alpha \doteq \tau\} \cup \mathcal{E}, \mathcal{I}, \mu)_\mathcal{B}^\mathcal{X} \rightsquigarrow \perp$

(st_1) $\qquad (\mathcal{E}, \{\{a : \gamma, \psi\} \lessdot \{a : \delta, \phi\}\} \cup \mathcal{I}, \mu)_\mathcal{B}^\mathcal{X} \rightsquigarrow (\{\gamma \doteq \delta\} \cup \mathcal{E}, \{\psi \lessdot \phi\} \cup \mathcal{I}, \mu)_\mathcal{B}^\mathcal{X}$

(st_2) $\qquad (\mathcal{E}, \{\psi \lessdot \phi\} \cup \mathcal{I}, \mu)_\mathcal{B}^\mathcal{X} \rightsquigarrow (\lambda\mathcal{E}, \{\psi \triangleleft \rho_{L''}'' \lessdot \rho_{L'}'\} \cup \lambda\mathcal{I}, \lambda\mu)_{\mathcal{B}'}^\mathcal{Y}$

where in

$(elim)$ $\alpha \notin var(\tau) \cup \mathcal{V}_{loc,}$, $\alpha \notin dom(\mu)$, $nm(\tau) \cap \mathcal{B}(\alpha) = \emptyset$, $\mathcal{B}'$ is the $[\tau/\alpha]$-closure of $\mathcal{B}$.

(loc_2) $\mathcal{Y} = \mathcal{X} \uplus \{\rho_{L''}''\}$, $\psi' = \psi \triangleleft \rho_{L''}''$, $\phi' = \phi \triangleleft \rho_{L''}''$ and $\lambda = [\psi'/\rho_{L'}', \phi'/\rho_L]$ with $\rho_L = \rho var(\psi), \rho_{L'}' = \rho var(\phi)$, and $L'' = (L - \mathcal{B}(\rho_{L'}')) \cup (L' - \mathcal{B}(\rho_L))$ and if

- $dom(\psi) \cap dom(\phi) = \emptyset$, $L' \cap dom(\psi) = \emptyset$ and $L \cap dom(\phi) = \emptyset$
- $nm(\psi) \cap \mathcal{B}(\rho_{L'}') = \emptyset$ and $nm(\phi) \cap \mathcal{B}(\rho_L) = \emptyset$
- $\rho_L \notin var(\phi) - \rho_{L'}'$ and $\rho_{L'}' \notin var(\psi) - \rho_L$
- $\mathcal{B}'$ is the λ-closure of $\mathcal{B}$.

$(clash)$ σ and τ are not type variables and have distinct top symbols, or are locality types with disjoint domains and conditions of (loc_2) fail.

(oc) $\alpha \in var(\tau)$.

(st_2) $\mathcal{Y} = \mathcal{X} \uplus \{\rho_{L''}''\}$, $\lambda = [\phi \triangleleft \rho_{L''}''/\rho_L]$ with $\rho_L = \rho var(\psi), \rho_{L'}' = \rho var(\phi)$, and if $\phi \notin \mathcal{V}_{loc}$, $dom(\psi) \cap dom(\phi) = \emptyset$, $L \cap dom(\phi) = \emptyset$, $\rho_L \notin var(\phi) - \rho_{L'}'$, $nm(\phi) \cap \mathcal{B}(\rho_L) = \emptyset$, $L'' = (L - \mathcal{B}(\rho_{L'}')) \cup (L' - \mathcal{B}(\rho_L))$, $\mathcal{B}' = \mathcal{B}'' \cup \mathcal{B}(\rho_{L'}') \times \{\rho_{L''}''\}$ where $\mathcal{B}''$ is the λ-closure of $\mathcal{B}$.

Fig. 6. Reduction relation for unification

Lemma 5.2. *If* $(\mathcal{E}, \mathcal{I}, \mu)_\mathcal{B}^\mathcal{X} \rightsquigarrow^* (\mathcal{E}', \mathcal{I}', \mu')_{\mathcal{B}'}^\mathcal{Y}$ *and* $(\mathcal{E}, \mathcal{I}, \mu)_\mathcal{B}^\mathcal{X}$ *is a well-formed configuration, then* $\mu' = \mu\mu''$ *and,*

1. *for all* λ *ground solution of* $\mathcal{E}$ *and* $\mathcal{I}$ *that respects* $\mathcal{B}$, *then there exists* λ' *such that* $\lambda =_\mathcal{X} \lambda'\mu''$ *and* λ' *is a ground solution of* $\mathcal{E}'$ *and* $\mathcal{I}'$ *that respects* $\mathcal{B}'$.
2. *For all solution* λ *of* $\mathcal{E}'$ *and* $\mathcal{I}'$ *that respects* $\mathcal{B}'$, $\lambda\mu''$ *is a solution of* $\mathcal{E}$ *and* $\mathcal{I}$ *that respects* $\mathcal{B}'$.

Lemma 5.3 (Termination). *All sequence of reductions*
$(\mathcal{E},\mathcal{I},\emptyset)^{\mathcal{X}}_{\mathcal{B}} \rightsquigarrow (\mathcal{E}',\mathcal{I}',\mu')^{\mathcal{Y}}_{\mathcal{B}'} \rightsquigarrow \ldots$ *terminates either with* $\perp$ *or with* $(\emptyset,\mathcal{A},\mu)^{\mathcal{Y}}_{\mathcal{B}''}$
where $\mathcal{A}$ *is a set of atomic subtyping assertions.*

We can finally state the soundness and completeness of our unification algorithm.

Proposition 5.1 (Soundness). *If* $(\mathcal{E},\mathcal{I},\emptyset)^{\mathcal{X}}_{\mathcal{B}}$ *is a well-formed and* $(\mathcal{E},\mathcal{I},\emptyset)^{\mathcal{X}}_{\mathcal{B}}$
$\rightsquigarrow^* (\emptyset,\mathcal{A},\mu)^{\mathcal{Y}}_{\mathcal{B}'} \not\rightsquigarrow$, *then* μ *is a principal solution of* $(\mathcal{E},\mathcal{I})_{\mathcal{B}}$ *on* $\mathcal{X}$ *and* μ *respects*
$\mathcal{B}'$.

Lemma 5.4. $(\mathcal{E},\mathcal{I},\emptyset)^{\mathcal{X}}_{\mathcal{B}} \rightsquigarrow^* \perp$ *iff* $\mathcal{E}$ *and* $\mathcal{I}$ *have no solution that respects* $\mathcal{B}$.

Proposition 5.2 (Completeness). *If* $\mathcal{E}$ *and* $\mathcal{I}$ *have a solution that respects*
$\mathcal{B}$, *if* $\mathcal{E} :: \mathcal{B}$ *and* $\mathcal{I} :: \mathcal{B}$, *then* $(\mathcal{E},\mathcal{I},\emptyset)^{\mathcal{X}}_{\mathcal{B}} \rightsquigarrow^* (\emptyset,\mathcal{A},\mu)^{\mathcal{Y}}_{\mathcal{B}'} \not\rightsquigarrow$ *where* $\mathcal{X} = \mathrm{var}(\mathcal{E},\mathcal{I})$.

6   Constraint Generation

In this section we describe the inference of types, that is starting from a network term and a minimal typing context, we generate a constraint whose principal solution applied to the initial context gives a principal typing. By initial context, for a term S, we mean the set of location names occurring free in S, associated with a row variable as type. The idea of the algorithm is to build incrementally the inference tree of the typing of a term, *i.e.* is the inference tree in the inference system described in section 3. This is done by means of a rewriting system which acts on tuples $(\mathcal{J},\mathcal{E},\mathcal{I})^{\mathcal{X}}_{\mathcal{B}}$ where $\mathcal{J}$ is a set of sequents involving context schemes and $(\mathcal{E},\mathcal{I})_{\mathcal{B}}$ is the constraint being generated. The reduction is very close to the inference system. Indeed, given a sequent in the tuple, the reduction mostly consists in replacing it by the sequents that are premises of the corresponding rule in the inference system. Possibly, constraints are also generated accordingly.

The rules are collected in figures 7 where an underscore (_) denotes an irrelevant component. We just comment the rules for the binding constructs, the others being relatively straightforward. For an input process the type system uses the auxiliary type system without weakening for names. Since it is very simple and completely deterministic, given a name u, a type τ and a location ℓ we can easily determine Γ such that $\Gamma \vdash_\ell u : \tau$. Actually, τ only needs to be a type variable and u a location or a compound name. We use $\mathrm{gen}(u : \alpha, \ell)$ to generate adequate context schemes and typing constraints for the typing of u.

Definition 6.1. *We define the function* $\mathrm{gen}(u : t, \ell) = (\Gamma, \mathcal{E}, \mathcal{X})$ *as follows:*

$$\mathrm{gen}(k : t, \ell) = (k : \rho_\emptyset, \{t \doteq \rho_\emptyset\}, \{\rho_\emptyset\})$$
$$\mathrm{gen}(a@k : t, \ell) = (k : \{a : h, \rho_\emptyset\}, \{t \doteq h@\rho_\emptyset\}, \{h, \rho_\emptyset\})$$

where $\ell \neq k$, $\rho_\emptyset$ *and* h *are fresh type variables.*

In the rule (p_{2b}), the body of an input (of a location or a compound name) is typed in the initial context extended with the context provided by gen. This extension is allowed since the name(s) received does not already occur in the context and all type variables of the extending context are assumed to be fresh.

(n_1) $(\{\Gamma \vdash_\ell^W k : t\} \cup \mathcal{J}, \mathcal{E}, \mathcal{I})_\mathcal{B}^\mathcal{X} \rightsquigarrow (\mathcal{J}, \mathcal{E} \cup \{t \doteq \rho_\emptyset\}, \mathcal{I} \cup \{\Gamma(k) \lessdot \rho_\emptyset\})_\mathcal{B}^{\mathcal{X} \uplus \{\rho_\emptyset\}}$

(n_2) $(\{\Gamma \vdash_\ell^W a : t\} \cup \mathcal{J}, \mathcal{E}, \mathcal{I})_\mathcal{B}^\mathcal{X} \rightsquigarrow (\mathcal{J}, \mathcal{E} \cup \{t \doteq h\}, \mathcal{I} \cup \{\Gamma(\ell) \lessdot \{a : h, \rho_{\{a\}}\}\})_\mathcal{B}^{\mathcal{X} \uplus \{\rho_{\{a\}}, h\}}$

(n_3) $(\{\Gamma \vdash_\ell^W a@k : t\} \cup \mathcal{J}, \mathcal{E}, \mathcal{I})_\mathcal{B}^\mathcal{X} \rightsquigarrow (\mathcal{J}, \mathcal{E} \cup \{t \doteq h@\rho_\emptyset'\},$
$\qquad\qquad\qquad\qquad\qquad\qquad\quad \mathcal{I} \cup \{\rho_{\{a\}} \doteq\!\equiv \rho_\emptyset', \Gamma(k) \lessdot \{a : h, \rho_{\{a\}}\}\})_\mathcal{B}^{\mathcal{X} \uplus \{h, \rho_{\{a\}}, \rho_\emptyset'\}}$

(p_0) $(\{\Gamma \vdash_\ell \mathbf{0}\} \cup \mathcal{J}, \text{-}, \text{-})_\mathcal{B}^\mathcal{X} \rightsquigarrow (\mathcal{J}, \text{-}, \text{-})_\mathcal{B}^\mathcal{X}$

(p_1) $(\{\Gamma \vdash_\ell \bar{a}u\} \cup \mathcal{J}, \mathcal{E}, \text{-})_\mathcal{B}^\mathcal{X} \rightsquigarrow (\mathcal{J} \cup \{\Gamma \vdash_\ell^W u : t\},$
$\qquad\qquad\qquad\qquad\qquad\quad \mathcal{E} \cup \{\Gamma(\ell) \doteq \{a : Ch(t), \rho_{\{a\}}\}\}, \text{-})_\mathcal{B}^{\mathcal{X} \uplus \{t, \rho_{\{a\}}\}}$

(p_{2a}) $(\{\Gamma \vdash_\ell a(b).P\} \cup \mathcal{J}, \mathcal{E}, \mathcal{I})_\mathcal{B}^\mathcal{X} \rightsquigarrow (\{\Delta \vdash_\ell P\} \cup \mathcal{J}, \{\Gamma(\ell) \doteq \{a : Ch(h), \rho_{\{a\}}''\}\} \cup \mathcal{E},$
$\qquad\qquad\qquad\qquad\qquad\quad \{\rho_\emptyset \doteq\!\equiv \rho_\emptyset'\} \cup \mathcal{I})_{\mathcal{B}'}^\mathcal{Y}$

(p_{2b}) $(\{\Gamma \vdash_\ell a(u).P\} \cup \mathcal{J}, \mathcal{E}, \mathcal{I})_\mathcal{B}^\mathcal{X} \rightsquigarrow (\{\Gamma, \Delta \vdash_\ell P\} \cup \mathcal{J},$
$\qquad\qquad\qquad\qquad\qquad\quad \{\Gamma(\ell) \doteq \{a : Ch(t), \rho_{\{a\}}\}\} \cup \mathcal{E} \cup \mathcal{E}', \mathcal{I})_{\mathcal{B}'}^\mathcal{Y}$

(p_3) $(\{\Gamma \vdash_\ell P \mid Q\} \cup \mathcal{J}, \text{-}, \text{-})_\mathcal{B}^\mathcal{X} \rightsquigarrow (\{\Gamma \vdash_\ell P, \Gamma \vdash_\ell Q\} \cup \mathcal{J}, \text{-}, \text{-})_\mathcal{B}^\mathcal{X}$

(p_4) $(\{\Gamma \vdash_\ell (\nu a) P\} \cup \mathcal{J}, \text{-}, \mathcal{I})_\mathcal{B}^\mathcal{X} \rightsquigarrow (\{\Delta \vdash_\ell P\} \cup \mathcal{J}, \text{-}, \{\rho_\emptyset \doteq\!\equiv \rho_\emptyset'\} \cup \mathcal{I})_{\mathcal{B}'}^{\mathcal{X} \uplus \{\rho_\emptyset', h\}}$

(p_5) $(\{\Gamma \vdash_k (\nu a@\ell) P\} \cup \mathcal{J}, \text{-}, \mathcal{I})_\mathcal{B}^\mathcal{X} \rightsquigarrow (\{\Delta \vdash_k P\} \cup \mathcal{J}, \text{-}, \{\rho_\emptyset \doteq\!\equiv \rho_\emptyset'\} \cup \mathcal{I})_{\mathcal{B}'}^{\mathcal{X} \uplus \{\rho_\emptyset', h\}}$

(p_6) $(\{\Gamma \vdash_\ell (\nu k) P\} \cup \mathcal{J}, \text{-}, \text{-})_\mathcal{B}^\mathcal{Y} \rightsquigarrow (\{k : \rho_\emptyset, \Gamma \vdash_\ell P\} \cup \mathcal{J}, \text{-}, \text{-})_\mathcal{B}^{\mathcal{X} \uplus \{\rho_\emptyset\}}$

(p_7) $(\{\Gamma \vdash_\ell \mathbf{go}\, k.P\} \cup \mathcal{J}, \text{-}, \text{-})_\mathcal{B}^\mathcal{X} \rightsquigarrow (\{\Gamma \vdash_k P\} \cup \mathcal{J}, \text{-}, \text{-})_\mathcal{B}^\mathcal{X}$

(p_8) $(\{\Gamma \vdash_\ell !P\} \cup \mathcal{J}, \text{-}, \text{-})_\mathcal{B}^\mathcal{X} \rightsquigarrow (\{\Gamma \vdash_\ell P\} \cup \mathcal{J}, \text{-}, \text{-})_\mathcal{B}^\mathcal{X}$

(s_0) $(\{\Gamma \vdash \mathbf{0}\} \cup \mathcal{J}, \text{-}, \text{-})_\mathcal{B}^\mathcal{X} \rightsquigarrow (\mathcal{J}, \text{-}, \text{-})_\mathcal{B}^\mathcal{X}$

(s_1) $(\{\Gamma \vdash \ell[\![P]\!]\} \cup \mathcal{J}, \text{-}, \text{-})_\mathcal{B}^\mathcal{X} \rightsquigarrow (\{\Gamma \vdash_\ell P\} \cup \mathcal{J}, \text{-}, \text{-})_\mathcal{B}^\mathcal{X}$

(s_2) $(\{\Gamma \vdash S \mid S'\} \cup \mathcal{J}, \text{-}, \text{-})_\mathcal{B}^\mathcal{X} \rightsquigarrow (\{\Gamma \vdash S, \Gamma \vdash S'\} \cup \mathcal{J}, \text{-}, \text{-})_\mathcal{B}^\mathcal{X}$

(s_3) $(\{\Gamma \vdash (\nu a@\ell) S\} \cup \mathcal{J}, \text{-}, \mathcal{I})_\mathcal{B}^\mathcal{X} \rightsquigarrow (\{\Delta \vdash S\} \cup \mathcal{J}, \text{-}, \{\rho_\emptyset \doteq\!\equiv \rho_\emptyset'\} \cup \mathcal{I})_{\mathcal{B}'}^{\mathcal{X} \cup \{t, \rho_\emptyset', h\}}$

(s_4) $(\{\Gamma \vdash (\nu \ell) S\} \cup \mathcal{J}, \mathcal{E}, \text{-})_\mathcal{B}^\mathcal{X} \rightsquigarrow (\{\ell : \rho_\emptyset, \Gamma \vdash S\} \cup \mathcal{J}, \mathcal{E}, \text{-})_\mathcal{B}^{\mathcal{X} \uplus \{\rho_\emptyset\}}$

(f) $\qquad\qquad\qquad (\mathcal{J}, \text{-}, \text{-})_\mathcal{B}^\mathcal{X} \rightsquigarrow \perp$

where in

(p_{2a}) $\Delta =_{\text{dom}(\Gamma)-\ell} \Gamma, \Delta(\ell) = [\{b : h, \rho_\emptyset'\}/\rho_\emptyset]\Gamma(\ell)$ with $\rho_\emptyset = \rho\text{var}(\Gamma(\ell))$,
$\qquad\quad \mathcal{Y} = \mathcal{X} \uplus \{h, \rho_\emptyset', \rho_{\{a\}}''\}$, and $\mathcal{B}' = \mathcal{B} \cup (\mathcal{B}(\rho_\emptyset) \times \{\rho_\emptyset'\}) \cup (\{b\} \times \mathcal{Y})$

(p_{2b}) $(\Delta, \mathcal{E}', \mathcal{X}') = \text{gen}(u : t, \ell), \mathcal{Y} = \mathcal{X} \uplus \mathcal{X}' \uplus \{t, \rho_{\{a\}}\}, \mathcal{B}' = \mathcal{B} \cup (\text{chan}(u) \times \mathcal{Y})$,

$(p_{4,5})$ (s_3) $\Delta =_{\text{dom}(\Gamma)-\ell} \Gamma$ and $\Delta(\ell) = [\{a : h, \rho_\emptyset'\}/\rho_\emptyset]\Gamma(\ell)$ with $\rho_\emptyset = \rho\text{var}(\Gamma(\ell))$,
$\qquad\quad$ and $\mathcal{B}' = \mathcal{B} \cup (\mathcal{B}(\rho_\emptyset) \times \{\rho_\emptyset'\}) \cup (\{a\} \times \mathcal{X} \uplus \{\rho_\emptyset', h\})$

(f) $\exists \Gamma \in \mathcal{J}$ that is not legal or if conditions of the previous rules fail.

Fig. 7. Constraints generation for processes and networks

Moreover, the binding relation is updated in order to forbid the substitution of any current type variables with a type in which the bound channel occurs. When the name received is simple (say b, in rule (p_{2a})), the type ψ assigned to the current location ℓ in Γ have to be extended with a type assignment for b. This is performed by the substitution of the row variable $\rho_\emptyset$ of ψ with a location type assigning a type (variable) to b. We have to maintain the coherence between the fresh row variable of the type assigned to ℓ in the new context (Δ) and the one in

$\boldsymbol{\Gamma}$ (that may still occurs in the remains tuple). This is achieved by equating those two row variables. As in (p_{2b}), we update the binding relation but so as to keep Δ well-formed with respect to the new binding relation. Rules for restrictions $(p_4, p_5$ and $s_3)$ are very similar.

We give some invariants and states the termination of the reduction. We denote by $bn(\mathcal{J})$ the set of bound names of terms in $\mathcal{J}$.

Definition 6.2. *We say that* $(\mathcal{J}, \mathcal{E}, \mathcal{I})_{\mathcal{B}}^{\mathcal{X}}$ *is a* well-formed configuration *if:*

1. $\mathrm{var}(\mathcal{J}, \mathcal{E}, \mathcal{I}) \subseteq \mathcal{X}$,
2. $\mathcal{E} :: \mathcal{B}$, $\mathcal{I} :: \mathcal{B}$ *and all types in* $\mathcal{J}$ *are well-formed with respect to* $\mathcal{B}$.
3. $bn(\mathcal{J}) \cap \mathrm{im}(\mathcal{B}) = \emptyset$,
4. *for all* $\boldsymbol{\Gamma} \in \mathcal{J}$ *we have* $\mathrm{dom}(\boldsymbol{\Gamma}) \cap bn(\mathcal{J}) = \emptyset$ *and for all* $\ell \in \mathrm{dom}(\boldsymbol{\Gamma})$ *we have* $\boldsymbol{\Gamma}(\ell)$ *has the form* $\{a_1 : h_1, \dots, a_n : h_n, \rho_\emptyset\}$ *with* $\mathcal{B}(\rho_\emptyset) = \mathrm{im}(\mathcal{B})$.

Lemma 6.1. *The property of well-formed configuration is preserved by* $\rightsquigarrow$.

Lemma 6.2. *All sequence of reductions* $(\mathcal{J}, \mathcal{E}, \mathcal{I})_{\mathcal{B}}^{\mathcal{X}} \rightsquigarrow (\mathcal{J}', \mathcal{E}', \mathcal{I}')_{\mathcal{B}'}^{\mathcal{X}'} \rightsquigarrow \cdots$ *terminates either with* $\bot$ *or with* $(\emptyset, \mathcal{E}'', \mathcal{I}'')_{\mathcal{B}''}^{\mathcal{Y}}$.

We say that a substitution λ is solution of $(\mathcal{J}, \mathcal{E}, \mathcal{I})$ if it is a solution of $\mathcal{E}$ and $\mathcal{I}$, and if it validates the sequents in $\mathcal{J}$.

Proposition 6.1. *Let* $(\mathcal{J}, \mathcal{E}, \mathcal{I})_{\mathcal{B}}^{\mathcal{X}}$ *be well-formed, and* $(\mathcal{J}, \mathcal{E}, \mathcal{I})_{\mathcal{B}}^{\mathcal{X}} \rightsquigarrow^*$ $(\mathcal{J}', \mathcal{E}', \mathcal{I}')_{\mathcal{B}'}^{\mathcal{Y}}$

1. *if* λ *is a ground solution of* $(\mathcal{J}, \mathcal{E}, \mathcal{I})$ *that respects* $\mathcal{B}$ *with* $nm(\mathrm{im}(\lambda)) \cap bn(\mathcal{J}) = \emptyset$, *then there exists* $\mu =_{\mathcal{X}} \lambda$ *with* $nm(\mathrm{im}(\mu)) \cap bn(\mathcal{J}') = \emptyset$, *and* μ *is a solution of* $(\mathcal{J}', \mathcal{E}', \mathcal{I}')$ *that respects* $\mathcal{B}'$.
2. *if* λ *is a ground solution of* $(\mathcal{J}', \mathcal{E}', \mathcal{I}')$ *that respects* $\mathcal{B}'$, *then* λ *is also a solution of* $(\mathcal{J}, \mathcal{E}, \mathcal{I})$.

The unification combined with this reduction provide a sound and complete type inference algorithm.

Theorem 6.1 (Soundness). *Let* $\boldsymbol{\Gamma}$ *be an initial context for* S, *and* $\mathcal{X} = \mathrm{var}(\boldsymbol{\Gamma})$, *if* $(\{\boldsymbol{\Gamma} \vdash S\}, \emptyset, \emptyset)_{\emptyset}^{\mathcal{X}} \rightsquigarrow^* (\emptyset, \mathcal{E}, \mathcal{I})_{\mathcal{B}}^{\mathcal{Y}}$ *and* $(\mathcal{E}, \mathcal{I}, \emptyset)_{\mathcal{B}}^{\mathcal{Y}} \rightsquigarrow^* (\emptyset, \mathcal{A}, \mu)_{\mathcal{B}'}^{\mathcal{Z}} \not\rightsquigarrow$ *then* $\mu\boldsymbol{\Gamma}; \mathcal{A}$ *is a principal typing for* S.

Lemma 6.3. *Let* $\boldsymbol{\Gamma}$ *be an initial context for* S, *if* $(\{\boldsymbol{\Gamma} \vdash S\}, \emptyset, \emptyset)_{\emptyset}^{\mathrm{var}(\boldsymbol{\Gamma})} \rightsquigarrow^* \bot$ *then* S *is not typable.*

Theorem 6.2 (Completeness). *Let* $\boldsymbol{\Gamma}$ *be a initial context for* S, *if* S *is typable then* $(\{\boldsymbol{\Gamma} \vdash S\}, \emptyset, \emptyset)_{\emptyset}^{\mathrm{var}(\boldsymbol{\Gamma})} \rightsquigarrow^* (\emptyset, \mathcal{E}, \mathcal{I})_{\mathcal{B}}^{\mathcal{X}}$ *and* $(\mathcal{E}, \mathcal{I}, \emptyset)_{\mathcal{B}}^{\mathcal{X}} \rightsquigarrow^* (\emptyset, \mathcal{A}, \mu)_{\mathcal{B}'}^{\mathcal{Y}} \not\rightsquigarrow$.

This completeness theorem combined with the soundness one allows us to say that, whenever a term is typable our algorithms of constraint generation and unification compute a principal typing for it.

7 Conclusion

In this paper we studied the problem of type inference for a distributed π-calculus with code migration and local communication. Using an explicit subtyping relation on location types we define a notion of *principal typing* leading to a *practical* type inference problem *à la* ML.

Technically, we proposed a unification algorithm that computes the principal solution of a constraint. We gave a sound and complete algorithm that, given a system S, generates a constraint whose solution yields a principal typing for S. Since we considered *dependant types*, we showed how to manage substitutions carefully with respect to bound names. To this aim we introduced the novel notion of *binding relation*. For the sake of simplicity, in this paper we considered a monadic calculus, however we could easily extend our results to the full polyadic version. In [8], we also deal with (mis)matching of values and recursion. We have not yet addressed the simplification of the atomic subtyping assertions generated by the algorithm ([9]).

We believe that this work could be easily adapted to the type system of [6]. Moreover, the presentation of algorithms by means of reduction relations, and the fact that we compute a principal type, should be useful for a formal definition of "dynamic" typing and its integration in process reduction. For instance, in [12], Hennessy and Reily, study a partial typing for open systems where only some sites may be typed. However, they informally assume the existence of a type checker, and their terms are explicitly typed. We think that their work could be extended to allow dynamic computation of type information.

References

[1] R. Amadio. On modeling mobility. *Journal of Theoretical Computer Science*, 240(1):147–176, 2000.

[2] R. Amadio, G. Boudol, and C. Lhoussaine. The receptive distributive π-calculus. Technical Report 4080, INRIA, Sophia Antipolis, 2000.

[3] G. Berry and G. Boudol. The Chemical Abstract Machine. In *POPL'90*, pages 81–94, San Francisco, California, January 17–19, 1990. ACM Press, New York.

[4] L. Cardelli and A.D. Gordon. Mobile ambients. In M. Nivat, editor, *FoSSaCS*, volume 1378, pages 140–155. Springer-Verlag, Berlin, Germany, 1998.

[5] C. Fournet, G. Gonthier, JJ. Lévy, L. Maranget, and D. Rémy. A calculus of mobile agents. In *CONCUR'96*, pages 406–421, Pisa, Italy, 1996. Springer-Verlag.

[6] M. Hennessy and J. Riely. Resource access control in systems of mobile agents. In *Information and Computation* 174(2): 143–179 (2002).

[7] L. Jategaonkar and J.C. Mitchell. Type inference with extended pattern matching and subtypes. *Fundamenta Informaticae*, 19(1/2):127–165, 1993.

[8] C. Lhoussaine. *Réceptivité, mobilité et π-calcul*. PhD thesis, Université de Provence, 2002.

[9] F. Pottier. Simplifying subtyping constraints: A theory. *INFCTRL: Information and Computation*, 170, 2001.

[10] Didier Rémy. Syntactic theories and the algebra of record terms. Research Report 1869, INRIA, Rocquencourt, 1993.

[11] Didier Rémy. Type inference for records in a natural extension of ML. In *Theoretical Aspects Of Object-Oriented Programming. Types, Semantics and Language Design*. MIT Press, 1993.

[12] James Riely and Matthew Hennessy. Trust and Partial Typing in Open Systems of Mobile Agents. In *POPL'99*, pages 93–104, 1999.

[13] M. Wand. Complete type inference for simple objects. In *Symposium on Logic in Computer Science, Ithaca, NY*, pages 37–44, 1987.

Type-Safe Update Programming

Martin Erwig and Deling Ren

Oregon State University
Department of Computer Science
{erwig,rende}@cs.orst.edu

Abstract. Many software maintenance problems are caused by using text editors to change programs. A more systematic and reliable way of performing program updates is to express changes with an update language. In particular, updates should preserve the syntax- and type-correctness of the transformed object programs.

We describe an update calculus that can be used to update lambda-calculus programs. We develop a type system for the update language that infers the possible type changes that can be caused by an update program. We demonstrate that type-safe update programs that fulfill certain structural constraints preserve the type-correctness of lambda terms.

1 Introduction

A major fraction of all programming activities is spent in the process of updating programs in response to changed requirements. The way in which these updates are performed has a considerable influence on the reliability, efficiency, and costs of this process. Text editors are a common tool used to change programs, and this fact causes many problems: for example, it happens quite often that, after having performed only a few minor changes to a correct program, the program consists of syntax and type errors. Even worse, logical errors can be introduced by program updates that perform changes inconsistently. These logical errors are especially dangerous because they might stay in a program undetected for a long time. These facts are not surprising because the "text-editor method" reveals a low-level view of programs, namely that of sequences of characters, and the operation on programs offered by text editors is basically just that of changing characters in the textual program representation.

Alternatively, one can view a program as an element of an abstract data type and program changes as well-defined operations on the program ADT. Together with a set of combinators, these basic update operations can then be used to write arbitrarily complex *update programs*. Update programs can prevent certain kinds of logical errors, for example, those that result from "forgetting" to change some occurrences of an expression. Using string-oriented tools like awk or perl for this purpose is difficult, if not impossible, since the identification of program structure generally requires parsing. Moreover, using text-based tools is generally unsafe since these tools have no information about the languages of the programs to be

P. Degano (Ed.): ESOP 2003, LNCS 2618, pp. 269–283, 2003.

transformed, which makes the correct treatment of variables impossible because that requires knowledge of the languages' scoping rules. In contrast, a promising opportunity offered by the ADT approach is that effectively checkable criteria can guarantee that update programs preserve properties of object programs to which they are applied; one example is type correctness. Even though type errors can be detected by compilers, type-safe update programs have the advantage that they document the performed changes well. In contrast, performing several corrective updates to a program in response to errors reported by a compiler leaves the performed updates hidden in the resulting changed program.

Generic updates can be collected in libraries that facilitate the reuse of updates and that can serve as a repository for executable software maintenance knowledge. In contrast, with the text-editor approach, each update must be performed on its own. At this point the safety of update programs shows an important advantage: whereas with the text-editor approach the same (or different) errors can be made over and over again, an update program satisfying the safety criteria will preserve the correctness for all object programs to which it applies. In other words, the correctness of an update is established once and for all. One simple, but frequently used update is the safe (that is, capture-free) renaming of variables. Other examples are extending a data type by a new constructor, changing the type of a constructor, or the generalization of functions. In all these cases the update of the definition of an object must be accompanied by corresponding updates to all the uses of the object. Many more examples of generic program updates are given by program refactorings [10] or by all kinds of so-called "cross-cutting" concerns in the fast-growing area of aspect-oriented programming [1], which demonstrates the need for tools and languages to express program changes.

The update calculus presented in this paper can serve as an underlying model to study program updates and as a basis on which update languages can be defined and into which they can be translated.

Our goal is *not* to replace the use of text editors for programming; rather, we would like to complement it: there will always be small or simple changes that can be most easily accomplished by using an editor. Moreover, programmers are used to writing programs with their favorite editor, so we cannot expect that they will instantly switch to a completely new way of performing program updates. However, there are occasions when a tedious task calls for automatic support. We can add safe update programs for frequently used tasks to an editor, for instance, in an additional menu.[1]

Writing update programs, like meta programming, is in general a difficult task—probably more difficult than creating "normal" object programs. The proposed approach does not imply or suggest that every programmer is supposed to *write* update programs. The idea is that update programs are written by a experts and used by a much wider audience of programmers (for example, through

---

[1] This integration requires resolving a couple of other non-trivial issues, such as how to preserve the layout and comments of the changed program and how to deal with syntactically incorrect programs.

a menu interface for text editors as described above). In other words, the update programming technology can be used by people who do not understand all the details of update programs.

In the next section we illustrate the idea of update programming with a couple of examples. In Section 3 we discuss related work. In Section 4 we define our object language. The update calculus is introduced in Section 5, and a type system for the update calculus is developed in Section 6. Conclusions given in Section 7 complete this paper.

2   Update Programming

To give an impression of the concept of update programming we show some updates to Haskell programs and how they can be implemented in HULA, the Haskell Update LAnguage [8] that we are currently developing.

Suppose a programmer wants to extend a module for binary search trees by a `size` operation giving the number of nodes in a tree. Moreover, she wants to support this operation in constant time and therefore plans to extend the representation of the tree data type by an integer field for storing the information about the number of nodes contained in a tree. The definition of the original tree data type and an insert function are as follows:

```
data Tree = Leaf | Node Int Tree Tree

insert :: Int -> Tree -> Tree
insert x Leaf          = Node x Leaf Leaf
insert x (Node y l r) = if x<y then Node y (insert x l) r
                               else Node y l (insert x r)
```

The desired program extension requires a new function definition `size`, a changed type for the `Node` constructor (since a leaf always contains zero nodes, no change for this constructor is needed), and a corresponding change for all occurrences of `Node` in patterns and expressions. Adding the definition for the size function is straightforward and is not very exciting from the update programming point of view. The change of the `Node` constructor is more interesting since the change of its type in the `data` definition has to be accompanied by corresponding changes in all `Node` patterns and `Node` expressions. We can express this update as follows.

```
con Node : {Int} t in
    (case Node {s} -> Node {succ s}
       | Leaf -> Node {1}); Node {1}
```

The update can be read as follows: the `con` update operation adds the type `Int` as a new first parameter to the definition of the `Node` constructor. The notation $a\{r\}\,b$ is an abbreviation for the rewrite rule $a\,b \leadsto a\,r\,b$. So $\{Int\}$ t means extend the type t on the left by `Int`. The keyword `in` introduces the updates that apply to the scope of the `Node` constructor. Here, a `case` update specifies how to change all pattern matching rules that use the `Node` constructor: `Node` patterns are extended by a new variable `s`, and to each application of the `Node` constructor in the return expression of that rule, the expression `succ s` is added as a new first argument (`succ` denotes the successor function on integers, which is predefined in Haskell). The `Leaf` pattern is left unchanged, and occurrences of the `Node` constructor within its return expression are extended by 1. As an alternative to the `case` update, the rule `Node {1}` extends all other `Node` expressions by 1.

The application of the update to the original program yields the new object program:

```
data Tree = Leaf | Node Int Int Tree Tree

insert :: Int -> Tree -> Tree
insert x Leaf          = Node 1 x Leaf Leaf
insert x (Node s y l r) =
        if x<y then Node (succ s) y (insert x l) r
               else Node (succ s) y l (insert x r)
```

It is striking that with the shown definition the `case` update is applied to all case expressions in the whole program. In our example, this works well since we have only one function definition in the program. In general, however, we want to be able to restrict `case` updates to specific functions or specify different `case` updates for different functions. This can be achieved by using a further update operation that performs updates on function definitions:

```
con Node : {Int} t in
    fun 'insert x y:
        (case Node {s} -> Node {succ s}
           | Leaf -> Node {1}); Node {1}
```

This update applies the `case` update only to the definition of the function `insert`. Here the backquote is used to distinguish Haskell variables from meta variables of the update language.[2] Uses of the function `insert` need not be updated, which is indicated by the absence of the keyword in and a following update. We can add further **fun** updates for other functions in the program to be updated each with its own `case` update. Note that the variables x and y of the update language are meta variables with respect to Haskell that match any object (that is, Haskell) variable.

We can observe a general pattern in the shown program update: a constructor is extended by a type, all patterns are extended at the (corresponding position) by a new variable, and expressions built by the constructor are extended either by a function which is applied to the newly introduced variable (in the case that

---

[2] The backquote is not needed for `succ` and `s` since they appear as free variables in RHSs of rules, which means that they cannot reasonably be meta variables since they would be unbound. Therefore they are automatically identified as object variables.

the expression occurs in the scope of a pattern for this constructor) or by an expression. We can define such a generic update, say `extCon`, once and store it in an update library, so that constructor extensions as the one for `Node` can be expressed as applications of `extCon` [8]. For example, the size update can then be expressed by:

```
extCon Node Int succ 1
```

which would have exactly the effect as the update shown above. We plan to implement extensions to text editors like Emacs or Vim that offer generic type-correctness preserving updates like renaming or `extCon` via menus.

Of course, it is very difficult (if not generally impossible) to write generic update programs that guarantee overall semantic correctness. Any change to a program requires careful consideration by the programmer, and this responsibility is still required when using update programs. We do not claim to free the update process from any semantics consideration; however, we do claim that update programs make the update process more reliable by offering type-preservation guarantees and consistency in updates.

Other examples, such as generalizing function definitions or a collection of updates to maintain variations of a lambda-calculus implementation are discussed in [9] where we also indicate how update programming could be applied to Java.

3   Related Work

There is a large body of work on impact analysis that tries to address the problems that come with performing changes to software [2,4]. However, we know of no work that attempts to exploit impact analysis to perform fully automated software changes.

Performing structured program updates is supported by program editors that can guarantee syntactic or even type correctness and other properties of changed programs. Examples for such systems are Centaur [6], the synthesizer generator [11], or *CYNTHIA* [15]. The view underlying these tools are either that of syntax trees or, in the case of *CYNTHIA*, proofs in a logical system for type information.

We have introduced a language-based view of program updates in [7]. Viewing programs as abstract data types goes beyond the idea of syntax-directed program editors because it allows a programmer to combine basic updates into update programs that can be stored, reused, changed, shared, and so on. The update programming approach has, in particular, the following two advantages: First, we can work on program updates offline, that is, once we have started a program change, we can pause and resume our work at any time without affecting the object program. Although the same could be achieved by using a program editor together with a versioning tool, the update program has the advantage of much better reflecting the changes performed so far than a partially changed object program that only shows the result of having applied a number of update steps. Second, independent updates can be defined and applied independently. For example, assume an update u_1 followed by an update u_2 (that does not depend on or interfere with u_1) is applied to a program. With the editor approach, we can undo u_2 and also u_2 and u_1, but we cannot undo just u_1 because the changes performed by u_2 are only implicitly contained in the final version that has to be discarded to undo u_1. In contrast, we can undo each of the two updates with the proposed update programming approach by simply applying only the other update to the original program.

Programs that manipulate programs are also considered in the area of meta programming [12]. However, existing meta programming systems, such as MetaML [13], are mainly concerned with the generation of programs and do not offer means for analyzing programs (which is needed for program transformation). Refactoring [10] is an area of fast-growing interest. Refactoring (like the huge body of work on program optimization and partial evaluation) leaves the semantics of a program unchanged. Program transformations that change the behavior of programs are also considered in the area of aspect-oriented programming [1], which is concerned with performing "cross-cutting" changes to a program.

Our approach is based in part on applying update rules to specific parts of a program. There has been some work in the area of term rewriting to address this issue. The ELAN logical framework introduced a strategy language that allows users to specify their own tactics with operators and recursion [5]. Visser has extended the set of strategy operators and has put all these parts together into a system for program transformation, called *Stratego* [14]. These proposals allow a very flexible specification of rule application strategies, but they do not guarantee type correctness of the transformed programs.

A related approach that is concerned with type-safe program transformations is pursued by Bjørner who has investigated a simple two-level lambda calculus that offers constructs to generate and to inspect (by pattern matching) lambda calculus terms [3]. In particular, he describes a type system for dependent types for this language. However, in his system symbols must retain their types over transformations whereas in our approach it is possible that symbols change their type (and name).

4   The Object Language

To keep the following description short and simple, we use lambda calculus together with a standard Hindley/Milner type system as the working object language. The syntax of lambda-calculus expressions and types is shown in Figure 1. In addition to expressions e, types t, and type schemas s, we use c to range over constants, v to range over variables, and b over basic types. The definition of the type rules is standard and is omitted for lack of space.

Since the theory of program updates is independent of the particular dynamic semantics of the object language (call-by-value, call-by-need, ...), we do not have to consider a dynamic semantics.

$$e ::= c \mid v \mid e\ e \mid \lambda v.e \mid \text{let } v = e \text{ in } e$$
$$t ::= b \mid a \mid t \to t$$
$$s ::= t \mid \forall \bar{a}.t$$

Fig. 1. Syntax and types of lambda calculus.

The main idea to achieve a manageable update mechanism is to perform somehow "coordinated" updates of the *definition* and all corresponding *uses* of a symbol in a program. We therefore consider the available forms of symbol definitions more closely. In general, a definition has the following form:

$$\text{let } v = d \text{ in } e$$

where v is the symbol (variable) being defined, d is the defining expression, and e is the scope of the definition, that is, e is an expression in which v will be used with the definition d (unless hidden by another nested definition for v). We call v the *symbol*, d the *defining expression*, and e the *scope* of the definition. If no confusion can arise, we sometimes refer to d also as the *definition* (of v). β-redexes also fit the shape of a definition since a (non-recursive) $\text{let } v = d \text{ in } e$ is just an abbreviation for $(\lambda v.e)\ d$.

Several extensions of lambda calculus that make it a more realistic model for a language like Haskell also fit the general pattern of a definition, for example, data type/constructor definitions and pattern matching rules. We will comment on this in Section 5.2.

5 The Update Calculus

The update calculus basically consists of rewrite rules and a scope-aware update operation that is able to perform updates of the definition and uses of a symbol. In addition, we need operations for composing updates and for recursive application of updates.

5.1 Rules

A rewrite rule has the form $l \rightsquigarrow r$ where l and r are expressions that might contain meta variables (m), that is, variables that are different from object variables and can represent arbitrary expressions. Expressions that possibly contain meta variables are called *patterns*. The type system for lambda calculus has to be extended by a rule for meta variables that is almost identical to the rule for variables (except that meta variables have monomorphic types).

An update can be performed on an expression e by applying a rule $l \rightsquigarrow r$ to e which means to match l against e, which, if successful, results in a binding σ (called *substitution*) for the meta variables in l. The fact that a pattern like l matches an expression e (under the substitution σ) is also written as: $l \succ e$ ($l \underset{\sigma}{\succ} e$). We assume that l is linear, that is, l does not contain any meta variable twice.

The result of the update operation is $\sigma(r)$, that is, r with all meta variables being substituted according to σ. If l does not match e, the update described by the rule is not performed, and e remains unchanged.

We use the matching definitions and notations also for types. If a type t matches another type t' (that is, $t \succ t'$), then we also say that t' is an instance of t.

5.2   Update Combinators

We can build more complex updates from rules by alternation and recursion. For example, the *alternation* of two updates u_1 and u_2, written as $u_1 ; u_2$, first tries to perform the update u_1. If u_1 can be applied, the resulting expression is also the result of $u_1 ; u_2$. Only if u_1 does not apply, the update u_2 is tried. *Recursion* is needed to move updates arbitrarily deep into expressions. For example, since a rule is always tried at the root of an expression, an update like $1 \rightsquigarrow 2$ has no effect when applied to the expression 1+(1+1). We therefore introduce a recursion operator $\downarrow$ that causes its argument update to be applied (in a top-down manner) to all subexpressions. For example, the update $\downarrow(1 \rightsquigarrow 2)$ applied to 1+(1+1) results in the expression 2+(2+2). (We use the recursion operator only implicitly in scope updates and do not offer it to the user.)

In a *scope update*, each element of a definition `let` $v = d$ `in` e, that is, v, d, or e, can be changed. Therefore, we need an update for each part. The update of the variable can just be a simple renaming, but the update of the definition and of the scope can be given by arbitrarily complex updates. We use the syntax $\{v \rightsquigarrow v' : u_d\} u_u$ for an update that renames v to v', changes v's definition by u_d, and all of its uses by u_u. (We also call u_d the *definition update* and u_u the *use update*.) Note that u_u is always applied recursively, whereas u_d is only applied to the root of the definition. However, to account for recursive `let` definitions we apply u_u also recursively to the result obtained by the update u_d. We use x to range over variables (v) and meta variables (m), which means that we can use a scope update to update specific bindings (by using an object variable) or to apply to arbitrary bindings (by using a meta variable). Either one of the variables (but not both) can be missing. These special cases describe the creation or removal of a binding. In both cases, we have an expression instead of a definition update. This expression is required in the case of binding removal where it is used to replace all occurrences of the removed variable. (Note that e must neither contain x nor a possible object variable that matches x in case x is a meta variable.) In the case of binding creation, e is optional and is used, if present, to create an expression `let` $v = e$ `in` e'' where e'' is the result of applying u to e'. Otherwise, the result is $\lambda v.e''$. The syntax of updates is shown in Figure 2.

We use an abbreviated notation for scope updates that do not change names, that is, we write $\{v : u_d\} u_u$ instead of $\{v \rightsquigarrow v : u_d\} u_u$. The updates of either the defining expression or the scope can be empty, which means that there is no update for that part. The updates are then simply written as $\{v : u_d\}$ and $\{v\} u_u$, respectively, and are equivalent to updates $\{v : u_d\} \iota$ and $\{v : \iota\} u_u$, respectively.

$$
\begin{array}{lll}
u ::= & \iota & \text{Identity (No Update)} \\
 \mid & p \rightsquigarrow p & \text{Rule} \\
 \mid & \{x \rightsquigarrow x : u\} u & \text{Change Scope} \\
 \mid & \{\rightsquigarrow v[= e]\} u & \text{Insert Scope} \\
 \mid & \{x \rightsquigarrow e\} u & \text{Delete Scope} \\
 \mid & u \, ; \, u & \text{Alternative} \\
 \mid & \downarrow u & \text{Recursion}
\end{array}
$$

Fig. 2. Syntax of updates.

Let us consider some examples. We already have seen examples for rules. A simple example for change scope is an update for consistently renaming variables $\{v \rightsquigarrow w\} v \rightsquigarrow w$. This update applies to a lambda- or let-bound variable v and renames it and all of its occurrences that are bound by that definition to w. The definition of v is usually not changed by this update. However, if v has a recursive definition, references to v in the definition will be changed to w, too, because the use update is also applied to the definition of a symbol.

A generalization of a function f can be expressed by the update $u = \{f : \{\rightsquigarrow w\} 1 \rightsquigarrow w\} f \rightsquigarrow f \ 1$. u is a change-scope update for f, which does not rename f, but whose definition update introduces a new binding for w and replaces all occurrences of a particular constant expression (here 1) by w in the definition of f. u's use update makes sure that all uses of f are extended by supplying a new argument for the newly introduced parameter. Here we use the same expression that was generalized in f's definition, which preserves the semantics of the program.

To express the size update example in the update calculus we have to extend the object language by constructors and **case** expressions and the update calculus by corresponding constructs, which is rather straightforward (in fact, we have already implemented it in our prototype). An interesting aspect is that each alternative of a **case** expression is a separate binding construct that introduces bindings for variables in the pattern. The scope of the variables is the corresponding right hand side of the **case** alternative. Since these variables do not have their own definitions, we can represent a **case** alternative by a lambda abstraction—just for the sake of performing an update. A **case** update can then be translated into an alternative of change-scope updates. For example, the translation of the size update yields:

```
{Node:t  ⤳  Int->t}
    ({Node}({⤳s}Node⤳Node (succ s));
    {Leaf}Node⤳Node 1);
    Node⤳Node 1
```

The outermost change-scope update expresses that the definition of the Node constructor is extended by Int. The use update is an alternative whose second part expresses to extend all Node expressions by 1 to accommodate the type change of the constructor. The first alternative is itself an alternative of two change-scope updates. (Since the ; operation is associative, the brackets are strictly not needed.) The first one applies to definitions of Node which (by way of translation) can only be found in lambda abstractions representing case alternatives. The new-scope update will add another lambda-binding for s, and the use update extends all Node expressions by the expression succ s. The other alternative applies to lambda abstractions representing Leaf patterns.

This last example demonstrates that the presented update calculus is not restricted to deal just with lambda abstractions or let bindings, but rather can serve as a general model for expressing changes to binding constructs of all kinds.

Due to space limitations we omit here the formal definition of the semantics that defines judgments of the form $[\![u]\!]_\rho(e) = e'$, see the extended version of this paper [9].

6   A Type System for Updates

The goal of the type system for the update calculus is to find all possible type changes that an update can cause to an *arbitrary* object program. We show that if these type changes "cover" each other appropriately, then the generated object program is guaranteed to be type correct.

6.1   Type Changes

Since updates denote changes of expressions that may involve a change of their types, the types of updates are described by *type changes*. A type change (δ) is essentially given by a pair of types $(t \leadsto t)$, but it can also be an alternative of other type changes $(\delta | \delta)$. For example, the type change of the update $1 \leadsto \text{True}$ is $\text{Int} \leadsto \text{Bool}$, while the type change of $1 \leadsto \text{True} ; \text{odd} \leadsto 2$ is $\text{Int} \leadsto \text{True} | \text{Int->Bool} \leadsto \text{Int}$.

Recursively applied updates might cause type changes in subexpressions that affect the type of the whole expression. Possible dependencies of an expression's type on that of its subexpressions are expressed using the two concepts of *type hooks* and *context types*. For example, the fact that the type of odd 1 depends on the type of 1 is expressed by the hook $\text{Int} \hookrightarrow \text{Bool}$, the dependency on odd is $\text{Int->Bool} \hookrightarrow \text{Bool}$. The dependency on the whole expression is by definition empty (ϵ), and a dependency on any expression that is not a subexpressions is represented by a "constant hook" $\hookrightarrow \text{Bool}$.

The application of a type hook C to a type t yields a *context type* denoted by $C\langle t \rangle$ that exposes t as a possible type in a type derivation. The meaning of a context type is given by the following equations.

$$\epsilon\langle t \rangle = t$$
$$\hookrightarrow t_2 \langle t \rangle = t_2$$
$$t_1 \hookrightarrow t_2 \langle t \rangle = \begin{cases} t_2 & \text{if } t \succ t_1 \\ \text{error} & \text{otherwise} \end{cases}$$

$$\begin{aligned}
\delta &::= \tau \rightsquigarrow \tau \quad | \quad \delta|\delta \\
\tau &::= b \mid a \mid \tau \rightarrow \tau \mid C\langle\tau\rangle \mid \tau_{|C} \\
C &::= \epsilon \mid \hookrightarrow t \mid t \hookrightarrow t
\end{aligned}$$

Fig. 3. Type changes.

The rationale behind context types is to capture changes of types that possibly happen only in subexpressions and do not show up as a top-level type change. Context types are employed to describe the type changes for use updates in scope updates. For example, the type change of the update $u' = 1 \rightsquigarrow w$ is $\text{Int} \rightsquigarrow a$. However, when u' is used as a use update of a scope update $u = \{\rightsquigarrow w\}1 \rightsquigarrow w$, it is performed recursively, so that the type change is described using a context type $C\langle\text{Int}\rangle \rightsquigarrow C\langle a\rangle$.

To describe the type change for u, the type for the newly introduced abstraction has to be taken into account. Here we observe that the type of w cannot be a in general, because w might be, through the recursive application of the rule, placed into an expression context that constrains w's type. For example, if we apply u to $\text{odd } 1$, we obtain $\lambda w.\text{odd } w$ where w's type has to be Int. In general, the type of a variable is constrained to the type of the subexpression that it replaces. We can use a type hook that describes a dependency on a type of a subexpression e to express a constraint on a type variable that might replace e. Such a *constraint type* is written as $a_{|C}$. Its meaning is to restrict a type variable a by the type of a subexpression (represented by the left part of a type hook):

$$\begin{aligned}
a_{|t_1 \hookrightarrow t_2} &= t_1 \\
t_{|C} &= t
\end{aligned}$$

The type change for u is therefore given by $C\langle\text{Int}\rangle \rightsquigarrow a_{|C}\text{->}C\langle a_{|C}\rangle$.

To see how type hooks, context types, and constrained types work, consider the application of u to 1, which yields $\lambda w.w$. The corresponding type change $\text{Int} \rightsquigarrow a\text{->}a$ is obtained using the type hook ϵ. However, applied to $\text{odd } 1$, u yields $\lambda w.\text{odd } w$ with the type change $\text{Bool} \rightsquigarrow \text{Int->Bool}$, which is obtained from the type hook $\text{Int} \hookrightarrow \text{Bool}$. As another example consider the renaming update $u = \{x \rightsquigarrow y\}x \rightsquigarrow y$. For the update we obtain a type change $C\langle a_{|C}\rangle \rightsquigarrow C\langle b_{|C}\rangle$ (which is the same as $C\langle a_{|C}\rangle \rightsquigarrow C\langle a_{|C}\rangle$). The type hook C results for the same reason as in the previous example. Applying u to the expression $\lambda x.1$ yields $\lambda y.1$ with a type change $a\text{->Int} \rightsquigarrow a\text{->Int}$, which can be obtained by using the type hook $\hookrightarrow a\text{->Int}$. Similarly, u changes $\lambda x.\text{odd } x$ to $\lambda y.\text{odd } y$ with a type change $\text{Int->Bool} \rightsquigarrow \text{Int->Bool}$. This type change is u's type change specialized for the type hook $\text{Int} \hookrightarrow \text{Int->Bool}$.

The syntax of contexts and type changes is summarized in Figure 3. Since the inference rules generate, in general, context constraints for arbitrary type changes, we have to explain how contexts are propagated through type changes to types:

$$\begin{aligned}
C\langle\tau \rightsquigarrow \tau'\rangle &:= C\langle\tau\rangle \rightsquigarrow C\langle\tau'\rangle \\
C\langle\delta|\delta'\rangle &:= C\langle\delta\rangle|C\langle\delta'\rangle
\end{aligned}$$

Types and type changes can be *applicative instances* of one another. This relationship says that a type t is an applicative instance of a function type $t' \to t$, written as $t \precsim t' \to t$. The rationale for this definition is that two updates u and u' of different types $t_1 \rightsquigarrow t_2$ and $t'_1 \rightsquigarrow t'_2$, respectively, can be considered well typed in an alternative $u \,; u'$ if one type change is an applicative instance of the other, that is, if $t_1 \rightsquigarrow t_2 \precsim t'_1 \rightsquigarrow t'_2$ or $t'_1 \rightsquigarrow t'_2 \precsim t_1 \rightsquigarrow t_2$, because in that case one update is just more specific than the other. For example, in the update

$$\{\texttt{f}\colon \texttt{succ} \rightsquigarrow \texttt{plus}\}\texttt{f } \underline{\texttt{x}} \rightsquigarrow \texttt{f } \underline{\texttt{x}} \texttt{ 1}; \texttt{f} \rightsquigarrow \texttt{f } \texttt{1}$$

the first rule of the alternative $\texttt{f } \underline{\texttt{x}} \rightsquigarrow \texttt{f } \underline{\texttt{x}} \texttt{ 1}$ has the type change $\texttt{Int} \rightsquigarrow \texttt{Int}$ whereas the second rule $\texttt{f} \rightsquigarrow \texttt{f } \texttt{1}$ has the type change $\texttt{Int->Int} \rightsquigarrow \texttt{Int->Int}$. Still both updates are compatible in the sense that the first rule applies to more specific occurrences of $\texttt{f}$ than the second rule. This fact is reflected in the type change $\texttt{Int} \rightsquigarrow \texttt{Int}$ being an applicative instance of $\texttt{Int->Int} \rightsquigarrow \texttt{Int->Int}$. The applicative instance relationship extends in a homomorphic way to all kinds of type changes and contexts.

Finally, note that a type change $t \rightsquigarrow t'$ does not necessarily mean that an update $u : t \rightsquigarrow t'$ maps an expression e of type t to an expression of type t', because u might not apply to e and thus we might get $[\![u]\!](e) = e$ of type t. Thus, the information about an update causing some type change is always to be interpreted as "optional" or "contingent on the applicability of the update".

6.2   Type-Change Inference

The type changes that are caused by updates are described by judgments of the form $\Delta \triangleright u \,:: \delta$ where Δ is a set of *type-change assumptions*, which can take one of three forms:

(1) $x \rightsquigarrow x' :: t \rightsquigarrow t'$ expresses that x of type t is changed to x' of type t'. The following constraint applies: if x' is a meta variable, then $x' = x$ and $t' = t$.
(2) $v :_r t$ expresses that v is a newly introduced (object) variable of type t.
(3) $x :_\ell t$ expresses that x is a (object or meta) variable of type t that is only bound in the expression to be changed.

Type-change assumptions can be extended by assumptions using the "comma" notation as in the type system.

The type-change system builds on the type system for the object language. In the typing rule for rules we make use of projection operations that project on the left and right part of a type-change assumption. These projections are defined as follows:

$$\Delta_\ell := \{x : t \mid x \rightsquigarrow x' :: t \rightsquigarrow t' \in \Delta\} \cup \{x : t \mid x :_\ell t \in \Delta\}$$
$$\Delta_r := \{x' : t' \mid x \rightsquigarrow x' :: t \rightsquigarrow t' \in \Delta\} \cup \{x' : t' \mid x' :_r t' \in \Delta\}$$

The type-change rules are defined in Figure 4. The rules for creating or deleting a binding have to insert a function argument type on either the right or the left

$$\rightsquigarrow_{\triangleright} \quad \frac{\Delta_\ell \vdash p : t \qquad \Delta_r \vdash p' : t'}{\Delta \triangleright p \rightsquigarrow p' :: t \rightsquigarrow t'} \qquad\qquad \iota_{\triangleright} \quad \frac{}{\Delta \triangleright \iota :: t \rightsquigarrow t}$$

$$;_{\triangleright} \quad \frac{\Delta \triangleright u :: \delta \quad \Delta \triangleright u' :: \delta' \quad \delta \gtrless \delta'' \quad \delta' \gtrless \delta''}{\Delta \triangleright u ; u' :: \delta''} \qquad \frac{\Delta \triangleright u :: \delta \qquad \Delta \triangleright u' :: \delta'}{\Delta \triangleright u ; u' :: \delta | \delta'}$$

$$\{:\}_{\triangleright}^{chg} \quad \frac{\Delta[, x \rightsquigarrow x' :: t_{|C} \rightsquigarrow t'_{|C}] \triangleright u_d :: t_{[|C]} \rightsquigarrow t'_{[|C]} \quad \Delta[, x \rightsquigarrow x' :: t_{|C} \rightsquigarrow t'_{|C}] \triangleright u_u :: \delta}{\Delta \triangleright \{x \rightsquigarrow x' : u_d\} u_u :: C\langle \delta \rangle}$$

$$\{:\}_{\triangleright}^{ins} \quad \frac{\{\bar{a}\} = FV(t) - FV(\Delta_r) \quad \Delta[, w : t_{[|C]}] \vdash e : \forall \bar{a}.t_{[|C]} \quad \Delta[, w :_r t_{|C}] \triangleright u :: \delta}{\Delta \triangleright \{\rightsquigarrow w = e\} u :: t_{[|C]} \overrightarrow{\tau} C\langle \delta \rangle}$$

$$\frac{\Delta[, w :_r t_{|C}] \triangleright u :: \delta}{\Delta \triangleright \{\rightsquigarrow w\} u :: t_{[|C]} \overrightarrow{\tau} C\langle \delta \rangle} \qquad \{:\}_{\triangleright}^{del} \quad \frac{\Delta[, x :_\ell t_{|C}] \triangleright u :: \delta \quad \Delta_r \vdash e : t_{[|C]}}{\Delta \triangleright \{x \rightsquigarrow e\} u :: t_{[|C]} \overrightarrow{\ell} C\langle \delta \rangle}$$

Fig. 4. Type change system.

part of a type change. This type insertion works across alternative type changes; we use the notation $\tau \overrightarrow{\ell} \delta$ ($\tau \overrightarrow{\tau} \delta$) to extend the argument (result) type of a type change to a function type. The definition is as follows.

$$\tau \overrightarrow{\ell}(\tau_l \rightsquigarrow \tau_r) := (\tau \rightarrow \tau_l) \rightsquigarrow \tau_r \qquad\qquad \tau \overrightarrow{\ell}(\delta | \delta') := (\tau \overrightarrow{\ell} \delta) | (\tau \overrightarrow{\ell} \delta')$$
$$\tau \overrightarrow{\tau}(\tau_l \rightsquigarrow \tau_r) := \tau_l \rightsquigarrow (\tau \rightarrow \tau_r) \qquad\qquad \tau \overrightarrow{\tau}(\delta | \delta') := (\tau \overrightarrow{\tau} \delta) | (\tau \overrightarrow{\tau} \delta')$$

The inference rule $\rightsquigarrow_{\triangleright}$ connects the type system of the underlying object language (lambda calculus) with the type-change system.

We have several rules for scope updates. To save space we combine two rules for each case by using square brackets for optional rule parts. For example, in the rule $\{:\}_{\triangleright}^{ins}$ if and only if the premise can be proved without using the assumption for w, then there is no type hook C on the type t in the conclusion.

6.3   Soundness of the Update Type System

In this section we define a class of *well-structured updates* that will preserve the well-typing of transformed object-language expressions. An update that, when applied to a well-typed expression, yields again a well-typed expression is called *safe*. In other words, we will show that typeable well-structured updates are safe. The structure condition captures the following two requirements:

(A) An update of the definition of a symbol that causes a change of its type or its name is accompanied by an update for all the uses of that symbol (with a matching type change).

(B) No use update can introduce a non-generalizing type change, that is, for each use update that has a type change $t \rightsquigarrow t' | \delta$ we require that t is a generic instance of t' or that one type, t or t', is an applicative instance of the other.

Condition (A) prevents ill-typed applications of changed symbols as well as un-bound variables whereas (B) prevents type changes from breaking the well typing of their contexts. An intuitive explanation of why these conditions imply safety for well-typed updates can be obtained by looking at all the possible ways in which an update can break the type correctness of an expression and how these possibilities are prevented by the type system or the well-structuring constraints. For a detailed discussion, see [9].

Let us now define the well-structuring constraint formally. We first iden-tify some properties of change-scope updates. Let $u = \{x \rightsquigarrow x' : u_d\} u_u$ and let $x \rightsquigarrow x' :: t \rightsquigarrow t'$ be the assumption that has been used in rule $\{:\}_{\triangleright}^{chg}$ to derive its type change, say $t_1 \rightsquigarrow t_2 | \delta$.

(1) u is *self-contained* iff $x \neq x' \lor t \neq t' \implies \exists u, u', p : u_u = u ; x \rightsquigarrow p ; u'.$
(2) u is *smooth* iff $t' \succ t$ or $t \gtrless t'$ or $t' \gtrless t$
(3) u is (at most) *generalizing* iff $t_2 \succ t_1$

An update u is *well structured* iff it is well typed and all of its contained change-scope updates are self-contained, smooth, and generalizing.

When we consider the application of a well-structured update u to a well-typed expression e, the following two cases can occur: (1) u does not apply to e. In this case e is not changed by u and remains well typed. (2) u applies to e and changes it into e'. In this case we have to show that from the result type of u we can infer the type of e'. We collect the results in the following two lemmas.

Lemma 1. *u does not apply to $e \land \Gamma \vdash e : t \implies \Gamma \vdash \llbracket u \rrbracket (e) : t$*

Lemma 2 (Soundness). *If u is well structured and applies to e, then*

$$\Delta \triangleright u :: \tau \rightsquigarrow \tau' | \delta \land \Delta_\ell \vdash e : \tau \implies \Delta_r \vdash \llbracket u \rrbracket (e) : \tau'$$

The lemma expresses that the derivation of a type change that includes an alternative $\tau \rightsquigarrow \tau'$ ensures for any expression e of type τ that u transforms e into an expression of type τ'. We have to use τ in the lemma because the type change for u is generally given by context types. For a concrete expression e, the type inference will fix any type hooks, which allows τ to be simplified to a type t. Finally, we can combine both lemmas in the following theorem.

Theorem 1. *If u is well structured, then*

$$\Delta \triangleright u :: \tau \rightsquigarrow \tau' | \delta \land \Delta_\ell \vdash e : \tau \implies \Delta_r \vdash \llbracket u \rrbracket (e) : t \land (t = \tau \lor t = \tau')$$

Let us consider the safety of some of the presented example updates. The function generalization update from Section 5.2 is safe, which can be checked by applying the definitions of "well structured" and the rules of the type-change system. The first size update (Section 2) is also safe, although to prove it we need the extension of lambda calculus by constructors and **case** expressions. In contrast, the second size update is *not* safe since the **case** update will be applied only to the definition of **insert** (and not to other functions).

7 Conclusions and Future Work

We have introduced an update calculus together with a type-change system that can guarantee the safety of well-structured updates, that is, well-typed, safe updates preserve the well typing of lambda-calculus expressions. The presented calculus can serve as the basis for type-safe update languages. Currently, we are working on the design and implementation of an update language for Haskell.

One area of future work is to relax the rather strict well-structuring conditions and facilitate larger classes of update programs under the concept of *conditional safety*, which means to infer constraints for object programs that are required for their type preservation under the considered update.

References

1. ACM. *Communications of the ACM*, volume 44(10), October 2001.
2. R. S. Arnold and S. A. Bohner. Impact Analysis – Towards a Framework for Comparison. In *IEEE Int. Conf. on Software Maintenance*, pages 292–301, 1993.
3. N. Bjørner. Type Checking Meta Programs. In *Workshop on Logical Frameworks and Meta-Languages*, 1999.
4. S. A. Bohner and R. S. Arnold, editors. *Software Change Impact Analysis*. IEEE Computer Society Press, Los Alamitos, CA, 1996.
5. B. Borovanský, C. Kirchner, H. Kirchner, P. E. Moreau, and M. Vittek. ELAN: A Logical Framework Based on Computational Systems. In *Workshop on Rewriting Logic and Applications*, 1996.
6. P. Borras, D. Clèment, T. Despereaux, J. Incerpi, G. Kahn, B. Lang, and V. Pascual. Centaur: The System. In *3rd ACM SIGSOFT Symp. on Software Development Environments*, pages 14–24, 1988.
7. M. Erwig. Programs are Abstract Data Types. In *16th IEEE Int. Conf. on Automated Software Engineering*, pages 400–403, 2001.
8. M. Erwig and D. Ren. A Rule-Based Language for Programming Software Updates. In *3rd ACM SIGPLAN Workshop on Rule-Based Programming*, pages 67–77, 2002.
9. M. Erwig and D. Ren. An Update Calculus for Type-Safe Program Changes. Technical Report TR02-60-09, Department of Computer Science, Oregon State University, 2002.
10. M. Fowler. *Refactoring: Improving the Design of Existing Code*. Addison-Wesley, Reading, MA, 1999.
11. T. W. Reps and T. Teitelbaum. *The Synthesizer Generator: A System for Constructing Language-Based Editors*. Springer-Verlag, New York, 1989.
12. T. Sheard. Accomplishments and Research Challenges in Meta-Programming. In *2nd Int. Workshop on Semantics, Applications, and Implementation of Program Generation*, LNCS 2196, pages 2–44, 2001.
13. W. Taha and T. Sheard. MetaML and Multi-Stage Programming with Explicit Annotations. *Theoretical Computer Science*, 248(1–2):211–242, 2000.
14. E. Visser. Stratego: A Language for Program Transformation Based on Rewriting Strategies. In *12th Int. Conf. on Rewriting Techniques and Applications*, 2001.
15. J. Whittle, A. Bundy, R. Boulton, and H. Lowe. An ML Editor Based on Proof-as-Programs. In *9th PLILP*, LNCS 1292, pages 389–405, 1997.

Type Error Slicing in Implicitly Typed Higher-Order Languages*

Christian Haack and J.B. Wells

Heriot-Watt University
http://www.cee.hw.ac.uk/ultra/

Abstract. Previous methods have generally identified the location of a type error as a particular program point or the program subtree rooted at that point. We present a new approach that identifies the location of a type error as a set of program points (a *slice*) all of which are necessary for the type error. We describe algorithms for finding minimal type error slices for implicitly typed higher-order languages like Standard ML.

1 Introduction

1.1 Previous Approaches to Identifying Type Error Locations

There has been a large body of work on explaining type errors in implicitly typed, higher-order languages with let-polymorphism (Haskell, Miranda, O'Caml, Standard ML (SML), etc.) [26,19,18,30,28,2,3,9,1,15,8,20,29]. This is much harder than in monomorphic, explicitly typed, first-order languages. None of the previous work on this is entirely satisfactory. In particular, the previous approaches do a poor job of identifying the *location* of type errors.

As an example, consider the following SML program fragment:

```
val f = fn x => fn y => let val w = x + 1 in w::y end
```

This defines a function f such that the function call (f 1 [2]) should compute the list [2,2]. Suppose the programmer erroneously typed this instead, making an error at the indicated spot:

```
val f = fn x => fn y => let val w = y + 1 in w::y end
```

When the $\mathcal{W}$ [6], $\mathcal{M}$ [18], or the $\mathcal{UAE}$ [28,30] type inference algorithms are used to identify the error location, the type inference algorithm traverses the program's abstract syntax tree and when it fails, the node of the tree currently being visited is blamed. The algorithms differ in how eagerly they check the

---

* This work was partially supported by EPSRC grant GR/R 41545/01, EC FP5 grant IST-2001-33477, NATO grant CRG 971607, NSF grants CCR 9988529 and ITR 0113193, Sun Microsystems equipment grant EDUD-7826-990410-US.

P. Degano (Ed.): ESOP 2003, LNCS 2618, pp. 284–301, 2003.

various type constraints, so they may fail at different nodes. When using either W or $\mathcal{UAE}$ for the example, this error location is identified:

```
val f = fn x => fn y => let val w = y + 1 in w::y end
```

Although $\mathcal{UAE}$ was designed with the intention that unlike W it would blame a location containing the error, it handles let-bindings in the same way as W so it fails in the same way on this error. It has been proposed to use $\mathcal{M}$ instead of W because this would yield more "accurate" error locations. For the example, $\mathcal{M}$ identifies this error location:

```
val f = fn x => fn y => let val w = y + 1 in w::y end
```

This example illustrates the general fact that W, $\mathcal{M}$, and $\mathcal{UAE}$ often fail to identify the real location of the error. They identify *one* node of the program tree which *participates* in the type error, but will often be the wrong node to *blame*. These approaches also often identify program subtrees that include many locations that do *not* participate in the type error, e.g., in the example both W and $\mathcal{UAE}$ include the occurrence of w in the blamed subtree. This problem can also happen for $\mathcal{M}$ in some cases, although it does not happen as often. For W and $\mathcal{M}$, this is not necessarily wrong because only the root of the subtree is being blamed, not necessarily all of the other nodes in the subtree, but the programmer will often not understand this distinction.

1.2   A New Notion of Type Error Location

In contrast, this paper locates errors not at single nodes or subtrees of the abstract syntax tree, but at program *slices*. For the example, our implementation finds this error location:

```
val f = fn x => fn y => let val w = y + 1 in w::y end
```

This correctly includes all of the parts of the program where changes can be made to fix the type error. Importantly, it also correctly *excludes* all of the parts of the program where changes can not fix the type error. The occurrences of + and :: are highlighted differently to show they are the "endpoints" of a clash between the int and list type constructors. As an alternative, the erroneous slice of the program can be presented separately by displaying a very small program that contains the same type error as the source program, and nothing but this type error. In many cases, this will make it easier for the programmer to understand the error, especially when the error spans multiple source files. Here is actual output from our implementation in this style for the example:[1]

```
Type of error: type constructor clash, endpoints int vs. list.
  (.. y => (.. y + (..) .. (..)::y ..) ..)
```

---

[1] The fn keyword is missing because SML has the *match* syntax. That x is bound in a fn-*match* as opposed to a case-*match* is irrelevant for the error.

Formally, a *type error slice* is a set of program points. It is *complete* if these program points together "form a type error". It is *accurate* if none these program points is irrelevant for the type error. Examples of incomplete type error slices include the locations that are returned in most error messages of, for example, the SML/NJ compiler. They consist of a single program point, namely the point where the type inference algorithm detects a failure. This program point by itself does not form a type error. As an example of an inaccurate type error slice, one could take the entire program if it contains a type error. If the type error locations produced by the $\mathcal{W}$, $\mathcal{M}$, or $\mathcal{UAE}$ algorithms are taken to be identifying a program *subtree*, then they will usually be inaccurate.

1.3   Related Work

Dinesh and Tip have applied slicing techniques for locating sources of type errors [8]. Their techniques are applicable to *explicitly* typed languages. Their approach depends on the fact that the type system can be expressed as a rewrite system, and they use techniques for origin and dependency tracking in rewrite systems to find error locations. Although type inference algorithms for implicitly typed languages can be phrased as rewrite systems, a large part of the rewrite rules would concern auxilliary functions, i.e., unification and constraint solving. For this reason, we do not believe that a direct application of Dinesh and Tip's methods results in accurate location of type error sources in languages with type inference.

Our work is based on Damas' type inference system [7]. This system differs from the more widely know type *scheme* inference system (i.e., the Hindley/Milner system) in the typing rule for let-expressions, but admits the same set of well-typed closed expressions. It can be seen as a restriction of a system of rank-2 intersection types. Jim [14] has proposed using rank-2 intesection types for accurate type error location. Bernstein and Stark [2] use Damas's type inference system for type error debugging of open terms.

Wand has presented an algorithm for finding the source of type errors in implicitly typed languages [26]. Similar methods have been used by Duggan and Bent [9]. Wand's algorithm uses a modified unification procedure that keeps track of constraint sets that have been used in the derivation of unsolvable constraints. However, there is no attempt to present the corresponding program slices and these constraint sets need not be minimally unsolvable. We use a similar method as a subroutine, but in addition, we minimize constraint sets and present the resulting minimal type error slices. Our slices are minimal in the sense that the omission of further program points yields a non-error. Johnson and Walz have a method which attempts to choose the location to blame by counting the number of sites which prefer one type over another [15].

Chopella and Haynes study type error diagnosis in a simply typed language [5,4]. Unlike our work, they do not actually treat let-polymorphism. They propose to present type error locations as program slices, but have no notation for slices. Moreover, they present a graph-based unification framework, based on work by Port [23], which could be used for finding minimal unsolvable constraint sets. However, the diagnostic unification algorithm that is eventually presented in [4] only computes a single unsolvable constraint set that is not necessarily minimal. In contrast, our algorithms are not graph-based but based on running a unification algorithm multiple times. A big advantage of our approach is simplicity of presentation and implementation. Unlike Chopella and Haynes, we give a detailed presentation of an algorithm that enumerates minimal unsolvable constraint sets. On the other hand, while our algorithm enumerates *some* minimal unsolvable subsets of a given constraint set, the algorithm is impractical for exhaustively enumerating *all* such sets. In the worst case, enumerating all such sets is intractable [27]. In some cases an algorithm based on Port's idea may find all minimal unsolvable subsets, whereas ours does not. In the future, we may adopt the algorithm that is sketched by Port.

Heeren and others propose constraint-based type inference for improved type error messages [13,12,11]. They treat let-polymorphism, and their type system is between a type inference system and a type scheme inference system. In addition to equality constraints, their inference algorithm generates type scheme instance constraints. As a result, the constraint solving order is restricted. We believe that a type inference system without type schemes would simplify their system and sometimes permit more accurate error messages. They do not attempt to compute type error slices.

MrSpidey is a static debugger for Scheme that is distributed with some versions of the DrScheme programming environment [10]. It is based on set-based flow analysis, constructs and, on demand, displays parts of flow graphs, and highlights critical program points at which runtime errors may occur.

Much related work on type error analysis has spent a great deal of effort on sophisticated ways for automatically generating type error *explanations* [3,9,20, 26,29,1,19]. Such explanations tend to be complicated and lengthy. We believe that it is most important to *accurately locate* type errors, and display type error *locations* in a user-friendly way. For *understanding* errors, programmers typically use additional semantic knowledge that cannot be provided automatically anyways. Our work is intended to be a step into this direction.

1.4   Outline of Paper

Section 3 gives an overview of Damas' type inference system. The methods for type error slicing proceed in three steps. The first step consists of assigning constraints to program points. In order to obtain accurate type error slices, it is important to follow a certain strategy. This strategy is described in section 4. The second step consist of finding minimal unsolvable subsets in the set of all constraints. Section 5 describes algorithms for doing this. Finally, section 6 describes how type error slices are computed from the results obtained in the previous step.

For concreteness, we describe our methodology in detail for the small model language shown in figure 1. The labels that superscript expressions mark pro-

$$
\begin{array}{lll}
l & \in \ \mathsf{Label} & \text{a fixed infinite set of labels}\\
L & \in \ \mathsf{LabelSet} & \text{all finite subsets of } \mathsf{Label}\\
x & \in \ \mathsf{Var} & \text{a fixed infinite set of variables}\\
n & \in \ \mathsf{Int} & \text{the set of integers}\\
lexp & \in \ \mathsf{LExp} & ::= \ x^l \ \mid \ n^l \ \mid \ (lexp \ \mathtt{+} \ lexp)^l \ \mid \ (\mathtt{fn} \ x^l \ \mathtt{=>} \ lexp)^l\\
& & \mid \ (lexp \ lexp)^l \ \mid \ (\mathtt{let\ val} \ x^l \ \mathtt{=} \ lexp \ \mathtt{in} \ lexp \ \mathtt{end})^l
\end{array}
$$

Restriction: The labels that occur in a labeled expression must be distinct.

Fig. 1. Labeled expressions

gram points. The labeled expression language is a sublanguage of Standard ML (SML) [21]. We have an implementation for a larger sublanguage of SML.[2]

Acknowledgments. We thank Sébastien Carlier for his help in making the web demonstration interface and Greg Michaelson, Phil Trinder, and Jun Yang for stimulating discussions.

2   Some Definitions and Notations

The symbols $\langle$ and $\rangle$ denote tuple braces. We use the terms "tuple" and "list" interchangeably. For a list $xs = \langle x_1, \ldots, x_n \rangle$, the expression $y :: xs$ denotes the list $\langle y, x_1, \ldots, x_n \rangle$. For each natural number i, the symbol π_i denotes the i-th projection operator, i.e., if $xs = \langle x_1, \ldots, x_n \rangle$ and $i \in \{1, \ldots, n\}$, then $\pi_i(xs) = x_i$. If f is a function, then $f[x \mapsto y]$ denotes the function $(f \setminus \{\langle x, f(x) \rangle\}) \cup \{\langle x, y \rangle\}$. If X is a set and $\rightarrow$ is a subset of $X \times X$, then $\rightarrow^*$ denotes its reflexive and transitive closure. An element x is called *irreducible* with respect to $\rightarrow$, if there is no element y such that $x \rightarrow y$. If X is a set of sets, then $\min(X)$ denotes the set of all elements of X that are minimal with respect to set inclusion. Two sets are called *incomparable* if neither of them is a subset of the other one. In definitions of rewrite systems, we use a form of pattern matching. The symbol $\cdot$ denotes a *wildcard* and is matched by any element of the appropriate domain. A *disjoint union pattern* is of the form $pat_1 \uplus pat_2$ and is matched by a set X, iff there are sets X_1, X_2 such that $X_1 \cup X_2 = X$, $X_1 \cap X_2 = \emptyset$, X_1 matches pat_1 and X_2 matches pat_2. Usually, X matches $pat_1 \uplus pat_2$ in more than one way.

3   Damas's Type Inference System

Types are defined as follows:

$$
\begin{array}{ll}
ty \ \in \ \mathsf{Ty} \ ::= \ a \mid \mathtt{int} \mid ty \ \mathtt{->} \ ty & \qquad ity \ \in \ \mathsf{IntTy} \ ::= \ \wedge S\\
\quad a \ \in \ \mathsf{TyVar} \quad \text{a fixed infinite set of type variables}\\
\quad S \ \in \ \mathsf{TySet} \quad \text{the set of all finite subsets of } \mathsf{Ty}
\end{array}
$$

---

[2] http://www.cee.hw.ac.uk/ultra/compositional-analysis/type-error-slicing

$$\Gamma[x \mapsto \wedge\{ty, \ldots\}] \vdash x^l : ty$$
$$\Gamma \vdash n : \texttt{int}$$

$(\Gamma \vdash lexp_1 : \texttt{int})$ and $(\Gamma \vdash lexp_2 : \texttt{int})$ $\quad \Rightarrow \Gamma \vdash (lexp_1 + lexp_2)^l : \texttt{int}$

$\Gamma[x \mapsto \wedge\{ty\}] \vdash lexp : ty'$ $\quad \Rightarrow \Gamma \vdash (\texttt{fn } x^l \texttt{ => } lexp)^{l'} : ty \texttt{ -> } ty'$

$(\Gamma \vdash lexp_1 : ty' \texttt{ -> } ty)$ and $(\Gamma \vdash lexp_2 : ty') \Rightarrow \Gamma \vdash (lexp_1 \ lexp_2)^l : ty$

$(n \geq 1)$ and $(\forall i \in \{1, \ldots, n\}.\ \Gamma \vdash lexp : ty_i)$ and $(\Gamma[x \mapsto \wedge\{ty_1, \ldots, ty_n\}] \vdash lexp' : ty)$
$\quad \Rightarrow \Gamma \vdash (\texttt{let val } x^l = lexp \texttt{ in } lexp' \texttt{ end})^{l'} : ty$

Fig. 2. Damas's typing rules

The elements of IntTy are called *intersection types*. The symbol $\wedge$ is syntax. For example, $\wedge\{a \texttt{ -> int}, \texttt{int -> } a\} \in$ IntTy. A *type environment* is a total function from Var to IntTy. Let Γ range over Env, the set of all type environments. Let empty be the type environment that maps all variables to $\wedge\{\}$.

Damas's type inference system is defined in figure 2. We will call it Damas's System T because it is used with Damas's algorithm T. It differs in the rule for let-expressions from the usual system for SML, which Damas called the type *scheme* inference system. Whereas the type *scheme* inference system requires the types of all occurrences of a let-bound variable to be substitution instances of a common type scheme, System T does not require this. However, Damas showed that the two approaches accept the same expressions. The following fact is a variation of proposition 2 in Damas's Ph.D. thesis [7, p. 85].

Fact 3.1 *For closed lexp,* (empty $\vdash lexp : ty$) *iff lexp has type ty in SML.*[3]   □

We use the system, because it is good for accurately locating sources of type errors. The use of closely related systems has been proposed previously for type error analysis [2,14] as well as separate compilation [24,14].

4   Assigning Constraints to Program Points

This section explains how constraints are assigned to program points. We will define a function that maps labeled expressions to finite sets of constraints associated with program points. An expression is typable if and only if the associated constraint set is solvable. The association between constraints and particular program points is important for an untypable expression *lexp*. All program points in *lexp* associated with a minimal unsolvable subset of the set of constraints generated for *lexp* jointly cause a type error, and we display these program points as the location of the type error.

A *labeled constraint* is a triple $\langle ty, ty', L \rangle$, which will be written as $ty \overset{L}{=\!=} ty'$. Such a labeled constraint is called *atomically labeled*, if L is a one-element set.

---

[3] Formally, some minor syntactic adjustments (omitted here) are needed to translate *lexp* into an *exp* of the SML definition [21].

Let $ty \overset{l}{=} ty'$ stand for $ty \overset{\{l\}}{=\!=} ty'$. Let C range over AtConstraintSet, the set of all finite sets of atomically labeled constraints. Let D range over ConstraintSet, the set of all finite sets of labeled constraints. A *type substitution* is a function from TyVar to Ty. If s is a type substitution and ty a type, then $s(ty)$ denotes the type that results from ty by replacing each type variable occurrence a in ty by $s(a)$. A *solution* to a constraint $ty \overset{L}{=} ty'$ is a type substitution s such that $s(ty)$ and $s(ty')$ are syntactically equal. A solution to a set of constraints is a type substitution that solves all constraints in the constraint set simultaneously. The projection operator Π_L is defined by $\Pi_L(C) = \{(ty \overset{l}{=} ty') \in C \mid l \in L\}$. Let Π_l stand for $\Pi_{\{l\}}$.

The total function $\Downarrow$ from LExp to Env $\times$ Ty $\times$ AtConstraintSet is defined as the least relation that satisfies the rules in figure 3. This function is a variation of Damas's type assignment algorithm T. We use the term "fresh variant" of an object involving type variables to denote the result of renaming the type variables occurring in it by fresh type variables. We define $(\wedge S) \wedge (\wedge S') = \wedge(S \cup S')$. The operation $\wedge$ on type environments is defined by $(\Gamma \wedge \Gamma')(x) = \Gamma(x) \wedge \Gamma'(x)$. We define $(\wedge S) \blacktriangleleft (\wedge S')$, iff $S \subseteq S'$, and $\Gamma \blacktriangleleft \Gamma'$, iff $\Gamma(x) \blacktriangleleft \Gamma'(x)$ for all x in Var. The following facts are variations of propositions 7 and 8 on pages 39 and 44 in Damas's Ph.D. thesis [7].

Fact 4.1 *Suppose* $(lexp \Downarrow \langle \Gamma, ty, C \rangle)$.

1. *If s is a solution of C, then $(s(\Gamma) \vdash lexp : s(ty))$.*
2. *If $(\Gamma' \vdash lexp : ty')$, then there is a solution s of C such that $s(\Gamma) \blacktriangleleft \Gamma'$ and $s(ty) = ty'$.* □

Example 4.1. Consider the following partially labeled expression. (We have omitted all labels that are irrelevant for this example.)

$$lexp = (\texttt{fn } \texttt{x}^{l_1} \texttt{ => } \texttt{f } (\texttt{x}^{l_2} \texttt{ 0})^{l_3} \texttt{ } (\texttt{x}^{l_4} \texttt{ + 0})^{l_5})$$

Note that this expression has an obvious type error. The bound variable x is used both as a function and as an integer. Formally, it is the case that $(lexp \Downarrow \langle \texttt{empty}[\texttt{f} \mapsto a], a', C \rangle)$ for some type variables a, a' and some constraint set C that has the following subset C'.

$$C' = \left\{ a_1 \overset{l_2}{=} a_2, \ a_2 \overset{l_3}{=} a_3 \text{ -> } a_4, \ a_5 \overset{l_4}{=} a_6, \ a_6 \overset{l_5}{=} \texttt{int}, \ a_7 \overset{l_1}{=} a_1, \ a_7 \overset{l_1}{=} a_5 \right\}$$

It is not hard to see that C' is unsolvable. Moreover, it is *minimally* unsolvable, i.e., every proper subset of C' is solvable. As a type error message, our implementation displays a program slice that contains all program points that are associated with C'. When applied to the declaration

```
val _ = fn x => f (x 0) (x + 0)
```

it displays a message like this one:

```
type constructor clash, endpoints: function vs. int
(.. fn x => (.. x (..) .. x + (..) ..) ..)
```
□

$$\frac{}{x^l \;\Downarrow\; \langle\; \mathsf{empty}[x \mapsto \wedge\{a_x\}],\; a,\; \{a_x \overset{l}{=} a\}\;\rangle} \quad \text{where } a_x, a \text{ fresh}$$

$$\frac{}{n^l \;\Downarrow\; \langle\; \mathsf{empty},\; a,\; \{\mathtt{int} \overset{l}{=} a\}\;\rangle} \quad \text{where } a \text{ fresh}$$

$$\frac{lexp_1 \Downarrow \langle \Gamma_1, ty_1, C_1 \rangle; \qquad lexp_2 \Downarrow \langle \Gamma_2, ty_2, C_2 \rangle}{(lexp_1 + lexp_2)^l \;\Downarrow\; \langle\; \Gamma_1 \wedge \Gamma_2,\; a,\; C_{new} \cup C_1 \cup C_2\;\rangle}$$
$$\text{where } a \text{ fresh},\; C_{new} = \{ty_1 \overset{l}{=} \mathtt{int},\; ty_2 \overset{l}{=} \mathtt{int},\; \mathtt{int} \overset{l}{=} a\}$$

$$\frac{lexp \Downarrow \langle \Gamma[x \mapsto \wedge\{ty_1, \ldots, ty_n\}],\; ty,\; C \rangle}{(\mathtt{fn}\; x^l \Rightarrow lexp)^{l'} \;\Downarrow\; \langle\; \Gamma[x \mapsto \wedge\{\}],\; a,\; C_{new} \cup C\;\rangle}$$
$$\text{where } a_x, a \text{ fresh},\; C_{new} = \{\; a_x \overset{l}{=} ty_1,\; \ldots,\; a_x \overset{l}{=} ty_n,\; a_x \to ty \overset{l'}{=} a\;\}$$

$$\frac{lexp_1 \Downarrow \langle \Gamma_1, ty_1, C_1 \rangle; \qquad lexp_2 \Downarrow \langle \Gamma_2, ty_2, C_2 \rangle}{(lexp_1\; lexp_2)^l \;\Downarrow\; \langle\; \Gamma_1 \wedge \Gamma_2,\; a,\; C_{new} \cup C_1 \cup C_2\;\rangle}$$
$$\text{where } a, a_1, a_2 \text{ fresh},\; C_{new} = \{\; ty_1 \overset{l}{=} a_1 \to a_2,\; ty_2 \overset{l}{=} a_1,\; a \overset{l}{=} a_2\;\}$$

$$\frac{lexp_1 \Downarrow \langle \Gamma_1, ty_1, C_1 \rangle; \qquad lexp_2 \Downarrow \langle \Gamma_2[x \mapsto \wedge\{ty'_1, \ldots, ty'_n\}],\; ty_2,\; C_2 \rangle}{(\mathtt{let\; val}\; x^l = lexp_1\; \mathtt{in}\; lexp_2\; \mathtt{end})^{l'} \;\Downarrow\; \langle\; \Gamma'_1 \wedge \Gamma_2[x \mapsto \wedge\{\}],\; a,\; C_{new} \cup C'_1 \cup C_2\;\rangle}$$
$$\text{where } \langle \Gamma_{1,1}, ty_{1,1}, C_{1,1} \rangle,\; \ldots,\; \langle \Gamma_{1,k}, ty_{1,k}, C_{1,k} \rangle \text{ are fresh variants of } \langle \Gamma_1, ty_1, C_1 \rangle,$$
$$\Gamma'_1 = \Gamma_{1,1} \wedge \ldots \wedge \Gamma_{1,k},\; C'_1 = C_{1,1} \cup \ldots \cup C_{1,k},\; C = \{ty_{1,1} \overset{l}{=} ty'_1, \ldots, ty_{1,n} \overset{l}{=} ty'_n\},$$
$$a \text{ fresh},\; C_{new} = \{a \overset{l'}{=} ty_2\} \cup C,\; k = \mathsf{max}(n, 1)$$

Fig. 3. Algorithm T

Unlike Damas's original algorithm, in our variation of algorithm T every expression's result type is a fresh type variable a equated to a type ty by a separate constraint. The additional constraints and type variables are vital for obtaining complete type error slices. For example, if the variable rule were replaced by

$$\frac{}{x^l \Downarrow \langle \mathsf{empty}[x \mapsto \wedge\{a_x\}], a_x, \emptyset\rangle} \quad \text{where } a_x \text{ fresh}$$

then in example 4.1 the generated constraint set would not mention the labels l_2 or l_4. Thus, these relevant program points would be wrongly omitted from the type error location. The resulting type error slice would be incomplete:

$$(.. \;\mathtt{fn}\; x \Rightarrow (.. \;(..) \;(..) \;.. \;(..) + (..) \;..) \;..)$$

The let-expression rule copies the constraint set C_1 for $lexp_1$ for each use of the variable x in $lexp_2$. In bad cases, the number of copies of a constraint set can be exponential in the size of the program. Consider, this example program:

```
let   val x₁ = lexp   in
let   val x₂ = f x₁ x₁   in
...
let   val xₙ = f xₙ₋₁ xₙ₋₁   in   f xₙ xₙ   end ... end
```

The resulting constraint set contains 2^n variants of *lexp*'s constraint set. Note, however, that this family of expressions is notorious also for algorithm $\mathcal{W}$: If $lexp = (\texttt{fn } x => x)$ and f's type scheme is assumed to be $(\forall a.\forall b.\ a \rightarrow b \rightarrow a \rightarrow b)$, then the principal type scheme of the entire expression contains $2^{(n+1)}$ distinct type variables. Remember also that Hindley/Milner (SML) typability in our small expression language is exponential time complete [16,17].

5   Finding Minimal Unsolvable Constraint Sets

We define a function that maps sets of atomically labeled constraints to sets of associated labels by $\mathsf{labels}(C) = \{\ l \mid (\exists ty, ty')((ty \overset{l}{=} ty') \in C)\ \}$. A set of labels L is called an *error* with respect to C, if C has an unsolvable subset C' such that $L = \mathsf{labels}(C')$. We denote the set of all such errors by $\mathsf{errors}(C)$. Moreover, $\mathsf{minErrors}(C)$ denotes the set of all those elements of $\mathsf{errors}(C)$ that are minimal with respect to set inclusion. This section shows how to find minimal errors in an unsolvable constraint set. We will present a greedy minimization algorithm that, given an unsolvable constraint set C, finds *a single* element of $\mathsf{minErrors}(C)$. This algorithm is reasonably efficient for practical purposes. It is not practical to always exhaustively enumerate *all* elements of $\mathsf{minErrors}(C)$, because this set has a worst-case size exponential in the size of C [27]. However, our simple enumeration algorithm seems to always find a few good candidates for some (but not all) minimal errors. These candidates are close to minimal and can be minimized with the minimization algorithm.

5.1   Labeled Unification

Unification can be viewed as a rewrite system on constraints. Our algorithms label each derived constraint with the labels of constraints used in deriving it. Our unification algorithm is similar to the one in [26]. Our *labeled unification algorithm* is a set of state transformation rules given in figure 4 which define the state transformation relation $\rightarrow$. Initial states are of the form $\mathsf{unify}(C)$ and final states of the form $\mathsf{Success}(E)$ or $\mathsf{Error}(L, l)$. Intermediate states are of the form $\mathsf{unify}(C, E)$ or $\mathsf{unify}(C, E, D, l)$ where the state components are as follows:

$C \in \mathsf{AtConstraintSet}$	initial constraints not yet considered
$E \in \mathsf{TyVar} \rightarrow ((\mathsf{Ty} \times \mathsf{LabelSet}) \cup \{\bot\})$	*environment*, contains derived bindings
$D \in \mathsf{ConstraintSet}$	*derived constraints* that are not bindings yet
$l \in \mathsf{Label}$	the label whose constraints are currently under inspection

Proposition 5.1 (Termination of unify). *Each state transformation sequence terminates. A state is irreducible iff it is a final state.*   □

We define a function app that maps environments to partial functions from TyVar to Ty. For every fixed E, the binary relation $\mathsf{app}(E)(\cdot) = \cdot$ is defined inductively as the least relation that satisfies the following conditions:

$$(E(a) = \bot) \Rightarrow (\mathsf{app}(E)(a) = a)$$
$$(E(a) = \langle ty, L \rangle) \Rightarrow (\mathsf{app}(E)(a) = \mathsf{app}(E)(ty))$$
$$(\mathsf{app}(E)(ty_1) = ty_1') \wedge (\mathsf{app}(E)(ty_2) = ty_2') \Rightarrow (\mathsf{app}(E)(ty_1 \mathrel{-\!\!>} ty_2) = ty_1' \mathrel{-\!\!>} ty_2')$$
$$(\mathsf{app}(E)(\texttt{int}) = \texttt{int})$$

$\mathsf{app}(E)$ is a partial function for every E. Although $\mathsf{app}(E)$ is not always total, because the second equation (for variables) is not size decreasing, it is only used in defined cases. For type substitutions s and s', their *composition* $s' \circ s$ is the type substitution that satisfies $(s' \circ s)(a) = s'(s(a))$ for all type variables a. A type substitution s is called a *most general unifier* of C, iff for every solution s' of C there exists a type substitution s'' such that $s' = s'' \circ s$.

Theorem 5.1 (Correctness of unify).

1. *If* $\mathsf{unify}(C) \to^* \mathsf{Success}(E)$, *then* $\mathsf{app}(E)$ *is a total function and a most general unifier of* C.
2. *If* $\mathsf{unify}(C) \to^* \mathsf{Error}(L, l)$, *then* $L \in \mathsf{errors}(C)$ *and* $L \setminus \{l\} \notin \mathsf{errors}(C)$.   □

If one ignores the labels, the labeled unification algorithm looks very much like standard presentations of unification. Note that the transformation system in figure 4 is non-deterministic. Arbitrary choices can be used for the label l in the fourth unify rule, the labeled constraint $(ty \overset{L}{=} ty')$ in the last ten unify rules, and the label set associated with an occurs-check failure in the last unify rule. Different choices may yield different final results. This is not a surprise, because the label sets that get returned in case of failure record parts of the histories of transformation sequences.

Example 5.1.

$$C = \{\, a_1 \overset{l_1}{=} a_2 \mathrel{-\!\!>} a_3,\; a_2 \overset{l_2}{=} \texttt{int} \mathrel{-\!\!>} a_4,\; a_1 \overset{l_3}{=} (a_5 \mathrel{-\!\!>} (a_6 \mathrel{-\!\!>} a_7)) \mathrel{-\!\!>} \texttt{int},$$
$$a_2 \overset{l_4}{=} a_8 \mathrel{-\!\!>} \texttt{int} \,\}$$

Both $\mathsf{unify}(C) \to^* \mathsf{Error}(\{l_1, l_2, l_3, l_4\}, l_4)$ and $\mathsf{unify}(C) \to^* \mathsf{Error}(\{l_1, l_3, l_4\}, l_4)$. The first result is obtained, for instance, if the constraints are inspected in the order l_1, l_2, l_3, l_4; the second result is obtained, for instance, if they are inspected in the order l_1, l_3, l_4. Note that this example shows that $\mathsf{unify}(C) \to^* \mathsf{Error}(L, l)$ does *not* imply that L is minimal.   □

Example 5.2.

$$C = \{\, a_1 \overset{l_1}{=} a_2 \mathrel{-\!\!>} a_3,\; a_1 \overset{l_2}{=} (a_4 \mathrel{-\!\!>} (a_5 \mathrel{-\!\!>} a_6)) \mathrel{-\!\!>} \texttt{int},$$
$$a_1 \overset{l_3}{=} (a_7 \mathrel{-\!\!>} (a_8 \mathrel{-\!\!>} a_9)) \mathrel{-\!\!>} \texttt{int},\; a_2 \overset{l_4}{=} \texttt{int} \mathrel{-\!\!>} \texttt{int} \,\}$$

Then, $\mathsf{unify}(C) \to^* \mathsf{Error}(\{l_1, l_2, l_4\}, l_4)$. The result is obtained, for instance, if the constraints are inspected in the order l_1, l_2, l_3, l_4. Note that, although l_3 is

dummy is some arbitrarily chosen fixed label

$\text{unify}(C)$ $\qquad\qquad\qquad\qquad\qquad\quad \rightarrow \text{unify}(C, (\lambda a \in \text{TyVar}.\bot))$

$\text{unify}(C, E)$ $\qquad\qquad\qquad\qquad\qquad \rightarrow \text{unify}(C, E, \emptyset, \text{dummy})$

$\text{unify}(\emptyset, E, \emptyset, l)$ $\qquad\qquad\qquad\qquad \rightarrow \text{Success}(E)$

$\text{unify}(C, E, \emptyset, l')$ $\qquad\qquad\qquad\qquad \rightarrow \text{unify}(C \setminus \Pi_l(C), E, \Pi_l(C), l),$
$\quad$ if $\Pi_l(C) \neq \emptyset$

$\text{unify}(C, E, \{ty \overset{L}{=} ty\} \uplus D, l)$ $\qquad\qquad \rightarrow \text{unify}(C, E, D, l)$

$\text{unify}(C, E, \{ty_1 \text{ -> } ty_2 \overset{L}{=} \text{int}\} \uplus D, l) \rightarrow \text{Error}(L, l)$

$\text{unify}(C, E, \{\text{int} \overset{L}{=} ty_1 \text{ -> } ty_2\} \uplus D, l) \rightarrow \text{Error}(L, l)$

$\text{unify}(C, E, \{\text{int} \overset{L}{=} a\} \uplus D, l)$ $\qquad\quad \rightarrow \text{unify}(C, E, \{a \overset{L}{=} \text{int}\} \cup D, l)$

$\text{unify}(C, E, \{ty_1 \text{ -> } ty_2 \overset{L}{=} a\} \uplus D, l)$ $\quad \rightarrow \text{unify}(C, E, \{a \overset{L}{=} ty_1 \text{ -> } ty_2\} \cup D, l)$

$\text{unify}(C, E, \{ty_1 \text{ -> } ty_2 \overset{L}{=} ty_1' \text{ -> } ty_2'\} \uplus D, l)$
$\quad \rightarrow \text{unify}(C, E, \{ty_1' \overset{L}{=} ty_1, ty_2 \overset{L}{=} ty_2'\} \cup D, l)$

$\text{unify}(C, E[a \mapsto \langle ty', L' \rangle], \{a \overset{L}{=} ty\} \uplus D, l)$
$\quad \rightarrow \text{unify}(C, E[a \mapsto \langle ty', L' \rangle], \{ty' \overset{L \cup L'}{=} ty\} \cup D, l)$

$\text{unify}(C, E[a \mapsto \bot], \{a \overset{L}{=} ty\} \uplus D, l)$
$\quad \rightarrow \begin{cases} \text{unify}(C, E[a \mapsto \langle ty, L \rangle], D, l) & \text{if } \text{occurs}(E, L, a, ty, 0) = \emptyset \\ \text{Error}(L', l) & \text{if } \langle L', n \rangle \in \text{occurs}(E, L, a, ty, 0) \text{ and } n \geq 1 \\ \text{unify}(C, E[a \mapsto \bot], D, l) & \text{otherwise} \end{cases}$

$\text{occurs}(E[a' \mapsto \langle ty, L' \rangle], L, a, a', i)$ $\quad = \text{occurs}(E[a' \mapsto \langle ty, L' \rangle], L \cup L', a, ty, i)$

$\text{occurs}(E[a' \mapsto \bot], L, a, a, i)$ $\qquad\quad = \{\langle L, i \rangle\}$

$\text{occurs}(E[a' \mapsto \bot], L, a, a', i)$ $\qquad\quad = \emptyset \qquad \text{if } a \neq a'$

$\text{occurs}(E, L, a, \text{int}, i)$ $\qquad\qquad\qquad = \emptyset$

$\text{occurs}(E, L, a, ty_1 \text{ -> } ty_2, i)$
$\quad = \text{occurs}(E, L, a, ty_1, i+1) \cup \text{occurs}(E, L, a, ty_2, i+1)$

Fig. 4. A non-deterministic labeled unification algorithm

---

inspected before the error is discovered, l_3 is not an element of the return set. This is so, because the constraint that is labeled by l_3 does not increment the knowledge that has already been accumulated as a result of inspecting l_1 and l_2.

It is also the case that $\text{unify}(C) \rightarrow^* \text{Error}(\{l_1, l_3, l_4\}, l_4)$. This result is obtained, for instance, if the constraints are inspected in the order l_1, l_3, l_2, l_4. It happens to be the case that $\text{minErrors}(C) = \{\{l_1, l_2, l_4\}, \{l_1, l_3, l_4\}\}$ $\qquad\qquad \square$

5.2   Error Minimization

Both our minimization and enumeration algorithms are based on the labeled unification algorithm; they execute it multiple times on different subsets of the initial constraint set. The minimization algorithm is based on the following idea: Remember that if $\text{unify}(C) \rightarrow^* \text{Error}(L, l)$, then L is an error and $L \setminus \{l\}$ is not

$$\mathsf{minimize}(C, L, l) \rightarrow \mathsf{minimize}(C, \lambda a \in \mathsf{TyVar}.\bot, L, l, \emptyset)$$

$$\frac{\mathsf{unify}(\ \Pi_l(C),\ E\ ) \rightarrow^* \mathsf{Error}(\cdot, \cdot)}{\mathsf{minimize}(C, E, L, l, L') \rightarrow \mathsf{MinError}(L' \cup \{l\})}$$

$$\frac{\mathsf{unify}(\ \Pi_l(C),\ E\ ) \rightarrow^* \mathsf{Success}(E_{new});\ \mathsf{unify}(\ \Pi_{L\backslash\{l\}}(C),\ E_{new}\ ) \rightarrow^* \mathsf{Error}(L_{new}, l_{new})}{\mathsf{minimize}(C, E, L, l, L') \rightarrow \mathsf{minimize}(C, E_{new}, L_{new}, l_{new}, L' \cup \{l\})}$$

Fig. 5. A non-deterministic error slice minimization algorithm

an error. It follows that l is an element of every minimal error that is contained in L. The minimization algorithm exploits this fact repetitively, and iteratively builds a minimal error.

In figure 5, the algorithm is presented as a set of state transformation rules. Initial states are of the form $\mathsf{minimize}(C, L, l)$ and final states of form $\mathsf{MinError}(L)$. Intermediate states are of the form $\mathsf{minimize}(C, E, L, l, L')$. The intention is that, if, initially, $L \in \mathsf{errors}(C)$ and $L \setminus \{l\} \notin \mathsf{errors}(C)$, and if $\mathsf{minimize}(C, L, l) \rightarrow^*$ $\mathsf{MinError}(L')$, then L' is a minimal error that is contained in L.

Proposition 5.2. *Suppose* $L_{in} \in \mathsf{errors}(C_{in})$, $L_{in} \setminus \{l_{in}\} \notin \mathsf{errors}(C_{in})$ *and* $\mathsf{minimize}(C_{in}, L_{in}, l_{in}) \rightarrow^* \mathsf{minimize}(C, E, L, l, L')$. *Then all of these hold:*

1. $C = C_{in}$, $l \in L$, $l_{in} \in L'$, $L \cap L' = \emptyset$ *and* $L \cup L' \subseteq L_{in}$.
2. $\mathsf{app}(E)$ *is a most general unifier of* $\Pi_{L'}(C)$.
3. $\mathsf{app}(E)(\Pi_L(C))$ *is not solvable.*
4. $\mathsf{app}(E)(\Pi_{L\backslash\{l\}}(C))$ *is solvable.* $\qquad\square$

Proposition 5.3 (Termination of $\mathsf{minimize}$**).** *Let* $L \in \mathsf{errors}(C)$ *and* $L \setminus \{l\} \notin \mathsf{errors}(C)$. *Every transformation sequence starting from* $\mathsf{minimize}(C, L, l)$ *terminates. If* $\mathsf{minimize}(C, L, l) \rightarrow^* s$, *then* s *is irreducible iff it is a final state.* $\qquad\square$

Lemma 5.1. *Suppose* $L_{in} \in \mathsf{errors}(C)$, $L_{in} \setminus \{l_{in}\} \notin \mathsf{errors}(C)$ *and* $\mathsf{minimize}(C, L_{in}, l_{in}) \rightarrow^* \mathsf{minimize}(C', E, L, l, L')$. *Then:*

$$\forall L_0 \in \mathsf{errors}(C). \ ((L_0 \subseteq L \cup L') \Rightarrow (L' \cup \{l\} \subseteq L_0)) \qquad\square$$

Theorem 5.2 (Correctness of $\mathsf{minimize}$**).** *If* $L \in \mathsf{errors}(C)$, $L \backslash \{l\} \notin \mathsf{errors}(C)$ *and* $\mathsf{minimize}(C, L, l) \rightarrow^* \mathsf{MinError}(L')$, *then* $L' \in \mathsf{minErrors}(C)$ *and* $L' \subseteq L$. $\qquad\square$

The transformation sequence $\mathsf{minimize}(C, L, l) \rightarrow^* \mathsf{MinError}(L')$ requires at most $2n$ calls to the labeled unification algorithm, where n is the size of $\Pi_L(C)$. In the worst case, our labeled unification algorithm takes exponential time in the the size of the constraint set, but linear time unification algorithms exist. Using a linear time unification algorithm, minimization would take quadratic time in the size of $\Pi_L(C)$. We apply the minimization algorithm only to label sets L returned by an initial run of labeled unification. Even for large input programs we expect these label sets, and also $\Pi_L(C)$, to be small.

5.3   Error Enumeration

Enumerating all minimal errors is harder than finding just one. In the worst case, the number of minimal errors is exponential in the size of the constraint set [27]. We use a simple algorithm that quickly finds a number of different errors that are close to minimal. In principle (but not in practice), this algorithm eventually returns the set of all minimal errors. However, we interrupt its execution after a short time. The interrupted algorithm returns an intermediate state that contains a list of candidates. These candidates are errors that are not guaranteed to be minimal yet. However, they are close to minimal and the minimization algorithm can be used to minimize them. Our algorithm has the property that it finds a few minimal errors fast, at the expense of behaving badly in the hypothetical limit case.[4] We do not think that, in practice, it is a great disadvantage that our algorithms only find some, but not all, minimal error slices of a program at once. Many of today's compilers report only a few type errors at a time. Even if they do report many type errors at once, most programmers correct only few of the reported errors before they try to recompile.

The (previously defined) function minErrors satisfies the following equations:

If $\mathsf{unify}(C) \to^* \mathsf{Success}(\cdot)$: $\mathsf{minErrors}(C) = \emptyset$

If $\mathsf{unify}(C) \to^* \mathsf{Error}(L, \cdot)$:
$\quad \mathsf{minErrors}(C) = \mathsf{min}(\, \bigcup \{\, \mathsf{minErrors}(\Pi_{\mathsf{labels}(C) \backslash \{l\}}(C)) \mid l \in L \,\} \cup \{L\} \,)$

A recursive implementation of these equations rediscovers identical errors many times. For instance, if $\mathsf{unify}(C) \to^* \mathsf{Error}(L, \cdot)$ and L' is a minimal error of C that is contained in $(\mathsf{labels}(C) \setminus L)$, then L' gets returned by each one of the recursive calls. Our enumeration algorithm suffers from such recomputations. For that reason, the algorithm is impractical for exhaustively enumerating all minimal errors, even in cases where $\mathsf{minErrors}(C)$ is small.

The algorithm in figure 6 is essentially an iterative version of the above recurrences presented as a set of state transformation rules. Initial states are of the form $\mathsf{enum}(C)$ and final states of the form $\mathsf{MinErrors}(Ls)$, where Ls is a set of pairwise incomparable label sets. Intermediate states are of the form $\mathsf{enum}(C, found, todo)$ where both *found* and *todo* are sets of pairwise incomparable label sets. At each state, the set *found* contains close approximations of some minimal errors of C ("candidate set"). Members of the set *todo* represent work items that still need to be done ("to-do set"). Specifically, for each label set L in the to-do set, the minimal errors that are contained in $(\mathsf{labels}(C) \setminus L)$ still need to be found. We usually interrupt the execution of $\mathsf{enum}(C)$ before it terminates but after it has found at least one error. In this case, the elements of the current *found*-set get minimized and then returned.

---

[4] An example of an algorithm that "behaves well" in the hypothetical limit case, but may often not even find a single minimal error in reality because of time or space limits, is a breadth-first exploration of all possible transformation sequences of labeled unification.

$$\mathsf{enum}(C) \;\to\; \mathsf{enum}(C, \emptyset, \{\emptyset\}); \qquad\qquad \mathsf{enum}(C, found, \emptyset) \;\to\; \mathsf{MinErrors}(found)$$

$$\frac{\mathsf{unify}(\Pi_{\mathsf{labels}(C)\setminus L}(C)) \;\to^*\; \mathsf{Success}(\cdot)}{\mathsf{enum}(C, found, \{L\} \uplus todo) \;\to\; \mathsf{enum}(C, found, todo)}$$

$$\frac{\mathsf{unify}(\Pi_{\mathsf{labels}(C)\setminus L}(C)) \;\to^*\; \mathsf{Error}(L', \cdot); \quad \mathsf{insertError}(L', found) \;=\; found_1;}{\mathsf{insertTodos}(\mathsf{distribute}(L', L), todo) \;=\; todo_1}{\mathsf{enum}(C, found, \{L\} \uplus todo) \;\to\; \mathsf{enum}(C, found_1, todo_1)}$$

$$\mathsf{insertError}(L, found) \;\overset{\mathrm{def}}{=\!=\!=}\; \begin{cases} found, & \text{if } (\exists L' \in found)(L' \subseteq L) \\ \{\, L' \in found \mid L \nsubseteq L' \,\} \cup \{L\}, & \text{otherwise} \end{cases}$$

$$\mathsf{insertTodos}(Ls, todo) \;\overset{\mathrm{def}}{=\!=\!=}\; todo \,\cup\, \{\, L \in Ls \mid (\forall L' \in todo)(L' \nsubseteq L) \,\}$$

$$\mathsf{distribute}(L', L) \;\overset{\mathrm{def}}{=\!=\!=}\; \{\, \{l'\} \cup L \mid l' \in L' \,\}$$

Fig. 6. A non-deterministic minimal error slice enumeration algorithm

Proposition 5.4 (Termination of enum). *Each state transformation sequence terminates. A state is irreducible iff it is a final state.* □

Theorem 5.3 (Correctness of enum). *If* $\mathsf{enum}(C) \to^* \mathsf{MinErrors}(Ls)$, *then* $Ls = \mathsf{minErrors}(C)$. □

6   Slicing the Program

Figure 7 defines the abstract syntax class of *slices*. The grammar extends the labeled expression grammar by the additional phrase

$$sl \quad ::= \; \ldots \quad | \quad \mathbf{dots}(sl_1, \ldots, sl_k) \quad | \quad \ldots$$

A **dots**-node in a slice's abstract syntax tree represents an irrelevant segment of the corresponding program's abstract syntax tree. Our experimental implementation displays $\mathbf{dots}(sl_1, sl_2, sl_3)$ as:

$$(.. \; sl_1 \; .. \; sl_2 \; .. \; sl_3 \; ..)$$

For instance, the type error slice

$$\mathtt{fn}\; \mathtt{x}^{l_1} \; \texttt{=>}\; \mathbf{dots}(\; (\mathtt{x}^{l_2}\; \mathbf{dots}())^{l_3}, \; (\mathtt{x}^{l_4} + \mathbf{dots}())^{l_5}\;)$$

computed for the erroneous program from example 4.1 is displayed as:

$$\mathtt{fn}\; \mathtt{x}\; \texttt{=>}\; (.. \; \mathtt{x}\; (..) \; .. \; \mathtt{x} + (..) \; ..)$$

Figure 7 defines additional typing rules for slices. A slice of the form $\mathbf{dots}(sl_1, \ldots, sl_k)$ is well-typed iff sl_1 through sl_k are. In this case, it has all types. The typing rules for other phrases are omitted, because they are the same as for expressions (see figure 2). Figure 7 also extends algorithm T. We need this extension, in order to formulate a statement that relates erroneous programs to

$$k \in \{0, 1, 2, \ldots\}$$
$$vsl \in \mathsf{VarSlice} \quad ::= \quad x^l \mid \mathtt{dots}()$$
$$sl \in \mathsf{Slice} \quad ::= \quad x^l \mid n^l \mid (sl + sl)^l \mid (\mathtt{fn}\ vsl\ \mathtt{=>}\ sl)^l \mid$$
$$(sl\ sl)^l \mid (\mathtt{let\ val}\ vsl\ \mathtt{=}\ sl\ \mathtt{in}\ sl\ \mathtt{end})^l \mid \mathtt{dots}(sl_1, \ldots, sl_k)$$

Typing rules

$$(\forall i \in \{1, \ldots, k\}.\ \Gamma \vdash sl_i : ty_i) \quad \Rightarrow \quad (\Gamma \ \vdash\ \mathtt{dots}(sl_1, \ldots, sl_k)\ :\ ty)$$
$$(\Gamma \vdash sl : ty') \quad \Rightarrow \quad (\Gamma \ \vdash\ (\mathtt{fn\ dots}()\ \mathtt{=>}\ sl)^l\ :\ ty\ \mathtt{->}\ ty')$$
$$(\Gamma \vdash sl' : ty')\ \text{and}\ (\Gamma \vdash sl : ty) \quad \Rightarrow \quad (\Gamma \ \vdash\ (\mathtt{let\ val\ dots}()\ \mathtt{=}\ sl'\ \mathtt{in}\ sl\ \mathtt{end})^l\ :\ ty)$$

Algorithm T

$$\frac{sl_i \Downarrow \langle \Gamma_i, ty_i, C_i \rangle \quad \text{for } i \text{ in } \{1, \ldots, k\}; \qquad a \text{ fresh}}{\mathtt{dots}(sl_1, \ldots, sl_k) \Downarrow \langle\ \Gamma_1 \wedge \ldots \wedge \Gamma_k,\ a,\ C_1 \cup \ldots \cup C_k\ \rangle}$$

$$\frac{sl \Downarrow \langle \Gamma, ty, C \rangle; \qquad a, a' \text{ fresh}}{(\mathtt{fn\ dots}()\ \mathtt{=>}\ sl)^l \Downarrow \langle \Gamma,\ a,\ \{a'\ \mathtt{->}\ ty \overset{l}{=} a\} \cup C\ \rangle}$$

$$\frac{sl_1 \Downarrow \langle \Gamma_1, ty_1, C_1 \rangle; \qquad sl_2 \Downarrow \langle \Gamma_2, ty_2, C_2 \rangle; \qquad a \text{ fresh}}{(\mathtt{let\ val\ dots}()\ \mathtt{=}\ sl_1\ \mathtt{in}\ sl_2\ \mathtt{end})^l \Downarrow \langle\ \Gamma_1 \wedge \Gamma_2,\ a,\ \{a \overset{l}{=} ty_2\} \cup C_1 \cup C_2\ \rangle}$$

Fig. 7. Additional rules for slices

their type error slices. The rule for dots-phrases does not generate any additional constraints. It merely propagates recursively computed results. The rules for other phrases are omitted, because they are exactly as in figure 3.

Figure 8 defines the function slice which takes a label set L and a labeled expression $lexp$ and returns a slice. This function replaces each node of $lexp$'s syntax tree by dots, if its node label is not in L. It also flattens nested dots. As a result of flattening, $\mathsf{slice}(L, lexp)$ does not have immediately nested dots.

Theorem 6.1 (Faithfulness). *If* $(lexp \Downarrow \langle \cdot, \cdot, C \rangle)$, $L \in \mathsf{errors}(C)$ *and* $(\mathsf{slice}(L, lexp) \Downarrow \langle \cdot, \cdot, C' \rangle)$, *then* $L \in \mathsf{errors}(C')$. $\qquad \square$

Let $\sqsubset$ be the least contextually closed and transitive relation on slices satisfying the following:

$$\mathtt{dots}() \sqsubset x^l; \qquad\qquad \mathtt{dots}(sl) \sqsubset (\mathtt{fn\ dots}()\ \mathtt{=>}\ sl)^l$$
$$\mathtt{dots}() \sqsubset n^l; \qquad\qquad \mathtt{dots}(sl_1, sl_2) \sqsubset (sl_1\ sl_2)^l$$
$$\mathtt{dots}(sl_1, sl_2) \sqsubset sl_1 + sl_2^l; \quad \mathtt{dots}(sl_1, sl_2) \sqsubset (\mathtt{let\ val\ dots}()\ \mathtt{=}\ sl_1\ \mathtt{in}\ sl_2\ \mathtt{end})^l$$
$$\left.\begin{matrix}(sl = \mathtt{dots}(sl_1, \ldots, sl_i, \ldots, sl_n)) \\ \text{and } (sl_i = \mathtt{dots}(sl'_1, \ldots, sl'_k))\end{matrix}\right\} \Rightarrow \left\{\begin{matrix}sl \sqsubset \mathtt{dots}(sl_1, \ldots, sl_{i-1}, \\ sl'_1, \ldots, sl'_k, sl_{i+1}, \ldots, sl_n)\end{matrix}\right.$$

Theorem 6.2 (Accuracy). *If* $(lexp \Downarrow \langle \cdot, \cdot, C \rangle)$, $L \in \mathsf{minErrors}(C)$ *and* $sl \sqsubset \mathsf{slice}(L, lexp)$, *then* sl *is well-typed.* $\qquad \square$

$$\frac{lexp \downarrow^L sl}{\text{slice}(L, lexp) = sl} \qquad \frac{l \in L}{x^l \downarrow^L x^l} \qquad \frac{l \notin L}{x^l \downarrow^L \text{dots}()} \qquad \frac{l \in L}{n^l \downarrow^L n^l} \qquad \frac{l \notin L}{n^l \downarrow^L \text{dots}()}$$

$$\frac{lexp_1 \downarrow^L sl_1; \quad lexp_2 \downarrow^L sl_2; \quad l \in L}{(lexp_1 + lexp_2)^l \downarrow^L (sl_1 + sl_2)^l} \qquad \frac{lexp_1 \downarrow^L sl_1; \quad lexp_2 \downarrow^L sl_2; \quad l \notin L}{(lexp_1 + lexp_2)^l \downarrow^L \text{merge}(\langle sl_1, sl_2 \rangle)}$$

$$\frac{x^{l_1} \downarrow^L vsl; \quad lexp \downarrow^L sl; \quad l_1 \in L \text{ or } l_2 \in L}{(\text{fn } x^{l_1} \Rightarrow lexp)^{l_2} \downarrow^L (\text{fn } vsl \Rightarrow sl)^{l_2}} \qquad \frac{lexp \downarrow^L sl; \quad l_1 \notin L \text{ and } l_2 \notin L}{(\text{fn } x^{l_1} \Rightarrow lexp)^{l_2} \downarrow^L \text{merge}(\langle sl \rangle)}$$

$$\frac{lexp_1 \downarrow^L sl_1; \quad lexp_2 \downarrow^L sl_2; \quad l \in L}{(lexp_1\ lexp_2)^l \downarrow^L (sl_1\ sl_2)^l L_2} \qquad \frac{lexp_1 \downarrow^L sl_1; \quad lexp_2 \downarrow^L sl_2; \quad l \notin L}{(lexp_1\ lexp_2)^l \downarrow^L \text{merge}(\langle sl_1, sl_2 \rangle)}$$

$$\frac{x^{l_1} \downarrow^L vsl; \quad lexp_1 \downarrow^L sl_1; \quad lexp_2 \downarrow^L sl_2; \quad l_1 \in L \text{ or } l_2 \in L}{(\text{let val } x^{l_1} = lexp_1 \text{ in } lexp_2 \text{ end})^{l_2} \downarrow^L (\text{let val } vsl = sl_1 \text{ in } sl_2 \text{ end})^{l_2}}$$

$$\frac{lexp_1 \downarrow^L sl_1; \quad lexp_2 \downarrow^L sl_2; \quad l_1 \notin L \text{ and } l_2 \notin L}{(\text{let val } x^{l_1} = lexp_1 \text{ in } lexp_2 \text{ end})^{l_2} \downarrow^L \text{merge}(\langle sl_1, sl_2 \rangle)}$$

. . . .

$$\frac{}{\text{merge}(\langle\rangle) = \text{dots}()} \qquad \frac{\text{merge}(sls) = \text{dots}(sl_1, \ldots, sl_n); \quad sl \neq \text{dots}(\cdot)}{\text{merge}(sl :: sls) = \text{dots}(sl, sl_1, \ldots, sl_n)}$$

$$\frac{\text{merge}(sls) = \text{dots}(sl'_1, \ldots, sl'_k)}{\text{merge}(\text{dots}(sl_1, \ldots, sl_n) :: sls) = \text{dots}(sl_1, \ldots, sl_n, sl'_1, \ldots, sl'_k)}$$

Fig. 8. Slicing

7 Conclusion

We have presented algorithms for type error slicing in an implicitly typed λ-calculus with let-polymorphism. These algorithms first generate type equality constraints using a version of Damas's type inference algorithm T, and then find minimal unsolvable subsets of the set of generated constraints. Type error slices are programs where irrelevant program points are masked.

In the future, we want to extend our implementation of type error slicing to full SML and improve its user interface. The user interface will both highlight program points in the source code and display separate type error slices. The separate slices will be especially useful, if relevant program points are far apart, possibly in multiple files. Hyperlinks will relate program points in the separate slice to the corresponding points in the source. The extension to full SML will require the treatment of additional issues. For instance, the presence of equality types and overloaded built-in operations requires an additional sort of constraints: kind constraints for type variables. Another important issue are explicit type and signature annotations. These will put natural boundaries on type error slices. For instance, if library modules are always annotated with explicit signatures, then type error slices for programs that use the library will never contain parts of the library implementation.

References

[1] M. Beaven, R. Stansifer. Explaining type errors in polymorphic languages. *ACM Letters on Programming Languages and Systems*, 2, 1993.

[2] K. L. Bernstein, E. W. Stark. Debugging type errors (full version). Technical report, State University of New York, Stony Brook, 1995.

[3] O. Chitil. Compositional explanation of types and algorithmic debugging of type errors. In *Proc. 6th Int'l Conf. Functional Programming*. ACM Press, 2001.

[4] V. Chopella. *Unification source-tracking with application to diagnosis of type inference*. PhD thesis, Indiana University, 2002.

[5] V. Chopella, C. T. Haynes. Diagnosis of ill-typed programs. Technical Report 426, Indiana University, 1995.

[6] L. Damas, R. Milner. Principal type schemes for functional programs. In *Conf. Rec. 9th Ann. ACM Symp. Princ. of Prog. Langs.*, 1982.

[7] L. M. M. Damas. *Type assignment in Programming Languages*. PhD thesis, University of Edinburgh, Edinburgh, Scotland, 1985.

[8] T. B. Dinesh, F. Tip. A slicing-based approach for locating type errors. In *Proceedings of the USENIX conference on Domain-Specific Languages*, Santa Barbara, California, 1997.

[9] D. Duggan, F. Bent. Explaining type inference. *Sci. Comput. Programming*, 27, 1996.

[10] C. Flanagan, M. Flatt, S. Krishnamurthi, S. Weirich, M. Felleisen. Catching bugs in the web of program invariants. In *Proc. ACM SIGPLAN '96 Conf. Prog. Lang. Design & Impl.*, 1996.

[11] B. Heeren, J. Hage. Parametric type inferencing for helium. Technical Report UU-CS-2002-035, University Utrecht, 2002.

[12] B. Heeren, J. Hage, D. Swierstra. Generalizing Hindley-Milner type inference algorithms. Technical Report UU-CS-2002-031, University Utrecht, 2002.

[13] B. Heeren, J. Jeuring, D. Swierstra, P. A. Alcocer. Improving type-error messages in functional languages. Technical Report UU-CS-2002-009, University Utrecht, 2002.

[14] T. Jim. What are principal typings and what are they good for? In POPL '96 [22].

[15] G. F. Johnson, J. A. Walz. A maximum flow approach to anomaly isolation in unification-based incremental type inference. In POPL '96 [22].

[16] P. Kanellakis, H. Mairson, J. C. Mitchell. Unification and ML type reconstruction. In J.-L. Lassez, G. Plotkin, eds., *Computational Logic: Essays in Honor of Alan Robinson*. MIT Press, 1991.

[17] A. J. Kfoury, J. Tiuryn, P. Urzyczyn. An analysis of ML typability. *J. ACM*, 41(2), 1994.

[18] O. Lee, K. Yi. Proofs about a folklore let-polymorphic type inference algorithm. *ACM Trans. on Prog. Langs. & Systs.*, 20(4), 1998.

[19] B. J. McAdam. On the unification of substitutions in type inference. In K. Hammond, A. J. T. Davie, C. Clack, eds., *Implementation of Functional Languages (IFL'98)*, vol. 1595 of *LNCS*, London, UK, 1998. Springer-Verlag.

[20] B. J. McAdam. Generalising techniques for type debugging. In Trinder et al. [25].

[21] R. Milner, M. Tofte, R. Harper, D. B. MacQueen. *The Definition of Standard ML (Revised)*. MIT Press, 1997.

[22] *Conf. Rec. POPL '96: 23rd ACM Symp. Princ. of Prog. Langs.*, 1996.

[23] G. S. Port. A simple approach to finding the cause of non-unifiability. In *Proc. Fifth International Conference on Logic Programming*. MIT Press, 1988.

[24] Z. Shao, A. Appel. Smartest recompilation. In *Conf. Rec. 20th Ann. ACM Symp. Princ. of Prog. Langs.*, 1993.

[25] P. Trinder, G. Michaelson, H.-W. Loidl, eds. *Trends in Func. Programming*. Intellect, 2000.

[26] M. Wand. Finding the source of type errors. In *Conf. Rec. 13th Ann. ACM Symp. Princ. of Prog. Langs.*, 1986.

[27] D. A. Wolfram. Intractable unifiability problems and backtracking. In *Proc. Third International Conference on Logic Programming*, vol. 225 of *LNCS*, 1986.

[28] J. YANG. Explaining type errors by finding the source of a type conflict. In Trinder et al. [25].

[29] J. YANG, G. Michaelson, P. Trinder. Explaining polymorphic types. *Computer Journal*, 200X. to appear.

[30] J. YANG, G. Michaelson, P. Trinder, J. B. Wells. Improved type error reporting. In *[Draft] Proc. 12th Int'l Workshop Implementation Functional Languages*, Aachen, Germany, 2000.

Core Formal Molecular Biology

Vincent Danos[1][*] and Cosimo Laneve[2]

[1] Équipe PPS, University Paris 7& CNRS
[2] Department of Computer Science, University of Bologna

Abstract. A core modeling language for Molecular Biology is introduced, where two simple forms of interaction are considered, *complexation* and *activation*. This core language is equipped with two sensible bisimulation-based equivalences, and it is shown that interactions involving complex reactants are superfluous up to these notions. Strong compilations in π-calculus are given, following Regev's principle of translating physical connection as private name sharing.

1   Introduction

The potential interest of formal models in molecular biology has been recognized for some time in the community of bioinformatics. Post-genomic biology is producing ever bigger networks of reactions at the molecular level. Soon, exhaustive descriptions of entire simple living organisms will be obtained, down to the minutest molecular cogs and rods. Any assistance in investigating and understanding these is welcome.

The sorts of computational models best suited for this task remain unclear. Cases, sometimes very convincing, have been made for the use of various analytic frameworks, from boolean analysis of ordinary differential equations [18] to model-checking of hybrid systems [8].

We take here a different stance by constructing a calculus *specifically designed for the task* of representing and studying biological networks at the molecular level. While it might sound strange to the ears of a computer scientist that no such calculus was given before, one has to understand that it is quite a surprise for a biologist that there is one at all! It's a long way from one's first readings in molecular biology to the realization that, at the appropriate level of description, it all relies on very few principles of interaction: complexation, activation, synthesis and degradation.

The first contribution of this paper is therefore to provide such a calculus. Of course, there is no such calculus without a demonstration of biological expressivity. One has to make sure the formalism is enough to model a significant part of molecular biology. We propose a few examples in the text, merely to illustrate the syntax. Our calculus was tested against Kohn's compilation of the vast network of molecular reactions controlling the cell cycle [10,11]. A system of about

---

[*] This research was partly funded by the INRIA ARC CPBIO project.

P. Degano (Ed.): ESOP 2003, LNCS 2618, pp. 302–318, 2003.

300 reactions —after correcting some notational ambiguities— and representing the 'logical' part of the system was obtained in [2].

With the formalism in place we may take a step beyond pure representational problems. The second contribution of this paper is to construct an encoding showing that *complex reactants are useless* in a suitable mathematical sense. Interestingly, this theorem can be construed as raising a biological question. Any such interpretation will, of course, depend on the extent to which our formal biology is biological and not only formal! But this could be said of any model, and one of the interests of building a calculus at all, as opposed to a mere model, is to have a formal counterpart to the phenomenon that can be exposed to precise criticism.

The third contribution is to provide *compilations of our formalism into π-calculus*. These compilations were used to provide guidance in defining reactions in the calculus and could be useful to enrich the model as well. Regev, with her coauthors, outlined in a series of papers [16,14,15] an alarmingly convincing dictionary between elementary biological events: binding, activation, transcriptional regulation, etc and π-calculus constructions. We were particularly keen here on giving compilations respecting *Regev's principle* of representing physical connectivity, a primitive notion in our formalism, as private name sharing. For want of a formal language to describe what was to be represented, Regev's dictionary had to stay informal and could really be understood only by following examples. Encoding of a particular portion of biological knowledge was not straightforward, could be done in many ways and would generally result in a biologically illegible code. Our language and compilations provide a layer of abstraction obviating this.

There is scope for extending the formalism. It is easy to add synthesis (transcription factors included) and degradation reactions. Decomplexation rules can be added too, but with a purely qualitative non-deterministic semantics, such as the one we have in this paper, this is probably not going to make any difference. On the other hand, if one equips solutions with the structure of a Markovian process following [14], decomplexations will make a difference. We still have to develop more theory to understand whether complex reactants are reducible to simple ones in such a quantitative framework.

Then comes the pressing question of whether model-checking methods would let us query the dynamics of our systems. What kind of biologically relevant questions can one crank out of a CTL or mu-calculus approach [3,4,9], or other symbolic toolsets as advocated in [6], when applied to some model of formal reactions ? Queries one can think of, for the time being, would be reachability, and reachability under constraints. Constraints are particularly interesting here because they might allow the model to represent higher-level knowledge for which no efficient molecular mechanism is known or even conjectured, a sort of epistemological cheat code. Another pressing question is to develop a notion of pseudo-metrics on such probabilistic (or differential, see below) systems, which would give a reasonable formal counterpart to the evasive concept of homology for biological processes. Finally, another breed of operational semantics can be imposed on the same calculus, namely continuous-time dynamics based on classical systems of multilinear differential equations (as explained for instance in [17]). One ought to understand when and how the stochastic and continuous-time deterministic operational semantics relate. This prompts us to remark that another advantage of having a calculus is to be able to plug in different dynamics calling on different tools and constraints. No matter how modest the contribution presented here, it is a preliminary step.

Related Work. A language, called "Pathway Logic", with quite similar concerns has been recently proposed by Lincoln and collaborators in [6]. Pathway Logic is a rewriting system formalism, where reactants are proteins and reactions are modeled by rewriting rules. As in κ, internal wirings of proteins are not modeled. The implementation of Pathway Logic in the Maude system may give access to useful analytic tools. This implementation is sequential, while our π calculus compilations exhibit at least the concurrency of the original biological systems, and are thus amenable to concurrent implementations.

Another language, the *biocalculus*, has been defined by Nagasaki and his colleagues [13]. The biocalculus is similar to Join [7], and therefore less abstract than the κ calculus —in fact, less intelligible for biologists— and could be used as a target language for compilation, similarly to π (see Section 5).

Acknowledgements. The first author gladly acknowledges numerous discussions about representation problems in systems biology with Marc Chiaverini, Magali Roux-Rouquié, Vincent Schächter, and with all the participants of the INRIA research action CPBIO.

2   The Calculus

Notations. We write $\tilde{x}$ for a (possibly empty) finite sequence $x_1 \cdots x_n$ of names, and $|\tilde{x}|$ for its length. Given a set S, $S^!$ will denote the set of multisets over S. We write $U + V$ for the multiset union, $V \subseteq U$ for the multiset inclusion and $V \subset U$ for the *strict* multiset inclusion; when $V \subseteq U$ we also write simply $U - V$ for the multiset $U \setminus V$. The empty multiset is denoted by $\varnothing$. The cardinality of a multiset U is denoted $|U|$. We use pattern matching to express set containment, *i.e.* $X = Y + \alpha$ means that $\alpha \subseteq X$. Variables X, Y range over multisets.

Sites, Proteins, and Signatures. We assume two countable sets of *sites* $\mathcal{N}$, and *protein names* $\mathcal{A}$ and a *signature* function $\mathfrak{s}(.) : \mathcal{A} \to \mathcal{N}^!$ from protein names to multiset of sites, mapping a protein name to its *static interface*. We ask further that $\mathfrak{s}(.)$ be countably onto, *i.e.* any static interface has an infinite number of associated protein names.

Sites and protein names will be ranged over by symbols such as r, s, t, and A, B, C, respectively. Sites will serve as both internal states and interfaces of the protein, through which the interactions between proteins may occur. We sort them accordingly in two separate infinite types, the *value* type $\mathcal{N}_v$ and the *proper* type $\mathcal{N}_p$.

A *formal protein*, or simply a *protein*, is a triple, written $A(\rho, \sigma)$, with $A \in \mathcal{A}$, and ρ, $\sigma \in \mathcal{N}^!$ such that $\rho + \sigma \subseteq \mathfrak{s}(A)$ and all sites in $\mathfrak{s}(A) - (\rho + \sigma)$ are of the proper type $\mathcal{N}_p$. In a given protein $A(\rho, \sigma)$, a site $r \in \mathfrak{s}(A)$ will be said *free* if $r \in \rho + \sigma$, *hidden* if $r \in \rho$, *visible* if $r \in \sigma$ and *bound* if not free.[1]

Take note that a site might be free and not visible, yet. The intended meaning is that, for instance, $A(\{r, s\}, \{t\})$ can interact at site t, and has also two other unoccupied sites r and s which are momentarily hidden; this could mean biologically that the particular folding A is assuming at the moment makes it impossible for another protein to dock on these sites, although they are *not* involved in any actual binding.

Complexes. Proteins may be composed into *protein complexes*, or simply *complexes* ranged over by C, D, ... and we denote the composition by the "⊙" operator, which is assumed to be associative and commutative (namely, the order of proteins inside the complexes is irrelevant). For instance, the complex

$$A_1(\rho_1, \sigma_1) \odot A_2(\rho_2, \sigma_2) \odot A_3(\rho_3, \sigma_3)$$

represents a compound made of A_1, A_2, and A_3. This notation is equivalent to $A_2(\rho_2, \sigma_2) \odot A_1(\rho_1, \sigma_1) \odot A_3(\rho_3, \sigma_3)$, as well as to any other permutation of A_1, A_2 and A_3.

Biologically, a complex is a bundle of proteins connected together by low energy bounds. Sometimes biologists are able to describe sub-components of the proteins which are instrumental in the binding. These are commonly called *domains*. Depending on the way proteins are folded in space, these domains can be active or not and the behaviour of the protein will be different. Both activations and complexations can modify the folding and therefore the subsequent behaviour. Sites are abstracting over both domains and folding states.

Well-formedness. A complex $A_1(\rho_1, \sigma_1) \odot \cdots \odot A_n(\rho_n, \sigma_n)$ is said to be *well-formed* if the following two conditions hold:

(a) for all $1 \leq i \leq n$, $\rho_i + \sigma_i \subset \mathfrak{s}(A_i)$, or $n = 1$ and $\rho_1 + \sigma_1 \subseteq \mathfrak{s}(A_1)$
(b) $\sum_{1 \leq i \leq n} |\mathfrak{s}(A_i) - (\rho_i + \sigma_i)| = 2m$, *for some* $m \geq n - 1$.

Both conditions work together to make sure that the complex is connected in the sense that there exists a wiring of the proteins participating in the complex, using all bound sites, that turns it into a connected graph. Condition (a) is *local*, and says that each protein must have at least one bound edge (unless $n = 1$), while condition (b) is *global* and says there is a big enough even number of bound edges, to connect the whole. All proteins and complexes will be taken to be well-formed from now on.

Both conditions are obviously necessary and an easy induction proves that they are also sufficient. So even if our complexation operator won't let us see the internal wiring, we still make sure that there is one.

---

[1] To be completely accurate, one should talk about an occurrence of $r \in \mathfrak{s}(A)$ since we're dealing with multisets here.

Examples. Consider the following complexes:

$$A(\{r,s\},\{r,t\}) \odot B(\varnothing,\varnothing) \qquad A(\{s\},\{r,t\})$$
$$A(\{s\},\{r,t\}) \odot B(\{t\},\varnothing) \odot B(\varnothing,\{t\})$$
$$B(\varnothing,\{t\}) \odot B(\varnothing,\{t\}) \odot B(\varnothing,\{t\}) \odot B(\varnothing,\{t\})$$

with $\mathfrak{s}(A) = \{2r,s,t\}$ and $\mathfrak{s}(B) = \{s,t\}$. All are ill-formed. Indeed, the first violates (a) at A, the second and the third violate the parity condition in (b), and the last doesn't have enough bound edges. On the contrary the following complexes are well-formed:

$$A(\{r,s\},\{r,t\}) \qquad A(\{r\},\{r,t\}) \odot B(\{s\},\varnothing) \qquad A(\varnothing,\{t\}) \odot B(\varnothing,\varnothing) \odot B(\varnothing,\{t\})$$

Solutions and Reactions. *Solutions*, ranged over by $\mathsf{S}, \mathsf{S}', \ldots$ are multisets of proteins and complexes. *Reactions* are defined by rewriting rules which have the shape $\mathsf{S} \longrightarrow \mathsf{S}'$. Following the chemical metaphor further, we'll call complexes present in the left hand side of a given rule *reactants*, and complexes present in the right hand side *products* of the rule. To define reactions we use metavariables X, Y, Z which range over multisets of sites. There are two kinds of *basic reactions*:

(ACTIVATION)   (COMPLEXATION)

$$\mathsf{C}_1, \ldots, \mathsf{C}_n \longrightarrow \mathsf{C}'_1, \ldots, \mathsf{C}'_n \qquad\qquad \mathsf{C}_1, \ldots, \mathsf{C}_n \longrightarrow \mathsf{C}'_1 \odot \ldots \odot \mathsf{C}'_n$$

and we ask for the following *conservation principles*, for activations:

$$\text{if } \mathsf{C}_i = \odot_{1 \le j \le k_i} A_{ij}(X_{ij} + \rho_{ij}, Y_{ij} + \sigma_{ij}), \text{ and}$$
$$\mathsf{C}'_i = \odot_{1 \le j \le k_i} A_{ij}(X_{ij} + \rho'_{ij}, Y_{ij} + \sigma'_{ij}),$$
$$\text{then, for every } j, \ \rho_{ij} + \sigma_{ij} = \rho'_{ij} + \sigma'_{ij},$$

and for complexations:

$$\text{if } \mathsf{C}_i = \odot_{1 \le j \le k_i} A_{ij}(X_{ij} + \rho_{ij}, Y_{ij} + \sigma_{ij} + \tau_{ij}), \text{ and}$$
$$\mathsf{C}'_i = \odot_{1 \le j \le k_i} A_{ij}(X_{ij} + \rho'_{ij}, Y_{ij} + \sigma'_{ij}), \text{ and } x_i = \sum_{1 \le j \le k_i} |\tau_{ij}|,$$
$$\text{then, for every } j, \ \rho_{ij} + \sigma_{ij} = \rho'_{ij} + \sigma'_{ij}, \text{ and } x_i > 0, \text{ and}$$
$$\sum_{1 \le i \le n} x_i = 2m \text{ for some } m \ge n - 1.$$

The condition for activation says that free sites may flip their visible/hidden status, but may not be bound by the reaction. The condition for complexation completely mirrors the well-formedness conditions (a) and (b) above and controls that the final product of the complexation rule:

$$\odot_{1 \le i \le n, 1 \le j \le k_i} A_{ij}(X_{ij} + \rho'_{ij}, Y_{ij} + \sigma'_{ij})$$

stays well-formed, knowing that the reactants were already so. We also ask the newly bound sites, namely the τ_{ij}, to be visible in the left hand side.

We could distinguish the case of self-complexation, where $n = 1$ and allow $\tau_1 = \varnothing$ but then self-complexation becomes exactly self-activation, so it doesn't make any difference and it feels better to have two disjoint sets of rules.

A basic reaction will be said *simple* if for all i, $k_i = 1$, that is to say if all the reactants are proteins; otherwise it will be said *complex*.

(CTX-ACT)

$$\frac{C_1, \ldots, C_n \ \longrightarrow \ C'_1, \ldots, C'_n}{D_1 \odot C_{i_1} \cdots C_{i_{j_1}}, \ldots, D_m \odot C_{i_m} \cdots C_{i_{j_m}} \ \longrightarrow \ D_1 \odot C'_{i_1} \cdots C'_{i_{j_1}}, \ldots, D_m \odot C'_{i_m} \cdots C'_{i_{j_m}}}$$

(CTX-CMP)

$$\frac{C_1, \ldots, C_n \ \longrightarrow \ C'_1 \odot \cdots \odot C'_n}{D_1 \odot C_{i_1} \cdots C_{i_{j_1}}, \ldots, D_m \odot C_{i_m} \cdots C_{i_{j_m}} \ \longrightarrow \ D_1 \odot C'_{i_1} \cdots C'_{i_{j_1}} \odot \cdots \odot D_m \odot C'_{i_m} \cdots C'_{i_{j_m}}}$$

Fig. 1. Contextual Reactions

Contextual Reactions. Basic transitions are made to act on generic solutions by means of suitable contextual rules. We need two such rules, (CTX-ACT) and (CTX-CMP), to define the action of a basic rule when the reactants are themselves embedded in super-complexes $D_1, \ldots, D_m$. In this sense these rules are allowing 'contextual reactions' where the context is precisely the multiset $D_1, \ldots, D_m$ of super-complexes hosting the reactants of the basic rules. The rules are given in Fig. 1, where $\{i_1, \ldots, i_{j_1}\}, \ldots, \{i_m, \ldots, i_{j_m}\}$ stands for any partition of $\{1, \ldots, n\}$. Take note that when one uses a partition which is not discrete, that is when $m < n$, then super-complexes hold more than one reactants. For instance, from the basic $C_1, C_2 \longrightarrow C'_1, C'_2$ one can derive $C_1 \cdot C_2 \longrightarrow C'_1 \cdot C'_2$. This is going to be crucial in the sequel. It also shows that our rules are not standard multiset rewriting rules; they're actually mixing two levels of multisets, the solution level associated to the operator "," and the complex level associated to the other operator "$\odot$".

Contextual reactions are readily seen to preserve well-formedness.

Systems. To complete the construction of our κ-calculus, we define a κ-*system* $\mathfrak{S}$ to be a pair $\langle S, R \rangle$ where S is a solution and R is a finite set of basic reactions. And we define also a transition relation over such κ-systems by $\langle (S_1, S), R \rangle \longrightarrow \langle (S_2, S), R \rangle$, if $S_1 \longrightarrow S_2$ according to some reaction, basic or contextual, that can be derived from R.

Most of the time, we will write $S \longrightarrow_R S'$ instead of $\langle S, R \rangle \longrightarrow \langle S', R \rangle$, or even better $S \longrightarrow S'$, when it's clear from the context which R is meant. We also write $\longrightarrow^*_R$ for the reflexive transitive closure of $\longrightarrow_R$.

Core κ-calculus. An interesting fragment of κ, the core κ-*calculus*, is obtained by restricting to simple systems, *i.e.* systems with no complex reactants in their basic rules. The simplest reaction which is not in the core calculus is:

$$A(\varnothing, \{r_1, r_2\}), B_1(\varnothing, \{r'_1\}) \cdot B_2(\varnothing, \{r'_2\}) \ \longrightarrow \ A(\varnothing, \varnothing) \cdot B_1(\varnothing, \varnothing) \cdot B_2(\varnothing, \varnothing).$$

We'll see in section 4 that, despite what seems a strong restriction, the core calculus is expressive enough to encode κ; but before, we're going to have a few examples and comments.

3   Discussion

Activation. The reader might ask how activation is implemented biologically. It could be a phosphorylation (or the converse reaction of dephosphorylation), a reaction whereby a protein is given (or taken) a phosphate group. Some change of conformation might then occur in the structure possibly revealing formerly hidden sites and hiding formerly visible ones:

(BIO-ACTIVATION)
$$A(X + \rho, Y + \sigma), B(X', Y') \longrightarrow A(X + \rho', Y + \sigma'), B(X', Y')$$

usually B is called a kinase (or the converse a phosphatase). Our activations are more general, but there doesn't seem to be any theoretical reward in restricting activations to have a closer fit.

Wiring doesn't matter? By hiding the complexes internal wirings, we seem to be assuming that the potential interactions of a given complex are not depending on the underlying graph, which happens to have been used to construct the complex. This is not true however. In case connections of a complex are making a difference regarding interaction, one may account for these differences using some sites as internal states. That said, dealing with explicit graphs and graph-rewriting reactions is an interesting option which we investigated in [5].

To illustrate further choices built in the formalism, we go now through a few small molecular stories (all true, although as usual the names have been changed).

Commuting and Competing behaviours. Suppose B is able to bind A, revealing a site r in A, and, independently, to bind C, then we write:

$$\mathfrak{r}_1 = A(X + r, Y + s), B(X', Y' + s') \longrightarrow A(X, Y + r) \odot B(X', Y')$$
$$\mathfrak{r}_2 = B(X, Y + t), C(X', Y' + t') \longrightarrow B(X, Y) \odot C(X', Y')$$

From an initial solution $\mathsf{S} = A(\{r\}, \{s\}), B(\varnothing, \{s', t\}), C(\varnothing, \{t'\})$ one gets two paths to the same final solution:

$$\mathsf{S} \longrightarrow A(\varnothing, \{r\}) \odot B(\varnothing, \{t\}), C(\varnothing, \{t'\}) \text{ by } \mathfrak{r}_1$$
$$\longrightarrow A(\varnothing, \{r\}) \odot B(\varnothing, \varnothing) \odot C(\varnothing, \varnothing) \quad \text{by } \mathfrak{r}_2 \text{ and (CTX-CMP)}$$

$$\mathsf{S} \longrightarrow A(\{r\}, \{s\}), B(\varnothing, \{s'\}) \odot C(\varnothing, \varnothing) \text{ by } \mathfrak{r}_2$$
$$\longrightarrow A(\varnothing, \{r\}) \odot B(\varnothing, \varnothing) \odot C(\varnothing, \varnothing) \quad \text{by } \mathfrak{r}_1 \text{ and (CTX-CMP)}$$

If, on the contrary, bindings to B are competing for the same binding site s' in B, we modify our second basic rule:

$$\mathfrak{r}_2' = B(X, Y + s'), C(X', Y' + t') \longrightarrow B(X, Y) \odot C(X', Y')$$

and starting from the same S, we get a 'deadlocked' solution:

$$\mathsf{S} \longrightarrow A(\varnothing, \{r\}) \cdot B(\varnothing, \{t\}), C(\varnothing, \{t'\})$$

because B has spent s' by binding with A. So both commuting and competing behaviours are expressible. In the latter case, when $A \odot B$, $A \odot C$ both exist, but $A \odot B \odot C$ doesn't, other mechanisms can be invoked and expressed. Instead of having A and C competing for the same docking site on B, A could be obstructing the site targeted by C, by moving that site into the hidden part of B's interface.

Synchronizing behaviours. So far, only simple reactants were used, but the real interest of complex formation is that some further event can be conditioned on two sites to be present on the same complex. For instance, some C' could bind only to A and B at the same time, and it easy to add a complex rule:

$$\mathfrak{r} = A(X, Y + r) \cdot B(X', Y' + t), C'(X'', Y'' + \{r', t'\})$$
$$\longrightarrow A(X, Y) \cdot B(X', Y') \cdot C'(X'', Y'')$$

and get:

$$A(\{r\}, \{s\}), B(\varnothing, \{s', t\}), C'(\varnothing, \{r', t'\}) \xrightarrow{\mathfrak{r}_1} A(\varnothing, \{r\}) \odot B(\varnothing, \{t\}), C'(\varnothing, \{r', t'\})$$
$$\xrightarrow{\mathfrak{r}} A(\varnothing, \varnothing) \odot B(\varnothing, \varnothing) \odot C(\varnothing, \varnothing)$$

So we can express competition, commutation and even some form of synchronization, and it seems natural to bring process algebra concepts in the picture.

4   Core κ-Calculus Is Enough

We've just said, in the example above, that complexes were useful. One may wonder whether they really are, formally speaking. In the following we show the existence of a non-uniform encoding $[\![\cdot]\!]$ of a complex biological system into a simple one. The encoding is non-uniform, namely $[\![S, S']\!] \neq [\![S]\!], [\![S']\!]$, because it depends on the initial solution. We suspect that uniform encodings of complex systems might not always exist.

To begin with, we introduce an extensional semantics, called *barbed bisimulation* [12], which equates systems if their transitions match and they are indistinguishable under global observations. The key of barbed bisimulation is the notion of observation. We provide two such notions, which define two different, uncomparable bisimulations.

Let a, b, c, $\cdots$ be a countable set of names—the *observations*—, and f be an injective mapping from protein names $\mathcal{A}$ to names. Let's remind that sites $\mathcal{N}$ are partitioned into *proper* sites $\mathcal{N}_p$ and value sites $\mathcal{N}_v$.

Definition 1. *The* complex barb $\downarrow_c$ *is the least relation satisfying the rules below.*

$$A(\rho, \sigma) \downarrow_c a \qquad\qquad \text{if } f(A) = a$$
$$A_1 \cdots A_n \downarrow_c a_1 \cdots a_n \qquad \text{if } f(A_i) = a_i \text{ for every } i$$
$$\mathsf{S}, \mathsf{S}' \downarrow_c \tilde{a} \qquad\qquad \text{if } \mathsf{S} \downarrow_c \tilde{a} \text{ or } \mathsf{S}' \downarrow_c \tilde{a}$$

The simple barb $\downarrow_s$ *is the least relation satisfying the rules below.*

$$A(\rho, \sigma) \downarrow_s a \qquad\qquad \text{if } \sigma \setminus \mathcal{N}_v \neq \varnothing \text{ and } f(A) = a$$
$$A_1 \cdots A_n \downarrow_s a \qquad\qquad \text{if there is an } i \text{ such that } A_i \downarrow_s a$$
$$S, S' \downarrow_s a \qquad\qquad \text{if } S \downarrow_s a \text{ or } S' \downarrow_s a$$

We write $S \Downarrow_c \tilde{a}$ *if* $S \longrightarrow^* T$ *and* $T \downarrow_c \tilde{a}$, *and* $S \Downarrow_s a$ *if* $S \longrightarrow^* T$ *and* $T \downarrow_s a$.

Definition 2. *A (weak) barbed bisimulation is a symmetric binary relation* $\mathcal{R}$ *on* κ-*systems such that if* $\langle S, R \rangle \; \mathcal{R} \; \langle S', R' \rangle$ *then:*

1. *If* $S \longrightarrow_R T$ *then, for some* T', $S' \longrightarrow_{R'}^* T'$ *and* $\langle T, R \rangle \; \mathcal{R} \; \langle T', R' \rangle$.
2. *If* $S \downarrow a$, *then* $S' \Downarrow a$.

Depending on whether $\downarrow$ *and* $\Downarrow$ *are* $\downarrow_c$, $\Downarrow_c$, *or* $\downarrow_s$, $\Downarrow_s$, *two* κ-*systems* $\mathfrak{S}$ *and* $\mathfrak{T}$ *will be said* complex (resp. simple) barbed bisimilar, *written* $\mathfrak{S} \approx_c \mathfrak{T}$ *(resp.* $\mathfrak{S} \approx_s \mathfrak{T}$*), if there exists a barbed bisimulation relating* $\mathfrak{S}$ *and* $\mathfrak{T}$.

We are ready to state our reducibility theorem:

Theorem 1. *Every* κ-*system is barbed bisimilar—both complex and simple—to a core* κ-*system.*

We explain the idea informally. Reactions with a complex reactant, say C, have to check whether each participant of C is present in a same supercomplex, and each with the appropriate internal state that would trigger the reaction. We have to achieve this synchronisation effect with 'bare hands' if complex reactants are forbidden. The gist of the proof is to use sites of value type to make elementary components 'aware' of the states of the partners they are in physical contact with, at any given moment. Both bisimulations will be blind to such manoeuvring since none is observing internal states—the value sites $\mathcal{N}_v$—and activation rules will provide the means to keep this local information consistent.

5   Compilations into Asynchronous π-Calculus

In this section we detail the compilation of core κ into asynchronous π-calculus [1]. We'll introduce an intermediate equivalent calculus κ_b with *explicit wirings*, that makes it easier to pin down the formal relationship with π-calculus.

We begin with a brief introduction to asynchronous π-calculus, then we introduce κ_b and prove it is equivalent to core κ, and from there we proceed to the compilations of κ_b into asynchronous π-calculus. We present two such compilations: the first fits with the standard pattern of encoding of chemical machines in process calculi, as in Join-calculus [7]; the second one follows Regev's idea that protein behaviours are described within the proteins [16].

5.1   The Asynchronous π-Calculus

The asynchronous π-calculus relies on three countable sets: 1) names, ranged over by a, b, c, x, y, z, ... 2) agent names, ranged over by A, B, ... and 3) variables X, Y, Z, ...; we use u, v to range over values, which may be names, natural numbers, tuples, written $\widetilde{u}$, or finite sets of names. Variables, which include names, represent formal parameters. Even if no explicit type system is given, our programs will be typable. Two syntactic categories are defined, *processes* written P and *boolean expressions* written M:

$$P \stackrel{def}{=} \mathbf{0} \mid \overline{x}\,\langle \widetilde{u} \rangle \mid \sum_{i \in I} x_i\,(\widetilde{Z_i}).P_i \mid P \mid P \mid (x)P \mid M\,P\,;\,P \mid \mathtt{A}(\widetilde{u})$$
$$M \stackrel{def}{=} [u = v] \mid [u \subseteq v] \mid MM$$

We see that a process P can be the inert process $\mathbf{0}$; a message $\overline{x}\,\langle \widetilde{u} \rangle$; a nondeterministic input $\sum_{i \in I} x_i\,(\widetilde{Z_i}).P_i$, where we assume I finite; a parallel composition of processes; a restricted process of the form $(x)P$ where (x) is the 'new' operator that limits the scope of x to P; a conditional $M\,P\,;\,Q$; or a defined agent $\mathtt{A}(\widetilde{u})$, and we ask for a unique defining equation $\mathtt{A}(\widetilde{X}) \stackrel{def}{=} P$ for each agent identifier.

Both restriction and input are binders: $(x)P$ binds name x in P and $x\,(\widetilde{Z}).P$ binds the variables $\widetilde{Z}$ in P. Names of P which are not bound are called *free* and we write $\mathrm{fn}(P)$ for the set of such names.

The conditional $M\,P\,;\,Q$ evaluates to P or Q depending on whether M is true or not. In our programs, M will be either $[u = v]$ or $[u \subseteq v]$ or sequences of such tests. We assume the existence of an evaluation function for terms in M which gives booleans, which we leave unspecified. Table 1 collects the semantics of π-calculus: there are three basic reductions which are then lifted to parallel contexts and scope contexts, up to the structural congruence defined above.

We consider a standard extensional semantics of π-calculus: (weak) barbed equivalence, written $\stackrel{.}{\approx}$. The definition parallels definition 2, with processes instead of solutions, and we only need to redefine the notion of observation.

Definition 3. *The observation relation on π-calculus processes is the least relation satisfying the rules below.*

$$\overline{a}\,\langle \widetilde{u} \rangle \downarrow a$$
$$P \mid Q \downarrow a \qquad \text{if } P \downarrow a \text{ or } Q \downarrow a$$
$$(x)P \downarrow a \qquad \text{if } x \neq a \text{ and } P \downarrow a$$
$$\mathtt{A}(\widetilde{u}) \downarrow a \qquad \text{if } \mathtt{A}(\widetilde{X}) \stackrel{def}{=} P \text{ and } P\{\widetilde{u}/\widetilde{X}\} \downarrow a$$

As usual, we write $P \Downarrow a$ if $P \longrightarrow^* Q$ and $Q \downarrow a$.

5.2   The κ_b-Calculus

Proteins and complexes. Besides *sites* $\mathcal{N}$, and *protein names* $\mathcal{A}$, we need a further disjoint set of names $\mathcal{V}$, called *connections*, and ranged over by x, y, z, ..., which are sorted by sites so as to have countably many connections for any given site.

Table 1. Operational semantics of the asynchronous π-calculus.

Structural congruence:

$$P \mid Q \equiv Q \mid P, \quad (P \mid Q) \mid R \equiv P \mid (Q \mid R), \quad P \mid \mathbf{0} \equiv P,$$
$$(x)\mathbf{0} \equiv \mathbf{0}, \quad (x)(y)P \equiv (y)(x)P,$$
$$(x)MP; Q \equiv M(x)P; (x)Q \quad \text{if } x \notin \mathrm{fn}(M)$$
$$P \mid (z)Q \equiv (z)(P \mid Q), \quad \text{if } z \notin \mathrm{fn}(P)$$
$$A(\tilde{u}) \equiv P\{\tilde{u}/\tilde{X}\} \quad \text{if } A(\tilde{X}) \stackrel{\text{def}}{=} P$$

Basic reductions:

$$\overline{x}\,\langle \tilde{u} \rangle \mid \sum_{i \in I} x_i\,(\tilde{Y_i}).P_i \longrightarrow P_j\{\tilde{u}/\tilde{Y_j}\} \quad (\text{if } x = x_j)$$
$$MP; Q \longrightarrow P \quad (\text{if } M \text{ is true}) \qquad MP; Q \longrightarrow Q \quad (\text{if } M \text{ is false})$$

Contextual reductions:

$$\frac{P \longrightarrow P'}{P \mid Q \longrightarrow P' \mid Q} \qquad \frac{P \longrightarrow P'}{(x)P \longrightarrow (x)P'} \qquad \frac{P \equiv P' \quad P' \longrightarrow Q' \quad Q' \equiv Q}{P \longrightarrow Q}$$

We need to adapt the definitions of Section 2. Protein names now carry three arguments: two multisets of sites ρ and σ, as before in κ, and an additional set ξ of connections. The connection set ξ represents the bound sites of a protein: every site in it is represented by a different connection. Let $\mathfrak{s}(\xi)$ be the multiset of sorts of the connections in ξ. We demand that a protein $A(\rho, \sigma, \xi)$ is such that $\mathfrak{s}(A) - (\rho + \sigma) = \mathfrak{s}(\xi)$ and also that for every complex $A_1(\rho_1, \sigma_1, \xi_1) \odot \cdots \odot A_n(\rho_n, \sigma_n, \xi_n)$:

1. for all $1 \le i \le n$, $\rho_i + \sigma_i \subseteq \mathfrak{s}(A_i)$, or $n = 1$ and $\rho_1 + \sigma_1 \subseteq \mathfrak{s}(A_1)$;
2. connections occur exactly twice in $\xi_1 + \ldots + \xi_n$.

To express the fact that names in the ξ arguments are local to the complex, we borrow the 'new' operator from π-calculus. So the general shape of a complex is $(\xi)A_1(\rho_1, \sigma_1, \xi_1) \odot \cdots \odot A_n(\rho_n, \sigma_n, \xi_n)$.

Solutions and Reactions. Solutions in κ_b must satisfy the additional constraint that *complexes have pairwise disjoint connection sets*.

We have now to adapt our basic reactions to handle correctly the connection sets. Activations don't modify connections:

(ACTIVATION)

$$
\begin{array}{ccc}
A_1(X_1 + \rho_1, Y_1 + \sigma_1, Z_1) & & A_1(X_1 + \rho_1', Y_1 + \sigma_1', Z_1) \\
, \ldots, & \longrightarrow & , \ldots, \\
A_n(X_n + \rho_n, Y_n + \sigma_n, Z_n) & & A_n(X_n + \rho_n', Y_n + \sigma_n', Z_n)
\end{array}
$$

But complexations, by definition, need to create new connections, and these have to be *fresh names* in the ambient solution:

(COMPLEXATION)

$$A_1(X_1 + \rho_1, Y_1 + \sigma_1 + \tau_1, Z_1)$$
$$,\ldots,$$
$$A_n(X_n + \rho_n, Y_n + \sigma_n + \tau_n, Z_n)$$

$$\longrightarrow$$

$$\begin{matrix}(\xi_1 \ldots \xi_n)\\ A_1(X_1 + \rho_1', Y_1 + \sigma_1', Z_1 + \xi_1)\\ \odot \cdots \odot\\ A_n(X_n + \rho_n', Y_n + \sigma_n', Z_n + \xi_n)\end{matrix}$$

Both kind of rules are subject to the side-conditions that $\rho_i + \sigma_i = \rho_i' + \sigma_i'$, and for complexations, we also demand that $\tau_i \neq \varnothing$, $\mathfrak{s}(\xi_i) = \tau_i$. Since the product of the reaction has to be a correct complex, new connections $\bigcup_{1 \leq i \leq n} \xi_i$ do not clash with existing connections in $\bigcup_{1 \leq i \leq n} Z_i$, and we observe that the 'big enough even number' side-condition is also taken care of automatically.

To move the new operator upwards, once it is created, we add the structural congruence: $\mathsf{S}, (\xi)\mathsf{S}' \equiv (\xi)(\mathsf{S}, \mathsf{S}')$, when ξ is not free in S. Additionally, we adapt rule (CTX-CMP) in Figure 1 such that names created in the subcomplex are also new in the host supercomplex. With these adaptations done, transitions between κ_b-systems are defined up to structural congruence and with the help of the following additional form of contextual reaction which we need for handling the 'new': $\mathsf{S} \longrightarrow \mathsf{T}$ implies $(\xi)\mathsf{S} \longrightarrow (\xi)\mathsf{T}$.

Equivalence with core κ. The notions of complex and simple barbs of Definition 1 can be easily extended to κ_b by discarding connections ξ. There is an observation preserving function U which maps a κ_b-solution to a κ-solution just by dropping the connections. This 'forgetful' map U is left inverse to a family of converse maps which make explicit the connections of the underlying graphs of complexes. Of course, there isn't a unique right inverse to U because many choices of internal wirings are possible for each complex.

Since reactions are not 'seeing' the internal wiring, any choices will end up to be complex and simple bisimilar. One easily sees that U commutes to transitions, and so does any of the converse maps. Therefore (with the obvious adaptation of weak barbed bisimilarity to include κ_b systems):

Proposition 1. *Every κ_b-system is barbed bisimilar—both complex and simple—to a core κ-system, and conversely.*

5.3   First Compilation: Proteins Encode States, Rules Are Outside

This first compilation is 'reaction-centric', proteins play a passive role and just encode the state of the solution. Contextual reactions are taken care of by contextual reductions in π, there is no need to translate them.

First, to each protein $A(\rho, \sigma, \xi)$, an agent $\mathsf{A}(\rho, \sigma, \xi)$ is associated with the following behaviour (we use the name $a = f(A)$, as defined in Section 4):

$$\mathsf{A}(\rho, \sigma, \xi) \stackrel{\text{def}}{=} [\sigma \setminus \mathcal{N}_v = \varnothing]\mathbf{0} \,;\, (x)(\overline{a} \langle \rho, \sigma, x \rangle \mid x (\rho', \sigma', \xi').\mathsf{A}(\rho', \sigma', \xi + \xi'))$$

By writing $\sigma \setminus \mathcal{N}_v$ we are cheating a little bit, because there is no such operation in the π-calculus of Section 5.1. But, we could easily implement this operation by partitioning σ in two different arguments of A, and keeping track of this difference in messages which exchange σ.

Second, given an activation reaction $\mathfrak{a}$:

$$A_1(X_1 + \rho_1, Y_1 + \sigma_1, Z_1), \cdots, A_n(X_n + \rho_n, Y_n + \sigma_n, Z_n) \longrightarrow$$
$$A_1(X_1 + \rho_1', Y_1 + \sigma_1', Z_1), \cdots, A_n(X_n + \rho_n', Y_n + \sigma_n', Z_n)$$

we define the agent $[\![\mathfrak{a}]\!] \overset{def}{=} (z)(\mathfrak{A}_1(\mathbf{0},\mathbf{0}) \mid \overline{z}\,\langle\rangle)$ with:

$$\mathfrak{A}_1(P,Q) \overset{def}{=} a_1\,(\ell_1', \ell_1'', x_1).$$
$$[\rho_1 \subseteq \ell_1', \sigma_1 \subseteq \ell_1'']$$
$$\mathfrak{A}_2(P \mid \overline{x_1}\,\langle(\ell_1' \setminus \rho_1) + \rho_1', (\ell_1'' \setminus \sigma_1) + \sigma_1', \varnothing\rangle, Q \mid \overline{a_1}\,\langle\ell_1', \ell_1'', x_1\rangle);$$
$$(Q \mid \overline{a_1}\,\langle\ell_1', \ell_1'', x_1\rangle \mid \mathfrak{A}_1(\mathbf{0},\mathbf{0}))$$
$$+z\,().(Q \mid [\![\mathfrak{a}]\!])$$

and similar definitions for $\mathfrak{A}_i$, with $i < n$, and:

$$\mathfrak{A}_n(P,Q) \overset{def}{=} a_n\,(\ell_n', \ell_n'', x_n).$$
$$([\rho_n \subseteq \ell_n', \sigma_n \subseteq \ell_n''](P \mid \overline{x_n}\,\langle\ell_n' \setminus \rho_n) + \rho_n', (\ell_n'' \setminus \sigma_n) + \sigma_n', \varnothing\rangle);$$
$$(Q \mid \overline{a_n}\,\langle\ell_n', \ell_n'', x_n\rangle) \mid \mathfrak{A}_1(\mathbf{0},\mathbf{0}))$$
$$+z\,().(Q \mid [\![\mathfrak{a}]\!])$$

Nondeterminism in the $\mathfrak{A}_i$s is introduced to avoid deadlocks which could occur when not all of $\mathfrak{a}$'s reactants are present and free to use.

Last, given a complexation reaction $\mathfrak{c}$:

$$A_1(X_1 + \rho_1, Y_1 + \sigma_1 + \tau_1, Z_1), \cdots, A_n(X_n + \rho_n, Y_n + \sigma_n + \tau_n, Z_n) \longrightarrow$$
$$(\xi_1 \ldots \xi_n)\,A_1(X_1 + \rho_1', Y_1 + \sigma_1', Z_1 + \xi_1) \odot \cdots \odot A_n(X_n + \rho_n', Y_n + \sigma_n', Z_n + \xi_n)$$

we define the agent $[\![\mathfrak{c}]\!] \overset{def}{=} (z)(\mathfrak{C}_1(\mathbf{0},\mathbf{0}) \mid \overline{z}\,\langle\rangle)$, with:

$$\mathfrak{C}_1(P,Q) \overset{def}{=} (\xi_1)\,a_1\,(\ell_1', \ell_1'', x_1).$$
$$[\rho_1 \subseteq \ell_1', \sigma_1 + \tau_1 \subseteq \ell_1'']$$
$$\mathfrak{C}_2(P \mid \overline{x_1}\,\langle(\ell_1' \setminus \rho_1) + \rho_1', (\ell_1'' \setminus (\sigma_1 + \tau_1)) + \sigma_1', \xi_1\rangle, Q \mid \overline{a_1}\,\langle\ell_1', \ell_1'', x_1\rangle);$$
$$(Q \mid \overline{a_1}\,\langle\ell_1', \ell_1'', x_1\rangle \mid \mathfrak{C}_1(\mathbf{0},\mathbf{0}))$$
$$+z\,().(Q \mid [\![\mathfrak{c}]\!])$$

and similar definitions for $\mathfrak{C}_i$, with $i < n$, and:

$$\mathfrak{C}_n(P,Q) \overset{def}{=} (\xi_n)\,a_n\,(\ell_n', \ell_n'', x_n).$$
$$([\rho_n \subseteq \ell_n', \sigma_n + \tau_n \subseteq \ell_n'']$$
$$(P \mid \overline{x_n}\,\langle(\ell_n' \setminus \rho_n) + \rho_n', (\ell_n'' \setminus (\sigma_n + \tau_n)) + \sigma_n', \xi_n\rangle);$$
$$(Q \mid \overline{a_n}\,\langle\ell_n', \ell_n'', x_n\rangle)) \mid \mathfrak{C}_1(\mathbf{0},\mathbf{0})$$
$$+z\,().(Q \mid [\![\mathfrak{c}]\!])$$

Observe that biological connections are explained in π-calculus in terms of bound names. In particular, two proteins are connected if they share a same bound name. We give now the action of $[\![\,\cdot\,]\!]$ on solutions and complexes:

$$[\![S, S']\!] = [\![S]\!] \mid [\![S']\!]$$
$$[\![(\xi)\,S']\!] = (\xi)\,[\![S]\!]$$
$$[\![A_1(\rho_1, \sigma_1, \xi_1) \odot \cdots \odot A_n(\rho_n, \sigma_n, \xi_n)]\!] = (\xi_1 \ldots \xi_n)\,(A_1(\rho_1, \sigma_1, \xi_1) \mid \cdots \mid A_n(\rho_n, \sigma_n, \xi_n))$$

Lemma 1. *Let* $\langle S, R \rangle$ *be a* κ_b-*system and set* $[\![R]\!] = \prod_{\mathfrak{r} \in R} [\![\mathfrak{r}]\!]$, *then:*

1. *(simulation) If* $S \longrightarrow_R S'$ *then* $[\![S]\!] \mid [\![R]\!] \longrightarrow^* [\![S']\!] \mid [\![R]\!]$.
2. *(catch-up) If* $[\![S]\!] \mid [\![R]\!] \longrightarrow^* Q$ *then* $Q \longrightarrow^* [\![S']\!] \mid [\![R]\!]$ *with* $S \longrightarrow_R^* S'$.

Next observe that, $S \downarrow_s a$ if and only if $[\![S]\!] \mid [\![R]\!] \downarrow a$, so the translation respects simple barbs. From there it is possible to deduce that (S, R) and $[\![S]\!] \mid [\![R]\!]$ are weakly bisimilar in their respective transition systems, and by transitivity, this gives a full abstraction result with respect to barbed equivalence:

Theorem 2. *Let* $\langle S, R \rangle$ *and* $\langle S', R' \rangle$ *be* κ_b-*systems, then* $\langle S, R \rangle \stackrel{.}{\approx}_s \langle S', R' \rangle$ *iff* $[\![S]\!] \mid [\![R]\!] \stackrel{.}{\approx} [\![S']\!] \mid [\![R']\!]$.

5.4 A Second Compilation: Rules Are inside Protein Agents

This second compilation will be protein-centric. In the previous compilation, proteins were just passive solution states and even if this is formally correct, we want to provide a more "natural" compilation, more in line with Regev's representations of various biological pathways [14,16].

Let R be the set of basic rules of a given κ_b-system, $\mathfrak{r} \in R$ be a rule, and $\ulcorner \mathfrak{r} \urcorner$ be the rule identifier (a number). A temporary network is set up between proteins by means of the agent $\text{LINK}_R \stackrel{def}{=} \prod_{\mathfrak{r} \in R} \text{link}(\ulcorner \mathfrak{r} \urcorner)$, where $\text{link}(\ulcorner \mathfrak{r} \urcorner)$ is defined below for activations and complexations. Suppose the reactant of $\mathfrak{r}$ are $A_1, \ldots, A_n$, we define:

$$\text{link}(\ulcorner \mathfrak{r} \urcorner) = a_1(z_1).(z)(\text{link}(\ulcorner \mathfrak{r} \urcorner, 2, z, z_1, \overline{a_1}\langle z_1 \rangle) \mid \overline{z}\langle\rangle)$$

$$(2 \leq i < n) \quad \text{link}(\ulcorner \mathfrak{r} \urcorner, i, z, \widetilde{y}, P) = a_i(z_i).\text{link}(\ulcorner \mathfrak{r} \urcorner, i+1, z, \widetilde{y}z_i, \overline{a_1}\langle z_1 \rangle)$$
$$+z().(P \mid \text{link}(\ulcorner \mathfrak{r} \urcorner))$$

while for $i = n$, there is a slight difference depending on whether $\mathfrak{r}$ is an activation or a complexation. Specifically for activations and complexations respectively, we define:

$$\text{link}(\ulcorner \mathfrak{r} \urcorner, n, z, z_1 \cdots z_{n-1}, P) =$$
$$a_n(z_n).(z'_1, \cdots z'_n)\left(\overline{z_1}\langle \ulcorner \mathfrak{r} \urcorner, z'_n, z'_2 \rangle \mid \cdots \mid \overline{z_n}\langle \ulcorner \mathfrak{r} \urcorner, z'_{n-1}, z'_1 \rangle \mid \overline{z'_n}\langle 1 \rangle \mid \text{link}(\ulcorner \mathfrak{r} \urcorner) \right)$$
$$+z().(P \mid \text{link}(\ulcorner \mathfrak{r} \urcorner))$$

$$\text{link}(\ulcorner \mathfrak{r} \urcorner, n, z, z_1 \cdots z_{n-1}, P) =$$
$$a_n(z_n).(z'_1, \cdots z'_n)\left(\overline{z_1}\langle \ulcorner \mathfrak{r} \urcorner, z'_n, z'_2 \rangle \mid \cdots \mid \overline{z_n}\langle \ulcorner \mathfrak{r} \urcorner, z'_{n-1}, z'_1 \rangle \mid (\widetilde{\xi})\overline{z'_n}\langle 1, \widetilde{\xi} \rangle \mid \text{link}(\ulcorner \mathfrak{r} \urcorner) \right)$$
$$+z().(P \mid \text{link}(\ulcorner \mathfrak{r} \urcorner))$$

In order to coordinate the reactants, link sets up a ring to support a *token ring protocol* and passes the token to the nth reactant. In addition, for complexations, link also creates the potential new connections. We observe that rules are attempted competitively, which is vaguely resembling the real thing.

The behaviour of a protein A depends on the activation and complexation rules it participates in. Let R_A be the set of rules the protein A may participate in (*i.e.*, is a reactant of). Then:

$$A(X, Y, Z, R) = [Y \setminus \mathcal{N}_v = \varnothing]\,\mathbf{0}\,;$$
$$(z)(\overline{a}\langle z \rangle \mid z(v, z', z'').\prod_{\mathfrak{r} \in R_A}[v = \ulcorner \mathfrak{r} \urcorner]\mathfrak{R}_A(X, Y, Z, z', z'', R);\mathbf{0})$$

(the same remark regarding the expression $Y \setminus \mathcal{N}_v$ applies here as well) and we define the agents $\mathfrak{R}_{A_1}(X, Y, Z, z', z'', \mathsf{R})$ for the activation rule $\mathfrak{a}$ and the complexation rule $\mathfrak{c}$ of Section 5.3. (The agents $\mathfrak{A}_{A_i}$ and $\mathfrak{C}_{A_i}$, for other i, are similar.)

$$
\begin{aligned}
\mathfrak{A}_{A_1}&(X, Y, Z, z', z'', \mathsf{R}) = \\
&[\rho_1 \subseteq X, \sigma_1 \subseteq Y] \\
&\quad z'(v).[v = 1] \\
&\qquad (\overline{z''}\langle v \rangle \mid z'(v').[v' = 1](\mathsf{A_1}((X \setminus \rho_1) + \rho_1', (Y \setminus \sigma_1) + \sigma_1', Z, \mathsf{R}) \mid \overline{z''}\langle 1 \rangle); \\
&\qquad\qquad (\mathsf{A_1}(X, Y, Z, \mathsf{R}) \mid \overline{z''}\langle 0 \rangle)); \\
&\quad (\overline{z''}\langle 0 \rangle \mid \mathsf{A_1}(X, Y, Z, \mathsf{R})); \\
&\quad z'(v).(\overline{z''}\langle 0 \rangle \mid \mathsf{A_1}(X, Y, Z, \mathsf{R}))
\end{aligned}
$$

$$
\begin{aligned}
\mathfrak{C}_{A_1}&(X, Y, Z, z', z'', \mathsf{R}) = \\
&[\rho_1 \subseteq X, \sigma_1 + \tau_1 \subseteq Y] \\
&\quad z'(v, \widetilde{\xi}).[v = 1] \\
&\qquad (\overline{z''}\langle v, \widetilde{\xi} \rangle \mid z'(v', \widetilde{\xi}').[v' = 1](\mathsf{A_1}(X', Y', Z', \mathsf{R}) \mid \overline{z''}\langle 1, \widetilde{\xi}' \rangle); \\
&\qquad\qquad (\mathsf{A_1}(X, Y, Z, \mathsf{R}) \mid \overline{z''}\langle 0, \widetilde{\xi}' \rangle)); \\
&\quad (\overline{z''}\langle 0, \widetilde{\xi} \rangle \mid \mathsf{A_1}(X, Y, Z, \mathsf{R})); \\
&\quad z'(v, \widetilde{\xi}).(\overline{z''}\langle 0, \widetilde{\xi} \rangle \mid \mathsf{A_1}(X, Y, Z, \mathsf{R}))
\end{aligned}
$$

where $X' = (X \setminus \rho_1) + \rho_1'$, $Y' = Y \setminus (\sigma_1 + \tau_1)) + \sigma_1'$, $Z' = Z + \widetilde{\xi}_1$

where $\widetilde{\xi}_1$ is the subsequence of $\widetilde{\xi}'$ containing names representing bound sites of the agent A_1. The token ring protocol used by reacting proteins consists in two steps. In the first, each protein sends 1 or 0 depending on whether its own sites satisfy the constraints of the rule or not. In the second step, 1 or 0 is propagated, depending on whether every protein satisfies the constraints of the rule or not. In case a protein receives 1 in the second step, the changes prescribed by the rule are performed, and the 1 is propagated. Otherwise the reduction is aborted, the initial state is restored, and the 0 is propagated.

The correctness of the compilation is established by means of an encoding $[\![\cdot]\!]$, which depends on solutions and basic rules:

$$
\begin{aligned}
[\![S, S']\!]_\mathsf{R} &= [\![S]\!]_\mathsf{R} \mid [\![S']\!]_\mathsf{R} \\
[\![A(\rho, \sigma, \xi)]\!]_\mathsf{R} &= \mathsf{A}(\rho, \sigma, \xi, \mathsf{R})
\end{aligned}
$$
$$
\begin{aligned}
[\![A_1(\rho_1, \sigma_1, \xi_1) \odot \cdots \odot A_n(\rho_n, \sigma_n, \xi_n)]\!]_\mathsf{R} = \\
(\xi_1, \cdots, \xi_n)(\mathsf{A_1}(\rho_1, \sigma_1, \xi_1, \mathsf{R}) \mid \cdots \mid \mathsf{A_n}(\rho_n, \sigma_n, \xi_n, \mathsf{R}))
\end{aligned}
$$

Lemma 2. *Let* (S, R) *be a* κ_b-*system and* LINK_R *be as above, then*

1. *if* $\mathsf{S} \longrightarrow_\mathsf{R} \mathsf{S}'$ *then* $[\![\mathsf{S}]\!]_\mathsf{R} \mid \mathrm{LINK}_\mathsf{R} \mid \mathfrak{G} \longrightarrow^* [\![\mathsf{S}']\!]_\mathsf{R} \mid \mathrm{LINK}_\mathsf{R} \mid \mathfrak{G}'$; *where* $\mathfrak{G}$ *and* $\mathfrak{G}'$ *are idle garbage agents;*
2. *if* $[\![\mathsf{S}]\!]_\mathsf{R} \mid \mathrm{LINK}_\mathsf{R} \mid \mathfrak{G} \longrightarrow^* Q$, *where* $\mathfrak{G}$ *is an idle garbage agent, then* $Q \longrightarrow^*$ $[\![\mathsf{S}']\!]_\mathsf{R} \mid \mathrm{LINK}_\mathsf{R} \mid \mathfrak{G}'$ *with* $\mathfrak{G}'$ *an idle garbage agent, and* $\mathsf{S} \longrightarrow^*_\mathsf{R} \mathsf{S}'$.

Our idle garbage agents are parallel compositions of processes like $(z)\overline{z}\langle u, \widetilde{\xi} \rangle$. These agents collect the last messages of our token ring protocol. Of course we could refine the protocol such that no garbage is ever produced.

As before, we observe that $\mathsf{S} \downarrow_s a$ iff $[\![\mathsf{S}]\!]_\mathsf{R} \mid \mathrm{LINK}_\mathsf{R} \downarrow a$, and from there one can prove the following:

Theorem 3. *Let* $\langle S, R \rangle$ *and* $\langle S', R' \rangle$ *be* κ_b-*systems, then* $\langle S, R \rangle \overset{.}{\approx}_s \langle S', R' \rangle$ *iff* $[\![S]\!]_R \mid \text{LINK}_R \overset{.}{\approx} [\![S']\!]_{R'} \mid \text{LINK}_{R'}$.

We conclude with two remarks. What is relevant in the former protocol—the token ring—is that it does not play a crucial role. Namely, our compilation may be abstracted from the protocol implementing the cooperation, still retaining the correctness. Our choice of the token ring protocol follows by its simplicity. But other reasons could be considered, such as efficiency, *i.e.* the number of channels used. In particular, our protocol doesn't use channels ξ_i which describe the underlying graph of connections of a complex. A clever protocol could make a profit of them, without introducing channels z_i. We keep this issue for future investigations. The second remark: barbed bisimilarity of our two compilations in π-calculus is an immediate consequence of Theorems 2 and 3.

6   Conclusions

We've presented a simple language of complexations and activations targeting core molecular biology. Synthesis and degradation were not considered, neither were decomplexations. No locations were introduced in the language either. We could have introduced all these. Though they certainly play a part in molecular biology, the idea here was to have the simplest meaningful language equipped with a barebone operational semantics and see if anything interesting happens.

What happens is that this language can be compiled in a even simpler fragment up to two different bisimulations. A simpler fragment which in turn can be compiled in two different styles in π-calculus. So the simplicity of the formalism pays off with this structured translation in π. In some sense the conclusion for now is that the formalism itself can be seen as a process algebra of its own. Further investigations will show if anything more practical comes out of it.

References

1. Roberto Amadio, Ilaria Castellani, and Davide Sangiorgi. On bisimulations for the asynchronous π-calculus. *Theoretical Computer Science*, 195(2):291–324, 1998.
2. Marc Chiaverini and Vincent Danos. A formalism for Kohn's molecular map. In *Proceedings of International Workshop on Computational Methods in Systems Biology*, LNCS. Springer-Verlag, 2003.
3. E. M. Clarke, E. Allen Emerson, and A. P. Sistla. Automatic verification of finite state concurrent systems using temporal logic specifications: A practical approach. *ACM Transactions on Programming Languages and Systems*, 8(2):244–263, 1986.
4. Edmund M. Clarke, Orna Grumberg, and Doron A. Peled. *Model Checking*. The MIT Press, Cambridge, Massachusetts, 1999.
5. Vincent Danos and Cosimo Laneve. Graphs for formal molecular biology. In *Proceedings of International Workshop on Computational Methods in Systems Biology*, LNCS. Springer-Verlag, 2003.
6. Steven Eker, Merrill Knapp, Keith Laderoute, Patrick Lincoln, José Meseguer, and Kemal Sonmez. Pathway logic: Symbolic analysis of biological signaling. In *Proceedings of the Pacific Symposium on Biocomputing*, pages 400–412, January 2002. To appear.

7. Cédric Fournet and Georges Gonthier. The reflexive chemical abstract machine and the join-calculus. In *23rd ACM Symposium on Principles of Programming Languages (POPL'96)*, 1996.

8. Ronojoy Ghosh and Claire J. Tomlin. Lateral inhibition through delta-notch signaling: A piecewise affine hybrid model? In *Proceedings of HSCC 2001*, volume 2034 of *LNCS*, pages 232–246. Springer, 2001.

9. Matthew Hennessy and Robin Milner. Algebraic laws for nondeterminism and concurrency. *Journal of the ACM (JACM)*, 32(1):137–161, 1985.

10. Kurt W. Kohn. Molecular interaction map of the mammalian cell cycle control and DNA repair systems. *Molecular Biology of the Cell*, n. 10:2703–2734, 1999.

11. Ron Maimon and Sam Browning. Diagrammatic notation and computational structure of gene networks. In *Proceedings of the 2nd International Conference on Systems Biology*, 2001.

12. Robin Milner and Davide Sangiorgi. Barbed bisimulation. In W. Kuich, editor, *Nineteenth Colloquium on Automata, Languages and Programming (ICALP) (Wien, Austria)*, volume 623 of *LNCS*, pages 685–695. Springer, 1992.

13. Masao Nagasaki, Shuichi Onami, Satoru Miyano, and Hiroaki Kitano. Bio-calculus: Its concept and molecular interaction. *Genome Informatics*, 10:133–143, 1999.

14. C. Priami, A. Regev, E. Shapiro, and W. Silverman. Application of a stochastic name-passing calculus to representation and simulation of molecular processes. *Information Processing Letters*, 80:25–31, 2001.

15. A. Regev and E. Shapiro. Cells as computation. *Nature*, 419, September 2002.

16. A. Regev, W. Silverman, and E. Shapiro. Representation and simulation of biochemical processes using the π-calculus process algebra. In R. B. Altman, A. K. Dunker, L. Hunter, and T. E. Klein, editors, *Pacific Symposium on Biocomputing*, volume 6, pages 459–470, Singapore, 2001. World Scientific Press.

17. Birgit Schoeberl, Claudia Eichler-Jonsson, Ernst-Dieter Gilles, and Gertraud Müller. Computational modeling of the dynamics of the map kinase cascade activated by surface and internalized EGF receptors. *Nature Biotechnology*, 20:370–375, 2002.

18. D. Thieffry and R. Thomas. Qualitative analysis of gene networks. In R. B. Altman, A. K. Dunker, L. Hunter, and T. E. Klein, editors, *Pacific Symposium on Biocomputing*, volume 3, pages 77–88, Singapore, 1998. World Scientific Press.

Requirements on the Execution of Kahn Process Networks*

Marc Geilen and Twan Basten

Dept. of Elec. Eng., Eindhoven University of Technology, The Netherlands
{m.c.w.geilen, a.a.basten}@tue.nl

Abstract. Kahn process networks (KPNs) are a programming paradigm suitable for streaming-based multimedia and signal-processing applications. We discuss the execution of KPNs, and the criteria for correct scheduling of their realisations. In [12], Parks shows how process networks can be scheduled in bounded memory; the proposed method is used in many implementations of KPNs. However, it does not result in the correct behaviour for all KPNs. We investigate the requirements for a scheduler to guarantee both correct and bounded execution of KPNs and present an improved scheduling strategy that satisfies them.

Keywords: Kahn process networks, Kahn Principle, dynamic scheduling, deadlock resolution, multi-processor architectures, media processing, signal processing, streaming

1 Introduction

Process networks are a popular model to express behaviour of data flow and streaming nature. This includes audio, video and 3D multimedia applications such as encoding and decoding of MPEG video streams. Using process networks, an application is modelled as a collection of concurrent processes communicating streams of data through FIFO channels. Process networks make task-level parallelism and communication explicit, have a simple semantics, are compositional and allow for efficient implementations without time-consuming synchronisations. There are several variants of process networks. One of the most general forms are Kahn process networks [7,8], where the nodes are arbitrary sequential programs, that communicate via channels of the process networks with blocking read and non-blocking write operations. Although harder to analyse than more restricted models, such as synchronous dataflow networks [11], the added flexibility makes KPNs a popular programming model. Where synchronous dataflow models can be statically scheduled at compile time, KPNs must be scheduled dynamically in general, because their expressive power does not allow them to be statically analysed. A run-time system is required to schedule the execution of processes and to manage memory usage for the channels. The goal is to create an execution that is as efficient as possible w.r.t. speed and memory and that is faithful to the process network specification.

---

* This work is supported in part by the IST-2000-30026 project, Ozone.

P. Degano (Ed.): ESOP 2003, LNCS 2618, pp. 319–334, 2003.

In this paper, we investigate the fundamental requirements for a run-time system for KPNs to be faithful to the semantics of the KPN specification and to use bounded memory resources when possible. In particular, we study the issues that arise when the conceptually unbounded FIFO channels of the KPN are realised using bounded FIFOs.

Related Work. Reasoning about realisations of KPNs touches on the Kahn Principle, stating that the solution to the network equations formulated by Kahn [7] is the same as the behaviour of a model of (sequential) programs reading and writing tokens on channels. The Principle was introduced, but not proved, by Kahn in [7]. It was proved [5,13] for an operational model of transition systems.

Scheduling process networks using static bounded channels is extensively addressed by Thomas Parks in [12], introducing an algorithm that uses bounded memory if possible. Based on this scheduling policy, a number of tools and libraries have been developed for executing KPNs. YAPI [9] is a C++ library for designing stream-processing applications. Ptolemy II [10] is a framework for codesign using mixed models of computation. The process-network domain is described in [6]. The Distributed Process Networks of [15] form the computational back end of the Jade/PAGIS system for processing digital satellite images. [14] covers an implementation of process networks in Java. [1] is another implementation for digital signal processing. Common among all these implementations is a multi-threading environment in which processes of the KPN execute in their own thread of control and channels are allocated a fixed capacity. Semaphores control access to channels and block the thread when reading from an empty or writing to a full channel. This raises the possibility of a deadlock when one or more processes are permanently blocked on full channels. A special thread (preempted by the other threads) is used to detect a deadlock and initiate a deadlock resolution procedure when necessary. This essentially realises the scheduling policy of [12]. The algorithm of Parks leaves some room for optimisation of memory usage by careful selection of initial channel capacities (using profiling) and clever selection of channels when the capacity needs to be increased; see [2]. [2] also introduces causal chains, also used in this paper to define deadlocks.

Contribution. All work on practical implementations of KPNs that we found builds on Parks' scheduling algorithm. We show that this algorithm does not execute all KPNs correctly and propose an improved scheduling strategy.

Organisation. Section 2 discusses the challenges related with implementing process networks, such as memory management, scheduling and deadlock detection and resolution. An operational semantics of process networks is introduced in Section 3 to enable reasoning about realisations of KPNs. Section 4 discusses the properties of realisations of process networks with bounded channels and Section 5 introduces a correct scheduling strategy. Section 6 concludes.

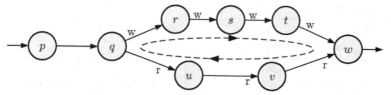

Fig. 1. An artificial deadlock

2   Implementing Kahn Process Networks

Conceptually, the FIFO communication channels of a KPN have an unbounded capacity. A realisation of a process network has to run within a finite amount of memory. Rather than dynamically allocating memory to channels when needed, it is for reasons of efficiency better to allocate fixed amounts of memory to channels and change this amount only sporadically, if necessary. An added advantage of the fixed capacity of channels is that one can use Parks' [12] model of execution, where a write action on a full FIFO blocks until there is room again in the FIFO. This gives an efficient intermediate form of data-driven and demand-driven scheduling [12,2] in which a process can produce output (in a data-driven way) until the channel it is writing to is full. Then it blocks and other processes take over. Unfortunately, it is undecidable in general, how much buffer capacity is needed in every channel [4]. If buffers are chosen too large, memory is wasted. If buffers are chosen too small, artificial deadlocks (i.e., processes being permanently blocked on a full channel) may occur that are not in the original KPN. Therefore, a scheduler is needed that determines the order of execution of processes and that manages buffer sizes at run-time.

In practice, such a scheduler should satisfy two requirements. Output should be complete; it must coordinate progress of all processes and manage channel capacity in such a way that the output produced by the KPN corresponds to the output predicted by the denotational semantics introduced in [7]. Secondly, it is important that this is achieved within bounded memory. Since memory usage of the individual processes is not under control of the scheduler, this amounts to keeping the FIFOs bounded, also in (conceptually) infinite computations.

An important aspect of a run-time scheduler for KPNs is dealing with deadlocks. One should discern different kinds of deadlocks. A process network is in *global deadlock* if none of the processes can make progress. In contrast, a *local deadlock* arises if some of the processes in the network cannot progress and their further progress cannot be initiated by the rest of the network. In a realisation of a KPN, processes may be blocked if an output channel is full. This is not the case for the conceptual KPNs. As a result, some of the deadlocks in realisations are *artificial* in the sense that they do not exist in the KPN. Figure 1 shows a process network in an artificial deadlock situation. Process w cannot continue because its input channel to process v is empty; it is blocked on a read action on the channel to v, denoted by the 'r' in the figure. The required input should be provided by v, but this is in turn waiting for input from u. u is waiting for q. Process q is blocked, because it is trying to output a token on the full channel to r; the block on the write action is denoted by a 'w'. Similarly processes r, s

322   M. Geilen and T. Basten

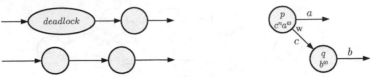

Fig. 2. A local deadlock   **Fig. 3.** Non effective network

and t are blocked by a full channel. Only w could start emptying these channels, but w is blocked. The processes are in artificial deadlock (q, r, s and t would not be blocked in the KPN) and can only continue if the capacity of one of the full channels is increased. The deadlock is local as long as process p can continue. To guarantee the correct output of a network, a run-time scheduler must detect and respond to artificial deadlocks. Parks proposes to respond to global artificial deadlocks. Detection is (in [1,6,9,14,15]) realised by detecting that all processes are blocked, some of which on a full FIFO. Although this guarantees that execution of the process network never terminates because of an artificial deadlock, it does not guarantee the production of *all* output required by the KPN semantics; output may not be complete. E.g., in the network of Figure 2, if the upper part reaches a local artificial deadlock, then the lower, independent part is not affected. Processes may not all come to a halt and the local deadlock is not detected and not resolved. The upper part may not produce the required output. Such situations exist in realistic networks. Further, when multiple KPNs are controlled by a single run-time scheduler, one entire process network may get stuck in a deadlock. A deadlock detection scheme has to detect local deadlocks.

It is well known that the Kahn Principle hinges on fair scheduling of processes [3,7,13]. Fairness means that all processes that can make progress should make progress at some point. This is often a tacit but valid assumption if the underlying realisation is truly concurrent, or fairly scheduled. In the context however of bounded FIFO channels where processes appear to be inactive while they are blocked for writing, fairness of a schedule is no longer evident. This issue is neglected in Parks' algorithm by responding to global deadlocks only, leading to a discrepancy with the behaviour of the conceptual KPN.

To come to an improved scheduling strategy, we must restrict our attention to particular classes of KPNs. It is observed in [12] that the scheduling requirements cannot always be met; some KPNs cannot be scheduled with bounded channel capacity meaning the second scheduling requirement cannot be achieved. Thus, the existence of a bounded execution must be required. We argue that one further restriction on KPNs is needed to meet the requirement of output completeness. A problem is posed by the production of data that is never used. This is illustrated with Figure 3. Process p writes n data elements (tokens) on channel c connecting p to process q; after that, it writes tokens to output channel a forever. q never reads tokens from c and outputs tokens to channel b forever. If the capacity of c is insufficient for n tokens, then output a will never be written to unless the capacity of c is increased. q doesn't halt and execution according to Parks' algorithm does not produce output on channel a. In the KPN however, infinite output is produced on both channels. The above suggests that a good scheduler should eventually increase the capacity of channel c so that it can contain all n tokens. However, such a scheduler fails to correctly schedule another KPN. Consider a process network with the same structure as the one of Figure 3, but this time, p continuously writes tokens on output a, mixed with infinitely many tokens to channel c. q writes infinitely many tokens to b and reads infinitely many tokens from c, but at a different rate than p writes tokens to c. Note that a bounded execution exists; a capacity of one token suffices for channel c. If process p writes to c faster than q reads, channel c may fill up and the scheduler, not knowing if tokens on channel c will ever be read, decides to increase channel capacity. A process q exists that always postpones the read actions until after the scheduler decides to increase the capacity; the execution will be unbounded, although a bounded execution exists. The above demonstrates that KPNs producing unread tokens cannot be scheduled correctly. Our solution is to assume that every token that is written to a channel, is eventually also read. We call such KPNs *effective*.

The development of a correct scheduling algorithm is based on the use of blocking write operations to full channels as in [12]. In order to deal with local deadlocks, we build upon the notion of causal chains as introduced in [2]. Any blocked process depends for its further progress on a unique other process that must fill or empty the appropriate channel. These dependencies give rise to chains of dependencies. If such a chain of dependencies is cyclic, it indicates a local deadlock; no further progress can be made without external help. In Figure 1, such a causal chain is indicated by the dashed ellipse indicating the cyclic mutual dependencies of the processes q, r, s, t, u, v and w.

3 An Operational Model of Process Networks

The denotational semantics of KPNs of [7] is attractive from a mathematical point of view, because of its abstractness and compositionality. It (purposely) abstracts from implementation related aspects such as scheduling, performance and resources such as channel capacities. In a realisation of a process network, FIFO sizes and contents play an important role and are influenced by a runtime environment that governs the execution of the network. It is for this reason that we give a simple operational semantics of process networks, similar to [5,13].

3.1 Labelled Transition Systems

We give an operational semantics to KPNs in the form of a labelled transition system (LTS). We use, more specifically, an LTS with an initial state, with designated input and output actions in the form of reads and writes of tokens on channels, as well as internal actions. For convenience, we assume a universal set $Chan$ of channels and for every channel $c \in Chan$ a corresponding channel alphabet Σ_c. We use Σ to denote the union of all channel alphabets, and A^* (A^∞) to denote the set of all finite (and infinite) strings over alphabet A. If i and j are functions from channels to strings over the corresponding alphabets, we write $i \preceq j$ iff for every channel c in the domain of i, $i(c)$ is a prefix of $j(c)$.

An LTS is a tuple $(S, s_0, I, O, Act, \rightarrow)$ consisting of a set S of states, an initial state $s_0 \in S$, a set $I \subseteq Chan$ of input channels, a set $O \subseteq Chan$ (distinct from I) of output channels, a set Act of actions consisting of input actions

$\{c?a \mid c \in I, a \in \Sigma_c\} \subseteq Act$, output actions $\{c!a \mid c \in O, a \in \Sigma_c\} \subseteq Act$ and (possibly) internal actions (all other actions), and a labelled transition relation $\to \subseteq S \times Act \times S$. Thus, $c!a$ is a write action to channel c with token a; $c?a$ models passing of a token from input channel c to the LTS. We write $s_1 \xrightarrow{\alpha} s_2$ if $(s_1, \alpha, s_2) \in \to$ and $s_1 \xrightarrow{\alpha}$ if there is some $s_2 \in S$ such that $s_1 \xrightarrow{\alpha} s_2$.

With a write operation, the token on the output channel is determined by the LTS. With a read operation, the token that appears on the input channel is determined by the environment of the LTS. Therefore, a read operation is modelled with a set of input actions that provides a transition for every possible token of the alphabet. Kahn process networks do not exhibit non-determinism. Transitions are deterministic and if multiple actions are available at the same time, then they are truly concurrent (i.e., they can be executed in any order with an identical result). We call such LTSes determinate.

Definition 1. (DETERMINACY) *LTS* $(S, s_0, I, O, Act, \to)$ *is determinate iff for any* $s, s_1, s_2 \in S$, $\alpha_1, \alpha_2 \in Act$, *if* $s \xrightarrow{\alpha_1} s_1$ *and* $s \xrightarrow{\alpha_2} s_2$, *the following hold:*

1. (DETERMINISM) *if* $\alpha_1 = \alpha_2$, *then* $s_1 = s_2$, *i.e., executing a particular action has a unique deterministic result;*
2. (CONFLUENCE) *if* α_1 *and* α_2 *are not two input actions on the same channel (i.e., instances of the same read operation), then there is some* s_3 *such that* $s_1 \xrightarrow{\alpha_2} s_3$ *and* $s_2 \xrightarrow{\alpha_1} s_3$.
3. (INPUT COMPLETENESS) *if* $\alpha_1 = c?a$ *for some* $c \in I$ *and* $a \in \Sigma_c$, *then for every* $a' \in \Sigma_c$, $s \xrightarrow{c?a'}$, *i.e., input tokens are completely defined by the environment, the LTS cannot be selective in the choice of tokens;*
4. (OUTPUT UNIQUENESS) *if* $\alpha_1 = c!a$ *and* $\alpha_2 = c!a'$ *for some* $c \in O$ *and* $a, a' \in \Sigma_c$, *then* $a = a'$, *i.e., output tokens are determined by the LTS.*

A sequential LTS is a determinate LTS with the additional property that

5. (SEQUENTIALITY) *if* $\alpha_1 = c \sharp a$ ($\sharp \in \{!, ?\}$), *for some* $c \in I \cup O$, $a \in \Sigma_c$, *then* $\alpha_2 = c \sharp a'$ *for some* $a' \in \Sigma_c$, *i.e., the LTS accepts at most one input/output operation at any point in time and no other (internal) actions.*

An execution of the transition system is a sequence $s_0 \xrightarrow{\alpha_0} s_1 \xrightarrow{\alpha_1} \dots$ of states $s_i \in S$ and actions $\alpha_i \in Act$, such that $s_i \xrightarrow{\alpha_i} s_{i+1}$ for all $i \geq 0$ (up to the length of the execution). If ρ is such an execution, then we use $|\rho| \in \mathbb{N} \cup \{\infty\}$ to denote the length of the execution. $|\rho| = \infty$ if ρ is infinite and $|\rho| = n$ if $\rho = s_0 \xrightarrow{\alpha_0} s_1 \xrightarrow{\alpha_1} \dots \xrightarrow{\alpha_{n-1}} s_n$. For $k \leq |\rho|$, we use ρ^k to denote the prefix of the execution up to and including state k.

3.2   Operational Semantics of Process Networks

We formalise an operational notion of a KPN as an LTS.

Definition 2. (KAHN PROCESS NETWORK) *A Kahn process network is a tuple* $(P, C, I, O, Act, \{LTS_p \mid p \in P\})$ *that consists of the following elements.*

- *A finite set* P *of* processes.
- *A finite set* $C \subseteq Chan$ *of internal channels, a finite set* $I \subseteq Chan$ *of input channels and a finite set* $O \subseteq Chan$ *of output channels, all distinct.*

- *The set Act of actions consisting of reads and writes of tokens on the channels c in $C \cup I \cup O$: $Act = \{c?a, c!a \mid c \in C \cup I \cup O, a \in \Sigma_c\}$.*
- *Every process $p \in P$ is defined by a sequential labelled transition system $LTS_p = (S_p, s_{p,0}, I_p, O_p, Act, \twoheadrightarrow)$, with $I_p \subseteq I \cup C$ and $O_p \subseteq O \cup C$.*
- *For every channel $c \in C \cup I$, there is exactly one process $p \in P$ that reads from it ($c \in I_p$) and for every channel $c \in C \cup O$, there is exactly one process $p \in P$ that writes to it ($c \in O_p$).*

To define the operational semantics of a KPN, we need a notion of global state of the network; this state is composed of the individual states of the processes and the contents of the internal channels.

Definition 3. (CONFIGURATION) *A configuration of a process network is a pair (π, γ) consisting of a process state π and a channel state γ, where*

- *a process state $\pi : P \to S = \bigcup_{p \in P} S_p$ is a function that maps every process $p \in P$ on a local state $\pi(p) \in S_p$ of its transition system;*
- *a channel state $\gamma : C \to \Sigma^*$ is a function that maps every internal channel $c \in C$ on a finite string $\gamma(c)$ over Σ_c.*

The set of all configurations is denoted by Confs and there is a designated initial configuration $c_0 = (\pi_0, \gamma_0)$, where π_0 maps every process $p \in P$ to its initial state $s_{p,0}$ and γ_0 maps every channel $c \in C$ to the empty string ϵ.

Definition 4. (OPERATIONAL SEMANTICS OF A KPN) *We assign to a KPN an operational semantics in the form of an LTS $(Confs, c_0, I, O, Act, \to)$. The labelled transition relation $\to$ is the smallest relation satisfying the following four induction rules. For reading from and writing to internal channels:*

$$\frac{\pi(p) \xrightarrow{c?a}_p s, \gamma(c) = a\sigma, c \in C}{(\pi, \gamma) \xrightarrow{c?a} (\pi\{s/p\}, \gamma\{\sigma/c\})} \qquad \frac{\pi(p) \xrightarrow{c!a}_p s, \gamma(c) = \sigma, c \in C}{(\pi, \gamma) \xrightarrow{c!a} (\pi\{s/p\}, \gamma\{\sigma a/c\})}$$

(The notation $f\{y/x\}$ denotes the function with the same domain as f and identical to f, except that $f(x) = y$.) Input channels and output channels are open to the environment:

$$\frac{\pi(p) \xrightarrow{c?a}_p s, c \in I}{(\pi, \gamma) \xrightarrow{c?a} (\pi\{s/p\}, \gamma)} \qquad \frac{\pi(p) \xrightarrow{c!a}_p s, c \in O}{(\pi, \gamma) \xrightarrow{c!a} (\pi\{s/p\}, \gamma)}$$

It is easy to show that if the labelled transition systems of the individual processes P are sequential, then the labelled transition system of the KPN is determinate. From a given execution ρ of a KPN, we extract the consumed input and the produced output on a set $D \subseteq C \cup I \cup O$ of channels as follows.

- For a channel $c \in D$, $\rho?_c$ is a (finite or infinite) string over Σ_c that results from projecting ρ onto *read* actions on c;
- similarly, $\rho!_c$ is a (finite or infinite) string over Σ_c that results from projecting ρ onto *write* actions on c;
- finally, $\rho?_D = \{(c, \rho?_c) \mid c \in D\}$ and $\rho!_D = \{(c, \rho!_c) \mid c \in D\}$.

Thus $\rho?_I$ denotes the input consumed by the network in execution ρ and $\rho!_O$ denotes the output of the network. To reason about the input *offered* to the network (consumed or not consumed), we say that ρ is an execution with input $i : I \to \Sigma^\infty$ iff $\rho?_I \preceq i$.

In the remainder, we assume that $(P, C, I, O, Act, \{LTS_p \mid p \in P\})$ is a Kahn process network with LTS $(Confs, c_0, I, O, Act, \to)$. We can now formalise the notions of fairness, maximality, effectiveness and boundedness.

Definition 5. $\rho = (\pi_0, \gamma_0) \xrightarrow{\alpha_0} (\pi_1, \gamma_1) \xrightarrow{\alpha_1} \dots$ *is an execution of the KPN.*

- (FAIRNESS) *Execution ρ with input i is fair iff it is finite, or it is infinite and if at some point an input, internal or output action is enabled, it must eventually be executed, i.e.,*
  - *if for some $n \in \mathbb{N}$, $c \in C$ and $a \in \Sigma_c$, $(\pi_n, \gamma_n) \xrightarrow{c?a}$, then there is some $k \geq n$ such that $\alpha_k = c?a$;*
  - *if for some $n \in \mathbb{N}$, $c \in I$ and $a \in \Sigma_c$, $(\pi_n, \gamma_n) \xrightarrow{c?a}$, and $i(c) = (\rho^n?_c)a\sigma$ for some $\sigma \in \Sigma_c^\infty$, then there is some $k \geq n$ such that $\alpha_k = c?a$;*
  - *if for some $n \in \mathbb{N}$, $c \in C \cup O$ and $a \in \Sigma_c$, $(\pi_n, \gamma_n) \xrightarrow{c!a}$, then there is some $k \geq n$ such that $\alpha_k = c!a$.*
- (MAXIMALITY) *Execution ρ with input i is called maximal iff it is infinite or, in its last configuration, only read actions on input channels from which all input of i has been consumed are possible, i.e., if $|\rho| = n$ and $(\pi_n, \gamma_n) \xrightarrow{\alpha}$ then $\alpha = c?a$ for some $c \in I$ and $a \in \Sigma_c$ and $\rho?_c = i(c)$.*
- (EFFECTIVENESS) *Execution ρ is effective iff every token produced on an internal channel is ultimately consumed, i.e., if $\rho?_C = \rho!_C$. A KPN is called effective iff for all inputs there exists an effective fair and maximal execution.*
- (BOUNDEDNESS) *Execution ρ is bounded iff for every internal channel there is an upper bound to the number of tokens that accumulate in it during the execution, i.e., $\forall c \in C : \exists n \in \mathbb{N} : \forall i \in \mathbb{N}, 0 \leq i \leq |\rho| : |\gamma_i(c)| \leq n$. A KPN is bounded iff for all inputs there is a bounded fair and maximal execution.*

Corollary 1. *Any two fair and maximal executions of a KPN with the same input execute the same actions.*

The question whether a KPN is bounded or effective is unfortunately undecidable in general; this follows immediately from the fact that processes are arbitrary sequential programs and thus Turing complete.

3.3   The Kahn Principle

The operational semantics given in the previous subsection is a model for a realisation of a KPN. Its behaviour corresponds to the function given by Kahn's semantics as the least solution to a set of network equations [7] for the KPN. This is referred to as the Kahn Principle. It was stated convincingly, but without proof, by Kahn in [7] and was later proved by Faustini [5] for an operational model similar to ours. Based on the operational semantics, we can derive a functional relation between inputs and outputs. This function can then be shown to correspond to the least solution of Kahn's network equations. The maximal and fair executions capture the input/output relation of the network.

Definition 6. (INPUT/OUTPUT RELATION) *The input/output relation IO of a KPN is the relation $\{(i, \rho!_O) \mid \rho$ is a maximal and fair execution with input $i\}$.*

IO is a so-called continuous function, which is the basis of the following theorem.

Theorem 1. (KAHN PRINCIPLE) *[7,5] The function IO of input strings and output strings for maximal and fair executions corresponds to the least solution of Kahn's network equations of [7].*

A proof of the Kahn Principle is beyond the scope of this paper and can be found in (for instance) [5] for a similar operational model and in [13] for an operational semantics in terms of so-called concurrent transition systems.

4   Process Networks with Channel Bounds

In this section, we study the effects of imposing channel bounds on KPNs. We consider what happens if we execute a process network when offered some fixed input i. We assume that all input offered is initially available, i.e., an input action only blocks if all input has been consumed. When we mention executions, we mean executions with input i.

4.1   Bounded Channels

The bounded memory requirement is enforced on a process network by bounds on the number of tokens that can accumulate in every channel. These bounds need not be the same for all channels. We can model a realisation by an LTS, as presented in the previous section, and an execution of the realisation by an execution of this LTS. Choices are resolved by a scheduling mechanism that controls when and how processes are executed on processors and that manages memory that is used for the channels. Hence, the scheduler is a mechanism that guides the execution through the LTS.

Definition 7. (CHANNEL BOUND) *A bound $\bar{b}$ on channel contents is a mapping $C \to \mathbb{N}^+$ that maps every internal channel to the (positive) maximum number of tokens it can simultaneously contain. If $\bar{b}_1$ and $\bar{b}_2$ are both channel bounds, we write $\bar{b}_1 \preceq \bar{b}_2$ to denote that for every $c \in C$, $\bar{b}_1(c) \leq \bar{b}_2(c)$.*

In the remainder, we refer to a KPN and a corresponding bound on its channel sizes as a *process network with bounds (PNB)*. The operational semantics of a PNB conforms to the operational semantics of the corresponding KPN except that those configurations (π, γ) are missing that do not respect the FIFO bounds, i.e., if $|\gamma(c)| > \bar{b}(c)$ for some $c \in C$. Also transitions from or to these configurations are removed. As a consequence, where the KPN may be able to write to a channel, a PNB may not be able to do the same if the channel is full. This write may have to be postponed, until there is room in the channel, but also, artificial deadlocks may arise in the transition system as a result of this [12]. We first show that PNBs also have determinate transition systems.

Proposition 1. *A PNB is determinate.*

Proof. The corresponding KPN is determinate. The LTS of the PNB is obtained from the LTS of the KPN by removing states and transitions; thus determinism is preserved. By a simple case analysis, one can show that the transitions of the PNB are confluent, i.e., that the configuration where actions from configurations respecting the bounds converge also stays within FIFO bounds. Since input and output actions do not touch internal channels, also input completeness and output uniqueness are preserved.

Note that executions of a PNB are also executions of the corresponding KPN.

Definition 8. *An execution of a PNB is fair (maximal, effective) iff it is fair (maximal, effective) in the corresponding KPN.*

Corollary 2. *An execution of a PNB is not fair or not maximal if it permanently blocks on a full channel; in its own LTS there is no enabled write transition corresponding to the blocked write action, but such an action exists in the LTS of the KPN implying that the execution is not fair/maximal in the KPN.*

4.2   Deadlocks

A PNB behaves the same as the corresponding KPN, except for the fact that certain write actions may be disabled by full channels. This may lead to artificial deadlock situations. Since the amount of memory required for channels cannot be decided upfront [4], a scheduler must provide the means to dynamically (at run-time) increase channel capacity where needed.

   If a process is blocked trying to read from an empty channel or trying to write to a full channel, this situation can only be resolved by a unique other process in the network or, in the latter case, by increasing FIFO capacity. These dependencies may give rise to a chain of blocked processes whose blocked condition depends on each other. In order for a process on this chain to make progress, a process further on the chain must first make progress. This is impossible however if the chain leads to an input and all input has been consumed, or if the chain is cyclic. In the latter case, it is clear that the processes in this cyclic causal chain are in local deadlock. If all channels in this chain are empty, the deadlock is real (i.e., also present in the KPN); if not, the deadlock is artificial and can be resolved by enlarging the capacity of a channel on that cycle.

Definition 9. (WAITING) *Let $p, q \in P$; process p is said to be waiting for process q in configuration (π, γ) of the PNB with bounds $\bar{b}$,*

 - *if it can read from an empty internal channel c and q is the process that writes to channel c; i.e., $\pi(p) \xrightarrow{c?a}_{p}$ for $a \in \Sigma_c$, $\gamma(c) = \epsilon$ and $c \in O_q$;*
 - *if it can write to a full internal channel c and q is the process that reads from channel c; i.e., $\pi(p) \xrightarrow{c!a}_{p}$ for some $a \in \Sigma_c$, $|\gamma(c)| = \bar{b}(c)$ and $c \in I_q$;*
 - *if $p = q$ and it has terminated; i.e., there is no $\alpha \in Act$ such that $\pi(p) \xrightarrow{\alpha}_{p}$.*

Note that in the third case the process p has terminated. Saying that in that case it is waiting for itself, simplifies further definitions. Since processes are sequential, a process is waiting for a unique other process. This gives rise to chains of waiting processes.

Definition 10. ((COMPLETE) CAUSAL CHAIN) *A causal chain (of waiting processes in configuration (π, γ) with bounds $\bar{b}$) is a sequence $\bar{p} = p_0 p_1 p_2 \ldots p_k$ of different processes such that for all $0 \leq n < k$, p_n is waiting for p_{n+1} (in configuration (π, γ) with bounds $\bar{b}$). Such a causal chain is called complete if p_k can read from an input channel, or it is waiting for some p_n $(0 \leq n \leq k)$ (in configuration (π, γ) with bounds $\bar{b}$).*

Based on causal chains, we can define what we consider to be a local deadlock.

Definition 11. (LOCAL DEADLOCK) *A local deadlock of a PNB is a complete causal chain forming a cycle, i.e., the last process waiting for the first. A local deadlock is artificial if there is a process p in the deadlock that has an enabled write action in the corresponding KPN to a channel that is full in the PNB. A local deadlock is called real if it is not artificial, i.e., if all FIFOs on the cycle are empty. With a local deadlock, we associate its impact as the set of processes that are waiting (via a causal chain) for a process in the deadlock.*

A deadlock is an inherent property of a process network with its particular FIFO bounds combined with the input provided to the network. As a direct consequence of Corollary 1, we know that it cannot be avoided by different scheduling (unless a schedule is unfair and slows progress so that the deadlock is never reached). Since an artificial local deadlock involves a blocking write to a full channel, the following proposition follows immediately from Corollary 2.

Proposition 2. *If a fair and maximal execution of a PNB exists, then none of its executions exhibits an artificial local deadlock.*

Now we can show that artificial local deadlocks are caused by a lack of capacity in the full channels of the corresponding cycle.

Proposition 3. *If a PNB with bounds $\bar{b}$ displays an artificial local deadlock and there exists a maximal and fair execution of the corresponding PNB with bounds $\bar{b}'$, then in the deadlock there is some full channel c such that $\bar{b}'(c) > \bar{b}(c)$.*

Proof. The fact that the execution with bounds $\bar{b}'$ is maximal and fair implies that the artificial deadlock is not encountered (Proposition 2). Let causal chain $\bar{p}$ be a reachable artificial deadlock of the PNB with bounds $\bar{b}$ and let $FC \subseteq C$ be the set of full channels on this chain. Assume towards a contradiction that there is a set $\bar{b}'$ of bounds with $\bar{b}'(c) \leq \bar{b}(c)$ for every $c \in FC$, allowing for a fair and maximal execution . Now we can imagine the set $\bar{b}''$ of FIFO bounds where $\bar{b}''(c) = \max(\bar{b}(c), \bar{b}'(c))$ for all $c \in C$. Note that both $\bar{b} \preceq \bar{b}''$ and $\bar{b}' \preceq \bar{b}''$. Then the execution leading to the deadlock with bounds $\bar{b}$ is also an execution in the PNB with bounds $\bar{b}''$. In that PNB, the causal chain $\bar{p}$ will occur in that execution (the full channels have the same capacity as in $\bar{b}$). But this contradicts by Proposition 2 the fact that the network with bounds $\bar{b}''$ has a fair and maximal execution (since the network with smaller bounds $\bar{b}'$ has one).

The previous two propositions demonstrate that the channel capacity on a causal chain causing an artificial deadlock is insufficient and needs to be increased. The deadlock is not caused by wrong scheduling (Proposition 2) and could not have been avoided if other buffers outside of the deadlock were larger (Proposition 3). It is not clear however which of the full FIFOs on the chain should be enlarged. As a consequence of Proposition 3, we do know that if there exist bounds large enough to prevent the artificial deadlock, then also for all PNBs with larger bounds, the artificial deadlock cannot occur.

Corollary 3. *If a process network with bounds $\bar{b}$ permits a maximal and fair execution, then on the same network with bounds $\bar{b}'$, with $\bar{b} \preceq \bar{b}'$, there is no execution that leads to an artificial deadlock.*

5   Schedulers

We view a scheduler for PNBs as a strategy that determines the order of execution of individual read and write actions of all processes as well as the increase (or decrease) of memory allocated to FIFOs. To define the result of a scheduling strategy, we imagine that it is applied to generate some (possibly infinite) execution. We capture a series of snapshots by repeatedly observing the PNB. The snapshots of the output $(\rho!_O)$ form chains of output strings. We can define the result of the scheduling strategy to be the supremum of this chain.

Definition 12. (SCHEDULER REQUIREMENTS) *A scheduling strategy should (if possible) satisfy the following constraints (taken from [2], adapted from [12]).*

- OUTPUT COMPLETENESS: *the output of the realisation should be equal to the output prescribed by the denotational semantics of KPNs.*
- BOUNDEDNESS: *The scheduler should realise an execution where a bounded amount of memory is used for channels.*

Based upon the observation made in Section 4.2, that an artificial deadlock indicates a lack of capacity in the corresponding cyclic chain, we can devise a deadlock resolution strategy, that establishes a bounded execution if one exists. Unfortunately, we do not know which of the full buffers on the local deadlock should be enlarged. Therefore, we employ a strategy, that will (eventually) enlarge all full FIFOs on a local deadlock if necessary.

Definition 13. (SCHEDULING STRATEGY) *A correct scheduling strategy is obtained by repeating the following steps forever.*

1. *Execute the processes of a PNB in a data-driven fashion until either an artificial (local) deadlock occurs or the PNB terminates. While executing, use a scheduling policy that guarantees progress for all processes that can continue within current FIFO bounds.*
2. *Resolve all artificial deadlocks by increasing the smallest full FIFO on that deadlock by a finite amount of tokens.*

Note the difference with the algorithm of Parks, where the network is executed until *all* processes are blocked. In our scheduling strategy, deadlock resolution is activated also for local artificial deadlocks.

We proceed to show that the proposed scheduling strategy satisfies the requirements of Definition 12. These requirements can only be met if the KPN is bounded and effective. Blocking because of a full channel must eventually be resolved when the channel is emptied by another process, or it must lead to a local artificial deadlock. To see this, consider a PNB where a process remains blocked on a full channel. The tokens in the channel are eventually read in an execution of the (effective) KPN. If this doesn't happen in the corresponding PNB, the process that reads the channel must also remain blocked, as well as the process on which this process waits, and so forth. The corresponding complete causal chain cannot end in an input; such a block can only be caused if all input has been consumed. But then the contents of the full channel will never be read contradicting effectiveness. Thus the causal chain must be cyclic, i.e., a local deadlock has occurred, and from effectiveness it follows that it must be artificial.

Lemma 1. *If a PNB of an effective KPN is scheduled according to the strategy of Definition 13 with bounds $\bar{b}$ and a process p is blocked on a write, then during step 1 of the scheduling strategy, either this write will become unblocked and subsequently scheduled, or p will eventually be in the impact of an artificial deadlock.*

Proof. Let (π, γ) be a configuration where process p is trying to write to a full channel $c \in C$, $\pi(p) \xrightarrow{c!a}{}_{p} s$ and $|\gamma(c)| = \bar{b}(c)$. Process p is waiting for process q reading from channel c. In any execution with bounds $\bar{b}$ passing through configuration (π, γ), a read action of q on channel c precedes the write action $c!a$ if it occurs. Effectiveness implies that an effective fair and maximal execution exists on the KPN. Corollary 1 implies that, in the KPN, q performs only a finite number of read and write operations before executing a read action from c. If during scheduling step 1, this action never occurs in the PNB, then q must from some point onward be permanently blocked, waiting for some other process r. It cannot be blocked because of termination of process q or on a read operation from an input channel, because that would contradict effectiveness of the KPN. The argument can be repeated for the processes q and r and so forth. Since the number of processes is finite, this implies that there is a set of processes that remain blocked and are waiting for each other, i.e., a local deadlock. Again, this deadlock must be artificial, because effectiveness of the KPN implies that the reading of tokens from the full channel c cannot depend on a real local deadlock.

Lemma 2. *The scheduling strategy of Definition 13 applied to a PNB of a bounded and effective KPN leads a finite number of times to an artificial deadlock.*

Proof. The KPN is bounded, thus there exists a capacity b of tokens, such that the PNB with bounds $\bar{b}$, where $\bar{b}(c) = b$ for all $c \in C$, has a fair and maximal execution. Then the sum of positive differences between b and the capacities of the full FIFOs in some deadlock is a measure that decreases with every resolution of *this* deadlock (Proposition 3) and does not increase with the resolution of other deadlocks. At the latest when this measure reaches zero, this deadlock can no more occur (Corollary 3). There is only a finite number of different deadlocks and thus at some point no more artificial deadlock can occur.

Lemma 3. *The scheduling strategy of Definition 13 applied to a PNB of a bounded and effective KPN produces a fair and maximal execution.*

Proof. Step 1 of the scheduling strategy guarantees progress on all actions, except write actions to full channels. That these blocking actions cannot persist follows from the fact that a persisting blocking write action leads to an artificial local deadlock (Lemma 1). The deadlock is resolved by the scheduling strategy. A new deadlock can occur only a finite number of times (Lemma 2). Thus eventually, the blocked write actions must become enabled thereby guaranteeing fairness and maximality.

This brings us to the main result, namely that the introduced scheduling strategy is correct for the class of KPNs that are bounded and effective.

Theorem 2. *The scheduling strategy of Definition 13 applied to a PNB of a bounded and effective KPN results in an execution that satisfies both correctness requirements of Definition 12.*

Proof. (OUTPUT COMPLETENESS) The output conforms to the denotational semantics if the execution is maximal and fair (Theorem 1). That the execution is maximal and fair follows from Lemma 3. (BOUNDEDNESS) First note that the strategy increases the buffer sizes with a finite amount with every deadlock detected. An unbounded schedule can only be the result of an infinite number of deadlocks. According to Lemma 2, only a finite number of times a deadlock can occur.

To conclude, we reflect on the restrictions of boundedness and effectiveness on the class of KPNs, and on the influence of fairness implicit in these restrictions.

Theorem 3. *There exists no scheduler that correctly schedules (i) all effective KPNs, (ii) all bounded KPNs, or (iii) all KPNs for which a maximal, bounded and effective (but possibly unfair) execution exists.*

Proof. (i) It is known [12] that there exist KPNs that are not bounded (but still effective). It is obvious that they cannot satisfy the boundedness and output completeness requirement. (ii) It follows from the example in Section 2 (Figure 3) that no scheduler exists that can schedule the described collection of KPNs in bounded memory *and* with complete output. (iii) A maximal, bounded and effective execution may exist that is not fair. It may be that it is bounded only because a part of the network is never scheduled. It may still be output complete if that part of the network does not produce any output. Then a bounded and effective execution may exist that doesn't execute that part of the network. A scheduler however cannot decide in general whether any part of the network contributes to the output and must schedule it, leading to unbounded memory usage.

6   Conclusions

(Kahn) process networks are a suitable model of computation and programming model for streaming-based multimedia applications. The Kahn Principle states that any operational implementation that respects some loose fairness constraints realises the behaviour specified by a KPN. The scheduling algorithm proposed in [12], and used for many implementations of KPNs [1,6,9,14,15], employs a scheduling and artificial-deadlock resolution strategy that does not guarantee fairness. In this paper, we have presented an alternative scheduling strategy that solves this problem and we have proved that for a very broad class of KPNs (called bounded and effective), this scheduler realises the correct behaviour. As future work, we would like to study an efficient implementation and the optimisation of scheduling as done in [2] for Parks' algorithm of [12]. We would also like to investigate the implications of distributed execution of KPNs.

References

1. G.E. Allen, B. Evans, and D. Schanbacher. Real-time sonar beamforming on a UNIX workstation using process networks and POSIX threads. In *Proc. of the 32nd Asilomar Conference on Signals, Systems and Computers*, pages 1725–1729. IEEE Computer Society, 1998.

2. T. Basten and J. Hoogerbrugge. Efficient execution of process networks. In A. Chalmers, M. Mirmehdi, and H. Muller, editors, *Proc. of Communicating Process Architectures 2001, Bristol, UK, September 2001*, pages 1–14. IOS Press, 2001.

3. S. Brookes. On the Kahn principle and fair networks. Technical Report CMU-CS-98-156, School of Computer Science, Carnegie Mellon University, 1998. Presented at FMPS'98. Submitted to Theoretical Computer Science.

4. J.T. Buck. *Scheduling Dynamic Dataflow Graphs with Bounded Memory Using the Token Flow Model*. PhD thesis, University of California, EECS Dept., Berkeley, CA, 1993.

5. A.A. Faustini. An operational semantics for pure dataflow. In M. Nielsen and E. M. Schmidt, editors, *Automata, Languages and Programming, 9th Colloquium, Aarhus, Denmark, July 12–16, 1982, Proceedings*, pages 212–224. Springer, 1982.

6. M. Goel. Process networks in Ptolemy II. Technical Memorandum UCB/ERL No. M98/69, University of California, EECS Dept., Berkeley, CA, December 1998.

7. G. Kahn. The semantics of a simple language for parallel programming. In J.L. Rosenfeld, editor, *Information Processing 74: Proceedings of the IFIP Congress 74, Stockholm, Sweden, August 1974*, pages 471–475. North-Holland, 1974.

8. G. Kahn and D.B. MacQueen. Coroutines and networks of parallel programming. In B. Gilchrist, editor, *Information Processing 77: Proceedings of the IFIP Congress 77, Toronto, Canada, August 8–12, 1977*, pages 993–998. North-Holland, 1977.

9. E.A. de Kock et al. YAPI: Application modeling for signal processing systems. In *Proc. of the 37th. Design Automation Conference, Los Angeles, CA, June 2000*, pages 402–405. IEEE, 2000.

10. E.A. Lee. Overview of the Ptolemy project. Technical Memorandum UCB/ERL No. M01/11, University of California, EECS Dept., Berkeley, CA, March 2001.

11. E.A. Lee and D.G. Messerschmitt. Synchronous data flow. *IEEE Proceedings*, 75(9):1235–1245, September 1987.

12. T.M. Parks. *Bounded Scheduling of Process Networks*. PhD thesis, University of California, EECS Dept., Berkeley, CA, December 1995.

13. E.W. Stark. Concurrent transition system semantics of process networks. In *Proc. of the 1987 SIGACT-SIGPLAN Symposium on Principles of Programming Languages, Munich, Germany, January 1987*, pages 199–210. ACM Press, 1987.

14. R.S. Stevens, M. Wan, P. Laramie, T.M. Parks, and E.A. Lee. Implementation of process networks in Java. Technical Memorandum UCB/ERL No. M97/84, University of California, EECS Dept., Berkeley, CA, 1997.
15. J. Vayssière, D. Webb, and A. Wendelborn. Distributed process networks. Technical Report TR 99–03, University of Adelaide, Department of Computer Science, South Australia 5005, Australia, October 1999.

Tagging, Encoding, and Jones Optimality

Olivier Danvy[1] and Pablo E. Martínez López[2]

[1] BRICS[**],
Department of Computer Science, University of Aarhus
Ny Munkegade, Building 540, DK-8000 Aarhus C, Denmark
(danvy@brics.dk)

[2] LIFIA
Universidad Nacional de La Plata
CC. 11 Correo Central, (1900) La Plata, Bs.As. Argentina
(fidel@info.unlp.edu.ar)

Abstract. A partial evaluator is said to be Jones-optimal if the result of specializing a self-interpreter with respect to a source program is textually identical to the source program, modulo renaming. Jones optimality has already been obtained if the self-interpreter is untyped. If the self-interpreter is typed, however, residual programs are cluttered with type tags. To obtain the original source program, these tags must be removed.

A number of sophisticated solutions have already been proposed. We observe, however, that with a simple representation shift, ordinary partial evaluation is already Jones-optimal, modulo an encoding. The representation shift amounts to reading the type tags as constructors for higher-order abstract syntax. We substantiate our observation by considering a typed self-interpreter whose input syntax is higher-order. Specializing this interpreter with respect to a source program yields a residual program that is textually identical to the source program, modulo renaming.

1 Introduction

Specializing an interpreter with respect to a program has the effect of translating the program from the source language of the interpreter to the implementation language (or to use Reynolds's words, from the defined language to the defining language [36]). For example, if an interpreter for Pascal is written in Scheme, specializing it with respect to a Pascal program yields an equivalent Scheme program. Numerous instances of this specialization are documented in the literature, e.g., for imperative languages [5,9], for functional languages [2], for logic languages [7], for object-oriented languages [27], for reflective languages [31], and for action notation [3]. Interpreter specialization is also known as the first Futamura projection [15,16,26].

[**] Basic Research in Computer Science (www.brics.dk), funded by the Danish National Research Foundation.

P. Degano (Ed.): ESOP 2003, LNCS 2618, pp. 335–347, 2003.

One automatic technique for carrying out program specialization is partial evaluation [6, 25]. An effective partial evaluator completely removes the interpretive overhead of the interpreter. This complete removal is difficult to characterize in general and therefore it has been characterized for a particular case, self-interpreters, i.e., interpreters whose source language is (a subset of) their implementation language. A partial evaluator is said to be *Jones optimal* if it completely removes the interpretation overhead of a self-interpreter, i.e., if the result of specializing a self-interpreter with respect to a well-formed source program is textually identical to the source program, modulo renaming. Jones optimality was obtained early after the development of offline partial evaluation for untyped interpreters, with lambda-Mix [18, 25].

A typed interpreter, however, requires a universal data type to represent expressible values. Specializing such an interpreter, e.g., with lambda-Mix, yields a residual program with many tag and untag operations. Ordinary, Mix-style, partial evaluation is thus not Jones optimal [24].

Obtaining Jones optimality has proven a source of inspiration for a number of new forays into partial evaluation, e.g., handwritten generators of program generators [19,1], constructor specialization [10,33], type specialization [11,21,20, 22,23,29], coercions [8], and more recently tag elimination [30,37,38] and staged tagless interpreters [34]. Furthermore, the term "identical modulo renaming" in the definition of Jones optimality has evolved into "at least as efficient" [17,25].

Here, we identify a simple representation shift of the specialized version of a typed lambda-interpreter and we show that with this representation shift, ordinary partial evaluation is already Jones optimal in the original sense.

Prerequisites and notation: We assume a basic familiarity with partial evaluation in general, as can be gathered in Jones, Gomard, and Sestoft's textbook [25]. We use Standard ML [32] and the notion of higher-order abstract syntax as introduced by Pfenning and Elliot [35] and used by Thiemann [39, 40]: Whereas the first-order abstract syntax of lambda-terms reads as

```
datatype foexp = FOVAR of string
               | FOLAM of string * foexp
               | FOAPP of foexp * foexp
```

the higher-order abstract syntax of lambda-terms reads as

```
datatype hoexp = HOVAR of string
               | HOLAM of hoexp -> hoexp
               | HOAPP of hoexp * hoexp
```

where the constructor HOVAR is only used to represent free variables. For example, the first-order abstract syntax of the K combinator $\lambda x.\lambda y.x$ reads as

```
FOLAM ("x", FOLAM ("y", FOVAR "x"))
```

and its higher-order abstract syntax reads as

```
HOLAM (fn x => HOLAM (fn y => x))
```

2   The Problem

The problem of specializing a typed interpreter is usually presented as follows [38]. Given

- a grammar of source expressions

```
datatype exp = LIT of int
             | VAR of string
             | LAM of string * exp
             | APP of exp * exp
             | ADD of exp * exp
```

- a universal type of expressible values

```
datatype univ = INT of int
              | FUN of univ -> univ
```

- an environment Env : ENV

```
signature ENV
= sig
    type 'a env
    val empty : 'a env
    val extend : string * 'a * 'a env -> 'a env
    val lookup : string * 'a env -> 'a
  end
```

- and two untagging functions app and add

```
exception TYPE_ERROR
(*  app : univ * univ -> univ  *)
fun app (FUN f, v)
    = f v
  | app _
    = raise TYPE_ERROR

(*  add : univ * univ -> univ  *)
fun add (INT i1, INT i2)
    = INT (i1 + i2)
  | add _
    = raise TYPE_ERROR
```

a typed lambda-interpreter is specified as follows:

```
(*  eval : exp -> univ Env.env -> univ  *)
fun eval (LIT i) env
    = INT i
  | eval (VAR x) env
    = Env.lookup (x, env)
  | eval (LAM (x, e)) env
    = FUN (fn v => eval e (Env.extend (x, v, env)))
  | eval (APP (e0, e1)) env
    = app (eval e0 env, eval e1 env)
  | eval (ADD (e1, e2)) env
    = add (eval e1 env, eval e2 env)
```

This evaluator is compositional, i.e., all recursive calls to eval on the right-hand side are on proper sub-parts of the term in the left-hand side [41, page 60]. Specializing this evaluator amounts to

1. unfolding all calls to eval while keeping the environment partially static, so that variables are looked up at specialization time, and
2. reconstructing all the remaining parts of the evaluator as residual syntax.

Unfolding all calls to eval terminates because the evaluator is compositional and its input term is finite.

Specializing the interpreter with respect to the term

```
LAM ("x", APP (VAR "x", VAR "x"))
```

thus yields

```
FUN (fn v => app (v, v))
```

This specialization is not Jones optimal because of the type tag FUN and the untagging operation app. (N.B. Danvy's type coercions and (depending on the annotations in the interpreter) Hughes's type specialization would actually not produce any result here [8, 21]. Instead, they would yield a type error because the source term is untyped. Raising a type error at specialization time or at run time is inessential with respect to Jones optimality.)

3   But Is It a Problem?

An alternative reading of

```
FUN (fn v => app (v, v))
```

is as higher-order abstract syntax [35]. In this reading, FUN is the tag of a lambda-abstraction and app is the tag of an application.

In that light, let us define the residual syntax as an ML data type by considering each branch of the evaluator and gathering each result into a data-type constructor:

```
datatype univ_res = INT_res of int
                  | FUN_res of univ_res -> univ_res
                  | APP_res of univ_res * univ_res
                  | ADD_res of univ_res * univ_res
```

The corresponding generating extension is a recursive function that traverses the source expression and constructs the result using the constructors of univ_res:

```
(*  eval_gen : exp -> univ_res Env.env -> univ_res  *)
fun eval_gen (LIT i) env
    = INT_res i
  | eval_gen (VAR x) env
    = Env.lookup (x, env)
```

```
  | eval_gen (LAM (x, e)) env
    = FUN_res (fn v => eval_gen e (Env.extend (x, v, env)))
  | eval_gen (APP (e0, e1)) env
    = APP_res (eval_gen e0 env, eval_gen e1 env)
  | eval_gen (ADD (e1, e2)) env
    = ADD_res (eval_gen e1 env, eval_gen e2 env)
```

The interpretation of univ_res elements is defined with a function eval_res that makes the following diagram commute:

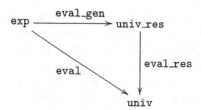

First of all, we need a conversion function u2ur and its left inverse ur2u to write eval_res:

```
exception NOT_A_VALUE

(*  u2ur : univ -> univ_res  *)
(*  ur2u : univ_res -> univ  *)
fun u2ur (INT i)
    = INT_res i
  | u2ur (FUN f)
    = FUN_res (fn r => u2ur (f (ur2u r)))
and ur2u (INT_res i)
    = INT i
  | ur2u (FUN_res f)
    = FUN (fn u => ur2u (f (u2ur u)))
  | ur2u (APP_res _)
    = raise NOT_A_VALUE
  | ur2u (ADD_res _)
    = raise NOT_A_VALUE
```

The corresponding evaluator reads as follows (the auxiliary functions app and add are that of Section 2):

```
(*  eval_res : univ_res -> univ  *)
fun eval_res (INT_res i)
    = INT i
  | eval_res (FUN_res f)
    = FUN (fn u => eval_res (f (u2ur u)))
  | eval_res (APP_res (r0, r1))
    = app (eval_res r0, eval_res r1)
  | eval_res (ADD_res (r1, r2))
    = add (eval_res r1, eval_res r2)
```

The generating extension, eval_gen, is an encoding function from first-order abstract syntax to higher-order abstract syntax. (In fact, it is the standard such encoding [35].) It maps a term such as

```
LAM ("x", APP (VAR "x", VAR "x"))
```

into the value of

```
FUN_res (fn v => APP_res (v, v))
```

With this reading of residual syntax as higher-order abstract syntax, ordinary partial evaluation (i.e., the generating extension) maps the first-order abstract-syntax representation of $\lambda x.x\,x$ into the higher-order abstract-syntax representation of $\lambda x.x\,x$, and it does so optimally.

(Incidentally, partial evaluation (of an interpreter in a typed setting) connects to Ershov's mixed computation, since the specialized version of an evaluator is both (1) a residual program and (2) the data type used to represent this residual program together with the interpretation of the constructors of the data type [12, 13, 14].)

4   An Interpreter for Higher-Order Abstract Syntax

Let us now verify that Jones optimality is obtained for a typed interpreter whose input syntax is higher order. It is a simple matter to adapt the representation of the input of the typed interpreter from Section 3 to be higher order instead of first order. In the fashion of Section 2, the grammar of source expressions and the universal type of expressible values read as follows:

```
datatype exp = LIT of int
             | LAM of exp -> exp
             | APP of exp * exp
             | ADD of exp * exp

datatype univ = INT of int
              | FUN of univ -> univ
```

The auxiliary functions app and add read just as in Section 2. As in Section 3, we need a conversion function u2e and its left inverse e2u:

```
exception NOT_A_VALUE

(*   u2e : univ -> exp   *)
(*   e2u : exp -> univ   *)
fun u2e (INT i)
    = LIT i
  | u2e (FUN f)
    = LAM (fn e => u2e (f (e2u e)))
```

```
and e2u (LIT i)
    = INT i
  | e2u (LAM f)
    = FUN (fn u => e2u (f (u2e u)))
  | e2u (APP _)
    = raise NOT_A_VALUE
  | e2u (ADD _)
    = raise NOT_A_VALUE
```

The corresponding evaluator reads as follows:

```
(*  eval : exp -> univ  *)
fun eval (LIT i)
    = INT i
  | eval (LAM f)
    = FUN (fn u => eval (f (u2e u)))
  | eval (APP (e0, e1))
    = app (eval e0, eval e1)
  | eval (ADD (e1, e2))
    = add (eval e1, eval e2)
```

As in Section 3, we define the residual syntax as an ML data type by enumerating each branch of the evaluator and gathering each result into a data-type constructor. The result and its interpretation (i.e., eval_res and its two auxiliary conversion functions) are the same as in Section 3:

```
datatype univ_res = INT_res of int
                  | FUN_res of univ_res -> univ_res
                  | APP_res of univ_res * univ_res
                  | ADD_res of univ_res * univ_res
```

As in Section 3, we need two conversion functions ur2e and e2ur to write the generating extension:

```
(*  ur2e : univ_res -> exp  *)
(*  e2ur : exp -> univ_res  *)
fun ur2e (INT_res i)
    = LIT i
  | ur2e (FUN_res f)
    = LAM (fn e => ur2e (f (e2ur e)))
  | ur2e (APP_res (e0, e1))
    = APP (ur2e e0, ur2e e1)
  | ur2e (ADD_res (e1, e2))
    = ADD (ur2e e1, ur2e e2)
and e2ur (LIT i)
    = INT_res i
  | e2ur (LAM f)
    = FUN_res (fn r => e2ur (f (ur2e r)))
  | e2ur (APP (e0, e1))
    = APP_res (e2ur e0, e2ur e1)
  | e2ur (ADD (e1, e2))
    = ADD_res (e2ur e1, e2ur e2)
```

The corresponding generating extension reads as follows:

```
(*  eval_gen : exp -> univ_res  *)
fun eval_gen (LIT i)
     = INT_res i
   | eval_gen (LAM f)
     = FUN_res (fn r => eval_gen (f (ur2e r)))
   | eval_gen (APP (e0, e1))
     = APP_res (eval_gen e0, eval_gen e1)
   | eval_gen (ADD (e1, e2))
     = ADD_res (eval_gen e1, eval_gen e2)
```

It should now be clear that `exp` and `univ_res` are isomorphic, since `ur2e` and `e2ur` are inverse functions, and that `eval_gen` computes the identity transformation up to this isomorphism. The resulting specialization is thus Jones optimal.

5   But Is It the Real Problem?

Jones's challenge, however, is not for any typed interpreter but for a typed self-interpreter. Such a self-interpreter, for example, is displayed in Taha, Makholm, and Hughes's article at PADO II [38]. We observe that the reading of Section 3 applies for this self-interpreter as well: its universal data type of values can be seen as a representation of higher-order abstract syntax.

6   A Self-Interpreter for Higher-Order Abstract Syntax

The second author has implemented a self-interpreter for higher-order abstract syntax in a subset of Haskell, and verified that its generating extension computes an identity transformation modulo an isomorphism [28].[1] Therefore, Jones's challenge is met.

7   Related Work

7.1   Specializing Lambda-Interpreters

The generating extension of a lambda-interpreter provides an encoding of a lambda-term into the term model of the meta language of this interpreter. For an untyped self-interpreter, the translation is the identity transformation, modulo desugaring. For an untyped interpreter in continuation-passing style (CPS), the translation is the untyped CPS transformation. For an untyped interpreter in state-passing style (SPS), the translation is the untyped SPS transformation. And for an untyped interpreter in monadic style, the translation is the untyped monadic-style transformation.

---

[1] The self-interpreter is available from the authors' web page.

In that light, what we have done here is to identify a similar reading for a typed self-interpreter, identifying its domain of universal values as a representation of higher-order abstract syntax. With this reading, type tags are not a bug but a feature and ordinary partial evaluation is Jones optimal. In particular, for a typed interpreter in CPS, the translation is the typed CPS transformation into higher-order abstract syntax, and similarly for state-passing style, etc.

7.2   Jones Optimality and Higher-Order Abstract Syntax

This article complements the first author's work on coercions for type specialization [8] and the second author's work on type specialization [29]. Our key insight is that a specialized interpreter is a higher-order abstract syntax representation of the source program. As pointed out by Taha in a personal communication to the first author (January 2003), however, this insight in itself is not new. Already in 2000, Taha and Makholm were aware that "A staged interpreter for a simply-typed lambda calculus can be modelled by a total map from terms to what is essentially a higher-order abstract syntax encoding." [37, Section 1.2]. Yet they took a different path and developed tag elimination and then tagless interpreters to achieve Jones-optimal specialization of typed interpreters.

7.3   Type Specialisation

The goal of type specialisation is to specialise both a source term and a source type to a residual term and a residual type. It was introduced by Hughes, who was inspired precisely by the problem of Jones optimality for typed interpreters [21, 20]. The framework of type specialisation, however, allows more than just producing optimal typed specialisers; traditional partial evaluation, constructor specialisation, firstification, and type checking are comprised in it (among other features). In contrast, we have solely focused on specializing (unannotated) typed interpreters here.

8   Conclusion

The statement of Jones optimality involves two ingredients:

1. an evaluator that is in direct style and compositional, i.e., that is defined by structural induction on the source syntax; and
2. a partial evaluator.

Our point is that if the partial evaluator, when it specializes the evaluator with respect to an expression,

- unfolds all calls to the evaluator,
- keeps the environment partially static, so that variables can be looked up at partial-evaluation time, and
- reconstructs everything else into a residual data type

then it computes a homomorphism, i.e., a compositional translation, from the source syntax (data type) to the target syntax (data type). When the source and target syntax are isomorphic, as in Section 4 and for lambda-Mix [18, 25], this homomorphism is an isomorphism and the partial evaluator is Jones optimal.

Acknowledgments. Our insight about higher-order abstract syntax occurred during the second author's presentation at ASIA-PEPM 2002 [29]. The topic of this article has benefited from discussions with Mads Sig Ager, Kenichi Asai, John Hughes, Neil Jones, Nevin Heintze, Julia Lawall, Karoline Malmkjær, Henning Korsholm Rohde, Peter Thiemann, and Walid Taha, with special thanks to Henning Makholm for a substantial as well as enlightening discussion in January 2003. We are also grateful to the anonymous reviewers for comments, with special thanks to Julia Lawall.

This work is supported by the ESPRIT Working Group APPSEM II (http://www.tcs.informatik.uni-muenchen.de/~mhofmann/appsem2/).

The second author is a PhD student at the University of Buenos Aires and is partially funded by grants from the ALFA-CORDIAL project Nr. ALR/B73011/ 94.04-5.0348.9 and the FOMEC project of the Computer Science Department, FCEyN, at the University of Buenos Aires.

References

1. Lars Birkedal and Morten Welinder. Handwriting program generator generators. In Manuel Hermenegildo and Jaan Penjam, editors, *Sixth International Symposium on Programming Language Implementation and Logic Programming*, number 844 in Lecture Notes in Computer Science, pages 198–214, Madrid, Spain, September 1994. Springer-Verlag.
2. Anders Bondorf. Compiling laziness by partial evaluation. In Simon L. Peyton Jones, Guy Hutton, and Carsten K. Holst, editors, *Functional Programming, Glasgow 1990*, Workshops in Computing, pages 9–22, Glasgow, Scotland, 1990. Springer-Verlag.
3. Anders Bondorf and Jens Palsberg. Compiling actions by partial evaluation. In Arvind, editor, *Proceedings of the Sixth ACM Conference on Functional Programming and Computer Architecture*, pages 308–317, Copenhagen, Denmark, June 1993. ACM Press.
4. Wei-Ngan Chin, editor. *ACM SIGPLAN Asian Symposium on Partial Evaluation and Semantics-Based Program Manipulation*, Aizu, Japan, September 2002. ACM Press.
5. Charles Consel and Olivier Danvy. Static and dynamic semantics processing. In Robert (Corky) Cartwright, editor, *Proceedings of the Eighteenth Annual ACM Symposium on Principles of Programming Languages*, pages 14–24, Orlando, Florida, January 1991. ACM Press.
6. Charles Consel and Olivier Danvy. Tutorial notes on partial evaluation. In Susan L. Graham, editor, *Proceedings of the Twentieth Annual ACM Symposium on Principles of Programming Languages*, pages 493–501, Charleston, South Carolina, January 1993. ACM Press.
7. Charles Consel and Siau-Cheng Khoo. Semantics-directed generation of a Prolog compiler. *Science of Computer Programming*, 21:263–291, 1993.

8. Olivier Danvy. A simple solution to type specialization. In Kim G. Larsen, Sven Skyum, and Glynn Winskel, editors, *Proceedings of the 25th International Colloquium on Automata, Languages, and Programming*, number 1443 in Lecture Notes in Computer Science, pages 908–917. Springer-Verlag, 1998.

9. Olivier Danvy and René Vestergaard. Semantics-based compiling: A case study in type-directed partial evaluation. In Herbert Kuchen and Doaitse Swierstra, editors, *Eighth International Symposium on Programming Language Implementation and Logic Programming*, number 1140 in Lecture Notes in Computer Science, pages 182–197, Aachen, Germany, September 1996. Springer-Verlag. Extended version available as the technical report BRICS-RS-96-13.

10. Dirk Dussart, Eddy Bevers, and Karel De Vlaminck. Polyvariant constructor specialisation. In William L. Scherlis, editor, *Proceedings of the ACM SIGPLAN Symposium on Partial Evaluation and Semantics-Based Program Manipulation*, pages 54–65, La Jolla, California, June 1995. ACM Press.

11. Dirk Dussart, John Hughes, and Peter Thiemann. Type specialization for imperative languages. In Mads Tofte, editor, *Proceedings of the 1997 ACM SIGPLAN International Conference on Functional Programming*, pages 204–216, Amsterdam, The Netherlands, June 1997. ACM Press.

12. Andrei P. Ershov. On the essence of compilation. In E. J. Neuhold, editor, *Formal Description of Programming Concepts*, pages 391–420. North-Holland, 1978.

13. Andrei P. Ershov. Mixed computation: Potential applications and problems for study. *Theoretical Computer Science*, 18:41–67, 1982.

14. Andrei P. Ershov, Dines Bjørner, Yoshihiko Futamura, K. Furukawa, Anders Haraldsson, and William Scherlis, editors. *Special Issue: Selected Papers from the Workshop on Partial Evaluation and Mixed Computation, 1987*, New Generation Computing, Vol. 6, No. 2-3. Ohmsha Ltd. and Springer-Verlag, 1988.

15. Yoshihiko Futamura. Partial evaluation of computation process – an approach to a compiler-compiler. *Higher-Order and Symbolic Computation*, 12(4):381–391, 1999. Reprinted from Systems · Computers · Controls 2(5), 1971.

16. Yoshihiko Futamura. Partial evaluation of computation process, revisited. *Higher-Order and Symbolic Computation*, 12(4):377–380, 1999.

17. Robert Glück. Jones optimality, binding-time improvements, and the strength of program specializers. In Chin [4], pages 9–19.

18. Carsten K. Gomard and Neil D. Jones. A partial evaluator for the untyped lambda-calculus. *Journal of Functional Programming*, 1(1):21–69, 1991.

19. Carsten K. Holst and John Launchbury. Handwriting cogen to avoid problems with static typing. In *Draft Proceedings, Fourth Annual Glasgow Workshop on Functional Programming, Skye, Scotland*, pages 210–218. Glasgow University, 1991.

20. John Hughes. An introduction to program specialisation by type inference. In *Functional Programming*, Glasgow University, July 1996. Published electronically.

21. John Hughes. Type specialisation for the lambda calculus; or, a new paradigm for partial evaluation based on type inference. In Olivier Danvy, Robert Glück, and Peter Thiemann, editors, *Partial Evaluation*, number 1110 in Lecture Notes in Computer Science, pages 183–215, Dagstuhl, Germany, February 1996. Springer-Verlag.

22. John Hughes. A type specialisation tutorial. In John Hatcliff, Torben Æ. Mogensen, and Peter Thiemann, editors, *Partial Evaluation – Practice and Theory; Proceedings of the 1998 DIKU Summer School*, number 1706 in Lecture Notes in Computer Science, pages 293–325, Copenhagen, Denmark, July 1998. Springer-Verlag.

23. John Hughes. The correctness of type specialisation. In Gert Smolka, editor, *Proceedings of the Ninth European Symposium on Programming*, number 1782 in Lecture Notes in Computer Science, pages 215–229, Berlin, Germany, March 2000. Springer-Verlag.

24. Neil D. Jones. Challenging problems in partial evaluation and mixed computation. In Dines Bjørner, Andrei P. Ershov, and Neil D. Jones, editors, *Partial Evaluation and Mixed Computation*, pages 1–14. North-Holland, 1988.

25. Neil D. Jones, Carsten K. Gomard, and Peter Sestoft. *Partial Evaluation and Automatic Program Generation*. Prentice-Hall International, London, UK, 1993. Available online at http://www.dina.kvl.dk/~sestoft/pebook/.

26. Neil D. Jones, Peter Sestoft, and Harald Søndergaard. MIX: A self-applicable partial evaluator for experiments in compiler generation. *Lisp and Symbolic Computation*, 2(1):9–50, 1989.

27. Siau Cheng Khoo and Sundaresh. Compiling inheritance using partial evaluation. In Paul Hudak and Neil D. Jones, editors, *Proceedings of the ACM SIGPLAN Symposium on Partial Evaluation and Semantics-Based Program Manipulation*, SIGPLAN Notices, Vol. 26, No 9, pages 211–222, New Haven, Connecticut, June 1991. ACM Press.

28. Pablo E. Martínez López. *Type Specialisation for Polymorphic Languages*. PhD thesis, Department of Computer Science, University of Buenos Aires, Buenos Aires, Argentina, 2003. Forthcoming.

29. Pablo E. Martínez López and John Hughes. Principal type specialisation. In Chin [4], pages 94–105.

30. Henning Makholm. On Jones-optimal specialization for strongly typed languages. In Walid Taha, editor, *Proceedings of the First Workshop on Semantics, Applications, and Implementation of Program Generation (SAIG 2000)*, number 1924 in Lecture Notes in Computer Science, pages 129–148, Montréal, Canada, September 2000. Springer-Verlag.

31. Hidehiko Masuhara, Satoshi Matsuoka, Kenichi Asai, and Akinori Yonezawa. Compiling away the meta-level in object-oriented concurrent reflective languages using partial evaluation. In *Proceedings of OOPSLA'91, the ACM SIGPLAN Tenth Annual Conference on Object-Oriented Programming Systems, Languages and Applications*, pages 300–315, Austin, Texas, October 1995. SIGPLAN Notices 30(10).

32. Robin Milner, Mads Tofte, Robert Harper, and David MacQueen. *The Definition of Standard ML (Revised)*. The MIT Press, 1997.

33. Torben Æ. Mogensen. Constructor specialization. In David A. Schmidt, editor, *Proceedings of the Second ACM SIGPLAN Symposium on Partial Evaluation and Semantics-Based Program Manipulation*, pages 22–32, Copenhagen, Denmark, June 1993. ACM Press.

34. Emir Pasalic, Walid Taha, and Tim Sheard. Tagless staged interpreters for typed languages. In Simon Peyton Jones, editor, *Proceedings of the 2002 ACM SIGPLAN International Conference on Functional Programming*, Pittsburgh, Pennsylvania, September 2002. ACM Press.

35. Frank Pfenning and Conal Elliott. Higher-order abstract syntax. In Mayer D. Schwartz, editor, *Proceedings of the ACM SIGPLAN'88 Conference on Programming Languages Design and Implementation*, SIGPLAN Notices, Vol. 23, No 7, pages 199–208, Atlanta, Georgia, June 1988. ACM Press.

36. John C. Reynolds. Definitional interpreters for higher-order programming languages. *Higher-Order and Symbolic Computation*, 11(4):363–397, 1998. Reprinted from the proceedings of the 25th ACM National Conference (1972).

37. Walid Taha and Henning Makholm. Tag elimination or type specialization is a type-indexed effect. In *Proceedings of the 2000 APPSEM Workshop on Subtyping and Dependent Types in Programming*, Ponte de Lima, Portugal, July 2000. http://www-sop.inria.fr/oasis/DTP00/.

38. Walid Taha, Henning Makholm, and John Hughes. Tag elimination and Jones-optimality. In Olivier Danvy and Andrzej Filinski, editors, *Programs as Data Objects, Second Symposium, PADO 2001*, number 2053 in Lecture Notes in Computer Science, pages 257–275, Aarhus, Denmark, May 2001. Springer-Verlag.

39. Peter Thiemann. Combinators for program generation. *Journal of Functional Programming*, 9(5):483–525, 1999.

40. Peter Thiemann. Higher-order code splicing. In S. Doaitse Swierstra, editor, *Proceedings of the Eighth European Symposium on Programming*, number 1576 in Lecture Notes in Computer Science, pages 243–257, Amsterdam, The Netherlands, March 1999. Springer-Verlag.

41. Glynn Winskel. *The Formal Semantics of Programming Languages*. Foundation of Computing Series. The MIT Press, 1993.

The Rely-Guarantee Method in Isabelle/HOL

Leonor Prensa Nieto

INRIA Sophia-Antipolis, France[**]
Leonor.Prensa@inria.fr

Abstract. We present the formalization of the rely-guarantee method in the theorem prover Isabelle/HOL. This method consists of a Hoare-like system of rules to verify concurrent imperative programs with shared variables in a compositional way. Syntax, semantics and proof rules are defined in higher-order logic. Soundness of the proof rules w.r.t. the semantics is proven mechanically. Also parameterized programs, where the number of parallel components is a parameter, are included in the programming language and thus can be verified directly in the system. We prove that the system is complete for parameterized programs. Finally, we show by an example how the formalization can be used for verifying concrete programs.

1 Introduction

The rely-guarantee method introduced by Jones [5] represents the first and most fundamental compositional method for correctness proofs of parallel imperative programs with shared variables. It consists of a set of axioms and inference rules that form a sound and complete system for the derivation of correct programs in the style of Hoare. It also has the classical advantages of Hoare logic, namely, it is syntax oriented and compositional. In a compositional proof system, the specification of a parallel program can be derived from the specification of the components without knowing the implementation of these components. This is important for the correct development of complex programs, where one would like to verify the design at stages where implementation details are still unknown.

The rely-guarantee method can be considered as a reformulation of the classical non-compositional Owicki-Gries method (also formalized in Isabelle/HOL [8]). To apply the Owicki-Gries method, programs have to be annotated with an assertion at every point of interference. The verification process requires proving that the annotations of each component be preserved by the atomic actions of the other components. This property, called *interference freedom*, makes the method non compositional because the particular implementation of the components must be known. The idea of the rely-guarantee method is to record the interference information in the specification of each component. Hence, besides the classical *pre* and *postcondition* of Hoare logic, each component

---

[**] This work has been realized as part of the author's PhD at the Computer Science Faculty of the Technical University of Munich.

P. Degano (Ed.): ESOP 2003, LNCS 2618, pp. 348–362, 2003.

is annotated with a *rely* and a *guarantee* condition, which describe the expected effect of the environment and of the component itself, respectively. Then, the verification process requires proving correctness of each component separately and some side conditions about their specifications, for which no knowledge of the internal implementation of the components is required. That is, the resulting proof method is compositional.

This paper presents the formalization in the theorem prover Isabelle/HOL of the rely-guarantee proof system. The main results are:

- A higher-order logic model of: parallel programs, a semantic definition of correctness and a proof system.
- A formalized theorem that the proof system is sound w.r.t. the semantics.

An interesting by-product of our formalization is that parameterized programs, where the number of components is a parameter n, are naturally included in the model. This is a consequence of the representation of parallel programs as lists of components. Our proof rule for parallel composition allows us to derive correct specifications of parameterized programs directly, without induction. A soundness and completeness proof for such a system is new in the literature.

Finally, we show by an example how the formalization can be used to verify concrete programs. In practice, the real challenge is to identify suitable rely and guarantee conditions. This requires a full understanding of the program and a detailed identification of the interactions that occur. Such verification exercises are tedious and error prone. A theorem prover is a great help in the iterative process of finding and adjusting the specifications; previous proofs can be easily reused and details are checked automatically. The user can then concentrate only on the most interesting steps.

The definitions and theorems shown in the paper are actual fragments of the Isabelle theories and we hope to convince the reader of the expressiveness of Isabelle's syntax. Due to lack of space we cannot show all the definitions and proofs. For a detailed exposition we refer to [11]. The full theories and proof scripts are available at http://isabelle.in.tum.de/library/HOL/HoareParallel/.

2 Related Work

The formalization presented here is mostly inspired by [15], where the system is proved to be sound and complete. The preciseness required by a theorem prover, however, leads to some simplifications and improvements over the original model. There exists a broad literature on the rely-guarantee and other related systems that we cannot survey here. The recent book [1] presents systematically and in a unified notation the work of more than a 100 publications and 15 dissertations on concurrency verification.

From the theorem prover angle, much work has been done on formalizing different concurrency paradigms like UNITY, CSP, CCS or TLA among others (see [8] for a list of references). Remarkable formalizations for compositional approaches are [2, 9] for the UNITY framework in Isabelle/HOL and the soundness proof of McMillan assume-guarantee rule [6] in PVS [12]. Surprisingly, there is not much work on embedding Hoare logics for parallelism in theorem provers. A Hoare-style compositional proof system for distributed real-time systems has been formalized and proved correct in PVS [4]. In this formalization, variables are local, i.e. not shared by parallel components and communication is achieved by means of events which are then used to model different forms of communication. Also a static checker for parallel programs has been presented in [3], where given a suitable rely-guarantee specification for a parallel program, the tool decomposes it in a verification problem for the sequential components, which can be checked by an automatic theorem prover. This tool is focused on the verification and no soundness proof has been formalized. To the best of our knowledge, the work presented in this paper is the first formalization in a theorem prover of a compositional system and its soundness proof for shared-variable parallelism in the style of Hoare.

3   Isabelle/HOL

Isabelle is a generic interactive theorem prover and Isabelle/HOL is its instantiation for higher-order logic. For a gentle introduction to Isabelle/HOL see [7]. Here we summarize the relevant notation and some predefined functions used in the paper. Others will be explained as they appear.

The product type $\alpha \times \beta$ comes with the projection functions *fst* and *snd*. Tuples are pairs nested to the right, e.g. $(a, b, c) = (a, (b, c))$. They may also be used as patterns like in $\lambda(x, y). f\ x\ y$. List notation is similar to ML (e.g. @ is 'append') except that the 'cons' operation is denoted by $\#$ (instead of $::$). The ith component of a list xs is written $xs\,!\,i$. The last element of a non-empty list is *last xs*. The functional $map :: (\alpha \Rightarrow \beta) \Rightarrow \alpha\ list \Rightarrow \beta\ list$ applies a function to all elements of a list. The syntax $xs[i := x]$ denotes the list xs with the ith component replaced by x.

The datatype $\alpha\ option = None\ |\ Some\ \alpha$ is frequently used to add a distinguished element to some existing type. It comes with the function *the* such that *the (Some x) = x*. Set comprehension syntax is $\{x.\ P\ x\}$ expressing the set of all elements that satisfy the predicate P. The complement of a set A is $-A$. The notation $[\![A_1; \ldots; A_n]\!] \Longrightarrow A$ represents an implication with assumptions $A_1, \ldots, A_n$ and conclusion A.

4   The Programming Language

We formalize a simple while-language augmented with shared-variable parallelism ($\|$) and synchronization via an await-construct. For simplicity, each P_i in **cobegin** $P_1 \| \ldots \| P_n$ **coend** must be a sequential command, i.e. nested parallelism is not allowed. We encode this stratification by defining the syntax in two layers, one for sequential component programs and another for parallel programs. We start by defining boolean expressions as sets of states, where the state is represented by the parameter α:

types α *bexp* $= \alpha$ *set*

The syntax of component programs is given by the following datatype:

datatype α *com* $= Basic\ (\alpha \Rightarrow \alpha)$
$\qquad\qquad$ | *Seq* $(\alpha\ com)\ (\alpha\ com)$ $\qquad\qquad$ (-; -)
$\qquad\qquad$ | *Cond* $(\alpha\ bexp)\ (\alpha\ com)\ (\alpha\ com)$
$\qquad\qquad$ | *While* $(\alpha\ bexp)\ (\alpha\ com)$
$\qquad\qquad$ | *Await* $(\alpha\ bexp)\ (\alpha\ com)$

The *Basic* command represents an atomic state transformation, for example, an assignment, a multiple assignment, or the *skip* command. The *Await* command executes the body atomically whenever the boolean condition holds. The rest are well-known. Parallel programs, on the other layer, are simply lists of component programs:

types α *par-com* $=$ $((\alpha\ com)\ option)\ list$

The option type is used to include the empty program *None* as a possible component program. For the moment, we only introduce concrete syntax of the form c_1; c_2 for sequential statements. Concrete syntax is nice for representing and proving properties of concrete programs. The main difficulty for defining concrete syntax lies in finding a convenient representation of the state, or more precisely, of program variables. We will come back to this issue in the example of section 10. The rest of the paper, however, deals with meta-theory, i.e. definitions and proofs about the language itself, so we use the abstract syntax and leave the state completely undetermined.

5   Operational Semantics

Semantics of commands is defined via transition rules between configurations. A configuration is a pair $(P,\ \sigma)$, where P is some program (or the empty program) and σ is a state. A transition rule has the form $(P,\ \sigma) - \delta \rightarrow (P',\ \sigma')$ where δ is a label indicating the kind of transition. A component program can perform two kinds of transitions: *component transitions* (labeled with c), performed by the component itself, and *environment transitions* (labeled with e), performed by a different component of the parallel composition or by an arbitrary environment.

5.1   Transition Rules

Rules for Component Programs: The rule for environment transitions is

$\quad$ *Env:* $(P,\ s) - e \rightarrow (P,\ t)$

Intuitively, a transition made by the environment of a component program P may change the state but not the program P. The program part is only modified by transitions made by the component itself. Such transitions are inductively defined by the following rules:

Basic: $(Some\ (Basic\ f),\ s)\ -c\rightarrow\ (None,\ f\ s)$

Await: $[\!\![\ s\in b;\ (Some\ P,\ s)\ -c*\rightarrow\ (None,\ t)\ ]\!\!]$
$\Longrightarrow\ (Some\ (Await\ b\ P),\ s)\ -c\rightarrow\ (None,\ t)$

*Seq*1: $(Some\ P_0,\ s)\ -c\rightarrow\ (None,\ t)\ \Longrightarrow\ (Some\ (P_0;\ P_1),\ s)\ -c\rightarrow\ (Some\ P_1,\ t)$
*Seq*2: $(Some\ P_0,\ s)\ -c\rightarrow\ (Some\ P_2,\ t)$
$\Longrightarrow\ (Some\ (P_0;\ P_1),\ s)\ -c\rightarrow\ (Some\ (P_2;\ P_1),\ t)$

CondT: $s\in b\ \Longrightarrow\ (Some\ (Cond\ b\ P_1\ P_2),\ s)\ -c\rightarrow\ (Some\ P_1,\ s)$
CondF: $s\notin b\ \Longrightarrow\ (Some\ (Cond\ b\ P_1\ P_2),\ s)\ -c\rightarrow\ (Some\ P_2,\ s)$

WhileF: $s\notin b\ \Longrightarrow\ (Some\ (While\ b\ P),\ s)\ -c\rightarrow\ (None,\ s)$
WhileT: $s\in b\ \Longrightarrow\ (Some\ (While\ b\ P),\ s)\ -c\rightarrow\ (Some\ (P;\ While\ b\ P),\ s)$

where $P\ -c*\rightarrow\ Q$ is the reflexive transitive closure of $P\ -c\rightarrow\ Q$. Basic actions and evaluation of boolean conditions are atomic. The body of an await-statement is executed atomically, i.e. without interruption from the environment, thus no environment transitions can occur.

Rules for Parallel Programs: Parallel programs may also interact with the environment, thus an analogous environment transition, labeled with *pe*, is defined:

ParEnv: $(Ps,\ s)\ -pe\rightarrow\ (Ps,\ t)$

Execution of a parallel program is modeled by a nondeterministic interleaving of the atomic actions of the components. In other words, a parallel program performs a component step when one of its non-terminated components performs a component step:

ParComp: $[\!\![\ i<length\ Ps;\ (Ps!i,\ s)\ -c\rightarrow\ (r,\ t)\ ]\!\!]\ \Longrightarrow\ (Ps,\ s)\ -pc\rightarrow\ (Ps[i:=r],\ t)$

$Ps[i:=r]$ is the list of programs Ps with the program i replaced by r. A parallel program terminates when all the components terminate, i.e. when all component programs are *None*.

5.2   Computations

A *computation* of a sequential program records the sequence of transitions. In [15] it is defined as any sequence of the form

$$(P_0,\sigma_0) - \delta_1 \rightarrow (P_1,\sigma_1) - \delta_2 \rightarrow \ldots - \delta_n \rightarrow (P_n,\sigma_n) - \delta_{n+1} \rightarrow \ldots, \quad \delta_i \in \{e,c\}$$

There are several ways to formalize this intuitive definition. We present two formalizations that are equivalent but serve different purposes. The first one directly follows the definition and is "obviously" the right one. The second one is more elaborated and is useful for the proofs.

Direct Definition of Computation: We define the set of computations, called *cptn*, as the set of lists of configurations inductively defined by the following rules:

One: $[(P, s)] \in cptn$

Env: $(P, t)\#xs \in cptn \Longrightarrow (P, s)\#(P, t)\#xs \in cptn$

Comp: $[\![(P, s) -c\rightarrow (Q, t); (Q, t)\#xs \in cptn]\!] \Longrightarrow (P, s)\#(Q, t)\#xs \in cptn$

The one-element list is always a computation. Two consecutive configurations are part of a computation if they are the initial and final configurations of an environment or a component transition. Computations of parallel programs (*par-cptn*) are defined analogously.

Modular Definition of Computation: The previous definition of computation clearly formalizes the one proposed in [15]. However, it represents the execution of a program in a simplified linear way without taking the structure of the development of a computation into account. For example, the computation of a sequential composition is formed by the computation of the two parts and the computation of a while-statement is formed by several computations of the body. Retrieving this information out of the linear representation of the computation is unnecessarily cumbersome. It can be elegantly avoided by defining computations in a modular way. We propose a new definition of computation which maintains the structure and considerably simplifies some proofs, especially those concerning properties of while-programs.

First, we define the auxiliary function *seq-with* that returns, given a program Q and a configuration (P, s), the same configuration where the program has been sequentially composed with Q. If the concerned program is finished, i.e. *None*, the returned program is just Q[1]:

$seq\text{-}with\ Q \equiv \lambda(P,s).\ if\ P{=}None\ then\ (Some\ Q, s)\ else\ (Some((the\ P); Q), s)$

We define the set of computations *mcptn* as the lists of configurations formed by the following rules:

MOne: $[(P, s)] \in mcptn$

MEnv: $(P, t)\#xs \in mcptn \Longrightarrow (P, s)\#(P, t)\#xs \in mcptn$

MNone: $[\![(Some\ P, s) -c\rightarrow (None, t); (None, t)\#xs \in mcptn]\!]$
$\Longrightarrow (Some\ P, s)\#(None, t)\#xs \in mcptn$

MCondT: $[\![(Some\ P_0, s)\#ys \in mcptn;\ s \in b]\!]$
$\Longrightarrow (Some\ (Cond\ b\ P_0\ P_1), s)\#(Some\ P_0, s)\#ys \in mcptn$

MCondF: $[\![(Some\ P_1, s)\#ys \in mcptn;\ s \notin b]\!]$
$\Longrightarrow (Some\ (Cond\ b\ P_0\ P_1), s)\#(Some\ P_1, s)\#ys \in mcptn$

---

[1] Isabelle's notation does not allow tuples as arguments on the left-hand side of a definition. Thus, λ-notation is used on the right-hand side.

$MSeq1$: $[\![$ $(Some\ P_0,\ s)\#xs \in mcptn;\ zs = map\ (seq\text{-}with\ P_1)\ xs\ ]\!]$
          $\implies (Some\ (P_0;\ P_1),\ s)\#zs \in mcptn$

$MSeq2$: $[\![$ $(Some\ P_0,\ s)\#xs \in mcptn;\ fst\ (last\ ((Some\ P_0,\ s)\#xs)) = None;$
          $(Some\ P_1,\ snd\ (last\ ((Some\ P_0,\ s)\#xs)))\#ys \in mcptn;$
          $zs = (map\ (seq\text{-}with\ P_1)\ xs)@ys\ ]\!] \implies (Some\ (P_0;\ P_1),\ s)\#zs \in mcptn$

$MWhile1$: $[\![$ $(Some\ P,\ s)\#xs \in mcptn;\ s \in b;\ zs = map\ (seq\text{-}with\ (While\ b\ P))\ xs\ ]\!]$
          $\implies (Some\ (While\ b\ P),\ s)\#(Some\ (P;\ While\ b\ P),\ s)\#zs \in mcptn$

$MWhile2$: $[\![$ $(Some\ P,\ s)\#xs \in mcptn;\ fst\ (last\ ((Some\ P,\ s)\#xs)) = None;$
          $s \in b;\ zs = (map\ (seq\text{-}with\ (While\ b\ P))\ xs)@ys;$
          $(Some\ (While\ b\ P),\ snd\ (last\ ((Some\ P,\ s)\#xs)))\#ys \in mcptn\ ]\!]$
          $\implies (Some\ (While\ b\ P),\ s)\#(Some\ (P;\ While\ b\ P),\ s)\#zs \in mcptn$

The first two rules are the same as in the set or rules defining *cptn*. The rule *Comp*, however, is now replaced by seven rules which correspond to different kinds of component transitions.

The rule *MNone* stands for the three possible component transitions where the program terminates, i.e. *Basic*, *Await* or *WhileF*. The two rules for the conditional are obvious. (Observe that for these five cases the new definition does not provide any richer information than the rule *Comp* with case analysis on the corresponding *c*-step.) Rule *MSeq1* represents the case where the second program of the sequential composition is not started, whereas *MSeq2* stands for the case where at least the first program is finished. *MWhile1* represents the computations where the body is started but not finished and *MWhile2* those where the body has been executed at least once.

The new definition is specially useful for the proof of soundness of the rule for while-programs. By using rule induction on *mcptn* we directly obtain the three following cases:

1. The while-body is not entered.
2. The execution of the body is at least started.
3. The body is executed completely at least once followed by a new computation of the same while-program, on which the induction hypothesis holds.

In contrast, the information obtained by using the same proof method on *cptn* was almost useless. The equivalence of both definitions is proven in the following theorem:

theorem *cptn-iff-mcptn*: $cptn = mcptn$

6   Validity of Correctness Formulas

In this section we formally define what it means for a program P to satisfy a rely-guarantee specification $(pre,\ rely,\ guar,\ post)$. These four conditions can be classified in two parts: *assumptions*, represented by the pre and rely condition, describe the conditions under which the program runs, and *commitments*, composed by the guarantee and postcondition, describe the expected behaviors of the program when it is run under the assumptions.

The pre and postcondition are, like in the traditional Hoare logic, sets of states. They impose conditions upon the initial and final states of a computation, respectively. The rely and guarantee conditions describe properties of transitions from the environment and transitions of the program, respectively. Thus, they are sets of pairs of states, formed by the state before and after the transition.

P satisfies its specification, written $\models P$ **sat** $[pre, rely, guar, post]$, if under the assumptions that

1. P is started in a state that satisfies *pre*, and
2. any environment transition in the computation satisfies *rely*,

then P ensures the following commitments:

3. any component transition satisfies *guar*, and
4. if the computation terminates, the final state satisfies *post*.

Formally, validity of a specification for a sequential component program is defined as follows:

$$\models P \text{ } \mathbf{sat} \text{ } [pre, rely, guar, post] \equiv \forall s. \text{ } cp \text{ } (Some \text{ } P) \text{ } s \cap assum \text{ } (pre, rely) \subseteq comm$$
$(guar, post)$

where $cp \text{ } (Some \text{ } P) \text{ } s$ represents the set of computations of the component program P starting from some initial state s, i.e. $cp \text{ } (Some \text{ } P) \text{ } s \equiv \{c. \text{ } c!0 = (Some \text{ } P, s) \land c \in cptn\}$. The definitions of *assum* and *comm* are:

$$assum \equiv \lambda(pre, rely). \{c. \text{ } snd \text{ } (c!0) \in pre \land (\forall i. \text{ } i+1 < length \text{ } c \longrightarrow$$
$$c!i -e\rightarrow c!(i+1) \longrightarrow (snd \text{ } (c!i), snd \text{ } (c!(i+1))) \in rely)\}$$
$$comm \equiv \lambda(guar, post). \{c. \text{ } (\forall i. \text{ } i+1 < length \text{ } c \longrightarrow$$
$$c!i -c\rightarrow c!(i+1) \longrightarrow (snd \text{ } (c!i), snd \text{ } (c!(i+1))) \in guar) \land$$
$$(fst \text{ } (last \text{ } c) = None \longrightarrow snd \text{ } (last \text{ } c) \in post)\}$$

In other words, P satisfies its specification iff all computations of P that satisfy the assumptions satisfy the commitments.

Validity of a specification of a parallel program Ps (of type α *par-com*), written $\models Ps$ **sat** $[pre, rely, guar, post]$, is defined analogously. (Note the syntactic difference between $\models$ used for component programs and $\models$ for parallel programs.)

Jones [5] first suggested that the rely and guarantee conditions be reflexive and transitive. However, for the soundness proof only the reflexivity of the guarantee condition is necessary. This is to ensure that transitions corresponding to the evaluation of boolean conditions (which do not affect the state) also satisfy the guarantee condition. If transitivity is also required another property, namely, observational equivalence, can be proven. In [14], the author discusses this point in more detail. Similarly, he requires only reflexivity since in practice finding guarantee conditions that are transitive is not easy.

7 The Proof System

First, we define *stable p q* $\equiv \forall x\, y.\ x \in p \longrightarrow (x,\, y) \in q \longrightarrow y \in p$. Thus, *stable pre rely* reads as "pre is stable when rely holds" meaning that if a state from the precondition performs a transition satisfying the rely condition, then the next state still satisfies the precondition.

The derivable correctness formulas $\vdash P$ **sat** $[pre,\ rely,\ guar,\ post]$ are inductively defined by the following set of rules:

Basic: $[\![\ pre \subseteq \{s.\ f\, s \in post\};\ \{(s,\, t).\ s \in pre \wedge (t = f\, s \vee t = s)\} \subseteq guar;$
    stable pre rely; stable post rely $]\!] \Longrightarrow \vdash Basic\, f$ **sat** $[pre,\ rely,\ guar,\ post]$

Seq: $[\![\ \vdash P$ **sat** $[pre,\ rely,\ guar,\ mid];\ \vdash Q$ **sat** $[mid,\ rely,\ guar,\ post]\ ]\!]$
    $\Longrightarrow \vdash P;\ Q$ **sat** $[pre,\ rely,\ guar,\ post]$

Cond: $[\![\ \vdash P_1$ **sat** $[pre \cap b,\ rely,\ guar,\ post];\ \vdash P_2$ **sat** $[pre \cap -b,\ rely,\ guar,\ post];$
    stable pre rely; $\forall s.\ (s,\, s) \in guar\ ]\!] \Longrightarrow \vdash Cond\, b\, P_1\, P_2$ **sat** $[pre,\ rely,\ guar,\ post]$

While: $[\![\ \vdash P$ **sat** $[pre \cap b,\ rely,\ guar,\ pre];\ pre \cap -b \subseteq post;\ $*stable post rely;*
    stable pre rely; $\forall s.\ (s,\, s) \in guar\ ]\!] \Longrightarrow \vdash While\, b\, P$ **sat** $[pre,\ rely,\ guar,\ post]$

Await: $[\![\ \forall V.\ \vdash P$ **sat** $[pre \cap b \cap \{V\},\ \{(s,\, t).\ s = t\},\ UNIV,$
    $\{s.\ (V,\, s) \in guar\} \cap post];\ $*stable pre rely; stable post rely* $]\!]$
    $\Longrightarrow \vdash Await\, b\, P$ **sat** $[pre,\ rely,\ guar,\ post]$

Conseq: $[\![\ pre \subseteq pre';\ rely \subseteq rely';\ guar' \subseteq guar;\ post' \subseteq post;$
    $\vdash P$ **sat** $[pre',\ rely',\ guar',\ post']\ ]\!] \Longrightarrow \vdash P$ **sat** $[pre,\ rely,\ guar,\ post]$

In the computation of a *Basic* command there is exactly one component transition that updates the state. Before and after this component transition there can be a number of environment transitions. The initial state satisfies *pre*, thus from *stable pre rely* it follows that *pre* holds immediately before the component transition takes place. From $pre \subseteq \{s.\ f\, s \in post\}$ it follows that *post* holds immediately after the component transition, and because *post* is stable when *rely* holds, *post* holds after any number of environment transitions.

The rules for the sequential composition and conditional statements are standard. In the while-rule the precondition plays the role of the invariant; it must hold before and after execution of the body at every iteration.

The rule for the await-statement is less obvious. By the semantics of the await-command, a positive evaluation of the condition and the execution of the body is done atomically. Thus, the state transition caused by the complete execution of P must satisfy the guarantee condition. This is reflected in the precondition and postcondition of P in the assumptions; since these are sets of single states, the relation between the state before and after the transformation is established by fixing the values of the first via a universally quantified variable V. The intermediate state changes during the execution of P must not guarantee anything, thus the guarantee condition is the universal set *UNIV*, defined as $\{s.\ True\}$. However, since they are executed atomically, the environment cannot change their values. This is reflected by the rely condition $\{(s,\ t).\ s = t\}$. To ensure that the postcondition holds at the end of the computation, regardless of possible environment transitions, *stable post rely* is required. Finally, the rule of consequence allows us to strengthen the assumptions and weaken the commitments.

We now introduce the proof rule for parallel composition. Recall that in a validity formula for a parallel program $\models$ *Ps* **sat** [*pre, rely, guar, post*], *Ps* has type α *par-com* with no information about the *pre, post, rely* and *guar* conditions of each component program. This is fine to define validity, however, for concrete verification of programs, we want to apply the rules backwards. Therefore, the conclusion of the rule should include all the information needed in the premises. Hence, in a derived formula for a parallel program, denoted $\Vdash$ *Ps* **sat** [*pre, rely, guar, post*], *Ps* is a list of tuples, each one formed by the code of the component program and its specification. The functions *Pre, Post, Rely, Guar* and *Com* (with obvious definitions) extract the different parts when applied to such a "component tuple".

Parallel:
$[\![\ \forall i{<}length\ Ps.\ \vdash\ Com(Ps!i)\ \mathbf{sat}\ [Pre(Ps!i),\ Rely(Ps!i),\ Guar(Ps!i),\ Post(Ps!i)];$
$\quad \forall i{<}length\ Ps.\ rely\ \cup\ (\bigcup j{\in}\{j.\ j{<}length\ Ps\ \wedge\ j{\neq}i\}.\ Guar\ (Ps!j))\ \subseteq\ Rely\ (Ps!i);$
$\quad (\bigcup j{\in}\{j.\ j{<}length\ Ps\}.\ Guar\ (Ps!j))\ \subseteq\ guar;$
$\quad pre\ \subseteq\ (\bigcap i{\in}\{i.\ i{<}length\ Ps\}.\ Pre\ (Ps!i));$
$\quad (\bigcap i{\in}\{i.\ i{<}length\ Ps\}.\ Post\ (Ps!i))\ \subseteq\ post\ ]\!]\ \Longrightarrow\ \Vdash\ Ps\ \mathbf{sat}\ [pre,\ rely,\ guar,\ post]$

We explain the five premises. The first one requires that each component together with its specification be derivable in the system for sequential program.

The second one is a constraint on the rely condition of component i. An environment transition for i corresponds to a component transition of another component j with $i{\neq}j$, or of a transition from the overall environment (which satisfies *rely*). Hence, the strongest rely condition for component i is *rely* $\cup$ $(\bigcup j{\in}\{j.\ j{<}length\ Ps\ \wedge\ j{\neq}i\}.\ Guar\ (Ps!j))$.

The third requirement imposes a relation among the guarantee conditions of the components and that of the parallel composition: since a component transition of the parallel program is performed by one of its components, the guarantee condition *guar* of the parallel program must be at least the union of the sets specified by the guarantee conditions of the components.

The forth premise requires that the precondition for the parallel composition imply all the component's preconditions. Finally, the overall postcondition must be a logical consequence of all postconditions.

This rule generalizes the particular case of composing two programs, as known from the literature [1, 15], to composing any number of programs. As a consequence, also parameterized parallel programs can be proved correct in a single derivation even though they represent an infinite family of programs (see section 9).

8   Soundness

To prove soundness of the rule for parallel composition we first need to prove soundness of the system of rules for sequential component programs:

theorem *sound:* $\vdash P$ **sat** $[pre, rely, guar, post] \Longrightarrow \models P$ **sat** $[pre, rely, guar, post]$

To state soundness of the parallel composition rule, we define a function *ParallelCom* which, given a list of "component tuples" formed by each component program's code and its corresponding four conditions it returns the same list with only the component programs, i.e. the parallel program. The soundness theorem is formulated using this function as follows:

theorem *par-sound:*

$\vdash Ps$ **sat** $[pre, rely, guar, post] \Longrightarrow \models ParallelCom\ Ps$ **sat** $[pre, rely, guar, post]$

Both proofs are done by rule induction. For the soundness of the system for component programs the most interesting case is the rule for while, where the use of the modular definition of computation results in an elegant and well-structured proof. Soundness of the parallel rule relies on an important lemma stating that the computation of a parallel program can be described in terms of the computations of its components, i.e. that the semantics is compositional. This result alone has the longest proof (about 500 lines).

9   Completeness for Parameterized Parallel Programs

By using lists to model parallel composition (see section 4) we can easily represent parameterized parallel programs via the predefined HOL functional *map* $:: (\alpha \Rightarrow \beta) \Rightarrow \alpha\ list \Rightarrow \beta\ list$, and the construct $[i..j]$, which represents the list of natural numbers from i to j. For example, the program **cobegin** $P\ 0 \parallel \dots \parallel P\ (n{-}1)$ **coend** representing the parallel composition of n components which differ only on the index number can be represented by $map\ (\lambda i.\ P\ i)\ [0..n{-}1]$, for which concrete syntax of the form **scheme** $[0 \leq i < n]\ P\ i$ has also been defined.

Consequently, the rule for parallel composition and its soundness proof also include the case of parameterized parallel programs. This means that correctness for such programs can be proven by a single derivation (typically parameterized by the number of components) which can then be instantiated for any parameter. This leads to the question whether finding such a derivation is always possible, i.e. whether the system is complete for this kind of programs.

In [10] we proved that the extended Owicki-Gries system of [8] is complete for parameterized programs. Using this result, we prove completeness of the rely-guarantee system for parameterized programs by reduction. The idea comes from [13], where the author proves that the rely-guarantee system is complete relative to the Owicki-Gries system, i.e. a rely-guarantee proof can be constructed from an Owicki-Gries proof of the same program. Thus, from the completeness of the Owicki-Gries system for parameterized programs it follows that the extended rely-guarantee system is also complete.

10   Example

We verify a simple parameterized parallel program presented in [13]. The program searches for the first element satisfying some predicate P in an array B of length m (represented by a list). If there is one, we call it *min-el*, otherwise *min-el* = m. Upon termination the program establishes the postcondition

$$min\text{-}el < m+1 \wedge (\forall i < min\text{-}el. \neg P(B!i)) \wedge min\text{-}el < m \longrightarrow P(B!min\text{-}el).$$

We use n concurrent programs, $S\ 0 \parallel \ldots \parallel S\ (n-1)$ (for simplicity let n divide m) such that $S\ i$ visits the array indices i, $n+i$, $2*n+i,\ldots$, $m+i$. Each $S\ i$ uses two variables x_i and y_i ranging over natural numbers. There exist several ways of formalizing program variables in such formalizations [9]. In the approach used here the state is represented by an Isabelle record type, whose fields are the program variables . For example, if a program has a boolean variable a and a variable b ranging over the natural numbers, the program state would be represented by the record:

record *Example* =
  a :: *bool*
  b :: *nat*

The advantages of this representation w.r.t. other approaches are discussed in [11]. In our example, parameterized variables are used. These can be implemented by lists or, more abstractly, functions from naturals into the corresponding value domain:

record *Parameterized-Example* =
  x :: *nat* $\Rightarrow$ *nat*
  y :: *nat* $\Rightarrow$ *nat*

Then, an indexed variable x_i in our program is represented by the function x applied to index i, i.e. $x\ i$. To distinguish program variables we write them in sans serif (e.g. x) in the following.

    Each component program $S\ i$ is a while-program which uses the variable x i, initially set to i, for searching. It terminates if

1. $P\ (B!(\mathsf{x}\ i))$ or,
2. x $i > m$ or,
3. $S\ k$, with $k \neq i$, has found that $P\ (B!(\mathsf{x}\ k))$ for x $k <$ x i.

Another variable y i is initially set to $m+i$ and, if $P(B!(\mathsf{x}\ i))$ holds, then y i is set to x i. Then, the termination condition for $S\ i$ is: $\exists j < n.$ y $j \leq$ x i. The code of the parameterized parallel program is:

    scheme $[0 \leq i < n]$
    while $(\forall j < n.$ x $i <$ y $j)$ **do**
    if $P\ (B!(\mathsf{x}\ i))$ **then** y := y $(i := $ x $i)$ **else** x := x $(i := ($x $i) + n)$ **fi** **od**

where f $(i := t)$ is Isabelle syntax for function update. Assignment to a parameterized variable is written $y := y$ $(i := x\ i)$ meaning that the variable $y\ i$ is updated to $x\ i$. The loop invariant is the predicate:

$$(x\ i)\ mod\ n = i \wedge (\forall z < x\ i.\ z\ mod\ n = i \longrightarrow \neg P\ (B\ !\ z)) \wedge$$
$$(y\ i < m \longrightarrow P\ (B\ !\ (y\ i)) \wedge y\ i \le m{+}i).$$

Now we need to find *rely* and *guar* conditions for each component program. Observe that for each $S\ i$ the following holds:

1. The variables $x\ i$ and $y\ i$ are only changed by component i, thus the environment cannot affect their values or increase $y\ j$ for $j{\ne}i$.
2. The program $S\ i$ cannot affect the variables $x\ j$ and $y\ j$ for $j{\ne}i$, and it does not increase the initial value of $y\ i$.

We represent the value of a variable x after a transition by $\bar{x}$. In the theorem below, we show each component i of the parallel composition as a tuple formed by the program code and its corresponding specification, i.e. the pre, rely, guar and postcondition. This theorem states that the full annotated program is derivable in the formalized rely-guarantee system:

theorem *Parameterized-Example*: $m\ mod\ n = 0 \Longrightarrow$
$\Vdash$ **cobegin**
scheme $[0 \le i < n]$
(**while** $(\forall j < n.\ x\ i < y\ j)$ **do**
  if $P\ (B\ !\ (x\ i))$ **then** $y := y\ (i := x\ i)$
  else $x := x\ (i := (x\ i){+}\ n)$ **fi**
od,
$\{\!|\ (x\ i)\ mod\ n = i \wedge (\forall z < x\ i.\ z\ mod\ n = i \longrightarrow \neg P\ (B\ !\ z)) \wedge$
  $(y\ i < m \longrightarrow P\ (B\ !\ (y\ i)) \wedge y\ i \le m{+}i)\ |\!\}$,
$\{\!|\ (\forall j < n.\ i \ne j \longrightarrow \bar{y}\ j \le y\ j) \wedge x\ i = \bar{x}\ i \wedge y\ i = \bar{y}\ i\ |\!\}$,
$\{\!|\ (\forall j < n.\ i \ne j \longrightarrow x\ j = \bar{x}\ j \wedge y\ j = \bar{y}\ j) \wedge \bar{y}\ i \le y\ i\ |\!\}$,
$\{\!|\ (x\ i)\ mod\ n = i \wedge (\forall z < x\ i.\ z\ mod\ n = i \longrightarrow \neg P\ (B\ !\ z)) \wedge$
  $(y\ i < m \longrightarrow P\ (B\ !\ (y\ i)) \wedge y\ i \le m{+}i) \wedge (\exists j < n.\ y\ j \le x\ i)\ |\!\})$
coend
sat $[\{\!|\ \forall i < n.\ x\ i = i \wedge y\ i = m{+}i\ |\!\},\ \{\!|\ x = \bar{x} \wedge y = \bar{y}\ |\!\},\ \{\!|\ True\ |\!\},$
  $\{\!|\ \forall i < n.\ (x\ i)\ mod\ n = i \wedge (\forall z < x\ i.\ z\ mod\ n = i \longrightarrow \neg P\ (B\ !\ z)) \wedge$
  $(y\ i < m \longrightarrow P\ (B\ !\ (y\ i)) \wedge y\ i \le m{+}i) \wedge (\exists j < n.\ y\ j \le x\ i)\ |\!\}]$

The expressions $\{\!|\ p\ |\!\}$ are concrete syntax for the set of states (or pairs of states) satisfying p. From the specifications of the components we establish the specification of the parallel program given by the four conditions after the keyword **sat**. The precondition of each component is the invariant shown above and the postcondition corresponds to the invariant and the negation of the loop guard.

The precondition $\{\!|\ \forall i{<}n.\ x\ i = i \wedge y\ i = m{+}i\ |\!\}$ of the parallel program gives the initial values of the variables. We consider the parallel program to be closed, meaning that the environment is empty. Thus, the corresponding *rely* condition simply states that the program variables are not modified by the environment. Analogously, the parallel program must not guarantee anything to the environment, so the guarantee condition is just *True*.

The proof is done by interactively applying the proof rules backwards until all the verification conditions are generated. It requires only one application of the consequence rule. The final verification conditions are proved with standard Isabelle tactics for simplification and natural deduction.

When all component programs terminate, the established postcondition implies that the element we were looking for, namely *min-el*, is the minimum of the set $\{y\ 0,\ \dots\ ,y\ (n-1)\}$. This is proven in the following lemma:

$$
\begin{aligned}
& [\![\forall i<n.\ (x\ i)\ mod\ n{=}i \wedge (\forall z < x\ i.\ z\ mod\ n{=}i \longrightarrow \neg P\ (B\ !\ z)) \wedge \\
& (y\ i < m \longrightarrow P(B\ !\ (y\ i)) \wedge y\ i \leq m{+}i \wedge (\exists j < n.\ y\ j \leq x\ i); \\
& min\text{-}el = minimum\ (map\ y\ [0..n{-}1])]\!] \Longrightarrow min\text{-}el < m{+}1\ \wedge \\
& (\forall i < min\text{-}el.\ \neg\ P\ (B\ !\ i)) \wedge min\text{-}el < m \longrightarrow P\ (B\ !\ min\text{-}el)
\end{aligned}
$$

where the function *minimum* returns the least element of a list, in this case the list $[y\ 0,\dots,\ y\ (n-1)]$. Hence, upon termination, the program establishes the postcondition announced at the beginning of the section for the indicated value of *min-el*.

11   Conclusions

We have presented the first formalization of the rely-guarantee system and its soundness proof in a theorem prover. This work represents another successful step towards the embedding of programming languages and their verification calculi in theorem provers. Another interesting contribution of this work is the extension of the formal treatment from the two-process to the n-process case, which is a technical challenge in formal verification, and whose soundness and completeness proofs have not been considered before.

The total number of specification lines for this formalization is 330. For the proof of soundness we proved 90 lemmas which were proven in 2200 lines (number of interactions with the theorem prover). Comparing it to the formalization of the Owicki-Gries system [8] with 220 lines of specification, 49 lemmas and 340 lines of proofs, it is clear that the rely-guarantee method is more involved. This is the price to obtain a compositional method: the underlying theory requires more work, but yields a simpler proof system.

Machine-checking soundness proofs is labour intensive, however, it produces not only highest confidence in the proof but also leads to optimizations and simpler formulations, which becomes crucial as languages are enriched with more complicated features. We hope that this work encourages further development in this area.

Acknowledgment. I wish to thank Tobias Nipkow for helpful comments on a previous version of the paper and Jozef Hooman and Qiwen Xu for their interest and useful feedback about their own and other related work.

References

1. W.-P. de Roever, F. S. de Boer, U. Hannemann, J. Hooman, Y. Lakhnech, M. Poel, and J. Zwiers. *Concurrency Verification: Introduction to Compositional and Non-compositional Methods*, volume 54 of *Tracts in Theoretical Computer Science*. Cambridge University Press, 2001.

2. S. O. Ehmety and L. C. Paulson. Program composition in Isabelle/UNITY. In M. Charpentier and B. Sanders, editors, *Formal Methods for Parallel Programming: Theory and Application*, 2002.

3. C. Flanagan, S. Freund, and S. Qadeer. Thread-modular verification for shared-memory programs. In *European Symposium on Programming*, volume 2305 of *LNCS*, pages 262–277. Springer-Verlag, 2002.

4. J. Hooman. Developing proof rules for distributed real-time systems with PVS. In *Proc. Workshop on Tool Support for System Development and Verification*, volume 1 of *BISS Monographs*, pages 120–139. Shaker Verlag, 1998.

5. C. B. Jones. Tentative steps towards a development method for interfering programs. *ACM Transactions on Programming Languages and Systems*, 5(4):596–619, 1983.

6. K. L. McMillan. Circular compositional reasoning about liveness. In *Advances in Hardware Design and Verification Methods: IFIP WG10.5 (CHARME'99)*, volume 1703 of *LNCS*, pages 342–345. Springer-Verlag, 1999.

7. T. Nipkow, L. C. Paulson, and M. Wenzel. *Isabelle/HOL — A Proof Assistant for Higher-Order Logic*, volume 2283 of *LNCS*. Springer-Verlag, 2002.

8. T. Nipkow and L. Prensa Nieto. Owicki/Gries in Isabelle/HOL. In J.-P. Finance, editor, *Fundamental Approaches to Software Engineering*, volume 1577 of *LNCS*, pages 188–203. Springer-Verlag, 1999.

9. L. C. Paulson. Mechanizing a theory of program composition for UNITY. *ACM Transactions on Programming Languages and Systems*, 23(6):1–30, 2001.

10. L. Prensa Nieto. Completeness of the Owicki-Gries system for parameterized parallel programs. In M. Charpentier and B. Sanders, editors, *6th International Workshop on Formal Methods for Parallel Programming: Theory and Applications. Held in conjunction with the 15th International Parallel and Distributed Processing Symposium*. IEEE CS Press, 2001.

11. L. Prensa Nieto. *Verification of Parallel Programs with the Owicki-Gries and Rely-Guarantee Methods in Isabelle/HOL*. PhD thesis, Technische Universität München, 2002. Available at http://tumb1.biblio.tu-muenchen.de/publ/diss/allgemein.html.

12. J. Rushby. Formal verification of McMillan's compositional assume-guarantee rule. Technical report, Sept. 2001.

13. C. Stirling. A generalization of Owicki-Gries's Hoare logic for a concurrent while language. *Theoretical Computer Science*, 58:347–359, 1988.

14. Q. Xu, W.-P. de Roever, and J. He. Rely-guarantee method for verifying shared variable concurrent programs. Technical Report 9502, Christian-Albrechts-Universität Kiel, March 1995.

15. Q. Xu, W.-P. de Roever, and J. He. The rely-guarantee method for verifying shared variable concurrent programs. *Formal Aspects of Computing*, 9(2):149–174, 1997.

Building Certified Libraries for PCC: Dynamic Storage Allocation*

Dachuan Yu, Nadeem A. Hamid, and Zhong Shao

Department of Computer Science, Yale University
New Haven, CT 06520-8285, U.S.A.
{yu,hamid-nadeem,shao}@cs.yale.edu

Abstract. Proof-Carrying Code (PCC) allows a code producer to provide to a host a program along with its formal safety proof. The proof attests a certain safety policy enforced by the code, and can be mechanically checked by the host. While this language-based approach to code certification is very general in principle, existing PCC systems have only focused on programs whose safety proofs can be automatically generated. As a result, many low-level system libraries (*e.g.,* memory management) have not yet been handled. In this paper, we explore a complementary approach in which general properties and program correctness are semi-automatically certified. In particular, we introduce a low-level language CAP for building certified programs and present a certified library for dynamic storage allocation.

1 Introduction

Proof-Carrying Code (PCC) is a general framework pioneered by Necula and Lee [13,12]. It allows a code producer to provide a program to a host along with a formal safety proof. The proof is incontrovertible evidence of safety which can be mechanically checked by the host; thus the host can safely execute the program even though the producer may not be trusted.

Although the PCC framework is general and potentially applicable to certifying arbitrary data objects with complex specifications, generating proofs remains difficult. Existing PCC systems [14,11,2,1] have only focused on programs whose safety proofs can be automatically generated. As a result, many low-level system libraries, such as dynamic storage allocation, have not been certified. Nonetheless, building certified libraries, especially low-level system libraries, is an important task in certifying compilation. It not only helps increase the reliability of "infrastructure" software by reusing provably correct program routines, but also is crucial in making PCC scale for production.

* This research is based on work supported in part by DARPA OASIS grant F30602-99-1-0519, NSF grant CCR-9901011, and NSF ITR grant CCR-0081590. Any opinions, findings, and conclusions contained in this document are those of the authors and do not reflect the views of these agencies.

P. Degano (Ed.): ESOP 2003, LNCS 2618, pp. 363–379, 2003.

On the other hand, Hoare logic [6,7], as a widely applied approach in program verification, allows programmers to express their reasonings with assertions and the application of inference rules, and can be used to prove general program correctness. In this paper, we introduce a conceptually simple low-level language for certified assembly programming (CAP) that supports Hoare-logic style reasoning. We use CAP to build a certified library for dynamic storage allocation, and further use this library to build a certified program whose correctness proof can be mechanically checked. Applying Hoare-logic reasonings at an assembly-level, our paper makes the following contributions:

- CAP is based on a common instruction set so that programs can be executed on real machines with little effort. The expected behavior of a program is explicitly written as a specification using higher-order logic. The programmer proves the well-formedness of a program with respect to its specification using logic reasoning, and the result can be checked mechanically by a proof-checker. The soundness of the language guarantees that if a program passes the static proof-checking, its run-time behavior will satisfy the specification.
- Using CAP, we demonstrate how to build certified libraries and programs. The specifications of library routines are precise yet general enough to be imported in various user programs. Proving the correctness of a user program involves linking with the library proofs.
- We implemented CAP and the dynamic storage allocation routines using the Coq proof assistant [18], showing that this library is indeed certified. The example program is also implemented. All the Coq code is available [19].
- Lastly, memory management is an important and error-prone part of most non-trivial programs. It is also considered to be hard to certify by previous researches. We present a provably correct implementation of a typical dynamic storage allocation algorithm. To the authors' knowledge, it is so far the only certified library for memory management.

2   Dynamic Storage Allocation

In the remainder of this paper, we focus on the certification and use of a library module for dynamic storage allocation. In particular, we implement a storage allocator similar to that described in [9,10]. The interface to our allocator consists of the standard `malloc` and `free` functions. The implementation keeps track of a *free list* of blocks which are available to satisfy memory allocation requests. As shown in Figure 1, the free list is a null-terminated list of (non-contiguous) memory blocks. Each block in the list contains a header of two words: the first stores a pointer to the next block in the list, and the second stores the size of the block. The allocated block pointer that is returned to a user program points to the useable space in the block, not to the header.

The blocks in the list are sorted in order of increasing address and requests for allocation are served based on a first-fit policy; hence, we implement an *address-ordered first-fit* allocation mechanism. If no block in the free list is big

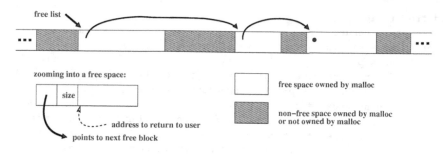

Fig. 1. Free list and free blocks.

enough, or if the free list is empty, then `malloc` requests more memory from the operating system as needed. When a user program is done with a memory block, it is returned to the free list by calling `free`, which puts the memory block into the free list at the appropriate position.

Our implementation in this paper is simple enough to understand, yet faithfully represents mechanisms used in traditional implementations of memory allocators [20,9,10]. For ease of presentation, we assume our machine never runs out of memory so `malloc` will never fail, but otherwise many common low-level mechanisms and techniques used in practice are captured in this example, such as use of a free list, in-place header fields, searching and sorting, and splitting and coalescing (described below). We thus believe our techniques can be as easily applied to a variety of other allocator implementations than described here.

In the remainder of this section, we describe in detail the functionality of the `malloc` and `free` library routines (Figure 2), and give some "pseudo-code" for them. We do not show the `calloc` (allocate and initialize) and `realloc` (resize allocated block) routines because they essentially delegate their tasks to the two main functions described below.

`free` This routine puts a memory block into the free list. It takes a pointer (`ptr`) to the useable portion of a memory block (preceded by a valid header) and does not return anything. It relies on the preconditions that `ptr` points to a valid "memory block" and that the free list is currently in a good state (*i.e.*, properly sorted). As shown in Figure 2, `free` works by walking down the free list to find the appropriate (address-ordered) position for the block. If the block being freed is directly adjacent with either neighbor in the free list, the two are *coalesced* to form a bigger block.

`malloc` This routine is the actual storage allocator. It takes the size of the new memory block expected by the user program, and returns a pointer to an available block of memory of that size. As shown in Figure 2, `malloc` calculates the actual size of the block needed including the header and then searches the free list for the first available block with size greater than or equal to what is required. If the size of the block found is large enough, it is *split* into two and a pointer to the tail end is returned to the user.

```
void free (void* ptr) {
    hp = ptr - header_size;                              // move to header
    for (prev = nil, p = flist; p <> nil; prev = p, p = p->next)
        if (hp < p) {                                    // found place
            if (hp + hp->size == p)      // join or link with upper neighbor
                hp->size += p->size, hp->next = p->next;
            else hp->next = p;
            if (prev <> nil)                  // join or link with lower neighbor
                if (prev + prev->size == hp)
                    prev->size += hp->size, prev->next = hp->next;
                else prev->next = hp;
            else flist = hp;
            return;
        }
    hp->next = nil;                      // block's place is at end of the list
    if (prev <> nil)                     // join or link with lower neighbor
        if (prev + prev->size == hp)
            prev->size += hp->size, prev->next = hp->next;
        else prev->next = hp;
    else flist = hp;
}
void* malloc (int reqsize) {
    actual_size = reqsize + header_size;
    for(prev = nil, p = flist; ; prev = p, p = p->next)
        if (p==nil) {                        // end of free list, request more memory
            more_mem(actual_size);
            prev = nil, p = flist;                   // restart the loop search
        } else if (p->size > actual_size + header_size) {
            p->size -= actual_size;          // found block bigger than needed
            p += p->size;                    //    by more than a header size,
            p->size = actual_size;           //             so split into two
            return (p + header_size);
        } else if (p->size >= actual_size) {      // found good enough block
            if (prev==nil) flist = p->next; else prev->next = p->next;
            return (p + header_size);
        }
}
void more_mem(int req_size) {
    if (req_size < NALLOC) req_size = NALLOC;     // request not too small
    q = alloc(req_size);                          // call system allocator
    q->size = req_size;
    free(q + header_size);                        // put new block on free list
}
```

Fig. 2. Pseudo code of allocation routines.

If no block in the free list is large enough to fulfill the request, more memory is requested from the system by calling more_mem. Because this is a comparatively expensive operation, more_mem requests a minimum amount of memory each time to reduce the frequency of these requests. After getting a new chunk of memory from the system, it is appended onto the free list by calling free.

These dynamic storage allocation algorithms often temporarily break certain invariants, which makes it hard to automatically prove their correctness. During intermediate steps of splitting, coalescing, or inserting memory blocks into the free list, the state of the free list or the memory block is not valid for one or two instructions. Thus, a traditional type system would need to be extremely specialized to be able to handle such code.

3 A Language for Certified Assembly Programming (CAP)

To write our certified libraries, we use a low-level assembly language CAP fitted with specifications reminiscent of Hoare-logic. The assertions that we use for verifying the particular dynamic allocation library described in this paper are inspired by Reynolds' "separation logic" [17,16].

The syntax of CAP is given in Figure 3. A complete program (or, more accurately, machine state) consists of a code heap, a dynamic state component made up of the register file and data heap, and an instruction sequence. The instruction set captures the most basic and common instructions of an assembly language, and includes primitive alloc and free commands which are to be viewed as system calls. The register file is made up of 32 registers and we assume an unbounded heap with integer words of unlimited size for ease of presentation.

Our type system, as it were, is a very general layer of specifications such that assertions can be associated with programs and instruction sequences. Our assertion language (*Assert*) is the calculus of inductive constructions (CiC) [18, 15], an extension of the calculus of constructions [3] which is a higher-order typed lambda calculus that corresponds to higher-order predicate logic via the Curry-Howard isomorphism [8]. In particular, we implement the system described in this paper using the Coq proof assistant [18]. Assertions are thus defined as Coq terms of type State → Prop, where the various syntactic categories of the assembly language (such as State) have been encoded using inductive definitions. We give examples of inductively defined assertions used for reasoning about memory in later sections.

3.1 Operational Semantics

The operational semantics of the assembly language is fairly straightforward and is defined in Figures 4 and 5. The former figure defines a "macro" relation detailing the effect of simple instructions on the dynamic state of the machine. Control-flow instructions, such as jd or bgt, do not affect the data heap or register file. The domain of the heap is altered by either an alloc command, which increases the domain with a specified number of labels mapped to undefined data, or by free, which removes a label from the domain of the heap. The ld and st commands are used to access or update the value stored at a given label.

$(Program)$	$\mathbb{P}$	$::=$	$(\mathbb{C}, \mathbb{S}, \mathbb{I})$
$(CodeHeap)$	$\mathbb{C}$	$::=$	$\{f \rightsquigarrow \mathbb{I}\}^*$
$(State)$	$\mathbb{S}$	$::=$	$(\mathbb{H}, \mathbb{R})$
$(Heap)$	$\mathbb{H}$	$::=$	$\{l \rightsquigarrow w\}^*$
$(RegFile)$	$\mathbb{R}$	$::=$	$\{r \rightsquigarrow w\}^*$
$(Register)$	r	$::=$	$\{r_k\}^{k \in \{0...31\}}$
$(Labels)$	f, l	$::=$	i (nat nums)
$(WordVal)$	w	$::=$	i (nat nums)
$(InstrSeq)$	$\mathbb{I}$	$::=$	$c; \mathbb{I} \mid$ jd $f \mid$ jmp r

$(Command)$ $c ::=$ add $r_d, r_s, r_t \mid$ addi r_d, r_s, i
$\mid$ sub $r_d, r_s, r_t \mid$ subi r_d, r_s, i
$\mid$ mov $r_d, r_s \mid$ movi r_d, i
$\mid$ bgt $r_s, r_t, f \mid$ bgti r_s, i, f
$\mid$ alloc $r_d[r_s] \mid$ ld $r_d, r_s(i)$
$\mid$ st $r_d(i), r_s \mid$ free r_s

$(CdHpSpec)$ $\Psi ::= \{f \rightsquigarrow a\}^*$
$(Assert)$ $a ::= ...$

Fig. 3. Syntax of CAP.

Since we intend to model realistic low-level assembly code, we do not have a "halt" instruction. In fact, termination is undesirable since it means the machine has reached a "stuck" state where, for example, a program is trying to branch to a non-existent code label, or access an invalid data label. We present in the next section a system of inference rules for specifications which allow one to statically prove that a program will never reach such a bad state.

3.2   Inference Rules

We define a set of inference rules allowing us to prove specification judgments of the following forms:

$\Psi \vdash \{a\} \mathbb{P}$ (well-formed program)
$\Psi \vdash \mathbb{C}$ (well-formed code heap)
$\Psi \vdash \{a\} \mathbb{I}$ (well-formed instruction sequence)

Programs in our assembly language are written in continuation-passing style because there are no call/return instructions. Hence, we only specify preconditions for instruction sequences (preconditions of the continuations actually serve as the postconditions). If a given state satisfies the precondition, the sequence of instructions will run without reaching a bad state. Furthermore, in order to check code blocks, which are potentially mutually recursive, we require that all labels in the code heap be associated with a precondition– this mapping is our code heap specification, Ψ.

Well-formed code heap and programs A code heap is well-formed if the code block associated with every label in the heap is well-formed under the corresponding precondition. Then, a complete program is well-formed if the code heap is well-formed, the current instruction sequence is well-formed under the precondition, and the precondition also holds for the dynamic state.

$$\frac{\mathrm{dom}(\Psi) = \mathrm{dom}(\mathbb{C}) \qquad \Psi \vdash \{\Psi(f)\} \, \mathbb{C}(f) \quad \forall f \in \mathrm{dom}(\Psi)}{\Psi \vdash \mathbb{C}} \qquad (1)$$

$$\frac{\Psi \vdash \mathbb{C} \qquad \Psi \vdash \{a\} \mathbb{I} \qquad (a \, \mathbb{S})}{\Psi \vdash \{a\} \, (\mathbb{C}, \mathbb{S}, \mathbb{I})} \qquad (2)$$

if c =	then AuxStep(c, $(\mathbb{H}, \mathbb{R})$) =
add r_d, r_s, r_t	$(\mathbb{H}, \mathbb{R}\{r_d \rightsquigarrow \mathbb{R}(r_s) + \mathbb{R}(r_t)\})$
addi r_d, r_s, i	$(\mathbb{H}, \mathbb{R}\{r_d \rightsquigarrow \mathbb{R}(r_s) + i\})$
sub r_d, r_s, r_t	$(\mathbb{H}, \mathbb{R}\{r_d \rightsquigarrow \mathbb{R}(r_s) - \mathbb{R}(r_t)\})$
subi r_d, r_s, i	$(\mathbb{H}, \mathbb{R}\{r_d \rightsquigarrow \mathbb{R}(r_s) - i\})$
mov r_d, r_s	$(\mathbb{H}, \mathbb{R}\{r_d \rightsquigarrow \mathbb{R}(r_s)\})$
movi r_d, w	$(\mathbb{H}, \mathbb{R}\{r_d \rightsquigarrow w\})$

Fig. 4. Auxiliary state update macro.

Well-formed instructions: Pure rules The inference rules for instruction sequences can be divided into two categories: pure rules, which do not interact with the data heap, and impure rules, which deal with access and modification of the data heap.

The structure of many of the pure rules is very similar. They involve showing that for all states, if an assertion a holds, then there exists an assertion a′ which holds on the state resulting from executing the current command and, additionally, the remainder of the instruction sequence is well-formed under a′. We use the auxiliary state update macro defined in Figure 4 to collapse the rules for arithmetic instructions into a single schema. For control flow instructions, we instead require that if the current assertion a holds, then the precondition of the label that is being jumped to must also be satisfied.

$$\frac{\begin{array}{c} c \in \{\mathsf{add}, \mathsf{addi}, \mathsf{sub}, \mathsf{subi}, \mathsf{mov}, \mathsf{movi}\} \\ \forall \mathbb{H}. \forall \mathbb{R}.\, a\,(\mathbb{H}, \mathbb{R}) \supset a'\,(\mathsf{AuxStep}(c, (\mathbb{H}, \mathbb{R}))) \qquad \varPsi \vdash \{a'\}\, \mathbb{I} \end{array}}{\varPsi \vdash \{a\}\, c;\, \mathbb{I}} \tag{3}$$

$$\frac{\begin{array}{c} \forall \mathbb{H}. \forall \mathbb{R}.\, (\mathbb{R}(r_s) \leq \mathbb{R}(r_t)) \supset a\,(\mathbb{H}, \mathbb{R}) \supset a'\,(\mathbb{H}, \mathbb{R}) \\ \forall \mathbb{H}. \forall \mathbb{R}.\, (\mathbb{R}(r_s) > \mathbb{R}(r_t)) \supset a\,(\mathbb{H}, \mathbb{R}) \supset a_1\,(\mathbb{H}, \mathbb{R}) \\ \varPsi \vdash \{a'\}\, \mathbb{I} \qquad \varPsi(f) = a_1 \end{array}}{\varPsi \vdash \{a\}\, \mathsf{bgt}\ r_s, r_t, f;\, \mathbb{I}} \tag{4}$$

$$\frac{\begin{array}{c} \forall \mathbb{H}. \forall \mathbb{R}.\, (\mathbb{R}(r_s) \leq i) \supset a\,(\mathbb{H}, \mathbb{R}) \supset a'\,(\mathbb{H}, \mathbb{R}) \\ \forall \mathbb{H}. \forall \mathbb{R}.\, (\mathbb{R}(r_s) > i) \supset a\,(\mathbb{H}, \mathbb{R}) \supset a_1\,(\mathbb{H}, \mathbb{R}) \\ \varPsi \vdash \{a'\}\, \mathbb{I} \qquad \varPsi(f) = a_1 \end{array}}{\varPsi \vdash \{a\}\, \mathsf{bgti}\ r_s, i, f;\, \mathbb{I}} \tag{5}$$

$$\frac{\forall \mathbb{S}.\, a\, \mathbb{S} \supset a_1\, \mathbb{S} \quad \text{where } \varPsi(f) = a_1}{\varPsi \vdash \{a\}\, \mathsf{jd}\ f} \tag{6}$$

$$\frac{\forall \mathbb{H}. \forall \mathbb{R}.\, a\,(\mathbb{H}, \mathbb{R}) \supset a_1\,(\mathbb{H}, \mathbb{R}) \quad \text{where } \varPsi(\mathbb{R}(r)) = a_1}{\varPsi \vdash \{a\}\, \mathsf{jmp}\ r} \tag{7}$$

	$(\mathbb{C}, (\mathbb{H}, \mathbb{R}), \mathbb{I}) \longmapsto \mathbb{P}$ where
if $\mathbb{I} =$	then $\mathbb{P} =$
jd f	$(\mathbb{C}, (\mathbb{H}, \mathbb{R}), \mathbb{I}')$ where $\mathbb{C}(\mathbf{f}) = \mathbb{I}'$
jmp r	$(\mathbb{C}, (\mathbb{H}, \mathbb{R}), \mathbb{I}')$ where $\mathbb{C}(\mathbb{R}(\mathbf{r})) = \mathbb{I}'$
bgt $\mathbf{r}_s, \mathbf{r}_t, \mathbf{f}; \mathbb{I}'$	$(\mathbb{C}, (\mathbb{H}, \mathbb{R}), \mathbb{I}')$ when $\mathbb{R}(\mathbf{r}_s) \leq \mathbb{R}(\mathbf{r}_t)$; and
	$(\mathbb{C}, (\mathbb{H}, \mathbb{R}), \mathbb{I}'')$ when $\mathbb{R}(\mathbf{r}_s) > \mathbb{R}(\mathbf{r}_t)$ where $\mathbb{C}(\mathbf{f}) = \mathbb{I}''$
bgti $\mathbf{r}_s, i, \mathbf{f}; \mathbb{I}'$	$(\mathbb{C}, (\mathbb{H}, \mathbb{R}), \mathbb{I}')$ when $\mathbb{R}(\mathbf{r}_s) \leq i$; and
	$(\mathbb{C}, (\mathbb{H}, \mathbb{R}), \mathbb{I}'')$ when $\mathbb{R}(\mathbf{r}_s) > i$ where $\mathbb{C}(\mathbf{f}) = \mathbb{I}''$
alloc $\mathbf{r}_d[\mathbf{r}_s]; \mathbb{I}'$	$(\mathbb{C}, (\mathbb{H}', \mathbb{R}\{\mathbf{r}_d \rightsquigarrow 1\}), \mathbb{I}')$
	where $\mathbb{R}(\mathbf{r}_s) = i$, $\mathbb{H}' = \mathbb{H}\{1 \rightsquigarrow \_, \ldots, 1+i-1 \rightsquigarrow \_\}$
	and $\{1, \ldots, 1+i-1\} \cap \mathrm{dom}(\mathbb{H}) = \emptyset$
free $\mathbf{r}_s; \mathbb{I}'$	$(\mathbb{C}, (\mathbb{H}', \mathbb{R}), \mathbb{I}')$ where $\forall 1 \in \mathrm{dom}(\mathbb{H}').\mathbb{H}'(1) = \mathbb{H}(1),$
	$\mathbb{R}(\mathbf{r}_s) \in \mathrm{dom}(\mathbb{H})$, and $\mathrm{dom}(\mathbb{H}') = \mathrm{dom}(\mathbb{H}) - \mathbb{R}(\mathbf{r}_s)$
ld $\mathbf{r}_d, \mathbf{r}_s(i); \mathbb{I}'$	$(\mathbb{C}, (\mathbb{H}, \mathbb{R}\{\mathbf{r}_d \rightsquigarrow \mathbb{H}(\mathbb{R}(\mathbf{r}_s) + i)\}), \mathbb{I}')$
	where $(\mathbb{R}(\mathbf{r}_s) + i) \in \mathrm{dom}(\mathbb{H})$
st $\mathbf{r}_d(i), \mathbf{r}_s; \mathbb{I}'$	$(\mathbb{C}, (\mathbb{H}\{\mathbb{R}(\mathbf{r}_d) + i \rightsquigarrow \mathbb{R}(\mathbf{r}_s)\}, \mathbb{R}), \mathbb{I}')$
	where $(\mathbb{R}(\mathbf{r}_d) + i) \in \mathrm{dom}(\mathbb{H})$
c; $\mathbb{I}'$ for remaining cases of c	$(\mathbb{C}, \mathtt{AuxStep}(c, (\mathbb{H}, \mathbb{R})), \mathbb{I}')$

Fig. 5. Operational semantics.

Well-formed instructions: Impure rules As mentioned previously, these rules involve accessing or modifying the data heap.

$$\frac{\forall \mathbb{H}. \forall \mathbb{R}. \, a \, (\mathbb{H}, \mathbb{R}) \supset a' \, (\mathbb{H}\{1 \rightsquigarrow \_, \ldots, 1+i-1 \rightsquigarrow \_\}, \mathbb{R}\{\mathbf{r}_d \rightsquigarrow 1\}) \quad \text{where } \mathbb{R}(\mathbf{r}_s) = i \text{ and } \{1, \ldots, 1+i-1\} \cap \mathrm{dom}(\mathbb{H}) = \emptyset \quad \Psi \vdash \{a'\} \mathbb{I}}{\Psi \vdash \{a\} \, \mathtt{alloc} \, \mathbf{r}_d[\mathbf{r}_s]; \mathbb{I}} \tag{8}$$

$$\frac{\forall \mathbb{H}. \forall \mathbb{R}. \, a \, (\mathbb{H}, \mathbb{R}) \supset ((\mathbb{R}(\mathbf{r}_s) + i) \in \mathrm{dom}(\mathbb{H})) \wedge (a' \, (\mathbb{H}, \mathbb{R}\{\mathbf{r}_d \rightsquigarrow \mathbb{H}(\mathbb{R}(\mathbf{r}_s) + i)\})) \quad \Psi \vdash \{a'\} \mathbb{I}}{\Psi \vdash \{a\} \, \mathtt{ld} \, \mathbf{r}_d, \mathbf{r}_s(i); \mathbb{I}} \tag{9}$$

$$\frac{\forall \mathbb{H}. \forall \mathbb{R}. \, a \, (\mathbb{H}, \mathbb{R}) \supset ((\mathbb{R}(\mathbf{r}_d) + i) \in \mathrm{dom}(\mathbb{H})) \wedge (a' \, (\mathbb{H}\{\mathbb{R}(\mathbf{r}_d) + i \rightsquigarrow \mathbb{R}(\mathbf{r}_s)\}, \mathbb{R})) \quad \Psi \vdash \{a'\} \mathbb{I}}{\Psi \vdash \{a\} \, \mathtt{st} \, \mathbf{r}_d(i), \mathbf{r}_s; \mathbb{I}} \tag{10}$$

$$\frac{\forall \mathbb{H}. \forall \mathbb{R}. \, a \, (\mathbb{H}, \mathbb{R}) \supset (\mathbb{R}(\mathbf{r}_s) \in \mathrm{dom}(\mathbb{H})) \wedge (a' \, (\mathbb{H}', \mathbb{R})) \quad \text{where } \mathrm{dom}(\mathbb{H}') = \mathrm{dom}(\mathbb{H}) - \mathbb{R}(\mathbf{r}_s) \text{ and } \forall 1 \in \mathrm{dom}(\mathbb{H}').\mathbb{H}'(1) = \mathbb{H}(1) \quad \Psi \vdash \{a'\} \mathbb{I}}{\Psi \vdash \{a\} \, \mathtt{free} \, \mathbf{r}_s; \mathbb{I}} \tag{11}$$

3.3   Soundness

We establish the soundness of these inference rules with respect to the operational semantics of the machine following the syntactic approach of proving type soundness [21]. From "Type Preservation" and "Progress" lemmas (proved by induction on $\mathbb{I}$), we can guarantee that given a well-formed program, the current instruction sequence will be able to execute without getting "stuck." Furthermore, at the point when the current instruction sequence branches to another code block, the machine state will always satisfy the precondition of that block.

Lemma 1 (Type Preservation). *If* $\Psi \vdash \{a\}\,(\mathbb{C}, \mathbb{S}, \mathbb{I})$ *and* $(\mathbb{C}, \mathbb{S}, \mathbb{I}) \longmapsto \mathbb{P}$, *then there exists an assertion* a' *such that* $\Psi \vdash \{a'\}\,\mathbb{P}$.

Lemma 2 (Progress). *If* $\Psi \vdash \{a\}\,(\mathbb{C}, \mathbb{S}, \mathbb{I})$, *then there exists a program* $\mathbb{P}$ *such that* $(\mathbb{C}, \mathbb{S}, \mathbb{I}) \longmapsto \mathbb{P}$.

Theorem 1 (Soundness). *If* $\Psi \vdash \{a\}\,(\mathbb{C}, \mathbb{S}, \mathbb{I})$, *then there exists a program* $\mathbb{P}$ *such that* $(\mathbb{C}, \mathbb{S}, \mathbb{I}) \longmapsto \mathbb{P}$, *and*
- *if* $(\mathbb{C}, \mathbb{S}, \mathbb{I}) \longmapsto^* (\mathbb{C}, \mathbb{S}', \mathsf{jd}\ f)$, *then* $\Psi(f)\,\mathbb{S}'$;
- *if* $(\mathbb{C}, \mathbb{S}, \mathbb{I}) \longmapsto^* (\mathbb{C}, (\mathbb{H}, \mathbb{R}), \mathsf{jmp}\ r_d)$, *then* $\Psi(\mathbb{R}(r_d))\,(\mathbb{H}, \mathbb{R})$;
- *if* $(\mathbb{C}, \mathbb{S}, \mathbb{I}) \longmapsto^* (\mathbb{C}, (\mathbb{H}, \mathbb{R}), (\mathsf{bgt}\ r_s, r_t, f))$ *and* $\mathbb{R}(r_s) > \mathbb{R}(r_t)$, *then* $\Psi(f)\,(\mathbb{H}, \mathbb{R})$;
- *if* $(\mathbb{C}, \mathbb{S}, \mathbb{I}) \longmapsto^* (\mathbb{C}, (\mathbb{H}, \mathbb{R}), (\mathsf{bgti}\ r_s, i, f))$ *and* $\mathbb{R}(r_s) > i$, *then* $\Psi(f)\,(\mathbb{H}, \mathbb{R})$.

It should be noted here that this soundness theorem establishes more than simple type safety. In addition to that, it states that whenever we jump to a block of code in the heap, the specified precondition of that code (which is an arbitrary assertion) will hold.

4   Certified Dynamic Storage Allocation

Equipped with CAP, we are ready to build the certified library. In particular, we provide provably correct implementation for the library routines `free` and `malloc`. The main difficulties involved in this task are: (1) to give precise yet general specifications to the routines; (2) to prove as theorems the correctness of the routines with respect to their specifications; (3) the specifications and theorems have to be modular so that they can interface with user programs. In this section, we discuss these problems for `free` and `malloc` respectively. From now on, we use the word "specification" in the wider sense, meaning anything that describes the behavior of a program. To avoid confusion, we call the language construct Ψ a *code heap spec*, or simply *spec*.

Before diving into certifying the library, we define some assertions related to memory blocks and the free list as shown in Figure 6. These definitions make use of some basic operators (which we implement as shorthands using primitive constructs) commonly seen in separation logic [17,16]. In particular, **emp** asserts that the heap is empty; $e \mapsto e'$ asserts that the heap contains one cell at address e which contains e'; and separating conjunction $p*q$ asserts that the heap can be split into two disjoint parts in which p and q hold respectively.

Memory block (MBlk $p\ q\ s$) asserts that the memory at address p is preceded by a pair of words: the first word contains q, a (possibly null) pointer to another

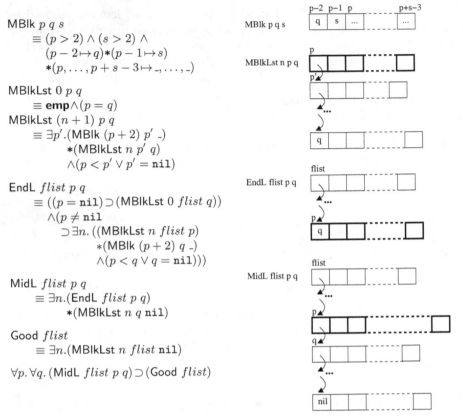

MBlk p q s
$\equiv (p > 2) \wedge (s > 2) \wedge$
$\quad (p - 2 \mapsto q) * (p - 1 \mapsto s)$
$\quad * (p, \ldots, p + s - 3 \mapsto \_, \ldots, \_)$

MBlkLst 0 p q
$\equiv \mathbf{emp} \wedge (p = q)$
MBlkLst $(n + 1)$ p q
$\equiv \exists p'.(\mathsf{MBlk}\ (p + 2)\ p'\ \_)$
$\quad * (\mathsf{MBlkLst}\ n\ p'\ q)$
$\quad \wedge (p < p' \vee p' = \mathbf{nil})$

EndL $flist$ p q
$\equiv ((p = \mathbf{nil}) \supset (\mathsf{MBlkLst}\ 0\ flist\ q))$
$\quad \wedge (p \neq \mathbf{nil}$
$\qquad \supset \exists n.\, ((\mathsf{MBlkLst}\ n\ flist\ p)$
$\qquad\quad * (\mathsf{MBlk}\ (p + 2)\ q\ \_)$
$\qquad\quad \wedge (p < q \vee q = \mathbf{nil})))$

MidL $flist$ p q
$\equiv \exists n.(\mathsf{EndL}\ flist\ p\ q)$
$\quad * (\mathsf{MBlkLst}\ n\ q\ \mathbf{nil})$

Good $flist$
$\equiv \exists n.(\mathsf{MBlkLst}\ n\ flist\ \mathbf{nil})$

$\forall p.\ \forall q.\ (\mathsf{MidL}\ flist\ p\ q) \supset (\mathsf{Good}\ flist)$

Fig. 6. Assertions on free list.

memory block, and the second word contains the size of the memory block itself (including the two-word header preceding p).

Memory block list (MBlkLst n p q) models an address-ordered list of blocks. n is the number of blocks in the list, p is the starting pointer and q is the ending pointer. This assertion is defined inductively and is a specialized version of the *singly-linked list* introduced by Reynolds [17,16]. However, unlike the somewhat informal definition of singly-linked list, MBlkLst has to be defined formally for mechanical proof-checking. Thus we use a Coq inductive definition for this purpose. In contrast, if the assertion language is defined syntactically, inductive definitions have to be defined in the assertion language, which is not shown in previous work.

A list with ending block (EndL $flist$ p q) is defined as a list $flist$ of memory blocks with p pointing at the last block whose forward pointer is q. In the special case that $flist$ is an empty list, p and q are $\mathbf{nil}$. (MidL $flist$ p q) models a list with a block B in the middle, where the list starts from $flist$, and the block B is specified by the position p and the forward pointer q. This assertion is defined as the separating conjunction of a list with ending block B and a null-terminated list starting from the forward pointer of B.

Finally we define a good free list (Good) as a null-terminated memory block list. It is easy to show the relation between MidL and Good as described.

free Putting aside the syntax for the moment, a specification which models the expected behavior of **free** can be written as the following Hoare triple:

$$\{PRE\} \; \mathtt{free}(fptr) \; \{POST\};$$
$$\text{where } PRE \equiv Pred * (\mathsf{MBlk} \; fptr \; \_\,\_) * (\mathsf{Good} \; flist)$$
$$POST \equiv Pred * (\mathsf{Good} \; flist)$$

Assertion PRE states the precondition. It requires that the heap can be separated into three disjoint parts, where $fptr$ points to a memory block to be freed; $flist$ points to a good free list; and the remaining part satisfies the user specified assertion $Pred$. Assertion $POST$ states the postcondition. Since the memory block is placed into the free list, the heap now can be separated into two disjoint parts: $flist$ still points to a good free list, and the remaining part of the heap still satisfies $Pred$ because it is untouched.

Note that this does not totally specify all the behaviors of **free**. For example, it is possible to add in the postcondition that the memory block that $fptr$ pointed to is now in the free list. However, this is irrelevant from a library user's point of view. Thus we favor the above specification, which guarantees that **free** does not affect the remaining part of the heap.

Now we write this specification in CAP, where programs are written in continuation-passing style. Before **free** completes its job and jumps to the return pointer, the postcondition should be established. Thus the postcondition can be interpreted as the precondition of the code referred to by the return pointer. Suppose $\mathbf{r_0}$ is the return pointer, a valid library call to **free** should require that $POST$ implies $\Psi(\mathbb{R}(\mathbf{r_0}))$ for all states (which we write as $POST \Longrightarrow \Psi(\mathbb{R}(\mathbf{r_0}))$). In fact, this condition is required for type-checking the returning code of **free** (*i.e.*, jmp $\mathbf{r_0}$). As a library routine, **free** is expected to be used in various programs with different code heap specs (Ψ). So the above condition has to be established by the user with the actually knowledge of Ψ. When proving the well-formedness of **free**, this condition is taken as a premise.

At an assembly-level, most non-trivial programs are expressed as multiple code blocks connected together with control flow instructions (jd, jmp and bgt). Type-checking these control flow instructions requires similar knowledge about the code heap spec Ψ. For instance, at the end of the code block **free**, an assertion A_{iter} is established about the current state, and the control is transferred to the code block **iter** with a direct jump. When type-checking this direct jump (*i.e.*, jd iter) against the assertion A_{iter}, the inference rule 6 requires that A_{iter} implies $\Psi(\mathtt{iter})$ for all states. These requirements are also taken as premises in the well-formedness theorem of **free**. Thus the specification of **free** is actually as follows:

$$\forall Pred. \, \forall \Psi. \, \forall \mathbf{f}. \, (POST \Longrightarrow \Psi(\mathbf{f})) \wedge (A_{iter} \Longrightarrow \Psi(\mathtt{iter}))$$
$$\supset \Psi \vdash \{PRE \wedge \mathbb{R}(\mathbf{r_0}) = \mathbf{f}\} \, \mathbb{C}(\mathtt{free})$$

where $\mathbb{C}(\texttt{free})$ is the code block labeled $\texttt{free}$, r_0 holds the return location, and universally quantified $Pred$ occurs inside the macros PRE and $POST$ as defined before. This is defined as a theorem and formally proved in Coq.

Following similar ideas, the well-formedness of all the other code blocks implementing the library routine $\texttt{free}$ are also modeled and proved as theorems, with the premises changed appropriately according to which labels they refer to.

Using the Coq proof-assistant, proving these theorems is not difficult. Pure instructions only affect the register file; they are relatively easy to handle. Impure instructions affect the heap. Nonetheless, commonalities on similar operations can be factored out as lemmas. For instance, writing into the "link" field of a memory block header occurs in various places. By factoring out this behavior as a lemma and applying it, the proof construction becomes simple routine work. The only tricky part lies in proving the code which performs coalescing of free blocks. This operation essentially consists of two steps: one to modify the size field; the other to combine the blocks. No matter which one is performed first, one of the blocks has to be "broken" from being a valid memory block as required by MBlk. This behavior is hard to handle in conventional type systems, because it tends to break certain invariants captured by the type system.

In a companion technical report [22] we give the routine $\texttt{free}$ written in CAP. This program is annotated with assertions at various program points. It contains the spec templates (the assertions at the beginning of every code block), and can be viewed as an outline of the proof. In this program, variables are used instead of register names for ease of understanding. We also assume all registers to be caller-saved, so that updating the register file does not affect the user customized assertion $Pred$. Typically relevant states are saved in activation records in a stack when making function calls, and $Pred$ would be dependent only on the stack. In the current implementation, we have not yet provided certified activation records; instead, we simply use different registers for different programs.

A certified library routine consists of both the code and the proof. Accordingly, the interface of such a routine consists of both the signature (parameters) and the spec templates ($e.g.,$ $PRE,POST$). When the routine is used by a user program, both the parameters and the spec templates should be instantiated properly. The well-formedness of $\texttt{free}$ is also a template which can be applied to various assertion $Pred$, code heap spec Ψ and returning label f. If a user program contains only one call-site to $\texttt{free}$, the corresponding assertion for $\texttt{free}$ should be used in Ψ. However, if a user program contains multiple call-sites to $\texttt{free}$, a "sufficiently weak" assertion for $\texttt{free}$ must be constructed by building a disjunction of all the individually instantiated assertions. The following derived Rule 12 (which is proved by induction on $\mathbb{I}$), together with the theorem for the well-formedness of $\texttt{free}$, guarantees that the program type-checks.

$$\frac{\Psi \vdash \{a_1\}\,\mathbb{I} \qquad \Psi \vdash \{a_2\}\,\mathbb{I}}{\Psi \vdash \{a_1 \vee a_2\}\,\mathbb{I}} \tag{12}$$

malloc Similarly as for **free**, an informal specification of **malloc** can be described as follows:

$$\{PRE\} \; \texttt{malloc}(nsize, mptr) \; \{POST\};$$
$$\text{where } PRE \equiv Pred * (\textsf{Good } flist) \wedge (nsize = s_0 > 0)$$
$$POST \equiv Pred' * (\textsf{Good } flist) * (\textsf{MBlk } mptr \lrcorner s) \wedge (s_0 + 2 \leq s)$$

The precondition PRE states that $flist$ points to a good free list, user customized assertion $Pred$ holds for the remaining part of the heap, and the requested size $nsize$ is larger than 0. The postcondition $POST$ states that part of the heap is the newly allocated memory block pointed to by $mptr$ whose size is at least the requested one, $flist$ still points to a good free list, and another assertion $Pred'$ holds for the remaining part of the heap. $Pred'$ may be different from $Pred$ because **malloc** modifies register $mptr$. The relation between these two assertions is described by $SIDE$ as follows:

$$SIDE \equiv \forall(\mathbb{H}, \mathbb{R}). \; Pred \; (\mathbb{H}, \mathbb{R}) \supset Pred' \; (\mathbb{H}, \mathbb{R}\{mptr \rightsquigarrow \lrcorner\})$$

Typically, $Pred$ does not depend on $mptr$. So $Pred'$ is the same as $Pred$ and the above condition is trivially established.

To type-check the control-flow instructions of routine **malloc** without knowing the actual code heap spec Ψ, we add premises to the well-formedness theorem of **malloc** similarly as we did for **free**. The specification in CAP is as follows:

$$\forall Pred. \, \forall Pred'. \, \forall s_0. \, \forall \Psi. \, \forall \mathtt{f}. \, SIDE \wedge (POST \Longrightarrow \Psi(\mathtt{f})) \wedge (A_{init} \Longrightarrow \Psi(\texttt{init}))$$
$$\supset \Psi \vdash \{PRE \wedge \mathbb{R}(\mathtt{r}_1) = \mathtt{f}\} \, \mathbb{C}(\texttt{malloc})$$

where $\mathbb{C}(\texttt{malloc})$ is the code block labeled **malloc**, universally quantified $Pred$, $Pred'$ and s_0 occurs inside the macros PRE, $POST$ and $SIDE$, init is the label of a code block that **malloc** refers to, and A_{init} is the assertion established when **malloc** jumps to init. Because **malloc** calls **free** during its execution, we use a different register $\mathtt{r}_1$ to hold the return location for routine **malloc**, due to the lack of certified activation records. The well-formedness of all the other code blocks implementing routine **malloc** are modeled similarly.

Proving these theorems is not much different than proving those of **free**. A tricky part is on the splitting of memory blocks. Similar to coalescing, splitting temporarily breaks certain invariants; thus it is hard to handle in conventional type systems. The annotated **malloc** routine in CAP is shown in the companion technical report [22] as an outline of the proof.

5   Example: Copy Program

With the certified implementation (*i.e.*, code and proof) of **free** and **malloc**, we now implement a certified program **copy**. As shown in Figure 7, this **copy** program takes a pointer to a list as the argument, makes a copy of the list, and disposes the original one.

Certifying the **copy** program involves the following steps: (1) write the plain code; (2) write the code heap spec; (3) prove the well-formedness of the code with

```
list* copy (list* src) {
   target = prev = nil;
   while (src<>nil) {
       p = malloc(2);                              \\ allocate for a new element
       p->data = src->data, p->link = src->link;          \\ copy an element
       old = src, src = src->link, free(old);            \\ dispose old one
       if (prev == nil) {target = p, prev = p}
       else {prev->link = p, prev=p}                  \\ link in new element
   }
   return target;
}
```

Fig. 7. Pseudo code of copy

respect to the spec, with the help of the library proofs. The companion technical report [22] shows the copy program with annotations at various program points, as well as discussions about the assertions used to handle the list data structure.

The spec for the code blocks that implement the copy program depends on what property one wants to achieve. In our example, we specify the partial correctness that if copy ever completes its task (by jumping to halt), the result list contains the same sequence as the original one.

We get the specs of the library blocks by instantiating the spec templates of the previous section with appropriate assertion $Pred$. The only place where malloc is called is in block nxt0 of copy. Inspecting the assertion at that place and the spec template, we instantiate $Pred$ appropriately to get the actual spec. Although free is called only once in program copy (in block nxt1), it has another call-site in block more of malloc. Thus for any block of free, there are two instantiated specs, one customized for copy (A_1) and the other for malloc (A_2). The actual spec that we use is the disjunction of these two ($A_1 \vee A_2$).

The well-formedness of the program can be derived from the well-formedness of all the code blocks. We follow the proof outline [22] to handle the blocks of copy. For the blocks of routine malloc, we directly import their well-formedness theorems described in the previous section. Proving the premises of these theorems (*e.g.*, $A_{init} \implies \Psi(\text{init})$) is trivial (*e.g.*, A_{init} is exactly $\Psi(\text{init})$). For routine free whose spec has a disjunction form, we apply Rule 12 to break up the disjunction and apply the theorems twice. Proving the premises of these theorems involves *or-elimination* of the form $A_1 \implies A_1 \vee A_2$, which is also trivial. We refer interested readers to our implementation [19] for the exact details.

6   Related Work and Future Work

Dynamic storage allocation Wilson *et al.* [20] categorized allocators based on *strategies* (which attempt to exploit regularities in program behavior), *placement policies* (which decide where to allocate and return blocks in memory), and mechanisms (which involve the algorithms and data structures that implement the policy). We believe that the most tricky part in certifying various allocators is on the low-level mechanisms, rather than the high-level strategies and policies. Most allocators share some subsidiary techniques, such as *splitting* and *coalescing*. Although we only provided a single allocation library implementing a particular policy, the general idea used to certify the techniques of splitting and coalescing can be applied to implement other policies.

Hoare logic. Our logic reasonings about memory properties directly follow Reynolds' separation logic [17,16]. However, being at an assembly level, CAP has some advantages in the context of mechanical proof-checking. CAP provides a fixed number of registers. So the dynamic state is easier to model than using infinite number of variables, and programs are free of variable shadowing. Being at a lower-level implies that the compiler is easier to build, hence it engages a smaller Trusted Computing Base (TCB). Defining assertions as CiC terms of type State → Prop, as opposed to defining assertions syntactically, is also crucial for mechanical proof-checking and thus for PCC. Another difference is that we establish the soundness property using a syntactic approach.

Filliâtre [4,5] developed a software certification tool *Why* which takes annotated programs as input and outputs proof obligations based on Hoare logic for proof assistants Coq and PVS. It is possible to apply *Why* in the PCC framework, because the proof obligation generator is closely related to the verification condition generator of PCC. However, it is less clear how to apply *Why* to Foundational PCC because the proof obligation generator would have to be trusted. On the other hand, if *Why* is applied to certify memory management, it is very likely to hit problems such as expressing inductively defined assertions. Our treatment of assertions in mechanical proof-checking can be used to help.

Certifying compilation. This paper is largely complementary to existing work on certifying compilation [14,11,2,1]. Existing work have only focused on programs whose safety proofs can be automatically generated. On contrast, we support general properties and partial program correctness, but we rely on the programmer to construct the proof. Nevertheless, we believe this is necessary for reasoning about program correctness. Automatic proof construction is infeasible because the problem in general is undecidable. Our language can be used to formally present the reasonings of a programmer. With the help of proof-assistants, proof construction is not difficult, and the result can be mechanically checked.

Future work. Exploring the similarity appeared between Hoare-logic systems and type systems, we intend to model types as assertion macros in CAP to ease the certifying task. For instance, a useful macro is the type of a memory block (MBlk). With lemmas (*c.f.,* typing rules) on how this macro interacts with commands, users can propagate it conveniently. If one is only interested in common properties, (*e.g.,* operations are performed only on allocated blocks), it is promising to achieve proof construction with little user directions, or automatically.

In the future, it would be interesting to develop high-level (*e.g.,* C-like or Java-like) surface languages with similar explicit specifications so that programs are written at a higher-level. "Proof-preserving" compilation from those languages to CAP may help retain a small trusted computing base.

7   Conclusion

Existing certifying compilers have only focused on programs whose safety proofs can be automatically generated. In complementary to these work, we explored in this paper how to certify general properties and program correctness in the PCC framework, letting programmers provide proofs with help of proof assistants. In particular, we presented a certified library for dynamic storage allocation — a topic hard to handle using conventional type systems. The logic reasonings on memory management largely follow separation logic. In general, applying Hoare-logic reasonings in the PCC framework yields interesting possibilities.

References

1. A. W. Appel. Foundational proof-carrying code. In *Proc. 16th Annual IEEE Symposium on Logic in Computer Science*, pages 247–258, June 2001.
2. C. Colby, P. Lee, G. Necula, F. Blau, M. Plesko, and K. Cline. A certifying compiler for Java. In *Proc. 2000 ACM Conf. on Prog. Lang. Design and Impl.*, pages 95–107, New York, 2000. ACM Press.
3. T. Coquand and G. Huet. The calculus of constructions. *Information and Computation*, 76:95–120, 1988.
4. J.-C. Filliâtre. Verification of non-functional programs using interpretations in type theory. Journal of Functional Programming (to appear), 2001.
5. J.-C. Filliâtre. The WHY certification tool, tutorial and reference manual. http://why.lri.fr/, July 2002.
6. C. A. R. Hoare. An axiomatic basis for computer programming. *Communications of the ACM*, Oct. 1969.
7. C. A. R. Hoare. Proof of a program: FIND. *Communications of the ACM*, Jan. 1971.
8. W. A. Howard. The formulae-as-types notion of constructions. In *To H.B.Curry: Essays on Computational Logic, Lambda Calculus and Formalism*. Academic Press, 1980.
9. B. W. Kernighan and D. M. Ritchie. *The C Programming Language (Second Edition)*. Prentice Hall, 1988.
10. D. E. Knuth. *The Art of Computer Programming (Second Edition)*, volume 1. Addison-Wesley, 1973.
11. G. Morrisett, D. Walker, K. Crary, and N. Glew. From System F to typed assembly language. In *Proc. 25th ACM Symp. on Principles of Prog. Lang.*, pages 85–97. ACM Press, Jan. 1998.
12. G. Necula. Proof-carrying code. In *Proc. 24th ACM Symp. on Principles of Prog. Lang.*, pages 106–119, New York, Jan. 1997. ACM Press.
13. G. Necula and P. Lee. Safe kernel extensions without run-time checking. In *Proc. 2nd USENIX Symp. on Operating System Design and Impl.*, pages 229–243, 1996.
14. G. Necula and P. Lee. The design and implementation of a certifying compiler. In *Proc. 1998 ACM Conf. on Prog. Lang. Design and Impl.*, pages 333–344, New York, 1998.
15. C. Paulin-Mohring. Inductive definitions in the system Coq—rules and properties. In M. Bezem and J. Groote, editors, *Proc. TLCA*, volume 664 of *LNCS*. Springer-Verlag, 1993.

16. J. C. Reynolds. Lectures on reasoning about shared mutable data structure. IFIP Working Group 2.3 School/Seminar on State-of-the-Art Program Design Using Logic, Tandil, Argentina, September 6-13, 2000.
17. J. C. Reynolds. Separation logic: A logic for shared mutable data structures. In *Proceedings Seventeenth Annual IEEE Symposium on Logic in Computer Science*, Los Alamitos, California, 2002. IEEE Computer Society.
18. The Coq Development Team. The Coq proof assistant reference manual. The Coq release v7.1, Oct. 2001.
19. The FLINT Project. Coq implementation for certified dynamic storage allocation. http://flint.cs.yale.edu/flint/publications/cdsa.html, Oct. 2002.
20. P. R. Wilson, M. S. Johnstone, M. Neely, and D. Boles. Dynamic storage allocation: A survey and critical review. In *Proc. Int. Workshop on Memory Management*, Kinross Scotland (UK), 1995.
21. A. K. Wright and M. Felleisen. A syntactic approach to type soundness. *Information and Computation*, 115(1):38–94, 1994.
22. D. Yu, N. A. Hamid, and Z. Shao. Building certified libraries for PCC: Dynamic storage allocation. Technical Report YALEU/DCS/TR-1247, Dept. of Computer Science, Yale Univeristy, New Haven, CT, Jan. 2003. http://flint.cs.yale.edu/.

Finite Differencing of Logical Formulas for Static Analysis*

Thomas Reps[1], Mooly Sagiv[2], and Alexey Loginov[1]

[1] Comp. Sci. Dept., University of Wisconsin; {reps,alexey}@cs.wisc.edu
[2] School of Comp. Sci., Tel-Aviv University; msagiv@post.tau.ac.il

Abstract. This paper concerns mechanisms for maintaining the value of an instrumentation predicate (a.k.a. *derived predicate* or *view*), defined via a logical formula over core predicates, in response to changes in the values of the core predicates. It presents an algorithm for transforming the instrumentation predicate's defining formula into a *predicate-maintenance formula* that captures what the instrumentation predicate's new value should be.

This technique applies to program-analysis problems in which the semantics of statements is expressed using logical formulas that describe changes to core-predicate values, and provides a way to reflect those changes in the values of the instrumentation predicates.

1 Introduction

This paper addresses a fundamental challenge in applying abstract interpretation, namely,

> Given the concrete semantics for a language and a desired abstraction, how does one create the associated abstract transformers?

The problem that we address arises in program-analysis problems in which the semantics of statements is expressed using logical formulas that describe changes to core-predicate values. When instrumentation predicates (defined via logical formulas over the core predicates) have been introduced to refine an abstraction, the challenge is to reflect the changes in core-predicate values in the values of the instrumentation predicates [8,5, 14,18,3]. The algorithm presented in this paper provides a way to create formulas that maintain correct values for the instrumentation predicates, and thereby provides a way to generate, completely automatically, the part of the transfer functions of an abstract semantics that deals with instrumentation predicates. The algorithm runs in time linear in the size of the instrumentation predicate's defining formula.

This research was motivated by our work on static analysis based on 3-valued logic [18]; however, any analysis method that relies on logic—2-valued or 3-valued—to express a program's semantics may be able to benefit from these techniques.

In our setting, we consider two related logics: an ordinary 2-valued logic, as well as a related 3-valued logic. A memory configuration, or store, is modeled by what logicians call a *logical structure*; an individual of the structure's universe either models a single

---

* Supported by ONR contract N00014-01-1-0796 and by the A. von Humboldt Foundation.

P. Degano (Ed.): ESOP 2003, LNCS 2618, pp. 380–398, 2003.

memory element or, in the case of a *summary individual*, it models a collection of memory elements. A run of the analyzer carries out an abstract interpretation to collect a set of structures at each program point. This involves finding the least fixed point of a certain set of equations. When the fixed point is reached, the structures that have been collected at program point P describe a superset of all the execution states that can occur at P. To determine whether a property always holds at P, one checks whether it holds in all of the structures that were collected there. Instantiations of this framework are capable of establishing nontrivial properties of programs that perform complex pointer-based manipulations of *a priori* unbounded-size heap-allocated data structures. The TVLA system (**T**hree-**V**alued-**L**ogic **A**nalyzer) implements this approach [11,1].

Summary individuals play a crucial role. They are used to ensure that abstract descriptors have an *a priori* bounded size, which guarantees that a fixed-point is always reached. However, the constraint of working with limited-size descriptors implies a loss of information about the store. Intuitively, some concrete individuals "lose their identity" when they are grouped together with other individuals in one summary individual. Moreover, a property can be true for some concrete individuals of the group but false for other individuals. It is for this reason that 3-valued logic is used; uncertainty about a property's value is captured by means of the third truth value, $1/2$.

An advantage of using 2- and 3-valued logic as the basis for static analysis is that the language used for extracting information from the concrete world and the abstract world is identical: *every* syntactic expression—i.e., every logical formula—can be interpreted either in the 2-valued world or the 3-valued world. The consistency of the 2-valued and 3-valued viewpoints is ensured by a basic theorem that relates the two logics. This provides a partial answer to the fundamental challenge posed above: formulas that define the concrete semantics when interpreted in 2-valued logic define a sound abstract semantics when interpreted in 3-valued logic [18].

Unfortunately, unless some care is taken in the design of an analysis, there is a danger that as abstract interpretation proceeds, the indefinite value $1/2$ will become pervasive. This can destroy the ability to recover interesting information from the 3-valued structures collected (although soundness is maintained). A key role in combating indefiniteness is played by *instrumentation predicates*, which record auxiliary information in a logical structure. They provide a mechanism for the user to fine-tune an abstraction: an instrumentation predicate, which is defined by a logical formula over the core predicate symbols, captures a property that an individual memory cell may or may not possess. In general, adding additional instrumentation predicates refines the abstraction, defining a more precise analysis that is prepared to track finer distinctions among stores. This allows more properties of the program's stores to be identified.

From the standpoint of the concrete semantics, instrumentation predicates represent cached information that could always be recomputed by reevaluating the instrumentation predicate's defining formula in the local state. From the standpoint of the abstract semantics, however, reevaluating a formula in the local (3-valued) state can lead to a drastic loss of precision. To gain maximum benefit from instrumentation predicates, an abstract-interpretation algorithm must obtain their values in some other way.

This problem, the *instrumentation-predicate-maintenance problem*, will be solved by incremental computation. The new value that instrumentation predicate p should have after a transition via abstract state transformer τ from state σ to σ' will be computed incrementally from the known value of p in σ.

The contributions of the work reported in this paper include the following:

- We give an algorithm for the predicate-maintenance problem; it creates a predicate-maintenance formula by applying a finite-differencing transformation to p's defining formula. The algorithm runs in time linear in the size of the defining formula.
- We present experimental evidence that our technique is an effective one, at least for the analysis of programs that manipulate acyclic singly-linked lists, doubly-linked lists, and binary trees, and for certain sorting programs. In particular, the predicate-maintenance formulas produced automatically using our approach are as effective for maintaining precision as the best available hand-crafted ones.
- This work is related to the view-maintenance problem in databases. Compared with that work, the novelty is the ability to create predicate-maintenance formulas that are suitable for use when abstraction has been performed.

The remainder of the paper is organized as follows: Sect. 2 introduces terminology and notation. Sect. 3 defines the predicate-maintenance problem. Sect. 4 presents a method for generating maintenance formulas for instrumentation predicates. Sect. 5 discusses extensions to handle instrumentation predicates that use transitive closure. Sect. 6 presents experimental results. Sect. 7 discusses related work.

2 Background

2 Valued First Order Logic with Transitive Closure. The syntax of first-order formulas with equality and reflexive transitive closure is defined as follows:

Definition 1. A *formula* over the *vocabulary* $\mathcal{P} = \{eq, p_1, \ldots, p_n\}$ is defined by

$$
\begin{aligned}
&p \in \mathcal{P} &\quad \varphi ::= \ &\mathbf{0} \mid \mathbf{1} \mid p(v_1, \ldots, v_k) \\
&\varphi \in \textit{Formulas} &\quad &\mid (\neg \varphi_1) \mid (\varphi_1 \wedge \varphi_2) \mid (\varphi_1 \vee \varphi_2) \mid (\exists v \colon \varphi_1) \mid (\forall v \colon \varphi_1) \\
&v \in \textit{Variables} &\quad &\mid (\mathbf{RTC}\ v_1', v_2' \colon \varphi_1)(v_1, v_2)
\end{aligned}
$$

The set of free variables of a formula is defined as usual. "**RTC**" stands for reflexive transitive closure. In $\varphi \equiv (\mathbf{RTC}\ v_1', v_2' \colon \varphi_1)(v_1, v_2)$, if φ_1's free-variable set is V, we require $v_1, v_2 \notin V$. The free variables of φ are $(V - \{v_1', v_2'\}) \cup \{v_1, v_2\}$.

We use several shorthand notations: $(v_1 = v_2) \overset{\text{def}}{=} eq(v_1, v_2)$; $(v_1 \neq v_2) \overset{\text{def}}{=} \neg eq(v_1, v_2)$; and for a binary predicate p, $p^*(v_1, v_2) \overset{\text{def}}{=} (\mathbf{RTC}\ v_1', v_2' \colon p(v_1', v_2'))(v_1, v_2)$. We also use a C-like syntax for conditional expressions: $\varphi_1\ ?\ \varphi_2\ :\ \varphi_3$.[1] The order of precedence among the connectives, from highest to lowest, is as follows: $\neg, \wedge, \vee, \forall$, and $\exists$. We drop parentheses wherever possible, except for emphasis.

---

[1] In 2-valued logic, one can think of $\varphi_1\ ?\ \varphi_2\ :\ \varphi_3$ as a shorthand for $(\varphi_1 \wedge \varphi_2) \vee (\neg\varphi_1 \wedge \varphi_3)$. In 3-valued logic, it becomes a shorthand for $(\varphi_1 \wedge \varphi_2) \vee (\neg\varphi_1 \wedge \varphi_3) \vee (\varphi_2 \wedge \varphi_3)$.

Definition 2. A *2-valued interpretation* over $\mathcal{P}$ is a *2-valued logical structure* $S = \langle U^S, \iota^S \rangle$, where U^S is a set of *individuals* and ι^S maps each predicate symbol p of arity k to a truth-valued function: $\iota^S(p) \colon (U^S)^k \to \{0, 1\}$. In addition, (i) for all $u \in U^S$, $\iota^S(eq)(u, u) = 1$, and (ii) for all $u_1, u_2 \in U^S$ such that u_1 and u_2 are distinct individuals, $\iota^S(eq)(u_1, u_2) = 0$.

An *assignment* Z is a function that maps variables to individuals (i.e., it has the functionality $Z \colon \{v_1, v_2, \dots\} \to U^S$). When Z is defined on all free variables of a formula φ, we say that Z is *complete* for φ. (We generally assume that every assignment that arises in connection with the discussion of some formula φ is complete for φ.)

The *(2-valued) meaning* of a formula φ, denoted by $[\![\varphi]\!]_2^S(Z)$, yields a truth value in $\{0, 1\}$; it is defined inductively as follows:

$$[\![0]\!]_2^S(Z) = 0 \qquad\qquad [\![\varphi_1 \wedge \varphi_2]\!]_2^S(Z) = \min([\![\varphi_1]\!]_2^S(Z), [\![\varphi_2]\!]_2^S(Z))$$
$$[\![1]\!]_2^S(Z) = 1 \qquad\qquad [\![\varphi_1 \vee \varphi_2]\!]_2^S(Z) = \max([\![\varphi_1]\!]_2^S(Z), [\![\varphi_2]\!]_2^S(Z))$$
$$[\![p(v_1, \dots, v_k)]\!]_2^S(Z) = \iota^S(p)(Z(v_1), \dots, Z(v_k)) \qquad [\![\exists v \colon \varphi_1]\!]_2^S(Z) = \max_{u \in U^S}[\![\varphi_1]\!]_2^S(Z[v_1 \mapsto u])$$
$$[\![\neg\varphi_1]\!]_2^S(Z) = 1 - [\![\varphi_1]\!]_2^S(Z) \qquad [\![\forall v \colon \varphi_1]\!]_2^S(Z) = \min_{u \in U^S}[\![\varphi_1]\!]_2^S(Z[v_1 \mapsto u])$$

$$[\![(\mathbf{RTC}\ v_1', v_2' \colon \varphi_1)(v_1, v_2)]\!]_2^S(Z)$$
$$= \begin{cases} 1 & \text{if } Z(v_1) = Z(v_2) \\[2ex] \max\limits_{\substack{n \geq 1, \\ u_1, \dots, u_{n+1} \in U, \\ Z(v_1) = u_1, \\ Z(v_2) = u_{n+1}}} \min\limits_{i=1}^{n}[\![\varphi_1]\!]_2^S(Z[v_1' \mapsto u_i, v_2' \mapsto u_{i+1}]) & \text{otherwise} \end{cases}$$

S and Z *satisfy* φ if $[\![\varphi]\!]_2^S(Z) = 1$. The set of 2-valued structures is denoted by 2-STRUCT[$\mathcal{P}$].

3 Valued Logic and Embedding.

In 3-valued logic, the formulas that we work with are identical to the ones used in 2-valued logic. At the semantic level, a third truth value—$1/2$—is introduced to denote uncertainty.

Definition 3. The truth values 0 and 1 are *definite values*; $1/2$ is an *indefinite value*. For $l_1, l_2 \in \{0, 1/2, 1\}$, the *information order* is defined as follows: $l_1 \sqsubseteq l_2$ iff $l_1 = l_2$ or $l_2 = 1/2$. We use $l_1 \sqsubset l_2$ when $l_1 \sqsubseteq l_2$ and $l_1 \neq l_2$. The symbol $\sqcup$ denotes the least-upper-bound operation with respect to $\sqsubseteq$.

Definition 4. A *3-valued interpretation* over $\mathcal{P}$ is a *3-valued logical structure* $S = \langle U^S, \iota^S \rangle$, where U^S is a set of individuals and ι^S maps each predicate symbol p of arity k to a truth-valued function: $\iota^S(p) \colon (U^S)^k \to \{0, 1/2, 1\}$. In addition, (i) for all $u \in U^S$, $\iota^S(eq)(u, u) \sqsupseteq 1$, and (ii) for all $u_1, u_2 \in U^S$ such that u_1 and u_2 are distinct individuals, $\iota^S(eq)(u_1, u_2) = 0$.

For an assignment Z, the *(3-valued) meaning* of a formula φ, denoted by $[\![\varphi]\!]_3^S(Z)$, yields a truth value in $\{0, 1/2, 1\}$. The meaning of φ is defined exactly as in Defn. 2, but interpreted over $\{0, 1/2, 1\}$. S and Z *potentially satisfy* φ if $[\![\varphi]\!]_3^S(Z) \sqsupseteq 1$. The set of 3-valued structures is denoted by 3-STRUCT[$\mathcal{P}$].

Defn. 4 requires that for each individual u, the value of $\iota^S(eq)(u, u)$ is 1 or $1/2$. An individual for which $\iota^S(eq)(u, u) = 1/2$ is called a *summary individual*. In the abstract-interpretation context, a summary individual is an abstract individual, and can represent more than one concrete individual.

Because $\varphi_1 ? \varphi_2 : \varphi_3$ is treated as a shorthand for $(\varphi_1 \wedge \varphi_2) \vee (\neg\varphi_1 \wedge \varphi_3) \vee (\varphi_2 \wedge \varphi_3)$ in 3-valued logic, the value of $1/2 ? V_1 : V_2$ equals $V_1 \sqcup V_2$.

Definition 5. Let $S = \langle U^S, \iota^S \rangle$ and $S' = \langle U^{S'}, \iota^{S'} \rangle$ be two structures, and let $f: U^S \to U^{S'}$ be a surjective function. We say that f *embeds* S in S' (denoted by $S \sqsubseteq^f S'$) if for every predicate symbol $p \in \mathcal{P}$ of arity k and for all $u_1, \dots, u_k \in U^S$, $\iota^S(p)(u_1, \dots, u_k) \sqsubseteq \iota^{S'}(p)(f(u_1), \dots, f(u_k))$. We say that S *can be embedded in* S' (denoted by $S \sqsubseteq S'$) if there exists a function f such that $S \sqsubseteq^f S'$.

The Embedding Theorem says that if $S \sqsubseteq^f S'$, then every piece of information extracted from S' via a formula φ is a conservative approximation of the information extracted from S via φ. To formalize this, we extend mappings on individuals to operate on assignments: if $f: U^S \to U^{S'}$ is a function and $Z: Var \to U^S$ is an assignment, $f \circ Z$ denotes the assignment $f \circ Z: Var \to U^{S'}$ such that $(f \circ Z)(v) = f(Z(v))$.

Theorem 1. (Embedding Theorem [18, Theorem 4.9]). Let $S = \langle U^S, \iota^S \rangle$ and $S' = \langle U^{S'}, \iota^{S'} \rangle$ be two structures, and let $f: U^S \to U^{S'}$ be a function such that $S \sqsubseteq^f S'$. Then, for every formula φ and complete assignment Z for φ, $[\![\varphi]\!]_3^S(Z) \sqsubseteq [\![\varphi]\!]_3^{S'}(f \circ Z)$.

Program Analysis Via 3 Valued Logic. The remainder of this section summarizes the program-analysis framework described in [18]. Stores are encoded as logical structures in terms of a fixed collection of *core predicates*, $\mathcal{C}$. Core predicates are part of the underlying semantics of the language to be analyzed; they record atomic properties of stores. For instance, Tab. 1 gives the definition of a C linked-list datatype, and lists the predicates that would be used to represent the stores manipulated by programs that use type List. (The core predicates are fixed for a given language; in general, different languages require different collections of core predicates.)

Table 1. (a) Declaration of a linked-list datatype in C. (b) Core predicates used for representing the stores manipulated by programs that use type List.

```
typedef struct node {
    struct node *n;
    int data;
} *List;
```

Predicate	Intended Meaning
$eq(v_1, v_2)$	Do v_1 and v_2 denote the same memory cell?
$q(v)$	Does pointer variable q point to memory cell v?
$n(v_1, v_2)$	Does the n field of v_1 point to v_2?

      (a)   (b)

Often only a restricted class of structures is used to encode stores; to exclude structures that cannot represent admissible stores, integrity constraints can be imposed. For instance, in program-analysis applications, a predicate like $q(v)$ of Tab. 1 captures whether pointer variable q points to memory cell v; q would be given the attribute "unique", which imposes the integrity constraint that q can hold for at most one individual in any structure.

A concrete operational semantics is defined by specifying, for each kind of statement st in the programming language, a structure transformer for each outgoing control-flow graph (CFG) edge $e = (st, st')$. A structure transformer is specified by providing a collection of *predicate-transfer formulas*, $\tau_{c,st}$, one for each core predicate c. These define how the core predicates of a logical structure S that arises at st is transformed by e to create a logical structure S' at st'.

Abstract stores are 3-valued logical structures. Concrete stores are abstracted to abstract stores by means of *embedding functions*—onto functions that map individuals of a 2-valued structure $S^\natural$ to those of a 3-valued structure S. The Embedding Theorem ensures that every piece of information extracted from S by evaluating a formula φ is a conservative approximation ($\sqsupseteq$) of the information extracted from $S^\natural$ by evaluating φ.

The finiteness of the abstract domain is assured by *canonical abstraction*, under which each individual of a 2-valued logical structure (representing a concrete memory cell) is mapped to an individual of a 3-valued logical structure according to the vector of values that the concrete individual has for a user-chosen collection of unary abstraction predicates. This mechanism ensures that each 3-valued structure is no larger than some fixed size, known *a priori*.

The abstraction function on which an analysis is based, and hence the precision of the analysis defined, can be tuned by (i) choosing to equip structures with additional *instrumentation predicates* to record derived properties, and (ii) varying which of the unary core and unary instrumentation predicates are used as the set of abstraction predicates. The set of instrumentation predicates is denoted by $\mathcal{I}$. Each arity-k predicate symbol $p \in \mathcal{I}$ is defined by an *instrumentation-predicate definition formula* $\psi_p(v_1, \dots, v_k)$. Instrumentation predicates may appear in the defining formulas of other instrumentation predicates as long as there are no circular dependences. Instrumentation predicates that involve reachability properties, which can be defined using **RTC**, often play a crucial role in the definitions of abstractions. For instance, in program-analysis applications, reachability properties from specific pointer variables have the effect of keeping disjoint sublists summarized separately. This is particularly important when analyzing a program in which two pointers are advanced along disjoint sublists.

For each kind of statement in the programming language, the abstract semantics is again defined by a collection of formulas: the *same* predicate-transfer formula that defines the concrete semantics, in the case of a core predicate, and, in the case of an instrumentation predicate p, by a *predicate-maintenance formula* $\mu_{p,st}$.[2]

Abstract interpretation collects a set of 3-valued structures at each program point. It can be implemented as an iterative procedure that finds the least fixed point of a certain set of equations [18]. (It is important to understand that although the analysis framework is based on logic, it is model theoretic, not proof theoretic: the abstract interpretation collects sets of 3-valued logical structures—i.e., abstracted models; its actions do not rely on deduction or theorem proving.)

Fig. 1 illustrates the abstract execution of the statement y = x on a 3-valued logical structure that represents concrete lists of length 2 or more.

The following graphical notation is used for depicting 3-valued logical structures:

- Individuals are represented by circles with names inside.
- A summary individual u has $eq(u, u) = 1/2$, and is represented by a double circle.

---

[2] In [18], predicate-transfer formulas and predicate-maintenance formulas are both called "predicate-update formulas". Here we use separate terms so that we can refer easily to predicate-maintenance formulas, which are the main subject of the paper.

	unary preds.			binary preds.						diagram
Structure before	indiv.	x	y	$is[n]$	n	u_1	u	eq	u_1	u	$x \to (u_1) \cdots n \cdots (u)$
	u_1	1	0	0	u_1	0	1/2	u_1	1	0	
	u	0	0	0	u	0	1/2	u	0	1/2	
Statement	$y = x$										
Predicate-transfer formulas	$\tau_{x,y=x}(v) = x(v)$ $\tau_{y,y=x}(v) = x(v)$ $\tau_{n,y=x}(v_1, v_2) = n(v_1, v_2)$										
Predicate-maintenance formula	$\mu_{is[n],y=x}(v) = \exists\, v_1, v_2 : n(v_1, v) \wedge n(v_2, v) \wedge v_1 \neq v_2$										
	unary preds.				binary preds.						diagram
Structure after	indiv.	x	y	$is[n]$	n	u_1	u	eq	u_1	u	$x, y \to (u_1) \cdots n \cdots (u)$
	u_1	1	1	0	u_1	0	1/2	u_1	1	0	$is[n]$
	u	0	0	1/2	u	0	1/2	u	0	1/2	

Fig. 1. The predicate-transfer formulas for x, y, and n express a transformation on logical structures that corresponds to the semantics of y = x. (The predicate $is[n]$ is discussed in Ex. 1.)

- A unary predicate p is represented by a solid arrow from p to each individual u for which $\iota(p)(u) = 1$, and by the absence of a p-arrow to each node u' for which $\iota(p)(u') = 0$. (If $\iota(p) = 0$ for all individuals, the predicate name p is not shown.)
- A binary predicate q is represented by a solid arrow labeled q between each pair of individuals u_i and u_j for which $\iota(q)(u_i, u_j) = 1$, and by the absence of a q-arrow between pairs u'_i and u'_j for which $\iota(q)(u'_i, u'_j) = 0$.
- Unary and binary predicates with value $1/2$ are represented by dotted arrows.

3   The Problem: Maintaining Instrumentation Predicates

The execution of a statement st transforms a logical structure S, which represents a store that arises just before st, into a new structure S', which represents the corresponding store just after st executes. The structure that consists of just the core predicates of S' is called a *proto-structure*, denoted by S'_{proto}. The creation of S'_{proto} from S, denoted by $S'_{proto} := [\![st]\!]_3(S)$, can be expressed as

$$\text{for each } c \in \mathcal{C} \text{ and } u_1, \dots, u_k \in U^S,$$
$$\iota^{S'_{proto}}(c)(u_1, \dots, u_k) := [\![\tau_{c,st}(v_1, \dots, v_k)]\!]_3^S([v_1 \mapsto u_1, \dots, v_k \mapsto u_k]). \quad (1)$$

In general, if we compare the various predicates of S'_{proto} with those of S, some tuples will have been added and others will have been deleted.

We now come to the crux of the matter: Suppose that ψ_p defines instrumentation predicate p; how should the static-analysis engine obtain the value of p in S'?

An instrumentation predicate whose defining formula is expressed solely in terms of core predicates is said to be in *core normal form*. Because there are no circular dependences, an instrumentation predicate's defining formula can always be put in core normal form by repeated substitution until only core predicates remain. When ψ_p is in core normal form, or has been converted to core normal form, it is possible to determine the value of each instrumentation predicate p by evaluating ψ_p in structure S'_{proto}:

for each $u_1, \ldots, u_k \in U^S$,

$$\iota^{S'}(p)(u_1, \ldots, u_k) := [\![\psi_p(v_1, \ldots, v_k)]\!]_3^{S'_{proto}}([v_1 \mapsto u_1, \ldots, v_k \mapsto u_k]). \quad (2)$$

Thus, in principle it is possible to maintain the values of instrumentation predicates via Eqn. (2). In practice, however, this approach does not work very well. As observed elsewhere [18], when working in 3-valued logic, it is usually possible to retain more precision by defining a special *instrumentation-predicate maintenance formula*, $\mu_{p,st}(v_1, \ldots, v_k)$, and evaluating $\mu_{p,st}(v_1, \ldots, v_k)$ in structure S:

for each $u_1, \ldots, u_k \in U^S$,

$$\iota^{S'}(p)(u_1, \ldots, u_k) := [\![\mu_{p,st}(v_1, \ldots, v_k)]\!]_3^S([v_1 \mapsto u_1, \ldots, v_k \mapsto u_k]). \quad (3)$$

The advantage of the predicate-maintenance approach is that the results of program analysis can be more accurate. In 3-valued logic, when $\mu_{p,st}$ is defined appropriately, the predicate-maintenance strategy can generate a definite value (0 or 1) when the evaluation of ψ_p on S'_{proto} generates the indefinite value $1/2$.

   To ensure that an analysis is conservative, however, one must also show that the following property holds:

Definition 6. Suppose that p is an instrumentation predicate defined by formula ψ_p. Predicate-maintenance formula $\mu_{p,st}$ *maintains p correctly for statement st* if, for all $S \in 2\text{-STRUCT}[\mathcal{P}]$ and all Z, $[\![\mu_{p,st}]\!]_2^S(Z) = [\![\psi_p]\!]_2^{[st]_2(S)}(Z)$.

   For an instrumentation predicate in core normal form, it is always possible to provide a predicate-maintenance formula that satisfies Defn. 6 by defining $\mu_{p,st}$ as

$$\mu_{p,st} \stackrel{\text{def}}{=} \psi_p[c \hookleftarrow \tau_{c,st} \mid c \in \mathcal{C}], \quad (4)$$

where $\varphi[q \hookleftarrow \varphi']$ denotes the formula obtained from φ by replacing each predicate occurrence $q(w_1, \ldots, w_k)$ by $\varphi'\{w_1, \ldots, w_k\}$, and $\varphi'\{w_1, \ldots, w_k\}$ denotes the formula obtained from $\varphi'(v_1, \ldots, v_k)$ by replacing each free occurrence of variable v_i by w_i.

Fig. 2.   Store in which u is shared;   i.e., $is[n](u) = 1$.

   The formula $\mu_{p,st}$ defined in Eqn. (4) maintains p correctly for statement st because, by the 2-valued version of Eqn. (1), $[\![\tau_{c,st}]\!]_2^S(Z) = [\![c]\!]_2^{S'_{proto}}(Z)$; consequently, when $\mu_{p,st}$ of Eqn. (4) is evaluated in structure S, the use of $\tau_{c,st}$ in place of c is equivalent to using the value of c when ψ_p is evaluated in S'_{proto}; i.e., for all Z, $[\![\psi_p[c \hookleftarrow \tau_{c,st} \mid c \in \mathcal{C}]]\!]_2^S(Z) = [\![\psi_p]\!]_2^{S'_{proto}}(Z)$. However—and this is precisely the drawback of using Eqn. (4) to obtain the $\mu_{p,st}$—the steps of evaluating $[\![\psi_p[c \hookleftarrow \tau_{c,st} \mid c \in \mathcal{C}]]\!]_2^S(Z)$ *mimic exactly* those of evaluating $[\![\psi_p]\!]_2^{S'_{proto}}(Z)$. Consequently, when we pass to 3-valued logic, for all Z, $[\![\psi_p[c \hookleftarrow \tau_{c,st} \mid c \in \mathcal{C}]]\!]_3^S(Z)$ yields exactly the same value as $[\![\psi_p]\!]_3^{S'_{proto}}(Z)$ (i.e., as evaluating Eqn. (2)). Thus, although $\mu_{p,st}$ that satisfy Defn. 6 can be obtained automatically via Eqn. (4), this approach does not provide a satisfactory solution to the predicate-maintenance problem.

Example 1. Eqn. (5) shows the defining formula for the instrumentation predicate $is[n]$ ("is-shared using n fields"),

$$is[n](v) \stackrel{\text{def}}{=} \exists\, v_1, v_2 : n(v_1, v) \wedge n(v_2, v) \wedge v_1 \neq v_2, \tag{5}$$

which captures whether a memory cell is pointed to by two or more pointer fields of memory cells, e.g., see Fig. 2.

Fig. 1 illustrates how execution of the statement y = x causes the value of $is[n]$ to lose precision when its predicate-maintenance formula is created according to Eqn. (4). The initial 3-valued structure represents all singly linked lists of length 2 or more in which all memory cells are unshared. Because execution of y = x does not change the value of core predicate n, $\tau_{n,y=x}(v_1, v_2)$ is $n(v_1, v_2)$, and hence the formula $\mu_{is[n],y=x}(v)$ created according to Eqn. (4) is $\exists\, v_1, v_2 : n(v_1, v) \wedge n(v_2, v) \wedge v_1 \neq v_2$. As shown in Fig. 1, the structure created using this maintenance formula is not as precise as we would like. In particular, $is(u) = 1/2$, which means that u can represent a shared cell. Thus, the final 3-valued structure also represents certain cyclic linked lists, such as

This sort of imprecision can usually be avoided by devising better predicate-maintenance formulas. For instance, when $\mu_{is[n],y=x}(v)$ is defined to be the formula $is[n](v)$—meaning that y = x does not change the value of $is[n](v)$—the imprecision illustrated in Fig. 1 is avoided (see Fig. 3). Hand-crafted predicate-maintenance formulas for a variety of instrumentation predicates are given in [18,11,1]; however, those formulas were created by *ad hoc* methods.

	unary preds.				binary preds.						
Structure before	**indiv.** x y $is[n]$ u_1 $\;$ 1 0 $\;$ 0 u $\;\;$ 0 0 $\;$ 0				n $\;u_1\;$ u u_1 0 1/2 u $\;$ 0 1/2			eq u_1 u u_1 1 0 u $\;$ 0 1/2			$x \rightarrow (u_1) \cdots^{n}\!\!\! \rightarrow (u)$ ^{n}
Statement	y = x										
Predicate-transfer formulas	$\tau_{x,y=x}(v) = x(v)$ $\tau_{y,y=x}(v) = x(v)$ $\tau_{n,y=x}(v_1, v_2) = n(v_1, v_2)$										
Predicate-maintenance formula	$\mu_{is[n],y=x}(v) = is[n](v)$										
Structure after	**indiv.** x y $is[n]$ u_1 $\;$ 1 1 $\;$ 0 u $\;\;$ 0 0 $\;$ 0				n $\;u_1\;$ u u_1 0 1/2 u $\;$ 0 1/2			eq u_1 u u_1 1 0 u $\;$ 0 1/2			x, y $\rightarrow (u_1) \cdots^{n}\!\!\! \rightarrow (u)$ ^{n}

Fig. 3. Example showing how the imprecision that was illustrated in Fig. 1 is avoided with the predicate-maintenance formula $\mu_{is[n],y=x}(v) = is[n](v)$. (Ex. 2 shows how this is generated automatically.)

To sum up, in past incarnations of our work, the user must supply a formula $\mu_{p,st}$ for each instrumentation predicate p and each statement st. In effect, the user must write down two *separate* characterizations of each instrumentation predicate p: (i) ψ_p, which defines p directly; and (ii) $\mu_{p,st}$, which specifies how execution of each kind of statement in the language affects p. Moreover, it is the user's responsibility to ensure that the two characterizations are mutually consistent. In contrast, with the new method for automatically creating predicate-maintenance formulas presented in Sects. 4 and 5, the user's only responsibility is to define the ψ_p.

4   A Finite Differencing Scheme for 3 Valued Logic

This section presents a finite-differencing scheme for creating predicate-maintenance formulas. A predicate-maintenance formula $\mu_{p,st}$ for $p \in \mathcal{I}$ is defined in terms of two finite-differencing operators, denoted by $\Delta_{st}^{-}[\cdot]$ and $\Delta_{st}^{+}[\cdot]$, which capture the negative and positive changes, respectively, that execution of statement st induces in an instrumentation predicate's value. The formula $\mu_{p,st}$ is created by combining p with $\Delta_{st}^{-}[\psi_p]$ and $\Delta_{st}^{+}[\psi_p]$ as follows: $\mu_{p,st} = p \; ? \; \neg\Delta_{st}^{-}[\psi_p] : \Delta_{st}^{+}[\psi_p]$.

Fig. 4 depicts how the static-analysis engine evaluates $\Delta_{st}^{-}[\psi_p]$ and $\Delta_{st}^{+}[\psi_p]$ in S and combines these values with the old value p to obtain the desired new value p''. The operators $\Delta_{st}^{-}[\cdot]$ and $\Delta_{st}^{+}[\cdot]$ are defined recursively, as shown in Fig. 5. The definitions in Fig. 5 make use of the following operator:

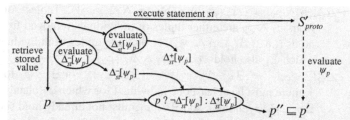

Fig. 4. How to maintain the value of ψ_p in 3-valued logic in response to changes in the values of core predicates caused by the execution of statement st.

$$\mathbf{F}_{st}[\varphi] \overset{\text{def}}{=} \varphi \; ? \; \neg\Delta_{st}^{-}[\varphi] : \Delta_{st}^{+}[\varphi]. \tag{6}$$

Thus, maintenance formula $\mu_{p,st}$ can also be expressed as $\mu_{p,st} = \mathbf{F}_{st}[p]$.

Eqn. (6) and Fig. 5 define a syntax-directed translation scheme that can be implemented via a recursive walk over a formula φ. The operators $\Delta_{st}^{-}[\cdot]$ and $\Delta_{st}^{+}[\cdot]$ are mutually recursive. For instance, $\Delta_{st}^{+}[\neg\varphi_1] = \Delta_{st}^{-}[\varphi_1]$ and $\Delta_{st}^{-}[\neg\varphi_1] = \Delta_{st}^{+}[\varphi_1]$. Moreover, each occurrence of $\mathbf{F}_{st}[\varphi_i]$ contains additional occurrences of $\Delta_{st}^{-}[\varphi_i]$ and $\Delta_{st}^{+}[\varphi_i]$.

Note how $\Delta_{st}^{-}[\cdot]$ and $\Delta_{st}^{+}[\cdot]$ for $\varphi_1 \vee \varphi_2$ and $\varphi_1 \wedge \varphi_2$ exhibit the "convolution" pattern characteristic of differentiation, finite-differencing, and divided-differencing.

Continuing the analogy with differentiation, it helps to bear in mind that the "independent variables" are the core predicates—which are being changed by the $\tau_{c,st}$ formulas; the dependent variable is the value of φ. A formal justification of Fig. 5 is stated later (Thm. 2); here we merely explain informally a few of the cases from Fig. 5:

$\Delta_{st}^{+}[1] = 0, \Delta_{st}^{-}[1] = 0.$ The value of atomic formula 1 does not depend on any core predicates; hence its value is unaffected by changes in them.

φ	$\Delta_{st}^+[\varphi]$	$\Delta_{st}^-[\varphi]$
1	0	0
0	0	0
$p(w_1,\dots,w_k)$, $p\in\mathcal{C}$, and $\tau_{p,st}$ is of the form $p\ ?\ \neg\delta_{p,st}^- : \delta_{p,st}^+$	$(\delta_{p,st}^+ \wedge \neg p)\{w_1,\dots,w_k\}$	$(\delta_{p,st}^- \wedge p)\{w_1,\dots,w_k\}$
$p(w_1,\dots,w_k)$, $p\in\mathcal{C}$, but $\tau_{p,st}$ is not of the form $p\ ?\ \neg\delta_{p,st}^- : \delta_{p,st}^+$	$(\tau_{p,st} \wedge \neg p)\{w_1,\dots,w_k\}$	$(p \wedge \neg\tau_{p,st})\{w_1,\dots,w_k\}$
$p(w_1,\dots,w_k)$, $p\in\mathcal{I}$	$((\exists v: \Delta_{st}^+[\varphi_1]) \wedge \neg p)\{w_1,\dots,w_k\}$ if $\psi_p \equiv \exists v: \varphi_1$ $\quad$ $\Delta_{st}^+[\psi_p]\{w_1,\dots,w_k\}$ $\quad$ otherwise	$((\exists v: \Delta_{st}^-[\varphi_1]) \wedge p)\{w_1,\dots,w_k\}$ if $\psi_p \equiv \forall v: \varphi_1$ $\quad$ $\Delta_{st}^-[\psi_p]\{w_1,\dots,w_k\}$ $\quad$ otherwise
$\neg\varphi_1$	$\Delta_{st}^-[\varphi_1]$	$\Delta_{st}^+[\varphi_1]$
$\varphi_1 \vee \varphi_2$	$(\Delta_{st}^+[\varphi_1] \wedge \neg\varphi_2) \vee (\neg\varphi_1 \wedge \Delta_{st}^+[\varphi_2])$	$(\Delta_{st}^-[\varphi_1] \wedge \neg\mathbf{F}_{st}[\varphi_2]) \vee (\neg\mathbf{F}_{st}[\varphi_1] \wedge \Delta_{st}^-[\varphi_2])$
$\varphi_1 \wedge \varphi_2$	$(\Delta_{st}^+[\varphi_1] \wedge \mathbf{F}_{st}[\varphi_2]) \vee (\mathbf{F}_{st}[\varphi_1] \wedge \Delta_{st}^+[\varphi_2])$	$(\Delta_{st}^-[\varphi_1] \wedge \varphi_2) \vee (\varphi_1 \wedge \Delta_{st}^-[\varphi_2])$
$\exists v: \varphi_1$	$(\exists v: \Delta_{st}^+[\varphi_1]) \wedge \neg(\exists v: \varphi_1)$	$(\exists v: \Delta_{st}^-[\varphi_1]) \wedge \neg(\exists v: \mathbf{F}_{st}[\varphi_1])$
$\forall v: \varphi_1$	$(\exists v: \Delta_{st}^+[\varphi_1]) \wedge (\forall v: \mathbf{F}_{st}[\varphi_1])$	$(\exists v: \Delta_{st}^-[\varphi_1]) \wedge (\forall v: \varphi_1)$

Fig. 5. Finite-difference formulas for first-order formulas.

$\Delta_{st}^-[\varphi_1 \wedge \varphi_2] = (\Delta_{st}^-[\varphi_1] \wedge \varphi_2) \vee (\varphi_1 \wedge \Delta_{st}^-[\varphi_2])$. Tuples of individuals removed from $\varphi_1 \wedge \varphi_2$ are either tuples of individuals removed from φ_1 for which φ_2 also holds (i.e., $(\Delta_{st}^-[\varphi_1] \wedge \varphi_2)$), or they are tuples of individuals removed from φ_2 for which φ_1 also holds, (i.e., $(\varphi_1 \wedge \Delta_{st}^-[\varphi_2])$).

$\Delta_{st}^+[\exists v: \varphi_1] = (\exists v: \Delta_{st}^+[\varphi_1]) \wedge \neg(\exists v: \varphi_1)$. For $\exists v: \varphi_1$ to change value from 0 to 1, there must be at least one individual for which φ_1 changes value from 0 to 1 (i.e., $\exists v: \Delta_{st}^+[\varphi_1]$ holds), and $\exists v: \varphi_1$ must not already hold (i.e., $\neg(\exists v: \varphi_1)$ holds).

$\Delta_{st}^+[p(w_1,\dots,w_k)] = (\exists v: \Delta_{st}^+[\varphi_1]) \wedge \neg p$, if $p\in\mathcal{I}$ and $\psi_p \equiv \exists v: \varphi_1$. This is similar to the previous case, except that the term to ensure that $\exists v: \varphi_1$ does not already hold (i.e., $\neg(\exists v: \varphi_1)$) is replaced by the formula $\neg p$. Thus, when $(\exists v: \Delta_{st}^+[\varphi_1]) \wedge \neg p$ is evaluated, the stored value of $\exists v: \varphi_1$, i.e., p, will be used instead of the value obtained by reevaluating $\exists v: \varphi_1$.

$\Delta_{st}^+[p(w_1,\dots,w_k)] = \Delta_{st}^+[\psi_p\{w_1,\dots,w_k\}]$, if $p\in\mathcal{I}$ and $\psi_p \not\equiv \exists v: \varphi_1$. To characterize the positive changes to p, apply Δ_{st}^+ to p's defining formula ψ_p.

One special case is also worth noting: $\Delta_{st}^+[v_1 = v_2] = 0$ and $\Delta_{st}^-[v_1 = v_2] = 0$ because the value of the atomic formula $(v_1 = v_2)$ (shorthand for $eq(v_1, v_2)$) does not depend on any core predicates; hence, its value is unaffected by changes in them.

Example 2. Consider the instrumentation predicate $is[n]$ ("is-shared using n fields"), defined in Eqn. (5). Fig. 6 shows the formulas obtained for $\Delta_{st}^+[is[n](v)]$ and $\Delta_{st}^-[is[n](v)]$.

For a particular statement, the formulas in Fig. 6 can usually be simplified. For instance, for $y = x$, the predicate-transfer formula $\tau_{n,y=x}(v_1, v_2)$ is $n(v_1, v_2)$; see Fig. 1. Thus, by Fig. 5, the formulas for $\Delta_{y=x}^-[n(v_1, v)]$ and $\Delta_{y=x}^+[n(v_1, v)]$ are both $n(v_1, v) \wedge \neg n(v_1, v)$, which simplifies to 0. (In our implementation, simplifications are performed greedily at formula-construction time; e.g., the constructor for $\wedge$ rewrites $0 \wedge p$ to 0, $1 \wedge p$ to p, $p \wedge \neg p$ to 0, etc.) The formulas in Fig. 6 simplify to $\Delta_{y=x}^+[is[n](v)] = 0$ and $\Delta_{y=x}^-[is[n](v)] = 0$. Consequently, $\mu_{is[n],y=x}(v) = \mathbf{F}_{y=x}[is[n](v)] = is[n](v) ?\ \neg 0 : 0 = is[n](v)$. As shown in Fig. 3, this definition of $\mu_{is[n],y=x}(v)$ avoids the imprecision that was illustrated in Ex. 1.

$$\Delta_{st}^{+}[is[n](v)] = \left(\exists v_1, v_2 : \begin{pmatrix} (\Delta_{st}^{+}[n(v_1,v)] \wedge F_{st}[n(v_2,v)]) \\ \vee\ (F_{st}[n(v_1,v)] \wedge \Delta_{st}^{+}[n(v_2,v)]) \end{pmatrix} \wedge v_1 \neq v_2 \right) \wedge \neg is[n](v)$$

$$\Delta_{st}^{-}[is[n](v)] = \begin{cases} \left(\exists v_1, v_2 : \begin{pmatrix} (\Delta_{st}^{-}[n(v_1,v)] \wedge n(v_2,v)) \\ \vee\ (n(v_1,v) \wedge \Delta_{st}^{-}[n(v_2,v)]) \end{pmatrix} \wedge v_1 \neq v_2 \right) \\ \wedge \\ \neg \left[\exists v_1, v_2 : \begin{matrix} ? \\ : \end{matrix} \neg \left(\begin{pmatrix} (n(v_1,v) \wedge n(v_2,v) \wedge v_1 \neq v_2) \\ \begin{pmatrix} (\Delta_{st}^{-}[n(v_1,v)] \wedge n(v_2,v)) \\ \vee\ (n(v_1,v) \wedge \Delta_{st}^{-}[n(v_2,v)]) \end{pmatrix} \wedge v_1 \neq v_2 \\ \begin{pmatrix} (\Delta_{st}^{+}[n(v_1,v)] \wedge F_{st}[n(v_2,v)]) \\ \vee\ (F_{st}[n(v_1,v)] \wedge \Delta_{st}^{+}[n(v_2,v)]) \end{pmatrix} \wedge v_1 \neq v_2 \end{pmatrix} \right) \right] \end{cases}$$

Fig. 6. Finite-difference formulas for the instrumentation predicate $is[n](v)$.

For 2-STRUCTs, the correctness of the finite-differencing transformation given in Fig. 5 is ensured by the following theorem.

Theorem 2. *Let S be a structure in 2-STRUCT, and let S'_{proto} be the proto-structure for statement st obtained from S. Let S' be the structure obtained by using S'_{proto} as the first approximation to S' and then filling in instrumentation predicates in a topological ordering of the dependences among them: for each arity-k predicate $p \in \mathcal{I}$, $\iota^{S'}(p)$ is obtained by evaluating $[\![\psi_p(v_1, \dots, v_k)]\!]_2^{S'}([v_1 \mapsto u'_1, \dots, v_k \mapsto u'_k])$ for all tuples $(u'_1, \dots, u'_k) \in (U^{S'})^k$. Then for every formula $\varphi(v_1, \dots, v_k)$ and complete assignment Z for $\varphi(v_1, \dots, v_k)$, $[\![F_{st}[\varphi(v_1, \dots, v_k)]]\!]_2^{S}(Z) = [\![\varphi(v_1, \dots, v_k)]\!]_2^{S'}(Z)$.*

For 3-STRUCTs, the soundness of the finite-differencing transformation given in Fig. 5 follows from Thm. 2 by the Embedding Theorem (Thm. 1).

Malloc and Free. In [18], the modeling of storage-allocation/deallocation operations is carried out with a two-stage statement transformer, the first stage of which changes the number of individuals in the structure. This creates some problems for the finite-differencing approach in establishing appropriate, mutually consistent values for predicate tuples that involve the newly allocated individual. Such predicate values are needed for the second stage, in which predicate-transfer formulas for core predicates and predicate-maintenance formulas for instrumentation predicates are applied in the usual fashion, using Eqns. (1) and (3).

However, there is a simple way to sidestep this problem, which is to model the free-storage list explicitly, making the following substructure part of every 3-valued structure:

$$\texttt{freelist} \rightarrow \overbrace{u_1} \xrightarrow{n} \cdots \xrightarrow{n} \overbrace{u}^{n} \tag{7}$$

A `malloc` is modeled by advancing the pointer `freelist` into the list, and returning the memory cell that it formerly pointed to. A `free` is modeled by inserting, at the head of `freelist`'s list, the cell being deallocated.

It is true that the use of structure (7) to model storage-allocation/deallocation operations also causes the number of individuals in a 3-valued structure to change; however, because the new individual is materialized using the usual mechanisms from [18] (namely, the *focus* and *coerce* operations), values for predicate tuples that involve the newly materialized individual will always have safe, mutually consistent values.

5   Reachability and Transitive Closure

Several instrumentation predicates that depend on **RTC** are shown in Tab. 2.

Table 2. Defining formulas of some instrumentation predicates that depend on **RTC**. (Recall that $n^*(v_1, v_2)$ is a shorthand for $(\mathbf{RTC}\ v_1', v_2' : n(v_1', v_2'))(v_1, v_2)$.)

p	IntendedMeaning	ψ_p
$t[n](v_1, v_2)$	Is v_2 reachable from v_1 along n fields?	$n^*(v_1, v_2)$
$r[z, n](v)$	Is v reachable from pointer variable z along n fields?	$\exists v_1 : z(v_1) \wedge t[n](v_1, v)$
$c[n](v)$	Is v on a directed cycle of n fields?	$\exists v_1 : n(v_1, v) \wedge t[n](v, v_1)$

Unfortunately, finding a good way to maintain instrumentation predicates defined using **RTC** is challenging because it is not known, in general, whether it is possible to write a first-order formula (i.e., without using a transitive-closure operator) that specifies how to maintain the closure of a directed graph in response to edge insertions and deletions. Thus, our strategy has been to investigate special cases for classes of instrumentation predicates for which first-order maintenance formulas do exist. Whenever these do not apply, the system falls back on safe maintenance formulas (which themselves use **RTC**).

In this paper, we confine ourselves to an important special case, namely, techniques to maintain instrumentation predicates specified via the **RTC** of a binary formula that defines an acyclic graph. (Some special cases for **RTC** of binary formulas that define possibly-cyclic graphs will be the subject of a future paper.)

Consider a binary instrumentation predicate p, defined by $\psi_p(v_1, v_2) \equiv (\mathbf{RTC}\ v_1', v_2' : \varphi_1)(v_1, v_2)$. If the graph defined by φ_1 is acyclic, it is possible to give a first-order formula that maintains p after the addition or deletion of a single φ_1-edge. The method we use is a minor modification of a method for maintaining non-reflexive transitive closure in an acyclic graph, due to Dong and Su [7].

In the case of an insertion of a single φ_1-edge, the maintenance formula is

$$\mathbf{F}_{st}[p](v_1, v_2) = p(v_1, v_2) \vee (\exists v_1', v_2' : p(v_1, v_1') \wedge \Delta_{st}^+[\varphi_1](v_1', v_2') \wedge p(v_2', v_2)). \quad (8)$$

The new value of p contains the old tuples of p, as well as those that represent two old paths connected with the new φ_1-edge.

The maintenance formula to handle the deletion of a single φ_1-edge is a bit more complicated. We first identify the tuples of p that represent paths that might rely on the edge to be deleted, and thus may need to be removed from p (S stands for *suspicious*):

$$S[p, \varphi_1](v_1, v_2) = \exists v_1', v_2' : p(v_1, v_1') \wedge \Delta_{st}^-[\varphi_1](v_1', v_2') \wedge p(v_2', v_2).$$

We next collect a set of p-tuples that definitely remain in p (T stands for *trusted*):

$$T[p, \varphi_1](v_1, v_2) = (p(v_1, v_2) \wedge \neg S[p, \varphi_1](v_1, v_2)) \vee \mathbf{F}_{st}[\varphi_1](v_1, v_2). \tag{9}$$

Finally, the maintenance formula for p for a single φ_1-edge deletion is

$$\mathbf{F}_{st}[p](v_1, v_2) = \exists\, v_1', v_2' : T[p, \varphi_1](v_1, v_1') \wedge T[p, \varphi_1](v_1', v_2') \wedge T[p, \varphi_1](v_2', v_2). \tag{10}$$

Maintenance formulas (8) and (10) maintain p when two conditions hold: the graph defined by φ_1 is acyclic, and the change to the graph is a single edge addition or deletion (but not both). To see that under these assumptions the maintenance formula for a φ_1-edge deletion is correct, suppose that there is a suspicious tuple $p(u_1, u_k)$, i.e., $S[p, \varphi_1](u_1, u_k) = 1$, but there is a φ_1-path $u_1, \ldots, u_k$ that does not use the deleted φ_1-edge. We need to show that $\mathbf{F}_{st}[p](u_1, u_k)$ has the value 1. Suppose that (a, b) is the φ_1-edge being deleted; because the graph defined by φ_1

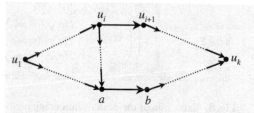

Fig. 7. Edge (a, b) is being deleted; u_i is the last node along path $u_1, \ldots, u_i, u_{i+1}, \ldots, u_k$ from which a is reachable.

is acyclic, there is a $u_i \neq u_k$ that is the last node along path $u_1, \ldots, u_i, u_{i+1}, \ldots, u_k$ from which a is reachable (see Fig. 7). Because $p(u_1, u_i)$ and $p(u_{i+1}, u_k)$ both hold, and because u_i cannot be reachable from b (by acyclicity), neither tuple is suspicious; consequently, $T[p, \varphi_1](u_1, u_i) = 1$ and $T[p, \varphi_1](u_{i+1}, u_k) = 1$. Because (u_i, u_{i+1}) is an edge in the new (as well as the old) graph defined by φ_1, we have $\mathbf{F}_{st}[\varphi_1](u_i, u_{i+1}) = 1$, which means that $T[p, \varphi_1](u_i, u_{i+1}) = 1$ as well, yielding $\mathbf{F}_{st}[p](u_1, u_k) = 1$ by Eqn. (10).

Fig. 8 extends the method for generating predicate-maintenance formulas to handle instrumentation predicates specified via the **RTC** of a binary formula that defines an acyclic graph. Fig. 8 makes use of the operator $T[p, \varphi_1](v, v')$ (Eqn. (9)), but recasts Eqns. (8) and (10) as finite-difference expressions $\Delta_{st}^{+}[\psi_p]$ and $\Delta_{st}^{-}[\psi_p]$, respectively.

To know whether this special-case maintenance strategy can be applied, for each statement st we need to know at analysis-generation time whether the change performed at st, to the graph defined by φ_1, always results in a single edge addition or deletion. If in any admissible 2-STRUCT[P] there is a unique satisfying assignment to the two free variables of $\Delta_{st}^{+}[\varphi_1]$ and no assignment satisfies $\Delta_{st}^{-}[\varphi_1]$, then the pair $\Delta_{st}^{+}[\varphi_1]$, $\Delta_{st}^{-}[\varphi_1]$ defines a change that adds exactly one edge to the graph. Similarly, if in any admissible 2-STRUCT[P] there is a unique satisfying assignment to the two free variables of $\Delta_{st}^{-}[\varphi_1]$ and no assignment satisfies $\Delta_{st}^{+}[\varphi_1]$, then the change is a deletion of exactly one edge from the graph.

Because answering these questions is in general undecidable, we employ a conservative approximation based on a syntactic analysis of logical formulas. The analysis uses a heuristic to determine a set of variables V such that for each admissible structure, the variables in V have a single possible binding in the formula's satisfying assignments. We refer to such variables as *anchored* variables. For instance, if predicate q has the

φ	$\Delta_{st}^{+}[\varphi]$	
	$((\exists v: \Delta_{st}^{+}[\varphi_1]) \wedge \neg p)\{w_1,\ldots,w_k\}$	if $\psi_p \equiv \exists v: \varphi_1$
$p(w_1,\ldots,w_k),$	$\left(\begin{array}{l} (\exists v_1', v_2': \Delta_{st}^{+}[\varphi_1](v_1', v_2')) \\ \wedge \left(\begin{array}{l} p(v_1, v_1') \\ \exists v_1', v_2': \wedge \Delta_{st}^{+}[\varphi_1](v_1', v_2') \\ \wedge p(v_2', v_2) \end{array} \right) \wedge \neg p(v_1, v_2) \end{array} \right)\{w_1, w_2\}$	if $\psi_p \equiv$ $(\textbf{RTC}\ v_1', v_2': \varphi_1)(v_1, v_2)$
$p \in \mathcal{I}$		
	$\Delta_{st}^{+}[\psi_p]\{w_1,\ldots,w_k\}$	otherwise

φ	$\Delta_{st}^{-}[\varphi]$	
	$((\exists v: \Delta_{st}^{-}[\varphi_1]) \wedge p)\{w_1,\ldots,w_k\}$	if $\psi_p \equiv \forall v: \varphi_1$
$p(w_1,\ldots,w_k),$	$\left(\begin{array}{l} (\exists v_1', v_2': \Delta_{st}^{-}[\varphi_1](v_1', v_2')) \\ \wedge \left(\begin{array}{l} T[p, \varphi_1](v_1, v_1') \\ \exists v_1', v_2': \wedge T[p, \varphi_1](v_1', v_2') \\ \wedge T[p, \varphi_1](v_2', v_2) \end{array} \right) \wedge p(v_1, v_2) \end{array} \right)\{w_1, w_2\}$	if $\psi_p \equiv$ $(\textbf{RTC}\ v_1', v_2': \varphi_1)(v_1, v_2)$
$p \in \mathcal{I}$		
	$\Delta_{st}^{-}[\psi_p]\{w_1,\ldots,w_k\}$	otherwise

Fig. 8. Extension of the finite-differencing method from Fig. 5 to cover **RTC** formulas, for unit-sized changes to an acyclic graph defined by φ_1.

attribute "unique", for each admissible structure there is a single possible binding for variable v in any assignment that satisfies $q(v)$; in a formula that contains an occurrence of $q(v)$, v is an anchored variable.

If both free variables of $\Delta_{st}^{+}[\varphi_1]$ are anchored and $\Delta_{st}^{-}[\varphi_1] = 0$, then the change adds one edge to the graph defined by φ_1. Similarly, if both free variables of $\Delta_{st}^{-}[\varphi_1]$ are anchored and $\Delta_{st}^{+}[\varphi_1] = 0$, then the change removes one edge from the graph. In these cases, the reflexive transitive closure of φ_1 can be updated using the method discussed above.

6   Experimental Evaluation

To evaluate the techniques presented in the paper, we extended TVLA to generate predicate-maintenance formulas, and applied it to a test suite of 5 existing analysis specifications, involving 26 programs (see Fig. 9).

The test programs consisted of various operations on acyclic singly-linked lists, doubly-linked lists, binary trees, and binary-search trees, plus several sorting programs [10]. The system was used to verify some partial-correctness properties of the test programs. For instance, Reverse, an in-situ list-reversal program, must preserve list properties and lose no elements; InsertSorted and DeleteSorted must preserve binary-search-tree properties; InsertSort must return a sorted list; Good Flow must not allow high-security input data to flow to a low-security output channel.

A few of the programs contained bugs: for instance, InsertSortBug2 is an insert-sort program that ignores the first element of the list; BubbleBug is a bubble-sort program with an incorrect condition for swapping elements, which causes an infinite loop if the input list contains duplicate data values; Non-tree creates a node whose left-child and right-child pointers point to the same subtree.

Category	Test Program	# of non-id maintenance-formula				Performance		
		schemas			instances	Analysis Time (sec.)		
		total	TC	non-TC		reference	FD	% increase
SLL Shape Analysis	Search	2	0	2	2	0.93	0.92	-0.11
	NullDeref	2	0	2	3	0.96	0.96	0.31
	GetLast	3	0	3	4	1.14	1.14	-0.44
	DeleteAll	11	2	9	15	0.79	0.81	3.30
	Reverse	12	2	10	16	1.33	1.39	4.49
	Create	11	2	9	21	0.73	0.76	3.68
	Swap	11	2	9	27	0.77	0.81	5.47
	Delete	12	2	10	39	3.78	4.81	27.15
	Merge	11	2	9	64	7.69	9.34	21.50
	Insert	12	2	10	72	3.67	4.47	21.69
DLL Shape Analysis	Append	15	2	13	50	7.66	8.81	14.96
	Delete	16	2	14	74	27.97	26.87	-3.93
	Splice	15	2	13	96	3.25	3.78	16.20
Binary Tree Shape Analysis	Non-tree	8	2	6	9	0.82	0.90	9.63
	InsertSorted	13	2	11	43	10.08	11.19	10.98
	Deutsch-Schorr-Waite	10	2	8	52	357.88	419.07	17.10
	DeleteSorted	13	2	11	554	284.50	406.30	42.81
SLL Sorting	ReverseSorted	18	2	16	23	1.62	1.69	4.13
	Bubble	18	2	16	80	36.08	41.88	16.07
	BubbleBug	18	2	16	80	34.68	39.85	14.90
	InsertSortBug2	18	2	16	87	29.95	43.52	45.29
	InsertSort	18	2	16	88	38.20	51.38	34.51
	InsertSortBug1	18	2	16	88	109.91	134.15	22.05
	MergeSorted	18	2	16	91	12.09	14.24	17.79
Information Flow	Good Flow	12	2	10	66	58.49	67.65	15.66
	Bad Flow	12	2	10	86	375.83	461.77	22.87

Fig. 9. Results from using hand-crafted vs. automatically generated maintenance formulas for instrumentation predicates.

In TVLA, the operational semantics of a programming language is defined by specifying, for each kind of statement, an *action schema* to be used on outgoing CFG edges. Action schemas are instantiated according to a program's statement instances to create the CFG. For each combination of action schema and instrumentation predicate, a *maintenance-formula schema* must be provided. The number of non-identity maintenance-formula schemas is reported in columns 3–5 of Fig. 9, broken down in columns 4–5 into those whose defining formula contains an occurrence of **RTC**, and those that do not. Predicate-maintenance formulas produced by finite differencing are generally larger than the hand-crafted ones. Because this affects analysis time, the number of instances of non-identity maintenance-formula schemas is a meaningful size measure for our experiments. These numbers appear in column 6.

For each program in the test suite, we first ran the analysis using hand-crafted maintenance formulas, to obtain a reference answer in which CFG nodes were annotated with their final sets of logical structures. We then ran the analysis using automatically generated maintenance formulas and compared the result against the reference answer.

For all 26 test programs, the analysis using automatically generated formulas yielded answers identical to the reference answers.

Columns 7–9 show performance data, which were collected on a 1Ghz AMD Athlon^{TM} workstation running Red Hat Linux version 7.1. In each case, five runs were made; the longest and shortest times were discarded from each set, and the remaining three averaged. (Figures do not report time spent on loading and initialization, which is not affected by our technique. We also exclude the overhead of formula differencing, because this is not an analysis-time cost.) The geometric mean of the slowdowns when using the automatically generated formulas was approximately 14%, with a median of 15%, mainly due to the fact that the automatically generated formulas are larger than the hand-crafted ones. The maximum slowdown was 45%.[3] A few analyses were actually faster with the automatically generated formulas; these speedups are either due to random variation or are accidental benefits of subformula orderings that are advantageous for short-circuit evaluation.

These results are encouraging. At least for abstractions of several common data structures, they suggest that the algorithm for generating predicate-maintenance formulas from Sect. 4 is capable of automatically generating formulas that (i) are as precise as the hand-crafted ones, and (ii) have a tolerable effect on runtime performance.

The extended version of TVLA also uncovered several bugs in the hand-crafted formulas. A maintenance formula of the form $\mu_{p,st}(v_1, \ldots, v_k) = p(v_1, \ldots, v_k)$ is called an *identity predicate-maintenance formula*. For each identity predicate-maintenance formula in the hand-crafted specification, we checked that (after simplification) the corresponding generated predicate-maintenance formula was also an identity formula. Each inconsistency turned out to be an error in the hand-crafted specification. We also found one instance of an incorrect non-identity hand-crafted maintenance formula. (The measurements reported in Fig. 9 are based on corrected hand-crafted specifications.)

7   Related Work

A weakness of past incarnations of TVLA has been the need for the user to define predicate-maintenance formulas that specify how each statement affects each instrumentation predicate. Recent criticisms of TVLA based on this deficiency are no longer valid [3,15], at least for analyses that can be defined using formulas that define acyclic relations (and also for some classes of formulas that define cyclic relations, using techniques not discussed in this paper). With the algorithm presented in Sects. 4 and 5, the user's responsibility is merely to write the ψ_p formulas; appropriate predicate-maintenance formulas are created automatically.

Graf and Saïdi [8] showed that theorem provers can be used to generate best abstract transformers [4] for abstract domains that are fixed, finite, Cartesian products of Boolean values. (The use of such domains is known as *predicate abstraction*; predicate abstraction is also used in SLAM [3] and other systems [5].) In contrast, the abstract transformers created using the algorithm described in Sects. 4 and 5 are not best transformers; however, this algorithm uses only very simple, linear-time, recursive tree-traversal procedures,

---

[3] We expect that some simple optimizations, such as caching the results from evaluating subformulas, could significantly reduce the slowdown.

whereas the theorem provers used in predicate abstraction are not even guaranteed to terminate. Moreover, our setting makes available much richer abstract domains than the ones offered by predicate abstraction, and experience to date has been that very little precision is lost (using only *good* abstract transformers) once the right instrumentation predicates have been identified.

Paige studied how finite-differencing transformations of applicative set-former expressions could be exploited to optimize loops in very-high-level languages, such as SETL [16]. Liu et al. used related program-transformation methods in the setting of a functional programming language to derive incremental algorithms for various problems from the specifications of exhaustive algorithms [13,12]. In their work, the goal is to maintain the value of a function $F(x)$ as the input x undergoes small changes. The methods described in Sects. 4 and 5 address a similar kind of incremental-computation problem, except that the language in which the exhaustive and incremental versions of the problem are expressed is first-order logic with reflexive transitive closure.

The finite-differencing operators defined in Sects. 4 and 5 are most closely related to a number of previous papers on logic and databases: finite-difference operators for the propositional case were studied by Akers [2] and Sharir [19]. Previous work on incrementally maintaining materialized views in databases [9], "first-order incremental evaluation schemes (FOIES)" [6], and "dynamic descriptive complexity" [17] has also addressed the problem of maintaining one or more auxiliary predicates after new tuples are inserted into or deleted from the base predicates. In databases, view maintenance is solely an optimization; the correct information can always be obtained by reevaluating the formula. In the abstract-interpretation context, where abstraction has been performed, this is no longer true: reevaluating a formula in the local (3-valued) state can lead to a drastic loss of precision. Thus, one aspect that sets our work apart from previous work is the goal of developing a finite-differencing transformation suitable for use when abstraction has been performed.

Not all finite-differencing transformations that are correct in 2-valued logic (i.e., satisfy Thm. 2), are appropriate for use in 3-valued logic. For instance, Fig. 10 presents an alternative finite-differencing scheme for first-order formulas. In this scheme, $\Delta_{st}[\varphi]$ captures both the negative and positive changes to φ's value. With Fig. 10, the maintenance formula for instrumentation predicate p is

$$\mu_{p,st} \overset{\text{def}}{=} p \oplus \Delta_{st}[\psi_p], \tag{11}$$

where $\oplus$ denotes exclusive-or. However, in 3-valued logic, we have $1/2 \oplus V = 1/2$, regardless of whether V is 0, 1, or $1/2$. Consequently, Eqn. (11) has the unfortunate property that if $p(u) = 1/2$, then $\mu_{p,st}$ evaluates to $1/2$ on u, and $p(u)$ becomes "pinned" to the indefinite value $1/2$; it will have the value $1/2$ in all successor structures S', in all successors of S', and so on. With Eqn. (11), $p(u)$ can *never* reacquire a definite value.

In contrast, the maintenance formulas created using the finite-differencing scheme of Fig. 5 do not have this trouble because they have the form $p ? \neg \Delta_{st}^-[\psi_p] : \Delta_{st}^+[\psi_p]$. The use of if-then-else allows $p(u)$ to reacquire a definite value after it has been set to $1/2$: if $p(u)$ is $1/2$, $\mu_{p,st}$ evaluates to a definite value on u if $[\![\Delta_{st}^-[\psi_p(v)]]\!]_3^S([v \mapsto u])$ is 1 and $[\![\Delta_{st}^+[\psi_p(v)]]\!]_3^S([v \mapsto u])$ is 0, or vice versa.

φ	$\Delta_{st}[\varphi]$
1	0
0	0
$p(w_1, \ldots, w_k), p \in \mathcal{C}$	$(\tau_{p,st} \oplus p)\{w_1, \ldots, w_k\}$
$p(w_1, \ldots, w_k), p \in \mathcal{I}$	$\Delta_{st}[\psi_p]\{w_1, \ldots, w_k\}$
$\varphi_1 \oplus \varphi_2$	$\Delta_{st}[\varphi_1] \oplus \Delta_{st}[\varphi_2]$
$\varphi_1 \wedge \varphi_2$	$(\Delta_{st}[\varphi_1] \wedge \varphi_2) \oplus (\varphi_1 \wedge \Delta_{st}[\varphi_2]) \oplus (\Delta_{st}[\varphi_1] \wedge \Delta_{st}[\varphi_2])$
$\forall v: \varphi_1$	$(\forall v: \varphi_1) ? (\exists v: \Delta_{st}[\varphi_1]) : (\forall v: \varphi_1 \oplus \Delta_{st}[\varphi_1])$

Fig. 10. An alternative finite-differencing scheme for first-order formulas.

Acknowledgments. We thank W. Hesse, N. Immerman, T. Lev-Ami and R. Wilhelm for their comments and suggestions concerning this work. R. Manevich provided invaluable help with TVLA.

References

1. TVLA system. Available at "http://www.math.tau.ac.il/~rumster/TVLA/".
2. S.B. Akers, Jr. On a theory of Boolean functions. *J. Soc. Indust. Appl. Math.*, 7(4):487–498, December 1959.
3. T. Ball, R. Majumdar, T. Millstein, and S.K. Rajamani. Automatic predicate abstraction of C programs. In *Conf. on Prog. Lang. Design and Impl.*, New York, NY, 2001. ACM Press.
4. P. Cousot and R. Cousot. Systematic design of program analysis frameworks. In *Symp. on Princ. of Prog. Lang.*, pages 269–282, New York, NY, 1979. ACM Press.
5. S. Das, D.L. Dill, and S. Park. Experience with predicate abstraction. In *Proc. Computer-Aided Verif.*, pages 160–171. Springer-Verlag, July 1999.
6. G. Dong and J. Su. Incremental and decremental evaluation of transitive closure by first-order queries. *Inf. and Comp.*, 120:101–106, 1995.
7. G. Dong and J. Su. Incremental maintenance of recursive views using relational calculus/SQL. *SIGMOD Record*, 29(1):44–51, 2000.
8. S. Graf and H. Saïdi. Construction of abstract state graphs with PVS. In *Proc. Computer-Aided Verif.*, pages 72–83, June 1997.
9. A. Gupta and I.S. Mumick, editors. *Materialized Views: Techniques, Implementations, and Applications*. The M.I.T. Press, Cambridge, MA, 1999.
10. T. Lev-Ami, T. Reps, M. Sagiv, and R. Wilhelm. Putting static analysis to work for verification: A case study. In *Int. Symp. on Software Testing and Analysis*, pages 26–38, 2000.
11. T. Lev-Ami and M. Sagiv. TVLA: A system for implementing static analyses. In *Static Analysis Symp.*, pages 280–301, 2000.
12. Y.A. Liu, S.D. Stoller, and T. Teitelbaum. Discovering auxiliary information for incremental computation. In *Symp. on Princ. of Prog. Lang.*, pages 157–170, January 1996.
13. Y.A. Liu and T. Teitelbaum. Systematic derivation of incremental programs. *Sci. of Comp. Program.*, 24:1–39, 1995.
14. K.L. McMillan. Verification of infinite state systems by compositional model checking. In *CHARME*, pages 219–234, 1999.
15. A. Møller and M.I. Schwartzbach. The pointer assertion logic engine. In *Conf. on Prog. Lang. Design and Impl.*, pages 221–231, 2001.
16. R. Paige and S. Koenig. Finite differencing of computable expressions. *Trans. on Prog. Lang. and Syst.*, 4(3):402–454, July 1982.
17. S. Patnaik and N. Immerman. Dyn-FO: A parallel, dynamic complexity class. *J. Comput. Syst. Sci.*, 55(2):199–209, October 1997.
18. M. Sagiv, T. Reps, and R. Wilhelm. Parametric shape analysis via 3-valued logic. *Trans. on Prog. Lang. and Syst.*, 24(3):217–298, 2002.
19. M. Sharir. Some observations concerning formal differentiation of set theoretic expressions. *Trans. on Prog. Lang. and Syst.*, 4(2):196–225, April 1982.

Register Allocation by Proof Transformation[*]

Atsushi Ohori

School of Information Science
Japan Advanced Institute of Science and Technology
Tatsunokuchi, Ishikawa 923-1292, JAPAN; ohori@jaist.ac.jp

Abstract. This paper presents a proof-theoretical framework that accounts for the entire process of register allocation – liveness analysis is proof reconstruction (similar to type inference), and register allocation is proof transformation from a proof system with unrestricted variable accesses to a proof system with restricted variable access. In our framework, the set of registers acts as a "working set" of the live variables at each instruction step, which changes during the execution of the code. This eliminates the ad-hoc notion of "spilling". The necessary memory-register moves are systematically incorporated in our proof transformation process. Its correctness is a direct corollary of our construction; the resulting proof is equivalent to the proof of the original code modulo treatment of structural rules. The framework yields a clean and powerful register allocation algorithm. The algorithm has been implemented, demonstrating the feasibility of the framework.

1   Introduction

Register allocation is a process to convert an intermediate language to another language closer to machine code. Such a process should ideally be presented as a language transformation system that preserves the meaning of a program – both its static and dynamic semantics. These results will not only yield robust and systematic compiler implementation but also serve as a basis for reasoning about formal properties of register allocation process such as preservation of type safety, which will complement recent results on verifying type safety of low-level code, e.g. [11,6,7,8]. Unfortunately, however, it appear to be difficult to establish such results for existing methods of register allocation.

The most widely used method for register allocation is *graph coloring* [3,2]. It first performs liveness analysis of a given code and constructs an interference graph. It then solves the problem by "spilling" some nodes from the graph and finding a "coloring" of the remaining subgraph. Although it is effective and practically feasible, there seems to be no easy and natural way to show type and semantics preservation of this process. There are also some other methods such as [10], but we do not know any attempt to establish a framework for reasoning about register allocation process.

---

[*] This work was partially supported by Grant-in-aid for scientific research on priority area "informatics" A01-08, grant no:14019403.

P. Degano (Ed.): ESOP 2003, LNCS 2618, pp. 399–413, 2003.

The goal of this work is to establish a novel framework for reasoning about register allocation process and also for developing a practical register allocation algorithm.

Our strategy is to present register allocation as a series of proof transformations among proof systems that represents code languages with different variable usage. In an earlier work [8], the author has shown that a low-level code language can be regarded as a sequent-style proof system. In that work, a proof system deduces typing properties of a code. However, it is also possible to regard each "live range" of a variable as a type, and to develop a proof system to deduce properties of variable usage of a given code. Such a proof system must admit *structural rules*, e.g. those of *contraction*, *weakening* and *exchange*, to rearrange assumptions. The key idea underlying the present work is to regard those structural rules as register manipulation instructions and to represent a register allocation process as a proof transformation from a proof system with implicit structural rules to one with explicit structural rules. In this paradigm, liveness analysis is done by proof reconstruction similarly to type inference. Different from ordinary type inference, however, it always succeeds for any code and returns a proof, which is the code annotated with variable liveness information. The reconstructed proof is then transformed to another proof where allocation and deallocation of registers, and memory-register moves are explicitly inserted. The target machine code is extracted mechanically from the transformed proof.

Based on this idea, we have worked out the details of proof transformations for all the stages of register allocation, and have developed a register allocation algorithm. The correctness of the algorithm is an obvious corollary of this construction itself. Since structural rules only rearrange assumptions and do not change the computational meaning of a program, the resulting proof is equivalent to the original proof representing the given source code. Moreover, as being a proof system, our framework can be easily combined with a static type system of low-level code. Compared with the conventional approaches based on graph coloring, our framework is more general in that it uniformly integrate liveness analysis and register-memory moves.

We believe that the framework can be used to develop a practical register allocation algorithm. In order to demonstrate its practical feasibility, we have implemented the proposed method. Although the current prototype is a "toy implementation" and does not incorporated any heuristics, our limited experimentation confirms the effectiveness of our framework.

The major source of our inspiration is various studies on proof systems in substructural logic [9] and in linear logic [5]. They have attracted much attention as logical foundations for "resource management". To the author's knowledge, however, there does not seem to exist any attempt to develop a register allocation method using proof theoretical or type-theoretical frameworks.

The rest of the paper is organized as follows. Section 2 defines a proof system for a simple source language and gives a proof reconstruction algorithm. Section 3 gives a proof normalization algorithm to optimize live ranges of variables. Section 4 presents a proof transformation to a language with a fixed number of registers, and gives an algorithm to assign register numbers. Section 5 discusses some properties of the method and concludes the paper.

2   Proof System for Code Language and Liveness Analysis

To present our method, we define a simple code language. Let $x, y, \ldots$ range over a given countably infinite set of variables and c range over a given set of atomic constants. We consider the following instructions (ranged over by I), basic blocks (ranged over by B), and programs (ranged over by P).

$$I ::= x = y \mid x = c \mid x = y + z \mid \text{if } x \text{ goto } l$$
$$B ::= \text{return} x \mid \text{goto } l \mid I; B$$
$$P ::= \{l : B, \ldots, l : B\}$$

There is no difficulty of adding various primitive operations other than $+$. It is also a routine practice to transform a conventional intermediate language into this representation by introducing necessary labels.

We base our development on a proof-theoretical interpretation of low-level code [8] where each instruction I is interpreted as an inference rule of the form

$$\frac{\Gamma' \rhd B : \tau}{\Gamma \rhd I; B : \tau}$$

indicating the fact that I changes machine state Γ to Γ' and continues execution of the block B. Note that a rule forms a bigger code from a smaller one, so the direction of execution is from the bottom to the top. If the above rule is the last inference step, then I is the first instruction to execute. The "return" instruction corresponds to an *initial sequent* (an axiom in the proof system) of the form

$$\Gamma, x : \tau \rhd \text{return } x : \tau$$

which returns the value of r to the caller. All the sequents in the same proof has the same result type determined by this rule.

Under this interpretation, each basic block becomes a proof in a sequent style proof system. A branching instruction is interpreted as a meta-level rule referring to an existing proof. For this purpose, we introduce a *label environment* (ranged over by $\mathcal{L}$) of the form $\{l_1 : \Gamma_1 \rhd \tau_1, \ldots, l_n : \Gamma_n \rhd \tau_n\}$ specifying the type of each label, and define a proof system relative to a given label environment. We regard $\mathcal{L}$ as a function and write $\mathcal{L}(l_i)$ for the l_i's entry in $\mathcal{L}$.

To apply this framework to register allocation, we make the following two refinements. First, we regard a type not as a property of values (such as being an integer) but as a property of variable usage, and introduce a *type variable* for each *live range* of a variable. Occurrences of the same variable with different type variables imply that the variable has multiple live ranges due to multiple assignments. Second, we regard *structural rules* in sequent style proof system as (pseudo) instructions for allocation and de-allocation of variables (registers). The left-weakening rule corresponds (in the sense of Curry-Howard isomorphism) to the rule for discarding a register:

$$\frac{\Gamma \rhd \tau_0}{\Gamma, \tau \rhd \tau_0} \quad \Longrightarrow \quad \frac{\Gamma, x : \text{nil} \rhd B : \tau_0}{\Gamma, x : \tau \rhd \text{discard } x; B : \tau_0}$$

$$\Gamma, x : t \triangleright \texttt{return } x \: : \: t \qquad \frac{\Gamma, x : \texttt{nil} \triangleright B \: : \: t_0}{\Gamma, x : t \triangleright \texttt{discard } x; B \: : \: t_0} \qquad \frac{\Gamma, x : t \triangleright B \: : \: t_0}{\Gamma, x : \texttt{nil} \triangleright x \: = \: c; B \: : \: t_0}$$

$$\frac{\Gamma, x : t_1, y : t_2 \triangleright B \: : \: t_0}{\Gamma, x : \texttt{nil}, y : t_2 \triangleright x \: = \: y; B \: : \: t_0} \qquad \frac{\Gamma, x : t_1, y : t_2, z : t_3 \triangleright B \: : \: t_0}{\Gamma, x : \texttt{nil}, y : t_2, z : t_3 \triangleright x \: = \: y \: + \: z; B \: : \: t_0}$$

$$\frac{\Gamma, x : t_1, y : t_2 \triangleright B \: : \: t_0}{\Gamma, x : t_3, y : t_2 \triangleright x \: = \: x \: + \: y; B \: : \: t_0} \qquad (\text{similarly for } x \: = \: y \: + \: x)$$

$$\frac{\Gamma, x : t \triangleright B \: : \: t_0}{\Gamma, x : t \triangleright \texttt{if } x \texttt{ goto } l; B \: : \: t_0} \qquad (\text{if } \mathcal{L}(l) = \Gamma' \triangleright t_0 \text{ such that } \Gamma' \subseteq \Gamma, x : t.)$$

$$\Gamma \triangleright \texttt{goto } l \: : \: t \quad (\text{if } \mathcal{L}(l) = \Gamma' \triangleright t \text{ such that } \Gamma' \subseteq \Gamma.)$$

Fig. 1. $\mathcal{SSC}(L)$: proof system for liveness information

where $x : \texttt{nil}$ indicates that x is not live at this point. Assuming that τ is a true formula (inhabited type), the following valid variant of the left-contraction rule corresponds to the rule for allocating a new register.

$$\frac{\Gamma, \tau \triangleright \tau_0}{\Gamma, \triangleright \tau_0} \quad \Longrightarrow \quad \frac{\Gamma, x : \tau \triangleright B \: : \: \tau_0}{\Gamma, x : \texttt{nil} \triangleright \texttt{alloc } x; B \: : \: \tau_0}$$

Later, we shall see that exchange rules represent register-memory moves.

We let t range over type variables. A *type* τ is either t or $\texttt{nil}$ (which is introduced to make type inference easier.) A *context* Γ is a mapping from a finite set of variables to types. For contexts Γ and Γ', we write $\Gamma \subseteq \Gamma'$ if Γ is included in Γ' as sets ignoring entries of the form $x : \texttt{nil}$. Fig. 1 gives the proof system for liveness. This is relative to a given label environment $\mathcal{L}$. A program $\{l_1 : B_1, \ldots, l_n : B_n\}$ is derivable under $\mathcal{L}$, if $\mathcal{L}(l_i) = \Gamma_i \triangleright \tau_i$ and $\Gamma_i \triangleright B_i : \tau_i$ for each $1 \le i \le n$. We call this proof system $\mathcal{SSC}(L)$[1]. We note that, in this definition, $\texttt{alloc}$ is implicitly included in the rules for assignment. Furthermore, if the target variable of an assignment is one of its operands, then the assignment rule also includes $\texttt{discard}$. For example, an inference step for $\texttt{x = x + y}$ discards the old usage of variable $\texttt{x}$ and allocates a new usage for $\texttt{x}$. This is reflected by the different type variables for $\texttt{x}$ in the rule.

We develop a proof reconstruction algorithm. For this purpose, we introduce *context variables* (denoted by ρ) and extend the set of contexts as follows.

$$\gamma ::= \Gamma \mid \rho \cdot \Gamma$$

For this set of terms, we can define a unification algorithm. We say that a set of context equations (i.e. a set of pairs of contexts) E is *well formed* if whenever $\rho \cdot \Gamma_1$ and $\rho \cdot \Gamma_2$ appear in E, $dom(\Gamma_1) = dom(\Gamma_2)$. Well-formedness is preserved by unification, and therefore it is sufficient to consider well formed equations. This

---

[1] The proof system for low-level code in [8] is called the *sequential sequent calculus*; hence the name. Also note that a program in general forms a cyclic graph, and therefore as a logical system it is inconsistent. It should be regarded as a type system of a recursive program, but we continue to use the term *proof system*.

property allows us to define a unification algorithm similarly to the standard unification. We note that although context terms are similar to record types, any extra machinery for record unification is not required. We can show the following.

Theorem 1. *There is an algorithm* CUNIF *such that for any set of well formed context equations* E, *if* CUNIF$(E) = S$ *then* S *is a unifier of* E, *and if there is a unifier* S *of* E *then* CUNIF$(E) = S'$ *such that* $S = S'' \circ S'$ *for some* S''.

We omit a simple definition of CUNIF and its correctness proof.

Using CUNIF and a standard unification algorithm UNIFY on types, we define a proof inference algorithm INFER. To present the algorithm, we first define some notations. We let Δ range over proofs. In writing a proof tree, we only include, at each inference step, the instruction that is introduced. We write $\dfrac{\Delta}{(\Gamma \rhd I \,:\, \tau)}$ if Δ is a proof whose end sequent is $\Gamma \rhd I \,:\, \tau$. If γ is a context containing x, $\gamma\{x : \tau\}$ is the context obtained from γ by replacing the value of x with τ. An *entry constraint* is a sentence of the form $l \ll \gamma \rhd \tau$ indicating the requirement that the block labeled with l must be a proof $\gamma' \rhd \tau$ such that $\gamma' \subseteq \gamma$. Let $\mathcal{L}$ be a label environment and $\mathcal{C}$ be a set of entry constraints. $\mathcal{L}(\mathcal{C})$ is the set of sentence of the form $\gamma' \rhd \tau' \ll \gamma \rhd \tau$ obtained from $\mathcal{C}$ by replacing each l appearing in $\mathcal{C}$ with $\mathcal{L}(l)$. We write $\overline{x}$ and $\overline{x : \tau}$ for a sequence of variables and a sequence of typed variables.

The algorithm INFER is given in Fig. 2. It takes a labeled set of basic blocks $\{l_1 : B_1, \ldots, l_n : B_n\}$ and returns a labeled set of proofs $\{l_1 : \Delta_1, \ldots, l_n : \Delta_n\}$. It first uses INFBLK to infer for each B_i its proof scheme (i.e. a proof containing context variables) together with a set of entry constraints. INFBLK proceeds by induction on the structure of B_i, i.e. it traverses B_i backward from the last instruction (**return** or **goto**). When it encounters a new variable, it introduces a fresh type variable for a new live range of the variable. When it encounters an assignment to x, it inserts **discard** x, and changes the type of x to **nil**, and continues toward the entry point of the code block. It generates an entry constraint for l for each branching instruction (**goto** l or **if** x **goto** l.) After having inferred proof schemes for blocks, the main algorithm gathers the set $\mathcal{L}(\mathcal{C})$ of constraints of the form $\gamma' \rhd t' \ll \gamma \rhd t$. The set of constraints is then solved by fixed point computation, where each iteration step picks one sentence $\rho' \cdot \Gamma' \rhd t' \ll \rho \cdot \Gamma \rhd t$ such that $\Gamma' \nsubseteq \Gamma$ or $t \neq t'$, and generates a minimal substitution S such that $S(\rho \cdot \Gamma) = \rho'' \cdot \Gamma''$, $S(\Gamma') \subseteq \Gamma''$ and $S(t') = S(t)$. Finally, the main algorithm INFER instantiates all the context variables with empty set to obtain a ground proof.

We establish the soundness of this algorithm. Let $\mathcal{C}$ be a set of entry constraints of $\mathcal{L}$; let $dom(\mathcal{C})$ be the set of labels mentioned in $\mathcal{C}$. We say that a substitution S is a solution of $\mathcal{C}$ under $\mathcal{L}$ if $dom(\mathcal{C}) \subseteq dom(\mathcal{L})$ and, for each constraint $l \ll \gamma \rhd \tau$ in $\mathcal{C}$, $\mathcal{L}(l) = \gamma' \rhd \tau'$, $S(\gamma') \subseteq S(\gamma)$, and $S(\tau') = S(\tau)$. From this definition, if S is a solution of $\mathcal{C}$ under $\mathcal{L}$, then $S(\mathcal{L})$ satisfies $S(\mathcal{C})$. We can show the following lemmas.

Lemma 1. *Let* B *be a code block. If* INFBLK$(B) = (\mathcal{C}, \Delta)$ *then for any solution* $(\mathcal{L}, S)$ *of* $\mathcal{C}$, $S(\Delta)$ *is a derivable proof under* $\mathcal{L}$.

$\text{INFBLK}(\texttt{return } x) = (\emptyset, \rho \cdot x : t \rhd \texttt{return } x : t) \quad (t, \rho \text{ fresh})$

$\text{INFBLK}(\texttt{goto } l) = (\{l \ll \rho \rhd t\}, \rho \rhd \texttt{goto } l : t) \quad (t, \rho \text{ fresh})$

$\text{INFBLK}(x \texttt{ = } v; B) =$

$\quad \text{let } (\mathcal{C}_1, \dfrac{\Delta_0}{(\gamma_0 \rhd I_0 : t_0)}) = \text{INFBLK}(B)$

$\qquad S = \text{CUNIF}(\gamma_0, \rho_1 \cdot \overline{y : t_2}) \quad (\overline{y} = FV(v) \cup \{x\}, \text{and } \rho_1, \overline{t_2} \text{ fresh})$

$\qquad \{y_1, \ldots, y_k\} = \{y' | (y' : \texttt{nil}) \in S(\gamma_0), y' \in \overline{y}\}$

$\qquad \dfrac{\Delta_1}{(\gamma_1 \rhd \tau_1)} = S(\Delta_0)$

$\qquad \dfrac{\Delta_{i+1}}{(\gamma_{i+1} \rhd \tau_{i+1})} = \dfrac{\Delta_i}{\gamma_i\{y_i : t_i'\} \rhd \texttt{discard } y_i : \tau_i} \quad (t_i' \text{ fresh for each } 1 \le i \le k)$

$\quad \text{in if } x \in FV(v) \text{ then } (S(\mathcal{C}_1), \dfrac{\Delta_{k+1}}{\gamma_{k+1}\{x : t_{k+1}\} \rhd x\texttt{=}v : S(t_0)}) \quad (t_{k+1} \text{ fresh})$

$\qquad \text{else } (S(\mathcal{C}_1), \dfrac{\Delta_{k+1}}{\gamma_{k+1}\{x : \texttt{nil}\} \rhd x\texttt{=}v : S(t_0)})$

$\text{SOLVE}(\mathcal{C}) =$

$\quad \text{if there is some } (\rho_1 \cdot \Gamma_1 \rhd \tau_1 \ll \rho_2 \cdot \Gamma_2 \rhd \tau_2) \in \mathcal{C} \text{ such that } \Gamma_1 \not\subseteq \Gamma_2 \text{ or } \tau_1 \ne \tau_2 \text{ then}$

$\qquad \text{let } S_1 = \text{UNIFY}(\{(\Gamma_1(x), \Gamma_2(x)) | x \in dom(\Gamma_1) \cap dom(\Gamma_1), \Gamma_1(x) \ne \texttt{nil}\} \cup \{(\tau_1, \tau_2)\})$

$\qquad\quad \Gamma_3 = \{x : \Gamma_1(x) | x \in (dom(\Gamma_1) \setminus dom(\Gamma_2)), \Gamma_1(x) \ne \texttt{nil}\}$

$\qquad\quad S_2 = [\rho_3 \cdot S_1(\Gamma_3)/\rho_2] \cup S_1 \quad (\rho_3 \text{ fresh})$

$\qquad \text{in SOLVE}(S_2(\mathcal{C})) \circ S_2$

$\quad \text{else } \emptyset$

$\text{INFER}(\{l_1 : B_1, \ldots, l_n : B_n\}) =$

$\quad \text{let } (\mathcal{C}_i, \dfrac{\Delta_i}{(\Gamma_i \rhd \tau_i)}) = \text{INFBLK}(B_i) \quad (1 \le i \le n)$

$\qquad (\mathcal{C}, \{l_1 : \Delta_1, \ldots, l_n : \Delta_n\}) = (\mathcal{C}_1 \cup \cdots \cup \mathcal{C}_n, \{l_1 : \Delta_1, \ldots, l_n : \Delta_n\})$

$\qquad \mathcal{L} = \{l_i : \gamma_i \rhd \tau_i | \Delta_i\text{'s end sequent is of the form } \gamma_i \rhd B_i : \tau_i\}$

$\qquad S = \text{SOLVE}(\mathcal{L}(\mathcal{C}))$

$\qquad P = S(\{l_1 : \Delta_1, \ldots, l_n : \Delta_n\})$

$\qquad \{\rho_1, \ldots, \rho_k\} = FreeContextVars(P)$

$\quad \text{in } [\emptyset/\rho_1, \ldots, \emptyset/\rho_k](P)$

Fig. 2. Some of the cases of proof reconstruction algorithm

Lemma 2. *If* $\text{SOLVE}(\mathcal{L}(\mathcal{C})) = S$ *and* $\{\rho_1, \ldots, \rho_k\}$ *is the set of free context variables in* $S(\mathcal{L}(\mathcal{C}))$ *then* $[\emptyset/\rho_1, \ldots, \emptyset/\rho_k] \circ S$ *is a solution of* $\mathcal{C}$ *under* $\mathcal{L}$.

Using these lemmas, we can show the following soundness theorem.

Theorem 2. *If* $\text{INFER}(\{\cdots, l_i : B_i \cdots\}) = \{\cdots, l_i : \dfrac{\Delta_i}{(\Gamma_i \rhd I_i : \tau_i)}, \cdots\}$ *then each* Δ_i *is a proof of* B_i *under the label environment* $\{l_1 : \Gamma_1 \rhd \tau_1, \ldots, l_n : \Gamma_n \rhd \tau_n\}$, *and therefore the program* $\{l_1 : B_1, \ldots, l_n : B_n\}$ *is derivable under* $\{l_1 : \Gamma_1 \rhd \tau_1, \ldots, l_n : \Gamma_n \rhd \tau_n\}$.

(1) An example source code

```
         i = 1
         s = 0
loop     c = i > n
         if c goto finish
         s = s + i
         i = i + 1
         goto loop
finish   return s
```

(2) The source program obtained by decomposing the source code into basic blocks

$\{l_1$: i = 1; s = 0; goto l_2,
l_2: c = i > n; if c goto l_4; goto l_3,
l_3: s = s + i; i = i + 1; goto l_2,
l_4: return s$\}$

(3) The inferred proof schemes of blocks, and the associated constraints

$$l_1: \quad \dfrac{\dfrac{\rho_1\{i : t_2, s : t_3\} \rhd \text{goto } l_2 : t_1}{\rho_1\{i : t_2, s : \text{nil}\} \rhd \text{s=0} : t_1}}{\rho_1\{i : \text{nil}, s : \text{nil}\} \rhd \text{i=1} : t_1}$$

$$\dfrac{\dfrac{\rho_3\{i : t_9, s : t_{10}\} \rhd \text{goto } l_2 : t_8}{\rho_3\{i : t_{11}, s : t_{10}\} \rhd \text{i=i+1} : t_8}}{l_3: \quad \rho_3\{i : t_{11}, s : t_{12}\} \rhd \text{s=s+i} : t_8}$$

$$l_2: \quad \dfrac{\dfrac{\rho_2\{c : t_5, i : t_6, n : t_7\} \rhd \text{goto } l_3 : t_4}{\rho_2\{c : t_5, i : t_6, n : t_7\} \rhd \text{if c goto } l_4 : t_4}}{\rho_2\{c : \text{nil}, i : t_6, n : t_7\} \rhd \text{c=i>n} : t_4}$$

$$l_4: \quad \rho_4\{s : t_{13}\} \rhd \text{return s} : t_{13}$$

$$l_2 \ll \rho_1\{i : t_2, s : t_3\} \rhd t_1 \qquad l_2 \ll \rho_3\{i : t_9, s : t_{10}\} \rhd t_8$$
$$l_3 \ll \rho_2\{c : t_5, i : t_6, n : t_7\} \rhd t_4 \qquad l_4 \ll \rho_2\{c : t_5, i : t_6, n : t_7\} \rhd t_4$$

(4) The reconstructed liveness proof of the program after constraint solving

$$l_1: \quad \dfrac{\dfrac{\{i : t_2, n : t_3, s : t_1\} \rhd \text{goto } l_2 : t_1}{\{i : t_2, n : t_3\} \rhd \text{s=0} : t_1}}{\{n : t_3\} \rhd \text{i=1} : t_1}$$

$$\dfrac{\dfrac{\{i : t_2, n : t_3, s : t_1\} \rhd \text{goto } l_2 : t_1}{\{i : t_2, n : t_3, s : t_1\} \rhd \text{i=i+1} : t_1}}{l_3: \quad \{i : t_2, n : t_3, s : t_1\} \rhd \text{s=s+i} : t_1}$$

$$l_2: \quad \dfrac{\dfrac{\{c : t_4, i : t_2, n : t_3, s : t_1\} \rhd \text{goto } l_3 : t_1}{\{c : t_4, i : t_2, n : t_3, s : t_1\} \rhd \text{if c goto } l_4 : t_1}}{\{i : t_2, n : t_3, s : t_1\} \rhd \text{c=i>n} : t_1}$$

$$l_4: \quad \{s : t_1\} \rhd \text{return s} : t_1$$

Fig. 3. Example code and the reconstructed liveness proof

Fig. 3 shows an example of proof reconstruction. It lists (1) a sample source code in an informal notation, (2) the source program obtained by decomposing the given source code into a set of basic blocks, (3) the inferred proof schemes of the basic blocks and the associated set of constraints, and (4) the reconstructed liveness proof after constraint resolution. In this final proof, empty entries of the form $x :$ nil are eliminated since they are no longer needed after the proof reconstruction have been completed.

We will use the sample source code (1) in Fig. 3 as the running example and will show examples of the proof transformation steps that follow (4) in Fig. 3. The examples above and those shown later are (reformatted) actual outputs of our prototype system.

3   Optimizing Liveness by Inserting Weakening Rule

The above proof inference algorithm always succeeds and returns a liveness proof for any given code. The resulting proof is, however, not the only possible one. The next step is to optimize the inferred proof by proof normalization.

The proof system has the freedom in terms of the places where discard is inserted. Our proof inference algorithm does not insert weakening rules (discard instructions) except for those required by assignments. All the necessary weakening rules are implicitly included in goto and return instructions. The optimization step is to introduce weakening rules explicitly and to move them toward the root of the proof tree (i.e. toward the entry point of the code) so that variables are discarded as early as possible. This is characterized as a proof normalization process with respect to the following commutative conversion (used in the specified direction) of proofs:

$$
\cfrac{\cfrac{\vdots}{\cfrac{\Gamma, x : \mathtt{nil} \vartriangleright B \; : \; \tau_0}{\Gamma, x : \tau \vartriangleright \mathtt{discard} \; x; B \; : \; \tau_0}}}{\Gamma, x : \tau \vartriangleright I; \mathtt{discard} \; x; B \; : \; \tau_0} \implies \cfrac{\cfrac{\cfrac{\vdots}{\Gamma, x : \mathtt{nil} \vartriangleright B \; : \; \tau_0}}{\Gamma, x : \mathtt{nil} \vartriangleright I; B \; : \; \tau_0}}{\Gamma, x : \tau \vartriangleright \mathtt{discard} \; x; I; B \; : \; \tau_0} \quad (\text{if } x \notin I)
$$

Fig. 4 gives the optimization algorithm WEAKEN. In these definitions, we used the notations $\Gamma|_V$ for the restriction of Γ to a set of variables V, and $\Gamma - V$ for the context obtained from Γ by removing the assumptions of variables in V.

We write ADDWEAKEN(Δ) for the proof obtained from Δ by adding all the discard instructions just before each branching instruction so that the proof conforms to the proof system where the axioms are restricted to the following:

$$\{x : t\} \vartriangleright \mathtt{return} \; x : t. \qquad \Gamma \vartriangleright \mathtt{goto} \; l : \tau \; (\text{if } \mathcal{L}(l) = \Gamma \vartriangleright \tau)$$

We write $\Delta \overset{*}{\longrightarrow} \Delta'$ if Δ' is obtained from Δ by repeated application of the conversion rule. We can show the following.

Theorem 3. *For any proof* Δ, *if* $\mathrm{WK}(\Delta) = \Delta'$ *then* ADDWEAKEN(Δ) $\overset{*}{\longrightarrow} \Delta'$.

Fig. 5 shows the optimized proof of the proof inferred for our running example in Fig. 3. Since discard is a pseudo instruction and is not needed in subsequent development, the algorithm erases them after the optimization is completed. In Fig. 5, discard step is shown in parenthesis to indicate this fact.

Let us review the results so far obtained. The labeled set of proofs obtained from a given program (a labeled set of basic blocks) by the combination of proof inference (INFER) and optimization (WEAKEN) is a code annotated with liveness information at each instruction step. The annotated liveness information is at least as precise as the one obtained by the conventional method. This is seen by observing the following property. If Δ contains a inference step $\Gamma \vartriangleright I \; : \; \tau$ then all the variables in Γ are live at I and the interference graph of P must contain a completely connected subgraph of the length of Γ. Significant additional benefit of our liveness analysis is that it is presented as a typing annotation to the original program. This enables us to change the set of the target variables for register allocation dynamically, to which we now turn.

$\text{WEAKEN}(\{l_1 : \Delta_1, \ldots, l_n : \Delta_n\}) =$
  let $\mathcal{E} = \{l_1 : \text{ENTRYVARS}(\Delta_1), \ldots, l_n : \text{ENTRYVARS}(\Delta_n)\}$
    $(V_i, \Delta'_i) = \text{WK}(\Delta_i) \quad (1 \le i \le n)$
  in $\{l_1 : \Delta'_1, \ldots, l_n : \Delta'_n\}$

$$\text{ENTRYVARS}(\frac{\Delta}{(\Gamma \triangleright I : \tau)}) = \{x | x \in dom(\Gamma), \Gamma(x) \ne \texttt{nil})\}$$

In the following definition, $\mathcal{E}$ is a global environment defined in the main algorithm.

$\text{WK}(\Gamma \triangleright \texttt{return } x : t) = (dom(\Gamma) \setminus \{x\}, \{x : \Gamma(x)\} \triangleright \texttt{return } x : t)$

$\text{WK}(\Gamma \triangleright \texttt{goto } l : \tau) = (dom(\Gamma) \setminus \mathcal{E}(l), \Gamma|_{\mathcal{E}(l)} \triangleright \texttt{goto } l : \tau)$

$$\text{WK}(\frac{\Delta}{\Gamma \triangleright x \texttt{ = } v : \tau}) =$$

  let $(V, \frac{\Delta_0}{(\Gamma_0 \triangleright I_0 : \tau)}) = \text{WK}(\Delta)$
    $\{x_1, \ldots, x_n\} = FV(v) \cap V$
    $V' = V \setminus \{x_1, \ldots, x_n\}$
    $$\frac{\Delta_i}{(\Gamma_i \triangleright \_ : \_)} = \frac{\Delta_{i-1}}{\Gamma_{i-1}\{x_i : \Gamma(x_i)\} \triangleright \texttt{discard } x_i : \tau} \quad \text{for each } x_i \ (1 \le i \le n)$$
  in $(V', \frac{\Delta_n}{\Gamma - V' \triangleright x \texttt{ = } v : \tau})$

$$\text{WK}(\frac{\Delta}{\Gamma \triangleright \texttt{discard } x : \tau}) = \text{let } (V, \Delta_0) = \text{WK}(\Delta) \text{ in } (V \cup \{x\}, \Delta_0)$$

Fig. 4. Some cases of weakening (discard pseudo instruction) insertion algorithm

$l_1:$
$$\frac{\dfrac{\{i : t_2, n : t_3, s : t_1\} \triangleright \texttt{goto } l_2 : t_1}{\{i : t_2, n : t_3\} \triangleright \texttt{s=0} : t_1}}{\{n : t_3\} \triangleright \texttt{i=1} : t_1}$$

$l_3:$
$$\frac{\dfrac{\{i : t_2, n : t_3, s : t_1\} \triangleright \texttt{goto } l_2 : t_1}{\{i : t_2, n : t_3, s : t_1\} \triangleright \texttt{i=i+1} : t_1}}{\{i : t_2, n : t_3, s : t_1\} \triangleright \texttt{s=s+i} : t_1}$$

$l_2:$
$$\frac{\dfrac{\dfrac{\dfrac{\{i : t_2, n : t_3, s : t_1\} \triangleright \texttt{goto } l_3 : t_1}{(\{c : t_4, i : t_2, n : t_3, s : t_1\} \triangleright \texttt{discard } c : t_1)}}{\{c : t_4, i : t_2, n : t_3, s : t_1\} \triangleright \texttt{if } c \texttt{ goto } l_4 : t_1}}{\{i : t_2, n : t_3, s : t_1\} \triangleright \texttt{c=i>n} : t_1}}{}$$

$l_4: \quad \{s : t_1\} \triangleright \texttt{return } s : t_1$

Fig. 5. The result of weakening insertion optimization for the example in Fig. 3

4   Assigning Registers

We have so far considered a language with unbounded number of variables. A conventional approach to register allocation selects a subset of variables for the target of register allocation, and "spills" the others out. The treatment of spilled variables require ad-hoc strategies. Our approach provides a systematic solution to this problem using the liveness annotated code itself. We consider the set of registers as a "working set" of the live variables at each instruction step, and maintain this working set. For this purpose, we define a new proof system whose sequents are of the form

$$\Sigma \mid \Pi \rhd_k B : \tau.$$

where Π is a *register context* whose length is bounded by the number k of available registers, and Σ is a *memory context* of unbounded length. We assume that k is no less than the number of assumptions needed for each instructions. In our case, instructions have at most 2 operands and therefore $k \geq 2$. Each logical rule (instruction) can only access assumptions in Π. To assess Σ, we introduce rules for `load` x and `store` x to move assumptions between Σ and Π:

$$\frac{\Sigma \mid \Pi, x : t_1 \rhd_k B : t}{\Sigma, x : t_1 \mid \Pi \rhd_k \text{load } x; B : t_0} \qquad \frac{\Sigma, x : t_1 \mid \Pi \rhd_k B : t_0}{\Sigma \mid \Pi, x : t_1 \rhd_k \text{store } x; B : t_0} \text{ (if } |\Pi| < k)$$

where $|\Pi|$ denotes the length of Π. The other rules do not change Σ and are the same as before. We call the new proof system $SSC(LE, k)$.

In a proof-theoretical perspective, the previous proof system $SSC(L)$ implicitly admits *unrestricted exchange* so that any assumptions in Γ is freely available, while the new proof system $SSC(LE, k)$ requires explicit use of the exchange rules to access some part of the assumptions. The next step of our register allocation method is to transform a proof obtained in the previous step into a proof in this new system. Since each inference rule only uses no more than k assumptions, the following is obvious.

Proposition 1. *There is an algorithm EXCHANGE such that, for any provable program P in $SSC(L)$, EXCHANGE(k, P) is a program provable in $SSC(LE, k)$, and if we ignore the distinction between Σ and Π, and erase `load` and `store`, then it is equal to P.*

EXCHANGE traverses the code block, and whenever it detects an instruction whose operands are not in Π, it exchanges the necessary operands in Σ with some variables in Π, which are selected according to some strategy. The algorithm is straightforward except for this strategy of selecting variables to be saved. With the existence of branches, developing an optimal strategy is a difficult problem. Our prototype system adopted a simple lookahead strategy: it selects one control flow and traverses the instructions (up to a fixed number) to form an ordered list of variables that are more likely to be used in near future, and select those variables that are not appearing in the beginning of this list. In practical, we need more sophisticated heuristics, which is outside of the scope of this paper.

Fig. 6 shows the result of exchange insertion against the optimized proof shown in Fig. 4.

The final stage of our development is to assign a register number to each type variable in Π at each instruction step. We do this by defining yet another proof system where a type variable in Π has an attribute of a register number (ranged over by p). The set of instructions in this final proof system is as follows.

$$I ::= x = y \mid x = c \mid x = x + x \mid \text{if } x \text{ goto } l$$
$$\mid \text{load } (p, x) \mid \text{store } (p, x) \mid \text{move } x[p_i \to p_j]$$

`load` (p, x) moves variable x from Σ to Π and loads register p with the content of x. `store` (p, x) is its converse. `move` $x[p_i \to p_j]$ is an auxiliary instruction

$$\cfrac{\cfrac{\emptyset \mid \{i : t_2, n : t_3, s : t_1\} \triangleright_3 \text{ goto } l_2 : t_1}{\emptyset \mid \{i : t_2, n : t_3\} \triangleright_3 \text{ s=0 } : t_1}}{l_1: \qquad \emptyset \mid \{n : t_3\} \triangleright_3 \text{ i=1 } : t_1}$$

$$\cfrac{\cfrac{\cfrac{\{s : t_1\} \mid \{i : t_2, n : t_3\} \triangleright_3 \text{ goto } l_3 : t_1}{\{s : t_1\} \mid \{c : t_4, i : t_2, n : t_3\} \triangleright_3 \text{ if } c \text{ goto } l_4 : t_1}}{\{s : t_1\} \mid \{i : t_2, n : t_3\} \triangleright_3 \text{ c=i>n } : t_1}}{l_2: \qquad \emptyset \mid \{i : t_2, n : t_3, s : t_1\} \triangleright_3 \text{ store } s : t_1}$$

$$\cfrac{\cfrac{\cfrac{\emptyset \mid \{i : t_2, n : t_3, s : t_1\} \triangleright_3 \text{ goto } l_2 : t_1}{\emptyset \mid \{i : t_2, n : t_3, s : t_1\} \triangleright_3 \text{ i=i+1 } : t_1}}{\emptyset \mid \{i : t_2, n : t_3, s : t_1\} \triangleright_3 \text{ s=s+i } : t_1}}{l_3: \{s : t_1\} \mid \{i : t_2, n : t_3\} \triangleright_3 \text{ load } s : t_1}$$

$$\cfrac{\emptyset \mid \{s : t_1\} \triangleright_3 \text{ return } s : t_1}{l_4: \{s : t_1\} \mid \emptyset \triangleright_3 \text{ load } s : t_1}$$

Fig. 6. Converting to the dual context calculus

that changes the register allocated to x, which corresponds to register-register copy instruction. The rules for **load**, **store** and **move** are given below.

$$\cfrac{\Sigma \mid \Pi, x : t[p_2] \triangleright_k I : t_0}{\Sigma \mid \Pi, x : t[p_1] \triangleright_k \text{ move } x[p_1 \to p_2] : t_0} \ (p_1 \notin \Pi) \qquad \cfrac{\Sigma \mid \Pi, x : t[p] \triangleright_k I : t_0}{\Sigma, x : t \mid \Pi \triangleright_k \text{ load } (p, x) : t_0}$$

$$\cfrac{\Sigma, x : t \mid \Pi \triangleright_k I : t_0}{\Sigma \mid \Pi, x : t[p] \triangleright_k \text{ store } (p, x) : t_0} \ (\text{if } |\Pi, x : t[p]| \leq k, \ p \notin \Pi)$$

The other rules are the same as those in $SSC(LE, k)$ except that in Π, each type variable has distinct register number attribute p. We call this proof system $SSC(LEA, k)$.

Within a block, proof transformation from $SSC(LE, k)$ to $SSC(LEA, k)$ is straightforwardly done by a simple tail recursive algorithm (starting from the entry point) that keeps track of the current register assignment of Π and a set of free registers, and updates them every time when Π is changed due to assignment, load or store instructions. Since the length of Π is bounded by k, it is always possible to assign registers. An extra work is needed to adjust register assignment before a branching instruction so that the assignment at the branching instruction agrees with that of the target block. If the target block is not yet processed, then we can simply set the current register assignment of Π as the initial assignment for the block. If an assignment has already been done for the target block and it does not agree on the current assignment, then we need to permutate some registers by inserting **move** instructions using one temporary register. If there is no free register, we have to save one and then load after the permutation. In our current prototype implementation, we adopt a simple strategy of trying to allocate the same register to the same liveness type whenever possible by caching the past allocation. Minimizing register-register moves at branching instructions requires certain amount of heuristics, which is left as future work.

It should be noted, however, that this problem is much simpler than the problem of combining independently colored basic blocks. Our liveness analysis and the subsequent decompositions of variables into Σ and Π are done globally, and therefore the set Π of register contexts are guaranteed to agree when control flows merge.

The remaining thing to be done is to extract machine code from a proof in $SSC(LEA, k)$. We consider the following target machine code.

$$I ::= \texttt{return } ri \mid \texttt{goto } l \mid ri = c \mid ri = rj \mid \texttt{if } ri \texttt{ goto } l$$
$$\mid \texttt{store } (ri, x) \mid \texttt{load } (ri, x) \mid ri = rj + rk$$

ri is the register identified by number i. $\texttt{store } (ri, x)$ stores the register ri to the memory location named x. $\texttt{load } (ri, x)$ loads the register ri with the content of the memory location x. Since in a proof of $SSC(LEA, k)$, each occurrence of variable in its register context Π is associate with a register number, it is straightforward to extract the target machine code by simply traversing a proof. For example, for the proof

$$\frac{\begin{array}{c} \Delta \\ (\Sigma \mid \Pi, x : t_1[1], y : t_2[2] \triangleright_k I : t_0) \end{array}}{\Sigma \mid \Pi, y : t_2[2] \triangleright_k x = y : t_0}$$

we emit instruction "$r1 = r2$" and then continue to emit code for the proof Δ.

Fig. 7 shows the proof in $SSC(LEA, k)$ and the machine code for our running example.

5   Conclusions and Discussions

We have presented a proof-theoretical approach to register allocation. In our approach, liveness analysis is characterized as proof reconstruction in a sequent-style proof system where a formula (or a type) represents a "live range" of a variable at each instruction step in a given code. Register manipulation instructions such as loading and storing registers are interpreted as *structural rules* in the proof system. Register allocation process is then regarded as a proof transformation from a calculus with implicit structural rules to one with explicit structural rules. All these proof transformation processes are effectively done, yielding a register allocation algorithm. The algorithm has been implemented, which demonstrates the practical feasibility of the method.

This is the first step toward proof theoretical framework for register allocation; there remain number of issues to be investigated – detailed comparisons with other approaches, relationship to other aspects of code generation such as instruction scheduling, robust implementation and evaluation etc. Below we include some discussion and suggestions for further investigation.

Correctness and other formal properties. In our approach, register allocation is presented as a series of proof transformations among proof systems that differ in their treatment of *structural rules.* Since structural rules do not affect the meanings, it is an immediate consequence that our approach preserves the meaning of the code. Since our method is a form of type system, it can smoothly be integrated in a static type system of a code language. By regarding liveness types as attribute of the conventional notion of types, we immediately get a register allocation method for a typed code language. Type-preservation is shown trivially by erasing liveness and register attributes, and merging the memory

The proof with register number annotation.

$$\frac{\emptyset \mid \{i : t_2[r1], n : t_3[r0], s : t_1[r2]\} \rhd_3 \text{goto } l_2 : t_1}{\emptyset \mid \{i : t_2[r1], n : t_3[r0]\} \rhd_3 \text{ s=0} : t_1}$$

$l_1:$ $\qquad \emptyset \mid \{n : t_3[r0]\} \rhd_3 \text{ i=1} : t_1$

$$\frac{\{s : t_1\} \mid \{i : t_2[r1], n : t_3[r0]\} \rhd_3 \text{goto } l_3 : t_1}{\{s : t_1\} \mid \{c : t_4[r2], i : t_2[r1], n : t_3[r0]\} \rhd_3 \text{if } c \text{ goto } l_4 : t_1}$$

$$\frac{\{s : t_1\} \mid \{i : t_2[r1], n : t_3[r0]\} \rhd_3 \text{ c=i>n} : t_1}{}$$

$l_2:$ $\qquad \emptyset \mid \{i : t_2[r1], n : t_3[r0], s : t_1[r2]\} \rhd_3 \text{ store } s : t_1$

$\emptyset \mid \{i : t_2[r1], n : t_3[r0], s : t_1[r2]\} \rhd_3 \text{goto } l_3 : t_1$

$\emptyset \mid \{i : t_2[r1], n : t_3[r0], s : t_1[r2]\} \rhd_3 \text{ i=i+1} : t_1$

$$\frac{\emptyset \mid \{i : t_2[r1], n : t_3[r0], s : t_1[r2]\} \rhd_3 \text{ s=s+i} : t_1}{}$$

$l_3:$ $\quad \{s : t_1\} \mid \{i : t_2[r1], n : t_3[r0]\} \rhd_3 \text{ load } s : t_1$

$$\frac{\emptyset \mid \{s : t_1[r0]\} \rhd_3 \text{ return } s : t_1}{}$$

$l_4:$ $\quad \{s : t_1\} \mid \emptyset \rhd_3 \text{ load } s : t_1$

The extracted machine code:

```
11 :    r1 = 1              13:        load r2,s
        r2 = 0                         r2 = r2 + r1
        goto 12                        r1 = r1 + 1
                                       goto 12
12:     store r2,s
        r2 = r1 > r0        14:        load r0,s
        if r2 goto 14                  return r0
        goto 13
```

Fig. 7. Example of register number assignment and code emission

and register context of each sequent. We also believe that our method can be combined with other static verification systems for low-level code.

Expressiveness. Our formalism covers the entire process in register allocation, and as a formalism, it appears to be more powerful than the one underlying the conventional method based on graph coloring. We have seen that liveness analysis is as strong as the conventional method using an interference graph. Since our formalism transforms the liveness annotated code, it provides better treatment for register-memory move than the conventional notion of "spilling". Although we have not incorporated various heuristics in our prototype implementation, our initial experimentation using our prototype system found that our method properly deals with the example of a "diamond" interference graph discussed in literature [1], for which the conventional graph coloring based approach cannot find an optimal coloring. Fig. 8 shows one simple example.

(1) The source program

```
L:    a = d + c
      b = a + d
      c = a + b
      d = b + c
      goto L
```

(2) The optimized liveness proof:

$$\frac{\{c:t_3,d:t_2\} \triangleright \text{goto } L : t_1}{}$$
$$\frac{\{b:t_4,c:t_3,d:t_2\} \triangleright \text{discard } b : t_1}{}$$
$$\frac{\{b:t_4,c:t_3\} \triangleright \text{d=b+c} : t_1}{}$$
$$\frac{\{a:t_5,b:t_4,c:t_3\} \triangleright \text{discard } a : t_1}{}$$
$$\frac{\{a:t_5,b:t_4\} \triangleright \text{c=a+b} : t_1}{}$$
$$\frac{\{a:t_5,b:t_4,d:t_2\} \triangleright \text{discard } d : t_1}{}$$
$$\frac{\{a:t_5,d:t_2\} \triangleright \text{b=a+d} : t_1}{}$$
$$\frac{\{a:t_5,c:t_3,d:t_2\} \triangleright \text{discard } c : t_1}{}$$
$$\frac{\{c:t_3,d:t_2\} \triangleright \text{a=b+d} : t_1}{}$$

(3) The proof without `discard`:

$$\frac{\{c:t_3,d:t_2\} \triangleright \text{goto } L : t_1}{}$$
$$\frac{\{b:t_4,c:t_3\} \triangleright \text{d=b+c} : t_1}{}$$
$$\frac{\{a:t_5,b:t_4\} \triangleright \text{c=a+b} : t_1}{}$$
$$\frac{\{a:t_5,d:t_2\} \triangleright \text{b=a+d} : t_1}{}$$
$$\frac{\{c:t_3,d:t_2\} \triangleright \text{a=b+d} : t_1}{}$$

(4) The proof in $SSC(LE,k)$:

$$\frac{\emptyset \mid \{c:t_3,d:t_2\} \triangleright_2 \text{goto } L : t_1}{}$$
$$\frac{\emptyset \mid \{b:t_4,c:t_3\} \triangleright_2 \text{d=b+c} : t_1}{}$$
$$\frac{\emptyset \mid \{a:t_5,b:t_4\} \triangleright_2 \text{c=a+b} : t_1}{}$$
$$\frac{\emptyset \mid \{a:t_5,d:t_2\} \triangleright_2 \text{b=a+d} : t_1}{}$$
$$\frac{\emptyset \mid \{c:t_3,d:t_2\} \triangleright_2 \text{a=b+d} : t_1}{}$$

(5) The proof in $SSC(LEA,k)$:

$$\frac{\emptyset \mid \{c:t_3[r0],d:t_2[r1]\} \triangleright_2 \text{goto } L : t_1}{}$$
$$\frac{\emptyset \mid \{b:t_4[r1],c:t_3[r0]\} \triangleright_2 \text{d=b+c} : t_1}{}$$
$$\frac{\emptyset \mid \{a:t_5[r0],b:t_4[r1]\} \triangleright_2 \text{c=a+b} : t_1}{}$$
$$\frac{\emptyset \mid \{a:t_5[r0],d:t_2[r1]\} \triangleright_2 \text{b=a+d} : t_1}{}$$
$$\frac{\emptyset \mid \{c:t_3[r0],d:t_2[r1]\} \triangleright_2 \text{a=b+d} : t_1}{}$$

(6) The extracted machine code

```
L:      r0 = r1 + r0
        r1 = r0 + r1
        r0 = r0 + r1
        r1 = r1 + r0
        goto L
```

Fig. 8. Example for a code whose interference graph forms a "diamond"

Liveness analysis and SSA-style optimization. The main strength of our method is the representation of liveness as type system of code itself. For example, as far as liveness analysis is concerned, our system already contains the effect of SSA (static single assignment) transformation [4] without actually performing the transformation. The effect of renaming a variable at each assignment is achieved by allocating a fresh type variable. The effect of ϕ function at control flow merge is achieved by unification of the type variables assigned to the same variable in different blocks connected by a branch instruction. Thanks to these effects, our liveness analysis achieves the accuracy of those that perform SSA transformation without introducing the complication of ϕ functions. Moreover, we believe that this property also allows us to combine various techniques of SSA-based optimization in our approach. For example, since each live range has distinct type variables, it is easy to incorporate constant propagation or dead code elimination. The detailed study on the precise relationship with our type-based approach and SSA transformation is beyond the scope of the current work, and we would like to report it elsewhere.

Acknowledgments. The author thanks Tomoyuki Matsumoto for his help in implementing the prototype system, and Sin-ya Katsumata for insightful discussion at early stage of this work while the author was in Kyoto University.

References

1. P. Briggs, K.D. Cooper, and L. Torczon. Improvements to graph coloring register allocation. *ACM Trans. Program. Lang. Syst.*, 16(3):428–455, 1994.
2. G. J. Chaitin. Register allocation & spilling via graph coloring. In *Proc. ACM Symposium on Compiler Construction*, pages 98–105, 1982.
3. G. J. Chaitin, M.A. Auslander, A.K. Chandra, J. Cocke, M.E. Hopkins, and P.W. Markstein. Register allocation via coloring. *Computer Languages*, 6(1):47–57, 1981.
4. R. Cytron, J. Ferrante, B.K. Rosen, M.N. Wegman, and F.K. Zadeck. Efficiently computing static single assignment form and the control dependence graph. *ACM Trans. Program. Lang. Syst.*, 13(4):451–490, 1991.
5. J.-Y. Girard. Linear logic. *Theoretical Computer Science*, 50(1):1–102, 1987.
6. G. Morrisett, D. Walker, K. Crary, and N. Glew. From system F to typed assembly language. In *Proc. ACM POPL Symposium*, 1998.
7. G. Necula and P. Lee. Proof-carrying code. In *Proc. ACM POPL Symposium*, pages 106–119, 1998.
8. A. Ohori. The logical abstract machine: a Curry-Howard isomorphism for machine code. In *Proc. International Symposium on Functional and Logic Programming*, Springer LNCS 1722, pages 300–318, 1999.
9. H. Ono and Y. Komori. Logics without the contraction rule. *Journal of Symbolic Logic*, 50(1):169–201, 1985.
10. M. Poletto and V. Sarkar. Linear scan register allocation. *ACM Trans. Program. Lang. Syst.*, 21(5):895–913, 1999.
11. R. Stata and M. Abadi. A type system for Java bytecode subroutines. In *Proc. ACM POPL Symposium*, pages 149–160, 1998.

Author Index

Lecture Notes in Computer Science

For information about Vols. 1–2523

please contact your bookseller or Springer-Verlag

Vol. 2567: Y.G. Desmedt (Ed.), Public Key Cryptography – PKC 2003. Proceedings, 2003. XI, 365 pages. 2002.

Vol. 2568: M. Hagiya, A. Ohuchi (Eds.), DNA Computing. Proceedings, 2002. XI, 338 pages. 2003.

Vol. 2569: D. Gollmann, G. Karjoth, M. Waidner (Eds.), Computer Security – ESORICS 2002. Proceedings, 2002. XIII, 648 pages. 2002. (Subseries LNAI).

Vol. 2570: M. Jünger, G. Reinelt, G. Rinaldi (Eds.), Combinatorial Optimization – Eureka, You Shrink!. Proceedings, 2001. X, 209 pages. 2003.

Vol. 2571: S.K. Das, S. Bhattacharya (Eds.), Distributed Computing. Proceedings, 2002. XIV, 354 pages. 2002.

Vol. 2572: D. Calvanese, M. Lenzerini, R. Motwani (Eds.), Database Theory – ICDT 2003. Proceedings, 2003. XI, 455 pages. 2002.

Vol. 2574: M.-S. Chen, P.K. Chrysanthis, M. Sloman, A. Zaslavsky (Eds.), Mobile Data Management. Proceedings, 2003. XII, 414 pages. 2003.

Vol. 2575: L.D. Zuck, P.C. Attie, A. Cortesi, S. Mukhopadhyay (Eds.), Verification, Model Checking, and Abstract Interpretation. Proceedings, 2003. XI, 325 pages. 2003.

Vol. 2576: S. Cimato, C. Galdi, G. Persiano (Eds.), Security in Communication Networks. Proceedings, 2002. IX, 365 pages. 2003.

Vol. 2578: F.A.P. Petitcolas (Ed.), Information Hiding. Proceedings, 2002. IX, 427 pages. 2003.

Vol. 2580: H. Erdogmus, T. Weng (Eds.), COTS-Based Software Systems. Proceedings, 2003. XVIII, 261 pages. 2003.

Vol. 2581: J.S. Sichman, F. Bousquet, P. Davidsson (Eds.), Multi-Agent-Based Simulation II. Proceedings, 2002. X, 195 pages. 2003. (Subseries LNAI).

Vol. 2583: S. Matwin, C. Sammut (Eds.), Inductive Logic Programming. Proceedings, 2002. X, 351 pages. 2003. (Subseries LNAI).

Vol. 2585: F. Giunchiglia, J. Odell, G. Weiß (Eds.), Agent-Oriented Software Engineering III. Proceedings, 2002. X, 229 pages. 2003.

Vol. 2586: M. Klusch, S. Bergamaschi, P. Edwards, P. Petta (Eds.), Intelligent Information Agents. VI, 275 pages. 2003. (Subseries LNAI).

Vol. 2587: P.J. Lee, C.H. Lim (Eds.), Information Security and Cryptology – ICISC 2002. Proceedings, 2002. XI, 536 pages. 2003.

Vol. 2588: A. Gelbukh (Ed.), Computational Linguistics and Intelligent Text Processing. Proceedings, 2003. XV, 648 pages. 2003.

Vol. 2589: E. Börger, A. Gargantini, E. Riccobene (Eds.), Abstract State Machines 2003. Proceedings, 2003. XI, 427 pages. 2003.

Vol. 2590: S. Bressan, A.B. Chaudhri, M.L. Lee, J.X. Yu, Z. Lacroix (Eds.), Efficiency and Effectiveness of XML Tools and Techniques and Data Integration over the Web. Proceedings, 2002. X, 259 pages. 2003.

Vol. 2591: M. Aksit, M. Mezini, R. Unland (Eds.), Objects, Components, Architectures, Services, and Applications for a Networked World. Proceedings, 2002. XI, 431 pages. 2003.

Vol. 2592: R. Kowalczyk, J.P. Müller, H. Tianfield, R. Unland (Eds.), Agent Technologies, Infrastructures, Tools, and Applications for E-Services. Proceedings, 2002. XVII, 371 pages. 2003. (Subseries LNAI).

Vol. 2593: A.B. Chaudhri, M. Jeckle, E. Rahm, R. Unland (Eds.), Web, Web-Services, and Database Systems. Proceedings, 2002. XI, 311 pages. 2003.

Vol. 2594: A. Asperti, B. Buchberger, J.H. Davenport (Eds.), Mathematical Knowledge Management. Proceedings, 2003. X, 225 pages. 2003.

Vol. 2595: K. Nyberg, H. Heys (Eds.), Selected Areas in Cryptography. Proceedings, 2002. XI, 405 pages. 2003.

Vol. 2597: G. Păun, G. Rozenberg, A. Salomaa, C. Zandron (Eds.), Membrane Computing. Proceedings, 2002. VIII, 423 pages. 2003.

Vol. 2598: R. Klein, H.-W. Six, L. Wegner (Eds.), Computer Science in Perspective. X, 357 pages. 2003.

Vol. 2599: E. Sherratt (Ed.), Telecommunications and beyond: The Broader Applicability of SDL and MSC. Proceedings, 2002. X, 253 pages. 2003.

Vol. 2600: S. Mendelson, A.J. Smola, Advanced Lectures on Machine Learning. Proceedings, 2002. IX, 259 pages 2003. (Subseries LNAI).

Vol. 2601: M. Ajmone Marsan, G. Corazza, M. Listanti, A. Roveri (Eds.) Quality of Service in Multiservice I Networks. Proceedings, 2003. XV, 759 pages. 2003.

Vol. 2602: C. Priami (Ed.), Computational Methods i Systems Biology. Proceedings, 2003. IX, 214 pages. 2003.

Vol. 2604: N. Guelfi, E. Astesiano, G. Reggio (Eds.), Sci entific Engineering for Distributed Java Applications. Pro ceedings, 2002. X, 205 pages. 2003.

Vol. 2606: A.M. Tyrrell, P.C. Haddow, J. Torresen (Eds. Evolvable Systems: From Biology to Hardware. Procee ings, 2003. XIV, 468 pages. 2003.

Vol. 2607: H. Alt, M. Habib (Eds.), STACS 2003. Pr ceedings, 2003. XVII, 700 pages. 2003.

Vol. 2609: M. Okada, B. Pierce, A. Scedrov, H. Tokud A. Yonezawa (Eds.), Software Security – Theories a Systems. Proceedings, 2002. XI, 471 pages. 2003.

Vol. 2612: M. Joye (Ed.), Topics in Cryptology – CT-RS 2003. Proceedings, 2003. XI, 417 pages. 2003.

Vol. 2614: R. Laddaga, P. Robertson, H. Shrobe (Eds Self-Adaptive Software: Applications. Proceedings, 200 VIII, 291 pages. 2003.

Vol. 2615: N. Carbonell, C. Stephanidis (Eds.), Univers Access. Proceedings, 2002. XIV, 534 pages. 2003.

Vol. 2618: P. Degano (Ed.), Programming Languages a Systems. Proceedings, 2003. XV, 415 pages. 2003.

Vol. 2619: H. Garavel, J. Hatcliff (Eds.), Tools and gorithms for the Construction and Analysis of Syster Proceedings, 2003. XVI, 604 pages. 2003.

Vol. 2621: M. Pezzè (Ed.), Fundamental Approach to Software Engineering. Proceedings, 2003. XIV, 4 pages. 2003.

Vol. 2622: G. Hedin (Ed.), Compiler Construction. P ceedings, 2003. XII, 335 pages. 2003.